S0-ACV-975

New Global Dangers:
Changing Dimensions of International Security

International Security Readers

Strategy and Nuclear Deterrence (1984)

Military Strategy and the Origins of the First World War (1985)

Conventional Forces and American Defense Policy (1986)

The Star Wars Controversy (1986)

Naval Strategy and National Security (1988)

Military Strategy and the Origins of the First World War, revised and expanded edition (1991)

—published by Princeton University Press

Soviet Military Policy (1989)

Conventional Forces and American Defense Policy, revised edition (1989)

Nuclear Diplomacy and Crisis Management (1990)

The Cold War and After: Prospects for Peace (1991)

America's Strategy in a Changing World (1992)

The Cold War and After: Prospects for Peace, expanded edition (1993)

Global Dangers: Changing Dimensions of International Security (1995)

The Perils of Anarchy: Contemporary Realism and International Security (1995)

Debating the Democratic Peace (1996)

East Asian Security (1996)

Nationalism and Ethnic Conflict (1997)

America's Strategic Choices (1997)

Theories of War and Peace (1998)

America's Strategic Choices, revised edition (2000)

Rational Choice and Security Studies: Stephen Walt and His Critics (2000)

The Rise of China (2000)

Nationalism and Ethnic Conflict, revised edition (2001)

Offense, Defense, and War (2004)

New Global Dangers: Changing Dimensions of International Security (2004)

—published by The MIT Press

New Global Dangers

Changing Dimensions of International Security

AN *International*
Security READER

EDITED BY

Michael E. Brown
Owen R. Coté Jr.
Sean M. Lynn-Jones
and Steven E. Miller

THE MIT PRESS
CAMBRIDGE, MASSACHUSETTS
LONDON, ENGLAND

The contents of this book were first published in *International Security* (ISSN 0162-2889), a publication of The MIT Press under the sponsorship of the Belfer Center for Science and International Affairs at Harvard University. Copyright in each of the following articles is owned jointly by the President and Fellows of Harvard College and of the Massachusetts Institute of Technology.

Barry R. Posen, "Command of the Commons: The Military Foundation of U.S. Hegemony," 28:1 (Summer 2003); Scott D. Sagan, "Why Do States Build Nuclear Weapons? Three Models in Search of a Bomb, " 21:3 (Winter 1996/97); Ariel E. Levite, "Never Say Never Again: Nuclear Reversal Revisited," 27:3 (Winter 2002); Sharon K. Weiner, "Preventing Nuclear Entrepreneurship in Russia's Nuclear Cities," 27:2 (Fall 2002); Gregory Koblentz, "Pathogens as Weapons: The International Security Implications of Biological Warfare," 28:3 (Winter 2003/04); Jessica Stern, "Dreaded Risks and the Control of Biological Weapons," 27:3 (Winter 2002/03); Dinshaw Mistry, "Beyond the MTCR: Building a Comprehensive Regime to Contain Ballistic Missile Proliferation," 27:4 (Spring 2003); Roland Paris, "Human Security: Paradigm Shift or Hot Air?" 26:2 (Fall 2001); Thomas F. Homer-Dixon, "Environmental Scarcities and Violent Conflict: Evidence from Cases," 19:1 (Summer 1994); Myron Weiner, "Security, Stability, and International Migration," 17:3 (Winter 1992/93); Valerie M. Hudson and Andrea Den Boer, "A Surplus of Men, A Deficit of Peace: Security and Sex Ratios in Asia's Largest States," 26:4 (Spring 2002); Stefan Elbe, "HIV/AIDS and the Changing Landscape of War in Africa," 27:2 (Fall 2002); Sarah Kenyon Lischer, "Collateral Damage: Humanitarian Assistance as a Cause of Conflict," 28:1 (Summer 2003); Michael Mousseau, "Market Civilization and Its Clash with Terror," 27:3 (Winter 2002/03); Audrey Kurth Cronin, "Behind the Curve: Globalization and International Terrorism," 27:3 (Winter 2002/03); Alexander Cooley and James Ron, "The NGO Scramble: Organizational Insecurity and the Political Economy of Transnational Action," 27:1 (Summer 2002); P.W. Singer, "Corporate Warriors: The Rise of the Privatized Military Industry and Its Ramifications for International Security," 26:3 (Winter 2001/02).

Selection and preface, copyright © 2004 by the President and Fellows of Harvard College and of the Massachusetts Institute of Technology.

All rights reserved. No part of this book may be reproduced in any form or by any means, electronic or mechanical, including photocopying, recording, or by any information storage and retrieval system, without permission in writing from The MIT Press. For information, please visit www.mitpress.com or please contact The MIT Press, Journals Department, Five Cambridge Center, 4th Floor, Cambridge, Mass. 02142.

Library of Congress Cataloging-in-Publication Data

New global dangers : changing dimensions of international security / edited by Michael E.
  Brown . . . [et al.].
    p. cm.—(International security readers)
    "First published in International security"—T.p. verso.
    Includes bibliographical references.
    ISBN 0-262-52430-9 (pbk. : alk. paper)
    1. Security, International. 2. World politics—1989– I. Brown, Michael E. (Michael
  Edward), 1954– II. International security. III. Series.

JZ6005.N49 2004
355'—dc22

2004050494

Contents

The Contributors

MICHAEL E. BROWN is Editor of *International Security* and Director of the Security Studies Program and the Center for Peace and Security Studies at the Edmund A. Walsh School of Foreign Service, Georgetown University.

OWEN R. COTÉ JR. is Editor of *International Security* and Associate Director of the Security Studies Program at the Massachusetts Institute of Technology.

SEAN M. LYNN-JONES is Editor of *International Security* and a Research Associate at the Belfer Center for Science and International Affairs (BCSIA), John F. Kennedy School of Government, Harvard University.

STEVEN E. MILLER is Editor-in-Chief of *International Security* and Director of the International Security Program at BCSIA.

ALEXANDER COOLEY is Assistant Professor of Political Science at Barnard College.

AUDREY KURTH CRONIN is a Specialist in International Terrorism at the Foreign Affairs, Defense and Trade Division in the Congressional Research Service, Library of Congress.

ANDREA DEN BOER is Lecturer in International Relations and Director of the Master of Arts in Human Rights, Ethics and International Relations program at the University of Kent in England.

STEFAN ELBE is Lecturer in International Relations in the Politics and International Studies Department at the University of Warwick in England.

THOMAS F. HOMER-DIXON is Associate Professor of Political Science and Director of the Centre for the Study of Peace and Conflict at the University of Toronto.

VALERIE M. HUDSON is Professor of Political Science at the David M. Kennedy Center for International Studies, Brigham Young University.

GREGORY KOBLENTZ is a doctoral candidate in political science with the Security Studies Program at the Massachusetts Institute of Technology.

ARIEL E. LEVITE is Principal Deputy Director General (Policy) of the Israeli Atomic Energy Commission.

SARAH KENYON LISCHER is Assistant Professor of Government at Sweet Briar College.

DINSHAW MISTRY is Assistant Professor of Political Science at the University of Cincinnati.

MICHAEL MOUSSEAU is Associate Professor of International Relations at Koç University in Istanbul, Turkey.

ROLAND PARIS is Assistant Professor of Political Science and International Affairs at the University of Colorado at Boulder.

BARRY R. POSEN is Ford International Professor of Political Science at the Massachusetts Institute of Technology and a member of its Security Studies Program.

JAMES RON is Associate Professor and Canada Research Chair in Conflict and Human Rights at McGill University.

SCOTT D. SAGAN is Professor of Political Science and Co-Director of the Center for International Security and Cooperation at Stanford University.

P.W. SINGER is Director of the Project on U.S. Policy Towards the Islamic World and John M. Olin Post-Doctoral Fellow at The Brookings Institution.

JESSICA STERN is Lecturer in Public Policy at the John F. Kennedy School of Government, Harvard University.

SHARON K. WEINER is a Research Associate in the Program on Science and Global Security at the Woodrow Wilson School, Princeton University.

MYRON WEINER, prior to his death in 1999, was Ford International Professor of Political Science at the Massachusetts Institute of Technology.

Acknowledgments

The editors gratefully acknowledge the assistance that has made this book possible. A deep debt is owed to all those at the Belfer Center for Science and International Affairs (BCSIA), Harvard University, who have played an editorial role at *International Security*. We are grateful for support from the Carnegie Corporation of New York. Special thanks go to Diane McCree, Sarah Buckley, and Jennifer Cook at BCSIA for their invaluable help in preparing this volume for publication.

Preface | *Michael E. Brown*

$\mathbf{W}$hen the Cold War ended, it is no exaggeration to say that hopes and expectations about the prospects for peace soared.[1] One of the most moving statements about the possibilities of the post-Cold War era came from U.S. President George H.W. Bush. Addressing a joint session of the U.S. Congress on September 11, 1990, he outlined his vision of a "new world order." He foresaw the advent of "a new era—freer from the threat of terror, stronger in the pursuit of justice, and more secure in the quest for peace, an era in which the nations of the worlds, East and West, North and South, can prosper and live in harmony." Bush maintained that a "new partnership of nations has begun."[2]

The end of the Cold War had tremendously important, positive effects on international security. With the collapse of the Soviet empire in Eastern Europe and the disintegration of the Soviet Union, the Soviet military threat that had loomed over Western Europe for decades vanished. At the same time, the threat of an all-out nuclear war between the United States and the Soviet Union faded. Many of the regional conflicts that had been fueled by superpower patronage—in Cambodia, El Salvador, Mozambique, Namibia, and Nicaragua, for example—wound down and began to move toward settlements.

At the same time, hopes for a new and predominantly peaceful world—so widespread at the beginning of the 1990s—were dashed by the deadly conflicts that followed. The leading powers did not form a new partnership of nations and create "a new world order." International responses to war, slaughter, and starvation in Bosnia, Somalia, and other lethal troublespots were appallingly inadequate. Nowhere was this more tragic than in Rwanda, where an esti-

---

1. This section is based on Michael E. Brown, "Security Challenges in the Twenty-first Century," in Brown, ed., *Grave New World: Security Challenges in the 21st Century* (Washington, D.C.: Georgetown University Press, 2003), pp. 1–13.
2. George Bush, "Presidential Address: Gulf Crisis an Opportunity for a 'New World Order'," (transcript), *Congressional Quarterly Weekly Report*, Vol. 48, No. 37 (September 15, 1990), pp. 2953–2955. Many have wondered if the terrorist attacks that took place on September 11, 2001 were timed to coincide with the anniversary of a previous political event. At this juncture, no one outside of Al Qaeda appears to know for sure. That said, there are two reasons for speculating that President Bush's 1990 speech might have figured in al-Qaeda's calculations. First, Bush was calling for the creation of a "new world order" that would inevitably be dominated by the West and based on Western values; this would not sit well with those who believed that Islam was already under siege from the West. Second, Bush's speech was one of the milestones in his effort to rally U.S. and international support for a campaign to overturn Iraq's August 1990 invasion of Kuwait. This ultimately led to a massive American and Western military build-up in Saudi Arabia. Al-Qaeda claims to see this military presence—which remained after the Gulf War of 1991 ended—as an assault on Islam's holiest lands.

mated 800,000 people were killed in a genocidal slaughter that went on for 100 days in the spring and summer of 1994. The world watched on CNN.

Two things are clear about the prospects for national and international security in the 21st century. First, security problems will continue to be widespread and deadly. It would be naive and irresponsible to assume that current problems will simply go away or that new problems will be neutralized by the positive benefits of globalization. In the first 12 years of the post-Cold War era, 57 major armed conflicts took place in 45 different countries. In the first half of this period, the number of conflicts in any given year ranged from 28 to 33; since 1998, the number of conflicts has held steady at around 25 conflicts per year. It is estimated that 6 million people were killed in armed conflicts in the 1990s.[3] As of 2004, armed conflicts simmered, seethed, and raged in places as diverse as Afghanistan, Burma, China, Colombia, the Democratic Republic of the Congo, Haiti, India, Indonesia, Iraq, Israel, Ivory Coast, Liberia, Nepal, Nigeria, Pakistan, the Philippines, Russia, Somalia, Spain, Sri Lanka, Sudan, Uganda, and Zimbabwe.[4]

Second, the security agenda will be far more complex than it has been in the past. If we want to develop a thorough understanding of the dynamics of security problems in the contemporary world, we must examine the full range of military and non-military factors that influence these problems around the world. Although the use of military force and the causes and consequences of wars are central issues in security affairs, security is not *just* a military issue. The origins of most security problems are not limited to military developments, and the solutions to security problems are rarely limited to military actions. In addition, transnational actors are increasingly influential in international security affairs. Coming to a determination about the likely impact of these actors is an important challenge for scholars and policymakers alike. Security problems in the 21st century will be multidimensional, and they have to be studied in broad, inclusive terms.

The editors of this volume have organized the book with these considerations in mind. The first part of the book focuses on "Weapons and Security," including the strategic implications of U.S. military hegemony and the chang-

3. IISS, Conflict Database Project, November 2002.
4. See Mikael Eriksson, Margareta Sollenberg, and Peter Wallensteen, "Patterns of Major Armed Conflicts, 1990–2001," in Stockholm International Peace Research Institute (SIPRI), *SIPRI Yearbook 2002: Armaments, Disarmament, and International Security* (Oxford: Oxford University Press, 2002), pp. 63–76. A "major armed conflict" is usually defined as one in which at least 1,000 people have been killed.

ing dynamics and dangers of weapons proliferation. The second part examines "Nonmilitary Aspects of Security," including the debate over the focus and scope of the international security agenda, and the role of important nonmilitary factors such as environmental change and resource competitions, demographic developments such as migration and gender imbalances, the impact of HIV/AIDS on political and military instability, and the complex effects of humanitarian assistance. The third and final part of the book turns to "Transnational Actors and Security." It examines the roots and ramifications of contemporary international terrorism, the driving forces behind the actions of nongovernmental organizations, and the emergence of private military firms on the international security scene. This volume is comprised primarily of articles that were recently published in the journal *International Security*, but it also includes three seminal articles that were first published in the 1990s.

Weapons and Security

The first part of this volume focuses on military aspects of national and international security. It begins with an analysis of the sources and strategic implications of U.S. military hegemony. It then examines the driving forces behind and the security implications of nuclear weapons proliferation, the dangers posed by biological weapons, and the challenges associated with the control of ballistic missile proliferation.

In "Command of the Commons: The Military Foundations of U.S. Hegemony," Barry Posen develops an innovative argument about the sources, nature, limitations, and implications of U.S. military hegemony. One of the keys to U.S. military preeminence, he says, is the country's unprecedented "command of the commons—command of the sea, space, and air." Although command of the commons gives the United States tremendous strategic advantages, it does not mean that the United States will go unchallenged everywhere. Posen notes that adversaries will be able to fight U.S. forces with "some hope of success" in several contested zones. These are arenas—"on land, in the air at low altitudes, and at sea in the so-called littorals"—where geography, knowledge of the local terrain, strong political motivations, and access to weaponry will enable adversaries to mount stiff resistance to U.S. military actions.

Posen argues that the U.S. command of the commons and the persistence of contested zones have important implications for U.S. grand strategy: "Even before the September 11 terrorist attacks, the foreign policy debate had narrowed to a dispute between primacy and selective engagement, between a nationalist, unilateralist version of hegemony, and a liberal, multilateral version of hegemony. U.S. command of the commons provides an impressive foundation for selective engagement. It is not adequate for a policy of primacy." The Bush administration's embrace of primacy is problematic, Posen argues, because it causes unease among allies and "may cause others to ally against the United States." A policy of selective engagement, on the other hand, would be more effective and more sustainable because it would help to "make U.S. military power appear less threatening and more tolerable."

In "Why Do States Build Nuclear Weapons? Three Models in Search of a Bomb," Scott Sagan challenges the conventional wisdom about the driving forces behind state decisions to acquire nuclear weapons. Most scholars and policymakers believe that these nuclear decisions are driven purely by security considerations. Sagan argues that the reality is more complex: "Nuclear weapons, like other weapons, are more than tools of national security; they are political objects of considerable importance in domestic debates and internal bureaucratic struggles and can also serve as international normative symbols of modernity and identity." Security concerns, domestic and bureaucratic politics, and concerns about state status must all be taken into account on a case by case basis. Sagan supports these arguments by examining nuclear decisions in the Soviet Union, China, France, India, South Africa, and the Ukraine. Although important developments have taken place since this article's original publication in 1996/97—in particular, India's and Pakistan's 1998 nuclear tests—these cases studies stand the test of time.

Nuclear weapons decisions and nuclear proliferation dynamics have profound implications for regional and international security. Sagan's analysis therefore has powerful practical ramifications. If state decisions to acquire nuclear weapons are driven by a range of factors that varies from case to case, it follows that nonproliferation policies have to be subtle. Nonproliferation campaigns have to address security concerns where they exist, but they cannot be limited to security considerations. These campaigns, moreover, have to be tailored to the idiosyncrasies of the state in question; they cannot be applied in cookie-cutter fashion from case to case. This will require an elevated level of analytic sophistication that is often lacking in policy circles.

In "Never Say Never Again: Nuclear Reversal Revisited," Ariel Levite argues that scholarship on nuclear proliferation issues has failed to devote sufficient attention to nuclear reversal—"the phenomenon in which states embark on a path leading to nuclear weapons acquisition but subsequently reverse course." Levite estimates that "nearly twenty states have chosen the path of nuclear reversal since 1945." As a result, the "nightmare proliferation scenarios" of the 1960s have not materialized. She argues that "no overarching explanation for nuclear reversal" explains all of these nuclear decisions. That said, "Nuclear hedging appears to have played a critical role in facilitating nuclear reversal in practically every case under examination." Nuclear hedging, according to Levite, is a "strategy of maintaining, or at least appearing to maintain, a viable option for the relatively rapid acquisition of nuclear weapons." Nuclear hedging is a strategy "that may be adopted either during the process of developing a bomb or as part of a rollback process, as a way of retaining the option of restarting a nuclear weapons program that has been halted or reversed." Although nuclear hedging and nuclear reversal have generated numerous nonproliferation successes in recent decades, Levite is far from sanguine about the future. Recent developments in Asia and the Middle East are worrisome, and the nuclear nonproliferation regime is fragile.

Sharon Weiner analyzes the proliferation dangers posed by tens of thousands of Russian nuclear experts who are working in the deteriorating Russian nuclear establishment. In "Preventing Nuclear Entrepreneurship in Russia's Nuclear Cities," Weiner argues that Russia is "the most likely source of black-market nuclear skills and materials" for would-be proliferators. She observes, "The end of the Cold War, the disintegration of the Soviet Union, and the subsequent collapse of the Russian economy brought misery to many of these once-revered members of the Soviet elite." Over the course of the 1990s, "increasing numbers of Russian nuclear scientists, engineers, and technicians were confronted with deteriorating living conditions and the threat of job loss. Many were owed months of back wages by the Russian government." These conditions are not conducive to nuclear containment.

Weiner goes on to analyze U.S. and Russian policy responses to these problems. Although the U.S. Congress, the first Bush administration, and the Clinton administration launched several nonproliferation programs in the 1990s, these initiatives have been hampered by intermittent high level attention, bureaucratic infighting, and mounting Congressional criticism. Weiner concludes that these efforts have nonetheless "helped to stabilize Russia's nuclear-related workforce." She argues that, unfortunately, these programs have not received the funding they need due to limited and sporadic political support. If these critical nonproliferation initiatives are to be successful in the long run, Weiner recommends that the United States abandon its narrow focus on private sector job creation and broaden its efforts to include retirement subsidies and creative use of short-term research contracts.

Biological weapons are also paramount national and international security concerns. In "Pathogens as Weapons: The International Security Implications of Biological Warfare," Gregory Koblentz provides a systematic overview of the pathogen problem. He breaks new ground by analyzing the implications of biological weapons for proliferation, deterrence, civil-military relations, and threat assessments. His appraisals are alarming: "First, it is extremely difficult to prevent the spread of biological warfare capabilities to actors motivated by a desire to challenge the status quo. Second, biological weapons do not confer the deterrent benefits associated with nuclear weapons and pose special difficulties for states seeking to prevent their use. Third, the intense secrecy that shrouds biological warfare programs impedes civilian control over them. Fourth, states tend to have flawed assessments of the biological warfare capabilities and intentions of their opponents."

Koblentz concludes with a sobering assessment: "The global diffusion of dual-use biotechnology, combined with strong incentives for revisionist states and extremist terrorist groups to harness this technology for malevolent purposes, poses a severe challenge to international peace and security." To minimize these dangers, Koblentz suggests that the barrier to the acquisition of biological weapons be raised, the norm against the development and use of biological weapons be strengthened, intelligence efforts be intensified, and defenses against biological weapons be bolstered.

Jessica Stern argues that policymakers have to be especially careful in crafting policy responses when security threats are particularly horrifying and when risks are difficult to quantify. Biological weapons generate "dreaded risks," she explains, because they are "mysterious, unfamiliar, indiscriminate, uncontrollable, inequitable, and invisible." She adds: "The effects of these weapons are also difficult to predict and poorly understood by science. They are physically disgusting, a factor associated with moral aversion. The media tend to highlight terrorist incidents, heightening dread and panic still further." This generates a powerful impetus for action, but not necessarily well-crafted action.

In "Dreaded Risks and the Control of Biological Weapons," Stern explains how, under these circumstances, policymakers are more likely to embrace policy options with excessive, long-term dangers. The dynamic, she says, is that "We feel a gut-level fear and are prone to trying to eradicate the risk with little regard for the costs involved." She worries that poorly crafted U.S. bioterrorism legislation could restrict the dissemination of basic biomedical research findings and diminish the ability of researchers to work with some biological agents. This, in turn, could reduce U.S. preparedness for biological weapons attacks or for the dangers posed by infectious diseases. "It is likely" she concludes, "that the countervailing dangers introduced by these proposed remedies exceed their benefits." The cure, in other words, could be worse than the disease. The challenge, therefore, is "to ensure that the revulsion invoked by these weapons does not push us to take actions with unacceptable adverse effects on competing interests, including the promotion of legitimate research, civil liberties, and public health."

In the final chapter of this section, "Beyond the MTCR: Building a Comprehensive Regime to Contain Ballistic Missile Proliferation," Dinshaw Mistry examines the security problems posed by the proliferation of ballistic missiles and the status of multilateral arms control efforts in this area. He argues that international efforts to control ballistic missile proliferation, centered on the Missile Technology Control Regime (MTCR), have a mixed record. Although countries such as Argentina, Brazil, Egypt, Iraq, Libya, South Africa, South Korea, Syria, and Taiwan have scaled back their ambitions, India, Iran, Israel, North Korea, and Pakistan have launched medium-range missiles, and other states have expanded their missile programs.

Mistry goes on to make two predictions about the prospects for ballistic missile proliferation and the MTCR. First, he argues that "the MTCR can considerably delay, but ultimately will not prevent, regional powers from building arsenals of intermediate- and long-range missiles." Second, he expects that "if regional powers maintain their missile programs (and, more ominously, if they export their missiles to other states), missile proliferation may greatly increase. As a result, the MTCR's past gains could be reversed." There are some reasons for being hopeful, however. Mistry maintains that "five measures—space service initiatives, regional missile-free zones, global intermediate-range missile bans, flight-test bans, and verification mechanisms—are available to expand the regime and provide firmer institutional barriers against missile proliferation." He contends that these measures are feasible and that their implementation would lead to the development of a more effective ballistic missile nonproliferation regime. The future of the MTCR, therefore, is up in the air.

Nonmilitary Aspects of Security

The second part of the volume turns to nonmilitary aspects of security. Although the nonmilitary dimensions of security have always been important, they have received more attention from scholars and policymakers since the end of the Cold War. This section begins with an overview of the debate over the focus and scope of the security studies agenda. It then examines several critical nonmilitary aspects of security, including environmental factors and resource competitions, demographic factors such as migration and gender balances, the impact of HIV/AIDS, and the unintended consequences of humanitarian assistance.

The boundaries of the security studies field have been the subject of an intense debate since the end of the Cold War. Some scholars and policymakers believe that the security studies field should continue to focus primarily on the military dimensions of security, and that national and international security policy agendas should be framed in similar terms. Other scholars and policymakers believe that both the security studies field and security policy agendas should be broadened considerably. Among the latter are advocates of the "human security" framework.[5] Roland Paris provides a thoughtful and balanced overview of this debate and the human security approach in "Human Security: Paradigm Shift or Hot Air?"

Paris argues that, although the human security approach makes important contributions to our understanding of security issues, it remains problematic. One difficulty is the concept's lack of clarity: "Existing definitions of human security tend to be extraordinarily expansive and vague, encompassing everything from physical security to psychological well-being, which provides policy makers with little guidance in the prioritization of competing policy goals and academics with little sense of what, exactly, is to be studied." Paris argues that some backers of human security prefer to keep the term expansive and vague because artful ambiguity "holds together a jumbled coalition of 'middle power' states, development agencies, and NGOs—all of which seek to shift attention and resources away from conventional security issues and toward goals that have traditionally fallen under the rubric of international development." Although these are formidable limitations, Paris does not reject the human security approach. Rather, he goes on to develop an innovative framework that situates human security issues more precisely within the parameters of the broader security studies field.

It is often said and widely believed that environmental problems have important security implications. In a pathbreaking article first published in 1994, "Environmental Scarcities and Violent Conflict: Evidence from Cases," Thomas

---

5. For more on the debate over the focus and scope of the security studies field, see Michael E. Brown, "Security Problems and Security Policy in a Grave New World," in Brown, ed., *Grave New World*, pp. 305–327.

Homer-Dixon argues that some environmental problems are more likely to generate social instability and violent conflict than others: "Of the major environmental changes facing humankind, degradation and depletion of agricultural land, forests, water, and fish will contribute more to social turmoil in coming decades than will climate change or ozone depletion." He contends that scholars and policymakers in the developed world focus "undue attention" on climate change and ozone depletion even though "vast populations in the developing world are already suffering from shortages of good land, water, forests, and fish."

Eschewing simple, single-factor explanations, Homer-Dixon outlines the causal mechanism by which environmental problems can have security ramifications.[6] Population growth and development, reduced supplies of key resources due to degradation and depletion ("environmental change"), and unequal distribution of resources ("ecological marginalization" and "resource capture") combine to generate environmental scarcities. These scarcities can have an array of pernicious effects, including intrastate and interstate migrations, declines in economic productivity, mounting social tensions, and faltering political institutions. These instabilities can, in turn, cause violent conflict, with subnational or intrastate conflict being more likely than interstate conflict. To support these arguments, Homer-Dixon examines the linkages between environmental scarcities and violent conflict in Bangladesh, China, Haiti, India, Israel and the West Bank, Lesotho, Mauritania, Peru, the Philippines, Senegal, and South Africa. Although developments in these countries have continued to unfold since the article's initial publication, Homer-Dixon's analysis is still compelling.

Homer-Dixon expects that scarcity-driven conflicts "will probably jump sharply in the next decades as scarcities rapidly worsen in many parts of the world." He worries that countries subjected to chronic discontent will be more inclined to either fragment or become more authoritarian. Neither outcome is to be welcomed: fragmenting countries will generate external migrations, and authoritarian regimes may launch attacks against other countries to divert domestic attention away from internal problems. These outcomes, Homer-Dixon concludes, "could seriously disrupt international security."

In a seminal article originally published in 1992–93, "Security, Stability, and

---

6. For another sophisticated analysis of the linkages between environmental factors and security, see J.R. McNeill, "Environmental Change and Security," in Brown, ed., *Grave New World*, pp. 178–196.

International Migration," the late Myron Weiner argued that the traditional political economy approach to the study of migration was useful but incomplete. Although economic factors are important driving forces behind many international population movements, economic explanations leave out critical political and security considerations. Weiner argued that "international population movements are often impelled, encouraged, or prevented by governments or political forces for reasons that may have little to do with economic conditions." Weiner maintained that a broader analytic framework was needed, one that focused "on state policies toward emigration and immigration as shaped by concerns over internal stability and international security."

Weiner argued that migration and security issues were linked in a number of ways. Some governments "may force emigration as a means of achieving cultural homogeneity or asserting the dominance of one ethnic community over another. Such flows have a long and sordid world-wide history." In addition, some governments have employed forced emigration as a way of eliminating political dissidents and group enemies. Some governments have used forced emigration as a means of putting political pressure on neighboring states. Weiner identified several sets of conditions under which immigrants and refugees were most likely to generate stability and security problems. He observed, "Conflicts create refugees, but refugees can also create conflicts." This is especially likely when immigrants and refugees pose political risks to host countries, when they are perceived as threats to the cultural identities of host countries, and when they place great social or economic burdens on host countries. Weiner broke important new ground by explaining how migration and refugee problems are not just economic and humanitarian issues, they are political and security issues.

Other demographic factors also have important security implications. In "A Surplus of Men, A Deficit of Peace: Security and Sex Ratios in Asia's Largest States," Valerie Hudson and Andrea Den Boer analyze an issue that has been largely neglected by scholars and policymakers: the impact of gender inequality on security dynamics. Although "there is probably no society in which women do not experience some gender inequality," Hudson and Den Boer are interested primarily in countries with exaggerated gender inequality. These are laces where, "because of gender, one child is allowed to live while another is actively or passively killed." In virtually every case, gender selection is in favor of male infants. The result is that more than 100 million females are "missing" in Asia, an estimated 62 to 68 million in China and India alone. Hudson and Den Boer estimate that a corresponding "surplus" of males is emerging: 29 to 33 million in China, and 28 to 32 million in India.

These "surplus males" will generate a range of social, economic, and political problems. In developing countries such as China and India, these surplus males will probably come from the lowest socioeconomic classes, they will probably be unemployed or underemployed, and they will be "losers" in competitions for spouses and families. These "bare branches" will be more prone to vice, crime, and organized violence. To deal with these problems, governments will be more inclined to embrace authoritarianism, to send surplus males to remote regions of the country, to encourage emigration, or to engage these men in military adventures. Hudson and Den Boer recognize that these "bare branches" are not the sole causes of violence; they argue that these demographic trends will amplify existing social, economic, and political instabilities, and that these developments will have important intrastate and perhaps interstate security ramifications.

In "HIV/AIDS and the Changing Landscape of War in Africa," Stefan Elbe starts with several grim observations: "Since the discovery of AIDS more than two decades ago, 60 million people have been infected with HIV, the virus that causes AIDS, and more than 20 million people have died from AIDS-related illnesses." The HIV/AIDS pandemic has been particularly devastating in sub-Saharan Africa, where HIV infection rates have reached 20 to 30 percent of the adult population in some countries and where AIDS "is now the primary cause of death." In addition to its humanitarian and social implications, Elbe argues that HIV/AIDS is having mounting but heretofore neglected effects on "the nature and conduct of armed conflict in Africa."

Elbe notes that armed forces in Africa have become a high-risk group for the transmission of HIV/AIDS. Infection rates among many African military organizations are 2 to 5 times greater than for corresponding civilian populations. According to Elbe, this has "already begun to diminish the operational efficiency of many of Africa's armed forces." This, in turn, can weaken the ability of these organizations to maintain intrastate and regional stability. It also has implications for African participation in regional and international peacekeeping operations. In addition, HIV/AIDS is providing African military organizations with a new instrument of war. Although rape has often been widespread in time of war, the expansion of organized rape campaigns and the use of HIV/AIDS as a weapon against civilian populations have taken this to a horrifying new level. This has led to a significant increase in the number of AIDS-related war casualties. Elbe concludes that "the AIDS pandemic should be understood not only as a global health issue but an international security issue."

In the final chapter in this part of the book, Sarah Kenyon Lischer observes that, although many people think of humanitarian activities as purely benign, humanitarian assistance to refugees can exacerbate conflict. Transcending the debate between reflexive defenders and unrelenting critics of humanitarian assistance, she develops a sophisticated argument about the conditions under which humanitarian assistance is most likely to be problematic. In "Collateral Damage: Humanitarian Assistance as a Cause of Conflict," Lischer explains that two factors are key. First, much depends on the level of politicization or political cohesion of refugee groups: "A highly politicized group is more likely to view humanitarian aid as a resource with which to further its political and military goals." Second, she argues, "misuse of aid is likely when the receiving state is unwilling or unable to impose political order and demilitarize the refugees." Lischer goes on to explain that humanitarian assistance can make conflicts worse through four mechanisms: "Refugee relief can feed militants; sustain and protect the militants' supporters; contribute to the war economy; and provide legitimacy to combatants."

Lischer's analysis has important policy implications. Although humanitarian aid organizations generally see themselves and their actions as impartial, Lischer contends that "it is virtually impossible for material assistance to have a neutral effect in a conflict situation." Humanitarian organizations need to develop a more realistic understanding of the roles they play in armed conflicts. In difficult cases, they must call for external political and military intervention to improve security conditions on the ground, or they must accept the harsh imperative to reduce or withdraw humanitarian assistance. "In militarized refugee crises," she concludes, "purity of intention cannot prevent the spread of conflict."

Transnational Actors and Security

The third and final part of this volume examines the changing roles that transnational actors are playing in international security. Although transnational terrorist organizations top the list of policy concerns in the developed world, the complex roles played by nongovernmental organizations and private military organizations are increasingly important.

In "Market Civilization and Its Clash with Terror," Michael Mousseau argues that al-Qaeda and its associated groups represent the values and beliefs of a substantial number of people and that, if the United States and its allies are to win the war against international terrorism, they must develop a better appreciation of the values and beliefs of those who directly and indirectly provide support to terrorist organizations. Although some scholars point to poverty and inequalities in the developing world as important root causes of terrorism, Mousseau believes that the social and economic origins of terrorism are more complex. He argues that globalization is injecting the liberal values of market democracies into countries with clientalist and autocratic systems. The increasing interaction of market and clientalist values and processes is a combustible mix. Mousseau argues that it is "triggering intense antimarket resentment directed primarily against the epitome of market civilization: the United States."

Mousseau warns that, contrary to what many in the United States have come to believe about the appropriate policy responses to international terrorism, the United States and its allies cannot solve the problem merely by signaling their good policy intentions, promoting democracy, or providing more exposure to appealing Western values. The key is to address more fundamental issues: "To win the war against terrorism, the United States and other market democracies must remove the underlying cause of terror: the deeply imbedded market rage brought on by the forces of globalization. To do this, the market democracies have only one option: to boost developing countries out of the mire of social anarchy and into market development." This, of course, is easier said than done.

Audrey Kurth Cronin builds on many of these themes. In "Behind the Curve: Globalization and International Terrorism," she notes that there have been several distinct waves of modern terrorism, and that the most recent wave represents a two-level challenge: "the religious fanatics who are the terrorists and the far more politically motivated states, entities, and people who would support them because they feel powerless and left behind in a globalizing world." Globalization, she observes, "including Westernization, secularization, democratization, consumerism, and the growth of market capitalism, represents an onslaught to less privileged people in conservative cultures repelled by the fundamental changes that these forces are bringing—or angered by the distortions and uneven distributions of benefits that result." Cronin argues that contemporary terrorist organizations are also facilitated by globalization. The use of modern communications and information technologies such as the internet has greatly enhanced the organizational capacities of these actors, as well as their ability to solicit support from donors. Globalization has made it easier for terrorist organizations to operate across international borders. Even more ominously, globalization has made it easier for terrorist organizations to acquire information about nuclear, biological, chemical, and radiological weapons—and perhaps access to such weapons.

Cronin believes that a two-track strategy is needed to counter international terrorism. The first track should focus on direct military actions to attack terrorists and policy actions designed to enhance homeland security. The second track should emphasize nonmilitary instruments "such as intelligence, public diplomacy, cooperation with allies, international legal instruments, and economic assistance and sanctions" to address the grievances of the supporters of terrorism. Unfortunately, Cronin concludes, the United States has emphasized the first track and neglected the second. This is unlikely to lead to success over the long term.

In "The NGO Scramble: Organizational Insecurity and the Political Economy of Transnational Action," Alexander Cooley and James Ron argue that most assessments of nongovernmental organizations are too optimistic in projecting the emergence of a benign international civil society based on liberal norms and values. The problem, they contend, is that most scholars and policy analysts fail to take into account the powerful, pernicious institutional and economic pressures that drive nongovernmental organizations. Drawing on a political economy approach to these issues and several case studies, Cooley and Ron maintain that these institutional and economic imperatives subvert NGO objectives, prolong inappropriate projects, and promote destructive forms of organizational competition among otherwise well-meaning actors. The problem is not a lack of moral character within these organizations. Rather, "dysfunctional organization behavior is likely to be a rational response to systemic and predictable institutional pressures."

The long-term trends are not encouraging. Cooley and Ron believe that the rise in the number of nongovernmental organizations "increases uncertainty, competition, and insecurity" for every NGO operating in that sector. This challenges the prevailing liberal view that increasing levels of NGO activity will lead to an increasingly robust and inherently benign international civil society. Cooley and Ron see competition prevailing over cooperation. They also believe that the growing use of competitive tenders, renewable contracts, and other forms of marketization will do more harm than good. They conclude, "Once established, transnationals are organizations like any other. To survive in a competitive world, they must justify their existence to donors, secure new contracts, and fend off competitors." Although one might hope for the best, "these imperatives will produce dysfunctional results."

In the book's final chapter, P.W. Singer argues that privatized military firms "represent the newest addition to the modern battlefield, and their role in contemporary warfare is becoming increasingly significant." He analyzes the emergence and global spread of these firms, and the reasons behind this expansion. These reasons include massive disruptions in the supply and demand in military forces after the end of the Cold War, changes in the nature of modern warfare, and what Singer calls "the power of privatization and the privatization of power." The number of firms operating today is "in the high hundreds," but a rapid consolidation of the industry into larger transnational firms is under way. The services provided by these firms range from support activities to consulting and training to "tip of the spear" command and control and battlefield capabilities.

Singer argues in "Corporate Warriors: The Rise of the Privatized Military Industry and Its Ramifications for International Security" that these firms have three main sets of implications for international security. First, they introduce contractual matters into security situations. Second, they introduce market dynamics and disruptions into international security. And third, they introduce new military actors into policymaking processes. In the most extreme cases, privatized military forms could be used to circumvent legislative or parliamentary control over the use of force. Singer concludes that the rise of this new security actor "challenges one of the basic premises of the study of international security: that states possess a monopoly over the use of force and that the study of security can therefore be based on the principle that states constitute the sole unit of analysis. Outdated assumptions about the exclusive role of the state in the military sphere should be reexamined."

Singer provides a fitting note on which to end this introductory essay. Narrow assumptions about the focus and scope of international security studies should indeed be reconsidered. In compiling this volume, the Editors hope to broaden understanding of the growing array of military, nonmilitary, and transnational factors that is shaping the international security landscape in the 21st century.

Part I:
Weapons and Security

Command of the Commons

Barry R. Posen

The Military Foundation of U.S. Hegemony

Since the end of the Cold War, scholars, commentators, and practitioners of foreign policy have debated what structure of world power would follow the bipolar U.S.-Soviet competition, and what U.S. foreign policy would replace containment. Those who hypothesized a long "unipolar moment" of extraordinary U.S. relative power have proven more prescient than those who expected the relatively quick emergence of a multipolar world.[1] Those who recommended a policy of "primacy"—essentially hegemony—to consolidate, exploit, and expand the U.S. relative advantage have carried the day against those who argued for a more restrained U.S. foreign policy.[2] One can argue that the jury is still out, the

Barry R. Posen is Professor of Political Science at the Massachusetts Institute of Technology and a member of its Security Studies Program. During the past academic year, he was a Transatlantic Fellow of the German Marshall Fund of the United States.

The author would like to thank Robert Art, Owen Coté, Etienne de Durand, Harvey Sapolsky, and the anonymous reviewers for their comments on earlier drafts of this article. Previous versions were presented at the U.S. Naval War College Current Strategy Forum, the Weatherhead Center Talloires conference "The Future of U.S. Foreign Policy," the Institut Français des Relations Internationales, the Centre for Defence Studies at King's College, and the European University Institute. An earlier version of this article, entitled "La maîtrise des espaces, fondement de l'hégémonie des Etats-Unis," appears in the spring 2003 issue of *Politique étrangère*, pp. 41–56.

1. The most comprehensive analysis of the extraordinary relative power position of the United States is William C. Wohlforth, "The Stability of a Unipolar World," *International Security*, Vol. 24, No. 1 (Summer 1999), pp. 5–41.
2. Barry R. Posen and Andrew L. Ross, "Competing Visions of U.S. Grand Strategy," *International Security*, Vol. 21, No. 3 (Winter 1996/97), pp. 5–53, summarizes the initial phase of the post–Cold War U.S. grand strategy debate. In that article, we discussed a policy called "primacy," a then popular term in U.S. foreign policy discourse. Primacy is one type of hegemony. A distinction should be made between a description of the structure of world politics—that is, the distribution of power among states—and the policies of a particular nation-state. The United States has more power in the world than any other state, and by a substantial margin. Wohlforth, "The Stability of a Unipolar World." This has become clear over the last decade. Thus it is reasonable to describe the world as "unipolar." Though this much power sorely tempts a state to practice a hegemonic foreign and security policy—that is, to further expand and consolidate its power position and to organize the world according to its own preferences—this is not inevitable. In terms of its potential capabilities, the United States has been a great power for at least a century, but it has followed foreign policies of varying activism. The U.S. national security elite (Democratic and Republican) did, however, settle on a policy of hegemony sometime in the late 1990s. The people of the United States did not play a significant role in this decision, so questions remained about how much they would pay to support this policy. The attacks of September 11, 2001, and the subsequent war on terror, have provided an important foundation of domestic political support for a hegemonic foreign policy. Debates between Democrats and Republicans now focus on the modalities of hegemony—whether

"moment" will soon pass, and the policy of hegemony enabled by great power will be fleeting. But the evidence does not support such predictions. Unipolarity and U.S. hegemony will likely be around for some time, though observers do suggest that the United States could hasten its own slide from the pinnacle through indiscipline or hyperactivity.[3]

The new debate on U.S. grand strategy is essentially about which variant of a hegemonic strategy the United States should pursue. The strategy proposed by President George W. Bush is, in caricature, unilateral, nationalistic, and oriented largely around the U.S. advantage in physical power, especially military power.[4] This is "primacy" as it was originally conceived. The last years of Bill Clinton's administration saw the emergence of a strategy that also depended heavily on military power, but which was more multilateral and liberal, and more concerned with international legitimacy. It aimed to preserve the dominant U.S. global position, including its military position, which was understood to be an essential underpinning of global activism.[5] That strategy has recently been elaborated, formalized, and defended under the rubric of "selective engagement" by Robert Art.[6] Though this is too big an argument to settle

---

the United States should work through multilateral institutions to exercise and increase its power or work outside them.

3. Stephen G. Brooks and William C. Wohlforth, "American Primacy," *Foreign Affairs,* Vol. 81, No. 4 (July/August 2002), pp. 20–33.

4. To be fair, Bush's *National Security Strategy of the United States of America* contains many allusions to alliances, cooperation, liberal values, and economic and political development. Nevertheless, the oldest and most powerful U.S. allies—the Europeans—are hardly mentioned in the document. Even allowing for the need for stern language to mobilize public support for the war on terror, the document has a martial tone—and is strongly committed to a wide variety of proactive uses of force. Also, the document has a vaguely nationalist flavor: "The U.S. national security strategy will be based on a distinctly American internationalism that reflects the union of our values and our national interests." Perhaps to drive home this point, the document devotes an entire paragraph to disassociating the United States from the International Criminal Court. President George W. Bush, *The National Security Strategy of the United States of America* (Washington, D.C.: White House, September 20, 2002), p. 30.

5. Posen and Ross, "Competing Visions of U.S. Grand Strategy," pp. 44–50, dubbed this strategy "selective (but cooperative) primacy."

6. Robert J. Art, *A Grand Strategy for America* (Ithaca, N.Y.: Cornell University Press, 2003). In the mid-1990s, most proponents of selective engagement had in mind a less ambitious strategy than Art now proposes. Formerly, the criteria for selective engagement were clear: Does an international problem promise significantly to increase or decrease the odds of great power war? Now the purpose of the strategy is to retain U.S. alliances and presence in Europe, East Asia, and the Persian Gulf "to help mold the political, military, and economic configurations of these regions so as to make them more congenial to America's interests." Included in the goals of the strategy are protection of the United States from grand terror attack, stopping the proliferation of weapons of mass destruction (nuclear, chemical, and biological), preserving peace and stability in Eurasia, securing access to oil, maintaining international economic openness, spreading democracy, protecting human rights, and avoiding severe climate change. Art does propose priorities among these objectives. See ibid., chap. 7.

on the sole basis of a military analysis, the understanding of U.S. military power developed below suggests that selective engagement is likely to prove more sustainable than primacy.

One pillar of U.S. hegemony is the vast military power of the United States. A staple of the U.S. debate about the size of the post–Cold War defense budget is the observation that the United States spends more than virtually all of the world's other major military powers combined, most of which are U.S. allies.[7] Observers of the actual capabilities that this effort produces can focus on a favorite aspect of U.S. superiority to make the point that the United States sits comfortably atop the military food chain, and is likely to remain there. This article takes a slightly different approach. Below I argue that the United States enjoys command of the commons—command of the sea, space, and air. I discuss how command of the commons supports a hegemonic grand strategy. I explain why it seems implausible that a challenge to this command could arise in the near to medium term. Then I review the arenas of military action where adversaries continue to be able to fight U.S. forces with some hope of success— the "contested zones." I argue that in the near to medium term the United States will not be able to establish command in these arenas. The interrelationship between U.S. command of the commons and the persistence of the contested zones suggests that the United States can probably pursue a policy of selective engagement but not one of primacy.

I purposefully eschew discussing U.S. military power in light of the metrics of the current and previous administrations. The Clinton administration planned to be able to fight two nearly simultaneous major theater wars; the Bush administration's emerging, and even more demanding, metric is the "4-2-1" principle—that is, deter in four places, counterattack in two, and if necessary, go to the enemy's capital in one of the two.[8] These metrics obscure the foundations of U.S. military power—that is, all the difficult and expensive things that the United States does to create the conditions that permit it to even consider one, two, or four campaigns.[9]

---

7. According to the Center for Defense Information, the fiscal year 2003 budget request of $396 billion "is more than the combined spending of the next 25 nations." See www.cdi.org/issues/wme.

8. U.S. Department of Defense, *Quadrennial Defense Review Report* (Washington, D.C.: U.S. Department of Defense, September 30, 2001), pp. 20–21.

9. This article does not review three military theoretical terms that have absorbed much attention over the last decade: the revolution in military affairs, net-centric warfare, and military transformation. To do so would require a major digression. I am trying to build an understanding of the overall U.S. military position and its strategic implications on the basis of a small number of empirical observations about familiar categories of conventional military activity.

Command of the Commons

The U.S. military currently possesses command of the global commons. Command of the commons is analogous to command of the sea, or in Paul Kennedy's words, it is analogous to "naval mastery."[10] The "commons," in the case of the sea and space, are areas that belong to no one state and that provide access to much of the globe.[11] Airspace does technically belong to the countries below it, but there are few countries that can deny their airspace above 15,000 feet to U.S. warplanes. Command does not mean that other states cannot use the commons in peacetime. Nor does it mean that others cannot acquire military assets that can move through or even exploit them when unhindered by the United States. Command means that the United States gets vastly more military use out of the sea, space, and air than do others; that it can credibly threaten to deny their use to others; and that others would lose a military contest for the commons if they attempted to deny them to the United States. Having lost such a contest, they could not mount another effort for a very long time, and the United States would preserve, restore, and consolidate its hold after such a fight.[12]

Command of the commons is the key military enabler of the U.S. global power position. It allows the United States to exploit more fully other sources

---

10. Kennedy distinguishes "naval mastery" from temporary, local naval superiority, or local command of the sea. "By . . . the term 'naval mastery', however, there is meant here something stronger, more exclusive and wider-ranging; namely a situation in which a country has so developed its maritime strength that it is superior to any rival power, and that its predominance is or could be exerted far outside its home waters, with the result that it is extremely difficult for other, lesser states to undertake maritime operations or trade without at least its tacit consent. It does *not* necessarily imply a superiority over all other navies combined, nor does it mean that this country could not temporarily lose local command of the sea; but it does assume the possession of an overall maritime power such that small-scale defeats overseas would soon be reversed by the dispatch of naval forces sufficient to eradicate the enemy's challenge. Generally speaking, naval mastery is also taken to imply that the nation achieving it will usually be very favourably endowed with many fleet bases, a large merchant marine, considerable national wealth, etc., all of which indicates influence at a global rather than a purely regional level." Paul M. Kennedy, *The Rise and Fall of British Naval Mastery* (London: Macmillan, 1983, first published in 1976 by Allen Lane), p. 9 (emphasis added).
11. Alfred Thayer Mahan called the sea "a wide common." Ibid., p. 2.
12. As is the case with much analysis of conventional military issues, for the sake of analytic simplicity, I do not treat the implications of the proliferation of weapons of mass destruction. Insofar as the main accomplishment of weapons of mass destruction is to increase significantly the costs and risks of any hegemonic foreign policy, the proliferation of these weapons for U.S. grand strategy should be considered independently of a treatment of their narrow tactical military utility. That said, broadly speaking the limited diffusion of these kinds of weapons would likely make the contested zone even more contested before they affect command of the commons.

of power, including its own economic and military might as well as the economic and military might of its allies. Command of the commons also helps the United States to weaken its adversaries, by restricting their access to economic, military, and political assistance. Command of the commons has permitted the United States to wage war on short notice even where it has had little permanent military presence. This was true of the 1991 Persian Gulf War, the 1993 intervention in Somalia, and the 2001 action in Afghanistan.

Command of the commons provides the United States with more useful military potential for a hegemonic foreign policy than any other offshore power has ever had. When nineteenth-century Britain had command of the sea, its timely power projection capability ended at the maximum range of the Royal Navy's shipboard guns. The Royal Navy could deliver an army many places around the globe, but the army's journey inland was usually difficult and slow; without such a journey, Britain's ability to influence events was limited. As the nineteenth century unfolded, the industrialization of the continental powers, improvements in land transportation, and the development of coastal warfare technologies such as the torpedo and mine reduced the strategic leverage provided by command of the sea.[13]

The United States enjoys the same command of the sea that Britain once did, and it can also move large and heavy forces around the globe. But command of space allows the United States to see across the surface of the world's landmasses and to gather vast amounts of information. At least on the matter of medium-to-large-scale military developments, the United States can locate and identify military targets with considerable fidelity and communicate this information to offensive forces in a timely fashion. Air power, ashore and afloat, can reach targets deep inland; and with modern precision-guided weaponry, it can often hit and destroy those targets. U.S. forces can even more easily do great damage to a state's transportation and communications networks as well as economic infrastructure. When U.S. ground forces do venture inland, they do so against a weakened adversary; they also have decent intelligence, good maps, and remarkable knowledge of their own position from moment to moment. Moreover, they can call on a great reserve of responsive, accurate, air-delivered firepower, which permits the ground forces considerable freedom of action. Political, economic, and technological changes since the 1980s have thus partially reversed the rise of land power relative to sea power that

---

13. Ibid., chap. 7.

occurred in the late nineteenth century and helped to erode Britain's formal and informal empire.

THE SOURCES OF COMMAND

What are the sources of U.S. command of the commons? One obvious source is the general U.S. superiority in economic resources. According to the Central Intelligence Agency, the United States produces 23 percent of gross world product (GWP); it has more than twice as many resources under the control of a single political authority as either of the next two most potent economic powers— Japan with 7 percent of GWP and China with 10 percent.[14] With 3.5 percent of U.S. gross domestic product devoted to defense (nearly 1 percent of GWP), the U.S. military can undertake larger projects than any other military in the world. The specific weapons and platforms needed to secure and exploit command of the commons are expensive. They depend on a huge scientific and industrial base for their design and production. In 2001 the U.S. Department of Defense budgeted nearly as much money for military research and development as Germany and France together budgeted for their entire military efforts.[15] The military exploitation of information technology, a field where the U.S. military excels, is a key element. The systems needed to command the commons require significant skills in systems integration and the management of large-scale industrial projects, where the U.S. defense industry excels. The development of new weapons and tactics depends on decades of expensively accumulated technological and tactical experience embodied in the institutional memory of public and private military research and development organizations.[16] Finally, the military personnel needed to run these systems are among the most highly skilled and highly trained in the world. The barriers to entry to a state seeking the military capabilities to fight for the commons are very high.

14. I calculated these percentages from the country entries in Central Intelligence Agency, *The World Factbook, 2001* (Washington, D.C.: CIA, 2001). The purchasing power parity method used by the CIA creates an exaggerated impression of China's current economic and technological capability. Measured by currency exchange rates, the United States had 29.5 percent of gross world product in 1999, Japan had 14 percent, and China had only 3.4 percent. See "World Gross Domestic Product by Region," *International Energy Outlook, 2002*, Report DOE/EIA-0484 (Washington, D.C.: Energy Information Administration, 2002), Table A3, Appendix A.
15. International Institute for Strategic Studies, *The Military Balance, 2002–2003* (London: IISS, 2002), pp. 241, 252–253. My colleague Harvey Sapolsky called this to my attention.
16. Harvey M. Sapolsky, Eugene Gholz, and Allen Kaufman, "Security Lessons from the Cold War," *Foreign Affairs*, Vol. 78, No. 4 (July/August 1999), pp. 77–89.

COMMAND OF THE SEA

U.S. nuclear attack submarines (SSNs) are perhaps the key assets of U.S. open-ocean antisubmarine warfare (ASW) capability, which in turn is the key to maintaining command of the sea.[17] During the Cold War, the Soviet Union challenged U.S. command of the sea with its large force of SSNs. The U.S. Navy quietly won the "third battle of the Atlantic," though the Soviet successes in quieting their nuclear submarines in the 1980s would have necessitated another expensive and difficult round of technological competition had the Cold War not ended.[18] At more than $1 billion each (more than $2 billion each for the new U.S. SSN), modern nuclear submarines are prohibitively expensive for most states. Aside from the United States, Britain, China, France, and Russia are the only other countries that can build them, and China is scarcely able.[19] Several partially built nuclear attack submarines remained in Russian yards in the late 1990s, but no new ones have been laid down.[20] Perhaps 20–30 Russian nuclear attack submarines remain in service.[21] Currently, the U.S. Navy has 54 SSNs in service and 4 under construction. It plans to build roughly 2 new boats every three years. It also has a program to convert 4 Ohio-class Trident ballistic missile submarines into nonnuclear cruise missile–carrying submarines for land attack. The U.S. Navy also dominates the surface of the oceans, with 12 aircraft carriers (9 nuclear powered) capable of launching high-performance aircraft.[22] The Soviet Union was just building its first true aircraft carrier when its political system collapsed. Aside from France,

---

17. The actual wartime missions of SSNs in the canonical major regional contingencies—aside from lobbing a few conventional cruise missiles and collecting electronic intelligence close to shore—are murky at best.

18. Owen R. Coté Jr., *The Third Battle: Innovation in the U.S. Navy's Silent Cold War Struggle with Soviet Submarines* (Newport, R.I.: Naval War College, 2003), pp. 69–78.

19. Construction of a new Chinese nuclear attack submarine has been delayed many times, and one is not expected to be completed until 2005. France does not have a nuclear attack submarine under construction, but it has a program planned for the 2010s. Britain has ordered three new nuclear attack submarines, and one is currently under construction. See A.D. Baker III, "World Navies in Review," *Naval Institute Proceedings*, Vol. 128 (March 2002), pp. 33–36.

20. According to A.D. Baker III, "Submarine construction in Russia had all but halted by the fall of 1998." At the time, there were four incomplete Akula-class nuclear attack submarines and one incomplete new-design attack submarine in Russian yards. Baker, "World Navies in Review," *Naval Institute Proceedings*, Vol. 125 (March 1999), pp. 3–4. See also Baker, "World Navies in Review," March 2002, pp. 35–36. One of the Akulas was finally commissioned at the end of 2001. One more may yet be completed.

21. IISS, *Military Balance, 2002–2003*, p. 113, suggests 22. Baker, "World Navies," (March, 2002), suggests about 30. I count Oscar-class cruise missile submarines as attack submarines.

22. For figures on the U.S. Navy and Marine Corps, see IISS, *Military Balance, 2002–2003*, pp. 18–21.

which has 1, no other country has any nuclear-powered aircraft carriers. At $5 billion apiece for a single U.S. Nimitz-class nuclear–powered aircraft carrier, this is no surprise.[23] Moreover, the U.S. Navy operates for the Marine Corps a fleet of a dozen large helicopter/VSTOL carriers, each almost twice the size of the Royal Navy's comparable (3 ship) Invincible class. To protect its aircraft carriers and amphibious assets, the U.S. Navy has commissioned 37 Arleigh Burke–class destroyers since 1991—billion-dollar multimission platforms capable of antiair, antisubmarine, and land-attack missions in high-threat environments.[24] This vessel is surely the most capable surface combatant in the world.

COMMAND OF SPACE

Though the United States is not yet committed to actual combat in or from space, it spends vast amounts on reconnaissance, navigation, and communications satellites.[25] These satellites provide a standing infrastructure to conduct military operations around the globe. According to Gen. Michael Ryan, the chief of staff of the U.S. Air Force, the United States had 100 military satellites and 150 commercial satellites in space in 2001, nearly half of all the active satellites in space.[26] According to Air Force Lt. Gen. T. Michael Moseley, air component commander in the U.S.-led invasion of Iraq in March 2003, more than 50 satellites supported land, sea, and air operations in every aspect of the campaign.[27] Secretary of Defense Donald Rumsfeld plans to emphasize the military exploitation of space, and has set the military the mission of "space

23. For costs of current U.S. warships, see Office of the Comptroller, U.S. Department of Defense, "Shipbuilding and Conversion," *National Defense Budget Estimates for the Amended FY 2002 Budget (Green Book), Procurement Programs (P1)*, pp. N. 17–18.
24. See http://www.globalsecurity.org/military/systems/ship/ddg-51-unit.htm.
25. The Pentagon has been hinting for some time that it would like to put weapons into space both for antisatellite attacks and for attacks on terrestrial targets. Many independent space policy analysts oppose this because the United States gets more out of space than any other state. They acknowledge that this makes U.S. space assets an attractive target, but they argue that hardening satellites, ground stations, and the links between them makes more sense than starting an expensive arms competition in space. Implicitly, they also rely on deterrence—the superior ability of the U.S. military to damage the other side's ground stations, links, and missile launch facilities, as well as to retaliate with nascent U.S. antisatellite systems against the other side's satellites. See, for example, Theresa Hitchens, *Weapons in Space: Silver Bullet or Russian Roulette* (Washington, D.C.: Center for Defense Information, April 19, 2002); Michael Krepon with Christopher Clary, *Space Assurance or Space Dominance? The Case against Weaponizing Space* (Washington, D.C.: Henry L. Stimson Center, 2003), chap. 3; and Charles V. Pena and Edward L. Hudgins, *Should the United States "Weaponize" Space?* Policy Analysis No. 427 (Washington D.C.: Cato Institute, March 18, 2002), pp. 5–10.
26. Vernon Loeb, "Air Force's Chief Backs Space Arms," *Washington Post*, August 2, 2001, p. 17.
27. Jim Garamone, "Coalition Air Forces Make Ground Gains Possible," American Forces Press Service, April 5, 2003, http://www.defenselink.mil/news/APR2003/n04052003_200304053.html.

control."[28] For fiscal years 2002–07, the Pentagon plans to spend $165 billion on space-related activities.[29]

Other states can and do use space for military and civilian purposes. Though there is concern that some commercial satellites have military utility for reconnaissance and communications, many belong to U.S. companies or U.S. allies, and full exploitation of their capabilities by U.S. enemies can be severely disrupted.[30] The NAVSTAR/GPS (global positioning system) constellation of satellites, designed and operated by the U.S. military but now widely utilized for civilian purposes, permits highly precise navigation and weapons guidance anywhere in the world. Full exploitation of GPS by other military and civilian users is permitted electronically by the United States, but this permission is also electronically revocable.[31] It will not be easy for others to produce a comparable system, though the European Union intends to try. GPS cost $4.2 billion (in 1979 prices) to bring to completion, significantly more money than was originally projected.[32]

---

28. According to the 2001 *Quadrennial Defense Review Report*, "The ability of the United States to access and utilize space is a vital national security interest." Moreover, "the mission of space control is to ensure the freedom of action in space for the United States and its allies and, when directed, to deny such freedom of action to adversaries." According to the report, "Ensuring freedom of access to space and protecting U.S. national security interests are key priorities that must be reflected in future investment decisions." Ibid., p. 45

29. General Accounting Office, *Military Space Operations: Planning, Funding, and Acquisition Challenges Facing Efforts to Strengthen Space Control*, GAO-02–738 (Washington, D.C.: GAO, September 2002), p. 3. It appears that U.S. military spending on space has nearly doubled since 1998, when it was estimated at $14 billion. See John Pike, "American Control of Outer Space in the Third Millennium," November 1998, http://www.fas.org/spp/eprint/space9811.htm.

30. Pike, "American Control of Outer Space."

31. The United States formerly corrupted the GPS satellite signals to reduce the accuracy that a nonmilitary user terminal could achieve. On May 1, 2000, President Clinton ended this policy due to the vast commercial possibilities of highly accurate positional information. At that time, the U.S. government believed that it could employ new techniques to jam the GPS signals regionally in a way that would prevent an adversary from exploiting them, but not dilute the accuracy elsewhere. See President Bill Clinton: "Improving the Civilian Global Positioning System (GPS)," May 1, 2000, http://www.ngs.noaa.gov/FGCS/info/sans_SA/docs/statement.html.

32. This is the cost of the development and deployment of the system, and the acquisition of sufficient satellites (118), to achieve and sustain a 24-satellite array. By 1997, $3 billion had been spent on "user equipment," the military terminals that calculate location on the basis of the satellites' signals. See U.S. Department of Defense, "Systems Acquisition Review Program Acquisition Cost Summary as of June 30, 1997." See also General Accounting Office, *Navstar Should Improve the Effectiveness of Military Missions—Cost Has Increased*, PSAD-80–91 (Washington, D.C.: GAO, February 15, 1980), p. 14. The European Union has decided to produce a competing system to GPS, called Galileo. It is estimated that 3 billion euros will be required to buy and operate 30 satellites. European advocates of Galileo explicitly argue that Europe must have its own satellite navigation systems or lose its "autonomy in defense." See Dee Ann Divis, "Military Role for Galileo Emerges," *GPS World*, Vol. 13, No. 5 (May 2002), p. 10.

The dependence of the United States on satellites to project its conventional military power does make the satellites an attractive target for future U.S. adversaries.[33] But all satellites are not equally vulnerable; low earth orbit satellites seem more vulnerable to more types of attack than do high earth orbit satellites.[34] Many of the tactics that a weaker competitor might use against the United States would probably not be usable more than once—use of space mines, for example, or so-called microsatellites as long-duration orbital interceptors. The U.S. military does have some insurance against the loss of satellite capabilities in its fleet of reconnaissance aircraft and unmanned aerial vehicles. A challenge by another country could do some damage to U.S. satellite capabilities and complicate military operations for some time. The United States would then need to put a new generation of more resilient satellites in orbit. One estimate suggests that the exploitation of almost every known method to enhance satellite survivability would roughly double the unit cost.[35]

The United States has had a number of antisatellite research and development programs under way for many years, and some are said to have produced experimental devices that have military utility.[36] The planned U.S. ballistic missile defense system will also have some antisatellite capability. U.S. conventional military capabilities for precision attack, even without the support of its full panoply of space assets, are not trivial. It is quite likely that an opponent's own satellites, and its ground stations and bases for attacking U.S. satellites, would quickly come under sustained attack. The most plausible outcome of a war over space is that the United States would, after a period of difficulty, rebuild its space assets. The fight would not only leave the adversary devoid of space capability, but would also cause the United States to insist on the permanent antisatellite disarmament of the challenger, which it would try to enforce. Finally, the United States would probably assert some special interest in policing space.

---

33. Tom Wilson, Space Commission staff member, "Threats to United States Space Capabilities," prepared for the *Report of the Commission to Assess United States National Security Space Management and Organization* (Washington, D.C.: Government Printing Office [GPO], January 11, 2001). Secretary of Defense Donald Rumsfeld chaired this commission.
34. A technically competent country with limited resources may be able to develop a capability to damage or destroy U.S. reconnaissance satellites in low earth orbit. See Allen Thomson, "Satellite Vulnerability: A Post–Cold War Issue," *Space Policy*, Vol. 11, No. 1 (February 1995), pp. 19–30.
35. This is based on my simple addition of the maximum estimated cost increases associated with hardening satellites, providing them the capability for autonomous operations, giving them some onboard attack reporting capability, making them maneuverable, supplying them with decoys, and providing them with some self defense capability. See Wilson, "Threats to United States Space Capabilities," p. 6.
36. Pike, "American Control of Outer Space in the Third Millennium."

COMMAND OF THE AIR

An electronic flying circus of specialized attack, jamming, and electronic intelligence aircraft allows the U.S military to achieve the "suppression of enemy air defenses" (SEAD); limit the effectiveness of enemy radars, surface-to-air missiles (SAMs) and fighters; and achieve the relatively safe exploitation of enemy skies above 15,000 feet.[37] Cheap and simple air defense weapons, such as antiaircraft guns and shoulder-fired lightweight SAMs, are largely ineffective at these altitudes. Yet at these altitudes aircraft can deliver precision-guided munitions with great accuracy and lethality, if targets have been properly located and identified. The ability of the U.S. military to satisfy these latter two conditions varies with the nature of the targets, the operational circumstances, and the available reconnaissance and command and control assets (as discussed below), so precision-guided munitions are not a solution to every problem. The United States has devoted increasing effort to modern aerial reconnaissance capabilities, including both aircraft and drones, which have improved the military's ability in particular to employ air power against ground forces, but these assets still do not provide perfect, instantaneous information.[38] Confidence in the quality of their intelligence, and the lethality and responsiveness of their air power, permitted U.S. commanders to dispatch relatively small numbers of ground forces deep into Iraq in the early days of the 2003 war, without much concern for counterattacks by large Iraqi army units.[39]

The U.S. military maintains a vast stockpile of precision-guided munitions and is adding to it. As of 1995, the Pentagon had purchased nearly 120,000 air-launched precision-guided weapons for land and naval attack at a cost of $18 billion.[40] Some 20,000 of these weapons were high-speed antiradiation missiles

---

37. Barry R. Posen, *Inadvertent Escalation: Conventional War and Nuclear Risks* (Ithaca, N.Y.: Cornell University Press, 1992), pp. 51–55. For a detailed description of a suppression operation, see Barry D. Watts and Thomas A. Keaney, *Effects and Effectiveness: Gulf War Air Power Survey*, Vol. 2, Pt. 2 (Washington, D.C.: GPO, 1993), pp. 130–145.
38. During Desert Storm, the United States employed one experimental JSTARS (joint surveillance target attack radar system) aircraft, a late Cold War project to develop an airborne surveillance radar capable of tracking the movements of large enemy ground forces at ranges of hundreds of kilometers. The U.S. Air Force has 15 such aircraft. Similarly, U.S. forces employed few if any reconnaissance drones in Desert Storm; the U.S. Air Force now operates both high- and low-altitude reconnaissance drones. Under the right conditions, drones allow U.S. forces to get a close and persistent look at enemy ground forces. For current U.S. Air Force holdings, see IISS, *Military Balance, 2002–2003*, pp. 22–23.
39. Lt. Gen. James Conway, U.S. Marine Corps, "First Marine Expeditionary Force Commander Live Briefing from Iraq," May 30, 2003, U.S. Department of Defense news transcript, http://www.defenselink.mil/transcripts/2003/tr20030530-0229.html.
40. General Accounting Office, *Weapons Acquisition: Precision-Guided Munitions in Inventory, Production, and Development*, GAO/NSIAD-95-95 (Washington, D.C.: GAO, June 1995), p. 12.

(HARMs), designed to home in on the radar emissions of ground-based SAM systems, a key weapon for the SEAD campaign. Thousands of these bombs and missiles were launched in Kosovo, Afghanistan, and Iraq, but tens of thousands more have been ordered.[41]

The capability for precision attack at great range gives the United States an ability to do significant damage to the infrastructure and the forces of an adversary, while that adversary can do little to harm U.S. forces.[42] Air power alone may not be able to determine the outcome of all wars, but it is a very significant asset. Moreover, U.S. air power has proven particularly devastating to mechanized ground forces operating offensively, as was discovered in the only Iraqi mechanized offensive in Desert Storm, the battle of al-Khafji, in which coalition air forces pummeled three advancing Iraqi divisions.[43] The United States can provide unparalleled assistance to any state that fears a conventional invasion, making it a very valuable ally.

THE INFRASTRUCTURE OF COMMAND

Two important Cold War legacies contribute to U.S. command of the commons—bases and command structure. Though the United States has reduced the number of its forces stationed abroad since the Cold War ended, and has abandoned bases in some places (such as Panama and the Philippines), on the whole the U.S. Cold War base structure remains intact.[44] Expansion of the

---

41. The U.S. military says that it needs 200,000 GPS satellite-guided bombs, the joint direct attack munition or JDAM—7,000 of which were used in the Afghan War. Six thousand five hundred JDAMs were used in the Iraq war. See Lt. Gen. T. Michael Moseley, commander, United States Central Command Air Forces, "Operation Iraqi Freedom—By the Numbers," Assessment and Analysis Division, USCENTAF, April 30, 2003, p. 3, http://www.iraqcrisis.co.uk/downloads/resources/uscentaf_oif_report_30apr2003.pdf. Boeing is producing this weapon at the rate of 2,000 per month, and the military wants to increase production to 2,800 per month. See Nick Cook, "Second-Source JDAM Production Line Moves Closer," *Jane's Defense Weekly*, October 16, 2002, p. 5.
42. Daryl G. Press, "The Myth of Air Power in the Persian Gulf War and the Future of Warfare," *International Security*, Vol. 26, No. 2 (Fall 2001), pp. 5–44, carefully and convincingly demonstrates that despite weeks of bombing, Iraqi mechanized ground forces in Kuwait and southern Iraq were still largely intact when the United States opened its ground attack. Perhaps 40 percent of Iraqi fighting vehicles were destroyed or immobilized by the air campaign, prior to the start of ground operations. Nevertheless, once the coalition ground operation began, Iraqi mechanized units managed to maneuver in the desert, in spite of U.S. command of the air. They did not suffer much damage from U.S. fixed-wing air attacks during the ground campaign. These forces were destroyed or enveloped by U.S. and allied mechanized ground forces. It should be noted, however, that army and marine attack helicopters destroyed much Iraqi armor.
43. Ibid., p. 12; and Michael R. Gordon and Bernard E. Trainor, *The Generals' War: The Inside Story of the Conflict in the Gulf* (Boston: Little, Brown, 1995), pp. 267–288.
44. The United States currently has military installations in three dozen foreign countries or special territories. See Office of the Deputy Undersecretary of Defense (Installations and Environ-

North Atlantic Treaty Organization has given the United States access to additional bases in eastern and southern Europe. These bases provide important stepping-stones around the world. The Pentagon has also improved the U.S. military's access in key regions. After the 1991 Gulf War, the United States developed a network of air base, port, and command and control facilities throughout the Persian Gulf, and cycled troops and aircraft through these bases. This base structure allowed the United States to attack Iraq successfully in 2003, despite the unwillingness of long-time NATO ally Turkey to permit the use of its territory to add a northern thrust to the effort. Though U.S. leaders were disappointed by Turkey's stance, it is noteworthy that sufficient bases were available in any case. After September 11, 2001, the U.S. government negotiated access to former Soviet air bases in the now independent states of Kyrgyzstan, Tajikistan, and Uzbekistan.[45]

The U.S. military has taken a number of other steps to improve its ability to send large forces across great distances. Munitions, support equipment, and combat equipment are prepositioned around the world, ashore and afloat. For example, the equivalent of 3 1/3 divisions' (10 brigades') worth of army and marine equipment was prepositioned at key spots in Asia, Europe, and the Persian Gulf during the 1990s. Perhaps 5 brigades of this equipment were employed in March 2003. In a crisis, troops fly to designated airfield-port combinations to marry up with this equipment. Since 1991 the United States has built

ment), Department of Defense, "Summary," *Base Structure Report (A Summary of DoD's Real Property Inventory), Fiscal Year 2002 Baseline,* http://www.defenselink.mil/news/Jun2002/basestructure2002.pdf.This report counts only installations in which the United States has actually invested federal dollars. Missing from the list are Kuwait and Saudi Arabia, so a peculiar definition of U.S. base must guide the report. Unfortunately, comparable time series data do not exist to permit comparison to the last days of the Cold War. Secretary of Defense William S. Cohen noted in 1997 that although the DoD had reduced active-duty military forces by 32 percent, it had reduced its domestic and overseas base structure by only 26 percent. See Secretary of Defense William S. Cohen, *Report of the Quadrennial Defense Review* (Washington, D.C.: Department of Defense, May 1997). The vast majority of overseas installations that were either reduced or closed, 878 out of 952, were in Europe. See Department of Defense, "Additional U.S. Overseas Bases to End Operations," Department of Defense, news release, April 27, 1995. From 1988 to 1997, the number of U.S. troops stationed abroad (on land) dropped from 480,000 to 210,000; 80 percent of the reduction came in Europe. See Secretary of Defense William S. Cohen, *Annual Report to the President and the Congress, 2000* (Washington, D.C.: Department of Defense, 2000), Appendix C, p. C-2.
45. Other post–Cold War allies offering overflight, port, or actual basing contributions to the war on terrorism include, among others, Albania, Bulgaria, the Czech Republic, Djibouti, Estonia, Ethiopia, Latvia, Lithuania, Pakistan, and Slovakia. See U.S. Department of Defense, *International Contributions to the War against Terrorism,* fact sheet, June 7, 2002. See also William M. Arkin, "Military Bases Boost Capability but Fuel Anger," *Los Angeles Times,* January 6, 2002, p. A-1, noting that U.S. military personnel were working at thirteen new locations in nine countries in support of the war on terror.

a fleet of 20 large, medium-speed, roll-on/roll-off military transport ships, to facilitate the movement of military matériel. Each ship can carry nearly 1,000 military vehicles and can off load this equipment at austere ports, if necessary.[46] These ships were extensively employed in the mobilization for the war to topple the Iraqi Ba'ath regime. Similarly, the United States has modernized its fleet of long-range airlift aircraft; 90 C17s of 180 on order have been delivered.[47] These aircraft are capable of carrying tank-sized cargo into relatively mediocre airfields. They in turn are supported by a fleet of aerial tankers. Finally, it is easy to forget that since World War II the U.S. Marine Corps has specialized in putting large ground and air forces ashore against opposition. The Marine Corps alone has as many personnel as the combined land and air forces of the United Kingdom, and the U.S. Navy operates almost 40 special-purpose combat ships for amphibious operations, roughly the same number of major surface combatants as the entire Royal Navy.[48]

Finally, all this capability is tied together by a seldom-mentioned Cold War legacy: the Unified Command Plan through which the U.S. military organizes the entire world for war. The U.S. military divides the world into both functional and regional commands. In most cases, the regional command elements are based in the theaters in which they would fight. PACOM is based in Hawaii and oversees U.S. forces in the Pacific. EUCOM, based in Europe, manages U.S. forces committed to NATO. CENTCOM oversees the Persian Gulf and Indian Ocean, but does so formally from Florida. Also in Florida, SOUTH-COM oversees Central and South America. These commands are each led by a four-star commander in chief (formerly referred to as a "CinC," pronounced "sink," they are now called "combatant commanders"). These are large multifunction military headquarters, to which are often attached significant operational forces. They engage in military diplomacy among the countries in

---

46. Military Sealift Command, U.S. Navy, fact sheet, "Large, Medium-Speed, Roll-on/Roll-off Ships (LMSRs)," October 2002. Thirty-three ships of various types, including 9 of the LMSRs, are employed to preposition equipment, ammunition, and fuel. See also Military Sealift Command, U.S. Navy, fact sheet, "Afloat Prepositioning Force," April 2003. A total of 87 dry cargo ships of various kinds, including 11 LMSRs and many other roll-on roll-off ships are based in the United States.

47. "Boeing and U.S. Air Force Sign $9.7 Billion C-17 Contract," news release, Boeing Corporation, August 15, 2002, http://www.boeing.com/news/releases/2002/q3/nr_020815m.html. This follow-on procurement contract added 60 C-17 Globemaster III transport aircraft to the 120 already on order.

48. IISS, *The Military Balance, 2002–2003*, pp. 18–21, 60–63. It is worth noting that Britain and France are the only two countries in the world, aside from the United States, with any global power projection capability.

their command and arrange joint exercises. They integrate the products of U.S. command of space, with the permissive conditions of command of the air and sea, to develop responsive war plans that can generate significant combat power in the far corners of the world on relatively short notice. That the geographical commands were barely touched by the passing of the Cold War is mute testimony to the quiet consensus among the foreign and security policy elite that emerged soon after the passing of the Soviet Union: The United States would hold on to its accidental hegemony.[49]

MAINTAINING COMMAND

U.S. command of the commons is the result of a Cold War legacy of both capabilities and bases, married to the disparity in overall economic power between the United States and its potential challengers. This disparity permits the United States to sustain a level of defense expenditure that dwarfs the spending of any of the world's other consequential powers. If grand strategists wish to pursue an activist global foreign policy, then they must preserve command of the commons. What then must the United States do? In the very long term, if a country comes to rival the United States in economic and technological capacity, it will be difficult to prevent a challenge, though it may be possible to out-compete the challenger. But in the short and medium terms, a successful challenge can be made highly impractical. In the short term, there is not much any other country can do to challenge the United States. In the medium term, through careful attention and resource allocation, the United States should be able to stay comfortably ahead of possible challengers. Indeed some of the more grandiose aspirations of the Pentagon may be realized: Pentagon documents in the early 1990s talked about deterring any effort to build a capability to challenge the United States.[50] The first full statement of the grand strategy of

---

49. Ronald H. Cole, Walter S. Poole, James F. Schnabel, Robert J. Watson, and Willard J. Webb, *The History of the Unified Command Plan, 1946–1993* (Washington, D.C.: Joint History Office, Office of the Chairman of the Joint Chiefs of Staff, 1995), http://www.dtic.mil/doctrine/jel/history/ucp.pdf; see especially pp. 107–117.
50. George H.W. Bush's administration reportedly issued draft defense planning guidance to the Pentagon in March 1992 with this objective. "Excerpts from Pentagon's Plan: 'Prevent the Emergence of a New Rival,'" *New York Times*, March 8, 1992, p. 14. For reportage, see Patrick E. Tyler, "U.S. Strategy Plan Calls for Insuring No Rivals Develop," *New York Times*, March 8, 1992, pp. 1, 14; and Barton Gellman, "The U.S. Aims to Remain First among Equals," *Washington Post National Weekly Edition*, March 16–22, 1992, p. 19. For examples of contemporary commentary, see Leslie Gelb, "They're Kidding," *New York Times*, March 9, 1992, p. A17; James Chace, "The Pentagon's Superpower Fantasy," *New York Times*, March 16, 1992, p. 17; and Charles Krauthammer, "What's Wrong with the 'Pentagon Paper'?" *Washington Post*, March 13, 1992, p. A25.

the administration of George W. Bush also declares, "Our forces will be strong enough to dissuade potential adversaries from pursuing a military build-up in hopes of surpassing, or equaling, the power of the United States."[51] This objective goes well beyond the traditional U.S. goal of deterring attacks. Yet it may be possible to create barriers to entry into the global military power club that are so high as to seem insurmountable.

MAINTAINING COMMAND AT SEA

Though the United States does not face a significant naval challenge to its supremacy in the open ocean, it should nevertheless preserve a scientific and technical capability to resume a sustained, large-scale, open-ocean anti-submarine warfare contest. Similarly, though the United States may not need the numbers of SSNs that it had during the Cold War, or even that it has today, it must nevertheless remain on the cutting edge of SSN design and production.

MAINTAINING COMMAND IN SPACE

In space, the United States has a more complicated political-military task. It benefits from the fact that those states capable of space activities have eschewed putting weapons in space. The United States has made the same decision, on the assumption that if it did, so would others. Ultimately the United States has more to lose than to gain from such a competition. The military does need to work aggressively on techniques to harden, hide, and maneuver satellites in case an adversary does try to interfere. An ability quickly to reconstitute some space capabilities should also be maintained, as should alternative reconnaissance means—aircraft and drones. The United States should also maintain some counteroffensive capabilities for purposes of deterrence and defense. The United States can leverage its long-range conventional attack capabilities to deny others the free use of space if they attack U.S. assets, and to reduce their offensive capabilities—mainly through direct and electronic attacks on an adversary's space launch, ground control, and tracking facilities. The United States should also maintain some antisatellite weapons research and development programs.

---

51. Bush, *The National Security Strategy of the United States of America*, p. 30. Accoding to the 2001 *Report of the Quadrennial Defense Review*, p. 12, "Well targeted strategy and policy can therefore dissuade other countries from initiating future military competitions"; see also ibid., p. 36.

MAINTAINING COMMAND OF THE AIR

Perhaps the most contested element of U.S. command of the commons is command of the air. Here, the air force buys weapons as if the principal challenge is adversary fighter aircraft. The U.S. Air Force, Navy, and Marine advantage in air-to-air combat is nearly overwhelming, however. It will be easier for others to challenge U.S. access above 15,000 feet with ground-based surface-to-air missiles of advanced design. The late–Cold War Soviet designs, and their follow-on systems, the so-called double-digit SAMs (with the SA-10 the best known and most lethal system) can offer real resistance to the U.S. military.[52] Fortunately for the United States, these systems are expensive, and Russian manufacturers sell only to those who can pay cash. China has purchased a significant number from Russia, and other countries will likely follow.[53] U.S. SEAD capabilities do not seem to be keeping up with this threat, much less staying ahead of it. The Pentagon needs to put more effort into SEAD if it hopes to retain command of the air.

Command of the commons is the military foundation of U.S. political preeminence. It is the key enabler of the hegemonic foreign policy that the United States has pursued since the end of the Cold War. The military capabilities required to secure command of the commons are the U.S. strong suit. They leverage science, technology, and economic resources. They rely on highly trained, highly skilled, and increasingly highly paid military personnel. On the whole, the U.S. military advantage at sea, in the air, and in space will be very difficult to challenge—let alone overcome. Command is further secured by the worldwide U.S. base structure and the ability of U.S. diplomacy to leverage other sources of U.S. power to secure additional bases and overflight rights as needed.

Command of the commons is so much a part of U.S. military power that it is seldom explicitly acknowledged, under this rubric or any other. And

---

52. Owen R. Coté Jr., "The Future of the Trident Force, Security Studies Program," Massachusetts Institute of Technology, May 2002, pp. 25–29, discusses air defense suppression generally, and the significant problems posed by the SA-10, specifically. See also Owen R. Coté Jr., "'Buying . . . From the Sea': A Defense Budget for a Maritime Strategy," in Cindy Williams, ed., *Holding the Line: U.S. Defense Alternatives for the Early Twenty-first Century* (Cambridge, Mass.: MIT Press, 2001), pp. 146–150.
53. IISS, *The Military Balance, 2002–2003*, p. 148, credits China with 144 SA-10s. This implies perhaps a dozen batteries. SA-10 is a NATO designation; Russia calls the weapon S-300. See Federation of American Scientists, "SA-10 Grumble," http://www.fas.org/nuke/guide/russia/airdef/s-300pmu.htm.

far too little attention is paid to the strategic exploitation of command of the commons. For example, many U.S. defense policy documents in recent years allude to the need for speed of deployment to distant theaters of operations and speed of decision in the theater contingency.[54] Among other things, this has caused the U.S. Army to become obsessed with "lightening" itself up, to better travel by air and to limit its logistics tail in the theater. This interest in speed seems misplaced. It underexploits the possibilities provided by command of the commons—the ability of the United States to muster great power; to militarily, economically, and politically isolate and weaken its adversaries; and to probe, study, and map the dimensions of the adversary to better target U.S. military power when it is applied. Full exploitation of command of the commons is rendered doubly necessary by the real problems presented once U.S. forces get close to the adversary. Below 15,000 feet, within several hundred kilometers of the shore, and on the land, a contested zone awaits them. The U.S. military hopes that it can achieve the same degree of dominance in this zone as it has in the commons, though this is unlikely to happen.

The Contested Zone

The closer U.S. military forces get to enemy-held territory, the more competitive the enemy will be. This arises from a combination of political, physical, and technological facts. These facts combine to create a contested zone—arenas of conventional combat where weak adversaries have a good chance of doing real damage to U.S. forces. The Iranians, the Serbs, the Somalis, and the still unidentified hard cases encountered in Operation Anaconda in Afghanistan have demonstrated that it is possible to fight the U.S. military. Only the Somalis can claim anything like a victory, but the others have imposed costs, preserved at least some of their forces, and often lived to tell the tale—to one another. These countries or entities have been small, resource poor, and often

---

54. The 2001 *Quadrennial Defense Review Report* seems to be preoccupied with swiftness: For example, the DoD seeks forces to "swiftly defeat aggression in overlapping major conflicts" (p. 17); "The focus will be on the ability to act quickly. U.S. forces will remain capable of swiftly defeating attack against U.S. allies and friends in any two theaters of operation in overlapping time frames" (p. 21); and "One of the goals of reorienting the global posture is to render forward forces capable of swiftly defeating an adversary's military and political objectives with only modest reinforcement" (p. 25; repeated on p. 26).

militarily "backward." They offer cautionary tales. The success of the 2003 U.S. campaign against the Ba'athist regime in Iraq should not blind observers to the inherent difficulty of fighting in contested zones.

Most of the adversaries that the United States has encountered since 1990 have come to understand U.S. military strengths, and have worked to neutralize them. The U.S. military often uses the term "asymmetric" threats to encompass an adversary's use of weapons of mass destruction, terrorism, or any mode of conventional warfare that takes into account U.S. strengths. This category is a kind of trap: Smart enemies get a special term, but by subtraction, many are expected to be stupid. This is unlikely to prove true; in any case it is a dangerous way to think about war.

The essential facts are as follows. First, local actors generally have strong political interests in the stakes of a war—interests that may exceed those of the United States. Their willingness to suffer is therefore often greater. Second, however small the local actors are, they usually have one resource in more plentiful supply than the all-volunteer U.S. military—males of fighting age. Though young men are no longer the most important ingredient of land warfare, they do remain critical, particularly in cities, jungles, and mountains. Third, local actors usually have some kind of "home-court advantage." Just as the U.S. military has built up an institutional memory over decades that has helped it to preserve command of the commons, local actors have often built up a similar institutional memory about their own arenas. They have intimate knowledge of the terrain and the meteorology and may have spent years adapting their military tactics to these factors. This advantage is magnified because the local actors are often on the defense, which permits their military engineers to disperse, harden, and camouflage their forces, logistics, and command and control. Fourth, foreign soldiers have studied how the U.S. military makes war. The Cold War saw a great deal of foreign military education as a tool of political penetration by both the U.S. and Soviet blocs. Potential adversaries have been taught Western tactics and the use of Western weaponry. There are even reports that those who have fought the U.S. forces share information on their experiences. Fifth, the weaponry of the close fight—on land, in the air at low altitudes, and at sea in the so-called littorals—is much less expensive than that required for combat in the commons. A great deal of useful weaponry was left over from the Cold War, especially Warsaw Pact designs, which are particularly cheap. Demand for weaponry has diminished greatly since the Cold War ended, so there is plenty of manufacturing capability looking for markets.[55] Moreover, the diffusion of economic and technological capabilities in the civil sector is paralleled in the military sector. New manufacturers are emerging, who themselves will seek export markets. Finally, weaponry for close-range combat is also being continuously refined. Old weapons are becoming more lethal because of better ammunition. New versions of old weapons are also more lethal and survivable. Because these weapons are relatively inexpensive, even some of the newer versions will find their way into the hands of smaller and poorer states.

Taken together, these mutually reinforcing factors create a "contested zone." In this zone, encounters between U.S. and local forces may result in fierce battles. This is not a prediction of U.S. defeat. The United States will be able to win wars in the contested zone, as it did in Afghanistan in 2002 and Iraq in 2003. It is a prediction of adversity. It is a prediction of a zone in which the U.S. military will require clever strategies and adroit tactics. It is a zone in which the U.S. military must think carefully and candidly about its own strengths and weaknesses, and how to leverage the former and buffer the latter.

LIMITS TO AIR POWER

Though U.S. aircraft possess significant potential destructive capacity, clever defenders can make it difficult to realize this potential. A combination of large numbers of inexpensive low-altitude air defense weapons; small numbers of intelligently organized and operated medium-altitude weapons; and systematic efforts at camouflage, protection, and concealment have permitted ground forces to survive the onslaught of modern U.S. air power under some circumstances.

Inexpensive weaponry drives U.S. fighters to high altitudes, where their effectiveness against ground forces is reduced. Below 15,000 feet, expensive tactical fighter aircraft are vulnerable to inexpensive weaponry—light-to-medium automatic cannon (antiaircraft artillery, or AAA) and relatively small and inexpensive short-range SAMS (mainly portable infrared-guided systems similar to the U.S. Stinger). Although some kinds of decoys work against some of the low-altitude SAMs, the effectiveness of AAA is essentially a function of how many weapons the adversary possesses, their location relative to important targets, and how much ammunition they are able and willing to expend. AAA is best thought of as a kind of aerial minefield. Vast numbers of AAA weapons

---

55. Daniel Williams and Nicholas Wood, "Iraq Finds Ready Arms Sellers from Baltic Sea to Bosnia," *International Herald Tribune*, November 21, 2002.

were built during the Cold War, especially by the Warsaw Pact, but also in the West. They seem not to wear out.[56] The majority of U.S. aircraft and helicopters lost in the Vietnam War were brought down by AAA.[57] Though coalition aircraft losses in the 1991 Persian Gulf War were very low, AAA and short-range infrared SAMs caused 71 percent of the attrition.[58] Currently, the U.S. military reports only 7 aircraft lost to enemy fire in the 2003 war—6 attack helicopters and an A-10. It is likely that all were victims of short-range air defense weapons.[59] In the only major success for Iraqi air defenses, 27 of 35 U.S. Army attack helicopters were damaged and one was lost in a single raid—all to AAA.[60] Even in South Vietnam, where North Vietnamese and Vietcong units had no radars for early warning, these weapons brought down 1,700 helicopters and aircraft between 1961 and 1968.[61] Generally, it is now the strategy of U.S. and

---

56. Prior to the start of the third Gulf War in March 2003, Iraq was reported to have had 3,000 antiaircraft guns. Many of Iraq's air defense duels with U.S. aircraft in the no-fly zones during the preceding decade depended on antiaircraft artillery. Iraq did not shoot down any Western aircraft before the war, but U.S. airmen nevertheless viewed these guns as a serious threat: "For years, the Iraqis used antiaircraft artillery (AAA), unguided rockets, and surface-to-air missiles against coalition aircraft in both the northern and southern no-fly zones. In fact, they started firing at our aircraft in 1992, and over the last three years Iraqi AAA has fired at coalition aircraft over 1,000 times, launched 600 rockets and fired nearly 60 SAMs." Secretary of Defense Donald H. Rumsfeld and Gen. Richard Myers, chairman, Joint Chiefs of Staff, news briefing, September 30, 2002. See IISS, *The Military Balance, 2002–2003,* p. 106, for Iraq's AAA inventory.

57. According to Kenneth P. Werrell, "Between 1965 and 1973 flak engaged one-fourth of all flights over North Vietnam and accounted for 66% of U.S. aircraft losses over the North." Werrell, *Archie, Flak, AAA, and SAM: A Short Operational History of Ground-Based Air Defense* (Maxwell Air Force Base, Ala.: Air University Press, 1988), p. 102.

58. Thomas A. Keaney and Eliot A. Cohen, *Gulf War Air Power Survey Summary Report* (Washington, D.C.: GPO, 1993), pp. 61–62. Thirty-eight aircraft were lost, and 48 were damaged. In explaining these low losses, Keaney and Cohen note: "Although some crews initially tried NATO-style low-level ingress tactics during the first few nights of Desert Storm, the sheer volume and ubiquity of barrage antiaircraft artillery, combined with the ability of Stinger-class infrared SAMs to be effective up to 12,000–15,000 feet, quickly persuaded most everyone on the Coalition side to abandon low altitude, especially for weapon release." See also General Accounting Office, *Operation Desert Storm: Evaluation of the Air Campaign,* GAO/NSIAD-97-134 (Washington, D.C.: GAO, June, 1997), Table II.7, p. 94. Fourteen aircraft were destroyed or damaged by radar SAMs, 28 by infrared SAMS, and 33 by AAA. AAA was much more likely than the other systems to damage rather than destroy a successfully engaged target.

59. Moseley, "Operation Iraqi Freedom—By the Numbers."

60. Rowan Scarborough, "Apache Operation a Lesson in Defeat," *Washington Times,* April 22, 2003, p. 1. This was apparently a clever Iraqi ambush. An Iraqi observer watched the helicopters take off and used a cell phone to alert some air defense units. On a prearranged signal, the local power grid was turned off for a few seconds to alert the rest. See Lt. Gen. William Scott Wallace, U.S. Army, "Fifth Corps Commander Live Briefing from Baghdad," May 7, 2003, U.S. Department of Defense news transcript, http://www.defenselink.mil/transcripts/2003/tr20030507-0157html.

61. Between 1961 and 1968, 1,709 U.S. aircraft were lost over South Vietnam, of which 63 percent were helicopters and the rest fixed-wing aircraft. During this period, AAA was the only air defense weapon available to the communists in the South. Werrell, *Archie, Flak, AAA, and SAM,* p. 112.

Western air forces to fly above 15,000 feet to avoid AAA. This reduces losses, but it also significantly reduces a pilot's ability to locate enemy forces on the ground, to distinguish targets from decoys, to distinguish undamaged targets from damaged ones, and more generally to develop a feel for the ground situation. A mobile adversary, with some knowledge of camouflage and deception, operating in favorable terrain, can exploit these problems. Thus inexpensive and simple air defense weapons help to protect ground forces even when they do not down many aircraft.

Operations above 15,000 feet can be further complicated by an integrated air defense system (IADS), which combines a communications system, early warning radars and signals intelligence collection devices, and medium-to-high-altitude SAM systems, as well as AAA.[62] An IADS does not have to shoot down many aircraft to lend assistance to ground forces. As discussed earlier, U.S. aircraft leverage technological advantages to suppress these integrated air defenses by jamming their radars and communications, by targeting SAMs with radar homing missiles, and by attacking communications nodes. More often than not, direct attacks on SAMs cause the gunners to shut down their radars, which makes the SAMs ineffective. At the same time, it usually ensures that the radar homing missiles fail to destroy the launchers—hence the term SEAD (suppression of enemy air defenses). Since 1972 both the Israeli air force and the U.S. air force(s) have proven this tactic, but it comes at a cost. It is safe to enter enemy airspace only when a host of expensive and scarce special assets are assembled.

Though the United States can command enemy airspace when it musters its SEAD capabilities, it cannot do so without them, and thus an adversary gets three benefits.[63] First, the scarcity of suppression assets slows the overall rate of

---

62. Passive electronic intelligence collection consists of radio receivers that track both radio and radar emissions. Without information on the precise content of coded communications, such systems may still develop an understanding of certain patterns of communications that are associated with certain kinds of operations. Occasional lapses in communications security may provide the actual content of communications to the receiver. Radio direction finding can provide indications of where certain patterns of electronic emissions occur, and where they are going. These can be cross-referenced with what radars may observe. The reports of spies and observers can also be integrated with this information. Over time, a competent adversary may build up a picture of U.S. procedures and tactics, which can prove invaluable. It is likely that this is how the Serbs were able to shoot down a U.S. F-117 stealth fighter in 1999. Because the Serbs destroyed so few U.S. aircraft, the magnitude of this particular achievement is underappreciated.

63. Some believe that the advent of stealth obviates this statement, but that does not seem to be the case. Stealth aircraft missions are generally planned to benefit from air defense suppression, though it appears that these missions rely on somewhat less direct suppressive support than do conventional bombing missions. Little more can be said, as the tactics of stealth missions are highly classified.

U.S. attack to the rate at which they can be assembled and organized.[64] Second, it is not safe to remain in airspace that is defended by an IADS, because it is difficult to sustain enough pressure to keep the defender's radars "off the air" for more than a short time. Finally, it seems that suppression operations generate lots of patterned activity—much of it emitting electronic signals. A dense network of reasonably good radars and passive electronic intelligence capabilities can develop a picture of such patterned activities, and thus provide early warning of U.S. attacks. Married to a decent communications system, the adversary's forces in the field can be alerted to take cover.[65] The defender may not shoot down many U.S. or other Western aircraft with this system; indeed the harder it tries, the more likely it is to suffer destruction. But by playing a game of cat and mouse, the defender can survive and achieve its minimum objective—it can ration U.S. attacks and gain useful early warning of those attacks. If patient, the defender may from time to time encounter tactical situations where it can score a kill.

In 1999 the Serb army demonstrated that AAA at low altitudes and a well-constructed, if obsolescent, IADS at medium to high altitudes can offer powerful assistance to an adversary ground force as it attempts to survive the attacks of U.S. air forces. NATO did little damage against Serb field forces in Kosovo in 1999.[66] It was no doubt discouraging to the adversary's air defense troops that they shot down so few U.S. aircraft. Nevertheless, when air defenses successfully defend key assets, they have done their job. Serbian forces presented a large array of small mobile targets. The adversary could easily camouflage tanks, tracks, and guns and could also offer a wide variety of decoys to attract the attention of U.S. pilots. Serbia's mobile SAMS also largely survived U.S. attempts to destroy them, so the United States was forced to continue mounting

---

64. Relying on accounts by Adm. James Ellis, commander in chief of Allied Forces Southern Europe during the Kosovo war, Timothy L. Thomas reports the Serbian strategy: "To prevent its air defense assets from being neutralized, the Serbian armed forces turned their assets on only as needed. They therefore presented a 'constant but dormant' threat. This resulted in NATO using its most strained assets (e.g., JSTARS, AWACS, or airborne warning and control system) to conduct additional searches for air defense assets and forced NATO aircraft to fly above 15,000 feet, making it difficult for them to hit their targets. Ellis noted that NATO achieved little damage to the Serbian integrated air defense system." see Thomas, "Kosovo and the Current Myth of Information Superiority," *Parameters*, Vol. 30, No. 1 (Spring 2000), pp. 14–29; quotation on p. 8 of the web version.
65. As Thomas notes, "Their [Serbian] offsets included deception, disinformation, camouflage, the clever use of radar, spies within NATO, helicopter movement NATO couldn't detect, and the exploitation of NATO's operational templating of information dominance activities (e.g., satellites, reconnaissance flights). See ibid., pp. 3, 9 of the web version.
66. On Serbia's air and ground strategies, as well as Serbia's tactical successes, see Barry R. Posen, "The War for Kosovo: Serbia's Political-Military Strategy," *International Security*, Vol. 24, No. 4 (Spring 2000), pp. 54–66.

elaborate suppression operations, providing the Serbs with useful early warning.

There were obvious limits to Serbian success. Large, fixed transportation targets (such as bridges) and economic infrastructure targets (such as power stations) cannot be moved, and they cannot easily be camouflaged. Only truly modern SAMs can possibly defend such targets from high-altitude aircraft armed with precision-guided munitions. In the end, it was the U.S. ability and demonstrated willingness to destroy Serbia's infrastructure and economy that coerced Slobodan Milošević into accepting a deal that satisfied NATO's war aims, but that deviated in important ways from NATO's original demands. The cautionary lesson is that a well-operated, if obsolescent, integrated air defense system can defend a ground force skilled at camouflage and deception.[67]

Iraqi air defenses and ground forces were apparently less successful at this game in 2003 than the Serbs were in 1999. Information is still limited, but several explanations seem plausible. First, Iraqi air defenses were in very poor shape on March 19, when the war officially began. The Iraqi air defense system was badly damaged in the 1991 war, damaged further during eleven years of engagements with U.S. and other Western air forces in the northern and southern no-fly zones, and largely prevented from replacing its losses or improving its technology by the twelve-year arms embargo. Existing Iraqi SAMs also seem to have been in disrepair, perhaps due to their age, the embargo, or operator incompetence.[68] Second, it appears that Iraqi SAM opera-

---

67. For a collection of deception tactics and countermeasures that the Serbs are said to have employed, see "Tactics Employed by the Yugoslav Army to Limit NATO Air Strikes' Effectiveness," Associated Press, November 18, 2002. Daryl Press notes that even in the deserts of Kuwait and southern Iraq, U.S. fighter aircraft experienced difficulties attacking a dug-in, camouflaged, ground force. See Press, "The Myth of Air Power in the Persian Gulf War," pp. 40–42. As of this writing, insufficient information has emerged to determine the effectiveness of these techniques in the U.S.-led war with Iraq that began in March 2003.

68. Lt. Gen. T. Michael Moseley, "Coalition Forces Air Component Command Briefing," April 5, 2003, U.S. Department of Defense news transcript, http://www.defenselink.mil/news/Apr2003/t04052003_t405mose.html, alludes to enforcement of the no-fly zones as an opportunity to degrade the Iraqi air defense system. He reports that after the first three or four days of the war, his flyers were able to switch from suppression to destruction of Iraqi air defenses, which suggests that the defenders suffered heavy losses in the early days, perhaps because they turned their radars on too often. Finally he said that "every time they move one of those things [a SAM or radar] they have a tendency to break something on them," which suggests unreliable and/or poorly maintained equipment. After the conventional phase of the war ended, an Iraqi air defense officer, Gen. Ghanem Abdullah Azawi, declared: "There has been practically no air defense since 1991. Nobody rebuilt it. We didn't receive any new weapons." Quoted in William Branigin, "A Brief, Bitter War for Iraq's Military Officers: Self-Deception a Factor in Defeat," *Washington Post*, April 27, 2003, p. A25.

tors were more aggressive in the early days of the war than was sensible, giving U.S. and British pilots excellent engagement opportunities. Third, Iraqi ground forces appear not to have enjoyed as much success at cover, concealment, and camouflage as did the Serbs. The terrain south of Baghdad may not have been favorable to such tactics, though opportunities did exist and much Iraqi equipment survived U.S. and British air attacks.[69] Perhaps as important, Iraqi forces had to concentrate and sometimes chose to maneuver en masse to try to meet U.S. ground attacks, creating better targets for U.S. aircraft.[70] Serb ground forces faced neither the necessity to concentrate nor the temptation to maneuver on a large scale because they faced no risk of a NATO ground attack.

The 1999 Kosovo war may provide other lessons as well. Militaries that have fought, or think they might fight, the United States now exchange lessons and technology. Serbs and Iraqis discussed tactics before the war in Kosovo began.[71] Iraq sought commercial communications technology to increase the re-

---

69. One journalist who toured Iraqi defenses south of Baghdad either in late March or early April reports that Iraqi units were well dispersed, dug in, and camouflaged. He saw some damaged equipment but more that had survived. Robert Fisk, "Saddam's Masters of Concealment Dig In, Ready for Battle," *Independent*, April 3, 2003, p. 1. On April 5, U.S. troops "found herds of tanks abandoned by the Iraqi Army and Republican Guard" in Karbala. See Jim Dwyer, "In Karbala, G.I.'s Find Forsaken Iraqi Armor and Pockets of Resistance," *New York Times*, April 6, 2003, sec. B, p. 4. One postwar report suggests that "fewer than 100 Republican Guard tanks were knocked out in the battles around Baghdad, so coalition officers say hundreds of modern T-72 main battle tanks and BMP infantry fighting vehicles are still to be found." Tim Ripley, "Building a New Iraqi Army," *Jane's Defence Weekly*, April 16, 2003, p. 3. Other journalists toured the same area after the end of conventional fighting and reported the existence of vast, but entirely unused, prepared defensive positions and the destruction of many reasonably well-camouflaged Iraqi combat vehicles, though they kept no count. They note little evidence of dead Iraqi soldiers and suggest that many units melted away. Terry McCarthy, "What Ever Happened to the Republican Guard?" *Time*, May 12, 2003, pp. 24–28. On the whole, it seems that large quantities of Iraqi armored vehicles and weapons survived concentrated Western air attacks, but Iraqi troops abandoned their equipment. One cannot know if better-led, more tactically proficient, and more politically committed troops would have found ways to employ this surviving equipment to offer stronger resistance to U.S. ground forces.

70. William M. Arkin, "Speed Kills," *Los Angeles Times*, June 1, 2003, pt. M, p. 1, suggests that the Iraqis suffered grievous damage when they tried to maneuver under cover of a late-March sandstorm. More generally, a U.S. Marine noncommissioned officer declared, "Every time they try to move their tanks even 100 yards, they get it from our aircraft. We are everywhere." See Matthew Fisher, "Skirmishes in Baghdad: Marines Blow Up Scores of Abandoned Iraqi Tanks and Armoured Vehicles," *Times Colonist* (Victoria, Canada), April 7, 2003, p. A5.

71. Philip Shenon, "The Iraqi Connection: Serbs Seek Iraqi Help for Defense, Britain Says," *New York Times*, April 1, 1999, p. A 16. This appears to have been two-way commerce. Until very recently, any companies in the former Yugoslavia apparently exported military equipment to Iraq in violation of the UN arms embargo. See Williams and Wood, "Iraq Finds Ready Arms Sellers from Baltic Sea to Bosnia."

silience of its air defense communications network.[72] This assistance seems to have come from Chinese firms, which suggests that Serb, Iraqi, and Chinese air defense experts have compared notes.[73] Serbia's mobile SA-6s largely survived NATO attacks, but its immobile SA-3s fared poorly.[74] Formerly immobile, obsolescent Iraqi SA-3 missiles turned up in domestically built mobile versions on the backs of trucks prior to the 2003 war.[75] The fact that Iraq did not profit from its contacts with Serbia does not undermine the central point—past and potential U.S. adversaries may exchange information. The Iraqis themselves demonstrated in the 1991 Gulf War that mobility pays: Though coalition forces chased Iraqi truck-mounted Scud surface-to-surface missiles all over the desert, it seems clear that none were destroyed during that war.[76] Scuds made no appearance in the 2003 war, but Iraq did possess many smaller, short-range tactical ballistic missiles. Though these were priority targets for U.S. forces because of their presumed ability to deliver chemical weapons, many of these systems survived attack. Indeed, on April 7, 2003, after nearly nineteen days of combat, a missile struck the headquarters of the Second Brigade of the 3d Infantry Division, just south of Baghdad.[77]

THE LIGHT INFANTRY CHALLENGE

The 1991 and 2003 Gulf Wars strongly suggest that there are few, if any, ground forces in the world that can challenge the U.S. Army in tank warfare in open country. But there are other possible ground fights—in cities, mountains, jungles, and marshes. And the United States needs to be cognizant of some of the difficulties that may lie ahead. The first is sheer numbers. The two remaining designated members of the "axis of evil," Iran and North Korea, have conscript

---

72. A fiber-optic network was reportedly added to Iraq's air defense command and control system. See IISS, *The Military Balance, 2002–2003,* p. 98.
73. Andrew Koch and Michael Sirak, "Iraqi Air Defences under Strain," *Jane's Defence Weekly,* February 28, 2001. The article also notes that while some Serbs have reportedly helped Iraq militarily over the years, others reportedly provided intelligence about Iraq to the United States and Britain.
74. Department of Defense, news briefing, June 10, 1999. See the slide "Air Defense BDA," http://www.defenselink.mil/news/Jun1999/990610-J-0000K-008.jpg.
75. IISS, *The Military Balance 2002–2003,* p. 98.
76. For reviews of the evidence supporting this point, see William Rosenau, *Special Operations Forces and Elusive Enemy Ground Targets: Lessons from Vietnam and the Persian Gulf War,* MR-1408-AF (Santa Monica, Calif.: RAND, 2001), pp. 40–44; and "The Great Scud Hunt: An Assessment," Centre for Defence and International Security Studies, Lancaster University, 1996, http://www.cdiss.org/scudnt6.htm.
77. Two soldiers and two journalists were killed, fifteen soldiers were wounded, and 17 military vehicles were destroyed. Steven Lee Myers, "A Nation at War: Third Infantry Division; Iraqi Missile Strike Kills Four at Tactical Operations Center," *New York Times,* April 8, 2003, sec. B, p. 3.

armies: Together these two countries have 13 million males between the ages of 18 and 32.[78] They do not train all these men for war; the training their soldiers get is almost certainly uneven; and for local political reasons, some of these young men would not necessarily fight. But this total does give some idea of the potentials: These men are an important military resource. This pattern can be expected elsewhere. The world's population is expected to grow from 6 billion to 8 billion by 2025, with most of that growth in the developing world.[79] Moreover, ground troops should have no trouble finding infantry weapons. According to one study, there are perhaps 250 million military and police small arms in the world, including mortars and shoulder-fired antitank weapons.[80]

U.S. strategists must also be cognizant of the significant police problem that would arise in the event the United States tried to conquer and politically reorganize some of these populous countries. The historical record suggests that stability operations require between two and twenty soldiers and/or policemen per 1,000 individuals, depending on the level of political instability.[81] The low figure is consistent with average U.S. police presence; the high figure with the height of the Troubles in Northern Ireland. Prior to the commencement of hostilities against Iraq in March 2003, many warned that the postwar occupation of the country could require significant troops. Gen. Eric Shinseki, then chief of staff of the U.S. Army, estimated before the Congress in late February 2003 that several hundred thousand troops would be required for several years to occupy Iraq with its 22 million people. Undersecretary of Defense Paul Wolfowitz derided this estimate.[82] By the end of April 2003, Pentagon planners were projecting that a force of 125,000 would be needed for at least a year.[83] As of early June, plans to withdraw troops of the hardworking 3d Infantry Divi-

78. IISS, *The Military Balance, 2002–2003*, pp. 103–105, 153–154, 279, 299. Nearly 10 million are in Iran, which conscripts perhaps only 125,000 of its 950,000 eligible males annually. North Korea appears to conscript virtually all of its eligible males.
79. U.S. Commission on National Security/21st Century, *New World Coming: American Security in the 21st, Supporting Research and Analysis*, September 15, 1999, p. 40.
80. Alexander Higgins, "UN-Backed Study Estimates 639 Million Small Arms in World," Associated Press, June 24, 2002; see also "Red Flags and Bucks: Global Firearm Stockpiles," chapter summary, *Small Arms Survey*, 2002, http://www.smallarmssurvey.org/Yearbook/EngPRkitCH2_11.06.02.pdf.
81. James T. Quinlivan, "Force Requirements in Stability Operations," *Parameters*, Vol. 25, No. 4 (Winter 1995–1996), p. 61.
82. Eric Schmitt, "Pentagon Contradicts General on Iraq Occupation Force's Size," *New York Times*, February 28, 2003, p. 1.
83. Tom Squitieri, "Postwar Force Could Be 125,000," *USA Today*, April 28, 2003, p. 1.

sion, which spearheaded the drive to Baghdad, had been shelved due to the deteriorating security situation, leaving 128,000 U.S. Army troops in Iraq and 45,000 more in Kuwait performing logistics functions. Perhaps another 30,000 U.S. Marines and British troops were also in Iraq. One unnamed U.S. Army officer averred that he has not seen the army so stretched in his thirty-one years of military service.[84] Yet with nearly 160,000 troops in Iraq, Maj. Gen. Tim Cross, the British deputy head of Reconstruction and Humanitarian Assistance, agreed that there were too few troops to keep order.[85]

U.S. military personnel, however, have almost become too expensive to hire. The Department of Defense completed a detailed study in summer 2002 suggesting that the military services cut 90,000 uniformed personnel.[86] It considered asking the army to cut one of its ten active divisions. At the time, the U.S. defense budget was going up, and the United States was already heavily engaged in the war on terror. The U.S. government had defined this war broadly, and the Pentagon civilian leadership favored extending it to Iraq. The demand for U.S. personnel would likely rise. Yet the sheer expense of uniformed personnel caused the Defense Department to briefly consider reducing the size of the armed forces.[87] This suggests that the United States must avoid lengthy military operations that require a large number of ground troops.

It is tempting to believe that heavily armed, high-technology ground forces can easily defeat large numbers of enemy infantry. But two vignettes, one from Somalia and the other from Afghanistan, suggest a different lesson. Elite U.S. Special Operations forces suffered high casualties in a mission gone awry in Mogadishu in 1993.[88] They were in part a victim of their own mistakes. But Somali gunmen fought with courage, and some skill, and were assisted by the ur-

---

84. Bradley Graham, "Iraq Stabilization Impinges on Army Rotation, Rebuilding," *Washington Post,* June 6, 2003, p. A21.

85. "'Too Few Troops' in Iraq," *BBC News,* May 26, 2003, http://news.bbc.co.uk/go/pr/fr/-/2/hi/middle_east/2938176.stm.

86. Tom Bowman, "Pentagon to Consider Large-Scale Troop Cuts," *Baltimore Sun,* July 10, 2001, p. 1A. A reduction of almost 90,000 soldiers, sailors, airmen, and marines is contemplated because "with personnel eating up a significant portion of the defense budget, and with Rumsfeld and his aides eager to harness the latest technology and weaponry, the Pentagon has begun to focus on cutting jobs among the 1.4 million people on active duty." See also Robert S. Dudney, "Hyper-extension," *Air Force Magazine,* August 2002, p. 2, noting Secretary of Defense Rumsfeld's reluctance to add manpower, which he considered to be "enormously expensive."

87. The final defense authorization for fiscal year 2003 approved a modest increase in the size of the U.S. active force.

88. Mark Bowden, *Black Hawk Down: A Story of Modern War* (New York: Atlantic Monthly Press, 1999), is the source for what follows.

ban environment. They clearly had "gone to school" on U.S. forces in preceding weeks, learning their patterns and tactics.[89] Their local intelligence apparatus may have provided some warning of the U.S. raids, and a crude communications system allowed them to mobilize and coordinate the movement of their forces.[90] The Somalis reportedly altered simple, Soviet-pattern RPG-7 antitank rockets to make them more effective weapons against U.S. helicopters.[91] Some observers suggest that al-Qaeda taught them this trick. Soviet AK-47 assault rifles, RPG-7 antitank rocket launchers, and ammunition for both appear to have been plentiful. And no wonder—millions of AK-47s had been manufactured and could be had for as little as $200 dollars apiece in Somalia.[92] The Somalis did, however, suffer grievous casualties, perhaps thirty times the eighteen U.S. dead.[93] The Somalis may be among the most individually courageous fighters U.S. soldiers have encountered since the North Vietnamese. But even better prepared and better armed urban infantry combatants do exist, as the Russians discovered in Grozny in 1995.

In recent years, the U.S. military has been working assiduously to improve its urban combat capability, but soldiers still expect fights against competent defenders in cities to be costly and difficult.[94] A military rule of thumb is that it takes one company, one day, and 30–40 percent casualties to take one well-

---

89. Ibid., p. 21.
90. Ibid., pp. 31, 230.
91. Ibid., pp. 110–111. The RPG-7, intended as a point-detonated antitank projectile, reportedly also has a time fuse to ensure that it will explode somewhere in the midst of the enemy in the event that the shooter misses his target. The Somalis may have somehow shortened the time setting on this fuse, to cause the projectile to burst in the air at relatively short range—essentially turning it into a medium-caliber antiaircraft artillery round. Alternatively, the Somalis may simply have learned the range at which this explosion would normally occur and fired at least some of their RPGs at helicopters at the appropriate range.
92. Ibid. p. 109.
93. Ibid. p. 333.
94. The 1968 Battle for Hue in South Vietnam offers a cautionary tale that is much studied by the U.S. military. Hue was not a particularly large city, with 140,000 people on sixteen square kilometers, though its heavy stone construction provided excellent defensive positions. It took twenty-five days for 11 South Vietnamese and 3 U.S. Marine Corps infantry battalions, with vastly superior firepower, to evict 16 to 18 Vietcong and North Vietnamese infantry battalions from the city. U.S. Army units assisted with critical supporting attacks outside the city. The U.S. and South Vietnamese troops suffered 600 killed and 3,800 wounded and missing to do so, and the fighting destroyed much of the city. Estimates of communist dead range from 1,000 to 5,000, out of a force of perhaps 12,000. See Abbott Associates, *Modern Experience in City Combat*, Technical Memorandum 5–87, AD-A180 999 (Aberdeen, Md.: U.S. Army Human Engineering Laboratory, 1987), pp. 67–68. Casualty estimates are from Jack Shulimson, Lt. Col. Leonard A. Blasiol, Charles R. Smith, and Captain David Dawson, *U.S. Marines in Vietnam: The Defining Year, 1968* (Washington, D.C.: History and Museums Division, Headquarters, U.S. Marine Corps, 1997), p. 213.

defended city block, which would usually be defended by a platoon one-third its strength.[95] It is generally believed that casualties of this magnitude would render a unit combat ineffective for some period. After two fights of this kind, it would likely take months to rebuild the unit's combat power—even if the infantry replacements could be found, which seems difficult given the U.S. voluntary recruitment system. The entire U.S. active Army has only about 60 infantry battalions (180 companies), so it would be stressed if it stumbled into a major, extended, urban campaign against an army of even modest size. Saddam Hussein's regime did not prepare to wage such a campaign in Baghdad in 2003, allowing its best units to be destroyed outside of the city.[96] But Iraqi infantry experienced their only successes in smaller cities across southern Iraq, most notably in an-Nasiriya, where they fought bloody battles with the U.S. Marines.[97] The marines suffered more than half of the U.S. casualties in the war, though they provided about a third of the ground forces. Their commander, Lt. Gen. James Conway, explained this anomaly as follows: "The forces that we had come up against were pretty much in the villages and towns along the single avenues of approach that we had that led into Baghdad. It was close-quarter fighting, in some cases hand-to-hand fighting."[98]

Captured documents from al-Qaeda training bases in Afghanistan show how competent infantry can be trained with relatively low-technology techniques.[99] Al-Qaeda trainers, many of whom appear to have served in regular

95. Barry R. Posen, "Urban Operations: Tactical Realities and Strategic Ambiguities," in Michael C. Desch, ed., *Soldiers in Cities: Military Operations on Urban Terrain* (Carlisle, Pa.: Strategic Studies Institute, U.S. Army War College, 2001), pp. 153–154. See also *Combined Arms Operations in Urban Terrain*, FM 3–06.11 (Washington, D.C.: Headquarters, Department of the Army, February 28, 2002), secs. 4–13, 4–37, 5–12.
96. According to Gen. Alaa Abdelkadeer, a Republican Guard officer interviewed after the war, the Iraqis had discussed the details of an urban defense of Baghdad before the war, "but none of this was carried out." Robert Collier, "Iraqi Military Plans Were Simplistic, Poorly Coordinated," *San Francisco Chronicle*, May 25, 2003, p. A-19.
97. Peter Baker, "A 'Turkey Shoot,' but with Marines as the Targets," *Washington Post*, March 28, 2003, p. A1; Dexter Filkins and Michael Wilson, "A Nation At War: The Southern Front; Marines, Battling in Streets, Seek Control of City in South," *New York Times*, "March 25, 2003, p. A1; John Roberts, "On the Scene: A Formidable Foe," March 26, 2003, http://www.cbsnews.com/stories/ 200 . . . 6/iraq/scene/printable546258.shtml; and Andrew North, "Nasiriya, 0941 GMT, " in "Reporters' Log: War in Iraq," *BBC News*, March 31, 2003, http://www.bbc.co.uk/reporters.
98. Conway, "First Marine Expeditionary Force Briefing."
99. Anthony Davis, "The Afghan Files: Al-Qaeda Documents from Kabul," *Jane's Intelligence Review*, Vol. 14, No. 2 (February 2002), p. 16. Davis visited Kabul shortly after its fall and collected many al-Qaeda documents. According to Davis, "Much of the literature also underlines the extent to which al-Qaeda was a highly organized military undertaking as well as a committed terrorist network. Detailed training manuals and student notebooks indicate that theoretical and on-the-job training involved not only small arms and assault rifles but a range of heavier weapons, including

forces, gathered tactical manuals from various armies. They distilled the information from these manuals into a syllabus. They lectured from the syllabus and insisted that each aspirant take copious notes, in effect copying a manual for himself. All procedures appear then to have been carefully drilled in the field. Bases were decorated with large training posters on various subjects.

Operation Anaconda (March 2–18, 2002) provides a sense of the success of this training, though it is unclear whether the adversary consisted entirely of al-Qaeda troops trained in Afghanistan.[100] Given the obvious skill of the defenders, it may be that these were the instructors, and not the troops, waging the fight. The adversary proved extremely skillful at camouflage; a motorized column of Afghan allies was ambushed at close range.[101] U.S. forces, though supported by reconnaissance and intelligence assets of all kinds, probably located not more than half of al-Qaeda's prepared positions in the Shah-e-Kot valley.[102] In at least one case, U.S. Special Forces helicopters landed practically on top of some of these positions, and were quickly shot up with heavy machine gun and RPG fire.[103] One Chinook transport helicopter was destroyed and another severely damaged. Every U.S. attack helicopter supporting the operation was peppered with bullet holes; four of seven AH-64s were damaged so severely that they ceased to fly sorties.[104] U.S. infantry were often brought under accurate mortar fire, which produced most of the two dozen U.S. casual-

---

12.7 millimeter machine guns, AGS-17 automatic grenade launchers, mortars, and even 107 mm BM-1 and BM-12 rocket systems." Ibid., p. 18

100. The section that follows relies largely on journalistic accounts of the battle. I have supplemented these accounts with some information gleaned in private conversations with U.S. military officers. See also the excellent study by Stephen Biddle, *Afghanistan and the Future of Warfare: Implications for Army and Defense Policy* (Carlisle, Pa.: U.S. Army Strategic Studies Institute, U.S. Army War College, November 2002), pp. 28–37.

101. Richard T. Cooper, "The Untold War: Fierce Fight in Afghan Valley Tests U.S. Soldiers and Strategy," *Los Angeles Times*, March 24, 2002, p. 1.

102. In the case of one communications bunker, an army intelligence specialist noted: "You wouldn't see it unless you looked directly on it. Predator wouldn't have been able to see it." The bunker contained a radio set up with "low probability of intercept techniques," which would have made it very difficult for U.S. electronic intelligence assets to detect its presence. See Thomas E. Ricks, "In Mop Up, U.S. Finds 'Impressive' Remnants of Fallen Foe," *Washington Post*, March 20, 2002, p. 1.

103. Cooper, "The Untold War," p. 1; see also Department of Defense, "Background Briefing on the Report of the Battle of Takur Ghar," May 24, 2002.

104. According to one reporter, "Five [AH-64] Apaches were present at the start of the battle, a sixth arrived later that morning and a seventh flew up from Kandahar to join the fight that afternoon. None of the helicopters was shot down, but four were so badly damaged they were knocked out of the fight. The fire the Apaches braved was so intense that when the day was over, 27 of the 28 rotor blades among the seven helicopters sported bullet holes, said Lt. Col. James M. Marye, the commander of the 7th Battalion, 101st Aviation Regiment." Sean D. Naylor, "In Shah-E-Kot, Apaches Save the Day—and Their Reputation," *Army Times*, March 25, 2002, p. 15.

ties on the first day of the fight.[105] After several days of combat, many al-Qaeda troops withdrew under cover of poor weather.[106] Few bodies were discovered in the valley, though U.S. officers believe that many al-Qaeda were killed and obliterated by powerful bombs. As far as one can tell, al-Qaeda waged this fight with the ubiquitous Soviet-pattern AK-47 assault rifle, RPG-7 shoulder-fired antitank grenade launcher, PKM medium machine gun, 12.7-millimeter DShK heavy machine gun, and 82-millimeter medium mortar. (There were no reliable reports of infrared-guided short-range air defense missiles fired, though a good many of them seem to have been found in Afghanistan.) Pictures of caches in Afghan caves often show crates of ammunition for these weapons stacked floor to ceiling.[107] It is important to note that better ammunition for existing Warsaw Pact–pattern infantry weapons will surely appear. Sophisticated, lightweight fire control systems, which can radically increase the lethality of such weapons, have also been designed. In addition, new generations of affordable infantry weapons will start reaching potential adversaries. Even in the Anaconda battle, night-vision devices were reportedly found in abandoned enemy positions.[108] If true, an important U.S. technical and tactical advantage has already waned. In short, large numbers of males of military age, favorable terrain, solid training, and plentiful basic infantry weapons can produce significant challenges for the U.S. military.

LITTORAL COMBAT

Since the Cold War ended, the U.S. Navy has been keen to show that it is relevant to the problems of the day. Thus, early in the 1990s it began to reorient it-

---

105. Sean D. Naylor, "What We Learned from Afghanistan," *Army Times,* July 29, 2002, p. 10. It appears to me that a problem with al-Qaeda mortar fuses saved some American lives; Soviet shells with point-detonated fuses occasionally bored into the mud without exploding. Western time or proximity fuses would not have had this problem and would have produced a more lethal explosion.
106. Walter Pincus, "Attacks on U.S. Forces May Persist, CIA, DIA Chiefs Warn of Afghan Insurgency Threat," *Washington Post,* March 20, 2002, p. 1. The director of the CIA, George Tenet, testified to Congress, "There are many, many points of exit that people in small numbers can get out. We're frustrated that people did get away." Quoted in ibid.
107. Ricks, "In Mop Up, U.S. Finds 'Impressive' Remnants of Fallen Foe" reports "sheaves of rocket-propelled grenades." Commenting on the lessons of the 2003 Iraq war, Col. Mike Hiemstra, director of the Center for Army Lessons Learned, notes, "The Proliferation of rocket-propelled grenades [RPGs] across the world continues to be huge." See "More 'Must-Have' Answers Needed," *Jane's Defence Weekly,* April 30, 2003, p. 25. The RPG was widely used by the Iraqis in the 2003 war; it seems to have been their only effective antiarmor weapon.
108. Ibid.; and Cooper, "The Untold War," p. 1, report night-vision devices being found in two separate al-Qaeda positions.

self toward affecting military matters ashore, insofar as it barely had any enemies left at sea. Its first public statements about this project were *From the Sea* and *Forward . . . From the Sea*.[109] The chief of naval operations reemphasized the navy's mission close to the adversary's shore as part of his *Sea Power 21* concept.[110] Though the navy leadership understands that combat in the littorals is a different kind of mission from its past specialization, and that this requires different assets and skills, not much progress has been made in the last decade.[111]

A properly constructed sea-denial capability in littoral combat combines several elements: bottom mines; diesel electric submarines; small, fast, surface attack craft; surveillance radars; passive electronic intelligence collectors; long-range mobile land-based SAMs; and long-range, mobile, land-based antiship missiles. Aircraft and helicopters also play important roles. These systems are inexpensive relative to the cost of U.S. warships and aircraft. There are a number of militaries worldwide with expertise in littoral combat.[112] Germany, Israel, Sweden, and perhaps South Korea are probably the best in terms of combining the most modern relevant technology and weaponry, with good training and appropriate tactics. (Only Germany and Sweden organized themselves to fight a superpower navy, however.) China, Iran, North Korea, and

---

109. U.S. Department of the Navy, . . . *From the Sea, Preparing the Naval Service for the 21st Century*, White Paper (Washington, D.C.: U.S. Department of the Navy, September 1992). See also *Forward . . . from the Sea*, U.S. Naval Institute Proceedings (Washington, D.C.: U.S. Department of the Navy, December 1994), pp. 46–49.

110. Adm. Vern Clark, U.S. Navy, "Sea Power 21 Series—Part I," National Institute *Proceedings*, Vol. 128, No. 196 (October 2002). The Pentagon recognizes the special problems of littoral warfare: "Anti-ship cruise missiles, advanced diesel submarines, and advanced mines could threaten the ability of U.S. naval and amphibious forces to operate in littoral waters." *Quadrennial Defense Review Report*, p. 31; see also p. 43. Recognition is not the same as solution, however. They recognized the problem in 1992: "Some littoral threats . . .tax the capabilities of our current systems and force structure. Mastery of the littoral should not be presumed. It does not derive directly from command of the high seas. It is an objective which requires our focused skills and resources." U.S. Department of the Navy, *Forward . . . From the Sea*, p. 4. Yet progress has been slow. According to the General Accounting Office, the Navy, "does not have a means for effectively breaching enemy sea mines in the surf zone; detecting and neutralizing enemy submarines in shallow water; defending its ships against cruise missiles, or providing adequate fire support for Marine Corps amphibious landings and combat operations ashore." General Accounting Office, *Navy Acquisitions: Improved Littoral War-Fighting Capabilities Needed*, GAO/NSIAD-01–493 (Washington, D.C.: GAO, May 2001), p. 2.

111. The problem of inexpensive technology complicating great power naval operations in the littorals is not new. This was a key fact of late nineteenth- and early twentieth-century naval life, which ended the practice of the "close blockade." See Kennedy, *The Rise and Fall of British Naval Mastery*, pp. 199–200.

112. This is my personal assessment. For suggestive, supporting material, see the various country entries in IISS, *The Military Balance, 2002–2003*.

Taiwan have all developed a considerable littoral capability, though each suffers some shortfalls. In recent years no great power has actually fought a first-class littoral navy, but there are examples of how damaging the various elements of littoral warfare can be.

Naval mines are very lethal and difficult to find and eliminate.[113] Iraq nearly blew the U.S. cruiser *Princeton* in half during Desert Storm with two modern bottom mines.[114] A more primitive Iraqi moored contact mine badly damaged and nearly sank the amphibious landing ship LPH *Tripoli* in the same engagement. In 1987 a $1,500, World War I–design, Iranian floating mine nearly sank the U.S. frigate *Samuel Roberts*.[115] Iraq still possessed some naval mines in the 2003 war, but few were deployed. Nevertheless, it took nearly a week for a combined force of British, U.S., and Australian mine-hunting units to clear the channel to the port of Umm Qasr of what was subsequently discovered to have been a total of eleven mines. It was learned, however, that the Iraqis had been preparing to lay another seventy-six mines as the war began, and commanders were very relieved that the outbreak of the war forestalled this action.[116]

Mobile land-based antiship missiles might prove as difficult to find as mobile Scuds or mobile SAMs. An improvised, land-based French-built Exocet badly damaged a British destroyer during the 1982 Falklands War.[117] Land-based Iranian Silkworm antiship missiles, of Chinese manufacture, damaged two tankers at a Kuwaiti oil terminal in 1987, from nearly 80 kilometers away.[118] Similar missiles were fired by Iraq in the same area in the 2003 war, though no shipping was hit and no serious damage was done. Iraqi antiship missiles instead struck a harborside shopping mall in Kuwait City on March

113. See Gregory K. Hartmann and Scott C. Truver, *Weapons That Wait: Mine Warfare in the U.S. Navy* (Annapolis, Md.: Naval Institute Press, 1991), pp. 254–262. These authors note that naval mine warfare has usually proven to be very cost effective. During World War II, U.S. forces damaged or sank five to nine Japanese ships per $1 million dollars of mine warfare expenditure. Ibid., pp. 236–237. See also "Appendix A: Mine Threat Overview," *U.S. Naval Mine Warfare Plan*, 4th ed., Programs for the New Millennium.
114. The mine was an Italian-manufactured "Manta," which cost perhaps $10,000. Edward J. Marolda and Robert J. Schneller Jr., *Shield and Sword: The United States Navy and the Persian Gulf War* (Washington, D.C.: Naval Historical Center, Department of the Navy, 1998), p. 267.
115. Ibid., p. 37.
116. "Minister of State for the Armed Forces and the First Sea Lord Admiral Sir Alan West: Press Conference at the Ministry of Defence," London, April 11, 2003, http://www.operations.mod.uk/telic/press_11april.htm.
117. Max Hastings and Simon Jenkins, *The Battle for the Falklands* (New York: W.W. Norton, 1983), pp. 296–297.
118. Robert W. Love, *A History of the U.S. Navy, 1942–1991* (Harrisburg, Pa.: Stackpole, 1992), p. 784.

29, and then struck near Umm Qasr on April 1. U.S. and British ground and air forces had been in southern Iraq for more than a week, yet these systems had eluded detection.[119] Antiship missiles fired from surface vessels and aircraft have damaged or sunk several large naval vessels. Two Exocets fired from an Iraqi aircraft nearly sank the U.S. frigate *Stark* in 1987, killing thirty-seven sailors.[120] Air-launched Exocets sank the British destroyer *Sheffield* and the container ship *Atlantic Conveyor* in the 1982 Falklands War.[121] U.S. ship-launched Harpoons sank two Iranian ships in Operation Praying Mantis in April 1988. Two Iranian ships managed to fire missiles in the same engagement, but neither was successful.[122]

Though they did not prove lethal against large ships, lightly armed (Swedish-built) Iranian Boghammer speedboats proved a nuisance in the Persian Gulf during the 1980–88 Iraq-Iran War. Their main mission was machine gun and rocket attacks on ships trading with the gulf states, especially Kuwait, which provided the money that fueled Saddam Hussein's war machine. Because the shallow waters of the northern gulf were considered too dangerous for large warships, due to mines and presumably land-based antiship missiles, the U.S. Navy built two floating bases aboard large, leased, commercial barges and used them for special operations helicopters and patrol boats to deal with this threat.[123] They did this successfully, though at some risk. The use of a small motorboat by suicide bombers against the U.S. destroyer *Cole* on October 14, 2000, has added a new dimension to this threat. Moreover, much more sophisticated fast-attack aircraft can be built.[124] Major navies now feel compelled to devise new weaponry to counter these cheap, nimble, and potentially deadly attackers. In a recent U.S war game, a defending "red force" navy con-

---

119. Paul Lewis and Steward Penney, "Timeline: Week Two," *Flight International*, April 8, 2003, p. 11.
120. Marolda and Schneller, *Shield and Sword*, p. 36.
121. Hastings and Jenkins, *Battle for the Falklands*, pp. 153–156, 227–228.
122. Love, *A History of the U.S. Navy*, pp. 787–789.
123. David B. Crist, "Joint Special Operations in Support of Earnest Will," *Joint Forces Quarterly*, No. 29 (Autumn/Winter 2001–02), pp. 15–22. Crist notes some forty-three attacks in 1986, though only one actually sank a ship.
124. Richard Scott, "UK Plans to Counter Threat of Terrorists at Sea," *Jane's Defence Weekly*, June 19, 20002, p. 8. According to Scott, "Staff in the UK Ministry of Defence's Directorate Equipment Capability . . . have identified a significant gap in the capability of ships to adequately defend themselves against fast attack craft (FACS) fast inshore attack craft (FIACS), and acknowledge a capability upgrade as an urgent priority." Ibid. In an act of perhaps unintentional irony, the second story on the same page of the magazine is "Taiwan to Launch Prototype Stealth PCFG," or fast- attack missile patrol boat. If Taiwan can build stealthy small craft, then so can many other small and middle-sized countries, and the threat can be expected to grow.

sisting of small boats and some aircraft, attacked the simulated U.S. Navy task force entering the Persian Gulf and sent much of it to the bottom.[125]

Finally, though modern diesel electric submarines have not sunk any major surface combatants of late, they have proven extremely difficult to catch. Hunting for diesel electric submarines in coastal waters is rendered difficult by the poor acoustical transmission properties of shallow water and the background noise of coastal traffic. When running on its battery, a diesel electric submarine is naturally very quiet. When recharging the battery, its diesel sounds much like any other diesel in coastal waters. Its snorkel may generate a heat and radar signature, which ASW aircraft could exploit, but not if they can in turn be engaged by SAMs based afloat or ashore. A German-designed Argentine submarine made several unsuccessful attacks against British aircraft carriers during the Falklands War. Large quantities of ASW munitions were used against it, without scoring a hit.[126] When the Iranians took their first Soviet-designed Kilo-class submarine out for its maiden voyage several years ago, the U.S. Navy is said to have quickly lost track of it.[127]

Treated separately, these weapons are not only annoying but also potentially deadly. Deployed together, they produce synergies that can be difficult to crack. These synergies become even more deadly when the "terrain" favors the defense (i.e., in constricted waters such as the Persian Gulf). Bottom mines are difficult enough to find and disable when one is not liable to attack. If the minefield is covered by fire, if it lies within the lethal range of shore-based antiship missiles, the work could be impossible. A maximum effort by a task force of heavily armed surface vessels may with difficulty defend mine hunters

---

125. Robert Burns, "Ex-General Says Wargames Were Rigged," Associated Press, August 16, 2002.

126. John Morgan, captain, U.S. Navy "Anti-Submarine Warfare: A Phoenix for the Future," *Undersea Warfare*, Vol. 1, No. 1 (Fall 1998), http://www.chinfo.navy.mil/navpalib/cno/n87/usw/autumn98/anti.htm. Morgan warns, "Finally, ASW is hard. The *San Luis* operated in the vicinity of the British task force for more than a month and was a constant concern to Royal Navy commanders. Despite the deployment of five nuclear attack submarines, twenty-four-hour-per-day airborne ASW operations, and expenditures of precious time, energy, and ordnance, the British never once detected the Argentine submarine. The near-shore regional/littoral operating environment poses a very challenging ASW problem. We will need enhanced capabilities to root modern diesel, air-independent, and nuclear submarines out of the 'mud' of noisy, contact-dense environments typical of the littoral, and be ready as well to detect, localize, and engage submarines in deep water and Arctic environments." Ibid.

127. I have heard this from several U.S. naval officers. Iran apparently began operating its first Kilo submarine in 1993. At the time Vice Admiral Henry Chiles, commander of the Atlantic Fleet's submarine force did not consider the Iranians to be a "serious military threat." He did expect that "a year from now I think they'll have a greatly improved military capability." Quoted in Robert Burns, "Admiral Calls Iranian Subs a Potential Threat to U.S. Interests," Associated Press, August 4, 1993.

working close to shore against antiship missile attack, but this will surely produce a signature that will attract the attention of surveillance assets ashore and perhaps draw the combined attention of surface, subsurface, and land-based assets.[128] The point here is not that the U.S. Navy could not ultimately take a competent littoral defense force apart. It probably could. The point is that it could take time, and may impose considerable costs.

Thus far, the United States has been fortunate in that it has encountered adversaries with perhaps only one of these three capabilities—air, land, or sea. And even when the adversary has had one of these specializations, it has not necessarily been the best of breed. Serbian air defense troops were extremely good, but their best weaponry was at least a generation old, maybe older. The Somalis fought with great tenacity and, candidly, drove the United States from the country. But they were neither as well armed nor as well trained as the al-Qaeda troops in the Shah-e-Kot valley during Operation Anaconda in Afghanistan. The al-Qaeda troops were still not as well armed as some adversaries that U.S. forces might encounter, and there were probably not more than a few hundred of them in the fight. Finally, the U.S. Navy's littoral engagements in the Persian Gulf have been fought under fortuitous conditions. Iraq did not take littoral warfare especially seriously. The Iranian navy suffered because it had lost many of its officers in the 1979 revolution and arguably had never fully focused on the littoral mission. The shah of Iran had delusions of grandeur and sought a blue water navy.

One cannot predict whether the United States will encounter an adversary with the full panoply of capabilities that make possible the contested zone, and the United States need not take up the challenge if it is presented with such an array. A decade from now, however, it seems plausible that China and Iran will have mastered a range of air, sea, and land combat capabilities. U.S. Naval authorities are already nervous about Iran's capabilities.[129] North Korea is probably quite good in the arena of close, ground combat, but only mediocre in the

---

128. Iraq's naval tactics were not adept during Operation Desert Storm: "Fortunately for the allies, the Iraqis had failed to activate many of the weapons, and chose not to cover the minefields with aircraft, naval vessels, artillery, or missiles. More expertly laid and defended mines would have sunk ships and killed sailors and marines." Marolda and Schneller, *Shield and Sword*, p. 267.
129. "U.S. Alarmed by Growing Iranian Might: U.S. Navy Commander," Agence France-Presse, February 4, 1996. Vice Adm. Scott Redd, then commander of the U.S. Fifth Fleet, declared, "Iran now poses a threat to navigation and aircraft flying over the Gulf." Referring to then new Iranian sea-launched antiship missiles he noted, "From a military point of view, I have to warn of the new threat, which is represented by Iran's ability to launch missiles from all directions and not only from its shores." Quoted in ibid.

realm of air defense and littoral warfare.[130] Russia will probably be the source of most of the best antiaircraft systems sold around the world to possible U.S. adversaries, though China will surely enter that market as its systems improve. Russia will also produce and sell deadly weapons for littoral warfare. It is likely that Russia itself will remain a master of antiair warfare, will develop (or arguably redevelop) mastery in littoral warfare, but will have problems generating land power, especially infantry power.

Implications

Military strategy that fully exploits command of the commons is not complicated in principle. From time to time, even a policy of selective engagement may necessitate offensive engagements; indeed they may necessitate fights in the contested zone. The main point is that time is usually on the side of the United States. U.S. military power resides mainly in North America, where it is largely safe from attack. Command of the sea allows the United States to marshal its capabilities, and those of its allies, from around the globe to create a massive local material superiority.

Command of the commons also permits the isolation of the adversary from sources of political and military support, further increasing the U.S. margin of superiority and further allowing the passage of time to work in favor of the United States. This is especially useful against adversaries who depend on exports and imports. U.S. allies have large numbers of good, small-to-medium, naval surface combatants, especially appropriate for maintaining a blockade.[131] These ships play important roles in the worldwide war on terror.[132]

---

130. North Korea exports several vessels designed for coastal operations, including miniature submarines. It has sold several such vessels to Iran. See Bill Gertz, "N. Korea Delivers Semi-submersible Gunships to Iran," *Washington Times,* December 16, 2002.

131. Britain, France, Germany, and Italy together operate 99 destroyers and frigates. The U.S. Navy operates 117 cruisers, destroyers, and frigates. European surface combatants are smaller and less capable than those of the U.S. Navy, but they permit the surveillance and control of a great deal of additional sea space. Moreover, these navies either possess significant littoral combat experience, such as Britain, or build some of the world's most lethal littoral weapons, such as France (antiship missiles) and Italy (bottom mines). IISS, *The Military Balance, 2002–2003,* country entries.

132. Michael R. Gordon, "Threats and Responses: Allies—German and Spanish Navies Take on Major Role Near Horn of Africa," *New York Times,* December 15, 2002, p. 36. Task Force 150 is an 8 ship flotilla conducting patrols in the Indian Ocean in search of al-Qaeda operatives. Its first commander was German, and its second was Spanish. This is part of a larger multinational operation in the region, which includes ships from Australia, Canada, France, Germany, Greece, Italy, Japan, the Netherlands, Spain, the United Kingdom, and the United States. "Greece Contributes Frigate to Anti-Terrorism Campaign," Xinhua news agency, March 12, 2002.

They played important roles in the isolation of Iraq, which was under economic embargo from 1990. Though Iraq illegally exported some oil and illegally imported some weapons and military technology between 1990 and 2003, its military capability suffered greatly in these years. It failed to modernize in any significant way and was prevented from recovering its ability to invade its neighbors. The erosion of Iraq's conventional combat power contributed to U.S. confidence as it considered an invasion of Iraq in the autumn of 2002. Once the third Persian Gulf War began in March 2003, it rapidly became clear that Iraqi conventional weapons had on the whole not improved since 1991. Iraqi tactics improved slightly, in part because U.S. forces could not avoid the contested zones. Over the last decade, the U.S. Navy and allied navies quietly helped to starve Iraq's army and air force. Had they not done so, U.S. casualties in the 2003 war in Iraq would surely have been higher.

Command of space allows the close study of the adversary and the tailoring of U.S. capabilities to fight that enemy, while command of the air permits a careful wearing away of the adversary's remaining strengths. There is little that an adversary can do to erode U.S. military capabilities or political will unless the United States engages on the enemy's terms. But the United States does not need to be in any rush to launch attacks into enemy-held real estate. Instead it can probe an adversary's defenses, forcing it to elicit the information that U.S. forces need. U.S. probes can also lure the adversary into using up some of its scarce and difficult-to-replace imported munitions. At the appropriate time, if necessary, quantitatively and qualitatively superior U.S. and allied forces can directly challenge the much-weakened adversary. The fight may still prove difficult, but the United States will have significantly buffered itself against the perils of the contested zone.

In land warfare, U.S. military capabilities are particularly lethal when defending against adversaries who have to move large amounts of heavy military equipment and supplies forward over long distances. Command of space, and command of the air, permit the United States to exact an immense toll on advancing ground forces and the air forces that support them. This means that the United States should have a good chance of deterring regional aggressors, and successfully defending against them in the event that deterrence fails, if it has some forces in the theater and is permitted to mobilize more forces in a timely fashion. Command of the sea helps the U.S. keep forces forward deployed, even in politically sensitive areas, and reinforce those forces quickly. Rapid response still, however, depends on good political relations with the threatened party. On the whole, states worry more about proximate threats than they do about distant ones. But the tremendous power projection capability of the United States can appear to be a proximate threat if U.S. policy seems domineering. So command of the commons will provide more influence, and prove more militarily lethal, if others can be convinced that the United States is more interested in constraining regional aggressors than achieving regional dominance.

Command of the commons and the enduring contested zones mean that allies remain useful, more useful than current U.S. strategic discourse would suggest. The allies provide the formal and informal bases that are the crucial stepping stones for U.S. power to transit the globe. The military power of these allies contributes modestly to maintenance and exploitation of command of the commons, but can contribute significantly to the close fights and their aftermath. The NATO allies, for example, have great expertise in sea mine clearance and possess many mine hunters; Britain and France together have nearly half again as many mine-hunting vessels as the U.S. Navy.[133] Several of the allies have good ground forces, and perhaps most critically, good infantry that seem able to tolerate at least moderate casualties. The British Army and Royal Marines have 43 infantry battalions—all professionals—nearly half as many as the United States; France has another 20.[134] Given the relative scarcity of U.S. infantry, allied ground forces are also particularly useful in the postconflict peace-enforcement missions necessary to secure the fruits of any battlefield victory.

IMPLICATIONS FOR GRAND STRATEGY

The nature and scope of U.S. military power should affect U.S. grand strategy choices. U.S. military power is very great; if it were not, no hegemonic policy would be practical, but that does not mean that every hegemonic policy is practical. Today, there is little dispute within the U.S. foreign policy elite about the fact of great U.S. power, or the wisdom of an essentially hegemonic foreign policy. Even before the September 11 terrorist attacks, the foreign policy debate had narrowed to a dispute between primacy and selective engagement, between a nationalist, unilateralist version of hegemony, and a liberal, multilateral version of hegemony. U.S. command of the commons provides an impressive foundation for selective engagement. It is not adequate for a policy of primacy.

---

133. IISS, *The Military Balance, 2002–2003,* country entries.
134. Ibid.

Primacy, in particular, depends on vast, omnicapable military power, which is why the Bush administration pushes a military agenda that aims self-confidently to master the "contested zones."[135] President Bush and his advisers believe that the United States need not tolerate plausible threats to its safety from outside its borders. These threats are to be eliminated. Insofar as preventive war is difficult to sell abroad, this policy therefore requires the ability to act alone militarily—a unilateral global offensive capability. The effort to achieve such a capability will cause unease around the world and will make it increasingly difficult for the United States to find allies; it may cause others to ally against the United States. As they do, the costs of sustaining U.S. military preeminence will grow. Perhaps the first problem that primacy will create for U.S. command of the commons is greater difficulty in sustaining, improving, and expanding the global base structure that the United States presently enjoys.

Current Pentagon civilian leaders understand that they do not yet have the military to implement their policy. They hope to create it. For political, demographic, and technological reasons, the close fights in the contested zones are likely to remain difficult—especially when the adversary is fighting largely in defense of its own country. Senior civilian and military planners in the Pentagon seem to believe that somehow the technological leverage enjoyed in the commanded zone can be made to apply equally well in the contested zone if only the Pentagon spends enough money. This seems a chimera. Although one doubts that the United States would lose many fights in the contested zones, the costs in lost U.S., allied, and civilian lives of one or more such fights could be great enough to produce significant political problems at home and abroad for an activist U.S. foreign policy of any kind.

Selective engagement aims above all to create conditions conducive to great power peace on the assumption that many other benefits flow from this blessing, the foremost being U.S. security. In return for their cooperation, others get U.S. protection. Command of the commons makes this offer of protection credible. Their cooperation, in turn, makes the protection easy for the United States

---

135. The Pentagon has set the goals of "defeating anti-access and area denial threats," and "denying enemies sanctuary by providing persistent surveillance, tracking, and rapid engagement with high-volume precision strikes . . . against critical mobile and fixed targets at various ranges and in all weather and terrains." *Quadrennial Defense Review Report*, p. 30. Moreover, "Likely enemies of the United States and its allies will rely on sanctuaries—such as remote terrain, hidden bunkers, or civilian 'shields'—for protection. The capability to find and strike protected enemy forces while limiting collateral damage will improve the deterrent power of the United States and give the president increased options for response if deterrence fails." Ibid., p. 44.

to deliver. Great powers typically chafe at such dependency relationships, so U.S. diplomacy must be particularly adroit to sustain their willingness to cooperate. Command of the commons gives the United States a tremendous capability to harm others. Marrying that capability to a conservative policy of selective engagement helps make U.S. military power appear less threatening and more tolerable.

Command of the commons creates additional collective goods for U.S. allies. These collective goods help connect U.S. military power to seemingly prosaic welfare concerns. U.S. military power underwrites world trade, travel, global telecommunications, and commercial remote sensing, which all depend on peace and order in the commons. Those nations most involved in these activities, those who profit most from globalization, seem to understand that they benefit from the U.S. military position—which may help explain why the world's consequential powers have grudgingly supported U.S. hegemony.

There is little question that the United States is today the greatest military power on the planet, and the most potent global power since the dawn of the age of sail. This military power is both a consequence and a cause of the current skewed distribution of power in the world. If the United States were not the dominant economic and technological power, it would not be the dominant military power. The fact of U.S. military dominance is also a consequence of choices—the choice to spend vast sums on armaments and the choice of how to spend those sums. Nevertheless, the immense U.S. military effort has not produced military omnipotence, and it probably cannot. Policymakers need a more nuanced understanding of the favorable U.S. military position to exploit it fully and to ensure that foreign and military policy are mutually supporting.

Why Do States Build Nuclear Weapons?

Scott D. Sagan

Three Models in Search of a Bomb

Why do states build nuclear weapons? Having an accurate answer to this question is critically important both for predicting the long-term future of international security and for current foreign policy efforts to prevent the spread of nuclear weapons. Yet given the importance of this central proliferation puzzle, it is surprising how little sustained attention has been devoted to examining and comparing alternative answers.

This lack of critical attention is not due to a lack of information: there is now a large literature on nuclear decision-making inside the states that have developed nuclear weapons and a smaller, but still significant, set of case studies of states' decisions to refrain from developing nuclear weapons. Instead, the inattention appears to have been caused by the emergence of a near-consensus that the answer is obvious. Many U.S. policymakers and most international relations scholars have a clear and simple answer to the proliferation puzzle: states will seek to develop nuclear weapons when they face a significant military threat to their security that cannot be met through alternative means; if they do not face such threats, they will willingly remain non-nuclear states.[1]

Scott D. Sagan is Associate Professor of Political Science and a faculty associate of the Center for International Security and Arms Control at Stanford University.

I greatly benefited from discussions about earlier drafts of this article at seminars at the Aspen Strategy Group, the Institute for Defense Analysis, the Lawrence Livermore National Laboratory, the Monterey Institute of International Studies, the Olin Institute for Strategic Studies, and the Stockholm International Peace Research Institute. For especially detailed comments and criticisms, I thank Itty Abraham, Eric Arnett, Michael Barletta, George Bunn, Colin Elman, Miriam Fendius Elman, Peter Feaver, Harald Müller, George Perkovich, Jessica Stern, and Bradley Thayer. Benjamin Olding and Nora Bensahel provided excellent research assistance. Support for this research was provided by the W. Alton Jones Foundation and the Institute for Defense Analysis.

1. Among policymakers, John Deutsch presents the most unadorned summary of the basic argument that "the fundamental motivation to seek a weapon is the perception that national security will be improved." John M. Deutsch, "The New Nuclear Threat," *Foreign Affairs*, Vol. 71, No. 41 (Fall 1992), pp. 124–125. Also see George Shultz, "Preventing the Proliferation of Nuclear Weapons," *Department of State Bulletin*, Vol. 84, No. 2093 (December 1984), pp. 17–21. For examples of the dominant paradigm among scholars, see Michael M. May, "Nuclear Weapons Supply and Demand," *American Scientist*, Vol. 82, No. 6 (November–December 1994), pp. 526–537; Bradley A. Thayer, "The Causes of Nuclear Proliferation and the Nonproliferation Regime," *Security Studies*, Vol. 4, No. 3 (Spring 1995), pp. 463–519; Benjamin Frankel, "The Brooding Shadow: Systemic Incentives and Nuclear Weapons Proliferation," and Richard K. Betts, "Paranoids, Pygmies, Pariahs, and Nonproliferation Revisited," both in Zachary S. Davis and Benjamin Frankel, eds. *The*

The central purpose of this article is to challenge this conventional wisdom about nuclear proliferation. I argue that the consensus view, focusing on national security considerations as the cause of proliferation, is dangerously inadequate because nuclear weapons programs also serve other, more parochial and less obvious objectives. Nuclear weapons, like other weapons, are more than tools of national security; they are political objects of considerable importance in domestic debates and internal bureaucratic struggles and can also serve as international normative symbols of modernity and identity.

The body of this article examines three alternative theoretical frameworks—what I call "models" in the very informal sense of the term—about why states decide to build or refrain from developing nuclear weapons: "the security model," according to which states build nuclear weapons to increase national security against foreign threats, especially nuclear threats; "the domestic politics model," which envisions nuclear weapons as political tools used to advance parochial domestic and bureaucratic interests; and "the norms model," under which nuclear weapons decisions are made because weapons acquisition, or restraint in weapons development, provides an important normative symbol of a state's modernity and identity. Although many of the ideas underlying these models exist in the vast case-study and proliferation-policy literatures, they have not been adequately analyzed, nor placed in a comparative theoretical framework, nor properly evaluated against empirical evidence. When I discuss these models, therefore, I compare their theoretical conceptions of the causes of weapons development, present alternative interpretations of the history of some major proliferation decisions, and contrast the models' implications for nonproliferation policy. The article concludes with an outline of a research agenda for future proliferation studies and an examination of the policy dilemmas produced by the existence of these three proliferation models.

It is important to recognize from the start that the nuclear proliferation problem will be a critical problem in international security for the foreseeable future. Despite the successful 1995 agreement to have a permanent extension of the Nuclear Nonproliferation Treaty (NPT), there will be continuing NPT review conferences assessing the implementation of the treaty every five years; each member state can legally withdraw from the treaty, under the "supreme national interest" clause, if it gives three months notice; and many new states

Proliferation Puzzle, special issue of *Security Studies*, Vol. 2, No, 3/4 (Spring/Summer 1993), pp. 37–38 and pp. 100–124; and David Gompert, Kenneth Watman, amd Dean Wilkening, "Nuclear First Use Revisited," *Survival*, Vol. 37, No. 3 (Autumn 1995), p. 39.

can be expected to develop a "latent nuclear weapons capability" over the coming decade. Indeed, some fifty-seven states now operate or are constructing nuclear power or research reactors, and it has been estimated that about thirty countries today have the necessary industrial infrastructure and scientific expertise to build nuclear weapons on a crash basis if they chose to do so.[2] The NPT encourages this long-term trend by promoting the development of power reactors in exchange for the imposition of safeguards on the resulting nuclear materials. This suggests that while most attention concerning proliferation in the immediate-term has appropriately focused on controlling nuclear materials in the former Soviet Union and preventing the small number of active proliferators (such as Iraq, Iran, Libya, and North Korea) that currently appear to have vigorous nuclear weapons programs from getting the bomb, the longer-term and enduring proliferation problem will be ensuring that the larger and continually growing number of latent nuclear states maintain their non-nuclear weapons status. This underscores the policy importance of addressing the sources of the political *demand* for nuclear weapons, rather than focusing primarily on efforts to safeguard existing stockpiles of nuclear materials and to restrict the *supply* of specific weapons technology from the "haves" to the "have-nots."

If my arguments and evidence concerning the three models of proliferation are correct, however, any future demand-side nonproliferation strategy will face inherent contradictions. For, in contrast to the views of scholars who claim that a traditional realist theory focusing on security threats explains all cases of proliferation and nuclear restraint,[3] I believe that the historical record suggests that each theory explains some past cases quite well and others quite poorly. Unfortunately, since the theories provide different and often contradictory lessons for U.S. nonproliferation policy, this suggests that policies designed to address one future proliferation problem will exacerbate others. As I discuss in more detail below, particularly severe tensions are likely to emerge in the future between U.S. extended deterrence policies designed to address security

---

2. See Steve Fetter, "Verifying Nuclear Disarmament," Occasional Paper No. 29, Henry L. Stimson Center, Washington, D.C., October 1996, p. 38; and "Affiliations and Nuclear Activities of 172 NPT Parties," *Arms Control Today*, Vol. 25, No. 2 (March 1995), pp. 33–36. For earlier pioneering efforts to assess nuclear weapons latent capability and demand, see Stephen M. Meyer, *The Dynamics of Nuclear Proliferation* (Chicago: University of Chicago Press, 1984); and William C. Potter, *Nuclear Power and Nonproliferation* (Cambridge, Mass: Oelgeschlager, Gunn and Hain, 1982).
3. For example, May, "Nuclear Weapons Supply and Demand"; Thayer, "The Causes of Nuclear Proliferation and the Nonproliferation Regime"; and Frankel, "The Brooding Shadow: Systemic Incentives and Nuclear Weapons Proliferation."

concerns of potential proliferators and U.S. NPT policies designed to maintain and enhance international norms against nuclear use and acquisition.

The Security Model: Nuclear Weapons and International Threats

According to neorealist theory in political science, states exist in an anarchical international system and must therefore rely on self-help to protect their sovereignty and national security.[4] Because of the enormous destructive power of nuclear weapons, any state that seeks to maintain its national security must balance against any rival state that develops nuclear weapons by gaining access to a nuclear deterrent itself. This can produce two policies. First, strong states do what they can: they can pursue a form of internal balancing by adopting the costly, but self-sufficient, policy of developing their own nuclear weapons. Second, weak states do what they must: they can join a balancing alliance with a nuclear power, utilizing a promise of nuclear retaliation by that ally as a means of extended deterrence. For such states, acquiring a nuclear ally may be the only option available, but the policy inevitably raises questions about the credibility of extended deterrence guarantees, since the nuclear power would also fear retaliation if it responded to an attack on its ally.

Although nuclear weapons could also be developed to serve either as deterrents against overwhelming conventional military threats or as coercive tools to compel changes in the status quo, the simple focus on states' responses to emerging nuclear threats is the most common and most parsimonious explanation for nuclear weapons proliferation.[5] George Shultz once nicely summarized the argument: "Proliferation begets proliferation."[6] Every time one state develops nuclear weapons to balance against its main rival, it also creates a

---

4. The seminal text of neorealism remains Kenneth N. Waltz, *Theory of International Politics* (New York: Random House, 1979). Also see Kenneth N. Waltz, "The Origins of War in Neorealist Theory," in Robert I. Rotberg and Theodore K. Rabb, eds., *The Origin and Prevention of Major Wars* (New York: Cambridge University Press, 1989), pp. 39–52; and Robert O. Keohane, ed., *Neorealism and Its Critics* (New York: Columbia University Press, 1986).

5. The Israeli, and possibly the Pakistani, nuclear weapons decisions might be the best examples of defensive responses to conventional security threats; Iraq, and possibly North Korea, might be the best examples of the offensive coercive threat motivation. On the status quo bias in neorealist theory in general, see Randall L. Schweller, "Bandwagoning for Profit: Bringing the Revisionist State Back In," *International Security*, Vol. 19, No. 1 (Summer 1994), pp. 72–107, and Richard Rosecrance and Arthur A. Stein, eds., *The Domestic Bases of Grand Strategy* (Ithaca, N.Y.: Cornell University Press, 1993).

6. Shultz, "Preventing the Proliferation of Nuclear Weapons," p. 18.

nuclear threat to another state in the region, which then has to initiate its own nuclear weapons program to maintain its national security.

From this perspective, one can envision the history of nuclear proliferation as a strategic chain reaction. During World War II, none of the major belligerents was certain that the development of nuclear weapons was possible, but all knew that other states were already or could soon be working to build the bomb. This fundamental fear was the central impetus for the United States, British, German, Soviet, and Japanese nuclear weapons programs. The United States developed atomic weapons first, not because it had any greater demand for the atomic bomb than these other powers but, rather, because the United States invested more heavily in the program and made the right set of technological and organizational choices.[7]

After August 1945, the Soviet Union's program was reinvigorated because the U.S. atomic attacks on Hiroshima and Nagasaki demonstrated that nuclear weapons were technically possible, and the emerging Cold War meant that a Soviet bomb was a strategic imperative. From the realist perspective, the Soviet response was perfectly predictable. Josef Stalin's reported request to Igor Kurchatov and B.L. Yannikov in August 1945 appears like a textbook example of realist logic:

A single demand of you comrades. . . . Provide us with atomic weapons in the shortest possible time. You know that Hiroshima has shaken the whole world. The balance has been destroyed. Provide the bomb—it will remove a great danger from us.[8]

The nuclear weapons decisions of other states can also be explained within the same framework. London and Paris are seen to have built nuclear weapons because of the growing Soviet military threat and the inherent reduction in the credibility of the U.S. nuclear guarantee to NATO allies once the Soviet Union was able to threaten retaliation against the United States.[9] China developed the bomb because Beijing was threatened with possible nuclear attack by the United States at the end of the Korean War and again during the Taiwan Straits

---

7. On the genesis of the atomic programs in World War II, see McGeorge Bundy, *Danger and Survival: Choices about the Bomb in the First Fifty Years* (New York: Random House, 1988) pp. 3–53; and Richard Rhodes, *The Making of the Atomic Bomb* (New York: Simon and Schuster, 1986).
8. A. Lavrent'yeva in "Stroiteli novogo mira," *V mire knig*, No. 9 (1970), in David Holloway, *The Soviet Union and the Arms Race* (New Haven, Conn.: Yale University Press, 1980), p. 20, also quoted in Thayer, "The Causes of Nuclear Proliferation," p. 487.
9. Important sources on the British case include Margaret Gowing, *Britain and Atomic Energy, 1939–1945* (London: Macmillan, 1964); Margaret Gowing, *Independence and Deterrence: Britain and Atomic Energy 1945–1952*, vols. 1 and 2 (London: Macmillan, 1974); and Andrew Pierre, *Nuclear*

crises in the mid-1950s. Not only did Moscow prove to be an irresolute nuclear ally in the 1950s, but the emergence of hostility in Sino-Soviet relations in the 1960s further encouraged Beijing to develop, in Avery Goldstein's phrase, the "robust and affordable security" of nuclear weapons, since the border clashes "again exposed the limited value of China's conventional deterrent."[10]

After China developed the bomb in 1964, India, which had just fought a war with China in 1962, was bound to follow suit. India's strategic response to the Chinese test came a decade later, when their Atomic Energy Commission successfully completed the long research and development process required to construct and detonate what was called a "peaceful nuclear explosion" (PNE) in May 1974. According to realist logic, India has maintained an ambiguous nuclear posture since that time—building sufficient nuclear materials and components for a moderate-sized nuclear arsenal, but not testing or deploying weapons into the field—in a clever strategic effort to deter the Chinese, while simultaneously not encouraging nuclear weapons programs in other neighboring states.[11] After the Indian explosion, however, the nascent Pakistani weapons program had to move forward according to the realist view: facing a recently hostile neighbor with both nuclear weapons and conventional military superiority, it was inevitable that the government in Islamabad would seek to produce a nuclear weapon as quickly as possible.[12]

Politics: The British Experience with an Independent Strategic Force, 1939–1970 (London: Oxford University Press, 1972). On the French case, see Lawrence Scheinman, *Atomic Energy Policy in France Under the Fourth Republic* (Princeton, N.J.: Princeton University Press, 1965) and Wilfred L. Kohl, *French Nuclear Diplomacy* (Princeton, N.J.: Princeton University Press, 1971).

10. Avery Goldstein, "Robust and Affordable Security: Some Lessons from the Second-Ranking Powers During the Cold War," *Journal of Strategic Studies*, Vol. 15, No. 4 (December 1992), p. 494. The seminal source on the Chinese weapons program, which emphasizes the importance of U.S. nuclear threats in the 1950s, is John W. Lewis and Xue Litai, *China Builds the Bomb* (Stanford, Calif.: Stanford University Press, 1988).

11. Recent estimates of the number of weapons India could deploy on short notice range from 25 to 105. See Mitchell Reiss, *Bridled Ambition: Why Countries Constrain Their Nuclear Capabilities* (Washington, D.C.: Woodrow Wilson Center Press, 1995), p. 185; Leonard S. Spector and Mark G. McDonough, *Tracking Nuclear Proliferation* (Washington, D.C.: Carnegie Endowment for International Peace, 1995), p. 89; and Eric Arnett, "Implications of the Comprehensive Test Ban," in Eric Arnett, ed., *Nuclear Weapons after the Comprehensive Test Ban* (Oxford: Oxford University Press, 1996), p. 13. Important sources on the Indian nuclear program include Ashok Kapur, *India's Nuclear Option: Atomic Diplomacy and Decision Making* (New York: Praeger, 1976); Brahma Chellaney, "South Asia's Passage to Nuclear Power," *International Security*, Vol. 16, No. 1 (Summer 1991), pp. 43–72; and T. T. Poulose, ed., *Perspectives of India's Nuclear Policy* (New Delhi: Young Asia Publications, 1978).

12. Valuable sources on Pakistan's program include Ziba Moshaver, *Nuclear Weapons Proliferation in the Indian Subcontinent* (Basingstoke, U.K.: Macmillan, 1991) and Ashok Kapur, *Pakistan's Nuclear Development* (New York: Croom Helm, 1987).

EXPLAINING NUCLEAR RESTRAINT

Given the strong deterrent capabilities of nuclear weapons, why would any state give up such powerful sources of security? The major recent cases of nuclear weapons restraint can also be viewed through the lens provided by the security model if one assumes that external security threats can radically change or be reevaluated. The case of South Africa has most often been analyzed in this light, with the new security threats that emerged in the mid-1970s seen as the cause of South Africa's bomb program and the end of these threats in the late 1980s as the cause of its policy reversal. As President F.W. de Klerk explained in his speech to Parliament in March 1993, the Pretoria government saw a growing "Soviet expansionist threat to southern Africa"; "the buildup of the Cuban forces in Angola from 1975 onwards reinforced the perception that a deterrent was necessary, as did South Africa's relative international isolation and the fact that it could not rely on outside assistance should it be attacked."[13] Six atomic weapons were therefore constructed, but were stored disassembled in a secret location, between 1980 and 1989, when the program was halted. The South African nuclear strategy during this period was designed to use the bomb both as a deterrent against the Soviets and as a tool of blackmail against the United States. If Soviet or Soviet-supported military forces directly threatened South Africa, the regime reportedly planned to announce that it had a small arsenal of nuclear weapons, dramatically testing one or more of the weapons if necessary by dropping them from aircraft over the ocean, hoping that such a test would shock the United States into intervention on behalf of the Pretoria regime.[14]

South Africa destroyed its small nuclear weapons arsenal in 1991, the theory suggests, because of the radical reduction in the external security threats to the regime. By 1989, the risk of a Soviet-led or sponsored attack on South Africa was virtually eliminated. President de Klerk cited three specific changes in military threats in his speech to Parliament: a cease-fire had been negotiated

13. F. W. de Klerk, March 24, 1993 address to the South African parliament as transcribed in Foreign Broadcast Information Service (FBIS), JPRS-TND-93-009, (March 29, 1993), p. 1 (henceforth cited as de Klerk, "Address to Parliament.") For analyses that focus largely on security threats as the cause of the program, see Darryl Howlett and John Simpson, "Nuclearization and Denuclearization in South Africa," *Survival*, Vol. 35, No. 3 (Autumn 1993), pp. 154–173; and J.W. de Villers, Roger Jardine, and Mitchell Reiss, "Why South Africa Gave up the Bomb," *Foreign Affairs*, Vol. 72, No. 5 (November/December 1993), pp. 98–109. For a more detailed and more balanced perspective see Reiss, *Bridled Ambition*, pp. 7–44.
14. Military planners nonetheless developed nuclear target lists in their contingency military plans and research was conducted on development of the hydrogen bomb until 1985. See Reiss, *Bridled Ambition*, p. 16.

in Angola; the tripartite agreement granted independence to Namibia in 1988; and most dramatically, "the Cold War had come to an end."[15]

Although the details change in different cases, the basic security model has also been used to explain other examples of nuclear restraint. For example, both Argentina and Brazil refused to complete the steps necessary to join the Latin American nuclear weapons-free zone (NWFZ) and began active programs in the 1970s that could eventually have produced nuclear weapons; however, their 1990 joint declaration of plans to abandon their programs is seen as the natural result of the recognition that the two states, which had not fought a war against one another since 1828, posed no fundamental security threat to each other.[16] Similarly, it has been argued that the non-Russian former states of the Soviet Union that were "born nuclear"—Ukraine, Kazakhstan, and Belarus—decided to give up their arsenals because of a mixture of two realist model arguments: their long-standing close ties to Moscow meant that these states did not perceive Russia as a major military threat to their security and sovereignty, and increased U.S. security guarantees to these states made their possession of nuclear weapons less necessary.[17] In short, from a realist's perspective, nuclear restraint is caused by the absence of the fundamental military threats that produce positive proliferation decisions.

POLICY IMPLICATIONS OF THE SECURITY MODEL

Several basic predictions and prescriptions flow naturally from the logic of the security model. First, since states that face nuclear adversaries will eventually develop their own arsenals unless credible alliance guarantees with a nuclear power exist, the maintenance of U.S. nuclear commitments to key allies, in-

---

15. See de Klerk, "Address to Parliament," p. 2.
16. Thayer, "The Causes of Nuclear Proliferation," p. 497; and May, "Nuclear Weapons Supply and Demand," pp. 534–535. For analyses of the Argentine-Brazilian decision, see Monica Serrano, "Brazil and Argentina," in Mitchell Reiss and Robert S. Litwak, eds. *Nuclear Proliferation After the Cold War* (Washington, D.C.: Woodrow Wilson Center Press, 1994), pp. 231–255; Jose Goldemberg and Harold A. Feiveson, "Denuclearization in Argentina and Brazil," *Arms Control Today*, Vol. 24, No. 2 (March 1994), pp. 10–14; Reiss, *Bridled Ambition*, pp. 45–88; and John R. Redick, Julio C. Carasales, and Paulo S. Wrobel, "Nuclear Rapprochement: Argentina, Brazil, and the Nonproliferation Regime," *Washington Quarterly*, Vol. 18, No. 1 (Winter 1995), pp. 107–122.
17. Sherman Garnett writes, for example, that "for many Ukrainian citizens—not just the ethnic Russians—it is difficult to conceive of Russia as an enemy to be deterred with nuclear weapons." Sherman W. Garnett, "Ukraine's Decision to Join the NPT," *Arms Control Today*, Vol. 25, No. 1 (January 1995), p. 8. Garnett also maintains that "the role that security assurances played in the creation of a framework for Ukrainian denuclearization is obvious. They were of immense importance." Sherman W. Garnett, "The Role of Security Assurances in Ukrainian Denuclearization," in Virginia Foran, ed., *Missed Opportunities?: The Role of Security Assurances in Nuclear Non-Proliferation* (Washington, D.C.: Carnegie Endowment for International Peace, forthcoming 1997).

cluding some form of continued first-use policy, is considered crucial.[18] Other efforts to enhance the security of potential proliferators—such as confidence-building measures or "negative security assurances" that the nuclear states will not use their weapons against non-nuclear states—can also be helpful in the short-run, but will likely not be effective in the long-term given the inherent suspicions of potential rivals produced by the anarchic international system.

Under the security model's logic, the NPT is seen as an institution permitting non-nuclear states to overcome a collective action problem. Each state would prefer to become the only nuclear weapons power in its region, but since that is an unlikely outcome if it develops a nuclear arsenal, it is willing to refrain from proliferation if, and only if, its neighbors remain non-nuclear. The treaty permits such states to exercise restraint with increased confidence that their neighbors will follow suit, or at a minimum, that they will receive sufficient advance warning if a break-out from the treaty is coming. It follows, from this logic, that other elements of the NPT regime should be considered far less important: specifically, the commitments that the United States and other nuclear states made under Article VI of the treaty—that the nuclear powers will pursue "negotiations in good faith on measures relating to cessation of the nuclear arms race at an early date and to nuclear disarmament"—are merely sops to public opinion in non-nuclear countries. The degree to which the nuclear states follow through on these Article VI commitments will not significantly influence the actual behavior of non-nuclear states, since it will not change their security status.

Under realist logic, however, U.S. nonproliferation policy can only slow down, not eliminate, the future spread of nuclear weapons. Efforts to slow down the process may of course be useful, but they will eventually be countered by two very strong structural forces that create an inexorable momentum toward a world of numerous nuclear weapons states. First, the end of the Cold War creates a more uncertain multipolar world in which U.S. nuclear guarantees will be considered increasingly less reliable; second, each time one state develops nuclear weapons, it will increase the strategic incentives for neighboring states to follow suit.[19]

---

18. See Lewis Dunn, *Controlling the Bomb* (New Haven, Conn.: Yale University Press, 1982); May, "Nuclear Weapons Supply and Demand," p. 535; and Frankel, "The Brooding Shadow," pp. 47–54.
19. See Kenneth N. Waltz, "The Emerging Structure of International Politics," *International Security,* Vol. 18, No. 2 (Fall 1993), pp. 44–79; and John J. Mearsheimer, "Back to the Future: Instability in Europe after the Cold War," *International Security,* Vol. 15, No. 1 (Summer 1990), pp. 5–56.

PROBLEMS AND EVIDENCE

What's wrong with this picture? The security model is parsimonious; the resulting history is conceptually clear; and the theory fits our intuitive belief that important events in history (like the development of a nuclear weapon) must have equally important causes (like national security). A major problem exists, however, concerning the evidence, for the realist history depends primarily on first, the statements of motivation by the key decision-makers, who have a vested interest in explaining that the choices they made served the national interest; and second, a correlation in time between the emergence of a plausible security threat and a decision to develop nuclear weapons. Indeed, an all too common intellectual strategy in the literature is to observe a nuclear weapons decision and then work backwards, attempting to find the national security threat that "must" have caused the decision. Similarly, scholars too often observe a state decision not to have nuclear weapons and then work backwards to find the change in the international environment that "must" have led the government to believe that threats to national security were radically decreasing.

These problems suggest that a more serious analysis would open up the black box of decision-making and examine in more detail how governments actually made their nuclear decisions. Any rigorous attempt to evaluate the security model of proliferation, moreover, also requires an effort to develop alternative explanations, and to assess whether they provide more or less compelling explanations for proliferation decisions. The following sections therefore develop a domestic politics model and a norms model of proliferation and evaluate the explanations that flow from their logic, versus the security model's arguments offered above, for some important cases of both nuclear proliferation and nuclear restraint.

The Domestic Politics Model: Nuclear Pork and Parochial Interests

A second model of nuclear weapons proliferation focuses on the domestic actors who encourage or discourage governments from pursuing the bomb. Whether or not the acquisition of nuclear weapons serves the national interests of a state, it is likely to serve the parochial bureaucratic or political interests of at least some individual actors within the state. Three kinds of actors commonly appear in historical case-studies of proliferation: the state's nuclear energy establishment (which includes officials in state-run laboratories as well as civilian reactor facilities); important units within the professional military (often within the air force, though sometimes in navy bureaucracies interested in nuclear propulsion); and politicians in states in which individual parties or the mass public strongly favor nuclear weapons acquisition. When such actors form coalitions that are strong enough to control the government's decision-making process—either through their direct political power or indirectly through their control of information—nuclear weapons programs are likely to thrive.

Unfortunately, there is no well-developed domestic political theory of nuclear weapons proliferation that identifies the conditions under which such coalitions are formed and become powerful enough to produce their preferred outcomes.[20] The basic logic of this approach, however, has been strongly influenced by the literature on bureaucratic politics and the social construction of technology concerning military procurement in the United States and the Soviet Union during the Cold War.[21] In this literature, bureaucratic actors are not seen as passive recipients of top-down political decisions; instead, they create the conditions that favor weapons acquisition by encouraging extreme perceptions of foreign threats, promoting supportive politicians, and actively lobbying for increased defense spending. This bottom-up view focuses on the formation of domestic coalitions within the scientific-military-industrial complex. The initial ideas for individual weapons innovations are often developed inside state laboratories, where scientists favor military innovation simply because it is technically exciting and keeps money and prestige flowing to their laboratories. Such scientists are then able to find, or even create, sponsors in the professional military whose bureaucratic interests and specific military responsibilities lead them also to favor the particular weapons system. Finally, such a coalition builds broader political support within the executive or legislative branches by shaping perceptions about the costs and benefits of weapons programs.

---

20. This is a serious weakness shared by many domestic-level theories in international relations, not just theories of proliferation. On this issue, see Ethan B. Kapstein, "Is Realism Dead? The Domestic Sources of International Politics," *International Organization*, Vol. 49, No. 4 (Autumn 1995), pp. 751–774.
21. The best examples of this literature include Morton H. Halperin, *Bureaucratic Politics and Foreign Policy* (Washington, D.C.: The Brookings Institution, 1974); Matthew Evangelista, *Innovation and the Arms Race: How the United States and Soviet Union Develop New Military Technologies* (Ithaca, N.Y.: Cornell University Press, 1988); and Donald MacKenzie, *Inventing Accuracy: A Historical Sociology of Nuclear Missile Guidance* (Cambridge, Mass.: MIT Press, 1990). For a valuable effort to apply insights from the literature on social construction of technology to proliferation problems, see Steven Flank, "Exploding the Black Box: The Historical Sociology of Nuclear Proliferation," *Security Studies*, Vol. 3, No. 2 (Winter 1993/94), pp. 259–294.

Realists recognize that domestic political actors have parochial interests, of course, but argue that such interests have only a marginal influence on crucial national security issues. The outcome of bureaucratic battles, for example, may well determine whether a state builds 500 or 1000 ICBMs or emphasizes submarines or strategic bombers in its nuclear arsenal; but a strong consensus among domestic actors will soon emerge about the need to respond in kind when a potential adversary acquires nuclear weapons. In contrast, from this domestic politics perspective, nuclear weapons programs are not obvious or inevitable solutions to international security problems; instead, nuclear weapons programs are solutions looking for a problem to which to attach themselves so as to justify their existence. Potential threats to a state's security certainly exist in the international system, but in this model, international threats are seen as being more malleable and more subject to interpretation, and can therefore produce a variety of responses from domestic actors. Security threats are therefore not the central cause of weapons decisions according to this model: they are merely windows of opportunity through which parochial interests can jump.

PROLIFERATION REVISITED: ADDRESSING THE INDIA PUZZLE

The historical case that most strongly fits the domestic politics model is the Indian nuclear weapons experience. In contrast to the brief realist's account outlined above, a closer look at the history of the Indian program reveals that there was no consensus among officials in New Delhi that it was necessary to have a nuclear deterrent as a response to the 1964 Chinese nuclear test. If that had been the case, according to realist logic, one of two events would likely have occurred. First, a crash weapons program could have been initiated; there is no evidence that such an emergency program was started, however, and indeed, given the relatively advanced state of Indian nuclear energy at the time, such an effort could have produced a nuclear weapon by the mid-to-late 1960s, relatively soon after the Chinese test, instead of in 1974.[22] Second, leaders in New Delhi could have made a concerted effort to acquire nuclear guarantees from the United States, the Soviet Union, or other nuclear powers. Indian officials, however, did not adopt a consistent policy to pursue security guaran-

---

22. In 1963, U.S. intelligence agencies estimated that India could test a nuclear weapon in four to five years (1967 or 1968). By 1965, U.S. estimates were that it would take one to three years additional years. See Peter R. Lavoy, "Nuclear Myths and the Causes of Proliferation," in Davis and Frankel, *The Proliferation Puzzle*, p. 202; and George Bunn, *Arms Control by Committee: Managing Negotiations with the Russians* (Stanford, Calif.: Stanford University Press, 1992), p. 68.

tees: in diplomatic discussions after the Chinese test, officials rejected the idea of bilateral guarantees because they would not conform with India's non-aligned status, refused to consider foreign bases in India to support a nuclear commitment, and publicly questioned whether any multilateral or bilateral guarantee could possibly be considered credible.[23]

Instead of producing a united Indian effort to acquire a nuclear deterrent, the Chinese nuclear test produced a prolonged bureaucratic battle, fought inside the New Delhi political elite and nuclear energy establishment, between actors who wanted India to develop a nuclear weapons capability as soon as possible and other actors who opposed an Indian bomb and supported global nuclear disarmament and later Indian membership in the NPT. Soon after the Chinese nuclear test, for example, Prime Minister Lal Bahadur Shastri argued against developing an Indian atomic arsenal, in part because the estimated costs ($42–84 million) were deemed excessive; Homi Bhabba, the head of the Atomic Energy Commission (AEC), however, loudly lobbied for the development of nuclear weapons capability, claiming that India could develop a bomb in 18 months and that an arsenal of 50 atomic bombs would cost less than $21 million (a figure that excluded the construction of reactors, separation plants, and the opportunity costs of diverting scientists from development projects).[24] Although Shastri continued to oppose weapons development and rebuked legislators in congressional debates for quoting Bhabba's excessively optimistic cost estimates, he compromised with the pro-bomb members of the Congress party and the AEC leadership, agreeing to create a classified project to develop an ability to detonate a PNE within 6 months of any final political decision.[25] However, even this compromise was short-lived, as Bhabba's successor at the AEC, Vikram Sarabhai, opposed the development of any Indian nuclear explosives, whether they were called PNEs or bombs, and ordered a halt to the PNE preparation program.[26]

---

23. See A.G. Noorani, "India's Quest for a Nuclear Guarantee," *Asian Survey,* Vol. 7, No. 7 (July 1967), pp. 490–502.
24. Frank E. Couper, "Indian Party Conflict on the Issue of Atomic Weapons," *Journal of Developing Areas,* Vol. 3, No. 2 (January 1969), pp. 192–193. Also see Lavoy, "Nuclear Myths and the Causes of Proliferation," p. 201.
25. See Shyam Bhatia, *India's Nuclear Bomb* (Ghaziabad: Vikas Publishing House, 1979), pp. 120–122. The director of the PNE study later wrote that "getting the Prime Minister to agree to this venture must have required great persuasion, as Shastriji was opposed to the idea of atomic explosions of any kind." Raja Ramanna, *Years of Pilgrimage: An Autobiography* (New Delhi: Viking, 1991), p. 74.
26. See Kapur, *India's Nuclear Option,* p. 195; Mitchell Reiss, *Without the Bomb: The Politics of Nuclear Nonproliferation* (New York: Columbia University Press, 1988), p. 221 and p. 325 (note 42); and Ramanna, *Years of Pilgrimage,* p. 75.

After Sarabhai's death in 1971, the pro-bomb scientists in the AEC began to lobby Prime Minister Indira Gandhi, and developed an alliance with defense laboratories whose participation was needed to fabricate the explosive lenses for a nuclear test.[27] Unfortunately, firm evidence on why Gandhi decided to approve the scientists' recommendation to build and test a "peaceful" Indian nuclear device does not exist: indeed, even nuclear scientists who pushed for the May 1974 test now acknowledge that it is impossible to know whether Gandhi was primarily responding to domestic motives, since she neither asked questions at the critical secret meetings in early 1974 nor explained why she approved their PNE recommendations.[28] A number of observations about the decision, however, do suggest that addressing domestic political concerns, rather than countering international security threats, were paramount. First, it is important to recognize that the decision was made by Prime Minister Gandhi, with the advice of a very small circle of personal advisers and scientists from the nuclear establishment. Senior defense and foreign affairs officials in India were not involved in the initial decision to prepare the nuclear device, nor in the final decision to test it: the military services were not asked how nuclear weapons would affect their war plans and military doctrines; the Defense Minister was reportedly informed of, but not consulted about, the final test decision only 10 days before the May 18 explosion; the Foreign Minister was merely given a 48-hour notice of the detonation.[29] This pattern suggests that security arguments were of secondary importance, and at a minimum, were not thoroughly analyzed or debated before the nuclear test. Second, the subsequent absence of a systematic program for either nuclear weapons or PNE development and testing, and New Delhi's lack of preparedness for Canada's immediate termination of nuclear assistance, suggest that the decision was taken quickly, even in haste, and thus may have focused more on immediate political concerns rather than on longer-term security or energy interests.

Third, it is important to recognize that domestic support for the Gandhi government had fallen to an all-time low in late 1973 and early 1974 due to a

27. Ramanna, *Years of Pilgrimage*, p. 89.
28. See George Perkovich, "Indian Nuclear Decision-Making and the 1974 PNE," unpublished manuscript, W. Alton Jones Foundation, Charlottesville, Va., 1996, p. 15; and Ramanna, *Years of Pilgrimage*, p. 89.
29. See Neil H.A. Joeck, *Nuclear Proliferation and National Security in India and Pakistan*, unpublished dissertation, UCLA, 1986, p. 229; and Kapur, *India's Nuclear Option*, p. 198. One former Indian Defense Secretary, K.B. Lall, has stated that the chairman of the chiefs of staff, the defense minister, and the defense secretary were not involved in the planning and argued therefore that "[the test] did not arise out of the Defense Ministry or on security grounds" since "if it was a defense project, there should have been some discussion." Lall interview quoted in Joeck, *Nuclear Proliferation and National Security*, p. 229.

prolonged and severe domestic recession, the eruption of large-scale riots in a number of regions, and the lingering effects of the splintering of the ruling Congress Party. From a domestic politics perspective, it would be highly surprising for a politician with such problems to resist what she knew was a major opportunity to increase her standing in public opinion polls and to defuse an issue about which she had been criticized by her domestic opponents.[30] Indeed, the domestic consequences of the test were very rewarding: the nuclear detonation occurred during the government's unprecedented crackdown on the striking railroad workers and contributed to a major increase in support for the Gandhi government. Indian public opinion polls taken in June 1974 reported, for example, that a full 91 percent of the adult literate population knew about the explosion and 90 percent of those individuals answered in the affirmative when asked if they were "personally proud of this achievement." The overall result was that public support for Mrs. Gandhi increased by one-third in the month after the nuclear test according to the Indian Institute of Public Opinion, leading the Institute to conclude that "both she [Gandhi] and the Congress Party have been restored to the nation's confidence."[31]

These arguments linking decision-making processes and domestic results to potential causes of proliferation clearly do not prove that the domestic politics model provides the correct explanation of the Indian case. But they do constitute stronger evidence than what has been offered in the literature to support a security model explanation, and provide an answer to what is otherwise the very puzzling occurrence of a state (India) *not* developing the bomb for ten years after one rival (China) tested a weapon, and then changing its proliferation policy and developing and testing a weapon less than three years after it attacked and dismembered its other rival state (Pakistan). In light of the domestic politics model, the unusual nature of Indian nuclear weapons policy since the 1974 test also becomes more understandable; it appears less like a calculated strategy of nuclear ambiguity and more like a political rationalization for latent military capabilities developed for other reasons. Finally, from

---

30. Although Gandhi denied, in a later interview, that domestic concerns influenced her 1974 decision, she did acknowledge that the nuclear test "would have been useful for elections." See Rodney W. Jones, "India," in Jozef Goldblat, ed., *Non-Proliferation: the Why and the Wherefore* (London: Taylor and Francis, 1985), p. 114.

31. The Institute's analysis was that the increase was the result of both "the demonstration of India's atomic capability and the decisive action on the Railway strike," though the data outlined above suggests that more emphasis should be placed on the weapons test. See "The Prime Minister's Popularity: June 1974," and "Indian Public Opinion and the Railway Strike," in *Monthly Public Opinion Surveys* (Indian Institute of Public Opinion), Vol. 19, No. 8 (May 1974), pp. 5–6 and pp. 7–11; and "Public Opinion on India's Nuclear Device," *Monthly Public Opinion Surveys*, Vol. 19, No. 9 (June 1974), Blue Supplement, pp. III–IV.

the domestic model's perspective, the 1974 test and subsequent building of significantly greater nuclear weapons capabilities are not seen as proud symbols of the success of an Indian national security program; instead, they are symbols of the failure of the Indian civilian nuclear power industry, which was forced to form an alliance with the pro-bomb lobby to justify its existence and funding after its failure to avoid cost overruns and prevent safety problems in its domestic energy program.[32]

DEVELOPMENT AND DENUCLEARIZATION: SOUTH AFRICA REVISITED

From the domestic model's perspective, one would expect that reversals of weapons decisions occur not when external threats are diminished, but rather when there are major internal political changes. There are a number of reasons why purely internal changes could produce restraint: a new government has an opportunity to change course more easily because it can blame failed policies of the previous regime; actors with parochial interests in favor of weapons programs may lose internal struggles to newly empowered actors with other interests; and the outgoing government may fear that the incoming government would not be a reliable custodian over nuclear weapons. It is important to note, however, that each of these domestic pathways to restraint can be relatively independent of changes in international security threats.

A quite different interpretation of the South African weapons program emerges when one reexamines the history with a focus on domestic political interests rather than national security. For example, President de Klerk's public explanation for the program stressed that it was caused by the need to deter "a Soviet expansionist threat to Southern Africa," especially after Cuban military forces intervened in Angola in October 1975. Yet the preliminary research needed to develop nuclear devices was started inside South Africa's Atomic Energy Board in 1971, on the independent authority of the Minister of Mines; a non-nuclear scale model of a gun-type explosive device was secretly tested in May 1974; and later in 1974, after the results of this test were known, Prime Minister John Voster approved plans to construct a small number of explosive devices and to build a secret testing site in the Kalahari desert.[33] Such evidence

---

32. For a detailed analysis, see Itty Abraham's *Atomic Energy and the Making of the Indian State,* unpublished manuscript, Center for International Security and Arms Control, Stanford University, 1996; and Itty Abraham, "India's 'Strategic Enclave': Civilian Scientists and Military Technologies," *Armed Forces and Society,* Vol. 18, No. 2 (Winter 1992), pp. 231–252.
33. See the chronology in Reiss, *Bridled Ambition,* p. 8 and p. 27; and Waldo Stumpf, "South Africa's Nuclear Weapons Program: From Deterrence to Dismantlement," *Arms Control Today,* Vol. 25, No. 10 (December 1995/January 1996), p. 4. Also see David Fischer, "South Africa," in Mitchell

strongly supports the claims of South African scientists that the nuclear program was originally designed to produce PNEs, and was championed within the government by the South African nuclear power and mining industries to enhance their standing in international scientific circles and to be utilized in mining situations.[34]

This explanation for the origin of the nuclear program helps in turn to explain South African nuclear doctrine, which otherwise appears so strange, as a *post hoc* development used to exploit devices that were originally developed for other purposes. (Testing a nuclear device in the event of a Soviet invasion might, after all, *reduce* the likelihood of U.S. intervention and would raise great risks of the use of Soviet nuclear weapons.) Senior officials in the program have stated, for example, that the military was not consulted about the bomb design and that operational considerations, such as the size and weight of the devices, were not taken into account.[35] As a result, the first South African nuclear device was actually too large to be deliverable by an aircraft and had to be redesigned because it did not meet the safety and reliability standards set by Armscor, the engineering organization run by the South African military, which took over the nuclear program in 1978.[36]

The timing and details of actions concerning the decision to dismantle and destroy the existing bomb stockpile also suggest that domestic political considerations were critical. In September 1989, de Klerk was elected president and immediately requested a high-level report on the possibility of dismantling the existing six nuclear devices. It is important to note that this request came before the Cold War was unambiguously over (the Berlin Wall fell in November 1989), and that de Klerk's action was considered by officials in South Africa as a sign that he had already decided to abandon the weapons program. Although possible concerns about who would inherit nuclear weapons are rarely discussed in the public rationales for the dismantlement decision, the de Klerk government's actions spoke more loudly than its words: the weapons components were dismantled *before* IAEA inspections could be held to verify the activities, and all the nuclear program's plans, history of decisions, and ap-

Reiss and Robert S. Litwak, eds., *Nuclear Proliferation After the Cold War* (Washington, D.C.: Woodrow Wilson Center Press, 1994), p. 208; and David Albright, "South Africa's Secret Nuclear Weapons," *ISIS Report* (Washington, D.C.: Institute for Science and International Security, May 1994), pp. 6–8.
34. See Mark Hibbs, "South Africa's Secret Nuclear Program: From a PNE to a Deterrent," *Nuclear Fuel*, May 10, 1993, pp. 3–6; and Stumpf, "South Africa's Nuclear Weapons Program," p. 4.
35. See Reiss, *Bridled Ambitions*, p. 12.
36. Albright, "South Africa's Secret Nuclear Weapons," p. 10.

proval and design documents were burned prior to the public announcement of the program's existence. This was a highly unusual step and strongly suggests that fear of ANC control of nuclear weapons (and perhaps also concern about possible seizure by white extremists) was critical in the decision.[37]

Domestic politics can also be seen as playing critical roles in other cases of nuclear restraint. In Argentina and Brazil, for example, the key change explaining the shift from nuclear competition to cooperative restraint in the 1980s could not have been a major reduction of security threats, since there was no such reduction. Indeed, a traditional realist view would predict that the experience of the 1982 Falklands/Malvinas War—in which Argentina was defeated by a nuclear power, Great Britain—would have strongly encouraged Argentina's nuclear ambitions. Instead, the important change was the emergence of liberalizing domestic regimes in both states, governments supported by coalitions of actors—such as banks, export-oriented firms, and state monetary agencies—who value unimpeded access to international markets and oppose economically unproductive defense and energy enterprises. Nuclear programs that were run as fiefdoms and served the interests of the atomic industry bureaucrats and the military were therefore abandoned by new civilian regimes with strong support of liberalizing coalitions.[38]

POLICY IMPLICATIONS OF THE DOMESTIC POLITICS MODEL

With respect to U.S. nonproliferation policy, a domestic politics approach both cautions modest expectations about U.S. influence and calls for a broader set of diplomatic efforts. Modest expectations are in order, since the key factors that influence decisions are domestic in origin and therefore largely outside the control of U.S. policy. Nevertheless, a more diverse set of tools could be useful to help create and empower domestic coalitions that oppose the development or maintenance of nuclear arsenals.

A variety of activities could be included in such a domestic-focused nonproliferation strategy. International financial institutions are already demand-

---

37. A rare public hint that concerns about domestic stability played a role in the decision is the acknowledgment by the head of the Atomic Energy Corporation that the government discussed issuing an immediate announcement revealing the existence of the weapons and thus permitting the IAEA to dismantle them because "the state of the country's internal political transformation was not considered conducive to such an announcement at the time." See Stumpf, "South Africa's Nuclear Weapons Program," p. 7.
38. The best analysis is Etel Solingen, "The Political Economy of Nuclear Restraint," *International Security*, Vol. 19, No. 2 (Fall 1994), pp. 126–169.

ing that cuts in military expenditures be included in conditionality packages for aid recipients. More direct conditionality linkages to nuclear programs— such as deducting the estimated budget of any suspect research and development program from IMF or U.S. loans to a country—could heighten domestic opposition to such programs.[39] Providing technical information and intellectual ammunition for domestic actors—by encouraging more accurate estimates of the economic and environmental costs of nuclear weapons programs and highlighting the risks of nuclear accidents[40]—could bring new members into anti-proliferation coalitions. In addition, efforts to encourage strict civilian control of the military, through educational and organizational reforms, could be productive, especially in states in which the military has the capability to create secret nuclear programs (like Brazil in the 1980s) to serve their parochial interests. Finally, U.S. attempts to provide alternative sources of employment and prestige to domestic actors who might otherwise find weapons programs attractive could decrease nuclear incentives. To the degree that professional military organizations are supporting nuclear proliferation, encouraging their involvement in other military activities (such as Pakistani participation in peacekeeping operations or the Argentine Navy's role in the Persian Gulf) could decrease such support. Where the key actors are laboratory officials and scientists, assistance in non-nuclear research and development programs (as in the current U.S.-Russian "lab-to-lab" program) could decrease personal and organizational incentives for weapons research.

A different perspective on the role of the NPT also emerges from the domestic politics model. The NPT regime is not just a device to increase states' confidence about the limits of their potential adversaries' nuclear programs; it is also a tool that can help to empower domestic actors who are opposed to nuclear weapons development. The NPT negotiations and review conferences create a well-placed elite in the foreign and defense ministries with considerable bureaucratic and personal interests in maintaining the regime. The IAEA creates monitoring capabilities and enforcement incentives against unregulated activities within a state's own nuclear power organizations. The network of

39. Etel Solingen, *The Domestic Sources of Nuclear Postures,* Institute of Global Conflict and Cooperation, Policy Paper No. 8, October 1994, p. 11.
40. On these costs and risks, see Kathleen C. Bailey, ed., *Weapons of Mass Destruction: Costs Versus Benefits* (New Delhi: Manohar Publishers, 1994); Stephen I. Schwartz, "Four Trillion and Counting," *Bulletin of the Atomic Scientists,* Vol. 51, No. 6 (November/December 1995); Bruce G. Blair, *The Logic of Accidental Nuclear War* (Washington, D.C.: The Brookings Institution, 1993); and Scott D. Sagan, *The Limits of Safety: Organizations, Accidents, and Nuclear Weapons* (Princeton, N.J.: Princeton University Press, 1993).

non-governmental organizations built around the treaty supports similar anti-proliferation pressure groups in each state.

According to this model, the U.S. commitment under Article VI to work for the eventual elimination of nuclear weapons is important because of the impact that the behavior of the United States and other nuclear powers can have on the domestic debates in non-nuclear states. Whether or not the United States originally signed Article VI merely to placate domestic opinion in non-nuclear states is not important; what is important is that the loss of this pacifying tool could influence outcomes in potential proliferators. In future debates inside such states, the arguments of anti-nuclear actors—that nuclear weapons programs do not serve the interests of their states—can be more easily countered by pro-bomb actors whenever they can point to specific actions of the nuclear powers, such as refusals to ban nuclear tests or the maintenance of nuclear first-use doctrines, that highlight these states' continued reliance on nuclear deterrence.

The Norms Model: Nuclear Symbols and State Identity

A third model focuses on norms concerning weapons acquisition, seeing nuclear decisions as serving important symbolic functions—both shaping and reflecting a state's identity. According to this perspective, state behavior is determined not by leaders' cold calculations about the national security interests or their parochial bureaucratic interests, but rather by deeper norms and shared beliefs about what actions are legitimate and appropriate in international relations.

Given the importance of the subject, and the large normative literature in ethics and law concerning the use of nuclear weapons, it is surprising that so little attention has been paid to "nuclear symbolism" and the development of international norms concerning the acquisition of nuclear weapons.[41] Sociologists and political scientists have studied the emergence and influence of international norms in other substantive areas, however, and their insights can

---

41. On nuclear ethics, see Joseph S. Nye, Jr., *Nuclear Ethics* (New York: Free Press, 1986); and Steven P. Lee, *Morality, Prudence, and Nuclear Weapons* (New York: Cambridge University Press, 1993). For a recent analysis of legal restraints on the use of nuclear weapons, see Nicholas Rostow, "The World Health Organization, the International Court of Justice, and Nuclear Weapons," *Yale Journal of International Law*, Vol. 20, No. 1 (Winter 1995), pp. 151–185. For a rare analysis of the symbolism of nuclear weapons, see Robert Jervis, "The Symbolic Nature of Nuclear Politics," in Jervis, *The Meaning of the Nuclear Revolution* (Ithaca, N.Y.: Cornell University Press, 1989), pp. 174–225.

lead to a valuable alternative perspective on proliferation. Within sociology, the "new institutionalism" literature suggests that modern organizations and institutions often come to resemble each other (what is called institutional isomorphism) not because of competitive selection or rational learning but because institutions mimic each other.[42] These scholars emphasize the importance of roles, routines, and rituals: individuals and organizations may well have "interests," but such interests are shaped by the social roles actors are asked to play, are pursued according to habits and routines as much as through reasoned decisions, and are embedded in a social environment that promotes certain structures and behaviors as rational and legitimate and denigrates others as irrational and primitive.

From this sociological perspective, military organizations and their weapons can therefore be envisioned as serving functions similar to those of flags, airlines, and Olympic teams: they are part of what modern states believe they have to possess to be legitimate, modern states. Air Malawi, Royal Nepal Airlines, and Air Myanmar were not created because they are cost-effective means of transport nor because domestic pressure groups pushed for their development, but rather because government leaders believed that a national airline is something that modern states have to have to be modern states. Very small and poor states, without a significant number of scientists, nevertheless have official government-sponsored science boards. From a new institutionalist perspective, such similarities are not the result of functional logic (actions designed to serve either international or domestic goals); they are the product of shared beliefs about what is legitimate and modern behavior.[43]

Within political science, a related literature has evolved concerning the development and spread of norms within international regimes. Although this norms perspective has rarely been applied to the proliferation problem, schol-

42. Among the most important sources are the essays collected in Walter W. Powell and Paul J. DiMaggio, eds., *The New Institutionalism in Organizational Analysis* (Chicago: University of Chicago Press, 1991); and John W. Meyer and W. Richard Scott, *Organizational Environments: Ritual and Rationality,* 2nd ed. (Newbury Park, Calif.: Sage Publications, 1992).

43. See Marc C. Suchman and Dana P. Eyre, "Military Procurement as Rational Myth: Notes on the Social Construction of Weapons Proliferation," *Sociological Forum,* Vol. 7, No. 1 (March 1992), pp. 137–161; Martha Finnemore, "International Organizations as Teachers of Norms: UNESCO and Science Policy," *International Organization,* Vol. 47, No. 4 (Autumn 1993), pp. 565–598; Francisco O. Ramirez and John Boli, "Global Patterns of Educational Institutionalization," in George M. Thomas, John W. Meyer, Francisco O. Ramirez, and John Boli, eds., *Institutional Structure: Constituting State, Society, and the Individual* (Newbury Park, Calif.: Sage Publications, 1987), pp. 150–172. For an excellent survey and critique, see Martha Finnemore, "Norms, Culture, and World Politics: Insights from Sociology's Institutionalism," *International Organization,* Vol. 50, No. 2 (Spring 1996), pp. 325–348.

ars have studied such important phenomena as the global spread of anti-colonialism, the abolition of the African slave trade, the near-total elimination of piracy at sea, and constraints against the use of chemical weapons.[44] There is a diverse set of ideas emerging in this field, producing a valuable debate about the role of global norms, but not a well-developed theory about their causal influence. Still, as one would expect of political scientists, coercion and power are seen to play a more important role in spreading norms than is the case in the sociologists' literature. Normative pressures may begin with the actions of entrepreneurial non-state actors, but their beliefs only have significant influence once powerful state actors join the cause. Religious and liberal opposition to slavery, for example, was clearly important in fueling American and British leaders' preferences in the nineteenth century, but such views would not easily have become an international norm without the bayonets of the Army of the Potomac at Gettysburg or the ships of the British Navy patrolling the high seas between Africa and Brazil.[45] Similarly, normative beliefs about chemical weapons were important in creating legal restrictions against their use in war; yet, the norm was significantly reenforced at critical moments by the fear of retaliation-in-kind and by the availability of other weapons that were believed by military leaders to be more effective on the battlefield.[46]

The sociologists' arguments highlight the possibility that nuclear weapons programs serve symbolic functions reflecting leaders' perceptions of appropriate and modern behavior. The political science literature reminds us, however,

---

44. For rare applications of the norms perspective to proliferation, see Harald Müller, "The Internationalization of Principles, Norms, and Rules by Governments: The Case of Security Regimes," in Volker Rittberger, ed., *Regime Theory and International Relations* (Oxford: Clarendon Press, 1995), pp. 361–390; and Müller, "Maintaining Non-Nuclear Weapon Status," in Regina Cowen Karp, ed., *Security With Nuclear Weapons?* (New York: Oxford University Press, 1991), pp. 301–339. Also see Robert H. Jackson, "The Weight of Ideas in Decolonization: Normative Change in International Relations," in Judith Goldstein and Robert O. Keohane, eds., *Ideas and Foreign Policy* (Ithaca, N.Y.: Cornell University Press, 1993), pp. 111–138; Neta C. Crawford, "Decolonization as an International Norm," in Laura W. Reed and Carl Kaysen, eds., *Emerging Norms of Justified Intervention* (Cambridge, Mass.: American Academy of Arts and Sciences, 1993), pp. 37–61; Ethan A. Nadelmann, "Global Prohibition Regimes: The Evolution of Norms in International Society," *International Organization*, Vol. 44, No. 4 (Autumn 1990), pp. 479–526; and Richard Price, "A Genealogy of the Chemical Weapons Taboo," *International Organization*, Vol. 49, No. 1 (Winter 1995), pp. 73–104.
45. Ethan Nadelman, who stresses this point about power, also adds, however, that "even among the laggards, indeed especially among the laggards, the consciousness of being perceived as primitive and deviant surely weighed heavily in the decisions of local rulers to do away with slavery." Nadelman, "Global Prohibition Regimes," p. 497.
46. See Price, "A Genealogy of the Chemical Weapons Taboo"; and Jeffrey Legro, *Cooperation Under Fire: Anglo-German Restraint During World War II* (Ithaca, N.Y.: Cornell University Press, 1995), pp. 144–216.

that such symbols are often contested and that the resulting norms are spread by power and coercion, and not by the strength of ideas alone. Both insights usefully illuminate the nuclear proliferation phenomenon. Existing norms concerning the non-acquisition of nuclear weapons (such as those embedded in the NPT) could not have been created without the strong support of the most powerful states in the international system, who believed that the norms served their narrow political interests. Yet, once that effort was successful, these norms shaped states' identities and expectations and even powerful actors became constrained by the norms they had created.[47] The history of nuclear proliferation is particularly interesting in this regard because a major discontinuity—a shift in nuclear norms—has emerged as the result of the NPT regime.

Although many individual case studies of nuclear weapons decisions mention the belief that nuclear acquisition will enhance the international prestige of the state, such prestige has been viewed simply as a reasonable, though diffuse, means used to enhance the state's international influence and security. What is missing from these analyses is an understanding of why and how actions are granted symbolic meaning: why are some nuclear weapons acts considered prestigious, while others produce opprobrium, and how do such beliefs change over time? Why, for example, was nuclear testing deemed prestigious and legitimate in the 1960s, but is today considered illegitimate and irresponsible? An understanding of the NPT regime is critical here, for it appears to have shifted the norm concerning what acts grant prestige and legitimacy from the 1960s notion of joining "the nuclear club" to the 1990s concept of joining "the club of the nations adhering to the NPT." Moreover, the salience of the norms that were made explicit in the NPT treaty has shifted over time. These arguments are perhaps best supported by contrasting two cases—the French decision to build and test nuclear weapons and the Ukrainian decision to give up its nuclear arsenal—in which perceptions of legitimacy and prestige appear to have had a major influence, albeit with very different outcomes.

PROLIFERATION REVISITED: FRENCH GRANDEUR AND WEAPONS POLICY
According to realist theory, the French decision to develop nuclear weapons has a very simple explanation: in the 1950s, the Soviet Union was a grave military threat to French national security, and the best alternative to building

---

47. For an excellent analysis of how such a process can work in other contexts, see Michael Byers, "Custom, Power, and the Power of Rules," *Michigan Journal of International Law,* Vol. 17, No. 1 (Fall 1995), pp. 109–180.

an independent arsenal—reliance on the United States's nuclear guarantee to NATO—was ruled out after the Soviet development of a secure second strike capability reduced the credibility of any U.S. nuclear first-use threats. According to this explanation, the need for a French arsenal was driven home by the 1956 Suez Crisis, when Paris was forced to withdraw its military intervention forces after a nuclear threat from Russia and under U.S. economic pressure. "The Suez humiliation of 1956 was decisive," writes David Yost. "It was felt that a nuclear weapons capability would reduce France's dependence on the U.S. and her vulnerability to Soviet blackmail."[48] The central realist argument for French nuclear weapons was clearly expressed in the rhetorical question Charles de Gaulle posed to Dwight Eisenhower in 1959: "Will they [future U.S. presidents] take the risk of devastating American cities so that Berlin, Brussels and Paris might remain free?"[49]

This explanation of French nuclear policy, however, does not stand up very well against either existing evidence or logic. Indeed, the two most critical decisions initiating the weapons program—Prime Minister Mendes-France's December 1954 decision to start a secret nuclear weapons research program inside the Commissariat à l'énergie atomique (CEA) and the May 1955 authorization by the Ministry of Defense for funds to be transferred to the CEA for the development of a prototype weapon—predated the 1956 Suez Crisis.[50] In addition, as Lawrence Scheinman has argued, it is by no means clear why French leaders would think that the traumatic Suez experience could have been avoided if there had been an independent French nuclear arsenal, since Great Britain had also been forced to withdraw from the intervention in Egypt under U.S. and Soviet pressure, despite its possession of nuclear weapons.[51] A simple exercise in comparative logic also raises doubts about the security model. If the critical cause of proliferation in France was the lack of credibility of U.S. nuclear guarantees given the growing Soviet threat in the mid-1950s, why then did other nuclear-capable states in Europe, faced with similar security threats at the time, not also develop nuclear weapons?[52] If one even briefly examines

---

48. David S. Yost, "France's Deterrent Posture and Security in Europe, Part I: Capabilities and Doctrine," Adelphi Paper No. 194 (London: International Institute for Strategic Studies [IISS], Winter 1984/85), p. 4. Also see Kohl, *French Nuclear Diplomacy*, p. 36.

49. Jean Lacouture, *De Gaulle: The Ruler 1945–1970* (New York: W.W. Norton, 1993), p. 421, as quoted in Thayer, "The Causes of Nuclear Proliferation," p. 489.

50. See Bertrand Goldschmidt, *The Atomic Complex* (La Grange Park, Ill.: American Nuclear Society, 1982), p. 131; and Scheinman, *Atomic Energy Policy in France Under the Fourth Republic*, pp. 120–122.

51. Scheinman, *Atomic Energy Policy in France Under the Fourth Republic*, pp. 171–173.

52. The British acquisition of nuclear weapons in 1952 predated the Soviet development of a secure second-strike capability.

the list of all the nuclear-capable states in Europe that were both threatened by Soviet military power and had reasons to doubt the credibility of the U.S. first-use pledge, France appears alone on the nuclear proliferation side of the ledger; West Germany, the Netherlands, Italy, Switzerland, Belgium, Norway, and Sweden were all on the nuclear restraint side. This presents a puzzle for the security model, since the Soviet Union's conventional and nuclear threat to most of these states' security was at least as great as the Soviet threat to France; the American nuclear guarantee should not have been not considered more credible by those states that had been U.S. enemies or neutrals in World War II, compared to France, a U.S. ally of long standing, and one which the United States had strongly aided once it entered the war in 1941.

A stronger explanation for the French decision to build nuclear weapons emerges when one focuses on French leaders' perceptions of the bomb's symbolic significance. The belief that nuclear power and nuclear weapons were deeply linked to a state's position in the international system was present as early as 1951, when the first French Five-Year Plan was put forward with its stated purpose being "to ensure that in 10 years' time France will still be an important country."[53] France emerged from World War II in an unusual position: it was a liberated victor whose military capabilities and international standing were not at all comparable to the power and status it had before the war. It should therefore not be surprising that the governments of both the Fourth and the Fifth Republics vigorously explored alternative means to return France to its historical great power status.[54] After the war, the initial French effort to restore its tarnished prestige focused on the fight to hold onto an overseas empire, yet as Michel Martin has nicely put it, "as the curtain was drawn over colonial domination, it became clear that the country's *grandeur* had to be nourished from other sources."[55]

After 1958, the Algerian crisis contributed greatly to Charles de Gaulle's obsession with nuclear weapons as the source of French *grandeur* and independence. In contrast, de Gaulle appeared less concerned about whether French nuclear forces could provide adequate deterrence against the Soviet

---

53. The document is quoted in Goldschmidt, *The Atomic Complex*, p. 126.
54. For detailed analyses of the French nuclear weapons decision which focus attention on political prestige as the central source of policy, see Scheinman, *Atomic Energy Policy in France Under the Fourth Republic;* and Kohl, *French Nuclear Diplomacy.* Also see Bundy, *Danger and Survival,* pp. 472–487, 499–503.
55. Michel L. Martin, *Warriors to Managers: The French Military Establishment Since 1945* (Chapel Hill, N.C.: University of North Carolina Press, 1981), p. 21.

military threat. For example, during both the Berlin crisis of 1958 (before the 1960 French nuclear weapons test) and the 1962 Cuban crisis (after the test, but before French nuclear forces were operational), de Gaulle expressed great confidence that the Soviets would not risk an attack on NATO Europe.[56] Wilfred Kohl also reports on a revealing incident in which a French military strategist sent de Gaulle a copy of a book on French nuclear doctrine and de Gaulle replied, "thanking the man for his interesting analysis of strategic questions, but stressing that for him the central and clearly the only important issue was: 'Will France remain France?'"[57] For de Gaulle, the atomic bomb was a dramatic symbol of French independence and was thus needed for France to continue to be seen, by itself and others, as a great power. He confided to President Dwight Eisenhower in 1959:

A France without world responsibility would be unworthy of herself, especially in the eyes of Frenchmen. It is for this reason that she disapproves of NATO, which denies her a share in decision-making and which is confined to Europe. It is for this reason too that she intends to provide herself with an atomic armament. Only in this way can our defense and foreign policy be independent, which we prize above everything else.[58]

When the French nuclear weapons arsenal is viewed as primarily serving symbolic functions, a number of puzzling aspects of the history of French atomic policy become more understandable. The repeated Gaullist declarations that French nuclear weapons should have world-wide capabilities and must be aimed in all directions (*"tous azimuts"*) are seen, not as the product of security threats that came from all directions, but rather because only such a policy could be logically consistent with global *grandeur* and independence. Similarly, the French strategic doctrine of "proportional deterrence" against the Soviet Union during the Cold War—threatening more limited destruction in a retaliatory strike than did the United States under its targeting doctrine—is seen as being produced, not by France's geographical position or limited economic resources, but rather because deterrence of the Soviet Union was a justification, and never the primary purpose of its arsenal. Finally, the profound French reluctance to stop nuclear testing in the mid-1990s is seen as being produced,

---

56. See Philip H. Gordon, "Charles de Gaulle and the Nuclear Revolution," *Security Studies,* Vol. 5, No. 1 (Autumn 1995), pp. 129–130.
57. Kohl, *French Nuclear Diplomacy,* p. 150, quoted in Bundy, *Danger and Survival,* p. 502.
58. Charles de Gaulle, *Memoirs of Hope: Renewal and Endeavor* (New York: Simon and Schuster, 1971), p. 209 (emphasis in the original), quoted in Yost, *France's Deterrent Posture and Security in Europe,* pp. 13–14.

not only by the stated concerns about weapons modernization and warhead safety, but also because weapons tests were perceived by Parisian leaders as potent symbols of French identity and status as a great power.

RESTRAINT REVISITED: THE NPT AND THE UKRAINE CASE
Stark contrasts exist between French nuclear decisions in the 1950s and Ukrainian nuclear decisions in the 1990s. When the Soviet Union collapsed in 1991, an independent Ukraine was "born nuclear" with more than 4,000 nuclear weapons on or under its soil. In November 1994, however, the Rada in Kiev voted overwhelmingly to join the NPT as a non-nuclear state, and all weapons were removed from Ukrainian territory by June 1996.

This decision to give up a nuclear arsenal is puzzling from the realist perspective: a number of prominent realist scholars, after all, maintained that given the history of Russian expansionist behavior and continuing tensions over the Crimea and the treatment of Russian minorities, Ukraine's independence was seriously threatened, and further argued that nuclear weapons were the only rational solution to this security threat.[59] The disarmament decision is also puzzling from a traditional domestic politics perspective. Despite the tragic consequences of the Chernobyl accident, public opinion polls in Ukraine showed rapidly growing support for keeping nuclear weapons in 1992 and 1993: polls showed support for an independent arsenal increasing from 18 percent in May 1992 to 36 percent in March 1993, to as much as 45 percent in the summer of 1993.[60] In addition, well-known retired military officers, such as Rada member General Volodomyr Tolubko, vigorously lobbied to maintain an arsenal and senior political leaders, most importantly Prime Minister (then President) Leonid Kuchma, came from the Soviet missile-building industry and would not therefore be expected to take an anti-nuclear position.[61]

An understanding of Ukraine's decision to eliminate its nuclear arsenal requires that more attention be focused on the role that emerging NPT nonproliferation norms played in four critical ways. First, Ukrainian politicians

---

59. See John J. Mearsheimer, "The Case for a Ukrainian Nuclear Deterrent," *Foreign Affairs*, Vol. 72, No. 3 (Summer 1993), pp. 50–66; and Barry R. Posen, "The Security Dilemma and Ethnic Conflict," *Survival*, Vol. 35, No. 1 (Spring 1993), pp. 44–45.
60. See William C. Potter, "The Politics of Nuclear Renunciation: The Cases of Belarus, Kazakhstan, and Ukraine," Henry L. Stimson Center, Occasional Paper No. 22, April 1995, p. 49.
61. For a detailed analysis see Bohdan Nahaylo, "The Shaping of Ukrainian Attitudes Toward Nuclear Arms," *RFE/RL (Radio Free Europe/Radio Liberty) Research Report*, Vol. 2, No. 8 (February 19, 1993), pp. 21–45.

initially adopted anti-nuclear positions as a way of buttressing Kiev's claims to national sovereignty. In one of its first efforts to assert an independent foreign policy from Moscow, Ukraine tried to accede to the NPT as a non-nuclear state in early 1990, attempting to use NPT membership as a way of separating itself from the Soviet Union.[62] In July 1990, this policy was underscored when the parliament in Kiev issued its Declaration of Sovereignty. Embedded in declarations about Ukraine's right to participate as a full member in all agreements concerning "international peace and security" was the proclamation that Ukraine would "become a neutral state that does not participate in military blocs and that adheres to three non-nuclear principles: not to maintain, produce, or acquire nuclear weapons." This extraordinary statement was an expedient designed to buttress Kiev's claim to independence from the Soviet Union, rather than a blueprint laying out Ukraine's long-term strategy: indeed, it was adopted by a vote of 355–4, without extensive debate, by the parliament in which conservative communists (many of whom would later take pro-nuclear positions) still held the majority of seats.[63] Nevertheless, the declaration placed the onus of reneging on an international commitment on the politicians and scholars who afterwards called for keeping an arsenal, and it is revealing that even many of the more hawkish analysts thereafter defensively advocated keeping the arsenal on a temporary basis until other sources of security could be found.[64] Second, although Ukrainian officials continued to be interested in enhancing the state's international prestige, the strength of the NPT regime created a history in which the most recent examples of new or potential nuclear states were so-called "rogue states" such as North Korea, Iran, and Iraq. This was hardly a nuclear club whose new members would receive international prestige, and during the debate in Kiev, numerous pro-NPT Ukrainian officials insisted that renunciation of nuclear weapons was now the best route to enhance Ukraine's international standing.[65] Third, economic pressures were clearly critical to the Ukrainian decision: the United States and NATO allies encouraged Kiev to give up the arsenal not by convincing officials that nuclear weapons could never serve as a military deterrent against Moscow, but by persuading them that not following the NPT norm would result in very

62. Potter, "The Politics of Nuclear Renunciation," p. 19.
63. See Nahaylo, "The Shaping of Ukrainian Attitudes," pp. 21–22.
64. Potter, "The Politics of Nuclear Renunciation," pp. 21–23; and Nahaylo, "The Shaping of Ukrainian Attitudes."
65. See Potter, "The Politics of Nuclear Renunciation," p. 44; and Garnett, "Ukraine's Decision to Join the NPT," p. 12.

negative economic consequences.[66] It is important to recognize, however, that the ability to coordinate such activities, and credibly to threaten collective sanctions and promised inducements for disarmament, were significantly heightened by the existence of the NPT norm against the creation of new nuclear weapons states. Fourth, the Kiev government and the Ukrainian public could more easily accept the economic inducements offered by the United States—such as Nunn-Lugar payments to help transport and destroy the weapons—with the belief that they were enabling Ukraine to keep an international commitment.

As with all counterfactuals, it is impossible to assess with certainty whether Ukraine would have made the same decision had the NPT norms not been in existence. Still, it is valuable to try to imagine how much more difficult a disarmament outcome would have been in the absence of the NPT and its twenty-five year history. Without the NPT, a policy of keeping a nuclear arsenal would have placed Ukraine in the category of France and China; instead, it placed Ukraine in the company of dissenters like India and Pakistan and pariahs like Iraq and North Korea. International threats to eliminate economic aid and suspend political ties would be less credible, since individual states would be more likely to defect from an agreement. Finally, without the NPT norm, U.S. dismantlement assistance would have been seen in Kiev as the crass purchase of Ukrainian weapons by a foreign government, instead of being viewed as friendly assistance to help Kiev implement an international agreement.

POLICY IMPLICATIONS OF THE NORMS MODEL

If the norms model of proliferation is correct, the key U.S. policy challenges are to recognize that such norms can have a strong influence on other states' nuclear weapons policy, and to adjust U.S. policies to increase the likelihood that norms will push others toward policies that also serve U.S. interests. Recognizing the possibility that norms can influence other states' behavior in complex ways should not be difficult. After all, the norms of the NPT have already influenced U.S. nuclear weapons policy in ways that few scholars or policymakers predicted ahead of time: in January 1995, for example, the Clinton administration abandoned the long-standing U.S. position that the Comprehensive Test Ban Treaty (CTBT) must include an automatic escape clause

---

66. An excellent analysis of U.S. policy appears in Garnett, "Ukraine's Decision to Join the NPT," pp. 10–12.

permitting states to withdraw from the treaty after ten years. Despite the arguments made by Pentagon officials that such a clause was necessary to protect U.S. security, the administration accepted the possibility of a permanent CTBT because senior decision-makers became convinced that the U.S. position was considered illegitimate by non-nuclear NPT members, due to the Article VI commitment to eventual disarmament, and might thereby jeopardize the effort to negotiate a permanent extension of the NPT treaty.[67]

Adjusting U.S. nuclear policies in the future to reenforce emerging nonproliferation norms will be difficult, however, because many of the recommended policies derived from the norms perspective directly contradict recommendations derived from the other models. Focusing on NPT norms raises especially severe concerns about how existing U.S. nuclear first-use doctrine influences potential proliferators' perceptions of the legitimacy or illegitimacy of nuclear weapons possession and use.[68] To the degree that such first-use policies create beliefs that nuclear threats are what great powers do, they will become desired symbols for states that aspire to that status. The norms argument against U.S. nuclear first-use doctrine, however, contradicts the policy advice derived from the security model, which stresses the need for continued nuclear guarantees for U.S. allies. Similarly, the norms perspective suggests that current U.S. government efforts to maintain the threat of first use of nuclear weapons to deter the use of biological or chemical weapons would have a negative impact on the nuclear nonproliferation regime.[69] Leaders of non-nuclear states are much less likely to consider their own acquisition of nuclear weapons to deter adversaries with chemical and biological weapons illegitimate and ill-advised if the greatest conventional military power in the world can not refrain from making such threats.

Other possible policy initiatives are less problematic. For example, if norms concerning prestige are important, then it would be valuable for the United States to encourage the development of other sources of international prestige

---

67. Douglas Jehl, "U.S. in New Pledge on Atom Test Ban," *New York Times*, January 31, 1995, p. 1; Dunbar Lockwood, "U.S. Drops CTB 'Early Out' Plan; Test Moratorium May Be Permanent," *Arms Control Today*, Vol. 25, No. 2 (March 1995), p. 27.

68. On this issue, see Barry M. Blechman and Cathleen S. Fisher, "Phase Out the Bomb," *Foreign Policy*, No. 97 (Winter 1994–95), pp. 79–95; and Wolfgang K.H. Panofsky and George Bunn, "The Doctrine of the Nuclear-Weapons States and the Future of Non-Proliferation," *Arms Control Today*, Vol. 24, No. 6 (July/August 1994), pp. 3–9.

69. For contrasting views on this policy, see George Bunn, "Expanding Nuclear Options: Is the U.S. Negating its Non-Use Pledges?" *Arms Control Today*, Vol. 26, No. 4 (May/June 1996), pp. 7–10; and Gompert, Watman, and Wilkening, "Nuclear First Use Revisited."

for current or potential proliferators. Thus, a policy that made permanent UN Security Council membership for Japan, Germany, and India conditional upon the maintenance of non-nuclear status under the NPT might further remove nuclear weapons possession from considerations of international prestige.

Finally, the norms model produces a more optimistic vision of the potential future of nonproliferation. Norms are sticky: individual and group beliefs about appropriate behavior change slowly, and over time norms can become rules embedded in domestic institutions.[70] In the short run, therefore, norms can be a brake on nuclear chain reactions: in contrast to more pessimistic realist predictions that "proliferation begets proliferation," the norms model suggests that such nuclear reactions to emerging security threats can be avoided or at least delayed because of normative constraints. The long-term future of the NPT regime is also viewed with more optimism, for the model envisions the possibility of a gradual emergence of a norm against all nuclear weapons possession. The development of such a norm may well have been inadvertent in the sense that the United States did not take its Article VI commitment to work in good faith for complete nuclear disarmament seriously, for quite understandable reasons, during the Cold War. But to the degree that other states believe that such commitments are real and legitimate, their perceptions that the United States is backsliding away from Article VI will influence their behavior over time. This emphasis on emerging norms therefore highlights the need for the nuclear powers to reaffirm their commitments to global nuclear disarmament, and suggests that it is essential that the U.S. and other governments develop a public, long-term strategy for the eventual elimination of nuclear weapons.[71] The norms model can not, of course, predict whether such efforts will ever resolve the classic risks of nuclear disarmament: that states can break treaty obligations in crises, that small arsenals produce strategic instabilities, and that adequate verification of complete dismantlement is exceedingly difficult. But the model does predict that there will be severe costs

---

70. For useful discussions, see Abram Chayes and Antonia Handler Chayes, *The New Sovereignty: Compliance with International Regulatory Agreements* (Cambridge, Mass.: Harvard University Press, 1995); and Andrew P. Cortell and James W. Davis Jr., "How Do International Institutions Matter?: The Domestic Impact of International Rules and Norms," *International Studies Quarterly,* Vol. 40, No. 4 (December 1996), pp. 451–478.
71. For important efforts to rethink the elimination issue, see "An Evolving U.S. Nuclear Posture," Report of the Steering Committee of the Project on Eliminating Weapons of Mass Destruction, Henry L. Stimson Center, Washington, D.C., December 1995; and Donald MacKenzie and Graham Spinardi, "Tacit Knowledge, Weapons Design, and the Uninvention of Nuclear Weapons," *American Journal of Sociology,* Vol. 101, No. 1 (July 1995), pp. 44–100.

involved if the nuclear powers are seen to have failed to make significant progress toward nuclear disarmament.

Conclusions: Causal Complexity and Policy Tradeoffs

The ideas and evidence presented in this article suggest that the widely held security model explanation for nuclear proliferation decisions is inadequate. A realist might well respond to this argument by asserting that evidence is always ambiguous in complex historical events, and that I underestimate foreign threats and thus provide a poor measure of the effects of security concerns on decision-makers. Moreover, it could be argued that the best theories are those that explain the largest number of cases and that the largest number of positive nuclear weapons decisions in the past (the United States, the Soviet Union, China, Israel, Pakistan) and the majority of the most pressing proliferation cases today (Iraq, Libya, and possibly North Korea and Iran) appear to be best explained by the basic security model.

I have no quarrel with the argument that the largest number of past and even current active proliferant cases are best explained by the security model. But the evidence presented above strongly suggests that multicausality, rather than measurement error, lies at the heart of the nuclear proliferation problem. Nuclear weapons proliferation and nuclear restraint have occurred in the past, and can occur in the future, for more than one reason: different historical cases are best explained by different causal models.

If this central argument is correct, it has important implications for future scholarship on proliferation as well as for U.S. nonproliferation policy. The challenge for scholars is not to produce increasing numbers of detailed, but atheoretical, case studies of states' nuclear proliferation and restraint decisions; it is to produce theory-driven comparative studies to help determine the conditions under which different causal forces produced similar outcomes. Predicting the future based on such an understanding of the past will still be problematic, since the conditions that produced the past proliferation outcomes may themselves be subject to change. But future scholarship focusing on how different governments assess the nuclear potential and intention of neighbors, on why pro-bomb and anti-bomb domestic coalitions form and gain influence, and on when and how NPT norms about legitimate behavior constrain statesmen will be extremely important.

For policymakers, the existence of three different reasons why states develop nuclear weapons suggests that no single policy can ameliorate all future proliferation problems. Fortunately, some of the policy recommendations derived from the models are quite compatible: for example, many of the diplomatic tools suggested by the domestic politics model, which attempts to reduce the power of individual parochial interests in favor of nuclear weapons, would not interfere with simultaneous efforts to address states' security concerns. Similarly, efforts to enhance the international status of some non-nuclear states need not either undercut deterrence or promote pro-nuclear advocates in those countries.

Unfortunately, other important recommendations from different models are more contradictory. Most importantly, a security-oriented strategy of maintaining a major role for U.S. nuclear guarantees to restrain proliferation among allies will eventually create strong tensions with a norms-oriented strategy seeking to delegitimize nuclear weapons use and acquisition. The final outcome of these alternative strategies, of course, is not under the control of the United States, as leaders of potential proliferators will decide for themselves whether to pursue or reject nuclear weapons programs. Yet U.S. policy will not be without influence, and intelligent decisions will not emerge if we refuse to recognize that painful tradeoffs are appearing on the horizon. U.S. decision-makers will eventually have to choose between the difficult non-proliferation task of weaning allies away from nuclear guarantees without producing new nuclear states, and the equally difficult task of maintaining a norm against nuclear proliferation without the U.S. government facing up to its logical final consequence.

Never Say Never Again | Ariel E. Levite

Nuclear Reversal Revisited

$\mathbf{A}$ serious gap exists in scholarly understanding of nuclear proliferation. The gap derives from inadequate attention to the phenomena of nuclear reversal and nuclear restraint as well as insufficient awareness of the biases and limitations inherent in the empirical data employed to study proliferation. This article identifies "nuclear hedging" as a national strategy lying between nuclear pursuit and nuclear rollback. An understanding of this strategy can help scholars to explain the nuclear behavior of many states; it can also help to explain why the nightmare proliferation scenarios of the 1960s have not materialized. These insights, in turn, cast new light on several prominent proliferation case studies and the unique role of the United States in combating global proliferation. They have profound implications for engaging current or latent nuclear proliferants, underscoring the centrality of buying time as the key component of a nonproliferation strategy.

The article begins with a brief review of contemporary nuclear proliferation concerns. It then takes stock of the surprisingly large documented universe of nuclear reversal cases and the relevant literature.[1] It proceeds to examine the empirical challenges that bedeviled many of the earlier studies, possibly skewing their theoretical findings. Next, it discusses the features of the nuclear reversal and restraint phenomena and the forces that influence them. In this context, it introduces and illustrates an alternative explanation for the nuclear behavior of many states based on the notion of nuclear hedging. It draws on this notion and other inputs to reassess the role that the United States

At the time this article was written, Ariel E. Levite was a Visiting Fellow at the Center for International Security and Cooperation (CISAC) at Stanford University.

The author is indebted to Sidney Drell, Alexander George, David Holloway, and Scott Sagan for their valuable input and support. Chaim Braun, Barry O'Neill, Jeremi Suri, and other affiliates of CISAC, as well as *International Security*'s anonymous reviewers, provided helpful feedback and suggestions. I also benefited greatly from comments received from several seasoned practitioners. Tracy Williams deserves much credit for her outstanding assistance. Nichole Argo, Jonathan Neril, Gil Reich, and Anca Ruhlen were exceptional in providing archival research; in addition, Megan Hendershott and Karen Stiller offered invaluable editorial assistance. This research was facilitated in part by a research grant from the Ploughshares Foundation.

1. "Annotated Bibliography of Nuclear Reversal," unpublished memo, Center for International Security and Cooperation, Stanford University, June 2002.

has played in influencing the nuclear behavior of other states. The conclusion explores some of the policy and research implications of the article's findings.

Current Proliferation Concerns

The nuclear proliferation phenomenon has taken many twists and turns over the years, with the pace, direction, and loci of action varying considerably. In the late 1950s and 1960s, it was widely believed that nuclear proliferation beyond the original club of five (i.e., China, France, Great Britain, the Soviet Union, and the United States) was likely to occur before long, and that it would be led mainly by countries in Europe (most prominently Germany, Italy, and Sweden).[2] With the establishment of the nuclear Nonproliferation Treaty (NPT) regime in 1968–70, however, international concern over nuclear proliferation in Europe began to wane, though worries about proliferation in the developing world persisted, with Latin America and South Africa becoming particular sources of anxiety. More recently, South Asia, East Asia, and the Middle East have become the primary foci of concern. In addition, overall confidence in the stability of the nuclear nonproliferation regime has been shaken by developments in the nuclear arena in India and Pakistan, as well as in Iran, Iraq, and North Korea.

These developments have led two observers to suggest that, despite the remarkable success in producing an indefinite extension of the NPT in 1995, the "complex [NPT] regime intended to contain the spread of nuclear technologies is disintegrating."[3] Moreover, the prevailing assumption is that Iran or Iraq (or both) is bound to cross the nuclear weapons threshold before long, while Libya is proceeding along the same path. If this happens, further "horizontal nuclear proliferation" (a spillover effect on other states) is likely to occur both in the Middle East and beyond. A similar process is considered likely if the security

2. According to the Harvard Nuclear Study Group, "In 1963 President [John F.] Kennedy envisioned a world in the 1970s with 15–25 nuclear weapon states." See Albert Carnesale, Paul Doty, Stanley Hoffmann, Samuel P. Huntington, Joseph S. Nye Jr., and Scott D. Sagan, *Living with Nuclear Weapons* (Cambridge, Mass.: Harvard University Press, 1983), p. 215. A similarly somber assessment ("The world is fast approaching a point of no return in the prospects of controlling the spread of nuclear weapons.") appeared in a secret U.S. report presented to President Lyndon Johnson in 1965. See the Committee on Nuclear Proliferation, "A Report to the President," January 21, 1965, http://www.gwu.edu/?nsarchiv/NSAEBB/NSAEBB1/nhch7_1.htm (accessed August 15, 2002).
3. Barry M. Blechman and Leo S. Mackay Jr., *Weapons of Mass Destruction: A New Paradigm for a New Century*, Occasional Paper No. 40 (Washington, D.C.: Henry L. Stimson Center, 2000), p. 4.

situation on the Korean Peninsula and the Indian subcontinent continues to deteriorate. These developments have rekindled interest both in identifying the factors that drive nuclear proliferation and in understanding the processes that govern them.[4]

Challenges to the Study of Nuclear Reversal

Most nuclear proliferation studies have focused on proliferation trends, their prospects, and means of dealing with the challenges they pose. A smaller body of research has focused on the motivations for acquiring or renouncing nuclear weapons. Relatively little has been written on nuclear reversal, although this phenomenon has attracted somewhat greater interest in recent years.[5] Nuclear reversal refers to the phenomenon in which states embark on a path leading to nuclear weapons acquisition but subsequently reverse course, though not necessarily abandoning altogether their nuclear ambitions. Using this definition, a preliminary survey suggests that nearly twenty states have chosen the path of nuclear reversal since 1945 (see Table 1).[6]

---

4. For leading works in this genre, see Scott D. Sagan, "Why Do States Build Nuclear Weapons? Three Models in Search of a Bomb," *International Security,* Vol. 21, No. 3 (Winter 1996/97), pp. 54–86; Bradley A. Thayer, "The Causes of Nuclear Proliferation and the Nonproliferation Regime," *Security Studies,* Vol. 4, No. 3 (Spring 1995), pp. 463–519; Benjamin Frankel, "The Brooding Shadow: Systemic Incentives and Nuclear Weapons Proliferation," and Richard K. Betts, "Paranoids, Pygmies, Pariahs, and Nonproliferation Revisited," both in Zachary S. Davis and Benjamin Frankel, eds., *The Proliferation Puzzle: Why Nuclear Weapons Spread (and What Results)* (Portland: Frank Cass, 1993), pp. 37–38 and pp. 100–124, respectively.
5. A study by Harald Muller, using somewhat different criteria, has identified a similar number of nuclear reversal cases. Most of the countries appear in both lists. See Muller, "Nuclear Nonproliferation: A Success Story," paper presented at the Thirteenth Annual Amaldi Conference on Problems of Global Security, Rome, Italy, November 30–December 2, 2000.
6. The most salient work in this area is T.V. Paul, *Power versus Prudence: Why Nations Forgo Nuclear Weapons* (Montreal: McGill-Queen's University Press, 2000). See also Mitchell Reiss, *Bridled Ambitions: Why States Constrain Their Nuclear Capability* (Washington, D.C.: Woodrow Wilson Center Press, 1995); Mitchell Reiss, *Without the Bomb: The Politics of Nuclear Nonproliferation* (New York: Columbia University Press, 1988); James Doyle, "Nuclear Rollback: A New Direction for United States Nuclear Policy?" Ph.D. dissertation, University of Virginia, 1997; Charles Edward Costanzo, "Returning from the Brink: Is There a Theory-Based Explanation for the Attenuation of Horizontal Nuclear Proliferation?" Ph.D. dissertation, University of Alabama, 1998; James Walsh, "Bombs Unbuilt: Power, Ideas, and Institutions in International Politics," Ph.D. dissertation, Massachusetts Institute of Technology, 2000; Barry R. Schneider and William L. Dowdy, eds., *Pulling Back from the Nuclear Brink: Reducing and Countering Nuclear Threats* (London: Frank Cass, 1998); Etel Solingen, "The Political Economy of Nuclear Restraint," *International Security,* Vol. 19, No. 2 (Fall 1994), pp. 126–169; Leonard S. Spector, "Repentant Nuclear Proliferants," *Foreign Policy,* No. 88 (Fall 1992), pp. 3–20; and William C. Potter, *The Politics of Nuclear Renunciation: The Cases of Belarus, Kazakhstan, and Ukraine,* Occasional Paper No. 22 (Washington, D.C.: Henry L. Stimson Center, 1995).

Table 1. Cases of Nuclear Reversal since 1945.

Never Tried (nuclear abstinence)	Tried but Gave Up (nuclear reversal)	Attained but Gave Up[a]	Still Trying	Attained and Maintained
All (?) other states	Argentina	Belarus[b]	Algeria[c]	China
	Australia	Kazakhstan[b]	Iran[d]	France
	Brazil	South Africa	Iraq[d]	Great Britain
	Canada[e]	Ukraine[b]	Libya	India
	Egypt		North Korea[f]	Pakistan
	Germany			Soviet Union/
	Indonesia			Russia
	Italy			United States
	Japan			-------
	Netherlands[c]			Israel[g]
	Norway[c]			
	Romania[c]			
	South Korea[d]			
	Sweden			
	Switzerland			
	Taiwan[d]			
	Yugoslavia[c]			

NOTE: There have been repeated assertions, but no hard publicly available data, that Finland, Greece, Spain, and Turkey may have also had nuclear weapons aspirations. In the absence of evidence to corroborate these assertions, these countries are excluded here from the category of nuclear weapons aspirants.

[a] For the purposes of this study, the states listed in this category are considered as having undergone nuclear reversal.

[b] These states had nuclear weapons deployed on their territory but not under their command. Only Ukraine appears to have had physical possession of Russian nuclear weapons deployed on its soil, although apparently not the codes necessary to launch them.

[c] The determination and intensity with which these states pursued nuclear weapons remain uncertain.

[d] These are states that appear to have sought to acquire nuclear weapons on more than one occasion.

[e] Canada's nuclear weapons–oriented activity began with its participation in the Manhattan Project in the 1940s. Subsequently, it remained principally tied to the U.S. and British programs.

[f] The status of the North Korean nuclear program remains uncertain, although the North Koreans are suspected of having produced one or two nuclear weapons in the mid-1990s. See National Intelligence Council, *Foreign Missile Developments and the Ballistic Missile Threat through 2015: Unclassified Summary of a National Intelligence Estimate* (Washington, D.C.: National Intelligence Council, December 2001). North Korea appears to have subsequently engaged in a clandestine enrichment project, and in late 2002 threatened to reactivate its plutonium production. But these actions apparently have not yielded any additional weapons-grade fissile material. See the Carnegie Endowment Nonproliferation Project's website at http://www.ceip.org/files/nonprolif/default.asp (accessed January 4, 2003).

[g] Israel's nuclear status is unconfirmed.

For all its accomplishments, the literature on nuclear reversal is plagued by a variety of theoretical and methodological problems. Some of these problems are inherent in the very nature of the reversal phenomenon. Consider, for example, the issue of equifinality. Previous studies have been unable to identify the necessary or sufficient conditions for nuclear reversal, in part because different factors and causal paths, none of which is fully understood, can produce it. In the 1980s and 1990s, for example, Libya apparently temporarily scaled back its pursuit of nuclear weapons (though not its nuclear aspirations).[7] Libya's problematic international standing has compounded its inability to find a willing foreign supplier for the finished product or key facilities,[8] while its weak indigenous technological base continues to preclude the development of a strictly domestic program. Nuclear reversals in Argentina and Brazil, on the other hand, are widely attributed to reduced external security threats and domestic regime changes.[9] In Sweden and Switzerland, another factor appears to have been at work—concern over incurring the wrath of hostile nuclear powers.[10] Also in the Swedish case, the implicit extension of the U.S. nuclear umbrella seems to have played an important role.

Previous studies have also had difficulty assessing the influence on nuclear behavior of factors such as sanctions and nonproliferation norms that have a delayed or "nonlinear" impact (i.e., they take effect only after a predetermined threshold is crossed). Nor have they been able to distinguish between factors that lead to nuclear reversal and those that lead toward proliferation. The case of Egypt is illustrative in this regard.

Egypt's interest in developing a nuclear weapons program in the early 1960s is widely attributed to one or more of the following factors: its perception of an evolving Israeli nuclear capability, an inability to defeat Israel using conventional weapons, a desire to lead the Arab world politically and technologically, and strong domestic support for an indigenous nuclear capability. Egypt ultimately decided not to develop a full-fledged nuclear weapons program, how-

---

7. See National Intelligence Council, *Foreign Missile Developments and the Ballistic Missile Threat through 2015: Unclassified Summary of a National Intelligence Estimate* (Washington, D.C.: National Intelligence Council, December 2001).
8. See Joshua Sinai, "Libya's Pursuit of Weapons of Mass Destruction," *Nonproliferation Review,* Vol. 4, No. 3 (Spring/Summer 1997), pp. 92–100; Leonard Spector, *Nuclear Ambitions: The Spread of Nuclear Weapons, 1989–1990* (Boulder, Colo.: Westview, 1990), p. 182; and Director of Central Intelligence, *Unclassified Report to Congress on the Acquisition of Technology Relating to Weapons of Mass Destruction and Advanced Conventional Munitions: 1 January through 30 June 2001* (Washington, D.C.: Central Intelligence Agency, January 2002).
9. See Paul, *Power versus Prudence,* p. 111.
10. Ibid., p. 97.

ever, because its successive leaders (initially President Gamal Abdel Nasser and later Presidents Anwar el-Sadat and Hosni Mubarak) appear to have concluded that it would be neither necessary nor desirable to do so based on three considerations: the magnitude of the technical and economic challenges involved in the development of such a program, Israel's counterproliferation effort against it, and most important, U.S. diplomatic initiatives toward Egypt employing both carrots (including, apparently, reassurances to Egypt that "Israel will not introduce" nuclear weapons into the Middle East) and sticks.[11] Thus, despite military defeats in 1967 and 1973 and the ongoing development of Israel's nuclear activity, Egypt chose not to join the nuclear club.[12]

Another shortcoming in the existing literature is its failure to explore the possibility that the rationale for developing (or for that matter retaining) nuclear weapons may change over time, with new rationales for doing so emerging to replace older ones that have lost some of their luster. As Alexander George has observed, "Once established, policies often acquire momentum that is difficult to control or reverse."[13] The studies have also failed to acknowledge that to bring about nuclear reversal, it is not enough merely to remove a state's original motivations for obtaining nuclear weapons. This explains why Britain, for example, continues to retain its nuclear arsenal, albeit one considerably smaller than it maintained at the height of the Cold War.

Empirical data on proliferation in general and nuclear reversal in particular often are incomplete or otherwise unreliable because of a combination of extraordinary secrecy, intentional cover-up, and deliberate misinformation. Yet the literature manifests little appreciation of the gravity of these data problems.

Even in democratic countries, nuclear weapons programs are typically compartmentalized (i.e., subjected to especially rigid need-to-know arrangements

---

11. For a discussion of the evolution of Egyptian thinking toward the Israeli nuclear option, see Ariel E. Levite and Emily Landau, *In Arab Eyes: Arab Perceptions of Israel's Nuclear Posture* (in Hebrew) (Tel Aviv: Papirus, 1994).

12. See Michael J. Siler, "Explaining Variation in Nuclear Outcomes among Southern States: Bargaining Analysis of U.S. Nonproliferation Policies towards Brazil, Egypt, India, and South Korea," Ph.D. dissertation, University of Southern California, 1992, pp. 63–97. See also Jan Prawitz, *From Nuclear Option to Non-Nuclear Promotion: The Sweden Case*, Research Report No. 20 (Stockholm: Swedish Institute of International Affairs, 1995), pp. 4, 12. According to Prawitz, among the factors that led to Sweden's reversal of its nuclear policy were the emerging taboo on nuclear weapons and the NPT, neither of which was an issue when Sweden began its nuclear program in the early 1990s.

13. Alexander L. George, *Presidential Decisionmaking in Foreign Policy: The Effective Use of Information and Advice* (Boulder, Colo.: Westview, 1980), p. 41.

even within the government) and shrouded in secrecy. This is intended to prevent potentially harmful information from making its way to prospective proliferants, foreign adversaries, and domestic political foes. The concealment of nuclear know-how, installations, personnel, and materials is often still deemed necessary long after a state reverses its nuclear program. This holds even for democracies such as Australia, Norway, and Sweden, all of which have subsequently become champions of nonproliferation. One reason why Sweden, as well as South Korea, Switzerland, and Taiwan, continue to maintain secrecy over their nuclear weapons programs is to leave open the possibility of restarting them, should circumstances change.[14]

But even where the logic of retaining a nuclear option no longer applies, states typically uphold secrecy for fear of the domestic and foreign political fallout that might result from information about past nuclear activities being made public. Of special concern is the potential of such information to undercut a state's stature as an advocate of nonproliferation. It might also be feared that the release of this information could inspire other countries' nuclear pursuits, whether as a model, source of legitimacy for activity, source of nuclear know-how, or basis for diplomatic leverage in nuclear reversal negotiations. For example, the publication of a semiofficial historical account of the Swedish nuclear weapons program and its later abandonment was designed to persuade Ukraine to give up the Russian nuclear weapons in its possession.[15] The publication, however, deliberately omitted reference to any parts of the Swedish program that could enhance Ukraine's bargaining position in nuclear negotiations with the United States and Russia.

The fear that revelations of past activity could be embarrassing or harmful is a reason frequently given by governments, corporations, and individuals that once were involved in nuclear programs for restricting transparency (Britain in the case of Australia, and Germany in the cases of Argentina and Brazil).[16] Some of the reasons behind nuclear reversal might also prove too politically embarrassing or counterproductive to reveal. For example, did South Africa

---

14. On the suspicions aroused by the secrecy surrounding Sweden's nuclear status, see Steve Coll, "Sweden's Quiet Quest: Nuclear Arms Option," *Washington Post*, November 25, 1994, p. A1. Although Prawitz, in *From Nuclear Option to Non-Nuclear Promotion*, rebutted Coll, even he was unable to penetrate fully the secrecy surrounding key aspects of the Swedish nuclear program.
15. See Prawitz, *From Nuclear Option to Non-Nuclear Promotion*.
16. For the most comprehensive discussion of Britain's long-concealed, extensive assistance to the Australian nuclear weapons program, see Wayne Reynolds, *Australia's Bid for the Atomic Bomb* (Melbourne: Melbourne University Press, 2000).

really give up its nuclear weapons because of U.S. concern over what might happen to them when the government was transferred to the black majority? Did Taiwan reverse course in response to intense U.S. pressure motivated by worries over China's likely reaction?

Worse still, data that reach the public domain may have been deliberately manipulated for one of two reasons: (1) to conceal the true nature of a state's nuclear program or to create the impression that the state has an advanced nuclear weapons program, perhaps that it has even reached a "threshold status" (or "standby capability"),[17] in order to deter would-be adversaries or encourage allies to provide greater security assistance;[18] or (2) to coerce allies into abandoning plans for scaling back their current security commitments, as in the cases of Japan, South Korea, and Taiwan.[19]

A reexamination of the data pertaining to the Italian nuclear program illustrates how inadequate awareness of these shortcomings and biases in the data can profoundly distort scholarly understanding of nuclear reversal. It dispels the commonly held belief that Italy's engagement in a nuclear weapons program in the 1950s was guided by a serious desire to acquire nuclear weapons. The Italians deliberately created this perception so they could use it as leverage in bargaining predominantly with the United States. Italy was able to parlay the suspension of its "nuclear weapons program" into greater external security (including nuclear-specific arrangements) as well as political and economic benefits.[20]

---

17. Nuclear "threshold status" is commonly understood to mean possession of the indigenous ability to acquire nuclear weapons within a relatively short time frame, ranging from a few hours to several months. It has much in common with the CIA's definition of "standby capability," which is the "possession as of now of all of the facilities needed to produce nuclear weapons." See Central Intelligence Agency, *Response to NSSM No. 9*, Vol. 7: *Disarmament and Miscellaneous*, February 20, 1969, p. 4. NSSM is the acronym for National Security Study Memorandum.
18. See, for example, Leopoldo Nuti, "'Me Too, Please': Italy and the Politics of Nuclear Weapons, 1945–1975," *Diplomacy & Statecraft*, Vol. 4, No. 1 (March 1993), pp. 114–148, especially pp. 120–122. Nuti suggests that the trilateral cooperation project created by France, Germany, and Italy in the mid-1950s for military applications of nuclear technology appears to have been intended, at least in part by the Italians, to apply pressure on the United States to disclose information on nuclear weapons to its European allies. Similar logic appears to have guided Gunnar Randers, who promoted transparency of the Norwegian nuclear program in the hope of motivating the United States to assist it. See Astrid Forland, "Norway's Nuclear Odyssey: From Optimistic Proponent to Nonproliferator," *Nonproliferation Review*, Vol. 4, No. 2 (Winter 1997), p. 8.
19. See, for example, Frankel, "The Brooding Shadow," p. 51.
20. Evidence to support such possibilities is difficult to uncover. Pakistan, South Korea, and Taiwan, however, are widely suspected of having used their nuclear programs as leverage in getting the United States to provide them with assistance.

What Constitutes Nuclear Reversal and Restraint?

In this study, I define nuclear reversal as a governmental decision to slow or stop altogether an officially sanctioned nuclear weapons program. At the core of this definition is the distinction between states that have launched (indigenously or with external assistance) a nuclear weapons program and then abandoned it and those that never had such a program in the first place. Nuclear reversal excludes both termination of unauthorized nuclear weapons–related activity within a government and private-sector research and development in a nuclear weapons–related field (e.g., nuclear fuel–cycle technologies) if the latter was not formally pursued as part of an effort either to create a bomb or at least to acquire standby status. As applied here, this definition does include, however, cases in which a governmental decision to acquire the bomb could not be ascertained (e.g., Argentina).

This definition of nuclear reversal is flexible enough to include cases in which neither the initial pursuit of the bomb nor the eventual rollback of the program was reflected in an explicit government decision. The rationale for this is grounded in the characteristics of most nuclear programs. Would-be proliferants rarely make formal decisions to acquire the bomb or for that matter to give it up before they absolutely have to (e.g., before they are on the verge of attaining or eliminating a nuclear capability), if then. National leaderships are usually reluctant to make a formal commitment to acquiring nuclear weapons (even if the intent is clear) until the technical feasibility, affordability, and political (internal as well as external) viability of this undertaking have been ascertained. Such premature decisions are widely seen as politically risky and, perhaps more important, politically and strategically unnecessary, because the absence of such a formal decision does not usually preclude development of a standby capacity to produce nuclear weapons, under the rationale of creating a nuclear "option."[21] Similarly, rollback processes often begin slowly and hesitantly and proceed incrementally. They are rarely if ever cemented until the trade-offs are apparent and the risks of the decision minimized (in part through nuclear hedging).

---

21. Ashok Kapur concurs with this observation in Kapur, "New Nuclear States and the International Nuclear Order," in T.V. Paul, Richard J. Harknett, and James J. Wirtz, eds., *The Absolute Weapon Revisited: Nuclear Arms and the Emerging International Order* (Ann Arbor: University of Michigan Press, 2000), p. 240.

Nuclear restraint is a phenomenon somewhat akin to nuclear reversal, whereby a state undertakes a policy or external commitment (commonly made to the United States) that, at least initially, falls short of nuclear rollback but nonetheless keeps it from proceeding with some prominent nuclear activities.[22] Such restraint typically pertains to refraining from the construction of certain facilities; the production (of certain or all fissionable materials), testing, assembly, or deployment of weapons; or proclamations of nuclear status. Until conducting their nuclear tests in May 1998, both India and Pakistan had adopted several of these measures—as had North Korea in the domains of plutonium production and reprocessing under the terms of its 1994 Agreed Framework with the United States.

What Drives Nuclear Reversal?

Earlier studies have considered a variety of factors in seeking to explain why states decide to roll back their nuclear weapons programs. Common to all is some diminution of the perceived utility of nuclear weapons either because (1) the external security situation of a state improves or alternatives to nuclear weapons emerge that make them unnecessary; (2) a change occurs within the domestic regime and the state's security and/or economic orientation (central planning vs. market economy); or (3) systemic or state-specific incentives, such as new norms, emerge that diminish the appeal of nuclear weapons.[23] Scholars differ in the weight they assign to one factor (or cluster thereof) over others in influencing the reversal decision. They also often disagree over which domestic entity (the military, the scientific community, a political leader or faction, an interest group) was the driving force for or against nuclear weapons acquisition.

T.V. Paul has argued that no single variable can explain nuclear reversal. According to Paul, the one that comes closest is a state's external security environment, which itself is composed of a variety of factors, including the number, scope, intensity, and duration of militarized disputes in which the state is involved. Paul has advanced instead an explanation based on the notion of "prudential realism," according to which states "balance their interests and capabilities so as to minimize the security challenges they pose to others

---

22. Other forms of restraint pertain to a commitment not to help disseminate further nuclear weapons–usable technology, as well as to refrain from first use of nuclear weapons.
23. For a comprehensive review and assessment of these factors, see Paul, *Power versus Prudence*, pp. 3–11.

and in expectation of reciprocal benign behavior in return." Prudential realism distinguishes itself from the worst-case thinking commonly attributed to hardcore realists by replacing it with a "most-probable" threat assessment.[24] Yet even Paul ultimately deemed this rather elaborate construct insufficient to explain certain cases of nuclear reversal, finding it necessary to weave in several additional (and often case-specific) variables to explain actual instances of nuclear reversal.

The nuclear-reversal case studies in this article reaffirm Paul's conclusion that no overarching explanation for nuclear reversal emerges from the literature. It also suggests that there is considerable variation among the characteristics of the reversal processes themselves. This is not surprising given the diversity of the cases in terms of the time frame, type of regime, economic orientation, geostrategic location, and external security environment. In sum, nuclear reversal is typically driven not by one factor but by a combination of factors, the exact combination of which varies between the cases (or clusters thereof) and over time. Moreover, nuclear reversal cannot be fully understood unless both the nuclear hedging phenomenon and the typical characteristics of a reversal process are considered.

NUCLEAR HEDGING
Nuclear hedging refers to a national strategy of maintaining, or at least appearing to maintain, a viable option for the relatively rapid acquisition of nuclear weapons, based on an indigenous technical capacity to produce them within a relatively short time frame ranging from several weeks to a few years. In its most advanced form, nuclear hedging involves nuclear fuel–cycle facilities capable of producing fissionable materials (by way of uranium enrichment and/ or plutonium separation), as well as the scientific and engineering expertise both to support them and to package their final product into a nuclear explosive charge. Nuclear hedging is a strategy that may be adopted either during the process of developing a bomb or as part of the rollback process, as a way of retaining the option of restarting a weapons program that has been halted or reversed.[25] Nuclear hedging may explain at least some of the difficulty encountered to date in efforts to understand nuclear reversal. Indeed, some of the

---

24. Ibid., p. 5.
25. In addition to Egypt and Japan, South Korea and Taiwan constitute more recent examples of nuclear hedging. In the South Korea and Taiwan cases, their reprocessing capabilities were at the center of the nuclear-hedging strategies that led both countries into confrontation with their U.S. ally. For a discussion of South Korea's pursuit of complete fuel-cycle technologies, see Jungmin

cases that have been assumed to involve nuclear reversal may on closer examination be cases of nuclear hedging.

Prime Minister Winston Churchill first articulated the essence of nuclear hedging in a November 1951 memorandum to Lord Cherwell, his ministerial adviser on nuclear matters. In the memorandum Churchill wrote, "I have never wished since our decision during the war that England should start the manufacture of atomic bombs. Research, however, must be energetically pursued. We should have the art rather than the article. A large sum of money will have to be provided for this." Churchill had naïvely expected that he could persuade officials in Washington to allocate some U.S. nuclear weapons to Britain in recognition of the latter's significant scientific contribution to the Manhattan Project.[26] After being rebuffed, Britain launched its own nuclear weapons program.

In the Swedish case, after a period of slow decline in the state's commitment to its nuclear program, the government officially eschewed any desire for nuclear weapons in the mid-1960s. But in practice, not much has changed. Research in all the relevant disciplines of bomb making that had originally been launched in the 1950s continued, under the guise of so-called nuclear defense programs carried out by the Swedish National Defense Research Establishment (FOA)—the same lead agency that had been responsible for Sweden's original nuclear weapons development program. This activity would continue long after Sweden joined the NPT in 1968 and became a champion of nonproliferation.[27] In addition, it means that Sweden is a mere two to three years away from acquiring a nuclear capability.[28]

Kang and H.A. Feiveson, "South Korea's Shifting and Controversial Interest in Spent Fuel Reprocessing," *Nonproliferation Review*, Vol. 8, No. 1 (Spring 2001), pp. 70–78. For a discussion of the Taiwan case, see David Albright and Corey Gay, "Taiwan: Nuclear Nightmare Averted," *Bulletin of the Atomic Scientists*, Vol. 54, No. 1 (January/February 1998), pp. 54–60.

26. Quoted in Margaret Gowing, *Independence and Deterrence: Britain and Atomic Energy, 1945–1952*, Vol. 1: *Policy Making* (New York: St. Martin's, 1974), p. 406. Cherwell's reply to Churchill is revealing: "If we are unable to make bombs ourselves and have to rely entirely on the United States army for this vital weapon, we shall sink to the rank of a second-class nation, only permitted to supply auxiliary troops, like the native levies who were allowed small arms but not artillery." Ibid., p. 407. I am indebted to David Holloway for drawing my attention to this correspondence.

27. For prominent accounts of the Swedish nuclear weapons program, see Jan Prawitz, "Non-Nuclear Is Beautiful, or Why and How Sweden Went Non-Nuclear," *Kungl Krigsventenskapsakademiens Handlingar och Tidskrift*, No. 198 (Stockholm: National Defense Research Establishment, June 1994); Reiss, *Without the Bomb*, pp. 37–77; Paul, *Power versus Prudence*, pp. 84–99; Paul M. Cole, *Atomic Bombast: Nuclear Weapons Decision Making in Sweden, 1945–1972*, Occasional Paper No. 26 (Washington, D.C.: Henry L. Stimson Center, 1996); and Wilhelm Agrell, "The Bomb That Never Was: The Rise and Fall of the Swedish Nuclear Weapons Programme," in Nils Peter Gleditsch and Olav Njolstad, eds., *Arms Races: Technological and Political Dynamics* (London: Sage, 1990).

28. See Central Intelligence Agency, *Response to NSSM No. 9*, p. 3.

Japan provides the most salient example of nuclear hedging to date. The Japan case illustrates how a state signatory to the NPT and a champion of nonproliferation and disarmament can legitimately maintain a nuclear fuel–cycle capability and possess huge quantities of weapons-grade fissile material. Moreover, according to an official British government report, Japan "has key bomb-making components, including plutonium and electronic triggers, and has the expertise to go nuclear very quickly."[29] Japan hardly tries to conceal its hedging strategy (though it does seek to keep some of its more specific features out of the public eye). This is evident in repeated statements by senior government officials that, under certain circumstances, Japan could revisit the issue of nuclear weapons acquisition. A statement by former Japanese Prime Minister Morihiro Hosokawa provides one such example: "It is in the interest of the United States, so long as it does not wish to see Japan withdraw from the NPT and develop its own nuclear deterrent, to maintain its alliance with Japan and continue to provide a nuclear umbrella."[30] Despite the long-term Japanese commitment to the "three nuclear principles" announced by Prime Minister Eisaku Sato in 1968 and formalized by the Diet in 1971 (banning the possession, production, or import of nuclear weapons) as well as provisions in the Japanese constitution that preclude the acquisition of a nuclear capability, senior Japanese officials have repeatedly indicated that these principles could be revised.[31] They have also stated that the constitution could be reinterpreted to permit Japanese possession of "defensive nuclear weapons."[32] In fact, the three principles are carefully worded so as to allow the development of a standby

---

29. "Japan May 'Go Nuclear,' Paper Says," *Japan Times*, August 11, 1993, p. 4, cited in Paul, *Power versus Prudence*, p. 51.

30. See Morihiro Hosokawa, "Are U.S. Troops in Japan Needed? Reforming the Alliance," *Foreign Affairs*, Vol. 77, No. 4 (July/August 1998), p. 5. This statement highlights the role that U.S. extended deterrence plays in restraining Japan's nuclear ambitions and reveals Japan's explicit preference for the U.S. nuclear umbrella over the development of an indigenous nuclear capability. It also demonstrates how Japan uses its advanced nuclear bomb–making potential both as leverage against the United States (lest it weaken its security commitment to Japan) and as a hedge should the United States do so. This case also underscores the limitations of the known universe of nuclear reversal cases, because it may include states that have all along pursued security offsets rather than nuclear weapons. See Yuri Kase, "The Costs and Benefits of Japan's Nuclearization: An Insight into the *1968/70 Internal Report*," *Nonproliferation Review*, Vol. 8, No. 2 (Summer 2001), pp. 55–68.

31. For the most recent official formulation of this position, see comments made on May 30, 2002, by a "high-ranking [Japanese] government official," later identified as Chief Cabinet Secretary Yasuo Fukuda, according to which Japan may reconsider its decade-long commitment to the three nuclear principles. See "Japan Official Hints at Review of Nonnuclear Policy," Jiji Press Ticker Service (Tokyo), May 31, 2002; and Howard W. French, " Koizumi Aide Hints at Change to No Nuclear Policy," *New York Times*, June 4, 2002, p. 10.

32. Paul, *Power versus Prudence*, p. 56.

nuclear capability that stops just short of actual weapons production—allowing Japan to remain within a few months of acquiring nuclear weapons. Under these circumstances, it is not surprising that South Korea has long referred to Japan as an "associate member of the nuclear club."[33]

Nuclear hedging appears to have played a critical role in facilitating nuclear reversal in practically every case under examination in this article, especially early in the reversal process. Its influence begins to subside only gradually if at all and only after the reversal process has gained momentum. What is striking about nuclear hedging as a strategy is its elasticity. Hedging does not translate into a uniform formula for action but merely into a general choice of strategic posture. The time frame that a state deems acceptable to acquire nuclear weapons depends, in turn, on three principal factors: (1) how the state defines the desired "nuclear capability" (e.g., the number of weapons it would have to produce, assemble, and deploy); (2) the amount of advance warning it expects to have of adverse developments that might necessitate nuclear weapons acquisition; and (3) its assessment of the risks, opportunities, and costs of stepping up nuclear preparedness, especially in terms of domestic and foreign reaction to its nuclear hedging posture.

The appeal of nuclear hedging goes well beyond the nuclear weapons option that it facilitates politically as well as technically. Its greatest appeal is the "latent" or "virtual" deterrence posture it generates toward nuclear weapons aspirants or potential aggressors,[34] and the leverage it provides in reinforcing a state's coercive diplomacy strategy, particularly against the United States.

A near-explicit endorsement of this logic found expression in a 1998 statement by President Mubarak of Egypt: "If the time comes when we need nuclear weapons, then we will not hesitate. I say if we have to, because this is the last thing we think about. We do not think now of joining the nuclear club." Mubarak then implied that neither technical nor financial barriers held Egypt back from getting nuclear weapons: "Acquiring material for nuclear weapons has become very easy and it can be bought."[35] Mubarak's warning regarding the potential for (re)activation of Egypt's nuclear weapons program was echoed by Nabil Fahmy, Egypt's ambassador to the United States, who linked it

---

33. Ibid., p. 54.
34. Ibid., p. 59.
35. Interview with the London-based newspaper *Al-Hayat*, quoted in "Egypt's Mubarak Says Egypt Can Join Nuclear Club," Reuters, October 5, 1998.

explicitly to weapons of mass destruction (WMD) proliferation trends in the Middle East.[36]

The Japanese and Egyptian cases underscore the complex relationship between the NPT and nuclear hedging. Contrary to widespread perceptions, the NPT appears to have had less to do with walking key states all the way back from nuclear weapons development to nuclear reversal and more to do with encouraging them (at least initially, and for some permanently) to trade nuclear development for nuclear hedging. This has resulted from a combination of flexibility implicit in NPT definitions of proscribed activities, the narrow focus on International Atomic Energy Agency (IAEA) safeguards as the core of its verification regime, and the NPT's provisions allowing members to engage in fuel-cycle activities. Their combined impact has been to convince many nations that it is easier to hedge and even push their nuclear weapons programs forward to a fairly advanced stage while being parties to the NPT. Both Iran and Iraq have been following this path for years, actively pursuing nuclear weapons while being members of the NPT.[37] All of these examples reaffirm Paul's observation that accession to the NPT is no more than a manifestation of a commitment to (rather than a practice of) nuclear nonproliferation, if that.[38]

CHARACTERISTICS OF THE NUCLEAR REVERSAL PROCESS

This analysis suggests that there is considerable variance in the motivations, direction, and pace governing nuclear reversal processes. The direction and speed of reversal are driven by complex motivations (not all of which may be explicit or widely shared among decisionmakers). Yet for all these differences,

36. Fahmy went on to write: "If this proliferation trend continues unabated, it will inevitably trigger a reevaluation on the part of regional states, prompting some to accelerate the development of their already existing WMD programmes, while forcing others to activate programmes that have so far remained dormant." Fahmy, "Special Comment," *Disarmament Forum*, No. 2 (2001), http://www.unog.ch/unidir/1-02-eSpecial_com.pdf (accessed January 4, 2003).
37. For authoritative assessments of the Iranian and Iraqi nuclear pursuits and ambitions, see the semiannual report submitted by the CIA to Congress on January 30, 2002, entitled *Unclassified Report to Congress on the Acquisition of Technology Relating to Weapons of Mass Destruction and Advanced Conventional Munitions, 1 July through 31 December 2001*, at http://www.cia.gov/cia/publications/bian/bian_jan_2003.htm#14 (accessed January 14, 2003), as well as the U.S. Department of Defense's *Proliferation: Threat and Response* (Washington, D.C.: Department of Defense, January 2001), pp. 34–41. A comprehensive account of past Iraqi nuclear pursuits is also provided by the IAEA reports to the UN Security Council. See, for example, IAEA, *Report by the Director General of the International Atomic Energy Agency in Connection with the Panel on Disarmament and Current and Future Ongoing Monitoring and Verification Issues*, GOV/INF/1999/4 (Vienna, Austria: IAEA, February 24, 1999), pp. 17–21.
38. Paul, *Power versus Prudence*, p. 57.

there are some important underlying similarities across the cases. They all seem to reaffirm the CIA's assessment that "political rather than economic and technical factors restrain most of the nations which are capable of developing nuclear weapons from doing so."[39] Economic resource constraints, technical hurdles, organizational behavior and bureaucratic politics, and even regime change appear to have much lesser roles in the overall direction of a state's nuclear weapons program, but they do typically influence its scope, pace, cost, efficiency, and technical parameters. Among the political factors that play a dominant role, external security considerations—however defined by different leaders—stand out as having consistently had a profound impact on states' nuclear choices. Moreover, although a favorable external security outlook appears necessary to bring about nuclear reversal, it rarely if ever appears to be sufficient, by itself, to produce this outcome. This is where the combination of domestic regime change and the availability of external incentives may tilt the balance in one direction or another.

Reversal processes also seem to share one of three characteristics (and often all three). First, nuclear weapons programs typically fizzle out in a gradual and nonlinear way rather than shut down abruptly and completely. South Africa is the sole known exception to this rule due to the unique circumstances of the handover of power to the country's black majority. Second, states contemplating nuclear reversal do not begin with a clearly articulated objective. This may reflect uncertainty over what that goal ought to be, or it may be a tactic to avoid or deflect counterpressures (where a consensus can be forged on the interim step but not necessarily on the desired result). Third, states considering nuclear reversal rarely assume that it is permanent and irreversible.[40] Indeed, the reversal process allows states both in theory and in practice to switch course and restart their nuclear weapons programs should conditions warrant it. This is especially true early in the process, a point that has been underscored by the recent revelations concerning North Korea's nuclear enrichment project.

Because capping, let alone walking back, from a nuclear weapons program is a momentous decision, typically fraught with political risks and surrounded by domestic controversy, governments have a powerful incentive to devise a process that minimizes risks and friction (through hedging) and generates domestic consensus in support of such a decision. This kind of consensus,

---

39. See Central Intelligence Agency, *Response to NSSM No. 9*, p. 1.
40. For a similar conclusion and an elaboration of the conditions that might result in such a reversal, see Paul, *Power versus Prudence*, pp. 147, 154–155.

whether cultivated entirely indigenously or, as is commonly the case, with some external support and (at times) prodding, typically requires the sophisticated use of offsets and incentives. These have to address the security, prestige, and bureaucratic appeal of a nuclear program. One prominent way in which this appears to have been done has been to offset, at least initially, a declining effort in acquiring nuclear weapons with an investment in peaceful nuclear activity, whether for power generation or further research. Notwithstanding any commercial or energy security rationales for building up the civilian nuclear infrastructure, in some of the countries of concern here, such investments—especially in enrichment and reprocessing technology and facilities—were designed at least in part to facilitate hedging at least for a while (Germany) or to this day (Japan and South Korea). For others, the construction of nuclear facilities could also have served to address issues of prestige and employment associated with nuclear activity, as was the case with Egypt and North Korea.[41] Civilian nuclear technology also underscores the important symbolic yet tangible benefits that accrue to a state for forswearing the nuclear option, of which access to modern reactors is tangible proof. Egypt and North Korea are once again cases in point.

The Role of the United States

Earlier sections have noted the importance of nuclear hedging as well as nuclear restraint in explaining the nuclear behavior of specific states. This discussion has also drawn attention to the centrality of these phenomena for shedding light on the process and not merely the outcome of nuclear reversal. These phenomena in turn yield new insights into the influence that the United States has had on the nuclear choices of key states. The United States has played a unique role in helping to move nuclear aspirants away from nuclear pursuits toward more benign behavior, be it nuclear restraint or hedging if not outright nuclear reversal. Toward that end, it has energetically employed a range of techniques since the early days of the Cold War.

The role of the United States in influencing the nuclear choices of a number of states has long been recognized in the literature on nuclear nonproliferation.

---

41. The United States, for example, promised to provide Egypt with a nuclear reactor in return for signing the NPT in 1981. North Korea was promised two light water reactors in return for signing the 1994 Agreed Framework, committing it to several verifiable steps of nuclear capping (freezing the reprocessing of plutonium and allowing inspections of nuclear waste storage sites).

James Doyle has provided the most comprehensive review of the efforts of successive U.S. administrations to stem the tide of nuclear proliferation and encourage would-be proliferants either to restrain or to abandon their programs altogether.[42] Some works have focused on specific initiatives taken by the United States either alone or with other states, the most recent example being the review by Robert Einhorn and Gary Samore, two former senior officials in President Bill Clinton's administration, of the U.S. effort to stem the tide of Russian nuclear assistance to Iran.[43] There is also extensive discussion of the traditional U.S. role in establishing and ultimately consolidating international nuclear nonproliferation norms and institutions and its efforts to persuade particular nuclear aspirants to desist from their pursuit of nuclear weapons.[44]

The nonproliferation literature, however, still lacks a systematic assessment of the vast array of nonproliferation instruments and assets employed by the United States across the cases of nuclear restraint and reversal. This is a glaring omission because the involvement of the United States in this area is unsurpassed in terms of the great quantity and diversity of resources that it has applied to an array of objectives—even if its policies have not always been consistently or coherently applied.

CHARACTERISTICS OF U.S. NONPROLIFERATION ACTIVITIES

U.S. nonproliferation efforts have four distinguishing characteristics, corresponding to the objectives, strategy, scope, and means of U.S. activity. First, the United States has sought to preserve its nuclear hegemony and diminish the appeal of nuclear weapons for others while improving overall international security. Second, although its stated goal in virtually all the cases has been to arrest or roll back nuclear proliferation, the United States has often settled for the more modest objective of nuclear restraint such as capping the production of fissionable material, banning nuclear testing, or preventing the deployment of nuclear capabilities (all of which it has attempted to apply in recent years to the Indian subcontinent). Third, the scope of U.S. efforts has been both global

---

42. For a comprehensive review of U.S. nonproliferation policies and instruments, see Doyle, "Nuclear Rollback," pp. 23–24. In addition to assessing the efficacy of the U.S. efforts generally, Doyle evaluates their influence in five prominent cases of nuclear rollback: Argentina, Brazil, South Africa, Sweden, and Ukraine.
43. Robert J. Einhorn and Gary Samore, "Ending Russian Assistance to Iran's Nuclear Bomb," *Survival*, Vol. 44, No. 2 (Summer 2002), pp. 51–70.
44. Perhaps the most salient study of this genre is McGeorge Bundy's *Danger and Survival: Choices about the Bomb in the First Fifty Years* (New York: Random House, 1988).

and regional, aiming to mold a nonproliferation regime as well as to influence the local and regional conditions (conflicts, stability) that inspire nuclear aspirations and regulate international trade of nuclear materials. Fourth, U.S. nonproliferation efforts have employed many unilateral but also bilateral, trilateral, and multilateral instruments (from dialogues and treaties to supplier regimes); softer measures (norms and rewards) and more coercive ones; and universal as well as case-specific means.

These distinctions are evident in my survey of nuclear reversal and restraint cases. In the security realm, the United States has repeatedly engaged in diplomatic initiatives aimed at settling or at least defusing conflicts that could fuel proliferation. It has also provided nonnuclear security assistance to increase the recipient's confidence that it can address its security concerns without nuclear weapons.[45] This assistance has appeared in the form of conventional arms transfers and other types of military assistance (e.g., training and education and military-to-military ties), as well as security guarantees.

POSITIVE AND NEGATIVE INDUCEMENTS. Security guarantees extended by the United States have varied greatly in scope, degree of formality, and level of commitment. These guarantees have included both positive and negative security assurances,[46] and pertain not only to U.S. conduct but also to the behavior of third countries of particular concern to the country that the United States is trying to dissuade from acquiring nuclear arms (e.g., providing reassurances to Egypt regarding Israeli nuclear behavior). The security assurances that the United States has made concerning its own behavior have ranged from the soft (less explicit and/or binding) variety (extended, for example, to Ukraine) to bilateral and multilateral collective security arrangements (Australia, Japan, the North Atlantic Treaty Organization, and South Korea), which often are reinforced by the presence of U.S. troops. In NATO, these have been accompanied

---

45. See Alexander Kelle, "Nonproliferation Decisions in Italy," paper prepared for the Workshop on Nonproliferation Decisions: Lessons from Lesser-Known Cases, Monterey Institute of International Studies, Monterey, California, August 19–20, 1996, p. 23; and Doyle, "Nuclear Rollback," p. 242. A good illustration of this point is Ukraine's attempts to procure security guarantees from both the United States and Russia in return for surrendering the nuclear weapons on its territory. This effort ultimately won it only modest guarantees. See James E. Goodby, *Europe Undivided: The New Logic of Peace in U.S.-Russian Relations* (Washington, D.C.: United States Institute of Peace, 1998), pp. 80–88. This case also illustrates the importance of most other incentives for securing nuclear reversal, including enhanced prestige and receipt of conventional arms and financial assistance.
46. Positive security assurances are commitments to extend help in the event of a nuclear attack; negative security assurances are reassurances against a first strike by a nuclear power.

by a promise not only to extend the U.S. nuclear umbrella to member states (and deploy nuclear weapons in some of them) but also to share information on these weapons. This has been coupled with some form of guaranteed formal (though, in practice, mostly symbolic other than as veto power) participation in nuclear weapons decisionmaking. In particular, such assurances have involved so-called dual-key arrangements,[47] bringing NATO countries into the process of U.S. nuclear contingency planning and providing them a veto right over certain pertinent scenarios for the employment of nuclear weapons. In the early 1960s, the United States considered (though never implemented) even more dramatic formulations of nuclear sharing, such as the 1960 proposal for the creation of a multilateral nuclear force.

The threat (or promise) of denying (or providing) economic and technological assistance, including the supply of civilian and nuclear weapons technology, has been another tool commonly (and successfully) used by the United States to encourage nuclear nonproliferation.[48] It has targeted suppliers, recipients, and developers of nuclear weapons–related capabilities, with special emphasis on denying the wherewithal to produce fissionable material.

In most cases, the United States has sought to downplay any explicit linkage between nuclear behavior and the provision (or denial) of economic assistance either unilaterally or through financial institutions such as the International Monetary Fund and the World Bank. Exceptions include the Argentinean case, in which the United States was widely suspected of linking external debt refinancing to Argentine nuclear reversal; energy assistance to North Korea by the Korean Peninsula Energy Development Organization; and bilateral and multilateral deals with Belarus, Kazakhstan, and Ukraine in the early to mid-1990s that facilitated the withdrawal of Russian nuclear weapons from their territory.[49] Most often, however, the quid pro quo is not as obvious, which sug-

---

47. Leopoldo Nuti recounts the importance of such arrangements at the time for the Italians, who were wavering between developing an indigenous nuclear weapons capability through participation in a French-German nuclear (including weapons) program and seeking cover and prestige under an Atlantic nuclear umbrella. See Nuti, "'Me Too, Please,'" pp. 120–132.

48. In addition to the more common U.S. offsets in the form of civilian nuclear technology (originally offered in its Atoms for Peace program of 1953), the United States has occasionally resorted to more direct forms of sharing nuclear weapons know-how and technology to induce the acceptance of nuclear restraints by Britain, France, and even China, most prominently in the domain of nuclear testing. For a reference to U.S. assistance to France, see Joseph S. Nye Jr., "New Approaches to Nuclear Proliferation Policy," *Science*, May 29, 1992, p. 1297. For the nature of the assistance, see Nicola Butler, "Sharing Secrets: Nuclear Weapons Information Exchange between France, Great Britain, and the United States," *Bulletin of the Atomic Scientists*, Vol. 53, No. 1 (January/February 1997), pp. 11–12.

49. In these cases, George H.W. Bush's administration and later the Clinton administration agreed to buy their supplies of highly enriched uranium. See Gilbert J. Brown, "From Nuclear Swords to

gests that a similar dynamic has been at work in many additional cases in which the extension of U.S. economic and security aid and/or other forms of U.S. engagement has coincided with nuclear reversal, or at least its formal codification (in the form of accession to a legally binding obligation prohibiting the production or purchase of nuclear weapons), with Argentina, Egypt, and Brazil being just three cases in point. In the Argentinean case, there appears to have been a linkage between the U.S. de-emphasis of the Carter administration's human rights initiative vis-à-vis Argentina and the (successful) U.S. effort to win the support of the military junta to terminate the country's nuclear weapons program.[50]

In 1976 President Gerald Ford's outgoing administration worked out a secret agreement with Brazil in which the latter agreed to annul a 1975 contract it had awarded to Germany for the purchase of reprocessing plants in return for U.S. security guarantees and promises of military sales. When the deal was leaked to the U.S. press by Jimmy Carter's incoming administration, Brazil's president backed out of the agreement and reverted to his earlier pronuclear stance, seriously straining U.S.-Brazil relations. Brazil canceled its mutual defense treaty with the United States and rejected $50 million in military sales credits.[51]

The U.S.-Brazil deal sheds light on the key role of the United States in facilitating nuclear reversal, but it also illustrates the difficulty, in the absence of reliable information on secret deals as well as on the reasoning of the leadership, of establishing causality in nuclear reversal cases. In part, countries such as Brazil may have been thinking about adopting nuclear reversal anyway, and wanted only to extract a U.S. offset or payoff before carrying out that policy.[52]

Nuclear Plowshares," *Washington Post*, September 1, 1992, p. A17; and Thomas W. Lippman, "Two Nuclear Accords Expected: U.S.-Russia Pact Involves Uranium Buy," *Washington Post*, March 21, 1999, p. A25. In addition, Congress passed the so-called Nunn-Lugar Act, which provides economic aid to these former Soviet republics to guarantee that none of them reneges on its promise to abstain from nuclear proliferation. See Theodor Galdi, *The Nunn-Lugar Cooperative Nuclear Threat Reduction Program for Soviet Weapons Dismantlement*, Congressional Research Service, 94-985-F (Washington, D.C.: Government Printing Office, December 6, 1994), pp. 1–6.

50. For a summary of recently declassified official U.S. documents on the policy toward the Argentinean nuclear program, see Paul Richter, "U.S. Feared a Nuclear Argentina," *Los Angeles Times*, August 23, 2002, http://www.latimes.com/news/printedition/front/la-fg-dirty23aug. story?null.

51. For information on the secret agreement, see A. David Rossin, "Plutonium," Stanford University, forthcoming. On the rejected mutual defense treaty and military sales credits, see Graham Hovey, "Carter Writes to Leader of Brazil," *New York Times*, March 31, 1977, p. 2. On the crisis in U.S.-Brazil relations, see, for instance, Hobart Rowen, "U.S. Shifted on Bonn-Brazil Nuclear Deal," *Washington Post*, May 9, 1977, p. A10. See also David Vidal, *New York Times*, Information Bank Abstract, June 14, 1977; and "Why Latin Americans Are Bitter about Carter," *Washington Post*, April 4, 1977, p. 33.

52. The Japanese case is a convincing example of extracting U.S. security guarantees as a condition for nuclear abstinence. Japan has repeatedly made it clear that the United States is a key player in

In addition, it is unclear whether these countries would have been able or willing to eschew nuclear weapons or to circumscribe their nuclear ambitions even if the United States had not responded to their demands. Moreover, there is evidence to suggest that at least some states (presently North Korea, but previously also Italy, Pakistan, South Korea, and Taiwan) may have deliberately moved ahead on the nuclear weapons path, by collecting information, conducting studies, procuring equipment, and constructing facilities, to attract or drive up the value of U.S. rewards offered to them in return for nuclear reversal.[53]

The extensive efforts by U.S. intelligence to track and analyze nuclear proliferation activities are relatively well documented, not in the least in scores of briefings, testimonies, and annual reports provided by the U.S. intelligence community to Congress. There have also been occasional references to some of the more creative and sophisticated means that U.S. intelligence agencies have employed to collect information, from using a civilian reconnaissance plane to fly over the South African nuclear test site in the Kalahari Desert in 1977 to planting an electronic monitoring device disguised as a rock near the Pakistani nuclear enrichment facility at Kahuta in the mid-1990s.[54]

CLANDESTINE TECHNIQUES. Clandestine techniques constitute additional U.S. tools employed to promote nuclear nonproliferation. Although they have been extensively used, and seem to be correlated with cases of nuclear restraint and even reversal, they have been neither well documented in the open literature nor systematically researched. Yet they merit serious consideration because they can help to put in perspective other explanations for the reversal phenomenon.

---

its security (and specifically) nuclear policy, both by emphasizing the importance of the U.S. extended deterrence guarantee and by notifying the United States of a Japanese report investigating the costs and benefits of Japanese nuclearization. See Kase, "The Costs and Benefits of Japan's Nuclearization," especially pp. 56, 60.

53. There is a correlation between two occasions in which the United States announced its intent to scale back its military presence on the Korean Peninsula (by President Richard Nixon in 1970 and President Carter in 1977) and the intensification of South Korea's efforts to develop a nuclear bomb option. In both cases the United States ended up largely reversing course, as did South Korea. See Kang and Feiveson, "South Korea's Shifting and Controversial Interest in Spent Fuel Reprocessing," pp. 71–72. A similar correlation is apparent between U.S. actions and Taiwan's nuclear weapons program, most prominently following the termination of diplomatic relations between the two countries on January 1, 1979. Then it culminated in a renewed U.S. commitment to the security of Taiwan in the form of the 1979 Taiwan Relations Act, public diplomacy to deter Chinese military invasion of the island, and massive conventional arms sales to Taiwan. For the ups and downs of Taiwan's nuclear program, see Albright and Gay, "Taiwan."

54. David Albright, "South Africa and the Affordable Bomb," *Bulletin of the Atomic Scientists*, Vol. 50, No. 4 (July–August 1994), http://www.thebulletin.org/issues/1994/ja94/Albright.html.

One cluster of U.S. clandestine activities to stop or slow foreign nuclear programs involves operations designed to recruit or trap foreign government agents engaged in procuring nuclear-related materials or foreign scientists engaged in nuclear research and development. Taiwan, for example, originally launched a secret nuclear weapons program in 1964 following China's first nuclear test earlier that year.[55] It abandoned the program in 1976 in response to extensive U.S. pressure. Taiwan restarted the program in 1987, however; and in violation of the 1976 agreement, its Institute for Nuclear Energy Research (INER) began construction of a hot cell facility. The United States apparently learned quickly of this development from Col. Chang Hsien-yi, the deputy director of INER and also a confirmed U.S. agent recruited by the CIA in the 1960s.[56] The United States proceeded to demand that Taiwan permanently disband this facility, which it did; Chang and his family were spirited to the United States shortly thereafter.[57]

Occasionally the U.S. government has also resorted to briefing foreign leaders about nuclear activities occurring in their own countries. The purpose has been to warn them that the United States is aware of the nuclear activity and to encourage them to terminate these activities or at least to scale them back. Perhaps the best-known case involves the June 1989 briefing provided by CIA Director William Webster to visiting Pakistani Prime Minister Benazir Bhutto. The briefing was meant to acquaint her with details of Pakistan's nuclear weapons program that the United States suspected were being withheld from her by the Pakistani military—in particular, Pakistan's transgression of its pledge to the United States concerning uranium enrichment. Although the briefing did not provide Bhutto with dramatic details of which she was previously unaware, it did impress her with the scope of U.S. knowledge of Pakistan's nuclear program, create a common base of knowledge between the U.S. government and the Pakistani premier on this delicate issue, and facilitate the establishment of a follow-up agenda for action. As a result of the meeting, Prime Minister Bhutto conceded her willingness to "work on any information or assessment" by the CIA of the Pakistani program.[58]

55. Albright and Gay, "Taiwan," p. 55.
56. See Tim Weiner, "How a Spy Left Taiwan in the Cold," *New York Times*, December 20, 1997, p. A7. According to the article, the CIA refused to disclose more information about Colonel Chang.
57. See Albright and Gay, "Taiwan," pp. 59–60.
58. David B. Ottaway, "U.S. Relieves Pakistan of Pledge against Enriching Uranium," *Washington Post*, June 15, 1989, p. A38.

The United States has also used public leaks to try, first, to embarrass governments engaged in clandestine nuclear weapons activities and, second, to galvanize opposition against them within the United States, inside their own country, and internationally. News leaks have dogged nearly all nuclear aspirants at one time or another. On many occasions the source can be traced back to a U.S. origin. Yet even when it is possible to establish a U.S. connection, it is all but impossible to ascertain whether this is part of an officially sanctioned policy or just another aspect of "doing business" in Washington.

There have also been a number of other initiatives designed to press U.S. administrations to take more forceful action.[59] The U.S. Congress, at times to the chagrin of the administration, has pushed some of these initiatives. One case in point is the 1985 Pressler amendment, which expressed concern over Pakistan's nuclear weapons development and required annual certification of its nuclear status as a condition of U.S. assistance. Another is former President Carter's negotiations with North Korea in 1993, which yielded an agreement in 1994 on the capping of the North Korean nuclear program and eventually also inspections of its facilities in return for providing North Korea with heavy fuel and modern nuclear reactors.

Given the tremendous resources at its disposal and its position as global leader, the United States has been able to exert more influence than any other country over nuclear proliferants and would-be proliferants. Its capacity for influence has been reinforced by the willingness of virtually every administration since World War II to employ U.S. clout to promote the cause of nuclear nonproliferation. Behind this willingness has been the belief that such involvement best serves U.S. (and broader) interests—even if Washington's policies were occasionally inconsistent (e.g., Pakistan), misguided (e.g., the Atoms for Peace initiative of Dwight Eisenhower's administration, which sought to provide states with peaceful nuclear technologies as a means of dissuading their pursuit of nuclear weapons), or otherwise uneven (e.g., France and India).

An understanding with the United States is, in fact, a hallmark of many cases of nuclear slowdown or reversal.[60] Lively debates about the impact of in-

---

59. One example is the consistent encouragement, and occasionally even direct financial assistance, provided in recent years by U.S. government agencies (primarily the Department of Energy, the Department of Defense, and the State Department) to bilateral and multilateral Middle East and South Asian track-two security and arms-control talks sponsored by several highly respected U.S. universities (e.g., Columbia, Stanford, and the University of California, Los Angeles) that do work in the field.

60. Some of the best-documented cases in point are those of Israel, North Korea, South Korea, and Taiwan.

digenous nuclear decisions on a country's relations with the United States have occurred within virtually every democratic nuclear aspirant, most prominently India and Israel. This has led Michael Siler to conclude that the actions of the United States can "make the critical difference," especially in dictating the particular course of a nuclear reversal process.[61] There is no evidence to suggest, however, that U.S. influence has ever been a sufficient factor for inducing nuclear reversal.[62]

U.S. INFLUENCE OVER DOMESTIC REGIMES

Some of the domestic calculations and forces affecting countries' nuclear ambitions have remained beyond the sphere of direct U.S. influence. As a result, although the United States has been able to encourage complete nuclear reversal in Europe and Latin America, and most saliently in South Africa, it has had more modest success in Egypt, Israel, Japan, South Korea, and Taiwan and much less success in India, North Korea, and Pakistan. In these cases, it has been able to limit their ambitions to some form of nuclear hedging and in the cases of India and Pakistan only to limited nuclear restraint. As for Iran, Iraq, and Libya, the United States has been unable to alter their nuclear aspirations, but it has been able to retard the progress of their nuclear programs, primarily by hindering access to fissionable materials and their production technologies and facilities.

The nature of domestic regimes is probably the most important factor affecting nuclear ambitions that remains largely outside the sphere of direct U.S. influence. It also provides some of the most fascinating illustrations of the delicate balance between the strength and limits of U.S. influence on foreign nuclear pursuits.

The studies of nuclear reversal and more broadly nuclear nonproliferation have been unable to establish a direct link between the nature of a regime and its nuclear orientation: Both democratic and totalitarian regimes have sought to produce or purchase nuclear weapons. Even changes in regime have not by themselves automatically yielded a reorientation of the state's nuclear pursuits.[63] Thus, even in those rare cases where the United States might be able to

61. Siler, "Explaining Variation in Nuclear Outcomes among Southern States," p. 244.
62. Etel Solingen convincingly demonstrates that U.S. "hegemonic protection," for example, has been neither a sufficient nor a necessary condition for nuclear reversal. But her analysis refers merely to the U.S. role in providing security guarantees. See Solingen, "The Political Economy of Nuclear Restraint."
63. The cases of democracies maintaining or renouncing nuclear weapons after pursuing a nuclear program are numerous (e.g., the United States and Australia, respectively). As for totalitarian re-

encourage a regime change, this would not guarantee, by itself, nuclear reversal or restraint. Regime change can create new opportunities for external influence, however, because it can buy precious time and favorably transform the international or regional security environment, thereby diminishing the need for nuclear weapons. Leaders of a new regime might also be less personally or politically committed to pursuing nuclear weapons, or more amenable than their predecessors to external persuasion and inducements to forgo them. U.S. nonproliferation policy toward Argentina and Brazil underscores this dynamic.

The South African case illustrates the interplay between external influence and regime change in the context of nuclear reversal.[64] The 1989 election of F.W. de Klerk as president led to huge changes in South Africa's foreign and domestic policies, facilitating the end of apartheid and improved international acceptance. And with the end of the Cold War, concern over a communist liberation movement poised to overthrow the South African government dissolved. These developments created a domestic climate more favorable to disassembling South Africa's nuclear weapons program, as "in the transformed [South African] security environment, security threats were no longer crucial, and nuclear weapons seemed unnecessary symbols of a bygone era."[65] By themselves, however, these developments did not suffice to bring about nuclear reversal, at least not the rapid and decisive manner in which it came about. Driving this decision was the determination of the outgoing apartheid regime not to pass on to its successors South Africa's nuclear or ballistic missile capability. There is some evidence to suggest that this position was heavily supported by the United States, which feared the consequences of South Africa's long-range ballistic missiles or nuclear weapons falling into the hands of the new South African government led by the African National Congress (and

---

gimes, Libya, Iraq, and North Korea continue to pursue a nuclear option. The issue of regime change is more intriguing and the effect more complex. Although some countries have reversed their nuclear policies after switching from military to civilian and more democratic rule, this change in policy often is directly linked to the more stable security situation accompanying the regime change. See the cases of Argentina and Brazil in Paul, *Power versus Prudence*, p. 111. Also, some states, such as India and Israel, have evolved to become more democratic while maintaining or intensifying their nuclear programs, but the changes in nuclear policy paralleled security changes rather than regime changes. Pakistan is a case in which a military coup could be associated with acceleration of its nuclear program, but security concerns are not the only factor that explains why other nations under military rule do not always seek to acquire nuclear weapons. See ibid., p. 141.
64. See Peter Liberman, "The Rise and Fall of the South African Bomb," *International Security*, Vol. 26, No. 2 (Fall 2001), pp. 45–86.
65. Paul, *Power versus Prudence*, pp. 115, 116.

by extension possibly the communist regimes with which it was allied, such as Cuba[66]) or nationalist white extremist groups.[67]

Regime change might also affect the way security is achieved, creating a preference for either indigenous reliance or alliance guarantees, thereby influencing the requirement for an indigenous nuclear weapons capability or its renunciation. Both Germany and Japan seem to fall into this category.[68] And once again the United States was ready to extend security guarantees to both.

More broadly, regime change may affect a regime's nationalistic tendencies and the preference for autarky or interdependence, economic liberalization or closure to the outside world. Different regimes may assign higher or lower priority to security concerns versus economic or social progress, potentially influencing the course of their nuclear programs. In fact, Etel Solingen has suggested that the openness and economic liberalization associated with democratic governance is the only regime-based explanation for nuclear reversal that has withstood the test of time.[69] Yet even if this is the case (which is not borne out by the absence of nuclear reversal in economically liberalizing India and Israel), it is clear that formidable outside assistance has also been necessary to facilitate economic liberalization.

Conclusion

The widely held fears of the 1960s of a world filled with dozens of nuclear weapons states grew out of a reality in which scores of countries were toying with, and in some cases actually pursuing, nuclear weapons capabilities. This nightmare scenario did not materialize, however, and since the mid-1960s the ranks of the nuclear powers have barely grown beyond the original five. Only India and Pakistan have tested their nuclear devices and proclaimed them-

---

66. See, for example, "S. Africa to Abandon Missile Launching Programme," in Agence France-Presse, June 30, 1993.
67. See David Albright and Mark Hibbs, "South Africa: The ANC and the Atom Bomb," *Bulletin of the Atomic Scientists,* Vol. 49, No. 3 (April 1993), pp. 32–37.
68. Yuri Kase's "The Costs and Benefits of Japan's Nuclearization," pp. 55–68, is particularly insightful on Japan's investigation of the nuclear option as an alternative method for attaining security. Although the investigation was not brought on by a regime change per se, Prime Minister Eisaku Sato and his administration were behind the creation of the report, which was intended to determine if nuclear weapons were a viable option for Japan. The conclusion of the report has a distinct hedging edge, placing great importance on the U.S. umbrella of extended deterrence as a condition for Japan's maintenance of a nonnuclear policy. Ibid., p. 60.
69. Solingen, "The Political Economy of Nuclear Restraint."

selves nuclear powers, while Israel and North Korea are widely suspected of having acquired the wherewithal to produce nuclear weapons.

This article has focused on nuclear reversal as a means of shedding new light on the gap between those expectations and the present reality. Nuclear reversal not only helps to explain why there are far fewer nuclear powers than once anticipated; it also generates fresh insight into the dynamics and patterns of proliferation, the factors that shape them, and the prospects for influencing them. In the process, this research has concluded that much of the success in curbing global nuclear proliferation has been attained by creating a favorable general as well as nation-specific political climate for restraining and even suppressing nuclear ambitions, as well as by converting many states' nuclear aspirations into a posture of nuclear hedging and, in a few other cases, nuclear restraint. Although this combination accounts for the considerable success in reversing proliferation trends, it also contains the seeds of its own undoing, should either of these conditions change for the worse. In fact, recent developments in both Asia and the Middle East attest to the highly precarious nature of the global order, as does the *U.S. National Strategy to Combat Weapons of Mass Destruction* report published in December 2002.

This leads us to consider the critical role that the United States has played in arresting nuclear proliferation. Obviously neither the United States by itself (or for that matter the Soviet Union at its peak) nor any group of powerful nations working together can impose nuclear reversal on a country that is adamantly opposed to it.[70] Nevertheless, the United States has been unique in its ability to create for most nations the favorable political climate necessary to encourage them to forgo the acquisition of nuclear weapons or, failing that, to transition toward nuclear hedging or at a minimum nuclear restraint. The opening for the United States to bring to bear its influence has been created by the acute demand facing virtually all nuclear programs for sustained, high-level domestic political support (to mobilize scarce resources, overcome bureaucratic and technical hurdles, and offset risks).

This study concludes that three factors have thus far combined to produce relative external success in bringing about nuclear reversal, hedging, or at a minimum restraint among the key nuclear aspirants: a change in the domestic

---

70. As an elaborate CIA analysis put it as early as 1969, "Neither the U.S. nor the USSR, however, could dictate a decision on the NPT to these nations [referring to the five major holdouts, of which three—India, Pakistan, and Israel—remain]. Even if the major powers were willing to employ drastic sanctions, the results might be counterproductive." See Central Intelligence Agency, *Response to NSSM No. 9*, p. 5.

perceptions of the nuclear aspirants of the utility of acquiring nuclear weapons; sustained U.S. encouragement of such perceptions, made possible by tracking, understanding, and ultimately addressing the nuclear aspirant's concerns and requirements; and a conscious U.S.-led effort to complicate the road to nuclear weapons acquisition for those who embark on it. Building a global norm against nuclear proliferation (using scarce resources to reinforce it), establishing comprehensive safeguards on nuclear facilities, developing restraints on the transfer of nuclear technology, and exercising restraint in its nuclear strategy (especially employing its own nuclear arsenal) have all been part of this overall U.S. approach. This approach, however, is currently undergoing profound change that both reflects the fragility of the nuclear nonproliferation regime and might further accelerate its transformation.

The study also yields one more conclusion, namely that time stands out as the most important variable in any effort to bring about nuclear turnaround. The long lead time from the moment a state launches its nuclear program until the capability emerges (typically measured in a decade or more) is what creates the opportunity to influence the program's course from the outside. It leaves room for the emergence of domestic conditions (leadership, political orientation, security situation) as well as external ones that might be either less conducive to the continuation of the nuclear weapons program or more receptive to external inducements to change the state's nuclear course. This underscores Joseph Nye's conclusion that "history shows that buying time to manage destabilizing effects [that motivate nuclear proliferation] is a feasible policy objective" for attaining nuclear reversal.[71]

Even in the easiest cases, however, merely placing obstacles in a state's path to nuclear weapons acquisition cannot attain success. As the case of Pakistan amply demonstrates, external inducements by themselves cannot prevent a determined regime from acquiring a nuclear weapons capability, even at significant cost and risk to itself and its people. Success is within reach only to the extent that foreign influence and domestic conditions converge, and the foreign effort is closely tuned (in terms of both agenda and timing) to the domestic context. External players need to aim at the key factors affecting domestic nuclear choices: the external security environment, the availability of alternative means to deal with the threats that this environment poses or to attain the other goals that the nuclear program is meant to achieve, and the

71. See Nye, "New Approaches to Nuclear Proliferation Policy," pp. 1293–1294.

balance between domestic proponents and opponents of nuclear weapons. They ought to seize on those opportunities in the nuclear program's evolution at which the program's proponents are either replaced, weakened, or otherwise undergo some transformation that may make them susceptible to external persuasion to consider at least nuclear restraint.

In closing, two suggestions for future research are in order. First, the concept of nuclear hedging, as well as the observations regarding the data limitations and their implications, should serve as a catalyst for a reexamination of nuclear reversal cases and further refinement of their theoretical findings. Second, it would be useful to broaden the scope of the empirical investigation of reversal processes beyond the nuclear domain, to compare the insights generated to date on nuclear reversal and restraint with similar processes in chemical and biological weapons programs and perhaps also ballistic missiles. The implementation in recent years of the Chemical Weapons Convention may well provide an opportunity and convenient platform for gaining new access into several such cases.

Preventing Nuclear Entrepreneurship in Russia's Nuclear Cities

Sharon K. Weiner

Since September 11, 2001, concern about an attack on the United States by terrorists using a stolen nuclear warhead or an improvised radiological weapon—a "dirty bomb"—has risen dramatically. In discussions about this threat, Russia is frequently mentioned as the most likely source of black-market nuclear skills and materials. In its 2002 report to Congress, for example, the National Intelligence Council noted that Russia's nuclear security measures are still primarily oriented toward external threats and "are not designed to counter the pre-eminent threat faced today—an insider who attempts unauthorized actions."[1] Reports of Russian weapons experts sharing their knowledge with other countries have also proliferated.[2] Whether through scientific exchange visits, conferences, or email, Russian nuclear experts may be sharing sensitive information with others. Although many of these reports are anecdotal and few have been rigorously documented since the early 1990s, the U.S. Central Intelligence Agency has consistently reported to Congress its suspicions that Russian scientists are helping foreign countries pursue nuclear weapons development programs.[3]

The nuclear experts of most concern are those living in Russia's ten "nuclear cities," which in the late 1980s employed an estimated 150,000 people in

Sharon K. Weiner is a Research Associate at the Program on Science and Global Security in Princeton University's Woodrow Wilson School of Public and International Affairs.

The author would like to thank Oleg Bukharin, Frank von Hippel, and three anonymous reviewers for their comments. Also, she gratefully acknowledges the support of the Carnegie Corporation of New York, which takes no responsibility for any statements or views expressed herein.

1. National Intelligence Council, *Annual Report to Congress on the Safety and Security of Russian Nuclear Facilities and Military Forces* (Washington, D.C.: Government Printing Office [GPO], February 2002), p. 2.
2. Such reports are scattered throughout the popular media. See, for example, Tim Beardsley, "Selling to Survive," *Scientific American,* Vol. 268, No. 2 (February 1993), pp. 92–100; Alan Cooperman and Kyrill Belianinov, "Moonlighting by Modem in Russia," *U.S. News and World Report,* April 17, 1995, pp. 45–48; and Michael Dobbs, "Collapse of Soviet Union Proved Boon to Iranian Missile Program," *Washington Post,* January 13, 2002, p. 19. One of the more comprehensive accounts is R. Adam Moody, "Report: Reexamining Brain Drain from the Former Soviet Union," *Nonproliferation Review,* Vol. 3, No. 3 (Spring–Summer 1996), p. 92.
3. See, for example, testimony of Robert Gates, director of Central Intelligence, House Committee on Foreign Affairs, *The Future of U.S. Foreign Policy in the Post–Cold War Era,* 102d Cong., 2d sess., February 25, 1992, pp. 205, 234–236; and testimony of George Tenet, director of central intelligence, Senate Select Committee on Intelligence, *Current and Projected National Security Threats to the U.S.,* 105th Cong., 2d sess., January 28, 1998, p. 135.

weapons-related work.[4] The end of the Cold War, the disintegration of the Soviet Union, and the subsequent collapse of the Russian economy brought misery to many of these once-revered members of the Soviet elite. As the 1990s wore on, increasing numbers of Russian nuclear scientists, engineers, and technicians were confronted with deteriorating living conditions and the threat of job loss. Many were owed months of back wages by the Russian government.

As reports of the theft of weapons-usable materials began to surface in the early 1990s, the U.S. government grew alarmed that some of Russia's nuclear weapons scientists would become "nuclear entrepreneurs," selling their expertise to the highest bidder or collaborating with others to steal nuclear weapons or their components. These concerns prompted Congress, the first Bush administration, and later President Bill Clinton to launch several nonproliferation programs between the United States and Russia.[5]

As the years wore on, however, the White House's interest in these programs diminished. Slow progress, bureaucratic infighting, and disagreements with Russia over access to its nuclear facilities led to much congressional criticism of these programs, especially among Republicans. After conducting their own critical internal review, President George W. Bush and his administration seemed poised to significantly reduce some of these programs and eliminate others.[6] The September 11 terrorist attacks, however, forced the administration and Congress to rethink this position. Amid renewed concerns that Russian nuclear weapons, materials, and expertise could leak out to terrorists, pundits and policymakers alike increasingly called for a greater U.S. commitment and more funding for U.S.-Russian nonproliferation programs.

This article analyzes U.S.-Russian nonproliferation efforts designed to help workers in Russia's nuclear cities.[7] The most important of these are the Nu-

---

4. Ministry of Atomic Energy of the Russian Federation (MinAtom), "Primary Objectives and Tasks of the Implementation of the Program on Restructuring and Conversion of Nuclear Industry Enterprises (of the Nuclear Weapons Complex), in 1998–2000," p. 3. In addition to nuclear weapons–related workers, MinAtom also employs people for nonnuclear defense–related and nuclear energy–related activities in the nuclear cities.
5. Most of these programs also included cooperation with other states of the former Soviet Union that inherited Soviet weapons of mass destruction or the scientists and facilities with which to design, test, or build them.
6. See Judith Miller with Michael R. Gordon, "U.S. Review of Russia Urges Keeping Most Arms Controls," *New York Times,* July 16, 2001, p. 1. The Bush administration was most critical of programs managed by the U.S. Department of Energy and especially the Nuclear Cities Initiative (NCI).
7. For a description and assessment of U.S. efforts to help Russia monitor and control its supply of fissile material, see Matthew Bunn, *The Next Wave: Urgently Needed New Steps to Control Warheads and Fissile Material* (Washington, D.C.: Managing the Atom Project, Belfer Center for Science and International Affairs, John F. Kennedy School of Government, Harvard University, and the Non-

clear Cities Initiative (NCI), Initiatives for Proliferation Prevention (IPP), and the International Science and Technology Center (ISTC). All three seek to create alternative nonmilitary jobs for nuclear weapons–related workers who might otherwise be driven to sell their nuclear knowledge or to steal weapons-related materials and components.[8]

I begin by describing Russia's nuclear cities and some of the proliferation problems that they present. I also assess how these cities and their role in nuclear weapons production have changed over the last decade and the impact of these changes on proliferation risk. Next I analyze the success of NCI, IPP, and ISTC in creating jobs for workers in the nuclear cities. I conclude with recommendations for ways to refocus these programs for greater effectiveness.

Russia's Nuclear Cities: Then and Now

Russia's nuclear cities contain the Soviet Union's principal nuclear weapons research, design, and production facilities.[9] Located in remote areas around the country, they began life as "company towns" with a nuclear mission. As in the past, decisions affecting the cities are made at the federal level, and the cities are funded directly by the Ministry of Atomic Energy (MinAtom).[10] If there were any private businesses, they existed only for the support of the local population. Each nuclear city continues to have a specific function (see Table 1).

Because of the sensitive nature of their work, the cities were "closed" during the Soviet era. Each city—including housing, schools, parks, and other facilities—was surrounded by double fences and guarded by troops from the ministry of internal affairs.[11] The nuclear facilities themselves were cordoned off with additional fences and guards. Access to and from the cities was tightly controlled by representatives of the KGB, the Soviet Union's intelligence

---

Proliferation Project of the Carnegie Endowment for International Peace, April 2000); and Oleg Bukharin, Matthew Bunn, and Kenneth N. Luongo, *Renewing the Partnership: Recommendations for Accelerated Action to Secure Nuclear Material in the Former Soviet Union* (Washington, D.C.: Russian American Nuclear Security Advisory Council, August 2000).

8. Another reason to help Russia downsize its nuclear production complex is the fear that it might rebuild its nuclear arsenal.

9. Some of the Soviet nuclear weapons production infrastructure was also located in open cities. For example, Moscow was and is home to the Institute of Automatics, which works on warhead design.

10. The Ministry of Atomic Energy is the successor to the Soviet Union's Ministry for Atomic Energy and Nuclear Power Engineering, which once performed these functions.

11. Oleg Bukharin, "What Are Russia's Closed Nuclear Cities?" in Bukharin, Frank N. von Hippel, and Sharon K. Weiner, *Conversion and Job Creation in Russia's Closed Nuclear Cities* (Princeton, N.J.: Program on Nuclear Policy Alternatives of the Center for International Studies and Center for Energy and Environmental Studies, Princeton University, November 2000), p. 73.

agency. Until the mid-1950s, residents were not allowed to leave except for official business.[12] Given the potential hardships of living under these conditions, residents were compensated by the Soviet government. Workers at the nuclear installations were generally paid higher wages and, more important, they and their families had greater access to quality health care, food, and consumer goods than most other Soviet citizens.[13] Until 1992 the existence of these cities was officially a secret. None appeared on Soviet maps, and they were known only by postal codes associated with large cities in the region.

THE SHIFT FROM WEAPONS WORK

At their peak in the mid-1980s, the nuclear cities employed 150,000 people in weapons-related work.[14] The cities began to shift from weapons work in the late 1980s when projected nuclear weapons reductions, excess stockpiles of fissile materials, and aging plutonium production reactors convinced the Soviet leadership to end the production of highly enriched uranium and plutonium for nuclear weapons.[15] Instead, the cities began to fill domestic and foreign orders for nuclear power–related activities including uranium enrichment and spent fuel management. The Soviet government also decided to scale back activities throughout the rest of the weapons-production complex but to avoid any major restructuring.[16]

By 1998, however, MinAtom decided that significant changes were no longer avoidable, and in June of that year, the government adopted the program "On Restructuring and Conversion of the Nuclear Weapons Complex." According

---

12. Ibid., p. 74. According to Anatoly Vevelovksy, *Nuclear Shield* (Sarov, Russia: RFYaTs-VNIIEF, 1999), p. 20, until 1954 people living in Sarov were not allowed to leave the city on vacation, nor were they permitted to make phone calls outside the city; mail was read by the security forces.
13. Kimberly Marten Zisk, *Weapons, Culture, and Self-Interest: Soviet Defense Managers in the New Russia* (New York: Columbia University Press, 1997), pp. 35–36; and Vevelovksy, *Nuclear Shield*, p. 25.
14. Ministry of Atomic Energy of the Russian Federation, "Primary Objectives and Tasks," p. 3.
15. Stockpiles of highly enriched uranium (HEU) and plutonium were much greater than what was required for the defense program. See Oleg Bukharin, "The Future of Russia's Plutonium Cities," *International Security*, Vol. 21, No. 4 (Spring 1997), p. 131. Also, by 1987 many of the Soviet Union's thirteen plutonium-producing reactors were more than thirty years old, thus raising questions about their safety. For a discussion of the history and characteristics of these reactors, see Pavel Podvig, ed., *Russian Strategic Nuclear Forces* (Cambridge, Mass.: MIT Press, 2001), pp. 90–98. The production of HEU for nuclear weapons ended in 1988, and between 1987 and 1992, ten plutonium production reactors were shut down. The three other reactors have remained open because they are still the primary sources of heat and electricity for two cities (Seversk and Zheleznogorsk). See Matthew Bunn and Frank N. von Hippel, "Saga of the Siberian Plutonium Production Reactors," *FAS Public Interest Report*, Vol. 53, No. 6 (November/December 2000), p. 1.
16. Oleg Bukharin, "Downsizing Russia's Nuclear-Warhead-Production Infrastructure," in Bukharin, von Hippel, and Weiner, *Conversion and Job Creation in Russia's Closed Nuclear Cities*, p. 62.

Table 1. The Soviet/Russian Nuclear Weapons Production Complex.

City (former name)	Main Defense Institute	Cold War Specialization (mid-1980s)	Current Nuclear Weapons–Related Missions
Lesnoy (Sverdlovsk-45)	Combine Electrochimpribor	Production of highly enriched uranium, lithium-6 separation, nuclear warhead assembly and disassembly	Nuclear warhead disassembly and possibly fissile material storage in the future
Novouralsk (Sverdlovsk-44)	Urals Electro-Chemical Combine	Production of highly enriched uranium	No weapons work
Ozersk (Chelyabinsk-65)	Production Association Mayak	Production of plutonium and tritium, fabrication of highly enriched uranium and plutonium weapon components	Tritium production, fabrication of highly enriched uranium and plutonium weapon components, possibly fissile material storage and management in the future
Sarov (Arzamas-16)	All-Russian Scientific Research Institute of Experimental Physics	Nuclear warhead research and development, stockpile support	Nuclear warhead research and development, stockpile support
	Electromechanical Plant AVANGARD	Nuclear warhead assembly and disassembly	All weapons work to end by 2003
Seversk (Tomsk-7)	Siberian Chemical Combine	Production of plutonium and highly enriched uranium, fabrication of highly enriched uranium and plutonium weapon components	Possibly fissile material storage and management in the future

Table 1. (continued)

City (former name)	Main Defense Institute	Cold War Specialization (mid-1980s)	Current Nuclear Weapons–Related Missions
Snezhinsk (Chelyabinsk-70)	All-Russian Scientific Research Institute of Technical Physics	Nuclear warhead research and development, stockpile support	Nuclear warhead research and development, stockpile support
Trekhgorny (Zlatoust-36)	Device-Building Plant	Nuclear warhead assembly and disassembly	Possibly fissile material storage in the future
Zarechny (Penza-19)	Production Association START	Nuclear warhead assembly and disassembly	Nuclear warhead dismantlement to end in 2003 and then no weapons work
Zelenogorsk (Krasnoyarsk-45)	Electro-Chemical Plant (EkhZ)	Production of highly enriched uranium	No weapons work
Zheleznogorsk (Krasnoyarsk-26)	Mining and Chemical Combine (GKhK)	Plutonium production	Possibly plutonium storage and management in the future

SOURCES: Adapted from Oleg Bukharin, "Downsizing Russia's Nuclear-Warhead-Production Infrastructure," in Bukharin, Frank N. von Hippel, and Sharon K. Weiner, *Conversion and Job Creation in Russia's Closed Nuclear Cities* (Princeton, N.J.: Program on Nuclear Policy Alternatives of the Center for International Studies and Center for Energy and Environmental Studies, Princeton University, November 2000), p. 68; and Oleg Bukharin, "Populations, Employment, and Conversion in Russia's Closed Nuclear Cities," in ibid., pp. 38–59.

to this initiative, the conversion of Russia's nuclear cities would cost U.S.$1 billion: $500 million to consolidate nuclear weapons activities and clean up buildings for commercial development and $500 million to create civilian jobs for excess workers.[17] According to MinAtom, the first phase of the conversion plan was completed in December 2001 at a cost of $500 million.[18] A revised conversion plan, scheduled to run through 2006, requires an additional investment of $600 million.[19]

MinAtom estimates that from 1998 to 2000 its conversion efforts generated 8,100 jobs.[20] This is far short, however, of the tens of thousands that will ultimately need to be created. Therefore MinAtom has delayed its plans to cut an additional 35,000 workers from the rolls.

FROM PRIVILEGE TO POVERTY

The government's decision to reduce the size of Russia's nuclear weapons production complex coincided with the near-total collapse of the Russian economy in the mid-1990s. Citing increased concerns about careless workers who had not been paid for months, authorities at the All-Russian Scientific Research Institute of Experimental Physics (VNIIEF in Russian) temporarily suspended some weapons work in 1993 and again in 1995.[21] Wage arrears prompted strikes and protests at several of Russia's nuclear weapons labs, most recently in 1998.[22]

Throughout the 1990s the economic situation in the nuclear cities mirrored that of Russia as a whole. Layoffs and reductions in government spending left nuclear weapons–related workers with greatly reduced incomes and a dearth of alternatives. Few new businesses were started in the nuclear cities because

17. Lev Ryabev, "Downsizing of the Nuclear Complex and Defense Conversion Programs," presentation at the Conference on Helping Russian Down-Size Its Nuclear Weapons Complex, Princeton, New Jersey, March 14–15, 2000. This amount does not include replacing the heat and power provided by the plutonium production reactors in Seversk and Zheleznogorsk. All dollar figures are in U.S. dollars.
18. Alexander Antonov, "Comments," presentation at the Second International Working Group Meeting of the European Nuclear Cities Initiative, Brussels, Belgium, February 25–26, 2002.
19. Ibid. This money is to come from the Russian federal government, taxes, private contributions, and international assistance.
20. Lev Ryabev, "Russia's Down-Sizing and Conversion Programs," presentation at the Sam Nunn/Bank of America Policy Forum, Atlanta, Georgia, March 26–27, 2001.
21. Zisk, *Weapons, Culture, and Self-Interest*, p. 130. At the All-Russian Institute of Technical Physics (VNIITF, in Russian), the director committed suicide, partly out of shame at his inability to support his workers. See Celestine Bohlen, "Putin Vows Russia Will Reinvigorate Its Nuclear Force," *New York Times*, April 1, 2000, p. 1.
22. Amy F. Woolf, "Nuclear Weapons in Russia: Safety, Security, and Control Issues," Congressional Research Service issue brief for Congress, November 21, 2000; and David Hoffman, "Russia's Nuclear Force Sinks with the Ruble," *Washington Post*, September 18, 1998, p. A01.

of government-imposed restrictions on investment and access. Moreover, workers from the nuclear cities seeking employment elsewhere had difficulty relocating, for three reasons. First, although many of the restrictions that once governed their behavior had been reduced, they still needed the government's permission to move.[23] Second, housing was a formidable obstacle. During the Soviet era, housing was provided by employers; as a result, Russia's rental market is extremely underdeveloped, and it is still very difficult to find affordable housing.[24] Third, as stories of economic fraud, organized crime, violence, and drug use multiplied, residents of the nuclear cities increasingly found comfort in their government-controlled isolation.[25]

The quality of life in the nuclear cities also declined because of a dramatic reduction in subsidies from the central government. From 1996 to 1998, every nuclear city except one experienced a decrease of between 4 percent and 50 percent in direct federal subsidies.[26]

Another huge problem was the delayed payment of wages not just to workers in the nuclear cities but to workers throughout Russia. Because of budget cuts, the central government was often unable to pay its workforce on time. In the early 1990s, MinAtom began to delay sending wages to the nuclear cities, and by the spring of 1997 most wage payments were behind by more than seven months.[27] By mid-1999 the delays averaged one to two months.[28] After 1999 the absence of reports to the contrary suggests that wages have been paid on time.[29]

Recent reports of wage increases for workers in the nuclear cities suggest some room for optimism, although reliable information is sparse. According to

23. Bukharin, "What Are Russia's Closed Cities?" pp. 74–75.
24. Maria Lodahl, "The Housing Market in Russia: Disappointing Results," *Economic Bulletin*, 6/ 2001 (Berlin: German Institute for Economic Research, 2001), p. 1.
25. Bukharin, "What Are Russia's Closed Cities?" p. 75; Glenn E. Schweitzer, *Swords into Market Shares: Technology, Economics, and Security in the New Russia* (Washington, D.C.: Joseph Henry Press, 2000), p. 186; and Judith Perera, "Opening the Closed Towns," *Nuclear Engineering International*, June 1995, p. 44.
26. Gregory Brock, "The ZATO Archipelago Revisited—Is the Federal Government Loosening Its Grip? A Research Note," *Europe-Asia Studies*, Vol. 52, No. 7 (November 2000), p. 1356. The exception was Zheleznogorsk, which saw a slight increase in subsidies.
27. Matthew Bunn, Oleg Bukharin, Jill Cetina, Kenneth N. Luongo, and Frank N. von Hippel, "Retooling Russia's Nuclear Cities," *Bulletin of the Atomic Scientists*, Vol. 54 (September/October 1998), p. 44.
28. Valentin Tikhonov, *Russia's Nuclear and Missile Complex: The Human Factor in Proliferation* (Washington, D.C.: Carnegie Endowment for International Peace, 2001), p. 38. As of July 1999, VNIIEF in Sarov was reporting wage delays of one month. See *RFNC–VNIIEF Quarterly Information Bulletin*, No. 1 (Sarov, Russia: Analytical Center for Nonproliferation, 1999), http:// www.ransac.org.
29. Since January 2000, *Atompressa*, MinAtom's newspaper, has not published any such reports.

one analysis, until 1994 the average wage for nuclear-related workers in the nuclear cities was about 20 percent higher than the national average in Russia.[30] By the end of the 1990s, however, wages in the nuclear cities remained constant while prices and inflation rose sharply.[31] As a result, the purchasing power of nuclear-related workers plummeted, both absolutely and in relation to Russia as a whole.[32] In 1999, when the average monthly wage in Russia was approximately $62,[33] about 60 percent of MinAtom's workforce in the nuclear cities was making less than $50 a month.[34] In June 1999, 60 percent of the nuclear workforce in the cities was moonlighting to make ends meet, and 84 percent believed that their financial situation was difficult or very difficult.[35] By 2000, however, when the average monthly wage in Russia had risen to $82,[36] average salaries in the nuclear cities were estimated to be $90–$150 per month and have continued to climb.[37] In late 2001, salaries at the nuclear facilities in Sarov averaged $200 a month, and those in several other nuclear cities were rumored to be higher.[38]

Although the wages of nuclear weapons workers have improved dramatically and are no longer in arrears, the future security of many nuclear weapons workers remains in doubt. Because of impending layoffs, the loss of government subsidies for the nuclear cities, and the almost complete lack of alternative employment, the risk that Russian nuclear expertise will be sold for profit remains significant.

A Proliferation Problem

The last ten years have been economically devastating for most Russians, yet workers in Russia's nuclear cities have an advantage that other Russians do

---

30. Tikhonov, *Russia's Nuclear and Missile Complex*, p. 36.
31. Ibid., pp. 9, 37, 38.
32. Ibid., pp. 9, 37. In Brock, "The ZATO Archipelago Revisited," p. 1357, the author uses personal income tax collection in the nuclear cities to show that between 1996 and 1998 per capita income in the nuclear cities fell by three times the national average in Russia.
33. This figure was calculated using information from the State Committee of the Russian Federation on Statistics, http://www.gks.ru/eng.
34. Tikhonov, *Russia's Nuclear and Missile Complex*, p. 37.
35. Ibid., pp. 9, 51.
36. This figure was calculated using information from the State Committee of the Russian Federation on Statistics.
37. S. Sachkova, *Atompressa*, No. 46 (December 1999); and press release by Yevgeny Adamov, minister of atomic energy, Russian Federation, January 2001.
38. "Former Atomic Minister Plays Down Possibility of Passing Nuclear Secrets Abroad," BBC Monitoring Service, November 23, 2001. According to interviews with U.S. national laboratory employees who work with either NCI or IPP, in 2002 wages in Seversk were close to $300 a month, while wages at VNIITF in Snezhinsk approached $600 a month.

not: the skills and equipment to build nuclear weapons. Although there have been confirmed cases of the theft of fissile materials from Russia's nuclear weapons complex, the sale of nuclear expertise, often referred to as "brain drain," is still largely unproven. A handful of Russian nuclear scientists emigrate each year, mostly to Germany, Israel, Sweden, and the United States.[39] So far the evidence is mostly anecdotal that Russian nuclear weapons experts are contributing to bomb programs in countries labeled by the United States as "proliferation concerns."[40] Nor is there proof that al-Qaeda or other terrorist organizations have acquired nuclear weapons and expertise from Russia.[41]

In the last decade, Russia reduced the size of its nuclear weapons design and production workforce from 150,000 to 60,000–67,000.[42] MinAtom's current plan calls for additional cuts of 35,000 workers from the nuclear cities between 2005 and 2012.[43] Although these reductions are proportionally similar, their impacts are likely to be quite different. The first round of cuts involved mostly younger workers who left voluntarily to seek employment in the private sector and the transfer of some functions and associated personnel away from the nuclear weapons complexes in some cities: For example, enrichment and reprocessing services were commercialized, and social, cultural, and other civil functions were shifted to the local government.[44]

---

39. Tikhonov, *Russia's Nuclear and Missile Complex*, pp. 63–64.
40. See, for example, testimony of Robert Gates, director of Central Intelligence, Senate Committee on Governmental Affairs, *Weapons Proliferation in the New World Order*, 102d Cong., 2d sess., January 15, 1992, p. 21; Senate Committee on Governmental Affairs, *The Proliferation Primer* (Washington, D.C.: GPO, January 1998), pp. 17–26; William C. Potter, "Nuclear Exports from the Former Soviet Union: What's New, What's True," *Arms Control Today*, Vol. 23, No. 1 (January/February 1993), pp. 7–9; and Office of Technology Assessment, *Proliferation and the Former Soviet Union*, OTA-ISS-605 (Washington, D.C.: GPO, September 1994), pp. 62–67.
41. See Michael Dobbs, "Senior Russian Official Reveals Nuclear Material Theft Attempt," *Washington Post*, November 13, 2001, p. 22; Jeffrey Kluger, "Osama's Nuclear Quest: How Long Will It Take before al-Qaeda Gets Hold of the Most Dangerous Weapons?" *Time*, November 12, 2001, p. 38; and Michael Dobbs and Peter Behr, "Analysts Debate Next Weapon in Al Qaeda Arsenal," *Washington Post*, November 16, 2001, p. 18.
42. Ryabev, "Russia's Down-Sizing and Conversion Programs." As of mid-2002, MinAtom's total nuclear-related workforce (in both open and closed cities) numbered around 75,000.
43. Ibid. MinAtom claims that with significant foreign assistance, it can reach this goal by 2005. Without foreign assistance, downsizing will take five additional years or more.
44. In the early 1990s, the city administrations of the closed cities took over such functions as the management of infrastructure, child care, and road maintenance, which were once performed by the nuclear weapons complexes. When these functions were transferred, so were the personnel who performed them. Various presentations from "Reorientation of Defense Enterprises, Scientific and Engineering Staff to Civil Production," Russian-U.S. Training and Consulting Workshop, Obninsk, Russia, June 27–29, 2000, summarized in Oleg Bukharin, "Populations, Employment, and Conversion in Russia's Closed Nuclear Cities," in Bukharin, von Hippel, and Weiner, *Conversion and Job Creation in Russia's Closed Nuclear Cities*, pp. 38–59.

Demographic and other changes in the nuclear cities since 1990 suggest that the next round of reductions will be harder to accommodate, for at least three reasons. First, the majority of nuclear weapons workers who want jobs in the private sector have already left.[45]

Second, the nuclear workforce is aging. In 1999 about 20 percent of the scientists, technicians, and engineers in the nuclear cities were older than fifty. Assuming current hiring, retirement, and demographic trends, this figure will rise to 30 percent by 2009.[46] The aging of Russia's soon-to-be-unemployed nuclear workers has significant implications for their future job prospects. Because older employees will work fewer years regardless of the jobs they take, the companies that hire and retrain them will see lower returns on their investment than if they hired younger employees in the first place. In addition, older workers in Russia are seen as having a greater sense of entitlement and less interest in changing jobs.[47] Generally, this is attributed to longer tenure in the Soviet system. Besides enjoying prestige based on their positions, older workers came of age in a system where paternalistic bonds between workers and their employers were common.[48] In addition to wages, employees were provided with housing, health care, day care, and a variety of other perks. They also lived, played, and raised their children in a community of coworkers. Older workers are thus much more reluctant about severing their connections to their old employers.

Third, changes in the legal status of Russia's nuclear cities have also had profound effects on the quality of life of their residents, on prospects for business development, and on opportunities for proliferation. In 1992 the Duma passed a law giving Russia's ten nuclear cities and approximately thirty other closed cities with defense-related functions status as ZATOs—that is, federally controlled "closed territorial-administrative formations." ZATOs require "a special regime of safe functions and protection of state secrets, including special residence conditions."[49]

The nuclear cities are still "closed," with movements in or out now controlled by the FSB, the KGB's successor. Unlike in the Soviet era, however, the number of foreign and Russian visitors to these cities has increased

---

45. Presentations from the Russian-U.S. Training and Consulting Workshop; and Tikhonov, *Russia's Nuclear and Missile Complex*, pp. 30–36.
46. Tikhonov, *Russia's Nuclear and Missile Complex*, p. 36.
47. Private communications with staff from several U.S. government programs.
48. For a discussion of the breadth and depth of these bonds, see Zisk, *Weapons, Culture, and Self-Interest*, pp. 35–39.
49. As quoted in Richard H. Rowland, "Russia's Secret Cities," *Post-Soviet Geography and Economics*, Vol. 37, No. 7 (September 1996), p. 427.

significantly. Indeed every closed city has been visited by foreigners, though many of their nuclear facilities remain off-limits.[50] Continued restrictions on access to the nuclear cities has been a deterrent to economic development. Both private companies and U.S. government programs seeking to encourage business development cite access restrictions as a major impediment to investment.[51] Besides having to obtain a visa for Russian entry, foreigners wanting to visit the nuclear cities must have an official letter of invitation from MinAtom or a Russian organization and must apply for permission to enter at least forty-five days in advance.[52] In selected cases, foreigners are given multiple-entry permits that require only two weeks' advance notice before a visit. Foreign visitors are usually escorted at all times.

Permission is also required to visit the nuclear weapons facilities themselves. In practical terms, this means that potential investors can meet the scientists they may want to employ, but they cannot inspect the premises where those scientists work. In deals involving private companies, access can be negotiated but with great difficulty.[53]

Russian access to the nuclear cities has also been liberalized, but this too has posed problems for job creation. The relocation of individual Russians to the nuclear cities is still contingent on employment by the nuclear facilities; however, relatives of current residents are now allowed to join them.[54] During the 1990s, when Russia's urban population was in decline, the population of the

---

50. This statement is based on information from the databases of various government and nongovernmental programs. See also L. Saratova, "Freedom for the Free: Regime in Sarov," *Gorodskoy Kuryer*, April 2, 1998, quoted in Bukharin, "What Are Russia's Closed Nuclear Cities?" p. 74. For example, in the first nine months of 2000, Sarov had nearly 300 foreign visitors. See *RFNC-VNIIEF Quarterly Information Bulletin*, Nos. 3, 4, 5 (Sarov, Russia: Analytical Center for Nonproliferation, 2000).

51. Interviews with NCI and IPP staff. See also Howard Baker and Lloyd Cutler, *A Report Card on the Department of Energy's Nonproliferation Programs with Russia* (Washington, D.C.: Secretary of Energy Advisory Board, U.S. Department of Energy, January 10, 2001), pp. ix, 22–23.

52. An additional impediment is that foreign visitors who are accompanied by U.S. government officials—including those whose jobs are to encourage business development in the nuclear cities—also require permission from the U.S. government. U.S. government officials traveling outside the United States usually need permission from their own agencies; those traveling to Russia need clearance from the U.S. embassy in Moscow. In the case of the nuclear cities, obtaining clearance takes about four weeks.

53. Private communications with officials from the U.S. national laboratories and DoE. One exception is the Avangard "technopark" in Sarov—an area where the U.S. government spent more than $1 million to relocate security fences so that four buildings would be in an "open" area. The technopark, however, remains inside the city of Sarov and thus is still governed by all the access restrictions that apply to the nuclear cities.

54. N. Kocheshkova, "Foreigners in Sarov," *Gorodskoy Kuryer*, February 1, 2001. For example, every month ten to twelve people from former Soviet republics move to Sarov to join their children or parents.

nuclear cities increased by an estimated 60,000 people, or slightly more than 8.5 percent.[55] The popularity of the nuclear cities and of the ZATOs in general has been attributed to the perception that they experience fewer crime and drug problems and better quality housing, schools, and public services.[56] According to Russian officials, in 1995, 95 percent of those living in the nuclear cities voted against opening them.[57]

These demographic changes mean that as jobs become fewer because of downsizing by MinAtom, unemployment will worsen as the working-age population increases. Throughout the 1990s the percentage of unemployment in the nuclear cities was approximately the same as it was in Russia as a whole.[58] However, while the demand for labor is growing in Russia, it is shrinking in the nuclear cities. As a result, from 2000 to 2009 the working-age population in the nuclear cities will increase by an estimated 50 percent, causing unemployment to skyrocket.[59]

U.S. Aid to the Nuclear Cities

Since the early 1990s, the United States has assisted Russia with its nuclear conversion and job creation efforts. Initially, temporary research contracts were used to provide wages to thousands of weapons workers in the nuclear cities, but permanent job creation outside of the nuclear weapons complex has increasingly become the goal. Only a handful of permanent jobs, however, have been created. Consequently, Congress, which authorized funding for these programs, has grown increasingly impatient and wants to tie future funding to demonstrable results. This has caused the programs to reinvigorate their efforts. Unfortunately, Congress and the programs involved are concentrating almost exclusively on the creation of private sector jobs and ignoring alternatives that may offer more immediate or long-lasting ways of providing security for Russia's nuclear weapons workforce.

---

55. Alexander Pikayev, "Russian Nuclear Insecurity," *Proliferation Brief,* Vol. 2, No. 3 (Washington, D.C.: Carnegie Endowment for International Peace, February 19, 1999); and Richard H. Rowland, "Secret Cities of Russia and Kazakhstan in 1998," *Post-Soviet Geography and Economics,* Vol. 40, No. 4 (June 1999), p. 290.
56. Bukharin, "What Are Russia's Closed Cities?" p. 75; and Schweitzer, *Swords into Market Shares,* p. 186.
57. Perera, "Opening the Closed Towns," p. 44.
58. Tikhonov, *Russia's Nuclear and Missile Complex,* p. 28.
59. Ibid., p. 25.

OVERVIEW OF U.S. ASSISTANCE PROGRAMS

Three programs—the Nuclear Cities Initiative, Initiatives for Proliferation Prevention, and the International Science and Technology Center—are responsible for the bulk of U.S. efforts to create alternative employment for Russia's nuclear workforce. The U.S. government also funds smaller programs to assist Russian nuclear weapons scientists with finding new jobs; U.S. foundations, universities, private businesses, and business consortia also have initiatives in the nuclear cities.[60]

NCI is the newest and smallest of the "the big three," but it has the broadest mandate. Established in 1998 within the Department of Energy (DoE), NCI is responsible not only for creating nonmilitary jobs for weapons-related personnel but also for helping Russia reduce the size of its weapons complex. NCI's efforts have also included community and infrastructure development in the nuclear cities, but criticism from members of Congress and the U.S. General Accounting Office (GAO) as well as a lack of funding forced it to curtail this activity in 2001.[61] According to the implementation agreement between the U.S. and Russian governments, NCI can work only with Sarov, Snezhinsk, and Zheleznogorsk. After it demonstrates success in these cities, it can engage other nuclear cities.

NCI's strategy is to encourage private industry and other U.S. government agencies to pursue business opportunities in the nuclear cities. It has worked with Western commercial businesses such as software developers, manufacturers of medical equipment, telecommunications providers, and others to invest in joint ventures in these cities. NCI representatives have also successfully lobbied several U.S. government agencies to provide resources or extend their programs to include the nuclear cities.[62]

The IPP and ISTC programs seek to engage nuclear weapons–related personnel in nonmilitary research and promote any promising commercial opportunities that may result. The clientele for IPP and ISTC projects includes

---

60. Some examples of other programs and groups engaged with the nuclear cities include the Russian American Nuclear Security Advisory Council, the Nuclear Threat Initiative, the Civilian Research and Development Foundation, the Pennsylvania-Russia Business Council, the Soros Foundation, the MacArthur Foundation, and Princeton University.
61. Private communications with NCI and DoE personnel, May 28, 29, and 30, 2002.
62. For example, the U.S. State Department's "sister cities" program has funded educational, health, and civic exchanges between the nuclear cities and their counterparts in the United States. See Nuclear Cities Initiative, "Community Development Working Group Briefing Update," July 23, 1999; "Idaho Falls Mayor Visits Russian Secret City," Associated Press Newswires, January 22, 2000; and "Russian Zheleznogrosk and U.S. Meryville to Be Sister Cities," ITAR Tass Newswire, June 2, 2000.

individuals throughout the former Soviet Union who have the knowledge or skills needed to make nuclear as well as chemical and biological weapons.

Created in 1994 and managed by DoE, IPP oversees projects that have been initiated through contacts between scientists in U.S. and Russian nuclear weapons laboratories. Through IPP projects, Russian scientists receive salaries for nonweapons work and are given the opportunity to interact with their U.S. counterparts. Projects with commercial potential move on to a second phase where U.S. scientists try to interest U.S. industry in cofunding additional research and development. The most promising projects move to a third phase in which IPP funding is supposed to be succeeded by a partnership between U.S. industry and Russian workers. To facilitate this process, IPP works with the United States Industrial Coalition, a nonprofit association of U.S. companies and universities created for this purpose.

ISTC shares NCI's and IPP's job creation mandate.[63] From the beginning, however, ISTC has been allowed greater leeway to fund pure scientific research with little concern for the commercial potential of the results. ISTC receives funding from the European Union, Japan, Norway, South Korea, and the United States, each of which decides how to allocate its money among the projects submitted to ISTC. U.S. participation is managed by the State Department, which coordinates with ISTC's permanent Moscow-based staff to vet proposals from weapons personnel and help them find Western collaborators.

AN ASSESSMENT OF U.S. ASSISTANCE

In one important area, U.S. nonproliferation assistance has been an overwhelming success: Tens of thousands of nuclear-related workers in the former Soviet Union have received wages through temporary research contracts, at times their only income during the years when their governments were months behind in paying wages.[64] Together IPP and ISTC have provided temporary research contracts to the nuclear cities that total 9,500 years of full-time work.[65] These projects have not only promoted interaction between Russia,

---

63. ISTC has a sister center in Kiev. The Science and Technology Center in Ukraine is ISTC's counterpart in Kiev. It works with former weapons of mass destruction scientists and engineers in Ukraine, Georgia, and Uzbekistan.
64. This statement is based on information from the ISTC (http://www.istc.ru) and IPP (http://www.ipp.lanl.gov) databases. As of August 2001, the Science Centers and IPP combined had given short-term work to an estimated 51,000 people from the former Soviet nuclear, biological, and chemical weapons complexes. See also Sharon K. Weiner, "International Cooperative Programmes," presentation at the Second International Working Group Meeting of the European Nuclear Cities Initiative, Brussels, Belgium, February 25–26, 2002.
65. These estimates are based on the amount of money that each program has transferred to Russia, after accounting for deductions for institute overhead, equipment costs, and other ex-

other parts of the former Soviet Union, and the West but have also contributed to making the nuclear cities much more open.

The creation of permanent employment in the nuclear cities has been far more problematic. IPP and ISTC have generated only a few permanent jobs in the nuclear cities.[66] As of 2001 NCI could claim responsibility for creating only about 300.[67]

Both IPP and ISTC have been criticized for funding "make work" projects that at best result in follow-on projects that do little to advance basic science or create jobs.[68] To increase its emphasis on commercialization and permanent job creation, in 1997 ISTC created "partner projects" that involve cost sharing with private industry and governmental and nongovernmental organizations. Similarly, IPP has renewed its emphasis on sustainable job creation by funding only projects that have an industry partner. As of 2002, however, only three ISTC partner projects have taken place in the nuclear cities, and only two IPP projects have been commercialized there.[69]

Given its limited resources, NCI has enjoyed some modest success. In addition to creating about 300 private sector jobs, it has also brokered an agreement with the Russian government to relocate security fences in Sarov, thus removing some buildings from the secret area of the Avangard warhead production plant and making this space available for commercial development. NCI has also worked with the European Bank for Reconstruction and Development (EBRD) and the U.S. Departments of State and Commerce to include the nuclear cities in some of their existing programs.[70]

---

penses. These personnel numbers refer not to individuals but to person years of full-time employment.

66. This is based on information from the ISTC and IPP databases and communications with ISTC and IPP staff. Two ISTC projects, one at Sarov and the other at Snezhinsk, have led to the creation of an estimated ten permanent jobs for nuclear weapons workers. Also, one IPP project in Snezhinsk looks quite promising.

67. The largest number of jobs has been created by the NCI-funded Open Computer Center at Sarov, which employs about 150 individuals. See General Accounting Office, *Nuclear Nonproliferation: DOE's Efforts to Assist Weapons Scientists in Russia's Nuclear Cities Face Challenges,* GAO-01-429 (Washington, D.C.: GPO, May 2001), p. 21; additional information provided by NCI, May 28, 29, and 30, 2002.

68. Kenneth N. Luongo, "Nuclear Cities: Problems and Opportunities in Building Commercially Viable Businesses," presentation at the Sam Nunn/Bank of America Policy Forum, Atlanta, Georgia, March 26–27, 2001. Also interviews with NCI, IPP and ISTC staff.

69. As of late 2001, there were approximately 130 ISTC Partner Projects, about 20 percent of the total. Out of approximately 400 IPP projects, only 20 have resulted in commercialization or were predicted to do so by 2002. "ISTC Projects By Funding Source," http://www.istc.ru (accessed November 5, 2001); and interviews with ISTC and IPP staff.

70. As explained above, the State Department has included some of the nuclear cities in its sister cities program. The Department of Commerce has included some of the cities in several business

Besides their failure to create more than a few hundred permanent jobs, NCI, IPP, and to a lesser extent ISTC have been criticized for several other reasons. One concern is that these programs might inadvertently contribute to Russia's own weapons programs. For example, the GAO found that some IPP, NCI, and possibly ISTC projects involved scientists who were also working on nuclear weapons projects for Russia and that a few IPP projects could unintentionally benefit Russia's defense efforts.[71] Another concern involves sloppy record keeping. For example, IPP's records often do not accurately record project budgets, the scientists involved, and whether key weapons scientists are taking part in projects.[72] GAO has also accused DoE of insufficient oversight of NCI expenditures in both the United States and Russia.[73]

Also at issue is determining who exactly benefits from these programs. Specifically, NCI and IPP have been criticized by Congress and the GAO for spending more money in U.S. weapons laboratories than in Russian ones. For example, in fiscal years 1999 and 2000, NCI received $16 million, of which about $5 million (or 30 percent) was spent on projects in Russia. The rest went mostly to U.S. national laboratories.[74] From FY 1994 through June 1998, 37 percent of IPP funding went to states of the former Soviet Union; 63 percent was spent in the United States, again, mostly in the U.S. national labs.[75] Since 2000, Congress has capped IPP spending at no more than 35 percent at the U.S. national labs; as of 2001, NCI must spend at least 51 percent of its funds in Russia.[76]

NCI, IPP, and ISTC are also increasingly sensitive to the highs and lows of U.S.-Russian relations. For example, in the spring of 2001, visits by DoE and State Department officials to the nuclear cities were put on hold pending the

---

development activities including the American Business Centers, and some trade development activities.

71. General Accounting Office, *Nuclear Nonproliferation: Concerns with DOE's Efforts to Reduce the Risks Posed by Russia's Unemployed Weapons Scientists*, GAO/RCED-99-54 (Washington, D.C.: GPO, February 1999), pp. 43–46; General Accounting Office, GAO-01-429, p. 3; and General Accounting Office, *Weapons of Mass Destruction: State Department Oversight of Science Centers Program*, GAO-01-582 (Washington, D.C.: GPO, May 2001), pp. 2, 15–20.

72. General Accounting Office, GAO/RCED-99-54, p. 3, 39–43; and comments from IPP program staff.

73. General Accounting Office, GAO-01-429, pp. 13–14.

74. Information provided by NCI, October 2000; and General Accounting Office, GAO-01-429, pp. 8–13.

75. General Accounting Office, GAO/RCED-99-54, p. 3.

76. *National Defense Authorization Act for Fiscal Year 2000*, House Report 106–301, 106th Cong., 1st sess., August 6, 1999, p. 427; and *Making Appropriations for Energy and Water Development for the Fiscal Year Ending September 30, 2001, and for Other Purposes*, House Report 106-907, 106th Cong., 2d sess., September 27, 2000, pp. 114–115.

resolution of allegations about Russian spying in the United States and the subsequent expulsion of selected diplomats from each country. Some members of Congress have called for making aid to Russia contingent on a variety of foreign policy issues including Russian assistance to Iran and missile sales to China.[77]

A CLOSER LOOK AT JOB CREATION EFFORTS. These concerns, along with Russia's poor economic conditions and problems of access to the nuclear cities, do little to assist U.S. programs in their job creation efforts. There are, however, additional roadblocks that arise from the choices that U.S. programs have made about how to create jobs in the nuclear cities.

One problem is the mismatch between the needs of Western industry and the technologies funded by ISTC and IPP.[78] Only about 30 percent of ISTC funding and 15 percent of IPP projects overlap with technologies identified as critically important to Western industry.[79] Second, job creation efforts have so far been directed exclusively at attracting investment in the nuclear cities themselves, ignoring possibilities in nearby cities or major metropolitan areas.[80] Third, partly in response to Russian concerns about secrecy, NCI, IPP, and ISTC have opted to work with virtually any employee of the Russian nuclear weapons establishment rather than devising a way to identify or assist only those with the most directly relevant nuclear weapons–related skills.[81] Fourth, despite their similar mandates, the three programs have a poor record of cooperation. Not only have they largely failed to learn from each other, but they have often worked at cross-purposes—for example, by negotiating separate agreements with the Russian government to solve the same or similar problems. Further, although MinAtom is sensitive about U.S. government em-

---

77. For example, in 1997 Representative Benjamin Gilman (R-N.Y.) introduced the Iran Missile Proliferation Sanctions Act, which prohibits U.S. assistance to any country that transfers missile technology or components to Iran; also that year, the House voted to cut off all aid to Russia if it sells antiship cruise missiles to China.
78. Luongo, "Nuclear Cities: Problems and Opportunities."
79. Ibid. This is based on a comparison of ISTC- and IPP- funded technologies and those identified in the National Critical Technologies List, Office of Science and Technology Policy, September 2000, http://www.ostp.gov/CTIformatted/AppA/appa.html (accessed November 1, 2001).
80. David Bernstein of Stanford University has suggested that Western investment could focus on expanding already existing high-technology businesses in nearby open cities. In return for investment, these businesses would agree to hire workers from the nuclear weapons complexes. See Bernstein, presentation at the Sam Nunn/Bank of America Policy Forum, Atlanta, Georgia, March 26–27, 2001. This criticism is less applicable to NCI because under its U.S.-Russian implementing agreement, NCI must limit its activities to the nuclear cities.
81. Both IPP and ISTC do rank scientists according to their knowledge and skills, and both prefer to fund projects in which at least half of the workers are nuclear weapons scientists. In practice, however, this ranking system is based on self-identification and does little to narrow the potential client base for IPP and ISTC projects.

ployees visiting the nuclear cities, NCI, IPP, and ISTC rarely coordinate or combine their delegations. Worse still, some in NCI and IPP believe that the State Department, which must approve their visits to Russia, will delay or deny approval because it sees these programs as competitive to and duplicative of its own ISTC efforts.[82]

A QUESTION OF FUNDING. Yet another problem shared by these programs is money. Figure 1 shows congressional funding for these programs from FY 1994 to 2002.[83] Including agreed and projected funding for FY 2002, the United States has spent $536 million on these three programs, of which $262 million has gone to the Science Centers (both the ISTC and its smaller sister center in Ukraine), $183 million to IPP, and $49 million to NCI. ISTC has enjoyed the most consistent congressional support, while NCI has consistently struggled the most for funding. In FY 2001, for example, $10 million (almost 40 percent) of NCI's budget was contingent on the negotiation of a U.S.-Russian agreement that Russia will permanently close some of its nuclear weapons assembly and disassembly facilities. In that year, NCI was required to spend most of its budget on projects that it certified would be commercially viable within three years, a criterion that is all but impossible to meet.

Regardless of the individual yearly appropriations, none of these programs has ever received more than a fraction of the funding needed for serious job creation efforts in the nuclear cities. Past attempts suggest that the true cost varies greatly.[84] For example, MinAtom has estimated that it costs $10,000 to create one job in a nuclear city, and this estimate is probably conservative.[85] Even assuming $10,000 per job, it would cost $350 million to create employment for the 35,000 people MinAtom intends to lay off over the next five years. Another funding benchmark was offered in a recent task force report, coauthored by Howard Baker and Lloyd Cutler, which provided an assessment of the DoE's nonproliferation programs with Russia. The Baker-Cutler report concluded that funding for these programs should be accelerated and

82. Interviews with IPP and NCI former and current staff.

83. IPP and NCI have specific accounts in the budget determined by Congress. ISTC, however, is funded as part of the congressional authorization for State Department assistance activities to the states of the former Soviet Union. The State Department then notifies Congress as to how much of this money will go to the ISTC. Final funding levels are determined by the resulting negotiations between Congress and the State Department.

84. Two estimates of the cost of creating one job are $17,000 (based on MinAtom's conversion expenditures from 1998 to 2000) and $24,000 (based on NCI's efforts to create an Open Computing Center in Sarov).

85. Comments by Lev Ryabev, first deputy minister, MinAtom, Princeton, New Jersey, April 15, 2000.

Figure 1. Funding from Congress by Fiscal Year, 1994–2002.

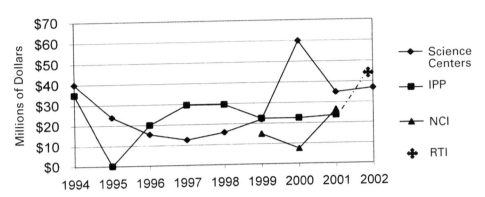

SOURCES: U.S. State Department, *U.S. Government Assistance to and Cooperative Activities with the New Independent States of the Former Soviet Union,* annual reports for FY 1994– FY 1999 (Washington, D.C.: Government Printing Office, January 1995, April 1996, January 1997, January 1998, January 1999, January 2000); U.S. Department of Energy, "IPP Program Briefing," March 2000; Russian American Nuclear Security Advisory Council, "Russian Nuclear Security and the Clinton Administration's Fiscal Year 2000 Expanded Threat Reduction Initiative: A Summary of Congressional Action," February 2000; and updates provided by William Hoehn, Washington office director, RANSAC.
NOTES: Science Centers include funding for both the ISTC in Moscow and the Science and Technology Center in Ukraine, located in Kiev. FY 1995 funding for IPP is $0 because in FY 1994 funding was transferred from the State Department late in the fiscal year, so there was no additional appropriation. In FY 2002, Congress approved $42 million for Russian Transition Initiatives, a joint account that includes both IPP and NCI. The division of funding between IPP and NCI was left to DoE.

increased, and that over the next eight to ten years, the cost of creating jobs in the nuclear cities could reach $700 million.[86]

Rather than funding increases, the current Bush administration initially sought significant cuts to some of these programs. The administration's 2001 review of U.S. nonproliferation assistance to Russia recommended a reduction in DoE cooperative nuclear security programs of 32 percent, cutting NCI by 75 percent and IPP by 10 percent.[87] Although these reductions were included in

---

86. Also recommended is an additional $2 billion to help Russia downsize its nuclear facilities and convert them to civilian use. See Baker and Cutler, *A Report Card on the Department of Energy's Nonproliferation Programs with Russia,* p. A-1.
87. According to John Fialka, these proposed cuts were the result of a budget battle between DoE and the Office of Management and Budget (OMB) that resulted in OMB successfully redirecting money from DoE's nonproliferation programs to upgrading DoE and nuclear weapons facilities. See Fialka, "U.S. Nuclear-Weapons Facilities Are Winner in Big Budget Battle," *Wall Street Journal,* March 30, 2001, p. A16.

the administration's FY 2002 budget request, Congress restored funding for IPP and NCI. Immediately after the September 11 attacks, the Bush administration requested $40 million in emergency funding—none of which was earmarked for nonproliferation activities in Russia. Initially, bipartisan congressional attempts to add funds, including money for nuclear security in Russia, were thwarted by President Bush's threat to veto any additional appropriations. Eventually, however, Congress added and approved $30 million for the Science Centers and $15 million for Russian Transition Initiatives (RTI), a new funding line that combines IPP and NCI into one account. In its FY 2003 budget request to Congress, the Bush administration asked for $39 million for RTI, slightly less than the FY 2002 appropriation, and $52 million for the funding line that includes the Science Centers.[88] More recently, in June 2002 at the urging of President Bush, the leaders from the Group of Eight committed their countries to spending $20 billion over the next ten years to fight the spread of weapons of mass destruction. Although creating jobs for weapons scientists was one of the tasks highlighted, the Bush administration has yet to identify how much of this money will go toward these efforts.[89]

A Refocused Effort

Increased U.S. concern about nuclear terrorism combined with MinAtom's planned layoffs warrant a renewed commitment to countering the proliferation of nuclear knowledge from Russia's nuclear cities. Although increased funding would no doubt be helpful, success will ultimately depend on the ability to learn from the past. More demonstrable results will in turn help to increase the political commitment necessary to sustain this effort into the next decade.

The creation of private sector jobs should not be the sole focus of U.S. nonproliferation programs or of NCI, IPP, or ISTC. Expansion of these programs requires new initiatives. The two most promising are investment in

---

88. The $30 million approved by Congress and the $52 million originally requested by the Bush administration include funding for the Science Centers and a separate program for biological weapons experts. Although the funding split between the two programs has yet to be decided, the funding requests are approximately equal to those from FY 2002. For more information on the administration's FY 2003 budget, see *Analysis of the Bush Administration's Fiscal Year 2003 Budget Requests for U.S.-Former Soviet Union Nonproliferation Programs,* April 2002; and *Update on Congressional Activity Affecting U.S.-Russian Cooperative Nonproliferation Programs,* June 17, 2002, both by William Hoehn (Washington, D.C.: Russian-American Nuclear Security Advisory Council, 2002).

89. Office of the Press Secretary, The White House, fact sheet, "G-8 Summit—Preventing the Proliferation of Weapons of Mass Destruction," June 27, 2002.

public goods and services that would benefit both the nuclear cities and the United States and retirement incentives that would provide a secure future for older nuclear workers. Additionally, NCI, IPP, and ISTC should each refocus on its comparative advantage. Better management and greater coordination are also needed from the executive branch.

PUBLIC GOODS AND SERVICES

The creation of private sector jobs in the nuclear cities is a difficult task. Although economic conditions in Russia are improving, investment—both foreign and domestic—remains low. Furthermore, Russian banking, private property, and intellectual property rules and practices have done little to encourage commercial development. Funding the production of public goods and services offers an opportunity to create jobs in the nuclear cities without the need to subsidize private industry investment.[90] U.S.-Russian cooperation is already under way on radioactive waste cleanup and on research and analysis useful for a variety of nonproliferation activities.

RADIOACTIVE WASTE. The production of nuclear weapons and nuclear energy has left a legacy of radioactive and chemical contamination and waste in the United States and Russia. Groundwater and soil in both countries have been contaminated with radioactive materials and vast amounts of highly radioactive wastes that need to be stored safely for thousands of years. Equipment and buildings also need to be decontaminated before they can be destroyed or retooled for other purposes.[91] In 2000, DoE estimated that it would cost the United States between $151 and $195 billion over seventy years to remediate its nuclear-related environmental problems.[92] Another study conducted by nongovernmental analysts puts the figure closer to $440 billion.[93]

---

90. Investing in public goods as a way of helping the nuclear cities is not a new idea. See Oleg Bukharin, Harold Feiveson, Frank N. von Hippel, Sharon K. Weiner, Matthew Bunn, William Hoehn, and Kenneth N. Luongo, *Helping Russia Downsize Its Nuclear Complex: A Focus on the Closed Nuclear Cities* (Princeton, N.J.: Program on Nuclear Policy Alternatives, Center for Energy and Environmental Studies, Princeton University, June 2000), pp. 28–30; and Bukharin, von Hippel, and Weiner, *Conversion and Job Creation*, pp. 25–33. Both publications discuss radioactive waste cleanup and nonproliferation activities specifically. See also Bunn, *The Next Wave*, pp. 90–94.
91. For information about environmental pollution that has resulted from nuclear weapons activities in both the United States and Russia, see Arjun Makhijani, Howard Hu, and Katherine Yih, eds., *Nuclear Wastelands: A Global Guide to Nuclear Weapons Production and Its Health and Environmental Effects* (Cambridge, Mass.: MIT Press, 1995).
92. Office of Environmental Management, U.S. Department of Energy, *Status Report on Paths to Closure* (Washington, D.C.: GPO, March 2000), p. 9.
93. Stephen I. Schwartz, ed., *Atomic Audit: The Costs and Consequences of U.S. Nuclear Weapons since 1940* (Washington, D.C.: Brookings, 1998), pp. 354–355, adjusted to current U.S. dollars.

Many of the scientists and engineers in Russia's nuclear cities have the skills and experience needed to tackle a variety of nuclear-related environmental issues. They can also be hired for around $2,000 a year. Moreover, in addition to providing research and development to aid the United States in cleaning up its environmental mess, these experts, with the proper support, could help Russia address its nonnuclear-related environmental problems as well.

An ongoing IPP project illustrates the potential of this partnership. Both the United States and Russia store high-level radioactive waste in above- and below-ground tanks, some of which leak and all of which need to be replaced due to erosion. The United States has more than 300 of these tanks at four sites, including 177 at DoE's Hanford nuclear facility in Washington state. Sandia National Laboratories has estimated that it will cost approximately $10 billion to clean these tanks.[94] The Mining and Chemical Combine at Zheleznogorsk, a Russian nuclear city that once specialized in plutonium production, has developed a system that can mobilize the radioactive sludge in these tanks, pump it out, and convert it into a more environmentally safe form for storage. Through the IPP project, Russian and U.S. scientists are seeking to apply this technology to clean out the tanks at Hanford and possibly also the Savannah River plutonium-production site in Georgia. Sandia estimates that this technology could save the U.S. government $10 million per tank.[95] By cooperating with Russia in this way, the United States can save billions of dollars over the long run. Future cooperation can also help Russia to more safely dispose of its nuclear waste by encouraging the development of technologies that Russia cannot afford to test and refine on its own.

NONPROLIFERATION ACTIVITIES. Since the end of the Cold War, the United States has devoted a small but growing share of its $300 billion annual defense budget to cooperative programs aimed at countering the proliferation of weapons of mass destruction. Cooperation with Russia and its nuclear cities can help by improving scientific research and analysis, fostering a mutual "nonproliferation culture," and improving the security of and accelerating reductions in fissile material inventories.

The United States and Russia are working together to improve the security of weapons-usable materials, develop mutually acceptable transparency and verification measures, and monitor and detect the proliferation of nuclear weapons–related materials. U.S.-Russian cooperative programs aimed at pro-

---

94. Private communication with Ralston Barnard, Sandia National Laboratories, November 2000.
95. Ibid.

tecting and accounting for weapons-usable materials total more than $260 million a year.[96] These efforts could be expanded to include a variety of nonproliferation applications. For example, the U.S. Defense Threat Reduction Agency is developing software to predict the movement and effect of hazardous materials in the atmosphere. The experiences of skilled mathematicians and programmers from the nuclear cities, particularly those who dealt with the 1986 nuclear reactor incident at Chernobyl, could be valuable in this effort. Other possibilities for U.S.-Russian cooperation include the detection of clandestine nuclear tests, the development of export controls, and the monitoring of worldwide production of fissile materials.

Cooperative nonproliferation research and analysis can help to spur the development of a post-Soviet nonproliferation culture in Russia. During the Soviet era, nuclear security focused on international borders and workers' fears that the KGB would detect and punish thefts. Inventories of fissile material stockpiles were either nonexistent or inadequate, nuclear facilities often lacked armed guards, and nuclear materials were in many cases inadequately secured. Although Russian government officials consider nuclear proliferation a threat, they do not view it with the same concern as their American counterparts. Therefore, the United States has a vested interest in working with Russia as a means of influencing and understanding Russian nonproliferation policy.

Another important nonproliferation project is reducing the size of fissile material inventories. Russia has an estimated 650 metric tons of weapons-usable plutonium and HEU, in addition to the fissile material in its nuclear weapons. A recent study by the Monterey Institute of International Studies and the Carnegie Endowment reports that weapons-usable fissile material can be found at more than fifty facilities in Russia and several other former Soviet states.[97]

Through the 1993 Russian HEU Purchase Agreement, the United States is helping to reduce the amount of weapons-grade uranium in Russia and provide jobs for nuclear cities where the blending-down of this uranium occurs.[98] Under the agreement, the U.S. government agreed to buy 500 metric tons of excess HEU from Russian dismantled nuclear weapons over a twenty-year pe-

---

96. This includes FY 2002 funding and projected funding for material protection, control and accounting activities, HEU and warhead transparency efforts, and transportation and security programs.
97. Jon Brook Wolfsthal, Cristina-Astrid Chuen, and Emily Ewell Daughtry, eds., *Nuclear Status Report: Nuclear Weapons, Fissile Material, and Export Controls in the Former Soviet Union* (Washington, D.C.: Monterey Institute of International Studies and the Carnegie Endowment for International Peace, June 2001), p. 75.
98. In Ozersk and Seversk, the HEU metal is converted into oxide; and in Seversk, Novouralsk, and Zelenogorsk, the HEU is down-blended to low enriched uranium.

riod. A portion of this income is a major source of funding for MinAtom's conversion efforts. At approximately $20 million per ton, even small additional purchases of HEU would provide tremendous income for Russia, create more jobs in the nuclear cities, and permanently remove more weapons-grade material from Russian inventories. The United States, either alone or in cooperation with other countries, could purchase additional excess HEU in exchange for guarantees that some of this money would be used for conversion and job creation in the nuclear cities.[99]

Expanding the HEU agreement would not be easy.[100] Periodically, Russian shipments of low enriched uranium (LEU) have been delayed because of disagreements over the disposition of the natural uranium contained in the LEU. Although an agreement on this issue was reached in 1999, concerns have been raised about the price to be paid for future enrichment work.[101] In the United States, the HEU agreement is managed by the U.S. Enrichment Corporation (USEC), a privatized company created by the U.S. government to manage U.S. enrichment operations. In early 2002, USEC completed renegotiating the terms of future enrichment services with Tenex, MinAtom's trade arm and Russia's executive agent for the HEU agreement.[102] Some analysts worry about insufficient government oversight of USEC and its activities.[103] Further, USEC has its own problems: Financial woes forced it to cut 20 percent of its workforce in 2000, and U.S. workers have accused the company of buying Russian uranium so it can eliminate more expensive U.S. enrichment jobs.[104]

---

99. Expanding the purchase of HEU has been proposed on numerous occasions. See, for example, Bukharin et al., *Helping Russia*, pp. 77–81, 98–104; Siegfried S. Hecker, "Thoughts about an Integrated Strategy for Nuclear Cooperation with Russia," *Nonproliferation Review*, Vol. 8, No. 2 (Summer 2001), p. 17; and Bunn, *The Next Wave*, pp. 99–102.
100. For a history of some of the problems with the HEU deal, see Thomas L. Neff, "Privatizing U.S. National Security: The U.S.-Russian HEU Deal At Risk," *Arms Control Today*, Vol. 28, No. 6 (August/September 1998), pp. 8–14.
101. See Elizabeth Martin-Alldred, "The Deal within the Deal," *Nukem*, May–June 1999, pp. 6–46; and "USEC Uranium Sales: Has the Big Wave Passed?" *Nukem*, May 2000, pp. 4–14.
102. Valeria Korchagina, "Russia, U.S. Extend Key Uranium Deal," *Moscow Times*, February 27, 2002, p. 5.
103. See, for example, Richard A. Falkenrath, "The HEU Deal and the U.S. Enrichment Corporation," *Nonproliferation Review*, Vol. 3, No. 2 (Winter 1996), pp. 62–66; and Thomas L. Neff, "Decision Time for the HEU Deal: U.S. Security vs. Private Interests," *Arms Control Today*, Vol. 31, No. 5 (June 2001), pp. 12–17.
104. Martha M. Hamilton, "Uranium Firm to Cut 20% of Jobs," *Washington Post*, February 4, 2000, p. E01; Joe Walker, "Analyst Says Uranium Enrichment Firms Deal Would Kill Paducah, Ky., Plants," *Paducah Sun*, May 25, 2000; and "PACE International Union Says Government Approval of Enriched Uranium Imports from Russia Will Jeopardize the Sole Remaining Uranium Enrichment Plant in the U.S.," PR Newswire, January 16, 2001. PACE is the Paper, Allied Industrial, Chemical and Energy (PACE) Workers International Union.

Before agreeing to additional purchases of HEU, the U.S. government needs to address two important issues. The first involves control. U.S. government oversight of USEC is weak, and there is no requirement for USEC to proactively report on its activities.[105] Further, oversight of USEC takes place outside the context of other U.S.-Russian cooperative security programs. This means that there is insufficient pressure on USEC to balance its own profits against U.S. national security interests. Second, expanding the HEU agreement is not revenue neutral. The world market for uranium and enrichment services is glutted, and any additional LEU that is sold may further depress the price. Any agreement to purchase additional HEU would require a way to keep the uranium off the market until after the current HEU deal ends (in approximately 2013).[106] This means that the U.S. government would have to purchase the HEU and hold it in storage until that date. An alternative approach is not to buy the HEU itself but to pay Russia the money necessary to speed up blend-down operations in the nuclear cities. Reportedly, these operations amount to about 20 percent of the cost of the HEU agreement.[107] The resulting LEU would then also be kept off the world market until later. This would serve the dual purposes of employing workers in the nuclear cities and eliminating additional quantities of weapons-grade uranium.

RETIREMENT INCENTIVES

MinAtom's nuclear cities employ 60,000–67,000 individuals, 20 percent of whom will be near retirement age (fifty-five for men, sixty for women) by 2005.[108] Russia's pension system, however, provides few incentives for older workers to retire, and the average pension is only about $300 per year.[109] Out of this money, retirees often have to support not only themselves but also children and grandchildren who are poorly paid or who do not have access to housing themselves. As a result, older workers are reluctant to leave their jobs, and thus far MinAtom has opted not to force them out.[110] Because the reemployment prospects for older workers are grim, subsidizing retirement is

---

105. Neff, "Privatizing U.S. National Security," pp. 10–11.
106. Bunn, *The Next Wave*, p. 101.
107. Communication from Thomas Neff, November 6, 2000.
108. Tikhonov, *Russia's Nuclear and Missile Complex*, p. 36, Figures 3–3 to 3–5.
109. Three hundred dollars was the Russian nationwide average in 2000; this figure was calculated using information from the State Committee of the Russian Federation on Statistics. Scientists in the nuclear cities most likely receive additional supplements.
110. Bukharin, von Hippel, and Weiner, *Conversion and Job Creation*, pp. 33–34.

an attractive option for securing the futures of older nuclear weapons–related personnel.[111]

By 2005, about 13,000 of MinAtom's employees in the nuclear cities will be older than fifty; some will possess critical skills that will have to be replaced. Assuming that three out of every four workers are not replaced, about 10,000 can be expected to retire—this is almost one-third of MinAtom's total planned reductions of 35,000.

The director of VNIIEF has estimated that his employees can be persuaded to retire for supplemental payments of $500 per year, in addition to the housing and other benefits currently provided by the Russian government.[112] For the purposes of illustration, assume that every retiree in the nuclear cities is fifty-five years old. According to current life expectancy estimates, a fifty-five-year-old in Russia will likely live to seventy-two years of age.[113] At $500 a year, the cost of providing financial security for each retiree for the rest of his or her life is $8,500, or about 75 percent of the estimated cost of creating one new job in a nuclear city ($10,000).[114] If 6,000 nuclear-related workers retired in 2001, an additional 1,000 retire every year through 2005, and all live for seventeen years past retirement, the total cost would be $85 million over twenty-two years. During peak years, the annual cost of the program would be about $5 million, which could be further reduced through the use of annuities.[115] Pension supplements could be paid through the ISTC, which already has a mechanism for setting up foreign currency bank accounts for individuals in the closed cities. The Russian government would only have to continue providing its meager pension payments as well as housing and social services to the retirees.

Retirement as an option for downsizing is not unproblematic. One issue is cultural sensitivities about aging and the social worth of retirees. One solution would be to offer retirees work in public service jobs—for example, as science or math teachers, conservationists, and so on. Also, retirement incentives can-

---

111. This idea is also discussed in ibid., pp. 33–35.

112. Communication with James Toevs, Los Alamos National Laboratory, about a discussion he had in 1999 with Radii I'lkaev, the director of VNIIEF.

113. The estimated life expectancy of seventy-two years is based on the World Health Organization, *1997–1999 World Health Statistics Annual* (Geneva: World Health Organization, 2000), http:// www.who.int (accessed November 14, 2001), Table 3. The total cost of retirement benefits will be much less because many would-be retirees are older than fifty-five, will live fewer years, and therefore will require smaller lifetime subsidies.

114. This assumes that every job created becomes sustainable. It is more likely that a high percentage of new businesses will fail and thus additional investment will be required to re-create those lost jobs.

115. Thomas L. Neff, "Accelerating Down-Sizing of the Russian Weapons Complex," Massachusetts Institute of Technology, October 2000.

not completely replace job creation. Russia's nuclear cities must develop healthy economies; they should not become retirement communities.

Another issue involves making sure that retirees do not continue to work within the nuclear complex. To prevent this, retirees could be required to give up their security badges or other papers that clear them for access to MinAtom facilities. They could also agree to random checks by an external third party that would verify that they are no longer working for the nuclear complex. Assurances must also be given that MinAtom is indeed downsizing and is not hiring new workers to replace all retirees. This might be accomplished by mutual disclosures by both the United States and Russia about the size of their nuclear workforces. These would then be verified by a third party, such as an accounting or auditing firm.

COORDINATION IN THE UNITED STATES

A persistent criticism of U.S. efforts to help the nuclear cities is that there is an absence of leadership at the executive branch level.[116] U.S. nonproliferation programs lack strategic direction, and despite their similar mandates, there is little coordination. Congress has also asked the executive branch to appoint a senior-level coordinator.[117]

The president should heed Congress's call and designate a coordinator for U.S. nonproliferation assistance to Russia at a senior level in the executive branch. This official would be responsible not only for coordinating the programs of the different agencies but also for articulating a coherent strategy for helping Russia's nuclear cities, assigning roles for implementing this strategy, and monitoring progress until these programs are no longer needed. This individual would also be responsible for raising public awareness about the value of these programs and building support among Congress and the American public. Without broader support, these programs are doomed to continued congressional micromanagement and inadequate funding.

The coordinator should first lead a review of how these programs have operationalized their goals.[118] The aim should not be to develop metrics by which individual programs can be measured, but rather to parse out the

---

116. See, for example, Baker and Cutler, *A Report Card on the Department of Energy's Nonproliferation Programs with Russia*, pp. 23–24, 25–26; Kenneth N. Luongo, "Improving U.S.-Russian Nuclear Cooperation," *Issues in Science and Technology*, Fall 2001, p. 90; and Bunn, *The Next Wave*, pp. 107–108.
117. See, for example, *National Defense Authorization Act for Fiscal Year 2000*, p. 429; and conference report, *Enactment of Provisions of H.R. 5408, the Floyd D. Spence National Defense Authorization Act for Fiscal Year 2001*, House Report 106-945, 106th Cong., 2d sess., October 6, 2000, p. 499.
118. I thank an anonymous reviewer for this suggestion and for providing very useful comments about the many questions that need to be addressed in such a discussion.

definitions and decisions that are needed to better link U.S. national security interests to programs in Russia's nuclear cities. Issues that need clarification include the kinds of nuclear knowledge to be controlled, how economically secure those who possess this knowledge need to be and for how long, the relationship between the well-being of these individuals and their families and surrounding communities, whether nuclear workers need to remain in the nuclear cities and for how long, and indeed, whether some of the nuclear cities should be allowed to stagnate or disappear. These goals need to be measured against the amount of money that the United States is willing to spend and the degree of intrusiveness Russia will permit, given its own security concerns.

The coordinator should then determine the roles of the NCI, IPP, and ISTC programs in fulfilling U.S. objectives. Although these programs have similar mandates, each has developed a comparative advantage that should be considered when deciding their future direction. Redundancy per se is not the problem, but each program should play to its strengths while continuing to work in concert with the others. For example, both ISTC and IPP provide nuclear workers with salaries through short-term research contracts. As MinAtom reduces the size of its nuclear complex, workers who are laid off need assurances that they will have incomes until they are reemployed or retire. Short-term contracts should therefore be continued. ISTC, however, is better suited for this effort than IPP. ISTC has a Moscow-based staff with which to more readily and efficiently oversee this effort. It also has in place an efficient mechanism for transferring salary payments to workers in the nuclear cities, and it has significantly lower overhead.[119]

IPP, on the other hand, should move away from funding short-term research contracts with little commercial potential.[120] Instead, U.S. nuclear scientists should concentrate on sifting through ISTC projects and identifying those that can further research of interest to the U.S. government. Determining the commercial potential of ISTC projects and other research from the nuclear cities should be the responsibility of the private sector. Entrepreneurs are better able to assess commercial feasibility and link Russian research and development with prospective partners. Further, business entrepreneurs might be convinced to participate in return for a nominal salary and the promise of a percentage of

---

119. Using information provided by ISTC and IPP, I estimate that the full-time cost of one Russian national ISTC staff person based in Moscow is $23,000 a year. One laboratory scientist working full-time for IPP in the United States costs an estimated $230,000 per year. If that person is working in Russia performing oversight for IPP projects, the estimated yearly cost goes up to $446,000.
120. Over the last few years, IPP has tried to do this with some success.

any future profits.[121] In addition, the conversion and economic development experiences of other countries should be exploited on a systematic basis for lessons that are applicable to the nuclear cities.[122]

Meanwhile, NCI should concentrate on developing an infrastructure in the nuclear cities that encourages business development and improves living standards. NCI should also continue to leverage relevant government programs in the United States and abroad, convincing them to devote a portion of their own finances to expanding their activities in the nuclear cities.

Until FY 2002, approximately half of NCI's funding went toward encouraging infrastructure and community development in the nuclear cities. NCI argues that such activities make the cities more attractive to potential investors. In contrast, a May 2001 report by the GAO concluded that NCI's community development efforts should be eliminated because they do little to further the goal of job creation.[123] GAO argues that "none of the industry officials whom we talked to during the course of our audit indicated that they would be more likely to invest in the nuclear cities because of municipal and social improvements."[124] The more relevant issue is whether nuclear experts are content to live in run-down cities with few social services. The purpose of U.S. assistance to the nuclear cities is to prevent proliferation. The decision to create new jobs was premised on the assumption that poorly paid weapons workers might be desperate enough to sell their skills to the highest bidder. Surely, weapons workers can also become desperate because they cannot provide for their children, because the only health care they can afford is of poor quality, or because they fear increased crime in their cities. Job creation alone will not solve these problems. Former weapons workers need to have secure and sustainable livelihoods.

NCI should not take on the task of completely transforming Russia's nuclear cities. The difficulty and expense of such an endeavor should not, however, be an excuse for doing nothing. Health care, for example, is one obvious area for cooperation. Funded by NCI and the State Department, the cities of Sarov and

---

121. There are already several U.S.-based business entrepreneurs who have their own initiatives for pairing Russian scientists with U.S. companies in return for a percentage of future profits. Some management consulting companies will also provide free or reduced-fee advice in return for shares of equity.
122. Although a discussion of the literature on conversion and economic development and its applicability to the nuclear cities is beyond the scope of this article, such an exploration should be made. Even the lessons from the United States' own conversion experience have yet to be exploited and have largely been limited to a few exchange visits between U.S. and Russian nuclear cities, conducted under NCI's now-terminated community development program.
123. General Accounting Office, GAO-01-429, pp. 19–21.
124. Ibid., p. 20.

Los Alamos are working together in several areas including adolescent and child health promotion, dental care, asthma control, cardiovascular risk management, diabetes control, and neonatal intensive care training.[125] Mayors and other local government officials from some of the nuclear cities have visited their counterparts in the United States to discuss issues of conversion and local governance. Officials from several nuclear cities have expressed an interest in learning about U.S. methods for treating drug addiction. NCI has also opened two International Development Centers (Snezhinsk and Zheleznogorsk) to offer business advice to local would-be entrepreneurs and provide internet access to the general population.

NCI should also continue to encourage other nongovernmental organizations and government agencies to include the nuclear cities in their own programs. For example, the State Department funds several sister city relationships between U.S. and Russian cities with nuclear facilities. The U.S. Department of Commerce has been approached about targeting some of its overseas business development resources on the nuclear cities. NCI outreach is also responsible for providing access to micro and small business loans in four nuclear cities. With seed money from NCI, in early 2001 the EBRD opened loan offices in Sarov, Snezhinsk, Zheleznogorsk, and Seversk, and as of April 2001, these offices had made more than 200 loans totaling more than $1.5 million.[126] According to a profile of borrowers in Snezhinsk, more than fifty new jobs are expected to result from EBRD loans of $225,000.

Finally, the coordinator should seek to resolve practical problems in the U.S.-Russian cooperative agenda. In the case of the nuclear cities, two of the more contentious issues are U.S. access to Russian facilities and linking Russian downsizing to U.S. assistance. U.S. programs frequently negotiate and renegotiate agreements pertaining to access and, in the case of NCI, reductions in Russian facilities. Often, U.S. requirements for both seem ad hoc or raise suspicions of espionage; and sometimes Russian intransigence is interpreted as ingratitude or a desire to obfuscate. Missing is U.S.-Russian agreement on the overall parameters to guide negotiations. Absent this guidance, cooperation is delayed as issues are repeatedly renegotiated. Assigning a senior-level executive branch official the responsibility for negotiating these issues with the Russian government would increase the likelihood that a meaningful agreement

---

125. Private communication from Robert Thomsen, director of the Los Alamos Medical Center, New Mexico, February 17, 2000; and private communication from Michael Johnson, Russia/New Mexico Secondary Schools Exchange and project leader, Critical Issues Program, Los Alamos, New Mexico, February 14, 2000.
126. Information provided by EBRD staff, April 2001.

can be reached, indicate renewed dedication on the part of the United States, and prompt Russia to respond in kind.

Conclusion

Since the collapse of the Soviet Union, the United States has worked to prevent the proliferation of nuclear expertise from Russia's nuclear cities. These efforts have helped to stabilize Russia's nuclear-related workforce. Nevertheless, Russia plans to lay off about 50 percent of this workforce over the next five to ten years. The pending unemployment of 35,000 workers with nuclear-related skills, plus U.S. fears of nuclear terrorism in the wake of the September 11 attacks, ensure that the proliferation of nuclear knowledge will remain a concern.

NCI, IPP, and to a lesser extent ISTC suffer from a lack of political clout on Capitol Hill, largely due to their lack of tangible results, poor oversight, and inadequate coordination. With inconsistent and narrowly based political support, these programs have fallen short of the funding necessary to accomplish their goals.

Much of the blame for this conundrum involves the means selected for achieving the goal—the United States has increasingly focused on countering the proliferation of nuclear knowledge by trying to create permanent private sector jobs for about half of Russia's current nuclear workforce. Permanent jobs, however, have been elusive.

This almost single-minded focus on job creation should be abandoned. Instead, U.S. efforts should be turned toward employing Russia's nuclear workforce in the production of public goods and services that the United States is already committed to purchasing. The areas of radioactive waste cleanup and nonproliferation offer two promising examples. Retirement subsidies present another way forward. Russia's nuclear workforce is aging. For about three-fourths of the cost of trying to create permanent jobs that may never materialize, the United States can provide retirement pensions to 10,000 Russian nuclear workers. Also, U.S. programs have excelled at using short-term research contracts to temporarily employ another 10,000 or more nuclear workers. Rather than decry the lack of commercial follow-ons to these contracts, they should be praised for what they are—a successful, cost-efficient way of keeping nuclear workers temporarily out of poverty.

These initiatives should be pursued while improvements are made in the coordination of these programs in the United States. Specifically, a senior-level executive branch official should be appointed to oversee U.S.-Russian nonproliferation programs, provide for strategic direction, and serve as an advocate and problem solver between these programs and both the U.S. Congress and the Russian government. Further, NCI, IPP, and ISTC should move away from their current duplication of effort and instead concentrate on the comparative advantage each has developed over time.

Pathogens as Weapons

Gregory Koblentz

The International Security Implications of Biological Warfare

$\mathbf{B}$iological weapons have become one of the key security issues of the twenty-first century.[1] Three factors that first emerged in the 1990s have contributed to this phenomenon. First, revelations regarding the size, scope, and sophistication of the Soviet and Iraqi biological warfare programs focused renewed attention on the proliferation of these weapons.[2] Second, the catastrophic terrorist attacks on September 11, 2001, and the anthrax letters sent to media outlets and Senate offices in the United States during the following month, demonstrated the desire of terrorists to cause massive casualties and heightened concern over their ability to employ biological weapons.[3] Third, significant advances in the life sciences have increased concerns about how the biotechnology revolution could be exploited to develop new or improved biological weapons.[4] These trends suggest that there is a greater need than ever to answer several fundamental questions about biological warfare: What is the nature of the threat? What are the potential strategic consequences of the proliferation of biological weapons? How ef-

Gregory Koblentz is a doctoral candidate in Political Science at the Massachusetts Institute of Technology.

I would like to thank Robert Art, Thomas Christensen, Linda Fu, Jeanne Guillemin, Kendall Hoyt, Milton Leitenberg, John Ellis van Courtland Moon, Julian Perry Robinson, Harvey Sapolsky, Margaret Sloane, Jonathan Tucker, and Stephen Van Evera for their support and discussion of previous drafts. I am also grateful for comments from the participants in seminars at the Massachusetts Institute of Technology's Security Studies Program, Harvard University's John M. Olin Institute for Strategic Studies, and the Fourth Annual New Faces Conference at the Triangle Institute for Security Studies, as well as the reviewers for *International Security*. I would also like to acknowledge the support of the MacArthur Foundation and the Carnegie Corporation.

1. The arguments made in this article are developed further in Gregory Koblentz, "Pathogens as Weapons: The International Security Implications of Biological Warfare," Ph.D. dissertation, Massachusetts Institute of Technology, forthcoming.
2. Ken Alibek with Stephen Handelman, *Biohazard: The Chilling True Story of the Largest Covert Biological Weapons Program in the World—Told from the Inside by the Man Who Ran It* (New York: Random House, 1999); and Raymond A. Zilinskas, "Iraq's Biological Weapons: The Past as Future?" in Joshua Lederberg, ed., *Biological Weapons: Limiting the Threat* (Cambridge, Mass.: MIT Press, 1999), pp. 137–158.
3. The letters, containing spores of *B. anthracis* (the organism that causes anthrax), killed five and infected another seventeen. Elin Gursky, Thomas V. Inglesby, and Tara O'Toole, "Anthrax 2001: Observations on the Medical and Public Health Response," *Biosecurity and Bioterrorism*, Vol. 1, No. 2 (2003), pp. 97–110.
4. Matthew Meselson, "Averting the Hostile Exploitation of Biotechnology," *CBW Conventions Bulletin*, No. 48 (June 2000), pp. 16–19; and Claire M. Fraser and Malcolm R. Dando, "Genomics and Future Biological Weapons: The Need for Preventive Action by the Biomedical Community," *Nature Genetics*, No. 29 (November 2001), pp. 253–256.

fective will traditional security strategies such as deterrence and arms control be in containing this threat? How do answers to these questions inform policies to reduce the danger of biological weapons?

A rich literature already exists on the history and capabilities of biological weapons.[5] In addition, the security studies community has begun to pay increased attention to the threat posed by these weapons.[6] Few attempts have been made, however, to apply theories from the field of security studies to assess the broader international security implications of biological weapons.[7] Previous studies addressed the potential lethality of biological weapons and concluded that state or terrorist use of these weapons in indiscriminant attacks on indefensible civilian populations represents the primary danger.[8] Biological weapons, however, possess other attributes that pose less obvious but more insidious threats to international security. These destabilizing features are mutu-

5. United Nations Secretary-General, *Chemical and Bacteriological (Biological) Weapons and the Effects of Their Possible Use* (Geneva: United Nations, 1969); World Health Organization (WHO), *Health Aspects of Chemical and Biological Weapons* (Geneva: WHO, 1970); Stockholm International Peace Research Institute (SIPRI), *The Problem of Chemical and Biological Warfare*, Vols. 1–6 (New York: Humanities, 1971–75); and Erhard Geissler and John Ellis van Courtland Moon, eds., *Biological and Toxin Weapons: Research, Development, and Use from the Middle Ages to 1945*, SIPRI Chemical and Biological Warfare Study No. 18 (Oxford: Oxford University Press, 1999).

6. Susan Wright, ed., *Preventing a Biological Arms Race* (Cambridge, Mass.: MIT Press, 1990); Marie I. Chevrier, "Deliberate Disease: Biological Weapons, Threats, and Policy Responses," *Environment and Planning C: Government and Policy*, Vol. 11, No. 4 (1993), pp. 395–417; Malcolm Dando, *Biological Warfare in the 21st Century: Biotechnology and the Proliferation of Biological Weapons* (New York: Brassey's, 1994); Brad Roberts, "The Proliferation of Biological Weapons: Trends and Consequences," in Oliver Thranert, ed., *Enhancing the Biological Weapons Convention* (Bonn, Germany: Dietz, 1996), pp. 57–70; John D. Steinbruner, "Biological Weapons: A Plague upon All Houses," *Foreign Policy*, No. 109 (Winter 1997–1998), pp. 85–96; Richard K. Betts, "The New Threat of Mass Destruction," *Foreign Affairs*, Vol. 77, No. 1 (January/February 1998), pp. 26–41; Christopher F. Chyba, "Toward Biological Security," *Foreign Affairs*, Vol. 81, No. 3 (May/June 2000), pp. 122–136; Lederberg, *Biological Weapons*; and Raymond Zilinskas, ed., *Biological Warfare: Modern Offense and Defense* (Boulder, Colo.: Lynne Rienner, 2000).

7. George H. Quester, "Chemical and Biological Warfare," *American Political Science Review*, Vol. 68, No. 3 (September 1974), pp. 1285–1291; Marie Isabelle Chevrier, "Impediment to Proliferation? Analysing the Biological Weapons Convention," *Contemporary Security Policy*, Vol. 16, No. 2 (August 1995), pp. 72–102; Peter R. Lavoy, Scott D. Sagan, and James J. Wirtz, eds., *Planning the Unthinkable: How New Powers Will Use Nuclear, Biological, and Chemical Weapons* (Ithaca, N.Y.: Cornell University Press, 2000); and Susan Martin, "The Role of Biological Weapons in International Politics: The Real Military Revolution," *Journal of Strategic Studies*, Vol. 25, No. 1 (March 2002), pp. 63–98.

8. Raymond A. Zilinskas, "Biological Warfare and the Third World," *Politics and the Life Sciences*, Vol. 9, No. 1 (August 1990), pp. 71–72; Steve Fetter, "Ballistic Missiles and Weapons of Mass Destruction: What Is the Threat? What Should Be Done?" *International Security*, Vol. 16, No. 1 (Summer 1991), pp. 22–26; Martin, "The Role of Biological Weapons in International Politics," p. 76; and Steinbruner, "Biological Weapons," pp. 85–86.

ally reinforcing and make biological weapons even more dangerous than suggested by assessments based solely on potential lethality.

The article begins with an examination of the major characteristics of pathogens as weapons. The next four sections assess the security implications of biological weapons in four key areas of concern for international security—proliferation, deterrence, civil-military relations, and threat assessment—and suggest the following conclusions. First, it is extremely difficult to prevent the spread of biological warfare capabilities to actors motivated by a desire to challenge the status quo. Second, biological weapons do not confer the deterrent benefits associated with nuclear weapons and pose special difficulties for states seeking to prevent their use. Third, the intense secrecy that shrouds biological warfare programs impedes civilian control over them. Fourth, states tend to have flawed assessments of the biological warfare capabilities and intentions of their opponents. A common theme throughout this article is that secrecy produces a variety of destabilizing effects: Not only does it impede verification, but it also undermines deterrence, hinders civilian oversight, and significantly complicates threat assessments.[9] After addressing potential objections to this analysis, I offer several policy prescriptions for reducing the biological weapons threat.

Pathogens as Weapons

Modern biological weapons are designed to disseminate pathogens or toxins in an aerosol cloud of microscopic particles that can be readily inhaled and retained in the lungs of the exposed population.[10] These aerosols are most effective when composed of particles ranging from 1 to 10 microns that can stay airborne longer and cause more severe cases of disease.[11] Aerosols are taste-

9. On the broader security implications of secrecy, see Stephen Van Evera, *Causes of War: Power and the Roots of Conflict* (Ithaca, N.Y.: Cornell University Press, 2000), pp. 140–141.
10. Disease-causing microorganisms such as bacteria, rickettsiae, viruses, and fungi are called pathogens. Another class of biological warfare agents are toxins, which are nonliving molecules that do no replicate in the body. For technical background on biological weapons, see Office of Technology Assessment (OTA), *Proliferation of Weapons of Mass Destruction: Assessing the Risks* (Washington, D.C.: U.S. Government Printing Office [U.S. GPO], 1993), pp. 71–117; Richard O. Spertzel, Robert W. Wannemacher, and Carol D. Linden, *Global Proliferation: Dynamics, Acquisition Strategies, and Response*, Vol. 4: *Biological Weapons Proliferation* (Washington, D.C.: Defense Nuclear Agency, September 1994); and William C. Patrick III, "Biological Warfare: An Overview," Director's Series on Proliferation No. 4 (Livermore, Calif.: Lawrence Livermore National Laboratory, May 1994), pp. 1–7.
11. Leroy Fothergill, "The Biological Warfare Threat," in American Chemical Society, *Nonmilitary*

less, odorless, and invisible, thus facilitating clandestine attacks. They can be generated either by bomblets loaded into cluster bombs or missile warheads or by spraying devices that are mounted on aircraft, helicopters, cruise missiles, ships, or vehicles, or that are carried by hand.[12] The key drawbacks to biological weapons include their delayed effects; their sensitivity to environmental and meteorological conditions, which could result in uncertain area coverage and effects; the risk of infecting friendly forces; and the prospect of long-term contamination. For example, wind speed and direction, humidity, atmospheric stability, and the presence of sunlight can all influence the performance of a biological weapon.[13] The careful selection of agents, delivery systems, and targets, however, as well as the timing of the attack, could compensate for most of these limitations.[14]

The offense-defense balance in biological warfare strongly favors the attacker because developing and using biological weapons to cause casualties is significantly easier and less expensive than developing and fielding defenses against them.[15] Whether the biotechnology revolution will strengthen the defender or allow attackers to maintain their edge in this competition is unknown.[16] The most common method of operationalizing the offense-defense balance is to construct a cost ratio of offense to defense: the more resources the attacker must invest to overcome the defender's investment in defensive forces, the greater the shift in the balance toward defense.[17] Qualitative factors that affect the ease of attack or defense are also important. Four factors help to determine the attacker's advantage in biological warfare: (1) the potency of

Defense: Chemical and Biological Defenses in Perspective, Advances in Chemistry Series No. 26 (July 1960), p. 26.

12. Spertzel, Wannemacher, and Linden, *Global Proliferation,* Vol. 4, pp. 28–30.

13. Patrick, "Biological Warfare," p. 5.

14. Graham S. Pearson, "Prospects for Chemical and Biological Arms Control: The Web of Deterrence," *Washington Quarterly,* Vol. 16, No. 2 (Spring 1993), pp. 147–148; and Patrick, "Biological Warfare."

15. This feature of biological warfare has been recognized for more than fifty years. Theodor Rosebury, *Peace or Pestilence: Biological Warfare and How to Avoid It* (New York: Whittlesey, 1946), p. 135; Stockholm International Peace Research Institute, *The Problem of Chemical and Biological Warfare,* Vol. 2: *CB Weapons Today* (New York: Humanities, 1973), p. 90; and Joshua Lederberg and George Whitesides, *Biological Defense: Report of the Defense Science Board/Threat Reduction Advisory Committee* (Washington, D.C.: Office of the Undersecretary of Defense for Acquisition, Technology, and Logistics, June 2001), p. 2, released under the Freedom of Information Act (FOIA).

16. Raymond A. Zilinskas, "Conclusion," in Zilinskas, *Biological Warfare,* pp. 247–254; and Lederberg and Whitesides, *Biological Defense.*

17. Charles L. Glaser and Chaim Kaufmann, "What Is the Offense-Defense Balance and Can We Measure It?" *International Security,* Vol. 22, No. 4 (Spring 1998), pp. 50–51.

biological weapons, (2) the diversity of threat agents, (3) the ease of surprise, and (4) the difficulty in defending against such an attack.

THE POTENCY OF BIOLOGICAL WEAPONS

Biological weapons combine a relatively low cost of production with the capability for infecting large numbers of people over a wide area. According to a 1969 United Nations study, the cost of causing one civilian casualty per square kilometer was about $2,000 with conventional weapons, $800 with nuclear weapons, $600 with chemical weapons, and only $1 with biological weapons.[18] The ability of biological weapons to cause mass casualties is well documented. A 1970 World Health Organization (WHO) study found that 50 kilograms of anthrax could result in 200,000 casualties in a medium-sized city such as Boston.[19] The U.S. Office of Technology Assessment (OTA) has estimated that an attack with less than 100 kilograms of aerosolized anthrax spores could cause as many as 3 million casualties, rivaling the lethality of a thermonuclear weapon.[20]

The creation of an offensive biological weapon capability is also relatively inexpensive, both in absolute terms and in comparison to the cost of developing defensive capabilities. According to OTA, a simple fermentation plant suitable for the production of biological warfare agents would cost $10 million to construct.[21] In 1999, the U.S. Defense Threat Reduction Agency built a small facility that could be used to produce biological warfare agents for only $1.6 million.[22] A comparison of the costs of modern state-sponsored biological warfare programs is also illustrative. In 1991, the U.S. Defense Intelligence Agency (DIA) put the cost of Iraq's biological warfare program at $100–$200 million.[23] In comparison, the Department of Defense's program to vaccinate U.S. soldiers

18. United Nations Secretary-General, *Chemical and Bacteriological (Biological) Weapons and the Effects of Their Possible Use,* p. 40. The methodology used to determine these figures is not known.
19. World Health Organization, *Health Aspects of Chemical and Biological Weapons,* p. 99.
20. Office of Technology Assessment, *Proliferation of Weapons of Mass Destruction,* pp. 53–54.
21. Office of Technology Assessment, *Technologies Underlying Weapons of Mass Destruction* (Washington, D.C.: U.S. GPO, 1993), p. 86. In contrast, nerve agent plants cost tens of millions of dollars, and fissile material production facilities cost hundreds of millions of dollars. Total program costs for these weapons are also significantly higher. Ibid., pp. 27, 156–158.
22. Judith Miller, Stephen Engelberg, and William Broad, *Germs: Biological Weapons and America's Secret War* (New York: Simon and Schuster, 2001), pp. 297–298.
23. The agency also estimated that a significant capability without the redundancy of the prewar program could be attained for less than $100 million. Defense Intelligence Agency, *Iraq's Chemical and Biological Warfare Capabilities: Surviving Assets and Lack of Use during the War,* Defense Intelligence Memorandum 88-91, March 1991, p. 3, declassified under FOIA.

against *Bacillus anthracis* has cost more than \$250 million over the past six years, and only a fraction of the force has been fully vaccinated.[24] In addition, developing a new biodefense vaccine costs \$300–\$400 million and typically takes eight to ten years; transforming a pathogen into a weapon takes only two to three years.[25] Although these comparisons are somewhat crude, they indicate the highly favorable cost ratio of offense to defense in biological warfare.

THE DIVERSITY OF BIOLOGICAL WARFARE AGENTS

Biological warfare agents are characterized by a relatively high degree of diversity, which provides terrorists and military planners with significant flexibility. The open literature discusses some thirty pathogens as having the physical and biological characteristics needed for a mass casualty–producing biological weapon. Most national biological warfare programs have focused on ten to fifteen agents.[26] Even this short list of biological warfare agents, however, offers a range of possibilities from the lethal *B. anthracis* to incapacitating agents such as *Coxiella burnetii* (which causes Q fever) and Venezuelan equine encephalitis. Pathogens that cause contagious diseases that have been developed as biological weapons include *variola major* (the causative agent of smallpox) and *Yersinia pestis* (the cause of plague).

This list of agents, however, reflects only known threats. Unexpected or novel pathogens may also emerge as threats. U.S. experts were surprised to learn of some of the agents that Iraq and the former Soviet Union had chosen to produce and weaponize.[27] Because biological terrorism is generally less sophisticated and less demanding than the military use of biological weapons,

---

24. As of January 2003, only 83,000 of 2.4 million service members had completed the six-shot series. Department of Defense, *Chemical and Biological Defense Program*, Vol. 1: *Annual Report to Congress* (Washington, D.C.: Department of Defense, April 2003), p. 59, http://www.acq.osd.mil/cp/vol1–2003cbdpannualreport.pdf.
25. Department of Defense, *Report on Biological Warfare Defense Vaccine Research and Development Programs* (Fort Belvoir, Va.: Defense Technical Information Center, July 2001), p. 2, http://www.acq.osd.mil/cp/bwdvrdp-july01.pdf; William Broad and Judith Miller, "Once He Devised Germ Weapons; Now He Defends against Them," *New York Times*, November 3, 1998, p. D1; and Kenneth Alibek, "Research Considerations for Better Understanding of Biological Threats," in Institute of Medicine, *Biological Threats and Terrorism: Assessing the Science and Response Capabilities* (Washington, D.C.: National Academy Press, 2002), p. 64.
26. Spertzel, Wannemacher, and Linden, *Global Proliferation*, Vol. 4, p. 11; and David R. Franz, "Medical Countermeasures to Biological Warfare Agents," in Alexander Kelle, Malcolm Dando, and Kathryn Nixdorff, eds., *The Role of Biotechnology in Countering BTW Agents* (Dordrecht, Netherlands: Kluwer, 2001), p. 228.
27. Chemical and Biological Arms Control Institute, *Responding to the Biological Weapons Challenge: Developing an Integrated Strategy* (Alexandria, Va.: Chemical and Biological Arms Control Institute, 2000), p. 43.

the range of possible agents for terrorists is even larger and more varied.[28] The application of molecular biology to the development of advanced biological weapons could significantly increase the diversity of biological warfare agents, but efforts along these lines are believed not to have advanced beyond the research stage.[29] As a result, because of the difficulty in assessing threat agents in a timely manner, defensive programs tend to lag behind offensive programs.[30]

THE EASE OF SURPRISE

The element of surprise is crucial for an effective biological weapon attack and is relatively easy to achieve. The small quantity of agent required for an attack, the ability to launch an attack with a spray system from several miles upwind from a target or to in some other way clandestinely deliver biological weapons, and the difficulty of detecting biological aerosols makes these weapons well suited for surprise attacks.[31] The nonspecific nature of the early symptoms of most diseases of concern can mask the beginning of a man-made outbreak and enhance the likelihood that such an attack will catch an adversary unprepared. Numerous exercises and simulations have demonstrated current U.S. vulnerability to clandestine attacks with biological weapons.[32]

This reliance on surprise, however, exposes an Achilles' heel of biological weapons. Accurate intelligence on an adversary's biological warfare capabilities can substantially reduce the effectiveness of a biological attack by providing the defender with sufficient information to organize public health and medical measures to mitigate the consequences of an attack.

---

28. This wider range of agents, however, may not be well suited to large-scale, outdoor aerosolization and would thus be limited to aerosol dissemination inside buildings or the contamination of food and water supplies.
29. Lederberg and Whitesides, *Biological Defense*, p. 12. This assessment is apparently based on information regarding the former Soviet biological weapons program. It is not known, however, to what extent Russia has continued the work initiated during the Soviet era or what other nations have accomplished in this field.
30. Edward Eitzen and Ernest Takafuji, "Historical Overview of Biological Warfare," in Frederick Sidell, Ernest Takafuji, and David Franz, eds., *Medical Aspects of Chemical and Biological Warfare* (Washington, D.C.: Office of the Surgeon General, 1997), pp. 443–444.
31. Field tests by the U.S. Army in the 1950s and 1960s demonstrated the ease of conducting covert attacks with biological weapons against buildings, subway systems, air bases, and cities. William C. Patrick III, "Biological Warfare Scenarios," in Scott P. Layne, Tony J. Beugelsdijk, and C. Kumar N. Patel, eds., *Firepower in the Lab: Automation in the Fight against Infectious Diseases and Bioterrorism* (Washington, D.C.: Joseph Henry Press, 2001), pp. 215–223.
32. Judith Miller, "Exercise Finds U.S. Unable to Handle Germ War Threat," *New York Times,* April 26, 1998, p. A1; Thomas V. Inglesby, Rita Grossman, and Tara O'Toole, "A Plague on Your City: Observations from TOPOFF," *Clinical Infectious Diseases,* Vol. 32, No. 3 (February 2001), pp. 436–445; and Tara O'Toole, Michael Mair, and Thomas V. Inglesby, "Shining Light on Dark Winter: Lessons Learned," *Clinical Infectious Diseases,* Vol. 34, No. 7 (April 2002), pp. 972–983.

THE DIFFICULTY OF DEFENSE

Defensive biological warfare includes measures to prevent, mitigate, and treat the effects of a biological weapon attack. Biological defenses include vaccines and other pharmaceuticals, early warning systems, and physical protection. Given the range of available agents, the agent-specific nature of most defenses, the time lag required to develop new vaccines, and the ease with which an attacker can achieve surprise, defending a large population against a significant number of threat agents is a daunting task that would require a huge investment. Biological weapons, however, are in some ways more vulnerable to countermeasures than high explosives, chemical weapons, or nuclear weapons. They are unique among weapon systems in that vaccines can protect soldiers and civilians before an actual attack.[33] Although licensed vaccines are currently available for only two of the most dangerous biological warfare agents—*B. anthracis* and *variola major*—the U.S. Department of Defense and the National Institutes of Health are developing more than twelve new biodefense vaccines.[34] Even though immunizing vulnerable populations against the full range of biological warfare threats is not feasible or desirable, the availability of sufficient stockpiles of appropriate vaccines is still valuable as a deterrent to potential attackers, as a defensive measure if warning of an attack is received, as a form of postexposure prophylaxis for anthrax and smallpox, and as a reassuring symbol of preparedness.

Given the limitations of vaccines, defenses against biological weapons rely more on early detection of a biological attack and postexposure prophylaxis with antimicrobial drugs. The incubation period following infection with a pathogen, typically several days, provides a window of opportunity for the detection of a biological attack and the preparation of a response.[35] Aerosol detection devices and public health surveillance systems can provide the early warning necessary to launch a medical intervention to mitigate the consequences of a biological attack. Although current systems do not yet offer rapid,

---

33. For vaccines to be effective, defenders must be able to meet the following conditions: identification of the target population, knowledge of the specific threat agent, availability of the appropriate vaccine, and time for the vaccine to be administered to the target population before an attack. David R. Franz, "Physical and Medical Countermeasures to Biological Weapons," Director's Series on Proliferation No. 4 (Livermore, Calif.: Lawrence Livermore National Laboratory, May 1994), pp. 59–60.

34. Department of Defense, *Chemical and Biological Defense Program*, Vol. 1, p. 62; and Tara Palmore, Greg Folkers, Carole Heilman, John R. La Montagne, and Anthony S. Fauci, "The NIAID Research Agenda on Biodefense," *ASM News*, Vol. 68, No. 8 (August 2002), pp. 376–377.

35. Arnold Kaufmann, Martin I. Meltzer, and George Schmid, "The Economic Impact of a Bioterrorist Attack: Are Prevention and Postattack Intervention Programs Justifiable?" *Emerging Infectious Diseases*, Vol. 3, No. 2 (April–June 1997), pp. 83–94.

accurate, and broad-spectrum detection and identification capabilities, new capabilities are under development.[36] Administered promptly after infection or the onset of symptoms, antibiotics can significantly reduce the morbidity and mortality of most bacterial and rickettsial agents. In contrast, there are few effective medical treatments for viral infections. Quarantine and vaccination can reduce the impact of contagious diseases such as smallpox.[37]

Physical defenses prevent exposure to biological warfare agents by filtering the air to remove dangerous particles. Simple masks, such as those used to prevent the inhalation of dust as well as more harmful materials, have been touted as being able to provide relatively inexpensive protection to civilian populations and military forces.[38] To be effective against a surprise attack, the use of these masks would have to be triggered by real-time detection of an attack, a capability that does not yet exist. Alternatively, military and health care personnel and others could wear masks when the threat of a biological attack is heightened, such as during a crisis or conflict. The prolonged use of such masks, however, would be difficult for several reasons: growing discomfort, especially during intense physical activity; the erosion of mask integrity and fit with rugged use; interference with face-to-face and radio communication; and the need to unmask to eat and drink.[39] Finally, masks do not prevent exposure if improperly fitted or if the concentration of agent goes beyond a certain level. Given the inability to detect a biological attack in real time, the most feasible type of physical defenses are buildings and vehicles equipped with filters and positive pressure systems that prevent the infiltration of biological aerosol clouds. Because of their expense, such systems are rare outside of the military. Nonetheless, they hold much promise for defending against biological attacks because they are not agent specific and can function continuously.[40]

---

36. Gregory Koblentz, "Biological Terrorism: Understanding the Threat and the Response," in Arnold Howitt and Robyn Pangi, eds., *Countering Terrorism: Dimensions of Preparedness* (Cambridge, Mass.: MIT Press, 2003), pp. 123–143.

37. Martin I. Meltzer, Inger Damon, James W. LeDuc, and J. Donald Millar, "Modeling Potential Responses to Smallpox as a Bioterrorism Weapon," *Emerging Infectious Diseases*, Vol. 7, No. 6 (November–December 2001), pp. 959–969.

38. Karl Lowe, Graham S. Pearson, and Victor Utgoff, "Potential Values of a Simple Biological Warfare Protective Mask," in Lederberg, *Biological Weapons*, pp. 263–281; and Stanley L. Weiner, "Strategies for the Prevention of a Successful Biological Warfare Aerosol Attack," *Military Medicine*, Vol. 161, No. 5 (May 1996), pp. 251–256.

39. See John Martyny, Craig S. Glazer, and Lee S. Newman, "Respiratory Protection," *New England Journal of Medicine*, September 12, 2002, p. 827.

40. Lester L. Yuan, "Sheltering Effects of Buildings from Biological Weapons," *Science and Global Society*, Vol. 8, No. 3 (2000), pp. 287–313; and Richard L. Garwin, Ralph E. Gomory, and Matthew S. Meselson, "How to Fight Bioterrorism," *Washington Post*, May 14, 2002, p. A21.

Proliferation to Dissatisfied Actors

Preventing the spread of biological warfare capabilities to dissatisfied actors seeking a means to challenge the status quo is extremely difficult. The proliferation of biological weapons is facilitated by the dual-use nature of biotechnology, which also complicates verification of the 1972 Biological Weapons Convention (BWC). The BWC prohibits the development, production, stockpiling, acquisition, and retention of biological weapons.[41] It does not include provisions for verification. In 2001, negotiations to develop a protocol to strengthen the BWC were halted after the United States announced that it would not accept the draft protocol. According to U.S. officials, the proposed protocol was not intrusive enough to detect clandestine biological weapons activities, yet it was too invasive to adequately safeguard proprietary and classified information.[42]

Actors pursuing biological weapons are motivated by a variety of factors.[43] The secrecy that shrouds biological weapons programs and the lack of reliable information regarding decisions to develop such programs, however, complicate efforts to study their motivations more thoroughly.[44] Nevertheless, an examination of the characteristics of biological weapons strongly suggests that they are attractive primarily to dissatisfied actors—whether states or terrorists. Biological weapons have military utility across the spectrum of conflict, rely on

---

41. The BWC does not prohibit research on biological and toxin agents, and it allows their development and production for protective, prophylactic, or other peaceful purposes. The convention, however, does not define activities that constitute research or are considered protective, prophylactic, or peaceful. Barend ter Haar, *The Future of Biological Weapons* (New York: Praeger, 1991), p. 16.
42. Ambassador Donald Mahley, "Statement by the United States to the Ad Hoc Group of Biological Weapons Convention States Parties," Geneva, Switzerland, July 25, 2001, http://www.state.gov/t/ac/rls/rm/2001/5497.htm.
43. See Chevrier, "Deliberate Disease," pp. 395–417; Jonathan B. Tucker, "Motivations For and Against Proliferation: The Case of the Middle East," in Zilinskas, *Biological Warfare*, pp. 27–52; and W. Seth Carus, "The Proliferation of Biological Weapons," in Brad Roberts, ed., *Biological Weapons: Weapons of the Future?* (Washington, D.C.: Center for Strategic and International Studies, 1993), pp. 19–27.
44. States also have an incentive to misrepresent their programs as being provoked by others or for the purpose of deterrence. In 1995, Iraq claimed that it developed strategic chemical and biological weapons as part of a deterrent strategy, but the United Nations Special Commission (UNSCOM) uncovered evidence that Iraq also planned on using these weapons for surprise attacks. United Nations Security Council, *Report of the Secretary-General on the Status of the Implementation of the Special Commission's Plan for the Ongoing Monitoring and Verification of Iraq's Compliance with Relevant Parts of Section C of Security Council Resolution 687 (1991)*, S/1995/864 (New York: United Nations, October 11, 1995), p. 11.

surprise, and do not destroy property. These characteristics favor the use of such weapons in offensive operations and asymmetric strategies against stronger opponents. The outlaw status of biological weapons renders them undesirable to status quo states interested primarily in self-defense. In addition, the relative ease of accessibility, high levels of potency, and potentially huge psychological impact combine to make biological weapons attractive to extremist religious terrorist groups interested in maximizing casualties and fear. In sum, dissatisfied actors—both states and terrorists—have the opportunity and motivation to acquire these weapons.

OPPORTUNITY TO OBTAIN BIOLOGICAL WEAPONS

Traditional arms control and nonproliferation measures are significantly less successful at halting the spread of biological weapons than other proscribed weapons. Effective biological disarmament faces two high hurdles: (1) the ease of acquiring the dual-use materials and technologies required to develop biological weapons, and (2) the difficulty in verifying that these resources are not being used for hostile purposes.

The dual-use nature of biotechnology means that materials, equipment, skills, and facilities designed for peaceful endeavors can also be exploited for hostile purposes. These resources are widely available on the open market and are highly sought by countries interested in economic development.[45] Export controls may slow national biological weapons programs and block access to the most advanced technologies, but they cannot prevent a determined state from acquiring a desired capability.[46] Although domestic access to dangerous pathogens in the United States has been regulated since 1996, these pathogens (with the exception of *variola major*) are available in nature and from a number of germ banks around the world.[47] In addition, domestic acquisition of dual-use equipment remains unfettered, greatly facilitating the development of biological weapons by terrorists.[48] This is not to say that the technical obstacles to

45. Brad Roberts, "Rethinking Export Controls on Dual-Use Materials and Technologies: From Trade Restraints to Trade Enablers," *Arena*, No. 2 (June 1995).
46. David A. Kay, "Denial and Deception Practices of WMD Proliferators: Iraq and Beyond," *Washington Quarterly*, Vol. 18, No. 1 (Winter 1995), pp. 85–105; and Gordon Vachon, "The Australia Group and Proliferation Concerns," *UNIDIR NewsLetter*, No. 33 (1996), pp. 59–61.
47. Michael Barletta, Amy Sands, and Jonathan B. Tucker, "Keeping Track of Anthrax: The Case for a Biosecurity Convention," *Bulletin of the Atomic Scientists*, Vol. 58, No. 3 (May/June 2002), pp. 58–59.
48. Barry Kellman, "Biological Terrorism: Legal Measures for Preventing Catastrophe," *Harvard Journal of Law and Public Policy*, Vol. 24, No. 2 (Spring 2001), pp. 457–462.

developing a biological weapon are trivial, but given the proper materials, skills, and equipment, these obstacles are surmountable.[49]

Preventing the acquisition of biological weapons through arms control and disarmament is extremely difficult.[50] Verification, the ability to confirm whether a nation is complying with its treaty obligations, is the foundation of effective arms control and disarmament.[51] The core problem in verifying compliance with biological disarmament is that the capabilities for conducting the research, development, production, and testing of biological weapons are virtually identical to those employed by defensive programs and in legitimate civilian enterprises.[52] There are few aspects of a biological weapons program that are unique to offensive applications and are readily detectable by outsiders. Advanced biotechnologies make it unnecessary to maintain large dedicated production plants, stockpiles of bulk agents, or filled munitions that would provide intelligence agencies or inspectors with a "smoking gun." States suspected of failing to meet their obligations under the BWC might seek to portray certain biotechnology-related capabilities and activities that cannot be justified as having a civilian purpose—such as working with dangerous pathogens or experimenting with aerosols of biological agents—as being part of a defensive program permissible under the BWC.[53] The BWC does not di-

---

49. On the difficulties of developing biological weapons outside of a state-run program, see General Accounting Office, *Need for Comprehensive Threat and Risk Assessments of Chemical and Biological Attacks*, GAO-NSIAD-99–163 (Washington, D.C.: GAO, September 1999).
50. For optimistic views on this issue, see Marie Isabelle Chevrier, "Verifying the Unverifiable: Lessons from the Biological Weapons Convention," *Politics and the Life Sciences*, Vol. 9, No. 1 (August 1990), pp. 93–105; Milton Leitenberg, "Biological Weapons and Arms Control," *Contemporary Security Policy*, Vol. 17, No. 1 (April 1996), pp. 1–79; Raymond A. Zilinskas, "Verifying Compliance to the Biological and Toxin Weapons Convention," *Critical Reviews in Microbiology*, Vol. 24, No. 3 (September 1998), pp. 195–218; and Malcolm Dando, *Preventing Biological Warfare: The Failure of American Leadership* (London: Palgrave, 2002). For pessimistic views, see Kathleen C. Bailey, "Problems with Verifying a Ban on Biological Weapons," Director's Series on Proliferation No. 3 (Livermore, Calif.: Lawrence Livermore National Laboratory, January 1994), pp. 59–63; Michael Moodie, "Arms Control Programs and Biological Weapons," in Roberts, *Biological Weapons*, pp. 47–57; and Robert P. Kadlec, Allan P. Zelicoff, and Ann M. Vrtis, "Biological Weapons Control: Prospects and Implications for the Future," in Lederberg, *Biological Weapons*, pp. 95–111.
51. Arms Control and Disarmament Agency, *Verification: The Critical Element of Arms Control* (Washington, D.C.: U.S. GPO, 1976); and Allan S. Krass, *Verification: How Much Is Enough?* (London: Taylor and Francis, 1985).
52. Office of Technology Assessment, *Technologies Underlying Weapons of Mass Destruction*, pp. 84–87; Zilinskas, "Verifying Compliance to the Biological and Toxin Weapons Convention," pp. 198–199; Susan Berger, "The Challenges of Chemical and Biological Weapons Arms Control Treaty Verification," in Elizabeth J. Kirk, W. Thomas Wander, and Brian D. Smith, eds., *Trends and Implications for Arms Control, Proliferation, and International Security in the Changing Global Environment* (Washington, D.C.: American Association for the Advancement of Science, 1993), pp. 175–189.
53. As a result of the ambiguities between prohibited and legitimate activities, making definitive

rectly address these types of activities.[54] Intrusive methods aimed at uncovering evidence of the development of biological weapons will inevitably require inspections of facilities engaged in biodefense and civilian activities. Defensive and civilian activities frequently have legitimate needs for a limited degree of secrecy to protect national security and proprietary business information.[55] The safeguards for protecting sensitive information insisted on by states uninterested in developing biological weapons necessarily makes it easier for noncompliant states to hide their illicit activities. The failure of the negotiations on the BWC protocol demonstrates the difficulty of striking a widely accepted balance between the competing needs of transparency and secrecy.

Even advocates of strengthening the BWC acknowledge that a verification regime that is sensitive to national security and commercial concerns will likely be unable to reliably detect violations of the treaty.[56] Instead, they contend that even a low probability of detection will deter states from violating the treaty because the costs and risks of such a violation being discovered would outweigh its benefits.[57] Proponents of this argument predicate it on the

---

judgments regarding the compliance of a state believed to be cheating could be difficult. Jonathan B. Tucker, "Strengthening the Biological Weapons Convention," *Arms Control Today*, April 1995, p. 11; and Berger, "The Challenges of Chemical and Biological Weapons Arms Control Treaty Verification," p. 185.

54. The *New York Times* highlighted this ambiguity in September 2001 when it revealed the existence of biodefense projects sponsored by the Department of Defense and Central Intelligence Agency that involved the construction of a small biological agent production facility, the testing of Soviet-designed biological bomblets, and the creation of a genetically engineered strain of *B. anthracis*. The agencies claimed that the purpose of these research projects was defensive and legal under the BWC, but the combination of capabilities under development and the secrecy of the work raised questions at home and abroad about the commitment of the United States to enforcing the treaty. Judith Miller, Stephen Engelberg, and William J. Broad, "U.S. Germ Warfare Research Pushes Treaty Limits," *New York Times*, September 4, 2001, p. A1; Judith Miller, "When Is a Bomb Not a Bomb? Germ Experts Confront U.S.," *New York Times*, September 5, 2001, p. A5; Elisa Harris, "Research Not to Be Hidden," *New York Times*, September 6, 20001, p. A27; and Barbara Hatch Rosenberg and Milton Leitenberg, "Who's Afraid of a Germ Warfare Treaty?" *Los Angeles Times*, September 6, 2001, p. B15.

55. In 1970, the U.S. government committed itself to conducting its defensive program as openly as possible, but determined that the performance of detection systems, threat assessments, and vulnerability studies may require classification. Interdepartmental Political Military Working Group, *Annual Review of United States Chemical Warfare and Biological Research Programs as of 1 November 1970*, December 5, 1970, pp. 23–24, http://foia.state.gov/documents/FOIADocs/000050DB.pdf. On industry concerns regarding the protection of intellectual property, see Al Homberg, "Industry Concerns Regarding Disclosure of Proprietary Information," Director's Series on Proliferation, No. 4 (Livermore, Calif.: Lawrence Livermore National Laboratory, May 23, 1994), pp. 91–100.

56. Chevrier, "Verifying the Unverifiable," p. 99; Zilinskas, "Verifying Compliance to the Biological and Toxin Weapons Convention," p. 211; and Barbara Rosenberg, "U.S. Policy and the BWC Protocol," *CBW Conventions Bulletin*, No. 52 (June 2001), p. 2.

57. Chevrier, "Impediment to Proliferation?" pp. 72–102; and Elisa Harris, "Bioweapons Treaty

assumption that biological weapons lack military utility and therefore are of marginal interest to most states.[58] The nature of international politics, however, provides a strong motivation to dissatisfied actors to pursue biological weapons, even if it means violating treaty commitments, because these weapons offer a potent means of challenging the status quo.

MOTIVATION TO OBTAIN BIOLOGICAL WEAPONS
Biological weapons appeal to both states and terrorists seeking a powerful, terrifying, and flexible weapon. This does not mean, however, that the widespread proliferation of these weapons is inevitable. Most states are satisfied with their overall security and position in the international system. However, deeply dissatisfied states that are willing to use violence to achieve their goals are likely to view biological weapons as a desirable force multiplier.[59] Similarly, among terrorist groups, only a limited number have the kind of radical religious philosophy or apocalyptic worldview that could justify the use of these weapons. This section challenges the myth that biological weapons lack military utility, it describes the properties of biological weapons that would appeal primarily to dissatisfied states, and it discusses the characteristics of terrorist groups interested in these weapons.

MILITARY UTILITY OF BIOLOGICAL WEAPONS. The widespread belief that biological weapons lack military utility is rooted in the United States' unilateral renunciation of biological weapons in 1969 and U.S. ratification of the BWC in 1975.[60] The government publicly justified these decisions in large part on the basis of the unpredictable and uncontrollable consequences of these weapons as well as their supposed lack of military utility.[61] It made these decisions at

Still a Good Idea," *Christian Science Monitor,* August 24, 2001, http://www.csmonitor.com/2001/0824/p11s3-coop.html.
58. Chevrier, "Impediment to Proliferation?" p. 95; Elisa Harris, "The Biological and Toxin Weapons Convention," in Albert Carnesale and Richard Haass, eds., *Superpower Arms Control: Setting the Record Straight* (Cambridge, Mass.: Ballinger, 1987), p. 205.
59. For a discussion of the role of revisionist states in international politics, see Randall L. Schweller, "Bandwagoning for Profit: Bringing the Revisionist State Back In," *International Security,* Vol. 19, No. 1 (Summer 1994), pp. 72–107; and Alastair Iain Johnston, "Is China a Status Quo Power?" *International Security,* Vol. 27, No. 4 (Spring 2003), pp. 8–11.
60. For the decisionmaking process leading to the 1969 decision, see Jonathan B. Tucker, "A Farewell to Germs: The U.S. Renunciation of Biological and Toxin Warfare, 1969–70," *International Security,* Vol. 27, No. 1 (Summer 2002), pp. 107–148.
61. "Remarks of the President on Announcing the Chemical and Biological Defense Policies and Programs," Office of the White House Press Secretary, The White House, November 25, 1969, Folder 5: Chemical, Biological Warfare (Toxins, etc.), Vol. 1, Box 310, National Security Council Subject Files, Nixon Presidential Materials, National Archives, College Park, Maryland [hereafter Nixon papers]; and Senate Committee on Foreign Relations, "Prohibition of Chemical and Biologi-

least in part, however, after concluding that the destructive power of these weapons and their relative accessibility posed a serious proliferation threat.[62] In addition, given its formidable nuclear and conventional forces, the United States did not believe that it needed biological weapons to cause massive civilian casualties or to deter the use of biological weapons by other states. For the United States, the contribution of these weapons to achieving other missions was not worth the price of a heightened risk of proliferation.[63] It is a mistake to extrapolate from this decision, however, that biological weapons are, in the words of Thomas Schelling, "ridiculous weapons that nobody is interested in having even if the other side is foolish enough to procure them."[64] Although biological weapons may have had marginal military utility for the United States in 1969, history has shown that this calculation is not universally applicable. Indeed, shortly after the U.S. decision to abandon these weapons, the Soviet Union decided to dramatically expand its own program and develop a new generation of biological weapons.[65] In addition, since 1972 the number of states suspected of developing these weapons has more than tripled from four to thirteen.[66]

Although biological weapons have not been used in modern times, it is possible to assess their military utility based on the characteristics of these weapons, the types of weapons developed and fielded, and the doctrines adopted. The diversity of available agents and the range of their effects could provide military planners with a flexible weapon system capable of carrying out a range of missions against a broad selection of targets.[67] At the tactical level, the

cal Weapons," 93d Cong., 2d sess., December 10, 1974, p. 10; and Arms Control and Disarmament Agency, *Verification*, pp. 17–18.
62. Matthew Meselson, "The Problem of Biological Weapons," undated, http://www.pugwash.org/reports/cbw/cbw5.htm; Julian P. Perry Robinson, "Some Political Aspects of the Control of Biological Weapons," *Science in Parliament*, Vol. 53, No. 3 (May/June 1996), pp. 6–11; Graham S. Pearson, "Biological Weapons: A Priority Concern," Director's Series on Proliferation No. 4 (Livermore, Calif.: Lawrence Livermore National Laboratory, May 1994), p. 42; and Gradon Carter, "Biological Warfare and Biological Defence in the United Kingdom, 1940–1979," *RUSI Journal*, Vol. 137, No. 6 (December 1992), p. 72.
63. Han Swyter, "Political Considerations and Analysis of Military Requirements for Chemical and Biological Weapons," *Proceedings of the National Academy of Sciences*, Vol. 65, No. 1 (January 15, 1970), pp. 261–270.
64. Thomas C. Schelling, *Choice and Consequence* (Cambridge, Mass.: Harvard University Press, 1984), p. 253, as cited in Chevrier, "Impediment to Proliferation?" p. 84.
65. Alibek, *Biohazard*; and Anthony Rimmington, "The Soviet Union's Offensive Program: The Implications for Contemporary Arms Control," in Susan Wright, ed., *Biological Warfare and Disarmament: New Problems/New Perspectives* (Lanham, Md.: Rowman and Littlefield, 2002), pp. 103–150.
66. General Accounting Office, *Arms Control: Efforts to Strengthen the Biological Weapons Convention*, GAO-02–1038 (Washington, D.C.: GAO, September 2002), pp. 10–11.
67. Brad Roberts, "Between Panic and Complacency: Calibrating the Chemical and Biological

delayed effects of biological agents and the susceptibility of aerosol clouds to vagaries in meteorological and environmental conditions limit their utility to static battles of attrition. The ability of aerosol clouds to penetrate fortifications and buildings could provide an attacker with a means of "softening up" a hardened enemy position before an assault.[68] The risk of infecting one's troops could be minimized by vaccinating them ahead of time, employing biological weapons far from friendly forces, or using only noncontagious or short-lived agents. States lacking precision-guided munitions and cluster bombs may find the cost effectiveness of these weapons attractive. Iraq under Saddam Hussein, for example, experimented with biological warheads for short-range artillery rockets during the final stages of its war of attrition with Iran (1980–88).[69]

Biological weapons may have their greatest military utility at the operational or theater level of warfare.[70] The goal of attacks on logistical networks, reinforcements, and command and control facilities is "to induce operational paralysis, which reduces the enemy's ability to move and coordinate forces in the theater."[71] At various times, the United States, the Soviet Union, and Iraq developed biological weapons and doctrines for their use at the operational level of warfare.[72] Targets in the enemy's rear area could be selected so that the effects of an attack were at their height when friendly forces plan on attacking the objective. The ability of some biological agents to sicken victims for weeks or months could also outweigh the delayed effects of such agents.[73] In addition, the use of incapacitating agents instead of lethal ones might allow an aggressor to seize its objectives without provoking regime-threatening retaliation

Warfare Problem," in Stuart E. Johnson, ed., *The Niche Threat: Deterring the Use of Chemical and Biological Weapons* (Washington, D.C.: National Defense University Press, 1997), pp. 9–41.

68. U.S. Army, *Employment of Chemical and Biological Agents,* Army Field Manual No. 3–10 (Washington, D.C.: Department of the Army, March 31, 1966), p. 47.

69. International Institute for Strategic Studies, *Strategic Survey, 1996/1997* (Oxford: Oxford University Press, 1997), p. 38.

70. This potential, however, has been ignored in many analyses of these weapons. Zilinskas, "Biological Warfare and the Third World"; and Richard Novick and Seth Shulman, "New Forms of Biological Warfare?" in Wright, *Preventing a Biological Arms Race,* pp. 105–106. An exception to this view is W. Seth Carus, *The Poor Man's Atomic Bomb? Biological Weapons in the Middle East,* Policy Paper No. 23 (Washington, D.C.: Washington Institute for Near East Policy, 1991), pp. 36–37.

71. Robert A. Pape, *Bombing to Win: Air Power and Coercion in War* (Ithaca, N.Y.: Cornell University Press, 1996), p. 72.

72. See, respectively, U.S. Army, *Employment of Chemical and Biological Agents;* Jonathan B. Tucker, "Biological Weapons in the Former Soviet Union: An Interview with Dr. Kenneth Alibek," *Nonproliferation Review,* Vol. 6, No. 3 (Spring–Summer 1999), p. 2; and Timothy McCarthy and Jonathan B. Tucker, "Saddam's Toxic Arsenal: Chemical and Biological Weapons in the Gulf Wars," in Lavoy, Sagan, and Wirtz, *Planning the Unthinkable,* p. 62.

73. The use of incapacitating agents instead of lethal ones would have the additional benefit of burdening the target with large numbers of wounded soldiers, who typically absorb more resources than fatalities.

from a nuclear-armed opponent. Power projection forces that rely on a small number of large facilities with primarily civilian workforces are particularly vulnerable to such disruptive attacks.[74] As a result, the employment of biological weapons against theater targets could serve as a potent force multiplier for a conventional military operation.[75] For this reason, the use of biological weapons as part of an asymmetric strategy to deter, prevent, or disrupt the intervention of U.S. forces in the Middle East or Northeast Asia is a major concern for American defense planners.[76]

At the strategic level of warfare, the goal is to reduce the willingness or ability of the enemy to continue to prosecute a war. States can achieve this objective either through attacks targeted at civilians, with the goal of increasing pressure on the government to yield, or through attacks aimed at damaging the enemy's economy to the point where the state can no longer effectively resist.[77] Biological warfare can target civilians directly with antipersonnel agents or indirectly with antilivestock or anticrop agents that could be used against agricultural targets to reduce an enemy's food supply. The ability of biological warfare agents to be disseminated over large areas and for agents such as *variola* virus and *y. pestis* to cause epidemics makes them well suited for strategic attacks.[78] The delayed effects of biological weapons and uncertainties surrounding the downwind travel of the aerosol cloud are less important for strategic attacks that do not require precision or immediate results. In addition, the disproportionate fear that these "dreaded" weapons evoke could amplify the psychological impact of even a small-scale biological attack.[79] In their offensive programs, the United States, the Soviet Union, and Iraq developed a

74. Robert J. Larsen and Robert P. Kadlec, *Biological Warfare: A Post–Cold War Threat to America's Strategic Mobility Forces*, Ridgway Viewpoint 95–3 (Pittsburgh, Penn.: Matthew B. Ridgway Center for Strategic Studies, 1995), pp. 12–15.
75. *Assessment of the Impact of Chemical and Biological Weapons on Joint Operations in 2010: A Summary Report* (McLean, Va.: Booz, Allen, and Hamilton, November 1997).
76. Department of Defense, *Report of the Quadrennial Defense Review* (Washington, D.C.: U.S. GPO, May 1997), p. 13; and George W. Bush, *National Security Strategy of the United States of America* (Washington, D.C.: White House, September 2002), pp. 13–16.
77. Pape, *Bombing to Win*, pp. 42–47.
78. There are also a number of viral agents and fungal agents that can cause epidemics among livestock and crops, respectively. See Simon M. Whitby, *Biological Warfare against Crops* (New York: Palgrave, 2002); and Terrance M. Wilson, Linda Logan-Henfrey, Richard Weller, and Barry Kellman, "Agroterrorism, Biological Crimes, and Biological Warfare Targeting Animal Agriculture," in Corrie Brown and Carole Bolin, eds., *Emerging Diseases of Animals* (Washington, D.C.: ASM Press, 2000), pp. 23–57.
79. Jessica Stern, "Dreaded Risks and the Control of Biological Weapons," *International Security*, Vol. 27, No. 3 (Winter 2002/03), pp. 102–106.

range of aircraft- and missile-delivered biological weapons and doctrines for use against urban populations and agricultural targets.[80] According to John Steinbruner, Soviet military planners "might have calculated that with judicious selection of the agents and timing of their delivery, the urban populations of Western Europe might be sufficiently weakened to allow an occupying army to accomplish an otherwise impossible task."[81]

ATTRACTIONS OF BIOLOGICAL WEAPONS TO DISSATISFIED STATES. Biological weapons are more attractive to dissatisfied states than status quo states for three reasons. First, pathogens and poisons have long been the subject of international opprobrium and efforts to control or eliminate them.[82] The 1925 Geneva Protocol banned the use of chemical and biological weapons, and the BWC prohibited the development and possession of biological weapons.[83] As a result, states that are satisfied with the status quo are unlikely to pursue these weapons. Not only are such states unlikely to develop these weapons, but they are also unlikely to use them during wartime to repulse an aggressor for fear of alienating the international community or key allies.[84] On the other hand, states that plan on using violence to challenge the status quo would not likely demonstrate similar respect for international treaties. The history of chemical warfare supports this proposition. During the twentieth century, the state that initiated hostilities was always the first to use lethal chemical weapons.[85]

---

80. See Ed Regis, *The Biology of Doom: The History of America's Secret Germ Warfare Project* (New York: Henry Holt, 1999), pp. 138–157; Christopher Davis, "Nuclear Blindness: An Overview of the Biological Weapons Programs of the Former Soviet Union and Iraq," *Emerging Infectious Diseases*, Vol. 5, No. 4 (July–August 1999), pp. 509–512; Zilinskas, "Iraq's Biological Weapons," p. 141; Whitby, *Biological Warfare against Crops*, pp. 10–21, 94–117; and Rimmington, "The Soviet Union's Offensive Program," pp. 113–115.
81. Steinbruner, "Biological Weapons," p. 90.
82. John Ellis van Courtland Moon, "Controlling Chemical and Biological Weapons through World War II," in Richard Burns, ed., *Encyclopedia of Arms Control and Disarmament*, Vol. 2 (New York: Charles Scribner's Sons, 1993), pp. 657–674.
83. Ironically, the development of biological weapons by revisionist states such as the Soviet Union and Imperial Japan may have been partly inspired by these agreements. On Japanese interest in chemical and biological weapons due to the Geneva Protocol, see Peter Williams and David Wallace, *Unit 731: Japan's Secret Biological Warfare in World War II* (New York: Free Press, 1989), pp. 7–8. The Soviet Union launched new efforts to develop biological weapons in the 1920s and 1970s following the creation of both the Geneva Protocol and the BWC. See Valentin Bojtzov and Erhard Geissler, "Military Biology in the USSR, 1920–1945," in Geissler and Moon, *Biological and Toxin Weapons*, pp. 156–157; and Rimmington, "The Soviet Union's Offensive Program," pp. 105–106.
84. States that do not expect external support in the event of an attack may not feel limited in their means of self-defense.
85. Confirmed cases of the use of chemical weapons initiated by the aggressor include Germany during World War I, the Allies during their intervention into the Russian civil war from 1919 to 1921, Italy against Ethiopia from 1935 to 1936, Japan against China between 1937 and 1945, Egypt

Second, biological weapons rely on surprise for much of their effectiveness. In general, attackers, not defenders, depend on surprise to achieve their objectives. As John Mearsheimer notes, "One important advantage held by the offense is the ability to choose the main point of attack for the initial battles, to move forces there surreptitiously, and to surprise the defender."[86] Aggressors are better prepared not only to employ biological weapons but also to defend against them, because they can anticipate enemy retaliation and prepare accordingly.[87] In addition, the need for surprise reduces the utility of these weapons for other strategies such as blackmail or deterrence. According to Robert Pape, "Military strategies that depend on surprise for their effectiveness have no coercive value because they cannot be used to *threaten* the target with defeat."[88] Robert Jervis uses a nineteenth-century newspaper commentary to illustrate the implications of a weapon that relies on surprise: "As a measure of defense, knives, dirks, and sword canes are entirely useless. They are fit only for attack, and all such attacks are of murderous character. Whoever carries such a weapon has prepared himself for homicide."[89]

Third, biological weapons do not damage or destroy property. By degrading enemy capabilities while preserving transportation infrastructure, biological weapons could be used to facilitate the advance of a blitzkrieg-style armored attack. Such weapons could also offer an expansionist state the means of seizing valuable resources such as cities and industrial facilities without risking their destruction. To reduce the chances of contaminating the desired assets, biological agents with a high decay rate that degrade rapidly upon release could be selected, and attacks could be timed to take place shortly before sunrise to minimize the agent's half-life.[90]

TERRORIST MOTIVATION. Terrorism experts have identified extremist religious groups, particularly those with an apocalyptic worldview, as the most

against Royalist forces in Yemen between 1963 and 1967, and Iraq against Iran during the 1980s. Stockholm International Peace Research Institute, *The Problem of Chemical and Biological Warfare*, Vol. 1: *The Rise of CB Weapons* (New York: Humanities, 1971), pp. 125–161.

86. John J. Mearsheimer, *Conventional Deterrence* (Ithaca, N.Y.: Cornell University Press, 1983), p. 26.

87. *Concepts for Employment of Antipersonnel Biological Warfare*, Information Report No. 1 (Edgewood, Md.: Chemical Corps Board, April 1, 1958), p. 12.

88. Pape, *Bombing to Win*, p. 14 (emphasis in original).

89. Quoted in Robert Jervis, "Cooperation under the Security Dilemma," *World Politics*, Vol. 30, No. 2 (January 1978), pp. 205–206.

90. On the limited risk of serious contamination, see Patrick, "Biological Warfare," p. 6; and Graham S. Pearson, "The Essentials of Biological Threat Assessment," in Zilinskas, *Biological Warfare*, p. 71.

likely terrorists to seek nuclear, biological, or chemical weapons for the purpose of causing mass casualties.[91] Traditional terrorists with ethnic, nationalist, or ideological grievances typically have political objectives that would be harmed if they were to use illegitimate weapons to kill large numbers of civilians. Extremist religious terrorist groups such as al-Qaeda and Japan's Aum Shinrikyo, on the other hand, have shown a proclivity for highly lethal attacks. These groups do not have broad constituencies that they risk alienating by using biological weapons, and their beliefs may permit the indiscriminant mass murder of nonbelievers. The association of disease and pestilence in sacred texts as forms of divine wrath and the dreaded nature of these weapons may further add to their appeal. In addition, some extremist groups may actually welcome severe government retaliation triggered by a biological attack as part of their plan to provoke an apocalyptic confrontation between the forces of good and evil.[92] To date, the very small number of terrorist groups that have had the motivation to use biological weapons on a large scale have been unable to develop the capability to do so.[93] A terrorist group that can combine the capability and motivation to use biological weapons will pose the novel threat of a nonstate actor capable of inflicting catastrophic damage against a perceived enemy.[94]

Biological Weapons Undermine Deterrence

Despite their frequent description as a "poor man's atomic bomb," biological weapons are not well suited to serving as a strategic deterrent.[95] Moreover, the

---

91. Bruce Hoffman, "Terrorists and WMD: Some Preliminary Hypotheses," *Nonproliferation Review*, Vol. 4, No. 3 (Spring/Summer 1997), pp. 45–53; Jessica Stern, "Terrorist Motivations and Unconventional Weapons," in Lavoy, Sagan, and Wirtz, *Planning the Unthinkable*, pp. 202–229; and Jerrold M. Post, "Psychological and Motivational Factors in Terrorist Decision-Making: Implications for CBW Terrorism," in Jonathan B. Tucker, ed., *Toxic Terror: Assessing Terrorist Use of Chemical and Biological Weapons* (Cambridge, Mass.: MIT Press, 2000), pp. 271–289.
92. Stern, "Terrorist Motivations and Unconventional Weapons," pp. 214–216.
93. Case studies of terrorist groups interested in biological weapons can be found in Tucker, *Toxic Terror*; and W. Seth Carus, *Bioterrorism and Biocrimes: The Illicit Use of Biological Agents in the 20th Century* (Washington, D.C.: National Defense University, April 2001).
94. Al-Qaeda is known to be interested in biological weapons and causing mass casualties, but it is not yet believed to have acquired the capability for conducting such an attack. Barton Gellman, "Al Qaeda Near Biological, Chemical Arms Production," *Washington Post*, March 23, 2003, p. A1.
95. Carus, *The Poor Man's Atomic Bomb?*; Neil C. Livingstone and Joseph D. Douglass Jr., *CBW: The Poor Man's Atomic Bomb* (Cambridge, Mass.: Institute for Foreign Policy Analysis, 1984); H. Lee Buchanan, "Poor Man's A-Bomb?" *U.S. Naval Institute Proceedings*, Vol. 123, No. 4 (April 1997), pp. 83–86; and Al J. Venter, "Biological Warfare: The Poor Man's Atomic Bomb," *Jane's Intelligence Review*, Vol. 11, No. 3 (March 1999), pp. 42–47.

accessibility of biological weapons and the ability to conduct anonymous bio-logical attacks reduce a state's ability to deter the use of these weapons.

POOR SUITABILITY FOR STRATEGIC DETERRENCE

The comparison of biological weapons with nuclear weapons is not without basis. Under the right conditions, a biological attack could kill as many people as a nuclear device.[96] This similarity is the basis for most analyses that suggest that biological weapons will have similar political effects as nuclear weapons.[97] According to Susan Martin, biological weapons enable even small states to de-ter threats to their vital interests and intervention by major powers. Because bi-ological weapons are more easily acquired than nuclear weapons, Martin predicts that the benefits of the "biological revolution" will be more wide-spread and have an even more profound impact on international affairs than the nuclear revolution.[98] I argue that despite their potential lethality, biological weapons do not possess the characteristics necessary for an effective strategic deterrent. They may, however, serve as an in-kind deterrent or contribute to a state's general deterrence posture. Nevertheless, the spread of biological war-fare capabilities is not likely to exert a stabilizing influence on international peace and security, as Martin asserts.[99]

The prerequisite for strategic deterrence is the capability of the target of a surprise attack to retaliate by inflicting unacceptable damage against its at-tacker.[100] During the Cold War, the possession of such forces by both super-powers gave rise to the situation of mutual deterrence described as mutual assured destruction. The nuclear revolution is a function not only of the de-structiveness of nuclear weapons but also of their reliability, the lack of effec-tive defenses, and the availability of survivable delivery systems.[101] Although biological weapons have the potential to inflict unacceptable damage against

96. Office of Technology Assessment, *Proliferation of Weapons of Mass Destruction*, pp. 53–54.
97. Fetter, "Ballistic Missiles and Weapons of Mass Destruction," pp. 22–26; and Martin, "The Role of Biological Weapons in International Politics," p. 77.
98. Martin, "The Role of Biological Weapons in International Politics," pp. 81–82, 86–87.
99. For additional analyses of the utility of biological weapons as deterrents, see Stockholm Inter-national Peace Research Institute, *The Problem of Chemical and Biological Warfare*, Vol. 2, pp. 155–159; and Chevrier, "Deliberate Disease," pp. 406–408.
100. Bernard Brodie, "Implications for Military Policy," in Brodie, ed., *The Absolute Weapon: Atomic Power and World Order: Statecraft and the Prospect of Armageddon* (New York: Harcourt, 1946), pp. 76–77, 89–91; and Robert Jervis, *The Meaning of the Nuclear Revolution* (Ithaca, N.Y.: Cornell University Press, 1989).
101. These characteristics are derived from Jervis, *The Meaning of the Nuclear Revolution*; Shai Feldman, *Israeli Nuclear Deterrence: A Strategy for the 1980s* (New York: Columbia University Press, 1982), pp. 32–33; and Van Evera, *Causes of War*, pp. 240–254.

an adversary, they are unable to offer states an "assured" capability for doing so; this shortfall undermines their suitability as a strategic deterrent. Biological weapons differ from nuclear weapons in two important ways that raise doubts about the applicability of strategic deterrence theory to biological warfare.

The first significant difference involves the level of uncertainty associated with the employment of these weapons. Based on a deep understanding of the fundamental scientific principles underlying nuclear weapons as well as extensive operational and experimental experience with them, experts have been able to document the levels of thermal radiation, nuclear radiation, and blast overpressure that cause specified effects in personnel and matériel.[102] Nuclear weapons deliver instantaneous and overwhelming destruction; the effects of biological weapons, on the other hand, are delayed, variable, and difficult to predict. There are ways to reduce this uncertainty by carefully selecting the agent, the delivery system, and the conditions under which an attack is conducted. States that plan on using their biological weapons as a strategic deterrent, however, may not have the luxury of choosing the time and place for a retaliatory strike.[103] In addition, the lack of operational experience with these weapons and the inability to realistically simulate their effects (short of massive human experimentation) impede the ability of states to substantially reduce this level of uncertainty.

The second major difference between nuclear and biological weapons concerns the availability of defenses. There are no effective defenses against the effects of a nuclear attack. As discussed earlier, however, there are countermeasures that can be taken prior to or following a biological attack. This creates two problems for relying on biological weapons as a strategic deterrent. First, the availability of defenses that could significantly mitigate the consequences of a biological attack is likely to reduce the confidence of states in their ability to reliably inflict unacceptable damage against an adversary in a retaliatory strike. The full panoply of defenses need not be deployed constantly at full readiness because the very availability of these defenses may be sufficient to dissuade a state from calculating that it can inflict unacceptable damage. Although civilian populations will remain more vulnerable to biological weapons than military forces, damage limitation remains a viable option for larger,

---

102. Samuel Gladstone and Dolan J. Philip, eds., *Effects of Nuclear Weapons* (Washington, D.C.: U.S. GPO, 1977).
103. In contrast, a state contemplating a first strike or surprise attack with biological weapons would have more flexibility in determining when, where, and how to employ these weapons.

more advanced states facing less sophisticated adversaries. The December 2002 initiative by the United States to vaccinate nearly 1 million soldiers, public health officials, and medical workers against smallpox in advance of the looming war with Iraq illustrates how states can adopt precautionary measures to blunt the effectiveness of an anticipated threat.[104]

Second, the availability of defenses against biological weapons also places a premium on surprise. Surprise requires strict secrecy, which reduces a state's ability to issue credible threats to inflict unacceptable damage against an adversary.[105] Credible deterrent threats would entail revealing details about the nature of a state's biological weapons capabilities. These revelations could reduce the effectiveness of these weapons by compromising the element of surprise and allowing the defender to take appropriate countermeasures. North Korea in the late 1960s and Iraq in the early 1990s employed deterrent strategies based on biological weapons only to have them compromised by secrecy.[106] Regardless of whether a state adopts a strategy of biological deterrence by denial or deterrence by punishment, neither will deter potential adversaries if the intention and capabilities to implement the strategy are unknown.

Secrecy may be an inexpensive and attractive way for gaining security for strategic forces, but it is also risky.[107] Forces that depend on secrecy for their protection are vulnerable to intelligence breakthroughs by an adversary. The

---

104. As of late 2003, fewer than 40,000 civilians had been vaccinated against smallpox, far short of the goal of 440,000. The military immunization campaign, however, was successful in vaccinating more than 500,000 soldiers and military health personnel. David Ruppe, "U.S. Military Official Praises Army Smallpox Vaccination Program," *Global Security Newswire*, October 23, 2003, http://www.nti.org/d_newswire/issues/2003_10_23.html#1AA0288D.

105. Avner Cohen and Benjamin Frankel, "Opaque Proliferation," *Journal of Strategic Studies*, Vol. 13, No. 3 (September 1990), pp. 31–32; and Feldman, *Israeli Nuclear Deterrence*, p. 19.

106. During the 1991 Gulf War, Iraq maintained a secret strategic reserve of mobile missiles armed with chemical and biological warheads. Launch authority for these weapons was predelegated in the event that a nuclear weapon struck Baghdad or that missile commanders lost contact with the leadership in the capital. This policy and the capabilities supporting it, however, were not known to Israel or the United States until revealed by Iraqi officials in 1995. McCarthy and Tucker, "Saddam's Toxic Arsenal," pp. 72–75; and Amatzia Baram, "An Analysis of Iraqi WMD Strategy," *Nonproliferation Review*, Vol. 8, No. 2 (Summer 2001), pp. 34–36. North Korea's aggressive behavior in the late 1960s was reportedly undertaken in the mistaken belief that the nation's new chemical and biological warfare capabilities would deter a strong U.S. response. The United States was not aware of these capabilities, however, and its forceful reaction led the North Korean leadership to moderate its behavior and reassess the deterrent value of their unconventional weapons. Joseph S. Bermudez Jr., "The Democratic People's Republic of Korea and Unconventional Weapons," in Lavoy, Sagan, and Wirtz, *Planning the Unthinkable*, pp. 186–187.

107. Thomas C. Schelling and Morton H. Halperin, *Strategy and Arms Control* (New York: Pergamon, 1985), p. 37.

loss of secrecy could be massive and occur without warning. If a defender has inside information about an attacker's intentions and capabilities, it could seek to develop and stockpile new vaccines and treatments, immunize the at-risk population, distribute protective masks and treatments, enhance public health surveillance, and take other precautions that could substantially miti-gate the impact of a biological weapon attack. Although such information is difficult to acquire, there have been a number of cases where high-level officials knowledgeable about their nation's biological weapons program have defected.[108]

THE DIFFICULTIES OF DETERRING BIOLOGICAL ATTACKS

The accessibility of biological weapons to a diverse set of actors and the ease of covert attacks complicate efforts to deter their use. The proliferation of biologi-cal weapons to nondeterrable actors and the prospect of anonymous attacks could undermine reliance on deterrence as a security strategy and lead states to adopt preventive or preemptive strategies.

ACCESSIBILITY OF BIOLOGICAL WEAPONS. Because of the global diffusion of dual-use biotechnology, biological weapons can be developed by a larger and more diverse group of actors than can nuclear weapons. Even states that are incapable of effectively managing the investment of large amounts of human, financial, and physical capital over the ten years typically required to produce nuclear weapons may still be able to develop biological weapons.[109] In 1993, the Office of Technology Assessment estimated that more than 100 states had the capability to develop biological weapons.[110] This greater accessibility raises the risk that biological weapons could be acquired by an actor that is insensi-tive to costs, values gains more than the status quo, and grossly misperceives the interests or capabilities of others. Such actors can be difficult to deter be-cause they "do not feel the pain of punishment, or they are willing to take great

---

108. In 1989 Vladimir Pasechnik, the director of a major Soviet biological weapons research insti-tute, defected to the United Kingdom. In 1992 Kenneth Alibek, a former deputy director of Biopreparat, the Soviet Union's biological weapons research and development agency, defected to the United States. In 1995 Hussein Kamel, the head of Iraq's weapons of mass destruction pro-grams, defected to Jordan. Tom Mangold and Jeff Goldberg, *Plague Wars: A True Story of Biological Warfare* (New York: St. Martin's, 1999), pp. 91–105, 177–195, 293–294.
109. On the ten-year rule for nuclear weapon's development, see Leonard S. Spector, "Strategic Warning and New Nuclear States," *Defense Intelligence Journal*, Vol. 3, No. 1 (Spring 1994), pp. 33–52. In contrast, Iraq went from biological weapons research to production in five years. See Mitch-ell B. Wallerstein, "Responding to Proliferation Threats," *Strategic Forum*, No. 138 (May 1998), http://www.ndu.edu/inss/strforum/SF138/forum138.html.
110. Office of Technology Assessment, *Technologies Underlying Weapons of Mass Destruction*, p. 85.

pains to gain their goals, or they fail to see the punishment coming."[111] The primary actors of concern in this regard are terrorists.[112] Although no terrorist group has yet succeeded in developing a mass casualty–producing biological weapon, groups such as Aum Shinrikyo and al-Qaeda have demonstrated the ability to employ sophisticated weapons, the desire to cause mass casualties, and an interest in using disease as a weapon.[113] Moreover, the possibility that a state sometime in the future might demonstrate some of these qualities cannot be excluded.[114]

PROSPECT OF ANONYMOUS USE. Biological weapons are relatively easy to develop in secret, are well suited for covert delivery, and do not provide signatures that can be used to identify the attacker. Aum Shinrikyo's dissemination of biological agents in Japan on a dozen separate occasions in the early 1990s went undetected until they were revealed years later during the trial of the cult's leadership.[115] As the Federal Bureau of Investigation's inability to identify the perpetrator of the 2001 anthrax letter attacks has demonstrated, forensic capabilities in this field are limited.[116] The potential accessibility of biological weapon capabilities to large number of actors also complicates efforts to identify the perpetrator of a biological attack. If a state or terrorist group believes that it could conduct an attack anonymously and thereby escape retaliation, deterrence would be ineffective.

A second potential consequence of the anonymous use of biological weapons is catalytic war: a war between two states secretly initiated by a third party. The spread of nuclear weapons in the 1960s created concern that a third party could attack either superpower and make it appear to be the work of its rival, sparking a crisis or war.[117] This worry faded in the 1970s with the signing of

---

111. Van Evera, *Causes of War*, p. 242.
112. On the difficulty of deterring terrorists, see Paul K. Davis and Brian M. Jenkins, *Deterrence and Influence in Counterterrorism: A Component in the War on al Qaeda* (Santa Monica, Calif.: RAND, 2002), pp. 3–8.
113. Gavin Cameron, "Multi-Track Microproliferation: Lessons from Aum Shinrikyo and Al Qaeda," *Studies in Conflict and Terrorism*, Vol. 22, No. 4 (November 1999), pp. 277–309.
114. The best illustration of this is Japan in December 1941. See Scott D. Sagan, "Origins of the Pacific War," *Journal of Interdisciplinary History*, Vol. 18, No. 4 (Spring 1988), pp. 893–922.
115. None of these attacks was successful because the group inadvertently used harmless versions of *B. anthracis* and botulinum toxin. Sheryl Wu Dunn, Judith Miller, and William J. Broad, "How Japan Germ Terror Alerted the World," *New York Times*, May 26, 1998, p. A1.
116. Martin Enserink, "Useful Data but No Smoking Gun," *Science*, May 10, 2002, pp. 1002–1003; and Laura Meckler, "Genetics Not Helping Anthrax Probe," Associated Press, June 19, 2002, http://www.ph.ucla.edu/epi/bioter/geneticsnothelpanthrax.html.
117. Henry S. Rowen, "Catalytic Nuclear War," in Graham T. Allison, Albert Carnesale, and Joseph S. Nye Jr., eds., *Hawks, Doves, and Owls: An Agenda for Avoiding Nuclear War* (New York: W.W. Norton, 1985), pp. 148–163.

the nuclear Nonproliferation Treaty, which helped to forestall the spread of nuclear weapons, and the advent of advanced early warning systems that allowed the superpowers to detect and track aircraft and ballistic missiles, the primary delivery systems for nuclear weapons. No such measures exist today with regards to biological weapons, so the possibility of a catalytic war sparked by the use of these weapons remains a possibility. For example, a hostile state or terrorist group in the Middle East could stage an attack on U.S. forces in the region that points to another state as the culprit.

PREVENTION AND PREEMPTION. States may adopt preventive or preemptive strategies to neutralize perceived threats posed by the prospect of anonymous biological attacks or the acquisition of biological weapons by nondeterrable actors.[118] After the September 11 terrorist attacks, preventive and preemptive strategies became central to U.S. national security planning.[119] These strategies, however, first emerged during President Bill Clinton's administration in response to the threat of mass casualty terrorism. In 1995, the White House issued a presidential decision directive stating that the acquisition of nuclear, biological, or chemical weapons by terrorists was "unacceptable." According to the directive, "There is no higher priority than preventing the acquisition of this capability or removing this capability from terrorist groups potentially opposed to the U.S."[120] This policy was first implemented on August 20, 1998, when the United States launched cruise missiles at the al-Shifa pharmaceutical plant in Sudan, which officials believed was linked to the development of chemical weapons for al-Qaeda.[121] Despite concerns within the administration about the legal and intelligence justifications for the attack, "the perception of imminent danger was powerful enough to overcome these concerns. At the Principals meeting, [National Security Adviser] Sandy Berger asked, 'What if we do not hit it [al-Shifa] and then, after an attack, nerve gas is released in the New York City subway? What will we say then?'"[122] Although this incident involved terrorist acquisition of chemical (not biological) weapons, it indicates

---

118. The goal of a preventive attack is to thwart a state or terrorist group from developing a threatening capability. Preemptive strikes are conducted when an enemy attack appears imminent. Richard K. Betts, *Surprise Attack: Lessons for Defense Planning* (Washington, D.C.: Brookings, 1982), p. 145.
119. Bush, *National Security Strategy of the United States of America*, pp. 15–16.
120. Memorandum for the Vice President, Subject: "U.S. Policy on Counterterrorism," June 21, 1995, http://www.fas.org/irp/offdocs/pdd39.htm.
121. Gregory Koblentz, "Countering Dual-Use Facilities: Lessons from Iraq and Sudan," *Jane's Intelligence Review*, Vol. 11, No. 3 (March 1999), pp. 48–53.
122. Quoted in Daniel Benjamin and Steven Simon, *The Age of Sacred Terror: Radical Islam's War against America* (New York: Random House, 2002), p. 260.

how states may respond to the specter of terrorist acquisition of even more le-thal weapons. Preventive and preemptive attacks against suspected biological weapons facilities present significant intelligence, military, and diplomatic challenges. The potential consequences of a biological attack and the limita-tions of defensive and deterrent strategies, however, may influence a decision-maker's calculation that the risks of inaction outweigh the costs of action.

Obstruction of Civilian Oversight

The intense secrecy that shrouds biological warfare programs distorts political decisionmaking and restricts civilian oversight. Secrecy also leads to the compartmentalization of information and increases the likelihood of corrup-tion and abuse by program managers. In announcing the results of a review of U.S. chemical and biological warfare programs in 1969, President Richard Nixon stated, "This has been the first thorough review ever undertaken of this subject at the Presidential level. . . . I recall during the eight years that I sat on the National Security Council in the Eisenhower Administration that these subjects, insofar as an appraisal of what the United States had, what our capa-bility was, what other nations had, were really considered taboo."[123] Within the obsessively secretive Soviet Union, the biological weapons program was "one of the best-guarded secrets."[124] It operated under the highest security classification in the Soviet system, even higher than the nuclear weapons pro-gram.[125] Although all weapon programs are subject to some level of secrecy to prevent adversaries from learning about capabilities and vulnerabilities, the secrecy surrounding biological weapons programs has been unusually high.[126]

States pursuing biological weapons have several reasons to subject these programs to stringent secrecy. The general revulsion against biological warfare has motivated states to conceal their research into these weapons. As a British study of chemical and biological weapons (CBW) policy noted, "For in order to avoid provoking the critics of CBW in peacetime, while forearming itself against charges of shortsightedness in case war should find the country unable to retaliate against CBW, a responsible government can hardly be blamed for

---

123. "Remarks of the President on Announcing the Chemical and Biological Defense Policies and Programs," p. 1, Nixon papers.
124. Russian Deputy Foreign Minister Grigory Berdennikov, quoted in John Barry, "Planning a Plague," *Newsweek*, February 1, 1993, p. 40.
125. Mangold and Goldberg, *Plague Wars*, p. 182.
126. Stockholm International Peace Research Institute, *The Problem of Chemical and Biological War-fare*, Vol. 5: *The Prevention of CBW* (New York: Humanities, 1974), p. 138.

procuring the weapons but keeping them dark."[127] Secrecy has become even more important since the creation of the 1972 BWC, which reinforces the norm against developing these weapons and raises the political costs of the discovery of a weapons program. Finally, there is a strategic motivation for wrapping biological weapons in secrecy. Military capabilities that strongly favor the offense, particularly those that rely on surprise, engender higher levels of secrecy.[128]

The intense secrecy surrounding biological weapons programs is inimical to effective decisionmaking and oversight. As described in the literature on opaque proliferation, the strict secrecy surrounding covert nuclear weapons programs leads to compartmentalization that restricts the information available to senior officials about the nature and conduct of these programs and limits the range and knowledge of participants involved in such oversight.[129] In addition, secrecy exacerbates existing information asymmetries between political leaders and military officers or scientists who run biological weapons programs. Such asymmetries enable subordinates to operate with too much autonomy, avoid accountability by concealing potentially embarrassing or damaging information from their superiors, and hinder the implementation of new policies with which they disagree. Large information asymmetries may allow program managers to take actions for their own benefit or for the benefit of their organization that are against the interests of their superiors.[130] Thus, programs escape review, decisions are made with incomplete or inaccurate information, and the exercise of appropriate oversight is hindered.

Three brief cases illustrate the adverse effects of secrecy on the management of major biological warfare programs. In 1975, a congressional investigation exposed a secret stockpile of toxins at the Central Intelligence Agency (CIA) that should have been destroyed years earlier when the United States decided to terminate its offensive biological warfare program.[131] The toxins were the result of cooperation between the CIA and the U.S. Army to develop biological

---

127. United Kingdom Foreign Office, Arms Control and Disarmament Research Unit, "The Arms Control Implications of Chemical and Biological Weapons: Analysis and Proposals," ACDRU 66(2), 2d draft, July 4, 1966, p. 25, FO 371/187448, Public Records Office, London, United Kingdom.

128. Van Evera, *Causes of War*, p. 137.

129. Cohen and Frankel, "Opaque Proliferation," pp. 22, 34; and Peter D. Feaver, "Proliferation Optimism and Theories of Nuclear Operations," *Security Studies*, Vol. 2, Nos. 3–4 (Spring/Summer 1993), pp. 175–178.

130. Peter D. Feaver, *Armed Servants: Agency, Oversight, and Civil-Military Relations* (Cambridge, Mass.: Harvard University Press, 2003), pp. 68–71.

131. Senate Select Committee to Study Governmental Operations with Respect to Intelligence Activities, *Hearings*, Vol. 1: *Unauthorized Storage of Toxic Agents* (Washington, D.C.: U.S. GPO, 1976).

agents and weapons for clandestine operations. An internal CIA review of the program found that it was "characterized by a compartmentation [*sic*] that was extreme even by CIA standards."[132] In contrast to the review of the Defense Department's plans to destroy its stocks of agents and munitions by appropriate federal, state, and local agencies, the destruction of the CIA's holdings of biological and toxin agents stored at Fort Detrick, Maryland, was not subject to any external oversight. As a result, CIA scientists were able to retain a small stockpile of toxins despite the presidential decision to destroy all such agents. The corrosive effects of too much secrecy on oversight was demonstrated again in 2001, when it was reported that the CIA and Defense Department were conducting classified projects to develop limited offensive capabilities for defensive purposes and that some of these activities had not been reported to the National Security Council or included in annual confidence-building declarations to the United Nations.[133]

Political leaders in Moscow in the 1990s experienced problems in obtaining accurate information from the military regarding biological warfare activities, making informed decisions about the future of the program, and ensuring the implementation of new policies. For example, in May 1990, under pressure from the United States and the United Kingdom, Soviet President Mikhail Gorbachev issued a secret decree halting the research, development, and testing activities of Biopreparat, an ostensibly civilian organization also responsible for the development and production of biological weapons. Gen. Yury Kalinin, the head of Biopreparat, and his allies in the military manipulated the formulation and implementation of the decree, however, to preserve as much of the program as possible. The final decree included a loophole inserted by Kalinin that allowed the continued funding of the full range of Biopreparat's activities. Kalinin then withheld the decree from the directors of Biopreparat's institutes so that they could act on it only under orders from headquarters, which were not forthcoming. As a result, the decree had a limited impact on Biopreparat's activities except to better conceal them from the civilians in the Kremlin.[134] According to Jack Matlock, U.S. ambassador to Moscow from 1987

---

132. *Summary Report on CIA Investigation of MKNAOMI*, undated (declassified September 15, 1975), p. 4, in Senate Committee on Human Resources, Subcommittee on Health and Scientific Research, "Biological Testing Involving Human Subjects by the Department of Defense," 95th Cong., 1st sess., March 8 and May 23, 1977, p. 247.
133. Tucker, "A Farewell to Germs," pp. 145–148.
134. Mangold and Goldberg, *Plague Wars*, pp. 109–110, 417, n. 20; and Alibek, *Biohazard*, pp. 190–191

to 1991, "From their behavior, I think the people at the top [in the Kremlin] probably did not know everything. There is plenty of evidence that shows these people were not able to get the information they wanted, because the system was so secret and the political authorities had so little control over the military and KGB. And they had no reliable way to check up on the information they did get."[135] Similar problems plagued efforts by President Boris Yeltsin to dismantle the former Soviet biological weapons program and bring Russia into compliance with the BWC.[136]

Problems of control and oversight also beset South Africa's chemical and biological weapons program that ran from 1981 to 1993. The Truth and Reconciliation Commission that investigated the program, called Project Coast, found that the military committee charged with oversight was "grossly negligent in approving programmes and allocating large sums of money for activities of which they had no understanding, and which they made no effort to understand."[137] This mismanagement resulted in scientific and financial fraud by a "nepotistic, self-serving and self-enriching group of people, misled by those who had a technical grasp of what was happening."[138] In addition, the program managers misled President F.W. de Klerk and later President Nelson Mandela about the offensive orientation of the program and its role in assassination operations.[139] As a result of this lack of oversight, the program's documents and materials were not properly destroyed or accounted for when the program was terminated and thus continued to present a proliferation risk many years later.[140]

These cases demonstrate the range of pathologies that secrecy can introduce into decisionmaking and oversight regarding biological weapons programs. The security implications are subtle but disturbing. Biological weapons programs managed by highly autonomous organizations could evade civilian oversight, manipulate ambiguous intelligence on foreign biological warfare ac-

---

135. Quoted in Mangold and Goldberg, *Plague Wars*, p. 109.
136. See ibid., pp. 158–169.
137. Truth and Reconciliation Commission, *Truth and Reconciliation Commission of South Africa Report*, Vol. 2 (Basingstoke, U.K.: Macmillan Reference Limited, March 1999), p. 522.
138. Ibid., p. 520.
139. Chandré Gould and Peter Folb, *Project Coast: Apartheid's Chemical and Biological Warfare Programme* (Geneva: United Nations, 2002), p. 118; and Marléne Burger, and Chandré Gould, *Secrets and Lies: Wouter Basson and South Africa's Chemical and Biological Warfare Programme* (Cape Town, South Africa: Zebra, 2002), pp. 9, 26.
140. Joby Warrick and John Mintz, "Lethal Legacy: Bioweapons for Sale," *Washington Post*, April 20, 2003, p. A1; and Joby Warrick, "Biotoxins Fall Into Private Hands," *Washington Post*, April 21, 2003, p. A1.

tivities or other information to mislead senior officials, and resist efforts to comply with international obligations. This lack of oversight could be especially dangerous if it allows unsafe or unauthorized experiments to develop new or improved biological weapons. In addition, decisionmakers denied the proper information and expertise may be poorly equipped to assess the strengths and limitations of these weapons. This in turn could lead them to miscalculate their ability to use these weapons covertly to avoid provoking regime-threatening retaliation or place undue confidence in them as a strategic deterrent. Finally, the lack of oversight increases the risk that such programs could become the source of expertise, materials, or weapons for terrorists or other states.

Flawed Threat Assessment

Accurate and timely intelligence has long been regarded as a crucial element in defending against biological weapons. In 1969, President Nixon stated that the unilateral renunciation of biological weapons would not "leave us vulnerable to surprise by an enemy who does not observe these rational restraints. Our intelligence community will continue to watch carefully the nature and extent of the biological programs of others."[141] Strict secrecy and the dual-use nature of biotechnology, however, make biological weapon programs a notoriously difficult target for intelligence agencies. According to the CIA's top nonproliferation analyst in 1999, "Biological weapons (BW) pose, arguably, the most daunting challenge for intelligence collectors and analysts."[142] Biological threat assessments must take into account not only capabilities that are challenging to monitor but also intentions that are even more difficult to discern. As a result, intelligence on foreign biological warfare programs is usually severely deficient. Indeed, the most significant intelligence breakthroughs have resulted from defections by knowledgeable insiders.[143] Only such insiders can provide the information on intent that is required for a comprehensive understanding of a state's biological warfare program.[144] Assessing the biological

---

141. "Statement by the President," Office of the White House Press Secretary, November 25, 1969, p. 2, Nixon papers.

142. Statement by Special Assistant to the DCI for Nonproliferation John A. Lauder to the House Permanent Select Committee on Intelligence, *Worldwide Biological Warfare Threat*, March 3, 1999, http://www.cia.gov/cia/public_affairs/speeches/archives/1999/lauder_speech_030399.html.

143. Prominent examples include Vladimir Pasechnik, Kenneth Alibek, and Hussein Kamel.

144. Intelligence from human sources can be difficult to verify. Moreover, such sources may pur-

threat posed by terrorists is likely to be even more difficult given the intensively secretive nature of such organizations. It is possible that a terrorist group with the motivation and capability to use these weapons will emerge with little or no warning.[145]

The historical record is replete with flawed biological threat assessments that have resulted in significant overestimates and underestimates of an adversary's biological warfare capabilities and intentions. During World War II, both the Allied and Axis powers had poor intelligence on the facilities, scientists, and agents involved in the biological warfare programs of the other side.[146] The U.S. military grossly underestimated the Japanese biological warfare program until it was able to interview personnel captured during and after the war.[147] In contrast, because of their misreading of German intentions, the Allies' fear of a German biological warfare program was greatly exaggerated.[148] Nonetheless, this fear spurred crash programs by the Allies to develop a range of defensive and offensive biological warfare capabilities.[149]

During the Cold War, the United States and its allies also lacked a clear understanding of the Soviet biological weapons program. According to a 1970 U.S. interagency report, "Useful intelligence on actual production, weaponization and stockpiling remains nonexistent, and information on the Soviet biological warfare program remains incomplete in almost all important details."[150] This lack of intelligence led to an underestimation of the size and sophistication of the Soviet biological warfare program that was revealed in 1989

---

posefully or inadvertently transmit false information, thus contributing to flawed assessments, as may have been the case prior to the 2003 U.S. invasion of Iraq. Bob Drogin, "U.S. Suspects It Received False Iraq Arms Tips," *Los Angeles Times,* August 28, 2003, p. A1; and Douglas Jehl, "Agency Belittles Information Given by Iraqi Defectors," *New York Times,* September 29, 2003, p. A1.
145. Neither the United States nor Japan identified Aum Shinrikyo as posing a biological threat prior to the cult's March 1995 sarin gas attack in the Tokyo subway system. Pearson, "The Essentials of Biological Threat Assessment," pp. 79–81.
146. Erhard Geissler, John Ellis van Courtland Moon, and Graham S. Pearson, "Lessons from the History of Biological and Toxin Warfare," in Geissler and Moon, *Biological and Toxin Weapons,* pp. 260–263.
147. Sheldon H. Harris, *Factories of Death: Japanese Biological Warfare, 1932–1945, and the American Cover Up* (London: Routledge, 1994), pp. 160–204.
148. Adolf Hitler had forbidden the development of biological weapons and, as a result, Germany conducted very little offensive biological research during the war. Erhard Geissler, "Biological Warfare Activities in Germany, 1923–1945," in Geissler and Moon, *Biological and Toxin Weapons,* pp. 99–102.
149. Geissler, Moon, and Pearson, "Lessons from the History of Biological and Toxin Warfare," in Geissler and Moon, *Biological and Toxin Weapons,* pp. 259–260.
150. Interdepartmental Political Military Working Group, *Annual Review of United States Chemical Warfare and Biological Research Programs as of 1 November 1970,* p. 19.

by Vladimir Pasechnik, a high-ranking member of Biopreparat and the director of a key biological weapons research institute, following his defection to the United Kingdom. Based on his information, British and U.S. intelligence doubled their estimates of the number of Soviet biological warfare facilities.[151]

Iraq's biological weapons program under Saddam Hussein had been subject to both underestimation and overestimation by the United States. After the 1991 Gulf War, the Pentagon acknowledged that in contrast to its understanding of Iraq's chemical weapons capabilities, "intelligence assessments of the BW threat were much more tenuous."[152] The United States had sufficient information to immunize portions of its forces against Iraq's primary biological warfare agents—*B. anthracis* and botulinum toxin.[153] The intelligence community, however, failed to identify many of Iraq's key biological facilities, including the main production plant at al-Hakam. According to a senior U.S. defense official, "Not even the most alarmed people thought Iraq was as advanced as they in fact were, that they had weaponized systems which were ready for use immediately. What it all adds up to is a program that was . . . very successfully hidden from the world's intelligence community."[154] In contrast, prior to the 2003 invasion of Iraq, the U.S. intelligence community believed that Iraq had stocks of biological agents as well as an active weapons program that was even larger and more advanced than it was in 1991.[155] Two trailers found after the invasion that resembled the mobile biological warfare production plants described by the United States before the war were called "the strongest evidence to date that Iraq was hiding a biological warfare program."[156] The State Department's intelligence bureau, engineers from DIA, and British biological weapons experts, however, have disputed this finding.[157] The controversy sur-

---

151. Bill Gertz, "Defecting Russian Scientist Revealed Biological Arms Efforts," *Washington Times*, July 4, 1992, p. A4; and R. Jeffrey Smith, "Russia Fails to Detail Germ Arms," *Washington Post*, August 31, 1992, p. A1.
152. Department of Defense, *Conduct of the Persian Gulf War: Final Report to Congress* (Washington, D.C.: U.S. GPO, 1992), p. 640.
153. Albert J. Mauroni, *Chemical-Biological Defense: U.S. Military Policies and Decisions in the Gulf War* (Westport, Conn.: Praeger, 1998), pp. 27, 86.
154. Quoted in R. Jeffrey Smith, "Iraq's Drive for a Biological Arsenal," *Washington Post*, November 21, 1997, p. A1.
155. Central Intelligence Agency, *Iraq's Weapons of Mass Destruction Programs* (Langley, Va.: Central Intelligence Agency, October 2002), pp. 2, 13–17.
156. Central Intelligence Agency and Defense Intelligence Agency, *Iraqi Mobile Biological Warfare Agent Production Plants*, May 28, 2003, p. 1, http://cia.gov/cia/reports/iraqi_mobile_plants/index.html.
157. The leading alternative explanation is that the trailers were used to produce hydrogen for weather balloons employed by artillery units. Judith Miller and William J. Broad, "Some Analysts

rounding the trailers highlights the ambiguity inherent in dual-use technologies and the challenges that this poses for conducting accurate and convincing threat assessments.

The difficulty in conducting such assessments has several implications. First, without adequate intelligence, it is more difficult to develop and deploy effective defenses. The agent-specific nature of most medical countermeasures and diagnostic and detection systems requires advance knowledge of the agents that an adversary is developing. As a result, it is "an established principle that offensive developments will always lead and drive defensive developments."[158] In addition, without reliable intelligence indicating that an adversary's biological warfare program poses a significant threat, it may not be possible to mobilize the resources for researching and fielding defenses against the threat.

Second, without credible intelligence, it is much more difficult to rally domestic and international support for diplomatic efforts to bring states into compliance with their biological disarmament obligations.[159] As the investigations into the Soviet and Iraqi biological weapons programs demonstrated, accurate intelligence is also crucial for planning and conducting inspections, as well as analyzing their results.[160]

Third, in the absence of reliable intelligence, governments may engage in worst-case planning and undertake an exaggerated reaction to perceived threats.[161] In light of the similarities between offensive and defensive biological warfare activities, interpreting uncertain intelligence in this way could lead

---

of Iraqi Trailers Reject Germ Use," *New York Times,* June 7, 2003, p. A1; Peter Beaumont, "Iraqi Mobile Labs Nothing to Do with Germ Warfare, Report Finds," *Observer,* June 15, 2003, http://observer.guardian.co.uk/international/story/0,6903,977853,00.html; Douglas Jehl, "Agency Disputes C.I.A. View on Trailers as Weapons Labs," *New York Times,* June 26, 2003, p. A1; and Douglas Jehl, "Iraqi Trailers Said to Make Hydrogen, Not Biological Arms," *New York Times,* August 9, 2003, p. A1.

158. Thomas Dashiell, "The Need for a Defensive Biological Research Program," *Politics and the Life Sciences,* Vol. 9, No. 1 (August 1990), p. 89

159. Paradoxically, the reluctance to share sensitive information may limit the utility of the most useful types of intelligence on foreign biological warfare programs, such as that provided by spies and defectors. According to a participant in the debate on how to confront the Soviet Union with the information provided by Pasechnik in 1989, "We were worried about not being able to convince people because our evidence was secret." Mangold and Goldberg, *Plague Wars,* p. 103.

160. David C. Kelly, "The Trilateral Agreement: Lessons for Biological Weapons Verification," in Trevor Findlay and Oliver Meier, eds., *Verification Yearbook, 2002* (London: VERTIC, 2002), p. 104; and Tim Trevan, "Exploiting Intelligence in International Organizations," in Zilinskas, *Biological Warfare,* pp. 207–224.

161. Robert Jervis, *Perception and Misperception in International Politics* (Princeton, N.J.: Princeton University Press, 1976), pp. 64–66.

to a security dilemma where states take actions to improve their own defense that inadvertently threaten other states.[162] As the number and size of national biological defense programs increases in response to the threat of biological terrorism, other states may perceive these activities as threatening, thereby providing a justification for initiating or continuing a biological weapons program. Timely and dependable intelligence will not negate the threat posed by biological weapons, but it will help to calibrate defensive and diplomatic responses to these threats and reduce the likelihood of counterproductive actions.

Rebuttals and Responses

There are three possible objections to the preceding analysis. The first objection is that terrorists, not states, pose the predominant biological threat.[163] This article's state-centric perspective may appear to be outmoded in the post-September 11 world, but it is both important and practical. National programs to develop biological weapons are both more numerous and more advanced than those of their terrorist counterparts. In addition, states that are hostile to the United States and its allies sponsor many of these programs. Further, as a result of declassification, defections, and investigations, there is much more information available regarding the history and conduct of national biological warfare programs.

The second potential rebuttal is that biological weapons will have their greatest impact on the relations and conflicts of smaller and nonnuclear states. This objection is based on the false premise that these are the only types of states interested in biological weapons and that the strategic consequences of these weapons can be contained to this group of states. Virtually all of the nuclear states, however, developed biological weapons at some point—for purposes ranging from counterinsurgency to operational military employment to strategic attack. Even nuclear states with weak conventional forces may be tempted to use these weapons as force multipliers. In addition, possession of

---

162. Jervis, "Cooperation under the Security Dilemma," pp. 169–170.
163. On the threat of biological terrorism, see Brad Roberts, ed., *Terrorism with Chemical and Biological Weapons: Calibrating Risks and Responses* (Alexandria, Va.: Chemical and Biological Arms Control Institute, 1997); Richard A. Falkenrath, Robert D. Newman, and Bradley A. Thayer, *America's Achilles' Heel: Nuclear, Biological, and Chemical Terrorism and Covert Attack* (Cambridge, Mass.: MIT Press, 1998); and Jessica Stern, *The Ultimate Terrorists* (Cambridge, Mass.: Harvard University Press, 1999).

nuclear weapons will not necessarily deter the use of biological weapons by actors that do not believe they will be identified or that are insensitive to retaliatory threats. Moreover, the use of biological weapons in a regional conflict is likely to involve the ally of a major power and lead to outside intervention or escalation. Like a contagious disease, the security implications of biological weapons will affect some states more than others, but they spread easily and no state is immune.

The third likely objection is that because biological weapons have been used so rarely, this restraint is likely to hold. Therefore, despite their potential military utility, biological weapons will remain marginal in most states' national security calculations. Although modern biological weapons based on aerosol dissemination technology have not been successfully employed by states or terrorists, cruder weapons have been used in modern times.[164] There are also disturbing signs that the normative, operational, and political restraints that have limited the use of these weapons are weaker now then they were thirty years ago. Most of the states currently suspected of developing biological weapons are parties to the 1972 BWC, which illustrates the permeability of the normative barrier to proliferation.[165] The 2001 anthrax letter attacks, the first overt use of biological weapons, weakened the taboo against using disease as a weapon. In addition, advanced biotechnologies that can ameliorate problems in safely producing, storing, and handling these weapons as well as effectively employing them in combat are becoming increasingly available.[166] Further-

---

164. Japan and South Africa employed biological agents for sabotage and counterinsurgency operations. The white-ruled government of Rhodesia, now Zimbabwe, has also been implicated in similar activities. On Japan, see Harris, *Factories of Death*. On Rhodesia and South Africa, see Gould and Folb, *Project Coast*, pp. 24–30, 159–167; and Burger and Gould, *Secrets and Lies*, pp. 15–16, 32–39. In addition, nonstate actors have used biological weapons at least twice in the past twenty years. In 1984 the Rajneeshee cult in Oregon sickened 750 with *Salmonella typhimurium*, and in 2001 an unidentified perpetrator caused twenty-two casualties and disrupted the operations of the U.S. Postal Service and U.S. Senate with five letters containing spores of *B. anthracis*. Ronald Atlas, "Bioterrorism before and after September 11," *Critical Reviews in Microbiology*, Vol. 27, No. 4 (January 2002), pp. 359–361.
165. The State Department lists eight states as not being in compliance with the BWC: China, Cuba, Iran, Iraq, Libya, North Korea, Russia, and Syria. Department of State, *Adherence to and Compliance with Arms Control and Nonproliferation Agreements and Commitments* (Washington, D.C.: Bureau of Verification and Compliance, 2002), http://www.state.gov/documents/organization/22466.pdf.
166. Department of Defense, *Biotechnology and Genetic Engineering: Implications for the Development of New Warfare Agents* (Washington, D.C.: U.S. GPO, 1996); Jonathan B. Tucker, "The Future of Biological Warfare," in W. Thomas Wander and Eric H. Arnett, eds., *The Proliferation of Advanced Weaponry* (Washington, D.C.: American Association for the Advancement of Science, 1992), pp. 61–71; Steven M. Block, "Living Nightmares: Biological Threats Enabled by Molecular Biology," in Sidney D. Drell, Abraham D. Sofaer, and George D. Wilson, eds., *The New Terror: Facing the Threat of Biolog-*

more, the overwhelming conventional superiority of Western states and their allies provides dissatisfied actors with strong incentives to employ biological weapons as part of an asymmetric strategy that may outweigh the political and strategic hazards of using these weapons.[167] Leaders may calculate that they can use their biological weapons as force multipliers to accomplish a fait accompli, tailor their use of these weapons to avoid provoking regime-threatening retaliation, or conduct anonymous attacks and avoid retaliation. Extremist religious terrorist groups such as al-Qaeda and its affiliates that have emerged as direct threats to the United States and its allies are among those most likely to resort to unconventional weapons in their drive to inflict as many casualties and as much terror as possible. As with nuclear weapons, the lack of large-scale use of biological weapons since 1945 is a cause for celebration, but not grounds for complacency.

Conclusion

The global diffusion of dual-use biotechnology, coupled with strong incentives for revisionist states and extremist terrorist groups to harness this technology for malevolent purposes, poses a severe challenge to international peace and stability in the twenty-first century. As biological weapons become more capable and more accessible to a wider range of players, the strategic consequences outlined in this article—proliferation to dissatisfied actors, undermining of deterrence, obstruction of civilian oversight, and flawed threat assessments—should become more evident. This analysis yields four policy prescriptions for countering the growing danger posed by biological weapons.

First, defenses against biological weapons should be strengthened to make these weapons less effective and less likely to be used in future conflicts. Robust defenses against the most threatening agents and further improvements in vaccines, detection, physical defense, diagnosis, surveillance, therapy, and forensics could create sufficient uncertainty in the minds of potential attackers about the likelihood of success to deter such attacks.[168] Besides the sub-

---

ical and Chemical Weapons (Stanford, Calif.: Hoover Institution Press, 1999), pp. 39–75; and Robert P. Kadlec and Alan P. Zelicoff, "Implications of the Biotechnology Revolution for Weapons Development and Arms Control," in Zilinskas, *Biological Warfare*, pp. 11–26.
167. Brad Roberts, *Biological Weapons in Major Theater War* (Alexandria, Va.: Institute for Defense Analysis, November 1998); and United States Commission on National Security/21st Century [Hart-Rudman Commission], *New World Coming: American Security in the 21st Century, Supporting Research and Analysis* (Washington, D.C.: United States Commission on National Security/21st Century, September 1999), p. 50.
168. For a biodefense research agenda, see National Research Council, *Making the Nation Safer: The*

stantial investment that must be made in research and development, medical countermeasures need to be stockpiled, and local public health and medical communities and military units need to be prepared to detect and respond to a biological attack.[169] At the same time, these efforts should be accompanied by transparency measures to ensure that these defensive programs are not misinterpreted by other states as threatening.[170] The use of biological weapons anywhere would further erode the taboo against these weapons everywhere. Therefore, these defensive innovations should also be made available internationally to reduce the incentives for any actor to develop or use these weapons.[171] To the extent that the tools and technologies developed to defend against biological weapons are also useful in combating naturally occurring infectious diseases, this initiative would have humanitarian as well as security benefits.

Second, the capability to detect clandestine offensive activities and distinguish them from defensive and civilian activities is needed for three reasons: (1) to establish a foundation for verification, (2) to provide policymakers with insights into the capabilities and intentions of other states, and (3) to improve the effectiveness of defenses. Accurate and timely intelligence is crucial to achieving these objectives. Therefore, the United States and its allies should enhance the collection and analysis of intelligence regarding biological warfare programs by aggressively seeking human sources, exploiting open sources, and recruiting more academic and industry biotechnology experts. In addition, a major research and evaluation program is required to develop techniques and technologies that could be employed to investigate allegations of noncompliance on an ad hoc basis or as part of a verification regime. The difficulty that the United States has had in confirming its prewar intelligence on Iraq's biological weapons program highlights the urgent need for improvements in this field.

Third, the barrier to the acquisition of biological weapons should be raised by limiting access to dangerous pathogens, techniques, and research results applicable to the development of biological weapons.[172] In addition, given the

---

Role of Science and Technology in Countering Terrorism (Washington, D.C.: National Academy Press, 2002), pp. 65–106.

169. For an overview of U.S. bioterrorism preparedness efforts, see Koblentz, "Biological Terrorism," pp. 97–173.

170. Barbara Hatch Rosenberg, "Defending against Biodefence: The Need for Limits," *Disarmament Diplomacy*, No. 69 (February–March 2003), http://www.acronym.org.uk/dd/dd69/69op03.htm.

171. I thank Paul Schulte for this point.

172. See Barletta, Sands, and Tucker, "Keeping Track of Anthrax," pp. 57–62; Gerald L. Epstein,

sophistication of the former Soviet biological weapons program, preventing the proliferation of biological weapons–related resources from Russia is essential.[173] Similar projects could also be useful in South Africa, Iraq, and other states unable to fully dismantle their former biological weapons programs. Enhanced cooperative nonproliferation efforts would complement efforts to strengthen biological defenses by slowing the progress of offensive programs and employing former weapons scientists in civilian or defensive research. These measures would not be able to prevent proliferation, but they could complicate terrorist access to biological weapons based on traditional pathogens and hinder the development of more sophisticated weapons by states.

Fourth, the norm against the development and use of biological weapons should be strengthened to reduce the motivations of states and terrorists to acquire these weapons and gain operational experience with them. One valuable step in this direction would be an international agreement that the development, production, transfer, and use of biological weapons, including unethical human experimentation, represents a crime against humanity and that perpetrators would be subject to international arrest and prosecution.[174]

"Controlling Biological Warfare Threats: Resolving Potential Tensions among the Research Community, Industry, and the National Security Community," *Critical Reviews in Microbiology*, Vol. 27, No. 4 (January 2002), pp. 321–354; and National Research Council, *Biotechnology Research in an Age of Terrorism: Confronting the "Dual Use" Dilemma* (Washington, D.C.: National Academies Press, 2003). On the potential drawbacks of these types of proposals, see Stern, "Dreaded Risks and the Control of Biological Weapons," pp. 89–123; and Kendall Hoyt and Stephen G. Brooks, "A Double-Edged Sword: Globalization and Biosecurity," *International Security*, Vol. 28, No. 3 (Winter 2003/04), pp. 123–148.

173. See Amy E. Smithson, *Toxic Archipelago: Preventing Proliferation from the Former Soviet Chemical and Biological Weapons Complexes* (Washington, D.C.: Henry L. Stimson Center, December 1999).

174. For proposals along these lines, see Matthew Meselson and Julian Robinson, *A Draft Convention to Prohibit Biological and Chemical Weapons under International Criminal Law* (Cambridge, Mass.: Harvard Sussex Program on CBW Armament and Arms Limitation, March 2003), http://www.sussex.ac.uk/spru/hsp/IntroConvRev1.pdf; and Jonathan Moreno, *Undue Risk: Secret State Experiments on Humans* (New York: Routledge, 2000), pp. 294–297.

Dreaded Risks and the Control of Biological Weapons

Jessica Stern

$\mathbf{O}$ne week after the September 11, 2001, terrorist attacks on the World Trade Center and the Pentagon, letters containing anthrax spores were mailed to the offices of NBC News, the *New York Post*, and the publisher of the *National Enquirer*. Contaminated letters were subsequently sent to, among others, then Senate Majority Leader Tom Daschle (D-S.D.) and Senator Patrick Leahy (D-Vt.). By the end of the year, anthrax- contaminated letters had infected eighteen people, five of whom died.[1] Although the anthrax attacks resulted in relatively few casualties, at least one poll suggested that public concern about biological terrorism had increased.[2] Some 10,000 people, actually or potentially exposed to virulent anthrax spores, were prescribed prophylactic antibiotics with unknown long-term effects on their health or the health of the public at large.[3]

In the aftermath of the September 11 attacks and anthrax mailings, U.S. policymakers scrambled to enact new legislation to address the terrorist threat. The urgency of the effort precluded careful balancing of competing interests, with potential adverse effects on civil liberties, public health, and national security. The U.S.A. Patriot Act, passed by both Houses of Congress in the space of weeks, was signed by President George W. Bush on October 26. Among its provisions, the act overrides laws in forty-eight states that made library re-

Jessica Stern is Lecturer in Public Policy at the John F. Kennedy School of Government, Harvard University.

The author is grateful to the following individuals for their assistance or comments: Christopher Chyba, Gerald Epstein, Jeanne Guillemin, Gregory Koblentz, Jason Sanchez, Nicole Simon, Monica Toft, Raymond Zilinskas, and an anonymous reviewer.

1. Centers for Disease Control, "Update: Investigation of Bioterrorism-Related Anthrax," *MMWR Weekly*, December 7, 2001, http://www.cdc.gov/mmwr/preview/mmwrhtml/mm5048a1.htm (accessed March 2, 2002). For more information, see Barbara Hatch Rosenberg's writings at http://www.fas.org/bwc/news/anthraxreport.htm (accessed June 28, 2002).
2. Harvard University School of Public Health/Robert Wood Johnson Foundation, *Survey Project on Americans' Response to Biological Terrorism*, November 8, 2001. Fifty-seven percent of those surveyed stated that they had taken one or more precautions in response to reports of bioterrorism.
3. Individuals were advised to take ciprofloxacin for up to sixty days. U.S. military researchers concluded, however, that increasing exposure to ciprofloxacin can result in fluoroquinolone resistance in *Bacillus anthracis*. Abstracts of Fourth International Conference organized by the U.S. Army Medical Research Institute, the British Defense Research Agency, the National Institutes of Health, and the Pasteur Institute. L. Price, A.G. Vogler, S. James, and P. Keim, Board 42A, "In Vitro Selection and Characterization of High-Level Fluoroquinolone Resistance in *Bacillus anthracis*." For treatment recommendations, see T.C. Dixon, M. Meselson, J. Guillemin, and P. Hanna, "*Bacillus Anthracis*: Infection Revisited," *New England Journal of Medicine*, September 9, 1999, pp. 815–825.

cords private.[4] In March 2002 the White House ordered all federal agencies to remove from their websites sensitive, but unclassified, documents that terrorists could use to produce weapons of mass destruction (WMD).[5] George Poste, a prominent biologist and science adviser to the U.S. Department of Defense urged that some aspects of basic microbiological research be made classified, prompting heated debate among biologists about the costs and benefits of openness in science.[6] The Patriot Act also criminalizes inappropriate possession of biological agents except for medical purposes or "bona fide" research and prohibits "restricted persons" from working with them.[7] Critics argue that these policies could hinder legitimate research on naturally occurring and deliberately disseminated infectious disease.[8]

Risk analysts have long observed a tendency for policymakers to respond rapidly to visible crises, even if the baseline rate of danger has not changed.[9] Examples include the enactment of Superfund in response to the furor over the 1978 declaration of Love Canal as a hazardous site and the Oil Pollution Act enacted after the Exxon *Valdez* oil spill of 1989, each of which was found to have serious drawbacks.[10] This tendency to respond quickly encourages reactive "risk of the month" policies crafted in the wake of visible or highly publicized events, resulting in ad hoc policymaking with little regard to competing interests, as John Graham and Jonathan Baert Wiener have observed in regard to environmental and health policy.[11] This dynamic may partly be explained

---

4. Bob Egelko, "FBI Checking Out Americans' Reading Habits: Bookstores Can't Do Much to Fend Off Search Warrants," *San Francisco Chronicle,* June 23, 2002, p. A5. See also Brad Smith, "FBI Can Check Out Reading Habits," *Tampa Tribune,* July 5, 2002, p. 1.
5. Bill Sammon, "Web Sites Told to Delete Data," *Washington Times,* March 21, 2002, p. A1.
6. Peter Aldhous, "Biologists Urged to Address Risk of Data Aiding Bioweapon Design," *Nature,* November 15, 2001, pp. 237–238.
7. The bill was signed into law as Public Law 107-56 (the *U.S.A. Patriot Act*), which became title 18, sec. 175B.
8. Egelko, "FBI Checking Out Americans' Reading Habits"; and Aldhous, "Biologists Urged to Address Risk of Data Aiding Bioweapon Design." The *Public Health Security and Bioterrorism Preparedness and Response Act of 2002* was signed as Public Law 107-188 on June 12, 2002.
9. In this article, the term "risk" is used to denote the possibility of an adverse outcome whose probability is between zero and one. It is important to point out at the outset that one school of thought, more prevalent in Europe, rejects many of the assumptions appealed to in this article. The alternative school questions the following assertions: that risk (other than actuarial risk) exists and can be quantified or that risk trade-off analysis can be accomplished; that experts and laypeople are different from one another; that "dread" is a property of risks; and that publics are anxious and irrational and that policy should compensate for these qualities. Sheila Jasanoff, email communication, August 18, 2002. I do not enter into this debate here.
10. John D. Graham and Jonathan Baert Wiener, eds., *Risk vs. Risk: Tradeoffs in Protecting Health and the Environment* (Cambridge, Mass.: Harvard University Press, 1995), p. 234.
11. Ibid.

by what Anthony Patt and Richard Zeckhauser refer to as "action bias"—that is, decisionmakers' penchant for taking action without necessarily considering its long-term effects, coupled with a tendency to choose those actions for which they are likely to receive the most credit.[12] At the same time, national attention often drifts once a crisis appears to be over. Perhaps then the biggest challenge for policymakers in responding to the fall 2001 terrorist strikes is to avoid overreacting while the strikes remain vivid in people's minds—what risk analysts refer to as "availability"—and to sustain the effort to reduce the threat, even during periods when the risk recedes from the national consciousness.

This article argues that effective policymaking requires an assessment of countervailing dangers introduced by remedies intended to decrease a target risk (the one the policy aims to reduce), even when it is particularly dreaded and when both target and countervailing risks are difficult to quantify. Such risk trade-off analysis has become commonplace in evaluations of medical procedures, health risks of pesticides, and policies for protecting the environment, but it is not yet practiced in foreign policy or national security decisionmaking.[13] Risk trade-off analysis differs from cost-benefit analysis, which Robert McNamara made popular in the U.S. Department of Defense during the Vietnam War. Cost-benefit analysis compares the benefits of policies with their financial costs, whereas risk trade-off analysis compares target and countervailing risks in nonfinancial terms. People make risk trade-offs regularly in their daily lives, for example, in deciding whether to take aspirin for a headache, despite the increased risk of stomach upset. Patients whose doctors prescribe a new medication will want statistics on purported benefits as well as possible side effects. Such statistics are less likely to be readily available to foreign policy and national security decisionmakers, but even a qualitative analysis of risk versus risk can improve policy design.

My goal is to demonstrate the utility of risk trade-off analysis to national security policy by applying it qualitatively to policies for reducing access to dangerous pathogens and related information. The framework developed in this article can also be applied to policy problems where both the target and the countervailing risks are difficult to quantify. As disciplines become more spe-

---

12. Anthony Patt and Richard Zeckhauser, "Behavioral Perceptions and Policies toward the Environment," in Rajeev Gowda and Jeffrey C. Fox, eds., *Judgments, Decisions, and Public Policy* (Cambridge: Cambridge University Press, 2002), pp. 265–302.
13. The concept of risk trade-off analysis was developed by Graham and Wiener, *Risk vs. Risk.*

cialized and government agencies more compartmentalized, decisionmakers are more prone to choose remedies that substitute new risks for old ones in the same population, transfer risks to new populations, or transform risks by creating new risks in new populations.[14] Among such countervailing dangers is the possibility that bioterrorism legislation could diminish researchers' willingness or ability to work with select agents, with the result of reducing U.S. preparedness for biological weapons (BW) attacks as well as infectious disease. Another possibility is that the risk could be transferred from the United States to the developing world, where diseases caused by select agents are endemic. The risk trade-off framework developed here entails determining whether emotions, such as dread, are influencing U.S. government decisionmaking; balancing competing policy priorities; taking core values explicitly into account, even if the demands of national security ultimately trump such concerns; and seeking "risk-superior" strategies.

I argue further that risk trade-off analysis is especially useful for assessing "dreaded risks," which evoke disproportionate fears and are likely to be maximally available in the sense defined above.[15] The image of a mad scientist spreading "weapons-grade" anthrax is difficult to forget, and the need to do something—anything—seemed critically important in the immediate aftermath of the anthrax mailings.[16] The countervailing long-term danger—a possi-

---

14. Graham and Wiener, *Risk vs. Risk*, lay out a four-part framework for considering trade-offs in health care and environmental policy, which is summarized in this sentence. In addition to these countervailing dangers, the framework I develop here assesses trade-offs in policy priorities and values.

15. In a survey comparing expert and lay judgment, experts ranked nuclear power twentieth on a list of thirty dangerous technologies and activities, whereas most lay respondents ranked it first. Paul Slovic, "Perception of Risk," *Science*, Vol. 236 (1987), pp. 280–281; Paul Slovic, Baruch Fischoff, and Sarah Lichtenstein, "Facts and Fears: Understanding Perceived Risk," in Richard Schwing and Walter Albers, eds., *Societal Risk Assessment: How Safe Is Safe Enough?* (New York: Plenum, 1980), pp. 181–216. In subsequent studies, Slovic and others have examined the emotional content of risks and its impact on assessment. See, for example, Paul Slovic, "Trust, Emotion, Sex, Politics, and Science: Surveying the Risk-Assessment Battlefield," *Risk Analysis*, Vol. 19. No. 4 (August 1999), pp. 689–701; and Melissa L. Finucane, Ali Alhakami, Paul Slovic, and Stephen M. Johnson, "The Affect Heuristic in Judgments of Risks and Benefits," *Journal of Behavioral Decision Making*, Vol. 13, No. 1 (January/March 2000), pp. 1–17. See also George F. Loewenstein, Christopher K. Hsee, Elke U. Weber, and Ned Welch, "Risk as Feelings," *Psychological Bulletin*, Vol. 127, No. 2 (March 2001), pp. 267–286; and Jonathan Baert Wiener, "Risk in the Republic," in *Duke Environmental Law and Policy Forum*, Vol. 8, No. 1 (Fall 1997), pp. 1–22, as well as the articles in part 3 of that issue.

16. Then House Democratic leader Richard Gephardt (D-Mo.) referred to the material as "weapons-grade" anthrax. Earl Lane, "America's Ordeal: Tracking the Anthrax," *Newsday*, October 18, 2001, p. A4. Laura Dohonue argues that heightened emotions are caused by the interplay between liberal democracy and terrorism. Donohue, "Fear Itself," in Russell D. Howard and Reid L. Saw-

ble chilling effect on research on natural and deliberately spread infectious disease—is less immediate, less visceral, and less likely to attract high-level governmental attention.

This article is not a comprehensive analysis of the bioterrorist threat, which has largely been covered elsewhere.[17] Rather it presents a framework for analyzing foreign and national security policy that takes countervailing risks explicitly into account. A more comprehensive analysis would require quantifying the risk of biological attacks as well as the countervailing risks to public health. I do not attempt such an assessment here. As more information about terrorists' intentions and capabilities becomes available, which is likely to happen only if the demand for human intelligence persists once the fall 2001 attacks lose their salience, a more complete analysis may become possible, especially for government agencies with access to classified information.

The first section of this article provides a brief overview of the threat of bioterrorism. The second section discusses risk analysis and explains why this threat is difficult to quantify. The third discusses dreaded risks and offers reasons why bioterrorism falls into this category. The fourth section introduces a framework for risk trade-off analysis for national security threats and applies it qualitatively to policies for controlling access to pathogens and related information. The conclusion proposes two ways to restrict terrorist access to biological weapons and related information while limiting the negative impact on legitimate scientific research.

---

yer, eds., *Terrorism and Counterterrorism: Understanding the New Security Environment* (Guilford, Conn.: McGraw-Hill, 2002), chap. 7.1.

17. See Jeffrey Simon, *Terrorists and the Potential Use of Biological Weapons* (Santa Monica, Calif.: RAND, 1989); W. Seth Carus, *Bioterrorism and Biocrimes: The Illicit Use of Biological Agents in the 20th Century: "The Poor Man's Atomic Bomb?" Biological Weapons in the Middle East*, Policy Papers No. 23 (Washington, D.C.: Washington Institute for Near East Policy, 1991); Jessica Stern, "Will Terrorists Turn to Poison?" *Orbis*, Vol. 37, No. 3 (Summer 1993) pp. 393–410; Ron Purver, "The Threat of Chemical/Biological Terrorism," *Commentary*, August 1995, http://www.csis-scrs.gc.ca/eng/comment/com60_e.html; Jonathan B. Tucker, "Chemical/Biological Terrorism: Coping with a New Threat," *Politics and the Life Sciences*, Vol. 15, No. 2 (September 1996), pp. 167–184; Leonard A. Cole, "The Specter of Biological Weapons," *Scientific American*, December 1996, pp. 17–21; Michael Moodie and Brad Roberts, eds., *Terrorism with Chemical and Biological Weapons: Calibrating Risks and Responses* (Alexandria, Va.: Chemical and Biological Arms Control Institute, 1997), pp. 71–90; Richard A. Falkenrath, Robert D. Newman, and Bradley A. Thayer, *America's Achilles' Heel: Nuclear, Biological, and Chemical Terrorism and Covert Attack* (Cambridge, Mass.: MIT Press, 1998); Joshua Lederberg, ed., *Biological Warfare: Limiting the Threat* (Cambridge, Mass.: MIT Press, 1999), Raymond A. Zilinskas, *Biological Warfare: Modern Offense and Defense* (Boulder, Colo.: Lynne Rienner, 1999); Jonathan B. Tucker, *Toxic Terror: Assessing Terrorist Use of Chemical and Biological Weapons* (Cambridge, Mass.: MIT Press, 2000); and Amy Smithson and Leslie Anne Levy, *Ataxia: The Chemical and Biological Terrorism Threat and the U.S. Response*, Report No. 35 (Washington, D.C.: Henry L. Stimson Center, October 2000).

Bioweapons and Bioterrorism: An Overview of the Threat

Four aspects of the bioterrorism threat are discussed below: supply-side issues; demand-side issues; changes in terrorist organizations that make them harder to penetrate and stop; and governments' inadequate preparations to meet the terrorist threat, including possible confusion about the source of a particular outbreak.

THE SUPPLY OF BIOLOGICAL AGENTS

Experts have been warning for some time that weapons of mass destruction are proliferating not only to states but also to subnational groups, and that the United States is particularly vulnerable to a bioterrorist strike.[18] On the supply side, several states known to sponsor terrorism have made improvements in their BW arsenals.[19] Iraq, in particular, was discovered to have produced a wide variety of lethal biological agents.[20] The Soviet Union was reported to have developed antibiotic-resistant pathogens for use as weapons.[21] Perhaps most troubling were revelations that the Soviet Union had produced several tons of smallpox—a particularly virulent biological weapon—and indications that both Iraq and North Korea may have acquired the virus.[22] Smallpox, which killed some 300 million people in the twentieth century alone, is highly contagious and lethal to 30 percent of those it infects. There is no treatment other than vaccination within four days of exposure. Since 1980, when

---

18. In addition to the material cited above on biological weapons, see also Brian Jenkins, "The Future Course of International Terrorism," *Futurist*, July–August 1987, p. 8; Bruce Hoffman, "Viewpoint: Terrorism and WMD—Some Preliminary Hypotheses," *Nonproliferation Review*, Vol. 4, No. 3 (Spring–Summer 1997), pp. 45–53; Philip B. Heymann, *Terrorism and America: A Commonsense Strategy for a Democratic Society* (Cambridge, Mass.: MIT Press, 1998); Ashton B. Carter, John Deutch, and Philip Zelikow, "Catastrophic Terrorism: Tackling the New Danger," *Foreign Affairs*, Vol. 77, No. 6 (November/December 1998), pp. 80–94; Gavin Cameron, *Nuclear Terrorism: A Threat Assessment for the 21st Century* (New York: Palgrave, 1999); and Ashton B. Carter and William J. Perry with David Aidekman, "Countering Asymmetric Threats," in Carter and John P. White, eds., *Keeping the Edge: Managing Defense for the Future* (Cambridge, Mass.: MIT Press, 2001).
19. A good source on biological weapons proliferation is the Henry L. Stimson Center website, http://www.stimson.org/cbw/?sn?CB2001121274 (accessed July 10, 2002).
20. Raymond A. Zilinskas, "Iraq's Biological Warfare Program: The Past as Future?" and Stephen Black, "Investigating Iraq's Biological Weapons Program," in Lederberg, *Biological Weapons: Limiting the Threat*, pp. 137–158 and 159–164, respectively.
21. Ken Alibek, *Biohazard: The Chilling True Story of the Largest Covert Biological Weapons Program in the World* (New York: Random House, 1999).
22. William Broad, "Smallpox: The Once and Future Scourge?" *New York Times*, June 15, 1999, p. F1.

the World Health Organization (WHO) certified that smallpox had been eradicated, few countries have maintained vaccine stocks. If smallpox were released, much of the world's population would be vulnerable.[23]

Another supply-side issue is that inputs to biological weapons are inherently dual-use. Unlike special nuclear materials (highly enriched plutonium and uranium), which are man-made at great expense and effort and produced only at government-sanctioned facilities, biological agents (with the single exception of variola virus, the causative agent of smallpox) exist in the environment.[24] Pathogens listed by the government as potential agents for terrorists are used in thousands of clinical and diagnostic laboratories.[25] The same equipment used to produce beer, for example, could be used to produce biological agents. The underlying research and technology base is available to a rapidly growing and increasingly international technical community.[26]

Until recently, germ banks routinely sent samples to virtually anyone who requested them in the belief that they were promoting public health. For example, during the 1980s the U.S. Commerce Department indiscriminately approved exports of *Bacillus anthracis*, the organism that causes anthrax, and *Clostridium botulinum*, the organism used to produce botulinum toxin, from the American Type Culture Collection.[27] The Centers for Disease Control (CDC) once sent cultures of West Nile virus to Iraq.[28] Because of growing concern about BW proliferation, in February 1989 the Commerce Department banned export of pathogen cultures to Iran, Iraq, Libya, and Syria; and in 1984 several

---

23. For a comprehensive analysis of the smallpox issue, see Jonathan B. Tucker, *Scourge: The Once and Future Threat of Smallpox* (New York: Atlantic Monthly Press, 2001).
24. Fomer Defense Department official Mitchell Wallerstein points out that the Russians have argued for years that smallpox may be found "in the environment in the form of bodies of deceased individuals trapped in the permafrost of Siberia. The concern may be real, imagined, or purposely made up during Soviet times as a cover for their illegal program." Email communication, December 17, 2002.
25. Lisa D. Rotz, Ali S. Khan, Scott R. Lillibridge, Stephen M. Ostroff, and James M. Hughes, "Public Health Assessment of Potential Biological Terrorism Agents," *Emerging Infectious Diseases*, Vol. 8, No. 2 (February 2002), pp. 225–230.
26. Gerald Epstein, "Controlling Biological Warfare Threats: Resolving Potential Tensions among the Research Community, Industry, and the National Security Community," *Critical Reviews in Microbiology*, Vol. 27, No. 4 (January 2001), pp. 321–354. For the impact on arms control, see Mark Wheelis, "Investigating Disease Outbreaks under a Protocol to the Biological and Toxin Weapons Convention," *Emerging Infectious Diseases*, Vol. 6, No. 6 (November–December 2000), pp. 595–600.
27. Kevin Merida and John Mintz, "Rockville Firm Shipped Germ Agents to Iraq, Riegle Says," *Washington Post*, February 10, 1994, p. A8.
28. Centers for Disease Control and Prevention, "Draft: West Nile Virus Strain, New York, 1999," CDC Media Relations 404 639-3286, April 2000, in files.

Western countries formed the Australia Group, which urges its members to restrict such exports.[29] In response to a neo-Nazi's acquisition of *Yersinia pestis* (the causative agent of plague) from an American germ bank in 1995, the U.S. government tightened the rules for shippers and receivers of select agents.[30] But cultures are also available from germ banks outside the United States; and according to one study, few of these are adequately regulated or secured.[31] And because of the difficulty of detecting biological agents, the ability of U.S. Customs to stop illegal imports of small quantities of pathogens, such as seed cultures, is minimal.[32]

Another problem is that the manufacture of biological weapons is relatively easy to hide. Enrichment and reprocessing of nuclear weapons materials emit chemical signatures that can be picked up by sensors placed at long distances from the production site. There are no equivalent, easily identifiable signatures for BW production.

THE DEMAND FOR BIOLOGICAL AGENTS

Several incidents before the 2001 anthrax attacks made clear that terrorists have been interested in acquiring and using WMD. Perhaps the most significant of these was the sarin gas attack by Aum Shinrikyo, a Japanese cult, on the Tokyo subway in 1995. During the 1990s the cult also attempted to use biological weapons, apparently unsuccessfully.[33] The U.S. government has repeatedly stated that Osama bin Laden is interested in acquiring biological agents.[34] George W. Bush and members of his administration continue to ex-

---

29. The Australia Group, composed of thirty-four countries plus the European Commission, lists twenty-four biological agents and eleven toxins (exports of which its members have agreed to control). See http://www.australiagroup.net/index.html (accessed June 25, 2001).
30. The Antiterrorism and Effective Death Penalty Act of 1996 requires the U.S. Department of Health and Human Services to regulate the transfer of "select agents." The CDC developed a list of twenty-four microbial pathogens and twelve toxins, which, if transferred to another facility, would require registration with the CDC. *Code of Federal Regulations*, title 42, pt. 72.
31. Michael Barletta, Amy Sands, and Jonathan B. Tucker, "Keeping Track of Anthrax: The Case for a Biosecurity Convention," *Bulletin of Atomic Scientists*, Vol. 58, No. 3 (May/June 2002), pp. 57–62.
32. Barry Kellman, "Biological Terrorism: Legal Measures for Preventing Catastrophe," *Harvard Journal of Law and Public Policy*, Vol. 24, No. 2 (Spring 2001), pp. 425–488.
33. William Rosenau, "Aum Shinrikyo's Biological Program: Why Did It Fail?" *Studies in Conflict and Terrorism*, Vol. 24, No. 4 (July 2001), pp. 289–302; and Milton Leitenberg, "The Experience of the Japanese Aum Shinrikyo Group and Biological Agents," in Brad Roberts, ed., *Hype or Reality? The "New Terrorism" and Mass Casualty Attacks* (Alexandria, Va.: Chemical and Biological Arms Control Institute, 2000), pp. 159–172.
34. Testimony by George Tenet, director of central intelligence, before the Senate Foreign Relations Committee, "The Formulation of Effective Nonproliferation Policy," 106th Cong., 2d sess., March

press concern that terrorist groups could join forces with states to carry out WMD attacks.[35] During the last decade, several American antigovernment individuals and groups were found to have acquired biological agents, revealing gaps in existing regulations regarding the sale or possession of lethal or incapacitating biological agents.[36]

THE TRANSFORMATION OF TERRORIST GROUPS

Another troubling development is that terrorist groups have begun organizing themselves into networks or virtual networks rather than large organizations, often with the explicit purpose of evading law enforcement detection.[37] International terrorist organizations, similarly, are forming loose affiliations that operate across national boundaries, making them harder to identify, penetrate, and stop. Ironically, the success of the U.S. operation in Afghanistan against the Taliban may have induced remaining al-Qaeda operatives to strengthen their ties with other groups, including Jaish-e-Mohammed in Pakistan and Jemaah Islamiyah in Southeast Asia, in effect creating franchise outfits around the world.[38] As a result, the leadership of the movement is more dispersed, and the network thereby made more robust.[39]

INADEQUATE PREPAREDNESS AGAINST THE TERRORIST THREAT

U.S. efforts to characterize the terrorist threat have entailed assessments of the country's vulnerability. Exercises in the 1990s tested the U.S. government's preparedness for responding to WMD attacks. The tests revealed that hospitals were likely to quickly exhaust their supplies of antidotes and vaccines; first responders (police, firefighters, and other emergency workers) were inadequately trained and likely to succumb themselves; and coordination among

---

21, 2000, Senate Serial 106-655, http://frwebgate.access.gpo.gov/cgi-bin/getdoc.cgi?dbname= 106_senate_hearings&docid=f:64521.wais (accessed September 29, 2002). See also Gavin Cameron, "Multi-track Microproliferation: Lessons from Aum Shinrikyo and Al Qaida," *Studies in Conflict and Terrorism,* Vol. 22, No. 4 (November 1999), pp. 277–309; and Kimberly Mclound and Matthew Osborne, *WMD Terrorism and Usama bin Laden* (Monterey, Calif.: Center for Nonproliferation Studies, Monterey Institute of International Studies, 2001), http://cns.miis.edu/pubs/reports/ binladen.htm (accessed September 29, 2002).

35. Lydia Adetunji, "Bush to Lay Out First-Strike Policy against Terrorism," *Financial Times* (London), June 11, 2002, p. 11.

36. Tucker, *Toxic Terror.*

37. L.R. Beam, "Leaderless Resistance," http://www2.mo-net.com/~mlindste/ledrless.html (accessed February 28, 2002).

38. Rohan Gunaratna, *Inside Al Qaeda: Global Network of Terror* (New York: Columbia University Press, 2002); and Jessica Stern, *Terror in the Name of God* (New York: HarperCollins, forthcoming).

39. For more on this, see Stern, *Terror in the Name of God.*

federal, state, and local officials was all but nonexistent. Hospital laboratories were poorly prepared for biological attacks. Secure communication links among doctors, veterinarians, and local and federal public-health officials were inadequate. Systems for ensuring that medication and personnel were distributed appropriately were undeveloped. The public health infrastructure was—and remains—unprepared for timely response and containment of outbreaks. Moreover, critics argue that the lack of a fully coordinated global disease surveillance system could obstruct early response to a bioterrorist attack. Congress enacted legislation to address some of these shortfalls, but many of these problems remain unresolved.[40]

A particularly frightening aspect of biological warfare or terrorism is that it may be difficult to distinguish from a natural outbreak. Although discerning natural from unnatural outbreaks proceeds more rapidly than in the past, suspicions and fears resulting from such outbreaks can still occur.

After Cuba suffered an epidemic of dengue hemorrhagic fever in 1981, it accused the United States of biological aggression. In 1997 Cuba made another allegation of biological warfare, charging that the United States had dropped crop-eating pests from a low-flying plane.[41] When West Nile encephalitis was first diagnosed in New York in the summer of 1999, CIA officials reportedly speculated that the virus, which had never been seen in the Western Hemisphere, might have been deliberately introduced.[42] Ultimately, the CDC concluded that the outbreak was not deliberate. But the difficulty of identifying the virus and its origin, exacerbated by the lack of communication between public health officials and the veterinary community, illustrates the complexity of distinguishing a BW attack from a natural outbreak of disease. This difficulty will grow as urbanization, crowding, travel, poverty, and misuse of

---

40. See Smithson and Levy, *Ataxia;* Tara O'Toole, Michael Mair, and Thomas V. Inglesby, "Shining Light on Dark Winter," *Clinical Infectious Diseases,* April 1, 2002, pp. 972–983; Christopher Chyba, "Biological Terrorism and Public Health," *Survival,* Vol. 43, No. 1 (Spring 2001), pp. 93–106; Christopher Chyba, "Toward Biological Security," *Foreign Affairs,* Vol. 81, No. 3 (May/June 2002), pp. 122–136; and Gregory Koblentz, "A Survey of Biological Terrorism and America's Domestic Preparedness Program," in Arnold Howitt and Robyn Pangi, eds., *Countering Terrorism: Dimensions of Preparedness* (Cambridge, Mass.: MIT Press, forthcoming), and much of that volume. For ongoing assessments, see the following websites: http://www.esdp.org; www.cns.miis. edu; and http://www.stimson.org/cbw/?SN=CB2001112951 (accessed August 14, 2002).
41. Raymond A. Zilinskas, "Cuban Allegations of Biological Warfare by the United States: Assessing the Evidence," *Critical Reviews in Microbiology,* Vol. 25, No. 3 (September 1999), pp. 173–227.
42. Richard Preston, "West Nile Mystery: How Did It Get Here? The CIA Would Like to Know," *New Yorker,* October 18–25, 1999, pp. 90–127. The virus was originally misdiagnosed as St. Louis encephalitis.

antibiotics continue to increase the incidence of infectious diseases once thought to be under control.

On the rare occasions when biological weapons were used or accidentally released, scientists and government officials often first assumed that the epidemics were natural outbreaks. For instance, when 751 people in Oregon became infected with salmonella in 1984, public health authorities suspected a natural outbreak, not bioterrorism. A year later, an unrelated law-enforcement investigation revealed that the Rajneeshee cult had deliberately spread pathogens causing the disease.[43] And when Robert Stevens, an avid outdoorsman and a photo editor for the supermarket tabloid *The Sun*, was found to have contracted anthrax, Florida State health officials initially attributed the source of the disease to a naturally occurring strain of the bacteria found in some soils.[44]

Terrorists have yet to employ successfully biological agents to carry out mass casualty attacks. Most incidents to date have involved readily available and easily deployed food-borne pathogens, resulting in relatively few casualties. Although the perpetrator of the fall 2001 attacks used a highly sophisticated powder, the letters in the envelopes identified the material as anthrax and warned recipients to seek treatment, suggesting that the intention was not to kill people. This could change if a state chose to sponsor a biological attack or if a group managed to secure assistance from former government scientists. Moreover, as aerosolization technologies continue to improve, high-casualty biological attacks will become easier to carry out.

Risk Analysis and the Bioterrorist Threat

Terrorist attacks are purposeful, unlike chemical hazards or earthquakes. Moreover, they threaten not only human lives but also political values, interests, and institutions. Government legitimacy is based on the state's monopoly over the use of force and protection of citizens. Terrorists threaten both of those norms.[45] Thus, there are inherent limits to our ability to assess the risk of ter-

43. Thomas J. Torok, Robert V. Tauxe, Robert P. Wise, John R. Livengood, Robert Sokolow, Steven Mauvais, Kristin A. Birkness, Michael R. Skeels, John M. Horan, and Laurence R. Foster, "A Large Community Outbreak of Salmonellosis Caused by Intentional Contamination of Restaurant Salad Bars," in Lederberg, *Biological Weapons*, pp. 167–184; and W. Seth Carus, "The Rajneeshee (1984)," in Tucker, *Toxic Terror*, pp. 115–138.
44. "Timeline: America Strikes Bioterrorism," *St. Petersburg Times*, October 14, 2001, p. 13A; and Laura Johannes, "Doctor Who Treated Florida Anthrax Case Criticizes Government's Early Reaction," *Wall Street Journal*, November 9, 2001, p. 8.
45. I am grateful to both Laura Donohue and Gregory Koblentz for encouraging me to make these differences clear.

rorism. Two additional kinds of uncertainties are discussed below. First, terrorists' capabilities and intentions are unknown. Second, there are uncertainties about the effects of the weapons themselves.

TERRORISTS' CAPABILITIES AND INTENTIONS

Terrorists rarely make their capabilities and intentions known. Their motivations and intentions also change over time in ways that are hard for analysts to predict. No statistically significant database of previous attacks exists that can be extrapolated, even if that were a valid technique for predicting future terrorist behavior. Terrorists may respond to risk-reduction strategies by finding more vulnerable targets or more effective or less detectable weapons. When metal detectors made it harder to bring guns onto airliners, terrorists began blowing up planes with plastic explosives or taking control of them by threatening pilots and passengers with box cutters.[46] Concrete barriers at U.S. embassies and government buildings have made driving onto these sites more difficult. Now terrorists use more powerful explosives. If cockpit doors are sealed, terrorists could put plastic explosives in luggage or attack other forms of mass transit or large buildings. If plastic-explosive detectors are deployed routinely at airports for checked-in luggage, terrorists might disseminate biological agents on planes or in other enclosed spaces.

TECHNICAL DIFFICULTIES WITH PREDICTING THE IMPACT OF BW ATTACKS

There are also technical problems with predicting the likely impact of a biological attack. Biological weapons are potentially as deadly as thermonuclear weapons. For example, one U.S. government study concluded that 100 kilograms of *Bacillus anthracis*, a fraction of the amount produced by Iraq, could kill from 1 to 3 million people if dispersed under optimal conditions.[47] In comparison, a Hiroshima-type fission bomb could kill as many as 80,000, while a more powerful hydrogen bomb could kill 600,000 to 2 million.[48] Contagious agents could kill even more people than anthrax. Joshua Lederberg calls the 1918 flu pandemic, which is estimated to have killed more than 20 million people worldwide, a model for the type of disaster that a biological weapon containing a contagious pathogen could wreak.[49] The public health infrastructure

46. According to Indian government officials, the group of Pakistani extremists who hijacked flight IC814 in December 1999 had box cutters, as did the September 11 attackers.
47. U.S. Congress, Office of Technology Assessment, *Proliferation of Weapons of Mass Destruction: Assessing the Risks*, OTA-ISC-559 (Washington, D.C.: Government Printing Office, 1993), p. 54.
48. Ibid.
49. Quoted in Dan Vergano, "Bioterrorism Defense Under Fire: Doctors Say Military Plans Are Wrong Approach," *USA Today*, June 21, 2000, p. 10D.

was overwhelmed in the first couple of weeks, despite the low case fatality rate of influenza compared with a typical biological warfare threat agent.[50]

Ideal conditions are unlikely to prevail in the field, making the actual results of a BW attack uncertain. The movement of aerosols, the virulence of micro-organisms, and the susceptibility of victims all depend on exogenous variables, some of which the perpetrator will be unable to influence and most of which government analysts will be unable to predict.[51] Warfare agents are killed by strong sunlight. Contagious viruses can mutate to become harmless, but they can also mutate to become more contagious and more lethal. Bacteria can be made—or may become—antibiotic resistant over time.

Even for traditional warfare agents such as anthrax, physicians remain uncertain about the dose response (the number of inhaled spores likely to cause infection in what percentage of the population) and the effectiveness of medical countermeasures.[52] There are ethical problems with carrying out the kinds of experiments that would be required to understand fully the effects of biological weapons. The gaps in physicians' knowledge about anthrax, which became clear during the fall 2001 attacks, suggest that even greater uncertainty would attend biological strikes employing less common disease agents.

Standard theories for evaluating risk—utility theory, for example—are not that useful for assessing risks of virtually unlimited cost and finite probability. Moreover, even if an attack were carried out successfully, the range of consequences runs from minor annoyance to society-altering catastrophe. The probability of infection for a given individual is the joint probability that a terrorist or terrorist group decides to use a biological agent; acquires an infectious agent in usable form; and disseminates it successfully in the vicinity of the

---

50. See Laurie Garrett, *The Coming Plague: Newly Emerging Diseases in a World Out of Balance* (New York: Farrar, Straus and Giroux, 1994); and Laurie Garrett, *Betrayal of Trust: The Collapse of Global Public Health* (New York: Hyperion, 2000).

51. On the varying susceptibility of victims, see Larry M. Bush, Barry H. Abrams, Anne Beall, and Caroline C. Johnson, "Bioterrorism in the United States," *New England Journal of Medicine*, November 29, 2001, pp. 1607–1610.

52. On the positive side, it was discovered that antibiotics may be effective even after symptoms appear; on the negative side, however, there may be no "safe" dose of inhaled spores. David Brown, "New Questions Raised on Anthrax Perils: Study Finds Spores in Daschle Office Easily Stirred Up, Complicating Risk Analysis," *Washington Post*, December 11, 2001, p. A15. See reference to Meselson in Jonathan Knight, "Bioweapons: Delivering Death in the Mail," *Nature*, December 20, 2001, pp. 719–720. Data from the largest recorded outbreak of inhalation anthrax, in 1979 in the Soviet city of Sverdlovsk, showed for the first time that anthrax spores could remain dormant in the human lung as long as six weeks after exposure, then germinate and cause fatal illness. See Matthew Meselson, Jeanne Guillemin, Martin Hugh-Jones, Alexander Langmuir, Ilona Popova, Alexis Shelokov, and Olga Yamploskaya, "The Sverdlovsk Anthrax Outbreak of 1979," *Science*, November 18, 1994, pp. 1202–1208.

person or, in the case of a contagious agent, in the vicinity of his contacts; and that the person is sensitive to the dosage received; medical countermeasures are not prescribed; or the medical countermeasures are not effective for that person.

Terrorists aim to make a target group feel vulnerable, and they often succeed. A key question for decisionmakers is whether policy responses should be based in part on perceptions of peril, including feelings of fright, or on a calculation that considers every potential casualty to be equal—whatever the emotional and symbolic content of the threat. Certain hazards evoke particular dread, which can lead to the overestimation of risks or the design of reactive policies whose costs may exceed their benefits.

Dreaded Risks

For more than a quarter century, psychologists and risk analysts have sought to identity the attributes of risks that are especially feared. They have found that fear is disproportionately evoked by certain characteristics of risks, including: involuntary exposure, unfamiliarity, and invisibility, as well as instances when victims may not realize that they were exposed or the effects are delayed, when the mechanism of harm is poorly understood, or when long-term effects or the number of people likely to be affected is difficult to predict.[53] In contrast, when risky activities are perceived as voluntary or familiar or when the actor feels—perhaps wrongly—that he or she is in control, danger is likely to be underappreciated.[54] On average, more than 100 Americans die in automobile accidents every day in the United States.[55] Yet because the risk is largely voluntary and seemingly under the driver's control, and because drivers perceive a direct benefit to themselves, most Americans blithely expose

---

53. Slovic, Fischoff, and Lichtenstein, "Facts and Fears"; and Slovic, "Perception of Risk," pp. 280–281.

54. N.D. Weinstein, "Optimistic Biases about Personal Risks," *Science*, December 8, 1989, pp. 1232–1233; and F.P. McKenna, "It Won't Happen to Me: Unrealistic Optimism or the Illusion of Control?" *British Journal of Psychology*, Vol. 84 (1993), pp. 39–50, cited in Lynn J. Frewer, Chaya Howard, Duncan Hedderley, and Richard Shepherd, "Methodological Approaches to Assessing Risk Perceptions Associated with Food-Related Hazards," *Risk Analysis*, Vol. 18, No. 1 (February 1998), pp. 95–102. According to Frewer et al., the more individuals feel they know about food-borne health hazards, the more they feel they have control over their exposure. Food deliberately contaminated with unknown biological agents could be expected to fall into the category of less controllable hazards.

55. The National Center for Statistics and Analysis (which reports to the National Highway Traffic Safety Administration) estimates there were 41,800 automobile-related fatalities in the year 2000, an average of 115 per day. See http://www.nhtsa.gov/ (accessed June 25, 2001).

themselves to this risk.[56] Bioterrorism is unusual in that it possesses all of the characteristics that psychologists have shown to be conducive to disproportionate dread.

Most of us rely on rules of thumb in calculating risks. Rather than carefully weighing pros and cons, we use heuristic devices. Supreme Court Justice Stephen Breyer explains, "We simplify radically; we reason with the help of a few readily understandable examples; we categorize (events and other people) in simple ways that tend to create binary choices—yes/no, friend/foe, eat/abstain, safe/dangerous, act/don't act."[57]

The media tend to focus on dramatic events, including tornadoes, fires, drownings, homicides, and accidents. Spectacular terrorist attacks—including those with biological agents—have become commonplace in literature and film, seeping into people's collective imagination. But as the September 11 terrorist strikes and the anthrax attacks that followed made clear, the threat is real. The U.S. Environmental Protection Agency observes that people tend to ignore hazards that seem routine, such as indoor air pollution, but fear those that are "high profile," such as hazardous waste sites, which actually pose lower aggregate risks to human health. Terrorist incidents are also high-profile events: They tend to be dramatic and generate media attention.[58] Studies show that people often exaggerate the likelihood of such events, which are easy to imagine or recall. We feel a gut-level fear of terrorism and are prone to trying to eradicate the risk with little regard to costs.[59]

Four aspects of dread: disgust, horror of disease, loss of faith in the ability of scientists to protect us, and implications for risk analysis and policy are particularly relevant to the discussion of the bioterror threat.

---

56. See J.K. Hammitt, "Evaluating Risk Communication: In Search of a Gold Standard," in M.P. Cottam, D.W. Harvey, R.P. Pape, and J. Tait, eds., *Foresight and Precaution,* proceedings of the ESREL 2000, SARS, and SRA-Europe annual conference (Rotterdam, the Netherlands: A.A. Balkema, 2000), pp. 15–19. See also Cass Sunstein, "A Note on 'Voluntary' versus 'Involuntary' Risks," *Duke Environmental Law and Policy Forum,* Vol. 8, No. 1 (Fall 1997), pp. 173–180.
57. Stephen Breyer, *Breaking the Vicious Circle: Toward Effective Risk Regulation* (Cambridge, Mass.: Harvard University Press, 1993), p. 35.
58. Amos Tversky and Daniel Kahneman, "Judgment under Uncertainty: Heuristics and Biases," *Science,* September 27, 1974, pp. 1124–1131; and Slovic, Fischoff, and Lichtenstein, "Facts and Fears." People also tend to be overconfident in the accuracy of their assessments, even when those assessments are based on nothing more than guesses. Moreover, people seem to desire certainty: They respond to the anxiety of uncertainty by blithely ignoring uncertain risks and by believing that although others may be vulnerable (to, for example, being involved in an automobile accident), they are not.
59. People are more willing to pay for risk reduction when they believe that zero risk is attainable, according to Kazuya Nakayachi, "How Do People Evaluate Risk Reduction When They Are Told Zero Risk Is Impossible?" *Risk Analysis,* Vol. 18, No. 3 (June 1998), pp. 235–242.

DISGUST

In *The Anatomy of Disgust,* William Miller explains that horror is "fear-imbued" disgust; it is a subset of disgust for which "no distancing or evasive strategies exist that are not themselves utterly contaminating."[60] As Miller observes, "Because the threatening thing is disgusting, one does not want to strike it, touch it, or grapple with it."[61]

Diseases infect us and inhabit us. We cannot physically remove them like a bullet; we cannot escape being defiled. In a conventional bombing campaign, we can run from collapsing structures; and we know immediately whether we have escaped. When biological agents spread, we may not know whether we have been poisoned, and we may not be able to escape no matter how fast we run.

The idea of involuntary exposure is inherently fear inducing. Nearly 40 percent of those queried in a recent study agreed with the statement that "if a person is exposed to a chemical that can cause cancer in humans, then that person will probably get cancer some day." The question provided no specifics about the magnitude of exposure. When the question referred to a specific quantity ("an extremely small amount"), 80 percent of respondents disagreed with the statement that the person exposed would "probably get cancer some day."[62] While the authors of the study conclude that inferences about chemical exposure relate to "the pragmatics of language interpretation,"[63] the study also reveals that the idea of exposure is inherently dread inducing, especially when specifics are not provided—as was the case with the 2001 anthrax attacks and could well be the case for future attacks.

HORROR OF DISEASE

Part of our fear of biological weapons attacks is related to fear of disease and contagion. Disease is familiar to us: We have all been sick and or seen loved ones suffer from disease. What makes bioterror particularly frightening, disgusting, and infuriating is the idea that someone would deliberately contaminate us, and that we in turn might contaminate others.

---

60. William Ian Miller, *The Anatomy of Disgust* (Cambridge, Mass.: Harvard University Press, 1998), p. 26; and Susan Miller, "Disgust: Conceptualization, Development, and Dynamics," *International Review of Psychoanalysis,* Vol. 13 (1986), pp. 295–307.
61. Miller, *The Anatomy of Disgust,* p. 26.
62. Donald G. MacGregor, Paul Slovic, and Torbjorn Malmfors, "How Exposed Is Exposed Enough? Lay Inferences about Chemical Exposure," *Risk Analysis,* Vol. 19, No. 4 (August 1999), pp. 649–659.
63. Ibid., p. 649.

Epidemic disease has killed more people than war. Thus far, fear of disease is a reasonable response to the threat. But people tend to fear unusual diseases more than well-known, more common killers. Malaria, an ancient disease, kills 1 million people a year worldwide. Marburg has killed only 10 people; Ebola has killed 891 since its discovery in 1976.[64] Yet it is Ebola and Marburg that have inspired terrifying books and movies. We respond to the likelihood of death in the event the disease is contracted, rather than the compound probability of contracting the disease and succumbing to its effects.[65] The pneumonic plague that broke out in Surat, India, in 1994 reportedly caused hundreds of thousands of people to flee in panic, including 80 percent of the city's private doctors. The disease is estimated to have cost India $2 billion because of its impact on tourism and exports, even though outside experts estimated that there were fewer than 100 cases of plague in Surat and fewer than 100 cases of plague in Beed.[66] Bioterrorism could involve diseases that seem exotic, especially in industrialized societies, increasing their hold on our imagination and increasing the dread factor.

LOSS OF FAITH IN THE ABILITY OF SCIENTISTS TO PROTECT US

In 1957 the National Association of Science Writers surveyed American views of science. Nearly 90 percent of those polled believed that the world was "better off because of science." Eighty-eight percent believed that science was "the main reason for our rapid progress," and 90 percent of those polled felt that there were no negative consequences of science.[67] Beginning in the 1970s, technological optimism began to erode. A series of environmental disasters, including those at Three Mile Island in 1979 and Chernobyl in 1986, contributed

---

64. See http://www.cdc.gov/ncidod/dvrd/spb/mnpages/dispages/ebotabl.htm (accessed February 20, 2002).
65. National BW programs have included work on Ebola and antibiotic-resistant bacteria. If terrorists do try to spread disease, they are probably more likely to choose more ordinary diseases. Still, the very idea of deliberately disseminated disease—whether ordinary or rare—is terrifying. Audrey Kurth Cronin points out that diseases for which there are no cures elicit particular dread, even if they are rare. Interview with Cronin, April 24, 2001.
66. Garrett, *Betrayal of Trust;* and Philip M. Boffey, "Lessons of the Plague," *New York Times,* November 14, 1994, p. 16. The response to the foot-and-mouth disease epidemic in the United Kingdom is perhaps a counterexample, in that there seems to have been little panic. The disease is fairly common but affects humans only very rarely. Perhaps these factors, together with the (possibly false) perception that the government was in control, fed into the public's response. This issue requires further study.
67. U.S. Congress, Office of Technology Assessment, *The Regulatory Environment for Science: A Technical Memorandum* (February 1986), pp. 130–132, cited in Charles Piller, *The Fail-Safe Society: Community Defiance and the End of American Technological Optimism* (New York: Basic Books, 1991), p. 5.

to the public's loss of faith. In a series of polls in the 1980s, 25 percent or more of those surveyed believed that technology would do more harm than good to the human race or that its risks outweighed its benefits.[68]

Kristin Shrader-Frechette argues that scientists contributed to the public's loss of faith in their work by presenting their opinions as established facts, noting that when scientists "present their own educated (but controversial) guesses as science, they can jeopardize the credibility of science. The result can be the anti-science sentiment that is widespread today."[69] Given this, it is perhaps not surprising that Europeans distrust the government scientists who are telling them that the outbreak of bovine spongiform encephalopathy (mad cow disease) is under control, and the risk of contracting its fatal human form, new-variant-Creutzfeldt-Jakob disease, is minimal.[70]

IMPLICATIONS FOR RISK ANALYSIS AND POLICY

What happens in risk versus risk trade-offs when the target risk evokes disproportionate fears? The literature provides few answers. But Americans' attitudes toward nuclear power provide some clues about the danger of overreaction.[71] The countervailing risk of relying on carbon fuels—air pollution and global warming—may be far more dangerous for human health than the target risk. But fear of radioactive hazards has made it difficult to increase reliance on nuclear power. The image of a mushroom cloud stays fixed in our subconscious—despite the physical impossibility of a nuclear power plant detonating like a nuclear bomb—whereas the dangers of relying on carbon fuels are far less graphic.

Bioterrorism is also a dreaded risk, suggesting that policymakers may rush to develop countermeasures to this terribly frightening threat without assessing countervailing dangers. They may feel politically vulnerable, knowing how their constituents would react if, after a BW attack, preparations were shown to be inadequate. They may also overestimate the risk of panic.[72] The

---

68. Piller, *The Fail-Safe Society*.

69. Kristin S. Shrader-Frechette, "Science versus Educated Guessing: Risk Assessment, Nuclear Waste, and Public Policy," *BioScience*, Vol. 46, No. 7 (July–August 1996), p. 498.

70. See Sheila Jasanoff, "Civilization and Madness: The Great BSE Scare of 1996," *Public Understanding of Science*, Vol. 6 (1997), pp. 221–232. For discussion of the impact of risk communication, see Nakayachi, "How Do People Evaluate Risk Reduction When They Are Told Zero Risk Is Impossible?" pp. 235–242; and MacGregor, Slovic, and Malmfors, "How Exposed Is Exposed Enough?"

71. Slovic, "Perception of Risk," pp. 280–281; and Slovic, Fischoff, and Lichtenstein, "Facts and Fears."

72. Social psychologists have shown that people tend to see others as overly emotional and to at-

purpose of this assessment is not to suggest that people should not fear terrorism, or that policymakers should not seek to reduce the risk, but to point out that fear can encourage "risk of the month" responses, without careful consideration of countervailing dangers.

The public's "irrational" overvaluation of dreaded risks may partly reflect ethical concerns (such as a desire for equity), concern about long-term effects on the environment, and the notion that people should be protected from involuntary risks more than from voluntary ones. Tensions between expert and lay communities are likely to rise unless each side fully understands the other's interests and values.

Moreover, one individual's expert is another's layperson. National security experts in the White House and Congress see microbiologists as naïve and reckless for publishing findings potentially of interest to terrorists. To them, microbiologists' attachment to the notion of openness in science looks like a dangerous indulgence. Microbiologists, on the other hand, are dismayed by government regulators' ignorance of basic science and of scientific methods. They see the publication of their results as the only way to develop better medical countermeasures for infectious disease.

There is a more general problem with the distinction between experts and laypersons: We all play both roles. As Sheila Jasanoff explains, although experts may consider fecal matter in breakfast cereal to be medically acceptable, provided the quantity is kept relatively low, the expert is likely to become a layperson if informed that the particular bowl of cereal his child is about to eat is contaminated with the maximally acceptable amount.[73]

The Need for Risk Trade-off Analysis

Americans are increasingly unwilling to accept involuntary risks. They demand cleaner water, tougher air-pollution standards, better treatment for disease, and safer cars. The effects of national risk-reduction campaigns are mixed, however, because remedies for reducing one danger often create new

---

tribute their reactions to their personalities, while judging themselves to be rational and flexible. See Lennart Sjoberg, "Worry and Risk Perception," *Risk Analysis*, Vol. 18, No. 1 (February 1998), p. 92. Thomas A. Glass and Monica Schoch-Spana, "Bioterrorism and the People: How to Vaccinate a City against Panic," *Clinical Infectious Diseases*, Vol. 34 (2002), pp. 217–223, http://www.journals.uchicago.edu/CID/journal/issues/v34n2/011333/011333.html (accessed September 30, 2002).

73. Interview with Sheila Jasanoff, science-studies scholar, Cambridge, Massachusetts, June 25, 2001.

ones. Doctors, regulators, and ordinary citizens make risk versus risk trade-offs every day, but sometimes it takes years before the adverse consequences of risk-reduction strategies become known.[74]

To prevent reactive, "risk of the month" responses to national security crises, decisionmakers could benefit from carrying out the kind of risk trade-off analysis employed to evaluate environmental and health policies. To this end, decisionmakers should ask themselves the following questions:

- What are the problems to be addressed?
- What are the proposed policy responses?
- In what ways might the policy affect other governmental priorities, for example, broader foreign policy objectives or domestic political concerns?
- In what ways might the policy adversely affect fundamental values, for example, civil liberties, fairness, or in the case of bioterror, the desire to promote cooperation among scientists conducting basic research? Are these values shared by the population at large or only by certain stakeholders?
- How effective is the proposed remedy: What percentage of the threat would be eradicated by the policy, with what probability?
- Do risk-superior strategies exist?

THE PROBLEMS TO BE ADDRESSED

Policymakers perceive two kinds of problems regarding access to biological agents. First, regulations governing access to pathogens are too lax. Second, information related to the production of biological agents is too loosely controlled.

PERCEIVED PROBLEMS IN REGULATING ACCESS TO PATHOGENS. Prior to September 11 and the anthrax scare, no law prohibited individuals from possessing biological agents. The Biological Weapons Act of 1989 makes it illegal knowingly to develop, produce, acquire, retain, or transfer biological agents, toxin, or delivery systems for use as a weapon. This law cannot be used to prosecute those who possess biological agents—even if they do not appear to have any legitimate reason to do so—unless the government can prove they intended to use those agents as weapons. Larry Wayne Harris, a neo-Nazi who ordered the causative agent of plague through the mail in 1995, was charged only with mail fraud because he claimed that he needed the plague for defensive purposes and the FBI could not prove otherwise.[75] Congressman Tom

---

74. Graham and Wiener, *Risk versus Risk*.
75. See Jessica Eve Stern, "Larry Wayne Harris (1998)," in Tucker, *Toxic Terror*, pp. 227–246.

Bliley (R-Va.) noted, "We permit anyone in this country—including felons, foreign nationals from sensitive countries, and members of extremists [*sic*] groups—to lawfully possess even the most deadly biological agents, including anthrax, the plague, and the Ebola virus. They don't even have to notify or register with any federal agency or gain government approval to possess them."[76]

The Antiterrorism and Effective Death Penalty Act of 1996 requires the Department of Health and Human Services to regulate the transfer of select agents. But the regulations apply only to those who acquire the agents through a self-disclosed transaction with a legitimate supplier. They do not apply to organizations or individuals who isolate threat agents from nature, who acquire them surreptitiously, or who possessed them prior to April 15, 1997, the date that the CDC issued the regulations. Animal and plant pathogens are not covered.[77] When individuals request to be registered to receive select agents, law enforcement personnel are not informed.[78]

Two laws passed in the wake of the anthrax mailings criminalize the possession of biological agents, except for medical purposes or "bona fide" research, and prohibit "restricted persons" from working with them.[79] But individuals known to have acquired biological agents in the past for questionable purposes might not have been included on the list. For example, Larry Wayne Harris was not a restricted person, as far as is publicly known. Thus he would presumably have been allowed to work with listed agents under the new rules.[80] And if the FBI is correct in its reported belief that the person responsi-

76. Statement by Congressman Tom Bliley of Virginia before the House Subcommittee on Oversight and Investigations of the Energy, and Commerce Committee, "Threat of Bioterrorism in America: Assessing the Adequacy of Federal Law Relating to Dangerous Biological Agents," 106th Cong., 1st sess., May 20, 1999, House Serial 106-19, http://com-notes.house.gov/cchear/hearings106.nsf/a317d879d32c08c2852567d3005399463/3aeb445f3c2d91e8852567cf0048bc27?OpenDocument (accessed September 29, 2002).
77. Epstein, "Controlling Biological Warfare Threats," p. 332.
78. Testimony by Robert Burnham, Federal Bureau of Investigation, "Threat of Bioterrorism in America: Assessing the Adequacy of the Federal Law Relating to Dangerous Biological Agents."
79. In Public Law 107-56 (the *U.S.A. Patriot Act*), a "restricted person" is defined as an individual who is under indictment for a crime punishable by imprisonment for a term exceeding one year; has been convicted in any course of a crime punishable by imprisonment for a term exceeding one year; is a fugitive from justice; is an unlawful user of controlled substances; is an illegal alien or an alien from a country that the State Department has designated as a sponsor of terrorism; has been adjudicated as having a mental defect or has been committed to a mental institution; or has been discharged dishonorably from the U.S. armed services. Public Law No. 107-188 repeated these restrictions and also required facilities that possess or transfer select agents to register.
80. See Stern, "Larry Wayne Harris (1998)." The Patriot Act's "restricted persons" definition does not address this case, but under Public Law 107-188, he would be required to register with the government.

ble for the 2001 mailings was a former government insider, he too would probably have been allowed to work with listed agents.[81] Some government
regulators believe that the law is still not strong enough.

PERCEIVED PROBLEMS IN CONTROLLING ACCESS TO INFORMATION. Advances
in molecular biology have yielded enormous breakthroughs for the treatment
of disease. Genome sequencing efforts are expected to deliver the complete sequence of more than seventy major bacterial, fungal, and parasitic pathogens
of humans, animals, and plants, with important implications for infectious disease research and comparative genomics.[82] Modern biomedical research is inherently dual-use, however. Advances in medicine and basic science—carried
out for commercial or defense purposes—can inevitably be put to hostile use.
Biophysicist Steven Block argues that these advances make possible the creation of entirely new biological weapons "endowed with unprecedented
power to destroy."[83]

A number of publications have alarmed some observers because of the
possibility that they could help a would-be producer of biological weapons—
whether a state or a subnational group.[84] The continuously expanding microbial genome databases, many of which are published on the internet,[85] now
provide a "parts-list of all potential genes involved in pathogenicity and virulence, adhesion and colonization of host cells, immune response evasion and

81. Dan Eggen and Joby Warrick, "FBI Still Lacks Identifiable Suspect in Anthrax Probe: Investiga-
tors Continue to Focus on People Connected to Labs That Had Strain Found in Letters," *Washington Post,* February 26, 2002, p. A7; and Guy Gugliotta, "Still No Arrests in Anthrax Probe, but
'Progress' Is Noted," *Washington Post,* August 4, 2002, p. A8.
82. Claire M. Fraser and Malcolm R. Dando, "Genomics and Future Biological Weapons: The Need
for Preventative Action by the Biomedical Community," *Nature Genetics,* November 1, 2001,
pp. 253–265.
83. Steven M. Block, "Living Nightmares: Biological Threats Enabled by Molecular Biology," in
Sydney D. Drell, Abraham D. Sofaer, and George D. Wilson, eds., *The New Terror: Facing the Threat
of Biological and Chemical Weapons* (Stanford, Calif.: Hoover Institution, 1999), pp. 39–75, at 42.
Mitchell Wallerstein points out that it is also possible that in the course of responding to biomedical and other terrorist threats, we may develop treatments, detection systems, and so on that are a
positive development for humanity. Email communication, December 17, 2002.
84. National BW programs and disgruntled government scientists can use information on cutting-
edge molecular biology more readily than terrorist groups, of course. "Possible Terrorist Use of
Modern Biotechnology Techniques," http://thayer.dartmouth.edu/%7Eethreats/ethreats6.html
(accessed September 30, 2002). For the purposes of this article, however, any use of BW against civilian populations is considered terrorism. For further discussion of definitions of terrorism, see
Jessica Stern, *The Ultimate Terrorists* (Cambridge, Mass.: Harvard University Press, 1999). Gregory
Koblentz reports that much of the Soviet Union's efforts to use molecular biology to create new or
improved weapons was inspired by research conducted by civilians in the United States for purely
scientific purposes. Koblentz, "Pathogens as Weapons: Biological Warfare and International Security," Ph.D. dissertation, Massachusetts Institute of Technology, forthcoming.
85. See http://www.tigr.org/tdb/mdb/mdbcomplete.html (accessed August 12, 2002).

antibiotic resistance from which to pick and choose the most lethal combinations," Clare Fraser and Malcolm Dando observe.[86]

In 1994 the smallpox genome was published. An article published in 2001 showed how a single gene modification can greatly increase the virulence of an influenza virus. Also in 2001, Australian researchers reported that they had inserted a gene into the mousepox genome, inadvertently converting the virus into a highly virulent strain. The recombinant virus was lethal even to mice that were genetically resistant to mousepox and to mice that had been vaccinated against the disease.[87]

In 2002 researchers reported that they had created infectious poliovirus "from scratch," using the published gene sequence for the virus and mail-order DNA.[88] This was the first demonstration that a published genome could be turned into an infectious virus. Gene sequences for Ebola, influenza, smallpox, HIV, and many other viruses are also published on the internet, prompting fears that terrorists could attempt to replicate the experiment with a more virulent agent.[89]

Also in 2002, researchers published an article that described a method for modifying the vaccinia virus (which is used as a vaccine against smallpox) to change a vaccinia protein into a version normally made by the related variola virus (which causes smallpox). The synthesized variola protein proved to be 100 times as potent as the original vaccinia version in inhibiting a component of the human immune system.[90] An editorial accompanying the article conceded that the idea that terrorists might attempt to replicate the experiment had been suggested as a "reason for considering it imprudent to publish observations of this nature." It insisted, however, that information that "can be ex-

---

86. Fraser and Dando, "Genomics and Future Biological Weapons."
87. Ronald J. Jackson, Alistair Ramsay, Carina D. Christensen, Sandra Beaton, Diana F. Hall, and Ian A. Ramshaw, "Expression of Mouse Interleukin-4 by a Recombinant Entromelia Virus Suppresses Cytolytic Lymphocyte Responses and Overcomes Genetic Resistance to Mousepox, " *Journal of Virology*, Vol. 75, No. 3 (February 2001), pp. 1205–1210; R. Nowak, "Disaster in the Making," *New Scientist*, January 13, 2002, p. 4; and Carina Dennis, "The Bugs of War," *Nature*, May 17, 2001, pp. 232–235. For analysis of why the results should not have been surprising, see Malcolm Dando, "Defining 'Potentially Dangerous' Biotechnology Research," University of Bradford, February 2002.
88. J. Cello, A.V. Paul, and E. Wimmer, *Science*, July 11, 2002, pp. 1016–1018.
89. Tom Clarke, "Polio Made from Scratch," *Nature: Science Update*, July 12, 2002. http://www.nature.com/nsu/020708/020708-17.html (accessed September 29, 2002).
90. Ariella M. Rosengard, Yu Liu, Zhiping Nie, and Robert Jimenez, "Variola Virus Immune Evasion Design: Expression of a Highly Efficient Inhibitor of Human Complement," *Proceedings of the National Academy of Sciences*, June 25, 2002, pp. 8808–8813.

ploited for beneficial ends" should not be censored "merely because it might give a potential terrorist ideas."[91]

Some observers are increasingly alarmed about the possibility that publications of this kind could be put to malign use. Bioethicist Arthur Caplan argues, "We have to get away from the ethos that knowledge is good, knowledge should be publicly available, that information will liberate us. . . . Information will kill us in the techno-terrorist age, and I think it's nuts to put that stuff on Web sites."[92] D.A. Henderson, a former adviser to President George W. Bush and director of the Center for Civilian Biodefense Studies at Johns Hopkins University, argues, "I can't for the life of me figure out how we are going to deal with this."[93] George Poste warns that biologists will have to regulate themselves or that controls will be imposed on them. Biology must "lose its innocence," he argues, calling the status quo "untenable."[94]

PROPOSED POLICY REMEDIES

Some policymakers would like to see the regulations controlling access to pathogens and related information tightened. The International Traffic in Arms Regulations (ITAR) regulates the export of certain munitions. If a project falls under ITAR, an export license is required before information can be shared with foreign nationals, including scientists and students. The design, development, engineering, and manufacture of defense articles (including chemical and biological agents) come under a provision entitled "defense services," which are also controlled for export.[95] "ITAR is comprehensive, complex, time-consuming, and often inconsistent," and often requires legal interpretation, explains Eugene Skolnikoff.[96] He expects that "it is only a matter of time before ITAR will be extended" to biological research that could be construed as having military applications.[97]

Representative Dave Weldon (R-Fla.) called the 2002 polio paper mentioned above "a blue print that could conceivably enable terrorists to inexpensively

91. P.J. Lachman, "Microbial Subversion of the Immune Response," *Proceedings of the National Academy of Sciences,* June 25, 2002, p. 8462.
92. Quoted in Ronald M. Atlas, "Bioterrorism: The ASM Response," *ASM News,* Vol. 68, No. 3 (2002), p. 118. Original in Eric Lichtblau, "Response to Terror: Rising Fears That What We Do Know Can Hurt Us," *Los Angeles Times,* November 18, 2001, p. 1.
93. Quoted in Nowak, "Disaster in the Making," p. 4.
94. Quoted in Aldhous, "Biologists Urged to Address Risk of Data Aiding Bioweapon Design."
95. International Traffic in Arms Regulations (22 CFR 120-13), March 2001.
96. Eugene Skolnikoff, "Research Universities and National Security: Can Traditional Values Survive?" p. 67, http://www.aaas.org/spp/yearbook/2003/stvwch6.pdf (accessed September 27, 2002).
97. Ibid., p. 68.

create human pathogens," and introduced a resolution criticizing the decision of the American Association for the Advancement of Science to publish it. The resolution, which did not pass, also called on government agencies that fund molecular biological research to reconsider classification rules.[98]

Poste has called for more classification of research with potential defense applications, as well as a requirement that proposals to the National Institutes of Health include a declaration that the researchers had considered the possibility that their findings could be used for malicious purposes. He has also urged that for projects considered especially risky, manuscripts be vetted prior to publication, with the possibility that permission to publish could be denied.[99] An editorial published in *Nature* together with an article describing Poste's recommendations observed that the "anguished reactions" to some of Poste's suggestions make clear that there are "no simple answers" to the dilemma about protecting information that could be used for malevolent purposes.[100]

OTHER POLICY PRIORITIES THREATENED BY THE PROPOSED REMEDIES

These proposed remedies threaten three policy priorities other than counterterrorism. The first is the fight against newly emerging and reemerging infectious disease. The second is arms control. The third is the promotion of advances in fundamental research and biotechnology.

According to a recent National Intelligence Estimate, "new and re-emerging infectious diseases will pose a rising global health threat that will complicate U.S. and global security over the next 20 years. These diseases will endanger U.S. citizens at home and abroad, threaten U.S. armed forces deployed overseas and exacerbate social and political instability in key countries and regions in which the United States has significant interests."[101] Every day, tens of thousands of people around the world die from infectious disease.[102] Thus, if citizens from non-NATO countries were prohibited from working on select

---

98. House Resolution 514, July 26, 2002, 107th Cong., 2d sess., http://www.fas.org/sgp/congress/2002/hres514.html. For arguments as to why it should not have been published (yet did not represent a security threat), see Steven M. Block and Donald Kennedy, "A Not-So-Cheap Stunt," *Science*, August 2, 2002, pp. 769–770. See also Jennifer Couzin, "Polio Paper Sparks Criticism from Congressional Representatives," *ScienceNOW*, July 29, 2002.
99. Aldhous, "Biologists Urged to Address Risk of Data Aiding Bioweapon Design."
100. "The End of Innocence?" *Nature*, November 15, 2001, p. 236.
101. Testimony by David Gordon, National Intelligence Council, before the House International Relations Committee, "Infectious Diseases: A Growing Threat to America's Health and Security," 106th Cong., 2d sess., June 29, 2000, House Serial 106-146, p. 35, http://www.house.gov/international_relations/fc062900.pdf (accessed September 29, 2002).
102. Testimony by Ronald Atlas, American Society of Microbiology, "Threat of Bioterrorism in America: Assessing the Adequacy of the Federal Law Relating to Dangerous Biological Agents."

agents, public health could suffer first in their countries and eventually worldwide. The potential adverse consequences for research on infectious disease transform the risk of biological terrorism against Americans into health risks worldwide.

Additional regulations could dampen researchers' enthusiasm for working on select agents at a time when such research is needed more than ever. It is important to realize that although most select agents pose an esoteric threat to NATO member countries, they cause endemic diseases in the developing world. As CDC scientist Stephen Ostroff argues, "There is a need to expand research involving select agents, not to constrain it. We must bring the best and brightest minds to bear on the development of better vaccines, antiviral agents, antibiotics, and other therapies for exposure to, or illness from, biological agents. To do so, we need to ensure that restrictions on possession or handling of biological agents do not have a chilling effect on the willingness of scientists and research establishments to take part."[103] Ronald Atlas warned in testimony before Congress, "We have to ensure that we do not take actions that will form roadblocks between us and the international community in our effort to in fact combat infectious disease."[104]

Censoring publication of biomedical research could also adversely affect work on infectious disease. Controlling dissemination of basic research findings could discourage research on virulence, transmissibility, pathogenesis, immunology, and other issues that are important for understanding and controlling the spread of infectious disease. This subversion of science could deter research in promising fields of inquiry. Dr. Ariella Rosengard, who modified a benign virus to make it more like the virus that causes smallpox, asks, "How do doctors talk about research if we don't publish it?" She argues that intellectual exchange promotes better science and better conclusions.[105]

Arms control experts also argue that classifying defensive bioweapons programs could give governments an excuse to hide offensive bioweapons research. Three *New York Times* reporters revealed in 2001 that three U.S.

---

103. Testimony by Stephen Ostroff, Centers for Disease Control and Prevention, "Threat of Bioterrorism in America: Assessing the Adequacy of the Federal Law Relating to Dangerous Biological Agents," p. 24.
104. Testimony by Ronald Atlas, American Society for Microbiology, before the Subcommittee on Technology, Terrorism, and Government Information of the Senate Judiciary Committee, "Germs, Toxins, and Terror: The New Threat to America," 107th Cong., 1st sess., November 6, 2001, http://judiciary.senate.gov/testimony.cfm?id=123&wit_id=49 (accessed September 29, 2002).
105. Quoted in Diana Jean Schemo, "Sept. 11 Strikes at Labs' Doors," *New York Times*, August 13, 2002, p. D2.

government agencies—the Central Intelligence Agency, the Defense Threat Reduction Agency, and the Defense Intelligence Agency—had been secretly engaged in biodefense projects that appeared to some arms control experts to come close to violating the Biological Weapons Convention (BWC), ratified by the United States in 1975.[106] President Bill Clinton was reportedly not informed of their existence.[107] In the course of the investigation of the source of the anthrax used in the 2001 attacks, the U.S. Army admitted that it had produced a small quantity of anthrax spores in a highly lethal powdered form.[108] "As long as the United States pursues classified projects, other members of the BWC have no way of knowing that these activities are treaty compliant and must accept U.S. assurances on faith," Jonathan Tucker argues.[109] Classifying such work could raise suspicions, creating a climate of fear with the potential to encourage proliferation.[110]

Applying ITAR regulations to biological research, as they have been to space-based technologies, would make American universities less hospitable to foreigners, which in turn could have adverse consequences not only for the advancement of molecular biology and medicine but also for the U.S. economy. More than half a million foreign students are studying at American universities, an increase of 35 percent in fifteen years. Foreign nationals account for more than 50 percent of engineering doctorates and more than 25 percent of science doctorates awarded by U.S. universities. Foreign students and researchers have become vital to the U.S. economy.[111]

VALUES PUT AT RISK BY PROPOSED REMEDIES
Three stakeholders' values need to be considered in contemplating possible remedies for controlling biological weapons agents: researchers, universities,

---

106. Judith Miller, Stephen Engelberg, and William J. Broad, *Germs: Biological Weapons and America's Secret War* (New York: Simon and Schuster, 2001), pp. 292–298; and Judith Miller, Stephen Engelberg, and William J. Broad, "U.S. Germ Warfare Research Pushes Treaty Limits," *New York Times*, September 4, 2001, p. A1.
107. Jonathan B. Tucker, "A Farewell to Germs: The U.S. Renunciation of Biological and Toxin Warfare, 1969–70," *International Security*, Vol. 27, No. 1 (Summer 2002), p. 147.
108. William J. Broad and Judith Miller, "U.S. Recently Produced Anthrax in a Highly Lethal Powder Form," *New York Times*, December 13, 2001, p. A1.
109. Tucker, "A Farewell to Germs," p. 148.
110. See quotes by Elisa D. Harris and Barbara Hatch Rosenberg in Broad and Miller, "U.S. Recently Produced Anthrax in a Highly Lethal Powder Form." See also Elisa D. Harris, "Research Not to Be Hidden," *New York Times*, September 6, 2001, p. 23. For more analysis, see http://www.fas.org/bwc/usbiodefense.htm (accessed September 30, 2002).
111. Skolnikoff, "Research Universities and National Security," p. 71.

and the public. Restricting foreign students' research choices and controlling dissemination of basic-research results represent a significant threat to the free exchange of ideas that scientists believe is essential. Research universities consider the commitment to openness and equal opportunity for all students regardless of national origin as essential for maintaining high-quality education and research.[112]

The debate about openness in science is not new. In 1982 the Department of Defense tried unsuccessfully to extend export controls on military hardware to research findings with possible military applications, arguing that controls were necessary because the Soviet Union had "organized a massive, systematic effort to get advanced technology from the West."[113] But a study commissioned by the Department of Defense concluded that the leadership of the United States was based on a scientific foundation, "whose vitality in turn depends on effective communication among scientists." The short-term security achieved by restricting the flow of information would be "purchased at a price." Moreover, "security by accomplishment may have more to offer as a general national strategy," and "openness helps to nurture" vitality in research efforts needed to ensure the long-term security of the United States.[114]

The study concluded that "no restriction of any kind limiting access of communication should be applied to any area of university research, be it basic or applied, unless it involves a technology meeting all the following criteria: 1. The technology is developing rapidly, and the time from basic science to application is short; 2. The technology has identifiable direct military applications; or it is dual-use and involves process or production-related techniques; 3. Transfer of the technology would give the [adversary] significant near-term military benefits; and 4. The U.S. is the only source of information about the technology, or other friendly nationals that could also be the source have control systems as secure as ours."[115] None of these conditions for restricting dissemination of research findings is met for molecular-biological basic-science

---

112. Skolnikoff, "Research Universities and National Security."
113. Don J. Deyoung, U.S. Naval Research Laboratory, White Paper on Proposed Security Controls on Defense Research, April 2, 2002, http://www.fas.org/sgp/othergov/deyoung.html (accessed August 13, 2002).
114. National Academy of Sciences, "Scientific Communication and National Security" (1982), p. ix; and Deyoung, White Paper on Proposed Security Controls on Defense Research.
115. National Academy of Sciences, "Executive Summary," *Scientific Communication and National Security* (1982), p. 5, http://www.nap.edu/books/0309033322.html. I replaced the acronym "USSR" with "[adversary]."

publications, such as the one on polio that was of particular concern to Congressman Weldon.

In 1985 President Ronald Reagan's administration issued a directive that reflected these findings. National Security Directive 189, which is still in force, argues that U.S. strength in science depends on "an environment conducive to creativity," in which the "free exchange of ideas is a vital component." It stipulates that products of fundamental research should remain unrestricted "to the maximum extent possible." The directive makes clear that no restrictions may be placed on the reporting of research results that are unclassified except as provided in applicable U.S. statutes. The only tool available to the government is classification; there can be no censoring of "sensitive" information that is not classified.[116] Executive Order 12958, issued in 1995, reiterates the prohibition against classifying "basic scientific research information not clearly related to the national security."[117] In November 2001, in a letter to former Defense Secretary Harold Brown, National Security Adviser Condoleezza Rice confirmed that National Security Directive 189 is still in place.[118] Nonetheless, four months later, the White House ordered government agencies to remove sensitive but unclassified documents from their websites.[119]

The public probably does not share the value of openness in science, at least not to the same degree. Policy solutions must be viewed as responsive to the public's concerns, biologist R. Timothy Mulcahy argues. Scientists "can ill afford to be perceived as 'intellectual Taliban,' aiding and abetting terrorists by perceived indifference or outright rejection of national security interests or public concerns."[120] It may be necessary for universities to get involved in educating the public about the contributions of biological science to national security, he argues.[121] Indeed the values and interests of the public, the national

---

116. "National Policy on the Transfer of Scientific, Technical, and Engineering Information," September 21, 1985, National Security Decision Directive 189, http://fas.org/irp/offdocs/nsdd/nsdd-189.htm (accessed August 12, 2002).
117. Rules for classification are spelled out in Executive Order 12958, April 17, 1995.
118. Letter to Dr. Harold Brown from Condoleezza Rice, November 1, 2001, in files.
119. The designation "sensitive but unclassified" is "potentially a catchall and it could be an invitation to abuse," argues secrecy expert Steven Aftergood, citing the Pentagon's removal of evaluation reports for procurement programs, which, although useless for terrorists, are "enormously useful for both congressional and public oversight of many large programs." Quoted in Sammon, "Web Sites Told to Delete Data."
120. R. Timothy Mulcahy, "The Response to Bioterrorism: Challenges for Universities and Scientists," in files.
121. Ibid.

security community, and the research community differ, and disputes among these communities are likely to grow in the absence of dialogue. "Arriving at a common understanding—the basis for sound policy—will therefore require each to understand the objectives and constraints of the others," Gerald Epstein argues.[122]

EFFECTIVENESS OF THE PROPOSED REMEDIES

All threat agents listed by the CDC, except variola, occur in nature.[123] For example, the CDC lists filoviruses, the causative agent of Ebola, which is endemic in Africa, as a high-priority category A organism with the potential to pose significant risks to national security.[124] Multidrug-resistant tuberculosis is listed in category C, which includes emerging, reemerging, and drug-resistant diseases that could be engineered for mass dissemination in the future. Multidrug-resistant tuberculosis is spreading rapidly through Russian prisons. No matter how tight the controls on laboratory research, determined terrorists could attempt to isolate these agents from sick persons' blood or from the soil. Also, as mentioned above, cultures are available from collections outside the United States.

Of course, the goal is to increase the difficulty of acquiring these agents: No regulatory regime, however, can prevent access to materials that exist in nature. The Aum Shinrikyo cult traveled to Zaire in search of Ebola but was apparently unsuccessful in isolating the agent, suggesting that controlling access to select agents can at least slow acquisition. Although everyone agrees that there will never be a leak-proof control system, it is important to compare the necessarily limited effectiveness of the controls with the countervailing dangers and to consider how these dangers can be minimized. Many scientists have voiced concerns that the regulations will impose heavy costs on the "good guys," who are unlikely to isolate cultures from nature or purchase them abroad to circumvent cumbersome regulations, with little effect on "bad guys," who may make such attempts and eventually succeed.[125]

Another consideration is that efforts to control the spread of information and technologies are ultimately doomed to fail. Diffusion of technologies to other

122. Epstein, "Controlling Biological Warfare Threats."
123. "Biological and Chemical Terrorism: Strategic Plan for Preparedness and Response," recommendations of the CDC Strategic Planning Group, *Morbidity and Mortality Weekly Report*, No. RR-04, April 21, 2000.
124. Ibid.
125. Interviews with CDC personnel, April 2000.

countries and even terrorists can only be delayed, not prevented. This is especially true for biological weaponry. The key questions are: How much delay, and at what cost? In this case, it is difficult to predict how new ideas will be applied—whether to cure diseases or create new, more lethal forms. This issue is particularly pertinent to the debate about whether to publish articles that discuss molecularly engineered pathogens and immune responses.

Toxicologist Eileen Choffnes, a senior program officer at the National Academy of Sciences (NAS), explains why restricting dissemination of basic microbiological research findings is different from classifying nuclear weapons–related information: "The United States had a virtual monopoly over the knowledge base, infrastructure, and processing technologies for nuclear weapons until the early 1950s. That knowledge base spread only very slowly, first to the Soviet Union, and later to other countries. But we have no comparable technological edge in molecular biology related to biological weapons. The technology, the infrastructure, the knowledge base—even the pathogens—are available globally."[126]

SEEKING RISK-SUPERIOR STRATEGIES

It is difficult to design risk-reduction strategies that do not create countervailing dangers. But sometimes it is possible to develop risk-superior policies that provide an equivalent level of benefit while minimizing countervailing dangers or even "coincident risk reductions," which Graham and Wiener define as an unexpected bonus risk reduction accompanying a policy for reducing the target risk.[127] To develop such risk-superior strategies, the needs and values of stakeholders must be known.

One such risk-superior policy would be to improve surveillance systems for human, animal, and plant diseases worldwide.[128] Laboratories need to be built

126. Interview with Eileen Choffnes, August 16, 2002. I am grateful to Eileen also for sharing the briefing books that she prepared for NAS panels that touch on these topics. Gerald Epstein points out that the arguments in favor of openness (which were derived in regard to nuclear weapons during the Cold War) may be sufficiently generic and robust to cover the current situation as well. But we need to reexamine them to convince ourselves (and others who may be pressing for more stringent restrictions) that they still apply. Email communication, August 28, 2002.
127. Graham and Wiener, *Risk versus Risk*, p. 232. Interestingly, there are a number of risk-coincident strategies for counterterrorism, although not necessarily regarding bioterror. Efforts to assist failed or failing states and removing import quotas on commodities produced in countries where terrorists thrive are but two examples. Raising the opportunity cost of young men's time and improving governance in failing states are likely to reduce the appeal of terrorism for the foot soldiers of terrorist groups.
128. Christopher Chyba, "Biological Terrorism, Emerging Diseases, and National Security," a report for the Rockefeller Brothers' Fund, http://www.rbf.org/Chyba_Bioterrorism.pdf (accessed

in the field; a system for transporting samples needs to be developed; and communication links among laboratories, national health ministries, WHO Collaborating Centers, hospitals, and private voluntary organizations need to be established. The revolution in communications technologies needs to be applied to disease surveillance and control.[129] Without such a system in place, physicians will be hard pressed to identify and respond to unusual disease outbreaks, whatever their source. The system would simultaneously assist in identifying bioterror sources and improving public health.

An arguably risk-superior approach to controlling access to pathogens might be to require institutions to register all individuals who work with select agents and to ban unregistered persons from entering laboratories where the agents are stored and used. Gerald Epstein points out that such a system would enable institutions to restrict access only to those whom they know to have a legitimate reason for using such agents and would also facilitate investigations of unlawful activity involving biological agents.[130]

A risk-superior approach to restricting dissemination of basic biomedical research would be to allow scientists to police themselves. John Collier argues that there is no bright line that would distinguish classified from unclassified material in molecular biology. "You can find a reason to censor almost any publication," he says. The only solution is to set up a committee of informed scientists willing to make a judgment about the benefits and costs of publication.[131] Malcolm Dando has proposed the creation of an international oversight board that would review potentially dangerous research projects to determine whether the benefits exceed the dangers and, for contentious projects with dangerous results that slip through the first filter, to determine whether publication of results should be allowed.[132] Epstein suggests a self-governance regime similar to the Asilomar process, which came out of a 1973 meeting of leading researchers studying recombinant DNA. Scientists from around the world agreed voluntarily not to carry out certain kinds of research and to put

August 16, 2002). See also Jessica Stern, "Reducing the Threat of WMD Terrorism: Opportunities for a New Foundation," recommendations to the Nuclear Threat Initiative, October 11, 2000; Jessica Stern, "Confronting Biological Terrorism," *Harvard International Review*, Vol. 23, No. 1 (Spring 2001), pp. 84–85; Christopher Chyba, "Biological Security in a Changed World," *Science*, September 28, 2001, p. 2349; and Chyba, "Toward Biological Security."
129. *Infectious Disease—A Global Health Threat*, report of the National Science and Technology Council Committee on International Science, Engineering, and Technology Working Group on Emerging and Re-emerging Infectious Disease, September 1995.
130. Epstein, "Controlling Biological Warfare Threats," p. 332.
131. Telephone interview, August 14, 2002.
132. Dando, "Defining 'Potentially Dangerous' Biotechnology Research," p. 23.

security and containment measures in place for other kinds. The challenge was to implement flexible constraints over potentially dangerous research without unnecessarily constraining it. Many of the restrictions put in place as a result of the scientists' concerns turned out to be technically unfounded and were ultimately removed. Asilomar serves as a good model for what is needed today, Epstein argues, in that the approach was voluntary, flexible, and effective.[133] Jonathan Tucker supports a similar approach, proposing that an international oversight board be created to assess potentially contentious research. Some research with direct offensive military applications would be forbidden outright, he proposes, but some would be allowed to go forward with close monitoring by the board.[134] Like Dando, Tucker suggests that the board conduct a prepublication review of research findings with potentially dangerous implications, such as the Australian mousepox discovery, for advice about whether publication should be allowed.[135]

Conclusion

Studies of perceived risk show that fear is disproportionately evoked by certain characteristics of risks. Biological agents are mysterious, unfamiliar, indiscriminate, uncontollable, inequitable, and invisible, all of which are characteristics of dreaded risks. The effects of these weapons are also difficult to predict and poorly understood by science. They are physically disgusting, a factor associated with moral aversion. The media tend to highlight terrorist incidents, heightening dread and panic still further (in a simultaneous relationship). We feel a gut-level fear and are prone to trying to eradicate the risk with little regard to the costs involved. This fear can influence our ability to assess with accuracy risk versus risk trade-offs, for example, between mundane (but common) risks to human health and those that are more spectacular. Experience with nuclear power, another dreaded risk, suggests that decisionmakers should be particularly careful when dealing with target risks that evoke dis-

133. Epstein, "Controlling Biological Warfare Threats," p. 338.
134. Jonathan B. Tucker, "Regulating Scientific Research of Potential Relevance to Biological Warfare," in Michael Barletta, ed., *After 9/11: Preventing Mass-Destruction Terrorism and Weapons Proliferation,* Occasional Paper 8 (Monterey, Calif.: Center for Nonproliferation Studies, Monterey Institute of International Studies, May 2002), pp. 24–27.
135. Tucker, "Regulating Scientific Research of Potential Relevance to Biological Warfare." See also publications and work in process by Elisa D. Harris and John Steinbruner, Controlling Dangerous Pathogens Project, University of Maryland, http://www.puaf.umd.edu/CISSM/Projects/AMCS/Pathogens.htm (accessed October 1, 2002).

proportionate dread, because there is a danger of choosing policies whose costs exceed their benefits. An assessment of countervailing dangers is thus particularly important for dreaded risks.

Risk trade-off analysis demands that decisionmakers think carefully about how to strike an appropriate balance between competing interests—in this case the desire to reduce the threat of terrorism while still promoting legitimate research. The article examined a particular policy remedy: controlling access to pathogens and related information as well as the possible countervailing risks.

Biological weapons are inherently dual-use commodities. All inputs to bioweapons production are used for legitimate purposes, including in medicine. Even variola virus, the causative agent of smallpox, is required for some biomedical research.[136] One of the most critical inputs—the pathogens—can be isolated from nature.[137] Another important input—information—is important to research on infectious disease. Even the tightest imaginable regime cannot prevent the production of biological weapons: The most policymakers can strive for is to make production more difficult. Efforts to frustrate BW production will inevitably affect both licit and illicit activities. Thus the limited effectiveness of the remedy must be balanced against the countervailing costs.

Two policy remedies currently under consideration—restricting dissemination of basic biomedical research findings and prohibiting citizens from non-NATO countries from working with select agents—could have an adverse impact on research on naturally occurring and deliberately disseminated infectious disease. It is likely that the countervailing dangers introduced by these proposed remedies exceed their benefits. Policies aimed at improving the public health infrastructure around the globe are critically important for addressing not only the threat of bioterror but also the threat of emerging, reemerging, and antibiotic-resistant disease. A better approach would be to allow scientists to police themselves by registering their laboratories and personnel with government agencies and by establishing an international oversight board that would review contentious research and publications.

Political scientist Leonard Cole observes that biological weapons have always been seen as "inherently sneaky, unfair, abhorrent," for reasons that are

---

136. The World Health Organization has decided not to destroy the official remaining live variola stocks, stored in repositories in Russia and the United States. The National Institute of Medicine recommended that stocks be retained because of their importance for developing antiviral medications and novel vaccines, as well as for use in studying the human immune system. See National Institute of Medicine, "Assessment of Future Needs for Variola (Smallpox) Virus," http://www.nap.edu/catalog/6445.html (accessed August 14, 2002).
137. Smallpox is the sole exception.

hard to explain.[138] Historian John Moon describes the revulsion as deep, mysterious, and ultimately inescapable.[139] As the technology for producing these weapons continues both to improve and to spread, those who oppose their use are in a race with those who would do us harm. Part of the race is technical—to develop better pharmaceuticals and diagnostics. And part of it involves developing better laws. But the challenge will be to ensure that the revulsion invoked by these weapons does not push us to take actions with unacceptable adverse effects on competing interests, including the promotion of legitimate research, civil liberties, and public health.

---

138. Leonard A. Cole, *The Eleventh Plague: The Politics of Biological and Chemical Warfare* (New York: W.H. Freeman and Co., 1997), p. 214.
139. John Moon, "Controlling Chemical and Biological Weapons through World War II," in Richard Dean Burns, ed., *Encyclopedia of Arms Control and Disarmament* (New York: Scribner's, 1993), pp. 657–674.

Beyond the MTCR | *Dinshaw Mistry*

Building a Comprehensive Regime to Contain Ballistic Missile Proliferation

The proliferation of ballistic missiles has been a major international security concern for many years.[1] Efforts to address this concern, centered on the Missile Technology Control Regime (MTCR), have had a mixed record.[2] The MTCR seeks to curb missile proliferation by denying regional powers the technology to build missiles. In the MTCR's first decade, Argentina, Brazil, Egypt, Iraq, Libya, South Africa, South Korea, Syria, and Taiwan were thwarted from advancing their missile ambitions. In light of these positive developments, MTCR members expressed satisfaction with the regime at its tenth anniversary in 1997. Yet in subsequent years, India, Iran, Israel, North Korea, and Pakistan launched medium-range missiles, and several other states have expanded their missile programs, demonstrating the MTCR's limitations. To augment the regime, MTCR members drafted the International Code of Conduct against Ballistic Missile Proliferation.[3] In November 2002 ninety-three countries signed the code, which calls on states to make their missile policies more transparent.

In this article I seek to answer two central questions: First, can the MTCR's technology barriers, along with the Code of Conduct's transparency initiatives, curb the spread of ballistic missiles? Second, if the MTCR and the code are inadequate, what additional measures are necessary to contain missile prolifer-

Dinshaw Mistry is Assistant Professor at the University of Cincinnati. This article draws from his book, Containing Missile Proliferation: Strategic Technology, Security Regimes, and International Cooperation in Arms Control *(Seattle: University of Washington Press, 2003).*

The author would like to thank Mark Smith, two anonymous reviewers, and participants at an October 2001 seminar at the Belfer Center for Science and International Affairs at Harvard University's John F. Kennedy School of Government for helpful comments on earlier drafts.

1. Ballistic missiles provide rapid delivery of weapons of mass destruction (WMD)—nuclear, biological, and chemical (NBC) weapons—over vast distances. Missile proliferation therefore exacerbates the WMD threat, weakens the WMD nonproliferation regime, and undermines international security. Conversely, containing missile proliferation strengthens the WMD nonproliferation regime.
2. For reviews of MTCR effectiveness, see Richard Speier, "How Effective Is the Missile Technology Control Regime?" *Proliferation Brief,* April 12, 2001; and Dinshaw Mistry, *Containing Missile Proliferation: Strategic Technology, Security Regimes, and International Cooperation in Arms Control* (Seattle: University of Washington Press, 2003).
3. Mark Smith, "Rules for the Road? The International Code of Conduct against Ballistic Missile Proliferation," *Disarmament Diplomacy,* No. 63 (March–April 2002), pp. 10–15; and Mark Smith, "On Thin Ice: First Steps for the Ballistic Missile Code of Conduct," *Arms Control Today,* Vol. 32, No. 5 (July/August 2002), pp. 9–13.

ation? The article offers three main conclusions: First, the MTCR can considerably delay, but ultimately will not prevent, regional powers from building arsenals of intermediate- and long-range missiles. Transparency initiatives are also insufficient to halt missile proliferation because they do not offer strong political and legal barriers against, and incentives to refrain from, missile activity. Second, if regional powers maintain their missile programs (and, more ominously, if they export their missiles to other states), missile proliferation may greatly increase. As a result, the MTCR's past gains could be reversed. Third, five measures—space service initiatives, regional missile-free zones, global intermediate-range missile bans, flight-test bans, and verification mechanisms—are available to expand the regime and provide firmer institutional barriers against missile proliferation.

The article begins by assessing the success of the MTCR in curbing regional power missile programs. Based on this assessment and on an analysis of trends in missile proliferation, the article explores whether a broader regime is required to halt the spread of missiles. The article then explains why the five above-mentioned measures can better contain missile proliferation. It concludes that two other options to counter missile threats—missile defenses and preemptive military strikes—are most viable in the context of a strong nonproliferation regime. In the end, despite other options against missile threats, strong security regimes are crucial to addressing the problem of ballistic missile proliferation.

The MTCR's Past Performance and Future Prospects

The MTCR is not a treaty that bans missiles.[4] Instead, it is a nontreaty regime that seeks to deny regional powers (1) access to complete missiles,[5] and (2)

---

4. The MTCR is thus different from the nuclear Nonproliferation Treaty (NPT) and the Chemical Weapons Convention (CWC), which prohibit states from possessing nuclear and chemical weapons, respectively. The NPT and CWC derive compliance in many ways, including through the logic of collective action: For any pair of states A and B, state A refrains from acquiring WMD and neighboring state B reciprocates, because if B did not reciprocate, this would cause A to reconsider its non-WMD decision, a step that could escalate into an undesired arms race between A and B. This dynamic of reciprocity and mutual restraint, backed by verification of compliance, is intended to address the security concerns of all parties and thereby persuade states to renounce their WMD programs. For more on the differences in scope and legalization between the MTCR and the NPT and CWC, as well as a related discussion on defining the MTCR as a regime, see Mistry, *Containing Missile Proliferation.*
5. Initially, the MTCR covered missiles capable of delivering 500 kilogram (kg) payloads (the estimated lightest weight of a regional power's nuclear warheads) as far as 300 kilometers (km). By mid-1993, the regime covered all missiles intended for WMD delivery. This extended scope covers

technology that would help them to build such missiles.[6] The MTCR has achieved substantial success in fulfilling the first objective and modest success regarding the second.[7]

RESTRICTING MISSILE EXPORTS AND TECHNOLOGY TRANSFERS

Two major former missile suppliers—China (which adheres to but has not formally joined the MTCR) and Russia—are not known to have exported ballistic missiles since the early 1990s. The only other major exporter, North Korea (which is not an MTCR member or adherent), supplied an estimated 400 Scud-B and Scud-C missiles to Iran and Syria in the late 1980s and early 1990s. Later it exported a smaller quantity of Scuds or Scud components such as engines to Egypt, Syria, Yemen, and possibly Libya, as well as Nodong missiles or components to Iran and Pakistan.[8]

Over the years MTCR members and adherents have sought to control their transfers of missile-relevant technology.[9] In the 1990s, for example, some Western states adopted strong national export controls to curb such transfers. Russia, which joined the MTCR in 1995, passed several laws to strengthen its

missiles such as China's M-11 that are declared to have ranges less than 300 km but can carry payloads lighter than 500 kg (such as biological and chemical payloads) over greater distances. The MTCR also covers cruise missiles, which this article does not discuss. For more on this topic, see Dennis Gormley, *Dealing with the Threat of Cruise Missiles*, Adelphi Paper No. 339 (London: International Institute for Strategic Studies, 2001).

6. Missile-relevant technology includes electronics for missile guidance systems, chemicals for propulsion systems, specialized steel for airframes, test equipment, and manufacturing equipment.

7. The MTCR's thirty-three member states implement the regime through their national export control legislation and policies (e.g., diplomacy and the use of sanctions). As of early 2003, the MTCR's members were Argentina, Australia, Austria, Belgium, Brazil, Canada, the Czech Republic, Denmark, Finland, France, Germany, Greece, Hungary, Iceland, Ireland, Italy, Japan, Luxembourg, the Netherlands, New Zealand, Norway, Poland, Portugal, the Russian Federation, South Africa, South Korea, Spain, Sweden, Switzerland, Turkey, Ukraine, the United Kingdom, and the United States. In addition, China, Israel, and Romania adhere to MTCR guidelines but are not formal members.

8. U.S. Central Intelligence Agency, *Unclassified Report to Congress on the Acquisition of Technology Relating to Weapons of Mass Destruction and Advanced Conventional Munitions, 1 January through 30 June 2001* (Washington, D.C.: Central Intelligence Agency, January 30, 2002); and Joseph Bermudez, *A History of Ballistic Missile Development in the DPRK* (Monterey, Calif.: Center for Nonproliferation Studies, Monterey Institute of International Studies, November 1999).

9. For a discussion of the extent to which suppliers have restricted their technology transfers, see U.S. Central Intelligence Agency, *Unclassified Report to Congress on the Acquisition of Technology Relating to Weapons of Mass Destruction and Advanced Conventional Munitions, 1 January through 30 June 2001*. See also similar earlier reports for July through December 2000 (September 7, 2001), and January through June 2000 (February 22, 2001). Additional assessments are found in Gary Bertsch and Michael Beck, *Nonproliferation Export Controls: A Global Evaluation* (Athens: Center for International Trade and Security, University of Georgia, 2001).

export control system.[10] Despite this, some Russian organizations continued to provide missile-relevant training and technology to other states, mainly Iran. China pledged to halt missile exports in 1992, 1994, 1998, and 2000.[11] In the mid- and late 1990s, Beijing also passed laws on and strengthened bureaucratic oversight of its export controls.[12] In spite of these steps, Chinese firms continued to transfer missile-related industrial technology to Iran, Libya, North Korea, Pakistan, and Syria. In August 2002, however, because of increased recognition of the threat that WMD posed to its own security, and after further talks with the United States, Beijing published a missile export control list that corresponded closely to MTCR guidelines.[13]

HINDERING TARGET MISSILE PROGRAMS

In the 1980s and 1990s, fourteen regional powers attempted to produce ballistic missiles. Nine either gave up their missile ambitions or restricted their missile programs to cruise missiles and short-range ballistic missiles (SRBMs) such as 300 km range Scud-Bs and 600 km range Scud-Cs that typically weigh 5–10 tons. These restraints in missile development, though partly a result of the MTCR's technological obstacles, were also induced by political considerations.

In general, the denial of foreign technology has been sufficient to thwart or considerably delay missile development in the two technologically weakest missile aspirants, Libya and Syria. Libya's missile development efforts are still thought to be generally unsuccessful. Syria did not build missiles in the 1990s,

---

10. Ibid. See also Robert J. Einhorn and Gary Samore, "Ending Russian Assistance to Iran's Nuclear Bomb," *Survival*, Vol. 44, No. 2 (Summer 2002), pp. 55–70; Alexander Pikayev, Leonard Spector, Elina Kirichenko, and Ryan Gibson, *Russia, the U.S., and the Missile Technology Control Regime*, Adelphi Paper No. 317 (London: International Institute for Strategic Studies, 1998); and Alexander Pikayev, "Russia and the Missile Technology Control Regime," in Gary K. Bertsch and William C. Potter, eds., *Dangerous Weapons, Desperate States: Russia, Belarus, Kazakhstan, and Ukraine* (New York: Routledge, 1999), pp. 188–212.
11. Beijing's early pledges covered only missiles that were within the primary parameters of the MTCR—that is, missiles with a range of at least 300 km with a 500 kg payload. Beijing had not committed to the MTCR revisions of 1993, which covered all WMD-relevant missiles and closed the range/payload loopholes.
12. Richard Cupitt, "Export Controls in the People's Republic of China," *Bulletin of Asia-Pacific Studies*, March 1999, pp. 29–72; Bates Gill and Evan Medeiros, "Foreign and Domestic Influences on China's Arms Control and Nonproliferation Policies," *China Quarterly*, No. 161 (March 2000), pp. 66–94; Evan Medeiros and Bates Gill, *Chinese Arms Exports: Policy, Players, and Process* (Carlisle, Pa.: Strategic Studies Institute, U.S. Army War College, August 2000); and Shirley Kan, *China's Proliferation of Weapons of Mass Destruction and Missiles* (Washington, D.C.: Congressional Research Service, March 12, 2001).
13. Phillip C. Saunders, *Preliminary Analysis of Chinese Missile Technology Export Control List* (Monterey, Calif.: Center for Nonproliferation Studies, Monterey Institute of International Studies, September 6, 2002).

though it may have built Scuds by 2000–01.[14] In Iraq, United Nations resolutions after the 1991 Gulf War constrained development to 150 km range missiles.[15] In six other regional powers—Argentina, Brazil, Egypt, South Africa, South Korea, and Taiwan—the MTCR's barriers generally hindered, raised the costs of, or delayed their missile programs.[16] During the time provided by MTCR-induced delays, two political factors restrained their missile programs:[17] (1) U.S. diplomacy and political and economic pressure, which influenced missile decisions in all the above-mentioned states, and (2) the easing of regional tensions, which reduced the security-related demand for missiles in Argentina, Brazil, and South Africa.[18]

The MTCR has not prevented five other regional powers—Israel, India, North Korea, Pakistan, and Iran—from testing intermediate-range ballistic missiles (IRBMs), which generally have ranges of 1,000–2,000 km and weigh 10–25 tons.[19] In the 1980s Israel tested for the first time two-stage solid-fuel 1,400 km range Jericho-2 missiles. It also developed more powerful Jericho-derived space launchers. India tested a two-stage solid- and liquid-fuel 1,000–1,500 km range Agni-1 missile in 1989 (the Agni was derived from India's SLV-3 satellite launch vehicle, which first flew in 1979). India tested a fully

---

14. In late 2001 the U.S. National Intelligence Council noted that "with considerable foreign assistance, Syria progressed to Scud production using primarily locally manufactured parts." National Intelligence Council, *Foreign Missile Developments and the Ballistic Missile Threat through 2015: Unclassified Summary of a National Intelligence Estimate* (Washington, D.C.: National Intelligence Council, December 2001), p. 12.
15. Iraq may have retained some 650 km range al-Hussein missiles; it also extended the range of its al-Samoud-2 missiles to beyond 150 km and constructed an engine test stand for IRBMs. For more on Iraq, see Joseph Cirincione, John Wolfsthal, and Miriam Rajkumar, *Deadly Arsenals: Tracking Weapons of Mass Destruction* (Washington, D.C.: Carnegie Endowment for International Peace, 2002), pp. 271–278, 286–287.
16. An exception to this trend is South Korea, where MTCR technology barriers have had a negligible impact. On the other hand, MTCR barriers were able to hinder Argentina's Condor missile program to a substantial degree.
17. Missile restraints do not imply missile elimination. Although technology barriers and U.S. pressure prevented some states (i.e., Argentina, Egypt, South Africa, and Taiwan) from building medium-range missiles or equivalent space rockets, these and other states continued to build or sought to build (and therefore had the infrastructure to build) SRBMs and space launchers. Iraq and Libya maintained some of their SRBM manufacturing infrastructure; Egypt and Syria built (and have the infrastructure to continue building) Scuds; Brazil scrapped its missile programs but built and launched a space rocket (as powerful as a medium-range missile); and South Korea is building 300 km range missiles as well as space launchers.
18. Further, Argentina and South Africa found space launchers unviable, and Argentina and Brazil anticipated fewer export opportunities for their missiles after the Iran-Iraq War. For more details on how security threats and political and economic pressures influenced regional power missile decisions, see Mistry, *Containing Missile Proliferation*.
19. For technical details of these missile programs, see the homepage of the Federation of American Scientists, http://www.fas.org/nuke/guide/index.html.

solid-fuel 2,000 km range Agni-2 in 1999 and also developed far more powerful space launchers. North Korea tested the single-stage liquid-fuel (estimated) 1,000 km range Nodong (built from Scud technology) in 1993. In 1998 it attempted a satellite launch aboard a three-stage version of the estimated 2,000 km range Taepodong-1 (which had a Nodong-derived first stage and a Scud-derived second stage). Pakistan and Iran first tested Nodong-derived missiles in 1998. In addition, Pakistan has tested a solid-fuel estimated 700 km range Shaheen-1 missile, and it may be building a two-stage solid-fuel 1,500–2,000 km range Shaheen-2 missile. Iran's as yet untested Shehab-4, which it declares to be a space launcher, is reportedly based on the RD-214 engine that powered Russia's SS-4 (the 30 ton liquid-fuel SS-4 had an estimated 2,000 km range with a 1.4 ton payload, or a greater range with a lighter payload). Reports of an Iranian Shehab-5, which may be derived from the Taepodong-1 or Taepodong-2, remain unconfirmed.

Although the MTCR has not stopped the proliferation of SRBMs and IRBMs, it has thwarted (or at least delayed) the proliferation of intercontinental ballistic missiles (ICBMs). As of early 2003, no regional power had flight-tested a dedicated ICBM, though this could change in the future: India's 275 ton polar satellite launch vehicle (PSLV) and Israel's 30 ton and Brazil's 50 ton satellite launchers can be modified into ICBMs. North Korea's 60–80 ton and estimated 4,000–6,000 km range Taepodong-2 was near a prototype test in 1999–2000. The Taepodong-2 could be exported to Iran and other countries, which may eventually develop similar long-range missiles indigenously.

CURBING THE PACE, SIZE, AND SOPHISTICATION OF MISSILE PROGRAMS
The option of stacking or clustering SRBM or IRBM engines to build an ICBM within a short time frame is generally not viable.[20] Therefore regional powers

---

20. The option of stacking an approximately 5 ton stage onto a 10–15 ton stage to produce a two-stage IRBM is viable and has been used in missiles such as the Taepodong-1 and the Agni. The option of clustering many 10–15 ton stages to produce a more powerful 40–50 ton system is challenging because regional powers must first perfect stage separation technologies. This option has been used in satellite launchers such as Brazil's vehiculo lancador de satellites (VLS), India's augmented satellite launch vehicle, and Iraq's Tammuz (which failed a 1990 launch attempt). Yet the resulting rocket is not optimal for use as a ballistic missile because it is unwieldy, difficult to transport, and cannot be rapidly launched. Therefore regional powers may have to develop a larger-diameter, more powerful engine (that typically weighs 30–60 tons) for a longer-range missile. Regional powers can then stack a single 10–15 ton stage onto a single 30–60 ton or larger stage to develop a two-stage, two-engine 40–70 ton missile with a range of 4,000–6,000 km—North Korea may have used this configuration in the Taepodong-2. Regional powers would still need longer-range missiles to reach the continental United States (the closest major U.S. cities are approxi-

may have to develop entirely new, more powerful, and more advanced propulsion systems and other subsystems for ICBMs.[21] Doing so would be difficult for many states, especially without foreign technical assistance. The MTCR's technology barriers can therefore continue to restrain regional powers from building long-range missiles, in three ways.

First, they can delay target states from producing advanced IRBMs and ICBMs. Regional powers typically take five years to build a short-range missile, and five to seven additional years to test more powerful missiles.[22] The Rumsfeld Commission noted that with "external help now readily available, a nation with a well-developed, Scud-based ballistic missile infrastructure would be able to achieve first flight of a long-range missile, up to and including intercontinental ballistic missile (ICBM) range (greater than 5,500 km), within about five years of deciding to do so."[23] Without external help, regional powers will take somewhat longer to build ICBMs.[24] For example, Iran's ICBM efforts, which it may initially pursue using an SLV, would also be delayed. U.S.

---

mately 7,500 km from Libya, 9,500 km from Iraq and Iran, and 8,000 km from North Korea). They could build one by adding a third stage to the Taepodong-2 missile. They could also cluster many 10–15 ton boosters alongside a 30–60 ton or larger booster and add a 10–15 ton or larger second stage. Both options, however, may not be optimal for ballistic missiles. Therefore regional powers may have to develop entirely new engines for a more viable ICBM.

21. In general, ICBMs require more advanced propulsion systems, reentry vehicles, and guidance systems than those found in IRBMs and SRBMs. Export controls can significantly hinder regional powers from mastering solid-fuel propulsion systems, which require large, solid-fuel engines; manufacturing equipment; and expertise that are difficult to indigenously develop. Export controls may not substantially hinder regional powers from building liquid-fuel systems because these are generally easier to develop. Regional powers cannot obtain much information on reentry systems from existing published sources and must instead begin research and development from scratch. Export controls on critical reentry materials and on high-speed wind tunnels (required for testing reentry vehicles) can therefore slow the development of such vehicles, especially those for long-range missiles, which have higher reentry temperatures and therefore require reentry vehicles with better heat shields. Guidance systems include several subcomponents such as advanced gyros, onboard computers, and rocket control mechanisms. Export controls can hinder regional powers from acquiring these subcomponents and developing high-performance guidance systems. Aaron Karp, *Ballistic Missile Proliferation: The Politics and Technics* (Oxford: Oxford University Press, 1996), pp. 99–131.
22. For example, North Korea took nine years to advance from testing the 300 km range Scud (1984) to testing the 1,000 km range Nodong (1993). It took five to seven more years to test the multiple-stage Taepodong-1 (1998) and to construct a prototype Taepodong-2 (1999–2000). India took fourteen years to progress from the 1979 test of its estimated 1,500 km range SLV-3 to the 1993 test of its estimated 8,000 km range PSLV.
23. Donald H. Rumsfeld, chairman, *Report of the Commission to Assess the Ballistic Missile Threat to the United States* (Washington, D.C.: Government Printing Office, July 15, 1998), Executive Summary, sec. 2.C.4.
24. National Intelligence Council, *Foreign Missile Developments and the Ballistic Missile Threat through 2015*, p. 10.

intelligence agencies note that Iran may test an SLV around 2005,[25] and add that "if Iran were to acquire complete TD-2 [Taepodong-2] systems from North Korea, it could conduct a flight test within a year of delivery. . . . In contrast, a halt or substantial decrease in [foreign technical] assistance would delay by years the development and flight-testing of these systems."[26]

Second, even after regional powers test any prototype ICBM or equivalent SLV, technology embargoes (and economic constraints) can considerably limit their volume of missile production. By denying regional powers large quantities of necessary missile components (e.g., engines that propel missiles and specialized alloys for missile bodies) and the manufacturing equipment for large-scale production, technology barriers would hinder them from initially building more than a few long-range missiles annually. This could mean that until it can indigenously produce large volumes of the necessary missile subcomponents, North Korea may not be able to build more than one or two Taepodong-2 missiles a year. The historical record from the 1980s and 1990s shows that regional powers annually built 50–100 short-range Scud-type missiles (this was North Korea's estimated Scud production rate) or 10–20 medium-range missiles (this was North Korea's estimated Nodong production rate). Yet they annually built only 1 or 2 intercontinental-range systems such as the 130 ton booster used on India's PSLV (launched six times between 1993 and 2001).

Third, technology embargoes can hinder regional powers from developing sophisticated targeting, guidance, and maneuvering systems. Crude ICBMs with primitive locally built guidance systems are likely to be highly inaccurate. Because missile inaccuracy increases with distance, ICBMs without good targeting and guidance may not be able to hit a target city when fired from halfway across the planet.

Ultimately, these three constraining effects will diminish over time, and regional powers could build better and greater quantities of ICBMs (5–10 or more) annually within a decade of their first ICBM tests. Further, regional powers could more rapidly advance their missile programs by pursuing the following four development strategies: acquiring new technologies and better-

---

25. This may be a test of the Shehab-4. The Shehab-4, if it is based on SS-4 or Taepodong-1 technology, would be the equivalent of a 2,000–3,000 km range IRBM. A Taepodong-2-derived SLV would be the equivalent of a 4,000–6,000 km range ICBM.
26. National Intelligence Council, *Foreign Missile Developments and the Ballistic Missile Threat through 2015*, p. 9.

trained workforces;[27] focusing on the development of simple rather than sophisticated technologies;[28] obtaining technology from other regional powers and increasing cooperation with them;[29] and allocating more resources to their states' missile programs.

Why a Broader Missile Nonproliferation Regime Is Necessary

If the MTCR can delay and constrain regional power long-range missile programs for five to ten years, is a broader regime necessary to contain missile proliferation? Four issues are likely to influence the outcome: trends in missile proliferation, norms and initiatives against missile possession, recent missile sales, and growth of the space sector.

TRENDS IN MISSILE PROLIFERATION
Two contradictory trends have emerged from recent developments in the area of missile proliferation. In a positive vein, as mentioned earlier, nine out of fourteen regional powers have restrained their missile programs and have not tested IRBMs. Further, even though other regional powers (e.g., India, Iran, and Pakistan) have tested IRBMs, they have not built them in large numbers. Moreover, North Korea's development of long-range missiles was slowed by its unilateral freeze on missile tests after 1999.

In addition, some states have eliminated substantial numbers of missiles, in three ways. First, under the Strategic Arms Reduction Talks (START) treaty, the United States and Russia had destroyed some 2,800 long-range missiles and submarine-launched missiles by 2001. They have also destroyed about 2,700 ballistic missiles and cruise missiles under the Intermediate Nuclear Force (INF) treaty. Second, the United States has bought dozens of short-range missiles from East European states for use in its antimissile tests. Third, several nonnuclear states that joined the MTCR were required to eliminate their offen-

---

27. Embargoes on soft-technology transfers (e.g., bans on training regional power personnel) become ineffective after regional powers develop pools of skilled technicians. Thus, if regional powers already have skilled personnel working on short-range missiles, they may not need to (or may not find it difficult to) train many more personnel to work on any new longer-range missiles. For a discussion of soft and hard technology, see Karp, *Ballistic Missile Proliferation*, pp. 51–81.
28. Peter Zimmerman, "Proliferation: Bronze Medal Technology Is Enough," *Orbis*, Vol. 38, No. 1 (Winter 1994), p. 71.
29. Janne E. Nolan elaborates on the advantages of technology sharing in Nolan, *Trappings of Power: Ballistic Missiles in the Third World* (Washington, D.C.: Brookings, 1991), p. 19.

sive missiles and related technology as a condition of entry. Under this policy, Argentina and South Africa destroyed missile components and manufacturing equipment. The Czech Republic, Hungary, and Poland eliminated tens of Scuds and SS-23 missiles. Slovakia and Bulgaria destroyed tens of SS-23s, and Bulgaria also agreed to scrap its Scuds and Frog artillery rockets. Slovakia may retain these systems, however; and Belarus, Kazakhstan, and Turkmenistan also retain Scuds, Frog artillery rockets, or SS-21 SRBMs.

The latter fact highlights the policy's limitations because it does not apply to states that are not (nor are interested in becoming) MTCR members. Moreover, the policy has encountered some prominent obstacles—for example, upon entering the MTCR Ukraine was allowed to retain its Scuds, and South Korea was allowed to build 300 km range missiles. The destruction of a few hundred missiles (mainly Scuds and SS-23s) by former East European states and new MTCR entrants was significant because it set a precedent for similar initiatives in the future. Yet the number of eliminated missiles was still less than the several hundred new missiles of comparable or longer ranges built by regional powers and by China and Russia in the 1990s.

There have also been negative trends in missile proliferation. For example, as Scud missiles acquired by several Middle Eastern states in the 1970s and 1980s (and CSS-2 missiles bought by Saudi Arabia) near retirement, the demand by these countries for such missiles has begun to increase as they seek to replenish their dwindling inventories. Several states in the region—including Egypt and Syria—are developing Scuds, while Iran pursues development of Shehab missiles. In time, regional powers could build 1,000 km range Nodong-type and longer-range Taepodong-type missiles and export them to new clients. If even a few states obtain these missiles, others may seek them as well (to replace their aging arsenals or to match their rivals' missile forces).[30] In addition, some states may acquire "strategic" chemical or biological weapons capabilities, which would greatly heighten security concerns among neighboring

---

30. States seek to match an adversary's missile programs not solely because of military requirements; they may also be driven by a competitive rivalry and a desire for prestige and parity. For example, North Korea and South Korea have sought to outdo each other since the 1970s. The acquisition and development of North Korea's Frog-7 (obtained in 1975), South Korea's NHK-1 (tested in 1978), North Korea's Scud-B (acquired from Egypt in the late 1970s and indigenously built and first tested in 1984), South Korea's NHK-2 (tested and deployed in 1986–87), and North Korea's Scud-C (tested in 1990) illustrate this missile rivalry. Further, Pyongyang's Scud activity and 1993 Nodong test influenced Seoul's 1995 request to Washington to scrap their bilateral missile restraint agreement. South Korea's 1993 launch of a satellite and its 1996 space plans may have prodded Pyongyang to upgrade its Taepodong into an SLV. This system's launch in 1998 influenced Seoul's 1999 decision to seek 500 km range missiles and to accelerate its space plans.

states and revive their demand (and development efforts) not only for ballistic missiles but also for a WMD-based deterrent.[31] In the absence of strong international commitments binding these countries and their neighbors to refrain from missile development, states that have renounced their missile aspirations could begin to rethink their decision. Because missile technology will be more easily available in the future, any renewed missile programs are unlikely to be halted by MTCR barriers. In such a situation, the few missile nonproliferation successes of years past could be reversed, and the missile nonproliferation regime (and possibly even other WMD control regimes) could collapse.

NORMS AND INITIATIVES AGAINST MISSILE PROLIFERATION

In contrast to global norms against NBC weapons activity, strong norms against missile possession, development, and testing do not exist. As a result, states can engage in missile activity without facing serious repercussions. The international community strongly condemned nuclear tests by China, France, India, and Pakistan in the period 1995–98, with some states imposing trade and aid sanctions against them. Yet in 1998 and 1999, missile tests by India, Pakistan, and Iran faced far less criticism (though North Korea's 1998 missile test did provoke an uproar). Neither the UN General Assembly nor the Security Council passed resolutions condemning these tests. Further, none of these states encountered major aid or trade sanctions (instead incurring only minor U.S. export control sanctions). Eventually, however, three instruments were introduced to address growing concern over missile proliferation: UN initiatives, the Russian-proposed Global Control System (GCS), and the MTCR-initiated Code of Conduct.

In 2001 and 2002, experts from twenty-three UN member states formed a group to discuss missile proliferation. At its April 2002 meeting, the group split over whether to seek modest or comprehensive initiatives to slow the disturbing trend in missile proliferation. Some states sought to focus on technol-

---

31. Ballistic missiles are optimal for nuclear delivery, whereas aircraft and cruise missiles have some advantages for delivering chemical and biological weapons. Chemical agents deteriorate at high temperatures and can become ineffective under the heat of ballistic missile reentry or impact. Chemical and biological agents have a greater effect when distributed over a wide area, a task better carried out by aircraft and cruise missiles. Despite these limitations, ballistic missiles can deliver chemical and biological agents, especially when these agents are placed in several small bomblets sheltered inside a larger, heat-shielded warhead. Steve Fetter, "Ballistic Missiles and Weapons of Mass Destruction: What Is the Threat? What Should Be Done?" *International Security,* Vol. 16, No. 1 (Summer 1991), pp. 22–23; and John R. Harvey, "Regional Ballistic Missiles and Advanced Strike Aircraft: Comparing Military Effectiveness," *International Security,* Vol. 17, No. 2 (Fall 1992), pp. 41–75.

ogy controls (and to accept missile defenses), while others sought an expanded nonproliferation regime.[32] The expert group's final report did not recommend specific ways to tackle missile proliferation, but instead suggested that ongoing approaches be further explored.[33]

Russian President Boris Yeltsin first proposed the GCS in June 1999 at the Group of Eight summit. Then in March 2000 and February 2001, Moscow hosted representatives from seventy-one states, including non-MTCR members, to discuss Yeltsin's proposal. The GCS concept had two core components. The first was a six-part nonproliferation cluster comprising the MTCR; the Code of Conduct; and an array of incentives, security assurances, nonproliferation measures, and diplomatic and economic enforcement measures. The second was a six-part transparency cluster, comprising the two missile and space transparency measures found in the Code of Conduct as well as launch notifications, provisions for technical monitoring of launches, an international data center, and additional confidence-building measures (CBMs).[34] Most states supported the transparency measures. Washington, however, hesitated about unconditionally endorsing the GCS's suggestions to offer to signatories that renounced missiles a set of satellite and space service incentives and unspecified security assurances (equivalent to those in the UN Charter). It hesitated partly because the details of these measures were unclear. Interestingly, Washington did not send representatives to any of the GCS meetings. By 2002 the Code of Conduct proposal prevailed over the GCS in international diplomatic circles.

MTCR members began working on the Code of Conduct in 1999. They outlined a draft code at their October 2000 plenary session and essentially completed their internal discussions on the draft at their September 2001 plenary meeting. France then took the lead in seeking to universalize the code in con-

---

32. "UN Missiles Panel Concludes Session," *Disarmament Diplomacy*, No. 64 (May–June 2002).
33. "The Issue of Missiles in All Its Aspects: Report of the Secretary General," UN General Assembly Document A/57/229, July 23, 2002. Subsequently, General Assembly resolution A/57/71 (November 22, 2002) welcomed the July 2002 report and is seeking a further experts' report on missiles by 2004.
34. The GCS was still in the concept stage in 2003. Its sponsors had not yet issued any draft negotiating texts or proposals for specific missile nonproliferation instruments. For more on the GCS, see Alexander Pikayev, "The Global Control System," in Michael Barletta, ed., *Missile Proliferation and Defenses: Problems and Prospects* (Monterey, Calif.: Center for Nonproliferation Studies, Monterey Institute of International Studies, May 2001), pp. 21–27; and Yuri E. Fedorov, "The Global Control System and the International Code of Conduct: Competition or Cooperation?" *Nonproliferation Review*, Vol. 9, No. 2 (Summer 2002), pp. 30–36.

sultation with other countries. Representatives from eighty-six states attended discussions in Paris in February 2002,[35] and ninety-six countries participated in follow-up consultations in Madrid in June 2002. Ninety-three countries adopted and signed the code at The Hague in November 2002.[36] Its most important provisions are two transparency-increasing CBMs. According to the first provision, countries must issue annual declarations explaining their ballistic missile and space launch vehicle policies. Such declarations could include information on test sites and on the number of missiles and space rockets launched during the preceding year. Second, countries must provide advance notice of missile and space rocket launches. The code also includes a "commitment by subscribing states to exercise maximum possible restraint in the development, testing, and deployment of ballistic missiles capable of delivering weapons of mass destruction, including, where possible, to reduce national holdings of such missiles."[37]

The Code of Conduct's missile transparency initiatives are pragmatic and useful short-term measures, but they do not establish strong legal barriers and norms against missile possession, development, and testing. Thus, even if states make declarations about their missile policies, such declarations by themselves would not necessarily cause these or other states to restrain their missile programs. Unless supported by a stronger overarching regime that would require states to more thoroughly restrain their missile programs, offer them incentives to do so, and include strong prospects for reciprocity, the code's CBMs are unlikely to halt missile proliferation.

---

35. At these discussions, some states wanted the code to ban missiles; others noted that the code did not offer enough incentives for states to renounce missiles; still others questioned whether MTCR members should offer space-launch technology to states that signed the code. States were also concerned that the code's transparency measures would legitimize rather than proscribe missile programs. Alex Wagner, "States Meet to Discuss Ballistic Missile Code of Conduct," *Arms Control Today*, Vol. 32, No. 3 (March 2002), p. 30.

36. Initial signatories of the code included European Union states, Libya, MTCR members, Russia, and the United States but not missile-possessing states such as China, Egypt, India, Iran, Israel, North Korea, Pakistan, Saudi Arabia, and Syria. The final code contains a preamble, a statement of adoption, and four sections on principles, general measures, transparency measures, and organizational aspects. These four sections were modified forms of four similar sections (concerning principles, commitments, confidence-building measures, and organizational aspects) found in the October 2000 draft code. This draft also had a section on incentives (for countries either to eliminate or forgo ballistic missile and space launch programs) that was eventually excluded from the final code.

37. International Code of Conduct against Ballistic Missile Proliferation, November 25, 2002, sec. 3c.

REVIVAL OF MISSILE SALES

Some of the MTCR's gains in curbing missile sales are being reversed. In recent years, France approved the sale of land attack cruise missiles to Bahrain; China and Russia offered cruise missiles for export; and the United States exported 100–200 km range Army Tactical Missile Systems to Bahrain, Greece, South Korea, and Turkey. If new suppliers enter the missile market, others will have fewer inhibitions about also exporting missiles. In this scenario, Russian Iskander SS-X-26 missiles (i.e., solid-fuel Scud successors with satellite and inertial guidance), Chinese M-11s and M-9s, Ukrainian Scuds, and North Korean Nodongs could all be offered for export. According to one report, Iran has already given missile assistance to Libya and possibly supplied Scuds to Congo in 1999;[38] Pakistan could sell Shaheen or Ghauri missiles to clients such as Saudi Arabia. Meanwhile India could sell its India-Russia Brahmos antiship cruise missiles. Although some of the above transactions involve missiles falling below the MTCR's 300 km/500 kg threshold, their export would still erode international norms against such sales.

THE NEED FOR A STRONGER REGIME AND GROWTH OF THE SPACE SECTOR

Even though regional powers have built only SRBMs and IRBMs rather than longer-range missiles, these SRBM and IRBM programs continue to be a concern. They provide states not only with skilled personnel (experienced in designing and building missile subsystems and complete missiles and with expertise in rocket operations), but also with some of the industrial infrastructure and components that could eventually be used to develop ICBMs. ICBMs are useful because, among other things, they can be a means to keep foreign powers out of regional conflicts. A stronger missile nonproliferation regime with verification measures would offer more certainty that regional powers' SRBM and space programs are not being expanded with an eye toward the development of ICBMs; however, such a regime has not yet been established.

Five Ways to Expand the MTCR

A more comprehensive arms control regime should include the following five elements: space service initiatives (and other incentives to dissuade rocket acquisition), regional missile-free zones and global intermediate-range missile

---

38. Bill Gertz, "Iran Sold Scud Missiles to Congolese," *Washington Times*, November 22, 1999, p. 1.

bans (both of which provide legal barriers to proliferation), flight-test bans, and verification mechanisms. Table 1 shows the architecture for an expanded missile nonproliferation regime containing the MTCR, the Code of Conduct, and these five initiatives.

SPACE SERVICE INITIATIVES

Nine states or agencies have satellite launchers—the United States and Russia, which have conducted hundreds of rocket launches; the European Space Agency (ESA), China, Japan, India, and Ukraine, which have conducted tens of launches; and Israel and Brazil, which have conducted fewer launches (see Table 2). Other states (Argentina, Iran, Italy, North Korea, South Korea, and Spain) also seek satellite launchers; yet these can be modified (with reentry vehicles and appropriate targeting systems) to become ballistic missiles.

On whether new space-launch programs should be permitted, the 1967 Outer Space Treaty notes that space is "free for exploration and use by all States without discrimination of any kind."[39] The Code of Conduct declares that although "states should not be excluded from utilizing the benefits of space for peaceful purposes," "space launch vehicle programs should not be used to conceal ballistic missile programs."[40]

For years the MTCR generally discouraged but did not fully address the development of space launchers. A September 1993 U.S. policy partly clarified the issue: It allowed new MTCR members to retain their space programs but required them to destroy their offensive ballistic missiles and related technology. In addition, Washington would not encourage new space programs that raised concerns on nonproliferation and economic viability grounds.[41] This policy allowed Brazil to continue with its VLS satellite launcher project upon joining the MTCR. (In later years Ukraine would be allowed to retain its space rocket program, and South Korea would be permitted to build liquid-fuel launchers.) Washington, however, did not permit Argentina and South Africa to retain their dual-use rocket programs. Both programs were eliminated

---

39. *Treaty on Principles Governing the Activities of States in the Exploration and Use of Outer Space, including the Moon and Other Celestial Bodies*, January 27, 1967, art. 1. Article 2 of the treaty adds that space is "not subject to national appropriation by claim of sovereignty, by means of use or occupation, or by any other means [such as regimes]," which suggests that international regimes may not prevent states from seeking access to space.
40. International Code of Conduct against Ballistic Missile Proliferation, November 25, 2002, secs. 2f, 2g.
41. "White House Fact Sheet on Non-Proliferation and Export Control Policy, September 27, 1993," *Arms Control Today*, Vol. 23, No. 9 (November 1993), p. 27.

Table 1. The Architecture for a Missile Nonproliferation Regime.

Missile Technology Control Regime	Code of Conduct	Space Service Regime	Regional Missile-Free Zones	Global Intermediate-Range Ballistic Missile Bans	Flight-Test Bans	Verification Measures
Key Suppliers	Universal	Suppliers: Space-faring states Recipients: Missile treaty members	Europe, Latin America, Southeast Asia, and Sub-Saharan Africa	North and South Korea, Middle East states, four of the permanent five members of the UN Security Council (France, Great Britain, Russia, and the United States)	Universal (test exceptions with verification)	Missile treaty and space regime members

NOTE: Missile programs in China, India, Israel, and Pakistan can be capped through agreements not to build new missiles; nuclear programs in these states can be frozen under a comprehensive test ban treaty and a fissile material cutoff treaty.

Table 2. A Comparative Study of Eight Space Programs.

Country/Agency	Number of Launches			Date of First Launch		Estimated Space Expenditure (average annual, 1990s)	
	1957–88	1989–99	2000–02	LEO	GEO	Million of Dollars	Percentage of GDP
Russia & CIS	2,107	506	90	1957	1967	1,000–6,000	1.0
United States	890	308	68	1958	1967	25,000	0.5
Europe/European Space Agency	23	93	31	1979	1980	3,200	0.10
China	23	41	11	1970	1984	>1,000	0.25
Japan	36	19	5	1970	1975	2,100	0.05
India	5	8	3	1980	2001	200–300	0.08
Israel	1	3	1	1988	—	>20	0.03
Brazil	—	2	—	1997	—	70–200	0.02

SOURCE: Table compiled from Andrew Wilson, ed., *Jane's Space Directory* (Alexandria, Va.: Jane's Information Group, 2000); and "Space Statistics," Office of Space Flight, National Aeronautics and Space Agency, http://www.hq.nasa.gov/osf/spacestat.html.
NOTE: LEO refers to low earth orbit; GEO refers to geostationary earth orbit (36,000 km altitude). U.S. totals include commercial, NASA, and space shuttle launches; Commonwealth of Independent States (CIS) totals are mostly Russian but include 3–5 Ukrainian launchers (including Zenit/Sea Launch) each year. The above space agencies conducted 58 launches (including 18 U.S., 22 CIS, and 2 failures) in 2001; 59 (including 22 U.S., 25 CIS, and 1 failure) in 2002; and 85 (including 29 U.S., 39 CIS, and 4 failures) in 2000.

because they were only in their initial phases (and therefore not economically viable) and because they were based on existing missile programs (which were of proliferation concern).

SPACE PROGRAM ECONOMICS. Space programs do not generate substantial economic gains. To develop a rudimentary low earth orbit (LEO) launcher, a state would have to spend at least several hundred million dollars; it would need a few billion dollars to produce the more powerful geostationary earth orbit (GEO) launcher.[42] Further, a state is unlikely to reap quick profits by building either an LEO or a GEO launcher: Revenues from LEO launches are low ($1–10 million); and although revenues are higher for GEO launches ($50–100 million), a new space entrant would conduct only a small number of launches (perhaps two LEO launches and one GEO launch annually), because the primary space suppliers largely fulfill the international demand for both LEO and GEO launches. In addition, although regional powers may reduce costs and save foreign exchange by using their own rockets to launch satellites, these savings are generally less than, and insufficient to recover, the substantial costs needed to initiate and operate a space launch program.

Although the absolute cost-benefit calculation for new space programs is unfavorable, the marginal cost-benefit analysis may be positive, especially in the long term. Thus, despite adverse short-term economic calculations, Argentina, Italy, South Korea, and Spain revived their space aspirations in the late 1990s, partly to acquire launch autonomy and with the expectation of long-term gains in the space industry. The long-term demand for satellite launches will depend on the competitiveness of existing launchers and on the demand for communications services. If the demand for communications satellites increases, the demand for rockets to launch these satellites could also increase.[43]

Moreover, if new types of LEO satellite constellations enter the market, regional powers could find a niche for LEO-capable rockets. Previously, com-

---

42. The costs of developing and launching communication satellite constellations were about $5 billion for Iridium, $3 billion for Globalstar, and $500 million for Orbcomm. The barriers to entry also apply to satellites. Firms may have to invest $100–500 million before collecting any revenue from remote sensing satellites, and revenue itself may be small. France's SPOT earned $40 million in 1998, but its development and launching cost $590 million. John G. Baker, Kevin M. O'Connell, and Ray A. Williamson, eds., *Commercial Observation Satellites: At the Leading Edge of Global Transparency* (Washington, D.C.: RAND, 1999), pp. 202, 442.
43. *Aviation Week* estimated that 149 satellites (worth $10.3 billion) would be launched in 2006, compared with 110 satellites (worth $9 billion) in 2002; the number of actual launches would be less because many satellites can be launched from a single rocket. "Satellite Industry Stalls in Standby Mode," *Aviation Week and Space Technology*, January 14, 2002, p. 15.

munications satellites were thrust into high-altitude GEO by heavy launchers (the equivalent of ICBMs) that were beyond the immediate technical capabilities of many regional powers. Yet new concepts such as Loral-Qualcomm's Globalstar and Motorola's Iridium involve placing lightweight communication satellites into LEO. Such LEO rockets (the equivalent of IRBMs) are within the technical and economic capabilities of many states. LEO communications satellites entered the market in the late 1990s but were commercially unviable, and Iridium declared bankruptcy in 1999–2000. If the industry should revive by, say, 2005–10, then an increased demand for technically attainable LEO rockets could spur additional states to enter the satellite-launch market and acquire IRBM capability.

TRANSPARENCY AND INCENTIVES. The verified space launch programs of states that have signed WMD nonproliferation treaties may not raise immediate proliferation concerns. Yet the rocket programs of states that have not joined or are suspected of violating WMD nonproliferation agreements, but still declare that they have peaceful space aspirations, present greater challenges. One approach to addressing the dual-use rocket dilemma would be to require greater transparency from national space programs and subject them to verification. This pragmatic approach could also discourage the creation of new space programs in return for providing space-related and other incentives.

Space-faring states could offer two types of space-related incentives to countries that renounce aspirations to acquire space launchers, without necessarily having to renounce their satellite programs. First, the major space agencies could launch satellites for other states at concessional prices. Second, global satellite providers could offer states data relevant to weather forecasting, natural resource management, and communications—again, on concessional terms. An international consortium of both suppliers and recipients could determine the technical parameters for such a space-service regime. These parameters would include membership fees and prices (based on easily determined demand and supply criteria); the duration of the regime (states would prefer a long-duration regime that ensures the supply of space services for several years, though prices would vary over time); and renegotiation provisions.

Such a space-service mechanism would have three advantages. First, it would not be discriminatory because it would apply the same conditions to all new space aspirants; it would strike a balance between existing space-faring states and new space aspirants; it would not encourage the emergence of new space-faring states, and in return would seek greater transparency from existing space programs[44]; and it would require them to share their services with new space aspirants. Second, it would be relatively inexpensive (costing only a few tens of millions of dollars annually for LEO launches). Third, the security benefits of limiting the spread of dual-use space technology would outweigh the small economic costs of this program.

The United States explored such a proposal with North Korea in 2000. Washington considered offering Pyongyang two to four launches annually if it renounced efforts to produce long-range rockets. Talks with North Korea stalled in 2001–02, but this does not preclude talks with other states. In addition, the lessons learned from ad hoc initiatives with a few states could be applied in building a more comprehensive space regime.[45]

States could also receive other economic incentives for joining missile nonproliferation treaties. Members of WMD-related supplier cartels could slightly relax technology embargoes, offer others technology-related services and products (without direct technology transfers), and consider trade concessions in relevant technology areas. Another set of incentives could be security related. The permanent five members of the UN Security Council (P-5) could offer negative security assurances to missile-free states, according to which the P-5 would agree not to launch ballistic missile attacks against countries that sign NBC and missile nonproliferation agreements and abide by their verification mechanisms.[46]

LEGAL BARRIERS: REGIONAL AND GLOBAL MISSILE NONPROLIFERATION TREATIES
Nonproliferation treaties that restrain missile development or call for the elimination of missiles can have either a regional or global focus. They may pertain to all missiles (SRBMs, IRBMs, and ICBMs) or just one type of missile.

---

44. Reflecting these views, a British statement at the UN noted that "making development of satellite launch vehicles more transparent would be a first step towards addressing more contentious issues" about the civil-military use of space launchers. UN General Assembly document A/55/116, July 6, 2000.

45. Further, in the absence of a global regime (or as an alternative to such a regime), existing space powers may form subregimes for select groups of states or regional organizations. In this type of consortium, some states could supply launchers; others could be partners in satellite development; and still others could share satellite data and services. Moreover, the space regime or subregime may include both national governments and firms. Current space-related cooperation includes space services for profit such as Intelsat and Inmarsat, as well as noncompetitive cooperation such as through the Committee on Earth Observation Satellites. These entities could be brought into a larger space-service regime.

46. The P-5 have offered qualified negative security assurances, and China and India have declared no-first-use policies, in the nuclear context. See George Bunn, "The Legal Status of U.S. Negative Security Assurances to Non-Nuclear Weapon States," *Nonproliferation Review*, Vol. 4, No. 3 (Spring–Summer 1997), pp. 1–17.

Science and technology expert groups have proposed a global ban on all missiles,[47] and one state—Canada—made a similar proposal at the 1993 MTCR plenary session.[48] Earlier, at the 1986 Reykjavik summit, Presidents Ronald Reagan and Mikhail Gorbachev raised the issue of eliminating strategic missiles under a zero ballistic missile regime.[49] A global missile ban would be politically difficult, however, because the five NPT-defined nuclear states (which are also the five permanent members of the UN Security Council) base the bulk of their nuclear arsenals on ICBMs. Although the United States has capable alternative delivery systems (long-range bombers and air-launched cruise missiles), the other P-5 members lack effective air delivery systems and instead rely heavily on long-range ballistic missiles. Nevertheless, the P-5 could undertake two important steps by agreeing to a policy of zero alerts and missile force reductions.[50] They could also support regional missile-free zones and join a global IRBM ban.

REGIONAL MISSILE-FREE ZONES AND A GLOBAL INTERMEDIATE-RANGE MISSILE BAN. Regional missile-free zones, which would ban all ballistic missiles in a given region, could be immediately introduced to Europe, Latin America, the Middle East Gulf Cooperation Council states, Southeast Asia and the Pacific, and sub-Saharan Africa. States in these regions show some willingness to accept missile restraints. During the Japanese-sponsored March 2001 talks on Asian security, the *Bangkok Post* endorsed such restraints, noting that

---

47. J. Jerome Holton, Lora Lumpe, and Jeremy J. Stone, "Proposal for a Zero Ballistic Missile Regime," *Science and International Security Anthology, 1993* (Washington, D.C.: American Association for the Advancement of Science, 1993), pp. 379–396; Alton Frye, "Banning Ballistic Missiles," *Foreign Affairs,* Vol. 75, No. 6 (November/December 1996), p. 106; Jonathan Dean, "Step-By-Step Control Over Ballistic and Cruise Missiles," *Disarmament Diplomacy,* No. 31 (October 1998); Randy Rydell, "Models for Missile Disarmament: In Search of a Political Foundation," *INESAP Information Bulletin,* No. 19 (March 2002), pp. 66–71; and Andrew Lichterman, Zia Mian, M.V. Ramana, and Jurgen Scheffran, "Beyond Missile Defense," INESAP Briefing Paper, No. 8 (2000).
48. Jing-dong Yuan, *The MTCR and Missile Proliferation: Moving toward the Next Phase* (Ottawa: Department of Foreign Affairs and International Trade, Government of Canada, May 2000).
49. For a related discussion, see Fred Charles Iklé, "Can Nuclear Deterrence Last Out the Century?" *Foreign Affairs,* Vol. 51, No. 2 (January 1973), pp. 267–285; and Randall Forsberg, "Abolishing Ballistic Missiles: Pros and Cons," *International Security,* Vol. 12, No. 1 (Summer 1987), pp. 190–196.
50. A global zero alert would deactivate most if not all ballistic missiles—so that they could not be redeployed without detectable preparations—and would be a key step toward eventually eliminating warheads and missiles altogether. See Harold A. Feiveson, ed., *The Nuclear Turning Point: A Blueprint for Deep Cuts and De-Alerting of Nuclear Weapons* (Washington, D.C.: Brookings, 1999), pp. 119–120. Although the P-5 would not presently agree to missile elimination, they could reduce their nuclear-capable missile stockpiles and place them under a no-increase ceiling until the missile reduction process meshes with deeper nuclear reductions. See Jonathan Dean, "Main Points of a Possible Treaty for Controlling the Global Missile Control Treaty," Union of Concerned Scientists, Washington, D.C., March 7, 2002.

"reasoned talks among reasonable nations can help stop such [missile] threats. . . . Such talks can build trust and confidence. They can help to establish a mood where countries can agree to stop building missiles, and start destroying them instead."[51] Regional missile bans are desirable even if they only appear to be "disarming the disarmed," because they offer institutional frameworks for the disarmed to stay disarmed. They also provide more verified certainty that missile-free states will not develop new missile programs in the future.

Over the long term, states in one region would be more inclined to maintain their missile-free status if states in other regions also restrain their missile programs. What alternative restraints might other states accept? Two P-5 members (Russia and the United States) have given up their IRBMs under the INF treaty. Two other P-5 states (Britain and France) have no IRBMs. Thus, a global IRBM ban appears feasible not only for four of the P-5 but also for regional powers.[52] Such a treaty could stem further proliferation on the Korean Peninsula and in the Middle East—South Korea and most Arab states have no pressing security requirements for longer-range missiles and could accept an IRBM ban. However, some states of concern (North Korea and Iran), and a few others whose missiles may not be covered by IRBM bans (India, Pakistan, China, and Israel), warrant further examination.

REGIONAL POWERS AND A GLOBAL IRBM BAN. Regional powers could be required to restrain procurement or development of ballistic missiles as a condition for better political relations and stronger economic links with the West. For example, they may consider curbing their ICBM and IRBM programs and retain only SRBMs against regional adversaries. And if they perceive reductions in their regional security threat levels, they may even be willing to renounce SRBMs. But if regional powers strongly prefer ballistic missile deterrence against the United States, its allies, and their regional rivals, they may continue their quest for IRBMs and ICBMs.[53] These general guidelines can

---

51. "Battling to Stop Dangerous Weapons," *Bangkok Post*, March 11, 2001.
52. In the 1990s, former Arms Control and Disarmament Agency (ACDA) Director Kenneth Adelman proposed a global INF-type treaty that would have banned both Scuds and intermediate-range missiles. In June 1994, ACDA Director John Holum suggested inviting all states to accept the INF's obligations. Kenneth Adelman, "How to Limit Everybody's Missiles," *New York Times*, April 7, 1991, p. 19; Kenneth Adelman, "Going Ballistic . . . Globally," *Washington Times*, June 3, 1992, p. G1; and *Arms Control Reporter, 1994* (Washington, D.C.: Institute for Defense and Disarmament Studies, 1994), pp. 603.B.225 (7-94), 706.B.170 (11-94).
53. A regional power's demand for long-range missiles is well illustrated in a statement by Muammar Qadhaffi, who noted: "If we had possessed a deterrent—missiles that could reach New York—we would have hit it at the same moment [as the 1986 U.S. air strike on Libya]. Conse-

indicate prospects for missile restraints in North Korea, Iran, and among other regional powers.

By late 2000 North Korea and the United States had come close to an agreement that "when completed, would both halt North Korea's exports of missiles and related technology and stop further production, deployment and testing of long-range missiles."[54] If U.S.–North Korea missile talks, which were frozen in 2001–02, resume, Pyongyang may negotiate missile restraints in several ways. It could agree to halt all missile exports in exchange for economic compensation (previously it sought $1 billion annually for three years, whereas Washington was prepared to offer a few hundred million dollars in food aid and other assistance); it may offer to scrap its long-range Taepodong rocket program if other states agreed to launch its satellites; and it may eliminate its medium-range Nodong missiles and keep only its Scud-class missiles if regional security threats diminish.[55]

Iran's Scud-B and Scud-C missiles enable it to counter its main strategic adversary, Iraq. Iran's Shehab-3 and Shehab-4 missiles provide options against Israel and other regional powers as well. Tehran's security rationale for maintaining its IRBMs is mixed. Pakistan, Russia, Saudi Arabia, Turkey, and the United States are all Iran's rivals for influence in Central Asia, the Persian Gulf, and the Middle East, but none has a major territorial dispute with Iran.[56] Yet, Iran has remained hostile toward both the United States and Israel since 1979, and its defense policy continues to be strongly influenced by hard-line lobbies seeking long-range missile options against both the United States and its allies.

---

quently, we should build this force so that they and others will no longer think about an attack." Speech by Muammar Qadhaffi, April 18, 1990, in Foreign Broadcast Information System, FBIS-NES-90-078, April 23, 1990, p. 8, cited in *Report of the Commission to Assess the Ballistic Missile Threat to the United States*, app. 3, p. 370.

54. Wendy Sherman, "Talking to the North Koreans," *New York Times*, March 7, 2001, p. 19A. See also Gary Samore, "U.S.-DPRK Missile Negotiations," *Nonproliferation Review*, Vol. 9, No. 2 (Summer 2002), pp. 16–20.

55. This regional security improvement would involve the normalization of relations with South Korea and Japan, accommodation with the United States, and continued support from North Korea's allies China and Russia. For more detailed assessments, see Leon V. Sigal, "North Korea Is No Iraq: Pyongyang's Negotiating Strategy," *Arms Control Today*, Vol. 32, No. 10 (December 2002), pp. 8–12; Victor D. Cha, "Hawk Engagement and Preventive Defense on the Korean Peninsula," *International Security*, Vol. 27, No. 1 (Summer 2002), pp. 40–78; and Selig S. Harrison, *Korean Endgame: A Strategy for Reunification and U.S. Disengagement* (Princeton, N.J.: Princeton University Press, 2002).

56. For recent discussions on the prospects for influencing Iran, see, for example, Shahram Chubin, *Whither Iran? Reform, Domestic Politics, and National Security*, Adelphi Paper No. 342 (London: International Institute for Strategic Studies, 2002); and James Bill, "The Politics of Hegemony: The United States and Iran," *Middle East Policy*, Vol. 8, No. 3 (September 2001), pp. 89–100.

In the middle term, however, three developments could influence an Iranian decision to restrain its missile program. The first would be greater domestic political reform and broader international engagement. The second would be if Iran's regional rivals such as Iraq were also under missile and WMD restraints. The third would be if restraint were not seen as the result of foreign pressure, but as part of a broader multilateral regime. On this issue, it is interesting to note that internationalist bodies such as Iran's foreign affairs ministry support multilateral agreements and that Tehran has signed the CWC, though hard-line groups are still suspected of engaging in chemical weapon activities.

Other states such India, Pakistan, China, and Israel may not be covered by an IRBM ban, though they could still accept alternative restraints—for example, agreeing not to produce any new missiles. India and Pakistan built IRBMs to enhance their nuclear deterrents, but they have no definitively known programs for building ICBMs. They could agree to cap their missile programs under two conditions (assuming that domestic political pressures do not also hinder nonproliferation efforts). First, they could accept restraints compatible with their security requirements for a minimum deterrent force. Such a force could comprise 100–150 nuclear weapons and necessary aircraft and IRBM delivery systems for India, as well as 20–40 nuclear weapons and associated delivery systems for Pakistan.[57] Second, restraints would be more feasible if they were part of a broader global regime and thereby addressed India's long-standing desire to include China in arms control negotiations. In particular, if a fissile material cutoff treaty (FMCT) were created and states (including China) joined it, then India and Pakistan might sign on as well. The FMCT would limit the size of member states' nuclear programs, thus reducing Delhi's and Islamabad's strategic need for additional delivery systems and making them more amenable to restraining their missile programs.[58] In the absence of an FMCT, however, Beijing could greatly expand its nuclear and missile forces (say in response to U.S. missile defenses), and Delhi (and consequently Islamabad) could reject new nuclear and missile limitations. Pakistan may also oppose missile restraints if India acquires theater missile defense (TMD) systems that would undermine Pakistan's deterrent.[59]

---

57. Ashley J. Tellis, *India's Emerging Nuclear Posture: Between Recessed Deterrent and Ready Arsenal* (Santa Monica, Calif.: RAND, 2001).
58. New Delhi is building a 3,000–5,000 km range Agni-3 to strengthen its deterrent capability against China. Under a South Asian strategic restraint regime, India would keep its Agni IRBMs but not build new missiles or modify existing missiles into ICBMs.
59. Pakistan has noted that it would support a regional-restraint regime "based on credible nuclear deterrence at the minimum possible level, including non-induction of anti-ballistic missiles

Beijing may decide to restrict its SRBM deployments if Taiwan curbs its missile defense plans and the United States restrains its arms transfers to Taiwan.[60] In the middle term, China might also consider agreements not to build new missiles, especially if regional rivals such as India are included, and if missile defenses do not undercut its deterrent.

On another front, Israel could renounce the development of new missiles under a memorandum of understanding with the United States. Israel anticipates that its neighbors will possess some 2,000 missiles by the end of this decade.[61] It could avert this development by offering to freeze its own missile production if other states reciprocated. Further, restraints on Israel would provide greater legitimacy to any broader Middle East nonproliferation initiative. Arab states with modern air forces such as Saudi Arabia and Jordan could feasibly renounce missiles under such regional initiatives. If its regional rivals accept missile restraints, Iran may more strongly consider restrictions on the production and testing of its Shehab-3s and on the development of new missiles.

THE FEASIBILITY AND ADVANTAGES OF LEGAL BARRIERS. IRBM bans and regional missile-free zones are feasible options for three reasons. First, conventionally armed ballistic missiles have limited military utility. Regional power missiles tend to be inaccurate and have a very low probability of hitting a military or industrial asset at a distance of hundreds of kilometers (though China has improved the accuracy of its SRBMs by using global positioning systems). Aircraft are generally more accurate delivery systems and can carry heavier payloads than missiles. Ballistic missiles have political utility mainly as national morale boosters and weapons of terror. Therefore, although new military doctrines in several states seek long-range strike capabilities, governments may not be averse to eliminating missiles with limited military utility, especially if their neighbors refrain from acquiring them and if international norms proscribe them. Second, in many cases states acquire missiles to enhance their

and submarine-launched ballistic missiles in the region." UN General Assembly document A/56/136/add.2, August 21, 2001.

60. In 1999–2000, both Taiwan's President Lee Teng-hui and Vice President Lien Chan noted that China's military buildup would be critical in Taiwan's TMD decision. Meanwhile Foreign Minister Tien Hung-mao asked Washington to discourage China from deploying missiles that could reach Taiwan. Karen E. House, "Taiwan Puts Onus on China in Arms Buildup," *Wall Street Journal,* June 25, 1999, p. 17A; and Russell Flannery, "Taiwan Wants U.S to Pressure Beijing on Deployment of Missiles," *Wall Street Journal,* April 17, 2000, p. 26A. Reversing this logic, China could restrain its SRBM deployments if Washington and Taipei made concessions on TMD and on U.S. arms transfers to Taiwan.

61. David A. Fulghum, "Advanced Threats Drive Arrow's Future," *Aviation Week and Space Technology,* October 12, 1998, pp. 56–57.

prestige (missiles are equated with technological advancement and modernization) and to attain parity with a neighbor's missile force. This logic implies that states would be willing to eliminate missiles if neighboring states did the same. Third, missile-free zones are, to a certain degree, verifiable.

Regardless of the logic favoring regional and global missile nonproliferation treaties, key states may opt not to sign them immediately. This would not necessarily be a major drawback: Key states did not sign and ratify the NPT in its first decade, but eventually it gained near-universal acceptance and was indefinitely extended in its twenty-fifth year.

Thus, despite initial obstacles, treaties that limit missile proliferation are not only viable in the middle term but can also have three major benefits.[62] First, they can constrain states from acquiring new missiles by checking domestic lobbies that seek them. Nonproliferation forces in a country can point to treaty obligations to counter missile- and WMD-seeking domestic lobbies. Second, states may be more likely to eliminate their missiles forces if neighboring states do not have similar missile forces or missile aspirations (which would be indicated by their signing a missile nonproliferation treaty). Third, a broader missile nonproliferation regime based on international law would provide greater legitimacy to, and consequently increase chances for the success of, U.S. nonproliferation talks with regional powers.

FLIGHT-TEST BANS

Two types of flight-test limitations—(1) test notifications and moratoriums and (2) test bans—can enhance the effectiveness of regional missile-free zones and intermediate-range bans. Test notifications, guidelines (e.g., agreements not to aim test missiles at neighboring states), and moratoriums form part of the Code of Conduct. These measures have important political and security benefits because they help to avert regional crises. Unannounced missile tests can shock neighboring states (as was the case with North Korea's 1998 Taepodong test) and increase their security concerns (and their demand for missiles). Test notifications remove the shock factor in any missile test. Further, test moratoriums allow the continuation of broader regional security dialogues. For example, any North Korean missile test in 1999 could have increased tensions and led to conflict. Instead, in September 1999 Pyongyang

---

62. For a broader discussion of legally binding agreements, see Miles Kahler, "The Causes and Consequences of Legalization," *International Organization*, Vol. 54, No. 3 (Summer 2000), pp. 661–683.

announced a freeze on tests as long as dialogue continued, an acceptable position to Washington, which increased its dialogue with the North Korean regime the next year.

More comprehensive flight-test bans (which are excluded from the Code of Conduct) would make the development of new missiles technologically harder and thus be a significant barrier to proliferation. Regional powers may henceforth not require any tests for developing Scud and Nodong-type missiles. They may also have advanced technologies to design and build more reliable missiles and missile components, which reduces the need for extensive testing. Yet flight testing is still necessary to prove stage separation for long-range missiles, to perfect guidance and targeting systems for any missile, and to boost confidence in the performance of new missiles.[63] A test ban can thus hinder states from developing long-range, multiple stage, and accurate missiles.

A flight-test ban may not immediately cover the P-5 states and regional missile powers that periodically test their missiles, nor would it cover U.S. missile defense tests. In these cases, advance notification may be provided, and tests may be nonintrusively monitored to verify that states are not testing new missiles.

VERIFICATION OF MISSILE CONTROLS

Verification of compliance is an important component of any missile nonproliferation agreement. Verification may appear difficult because a determined violator can clandestinely build missiles in underground factories and store them in underground facilities. Even above ground, missiles can be concealed. Yet several points suggest that verification is feasible. First, an international agreement would require parties to cooperate by declaring production facilities and inventories and allowing monitoring. Second, verification is technologically possible through satellite observation. Third, the experience of the START and INF treaties, and of UN inspectors in Iraq, has demonstrated the feasibility of verification mechanisms such as on-site inspections and portal and perimeter monitoring.[64]

---

63. Test bans are useful because some problems associated with predicting ballistic trajectory bias, multiple warhead maneuvering, and warhead reentry can be resolved only through actual tests. Even if missile components are tested outside of flight tests, there are numerous instances when the components worked well by themselves and yet revealed problems when tested together. Lora Lumpe, "A Flight Test Ban as a Tool for Curbing Ballistic Missile Proliferation," in Peter Hayes, ed., *Space Power Interests* (Boulder, Colo.: Westview, 1996), pp. 146–182.
64. For a more detailed treatment of verification, see Peter Zimmerman, "Verification of Ballistic Missile Activities: Problems and Possible Solutions," in ibid., pp. 207–232; and Jurgen Scheffran,

Verification can still be challenging. One potential drawback is that a missile ban would not preclude states from testing many missile components in a space program. As a result, states could test key components and major boosters up to the threshold of a breakout, and could also gain experience in building and handling rockets. But states would require additional testing to have confidence in missile reentry and targeting systems that are not part of space launchers. Another drawback is that some uncertainty may persist in monitoring a missile nonproliferation zone. Yet although some missile development activities can be successfully hidden, others such as testing can be easily detected, and states cannot confidently develop accurate and long-range missiles without testing. Further, low levels of uncertainty may be tolerable, because a violator may clandestinely build only a small number of missiles—any large-scale program is more likely to be detected.

Arms Control Regimes and Missile Defense

This article has examined ways to contain missile proliferation. It has not dealt with another approach against the missile threat—missile defense—whose pros and cons have been extensively discussed elsewhere.[65] Yet it is worth emphasizing that missile nonproliferation initiatives have important implications for missile defense. A significant concern with national missile defense (NMD) is that it could undermine Beijing's (and eventually Moscow's) deterrent against the United States. This in turn would pressure Beijing (and in the middle term Moscow) to maintain large offensive forces and reject deeper arms control accords.[66] An expanded Chinese nuclear buildup could also trigger much greater nuclearization by India, and consequently by Pakistan, and

"Verification of Ballistic Missile Bans and Space Technologies," in Wolfgang Liebert and Scheffran, eds., *Against Proliferation—Towards General Disarmament* (Munster, Germany: Agenda, 1995), pp. 156–164. For more on INF and START verification, see the homepage of the Defense Threat Reduction Agency, http://www.dtra.mil/os/ops/os_ops.html. See also Annette Schaffer, "Verifying Nuclear Arms Control and Disarmament," in Trevor Findlay, ed., *Verification Yearbook, 2000* (London: Vertic, 2000), p. 60; and Edward Ifft, "Verifying Nuclear Arms Control and Disarmament," in Trevor Findlay and Oliver Meier, eds., *Verification Yearbook, 2001* (London: Vertic, 2001), pp. 25–42. For UNSCOM, see Stephen Black, "Verification Under Duress: The Case of UNSCOM," in Findlay, *Verification Yearbook, 2000*, pp. 115–129.
65. Dean A. Wilkening, *Ballistic Missile Defense and Strategic Stability*, Adelphi Paper No. 334 (London: International Institute for Strategic Studies, 2000); James M. Lindsay and Michael E. O'Hanlon, *Defending America: The Case for a Limited National Missile Defense* (Washington, D.C.: Brookings, 2001); and Charles L. Glaser and Steve Fetter, "National Missile Defense and the Future of U.S. Nuclear Weapons Policy," *International Security*, Vol. 26, No. 1 (Summer 2001), pp. 40–92.
66. To counter NMD, Beijing may build a few hundred multiple-warhead ICBMs by 2015, compared to its 20 single-warhead liquid-fuel ICBMs that would be replaced by 75–100 solid-fuel

would spur an arms race creating a more nuclearized Asia. These developments would seriously undermine the broader nuclear arms control and nonproliferation regime.

A strong missile nonproliferation regime could avert such grave negative strategic developments. A regime that considerably contains the missile threat would permit NMD to be significantly limited as well, and thereby make it less strategically destabilizing. For example, NMD could then be limited to research and testing without deployment, or to small-sized 100 interceptor deployments (the former ABM treaty originally permitted 100 interceptors at two sites). A very limited defense would allow Beijing and Moscow (and consequently Delhi and Islamabad) to considerably curb their nuclear and missile expansion.

Initiatives that contain missile proliferation would complement defenses in several additional ways. First, they would minimize not only the adverse strategic consequences of NMD but also the negative consequences of TMD. Although a state may seek TMD to counter an adversary's missile buildup, TMD deployments could cause the adversary to seek additional missiles to counter TMD. Such an expanded missile buildup among several regional powers could increase interstate tensions and undermine regional security. This regional rivalry could be averted if missile proliferation were restrained so that TMD deployments (that would stimulate a further missile buildup) could be minimized. Second, a strong missile nonproliferation regime can reduce the costs of defense; by keeping the missile threat small, it averts the need for large, more expensive defenses. Third, an effective missile nonproliferation regime can provide a safety net for defense or an additional option against missiles that would be necessary if defensive technology cannot be perfected.[67]

ICBMs and SLBMs under a modest modernization program. It could also reject any fissile material cutoff treaty (i.e., a treaty that would halt production of nuclear weapons material). Moreover, Moscow may hesitate to reduce its nuclear force much below levels of about 2,000 strategic warheads—especially if political ties with the United States deteriorate. (Although Russia may not have budgetary resources to deploy more than 1,000 warheads by 2010–15, it could still maintain thousands of warheads in storage.) The introduction of defensive technology does not always cause expansions in offense forces—for example, during the Cold War, U.S. bomber force megatonnage declined despite increases in Soviet air defense—but observers note that "there is, should be, and predictably will be a close relation between offense and defense whenever defenses threaten to take away something the offense really values. . . . Where defenses do not bother offensive missiles much, they might not be countered." Ashton B. Carter, "Introduction," in Herbert F. York, *Does Strategic Defense Breed Offense?* (Cambridge, Mass.: Center for Science and International Affairs, John F. Kennedy School of Government, Harvard University, 1987), pp. 2, 4.

67. Although ground-based midcourse phase interceptors successfully hit targets in their last four tests in 2002 (after failing in two of their first three tests), these tests did not fully accounted for decoys, countermeasures, and battlefield conditions. Further, some defenses such as boost-phase sys-

Fourth, a missile nonproliferation regime can enhance the technological effectiveness of defenses; for any given combat engagement, defenses have a better chance of success against a smaller number of target missiles.

These four benefits would be substantially forfeited in the absence of strong regimes to contain the missile threat. Further, in the absence of a strong arms-control regime, target missile arsenals are likely to grow in quantity and quality, and this would seriously undercut defenses. Larger and more sophisticated target missile arsenals would be able to overwhelm and evade missile defenses. Moreover, other tactical-level options such as preemptive strikes would also fail against larger missile arsenals. Military strikes may substantially eliminate small-sized target missile arsenals, but they may have little impact on larger ones.

In short, although missile defense and preemptive strikes provide some leverage against missile threats, they become more costly, technologically harder, and strategically destabilizing if they are not complemented by a strong security regime that contains target missile programs. Security and nonproliferation regimes can counter the missile threat with few negative strategic consequences and much less expensively than missile defense.[68]

A stronger missile nonproliferation regime is not merely desirable; it is also politically attainable. As a result of recent initiatives (UN initiatives, the GCS proposal, and the Code of Conduct), there is increased "knowledge" in diplomatic circles about the perils of missile proliferation and the need to contain it.[69] The issue is more pressing because other options against missiles—such as expanded missile defense initiatives—may undermine strategic nuclear arms control. This knowledge has generated substantial international interest in a stronger missile nonproliferation regime (as previously mentioned, ninety-three states have signed the Code of Conduct). A stronger regime can be nego-

---

tems remain largely untested. For more on technological obstacles to defenses, see Theodore A. Postol, "Why Missile Defense Won't Work," *Technology Review*, April 2002, pp. 42–51.

68. Although defenses are not entirely unaffordable (their projected annual costs of $5–7 billion are only 1–2 percent of an approximately $400 billion U.S. defense budget), lowering their costs is still advantageous because this would release billions of dollars for other programs. Further, missile nonproliferation initiatives such as space service sharing and verification mechanisms would cost an estimated few hundred million dollars annually, an order of magnitude less than the cost of missile defense.

69. Regime politics often involve the interaction between power, interests, and knowledge. These dynamics were instrumental in the MTCR's creation and expansion. During the 1980s and 1990s, increasing and more widely accepted knowledge about the perils of proliferation generated an interest in a missile control regime. When suppliers did not fully comply with the regime, however, power politics—in the form of U.S. pressure and incentives—influenced key suppliers to more strongly curb their technology exports. On regimes, see Andreas Hasenclever, Peter Mayer, and Volker Rittberger, *Theories of International Regimes* (Cambridge: Cambridge University Press, 1997).

tiated in several venues. The Conference on Disarmament is the most appropriate forum for negotiating a global IRBM ban with verification protocols (the conference has been deadlocked, however, since the late 1990s).[70] Alternatively, an IRBM ban could be created through discussions hosted by a few states but open to all relevant parties.[71]

The MTCR's technology barriers and the Code of Conduct's CBMs are useful and practical short-term arms control measures. They are not sufficient, however, to contain missile proliferation in the long term. A broader and deeper missile nonproliferation regime having incentives, legal barriers, and verification mechanisms would better address all issues relevant to missile proliferation.[72] Although a wider regime could have drawbacks (it would not immediately or completely eliminate regional missile forces and may not be completely verifiable), it could still considerably contain proliferation and be effective over the long term. The establishment of space service incentives, regional missile-free zones, global intermediate-range missile bans, flight-test bans, and verification initiatives are five feasible ways to strengthen the missile nonproliferation regime. Such an expanded regime would offer a firmer institutional framework to contain missile proliferation.

---

70. Rebecca Johnson, "CD Closes 2002 Still Deadlocked," *Disarmament Diplomacy*, No. 67 (October–November 2002).

71. The Landmine Convention was furthered by a small core group of states influenced by an active nongovenmental movement. Epistemic communities and groups of specialists can also be influencial in treaty negotiations. For the role of epistemic communities, see Peter M. Haas, ed., *Knowledge, Power, and International Policy Coordination* (Columbia: University of South Carolina Press, 1997). For a discussion of the paths to regime formation and the depth of cooperation, see, for example, George Downs, David Rocke, and Peter Barsoom, "Managing the Evolution of Multilateralism," *International Organization*, Vol. 52, No. 2 (Spring 1998), pp. 397–419.

72. Other arms control arrangements such as the Comprehensive Test Ban Treaty (CTBT) would crucially reinforce a missile nonproliferation regime. The CTBT would limit the ability of states to develop new types of (and to reduce the size and weight of their) warheads. It could thereby hinder China from expanding and adding multiple independently targetable reentry vehicles to its strategic missile forces. It could also prevent India and Pakistan from perfecting boosted fission and thermonuclear weapons, and thus limit the destructive power they could deliver on a given force of missiles. National Academy of Sciences, *Technical Issues Related to the Comprehensive Nuclear Test Ban Treaty* (Washington, D.C.: National Academy Press, 2002), p. 8.

Part II:
Nonmilitary Aspects of Security

Human Security

Paradigm Shift or Hot Air?

Roland Paris

Human security is the latest in a long line of neologisms—including common security, global security, cooperative security, and comprehensive security—that encourage policymakers and scholars to think about international security as something more than the military defense of state interests and territory. Although definitions of human security vary, most formulations emphasize the welfare of ordinary people. Among the most vocal promoters of human security are the governments of Canada and Norway, which have taken the lead in establishing a "human security network" of states and nongovernmental organizations (NGOs) that endorse the concept.[1] The term has also begun to appear in academic works,[2] and is the subject of new research projects at several major universities.[3]

Roland Paris is Assistant Professor of Political Science and International Affairs at the University of Colorado, Boulder.

My thanks to Michael Barnett, Francis Beer, Stephen Brooks, Steve Chan, Claudio Cioffi, Daniel Drezner, Colin Dueck, Natalie Goldring, Ian Hurd, Peter Viggo Jakobsen, David Leblang, Daniel Lindley, Michael Lipson, and Thomas Weiss for comments on previous drafts. An earlier version of this article was presented to the joint meeting of the International Security and Arms Control section of the American Political Science Association and the International Security Studies section of the International Studies Association in Denver, Colorado (November 9–11, 2000), and at the annual conference of the International Studies Association in Chicago, Illinois (February 20–24, 2001).

---

1. Other states in the network include Austria, Chile, Greece, Ireland, Jordan, Mali, the Netherlands, Slovenia, Switzerland, and Thailand. See "Chairman's Summary," Second Ministerial Meeting of the Human Security Network, Lucerne, Switzerland, May 11–12, 2000, http://www.dfait-maeci.gc.ca/foreignp/humansecurity/Chairman_summary-e.asp (accessed on February 14, 2001).
2. For example, Yuen Foong Khong, "Human Security: A Shotgun Approach to Alleviating Human Misery?" *Global Governance*, Vol. 7, No. 3 (July–September 2001); Oliver Richmond, "Human Security, the 'Rule of Law,' and NGOs: Potentials and Problems for Humanitarian Intervention," *Human Rights Review*, Vol. 2, No. 4 (July–September 2001); Astri Suhrke, "Human Security and the Interests of States," *Security Dialogue*, Vol. 30, No. 3 (September 1999), pp. 265–276; Peter Stoett, *Human and Global Security: An Exploration of Terms* (Toronto: University of Toronto Press, 1999); Caroline Thomas and Peter Wilkin, eds., *Globalization, Human Security, and the African Experience* (Boulder, Colo.: Lynne Rienner, 1999); Jorge Nef, *Human Security and Mutual Vulnerability: The Global Political Economy of Development and Underdevelopment*, 2d ed. (Ottawa: International Development Research Centre, 1999); Majid Tehranian, ed., *Worlds Apart: Human Security and Global Governance* (London: I.B. Tauris, 1999); Heather Owens and Barbara Arneil, "The Human Security Paradigm Shift: A New Lens on Canadian Foreign Policy? Report of the University of British Columbia Symposium on Human Security," ibid., pp. 1–12; Ramesh Thakur, "The United Nations and Human Security," ibid., pp. 51–60; and Tatsuro Matsumae and L.C. Chen, eds., *Common Security in Asia: New Concept of Human Security* (Tokyo: Tokai University Press, 1995).
3. These include Harvard University's Program on Human Security, the University of Denver's

Some commentators argue that human security represents a new paradigm for scholars and practitioners alike. Despite these claims, however, it remains unclear whether the concept of human security can serve as a practical guide for academic research or governmental policymaking. As Daniel Deudney has written in another context, "Not all neologisms are equally plausible or useful."[4] Two problems, in particular, limit the usefulness of the human security concept for students and practitioners of international politics. First, the concept lacks a precise definition. Human security is like "sustainable development"—everyone is for it, but few people have a clear idea of what it means. Existing definitions of human security tend to be extraordinarily expansive and vague, encompassing everything from physical security to psychological well-being, which provides policymakers with little guidance in the prioritization of competing policy goals and academics little sense of what, exactly, is to be studied.

Second, the most ardent backers of human security appear to have an interest in keeping the term expansive and vague. The idea of human security is the glue that holds together a jumbled coalition of "middle power" states, development agencies, and NGOs—all of which seek to shift attention and resources away from conventional security issues and toward goals that have traditionally fallen under the rubric of international development. As a unifying concept for this coalition, human security is powerful precisely because it lacks precision and thereby encompasses the diverse perspectives and objectives of all the members of the coalition. The term, in short, appears to be slippery by design. Cultivated ambiguity renders human security an effective campaign slogan, but it also diminishes the concept's usefulness as a guide for academic research or policymaking.

This is not to say that human security is merely "hot air" or empty rhetoric. The political coalition that now uses human security as a rallying cry has chalked up significant accomplishments, including the signing of an antipersonnel land mines convention and the imminent creation of an international criminal court. The alliance of some states and advocacy groups has altered the landscape of international politics since the end of the Cold War, as Richard Price and others have shown.[5] But to say that human security has

Graduate School of International Studies, the University of New South Wales's Asia-Australia Institute, and the University of British Columbia's Institute of International Relations.
4. Daniel Deudney, "Environment and Security: Muddled Thinking," *Bulletin of the Atomic Scientists*, Vol. 47, No. 3 (April 1991), p. 23.
5. Richard Price, "Reversing the Gun Sights: Transnational Civil Society Targets Land Mines," *International Organization*, Vol. 52, No. 3 (Summer 1998), pp. 613–644; and Craig Warkentin and Karen

served as an effective rallying cry is different from claiming that the concept offers a useful framework for analysis, as some of its proponents maintain.[6] Campaign slogans can be consequential without being well defined. The impact of Lyndon Johnson's Great Society rhetoric, for example, was arguably significant—serving as a focal point for political supporters of his reformist social agenda—but the exact meaning of the term "great society" was obscure. Similarly, one can support the political goals of the human security coalition while recognizing that the idea of human security itself is a muddle.

This article proceeds as follows. First, I examine existing definitions of human security. Second, I explore the limits of human security as a practical guide for academic research and policymaking. Third, I examine recent efforts to narrow the definition of human security. Fourth, I consider ways in which the concept might, despite its limitations, make a contribution to the study of international relations and security.

What Is Human Security?

The first major statement concerning human security appeared in the 1994 *Human Development Report*, an annual publication of the United Nations Development Programme (UNDP). "The concept of security," the report argues, "has for too long been interpreted narrowly: as security of territory from external aggression, or as protection of national interests in foreign policy or as global security from the threat of nuclear holocaust. . . . Forgotten were the legitimate concerns of ordinary people who sought security in their daily lives."[7] This critique is clear and forceful, but the report's subsequent proposal for a new concept of security—*human* security—lacks precision: "Human security can be said to have two main aspects. It means, first, safety from such chronic threats as hunger, disease and repression. And second, it means protection from sudden and hurtful disruptions in the patterns of daily life—whether in homes, in jobs or in communities."[8] The scope of this definition is vast: Virtually any kind of unexpected or irregular discomfort could conceivably constitute a threat to one's human security. Perhaps anticipating this criticism, the authors

---

Mingst, "International Institutions, the State, and Global Civil Society in the Age of the World Wide Web," *Global Governance*, Vol. 6, No. 2 (April–June 2000), pp. 237–257.
6. Laura Reed and Majid Tehranian, "Evolving Security Regimes," in Tehranian, *Worlds Apart*, p. 35.
7. United Nations Development Programme, *Human Development Report, 1994* (New York: Oxford University Press, 1994), p. 22.
8. Ibid., p. 23.

of the report identify seven specific elements that comprise human security: (1) economic security (e.g., freedom from poverty); (2) food security (e.g., access to food); (3) health security (e.g., access to health care and protection from diseases); (4) environmental security (e.g., protection from such dangers as environmental pollution and depletion); (5) personal security (e.g., physical safety from such things as torture, war, criminal attacks, domestic violence, drug use, suicide, and even traffic accidents); (6) community security (e.g., survival of traditional cultures and ethnic groups as well as the physical security of these groups); and (7) political security (e.g., enjoyment of civil and political rights, and freedom from political oppression). This list is so broad that it is difficult to determine what, if anything, might be excluded from the definition of human security. Indeed the drafters of the report seem distinctly uninterested in establishing any definitional boundaries. Instead they make a point of commending the "all-encompassing" and "integrative" qualities of the human security concept, which they apparently view as among the concept's major strengths.[9]

Today the UNDP's 1994 definition of human security remains the most widely cited and "most authoritative" formulation of the term,[10] although different members of the human security coalition have customized the definition to suit their own particular interests. According to the government of Japan, for example, the concept of human security "comprehensively covers all the measures that threaten human survival, daily life, and dignity—for example, environmental degradation, violations of human rights, transnational organized crime, illicit drugs, refugees, poverty, anti-personnel landmines and . . . infectious diseases such as AIDS—and strengthens efforts to confront these threats."[11] Other states, such as Canada, have promoted a more restrictive definition of human security as "freedom from pervasive threats to people's rights, safety or lives."[12] But even this slightly narrower con-

9. Ibid., p. 24.
10. John G. Cockell, "Conceptualising Peacebuilding: Human Security and Sustainable Peace," in Michael Pugh, ed., *Regeneration of War-Torn Societies* (London: Macmillan, 2000), p. 21.
11. Japanese Ministry of Foreign Affairs, *Diplomatic Bluebook, 1999*, chap. 2, sec. 3. See also "Statement by Director-General Yukio Takasu at the International Conference on Human Security in a Globalized World," Ulan Bator, May 8, 2000. Both documents are reproduced on the Japanese foreign ministry's web site at http://www.mofa.go.jp (accessed on February 14, 2001).
12. Canadian foreign ministry web site: http://www.dfait-maeci.gc.ca/foreignp/humansecurity/menu-e.asp (accessed on February 14, 2001). See also the statement by former Canadian Foreign Minister Lloyd Axworthy, "Canada and Human Security: The Need for Leadership," *International Journal*, Vol. 52, No. 2 (Spring 1997), pp. 183–196. Since leaving his post as foreign minister in 2000, Axworthy has continued to espouse the concept of human security; see Lloyd Axworthy, "Human Security and Global Governance: Putting People First," *Global Governance*, Vol. 7, No. 1 (January–March 2001), pp. 19–23.

ceptualization of human security is sweeping and open-ended: Among other things, the Canadian formulation includes safety from physical threats, the achievement of an acceptable quality of life, a guarantee of fundamental human rights, the rule of law, good governance, social equity, protection of civilians in conflicts, and sustainable development.[13] Meanwhile the human security network—which, in addition to Canada, Norway, and Japan, includes several other states and a broad assortment of international NGOs—has committed itself to the goal of "strengthening human security with a view to creating a more humane world where people can live in security and dignity, free from want and fear, and with equal opportunities to develop their human potential to the full."[14] The sentiments embodied in these statements are honorable, but they do little to clarify the meaning or boundaries of the human security concept.

Some academic writings on the subject have been similarly opaque. Many works amount to restatements or revisions of the UNDP's laundry list of human security issues. Jorge Nef, for example, devises a fivefold classification scheme, arguing that human security comprises (1) environmental, personal, and physical security, (2) economic security, (3) social security, including "freedom from discrimination based on age, gender, ethnicity, or social status," (4) political security, and (5) cultural security, or "the set of psychological orientations of society geared to preserving and enhancing the ability to control uncertainty and fear."[15] Laura Reed and Majid Tehranian offer their own list of human security's ten constituent elements—including psychological security, which "hinges on establishing conditions fostering respectful, loving, and humane interpersonal relations," and communication security, or the importance of "freedom and balance in information flows."[16] Other scholars avoid the laundry list approach, but offer equally expansive definitions. According to Caroline Thomas, human security refers to the provision of "basic material needs" and the realization of "human dignity," including "emancipation from oppressive power structures—be they global, national, or local in origin and scope."[17] For Robert Bedeski, human security includes "the totality of knowledge, technology, institutions and activities that protect, defend and preserve the biological existence of human life; and the processes which protect and

13. Axworthy, "Canada and Human Security," p. 184.
14. "Chairman's Summary," Second Ministerial Meeting of the Human Security Network.
15. Nef, *Human Security and Mutual Vulnerability*, p. 25.
16. Reed and Tehranian, "Evolving Security Regimes," pp. 39 and 47.
17. Caroline Thomas, "Introduction," in Thomas and Wilkin, *Globalization, Human Security, and the African Experience*, p. 3.

perfect collective peace and prosperity to enhance human freedom."[18] Again, if human security is all these things, what is it *not*?

A Guide for Research and Policymaking?

Policymakers and scholars face different, but related, problems in attempting to put these definitions of human security into practical use. For policymakers, the challenge is to move beyond all-encompassing exhortations and to focus on specific solutions to specific political issues. This is a difficult task not only because of the broad sweep and definitional elasticity of most formulations of human security but also—and perhaps even more problematically—because the proponents of human security are typically reluctant to prioritize the jumble of goals and principles that make up the concept. As noted above, part of the ethic of the human security movement is to emphasize the "inclusiveness" and "holism" of the term, which in practice seems to mean treating all interests and objectives within the movement as equally valid. Reed and Tehranian, for instance, after presenting their list of ten constituent categories of human security, conclude with this caveat: "It is important to reiterate that these overlapping categories do not represent a hierarchy of security needs from personal to national, international, and environmental rights. On the contrary, each realm impinges upon the others and is intrinsically connected to wider political and economic considerations."[19] The observation that all human and natural realms are fundamentally interrelated is a truism, and does not provide a very convincing justification for treating all needs, values, and policy objectives as equally important. Nor does it help decisionmakers in their daily task of allocating scarce resources among competing goals: After all, not everything can be a matter of national security, with all of the urgency that this term implies. To put it simply, human security "is too broad and vague a concept to be meaningful for policymakers, as it has come to entail such a wide range of different threats on one hand, while prescribing a diverse and sometimes incompatible set of policy solutions to resolve them on the other."[20]

For those who study, rather than practice, international politics, the task of transforming the idea of human security into a useful analytical tool for schol-

---

18. Robert Bedeski, "Human Security, Knowledge, and the Evolution of the Northeast Asian State," Centre for Global Studies, University of Victoria, February 8, 2000, http://www.globalcentres.org/docs/bedeski.html (accessed on February 14, 2001).
19. Reed and Tehranian, "Evolving Security Regimes," p. 53.
20. Owens and Arneil, "The Human Security Paradigm Shift," p. 2.

arly research is also problematic. Given the hodgepodge of principles and objectives associated with the concept, it is far from clear what academics should even be studying. Human security seems capable of supporting virtually any hypothesis—along with its opposite—depending on the prejudices and interests of the particular researcher. Further, because the concept of human security encompasses both physical security and more general notions of social, economic, cultural, and psychological well-being, it is impractical to talk about certain socioeconomic factors "causing" an increase or decline in human security, given that these factors are themselves part of the definition of human security. The study of causal relationships requires a degree of analytical separation that the notion of human security lacks.[21]

To illustrate these problems, consider John Cockell's efforts to apply the human security concept to the phenomenon of international peacebuilding operations in countries at risk of slipping into, or just emerging from, civil war.[22] After embracing the open-ended UNDP definition of human security, Cockell states that "peacebuilding is a sustained process of preventing internal threats to human security from causing protracted, violent conflict."[23] Yet because the UNDP definition of human security includes safety from violence as a central component of human security, Cockell is effectively saying that peacebuilding seeks to prevent a decline in human security from causing a decline in human security, which makes little sense. He then identifies "four basic parameters," based on the principles of human security, for the conduct of peacebuilding operations: Peacebuilders should focus on root causes of conflicts, pay attention to the differences in local conditions from one operation to the next, seek sustainable and durable results, and mobilize local actors and resources in support of peace. Although these guidelines seem reasonable, the sprawling concept of human security could support many more—and quite different—principles for peacebuilding. Indeed Cockell himself acknowledges that his policy prescriptions are "arbitrary," which belies the notion that human security entails a particular "orientation" toward peacebuilding, as Cockell claims.[24] More generally, if human security means almost anything, then it effectively means nothing.[25]

---

21. Suhrke makes a similar point in "Human Security and the Interests of States," pp. 270–271.
22. Cockell, "Conceptualising Peacebuilding."
23. Ibid., p. 21.
24. Ibid., pp. 26, 21.
25. On the problem of "conceptual stretching," see Giovanni Sartori, "Concept Misinformation in Comparative Politics," *American Political Science Review*, Vol. 64, No. 4 (December 1970), pp. 1033–1053.

Attempts to Narrow the Concept

One possible remedy for the expansiveness and vagueness of human security is to redefine the concept in much narrower and more precise terms, so that it might offer a better guide for research and policymaking. This is the approach that Gary King and Christopher Murray have adopted in their ongoing project on human security.[26] King and Murray offer a definition of human security that is intended to include only "essential" elements, meaning elements that are "important enough for human beings to fight over or to put their lives or property at great risk."[27] Using this standard, they identify five key indicators of well-being—poverty, health, education, political freedom, and democracy—that they intend to incorporate into an overall measure of human security for individuals and groups. Similarly, another scholar, Kanti Bajpai, proposes construction of a "human security audit" that would include measures of "direct and indirect threats to individual bodily safety and freedom," as well as measures of different societies' "capacity to deal with these threats, namely, the fostering of norms, institutions, and . . . representativeness in decisionmaking structures."[28] Although both projects are still in the early stages of development, they represent welcome efforts at operationalizing the concept of human security with a more precise definition of the term. A clear measure or audit of human security would allow scholars to assess the factors that lead to declines or increases in the human security of particular groups or individuals.[29]

Both of these projects, however, face problems that seem endemic to the study of human security. First, they identify certain values as more important than others without providing a clear justification for doing so. Bajpai, for instance, proposes inclusion of "bodily safety" and "personal freedom" in his human security audit, and argues that this audit would draw attention to the fact that "threats to safety and freedom are *the most important*" elements of hu-

26. Gary King and Christopher Murray, "Rethinking Human Security," Harvard University, May 4, 2000, http://gking.harvard.edu/files/hs.pdf (accessed on February 14, 2001).
27. Ibid., p. 8.
28. Kanti Bajpai, "Human Security: Concept and Measurement," Kroc Institute Occasional Paper No. 19:OP:1 (Notre Dame, Ind.: University of Notre Dame, August 2000), http://www.nd.edu/?krocinst/ocpapers/op_19_1.PDF (accessed on February 14, 2001).
29. In addition to these projects, on January 24, 2001, the United Nations and the government of Japan announced plans to establish a Commission on Human Security, which will be cochaired by Nobel laureate Amartya Sen and former UN High Commissioner for Human Rights Sadako Ogata. See "Independent Panel on 'Human Security' To Be Set Up," Agence France-Presse, January 24, 2001.

man security.[30] He does not explain, however, why other values are not equally, or perhaps even more, important than the values he champions. What about education? Is the ability to choose one's marriage partner, which is one of Bajpai's examples of personal freedom, really more important than, say, a good education? Perhaps it is, but Bajpai does not address this issue. Similarly, King and Murray state that their formulation of human security includes only those matters that people would be willing to fight over. But they neglect to offer evidence that their five indicators are, in fact, closely related to the risk of violent conflict. In other words, they favor certain values as representative of human security without offering a clear justification for doing so. Additionally, their decision to exclude indicators of violence from their composite measure of human security creates a de facto distinction between human security and physical security, thereby purging the most familiar connotation of security—safety from violence—from their definition of human security. Under the King-Murray formulation, individuals could find themselves in the strange position of enjoying a high level of human security (low poverty, reasonable health care, good education, political freedom, and democracy), while facing a relatively high risk of becoming victims of deadly violence. One need only think of residents of certain neighborhoods in Belfast, who might not consider themselves very "secure." Thus the challenge for these scholars is not simply to narrow the definition of human security into a more analytically tractable concept, but to provide a compelling rationale for highlighting certain values.

This raises another problem. Defining the core values of human security may be difficult not only because there is so little agreement on the meaning of human security, but because the term's ambiguity serves a particular purpose: It unites a diverse and sometimes fractious coalition of states and organizations that "see an opportunity to capture some of the more substantial political interest and superior financial resources" associated with more traditional, military conceptions of security.[31] These actors have in effect pursued a political strategy of "appropriating" the term "security," which conveys urgency, demands public attention, and commands governmental resources.[32] By main-

---

30. Ibid., p. 53 (emphasis added).
31. King and Murray, "Rethinking Human Security," p. 4. See also Mahbub ul Haq, *Reflections on Human Development,* exp. ed. (Delhi: Oxford University Press, 1998). On the strategic use of the term "security" as a tool for changing policy or obtaining resources, see Emma Rothschild, "What Is Security?" *Dædalus,* Vol. 124, No. 3 (Summer 1995), pp. 58–59.
32. On the urgency that is automatically associated with the concept of national security, see David E. Sanger, "Sometimes National Security Says It All," *New York Times,* Week in Review, May 7, 2000, p. 3.

taining a certain level of ambiguity in the notion of human security, moreover, the members of this coalition are able to minimize their individual differences, thereby accommodating as wide a variety of members and interests in their network as possible.[33] Given these circumstances, they are unlikely to support outside calls for greater specificity in the definition of human security, because definitional narrowing would likely highlight and aggravate differences among them, perhaps even to the point of alienating certain members and weakening the coalition as a whole.

Why, then, should scholars bother trying to transform the concept of human security into a serviceable analytical tool at all? Why embark on what could well be a quixotic quest to wrest the definition of human security away from those who have an interest in keeping it vague and expansive? Perhaps a more sensible alternative would be to employ a less politically encumbered terminology, or to think about other ways in which the concept of human security could contribute to the field of security studies.

Human Security as a Category of Research

To recapitulate my argument so far: Human security does not appear to offer a particularly useful framework of analysis for scholars or policymakers. But perhaps there are other avenues by which the idea of human security can contribute to the study of international relations and security. I would like to suggest one such possibility: Human security may serve as a *label* for a broad category of research in the field of security studies that is primarily concerned with nonmilitary threats to the safety of societies, groups, and individuals, in contrast to more traditional approaches to security studies that focus on protecting states from external threats. Much of this work is relatively new, and our understanding of how such research "fits" within the larger field of security studies is still limited. In other words, even if the concept of human secu-

---

33. The communiqués of the human security network, for example, describe the concept of human security more vaguely than do Canadian or Japanese government documents on the subject. Compare "Chairman's Summary," Second Ministerial Meeting of the Human Security Network, to the Government of Canada's "Human Security: Safety for People in a Changing World," Department of Foreign Affairs and International Trade, May 1999, and the "Statement by Director-General Yukio Takasu." Bajpai also discusses some of these differences in "Human Security: Concept and Measurement," as does Fen Osler Hampson, "The Axworthy Years: An Assessment," presentation prepared for delivery to the Group of 78, National Press Club, Ottawa, October 31, 2000, http://www.hri.ca/partners/G78/English/Peace/hampson-axworthy.htm (accessed on February 14, 2001).

rity itself is too vague to generate specific research questions, it could still play a useful taxonomical role in the field by helping to classify different types of scholarship. Using human security in this manner would be compatible with the *spirit* of the term—particularly its emphasis on nonmilitary sources of conflict—while recognizing that there is little point in struggling to operationalize the quicksilver concept of human security itself.

Despite resistance from some scholars, such as Stephen Walt, the field of security studies has developed beyond its traditional focus on the "threat, use and control of military force" primarily by states.[34] Since the end of the Cold War, in particular, the subject matter of security studies has undergone both a "broadening" and a "deepening."[35] By broadening, I mean the consideration of nonmilitary security threats, such as environmental scarcity and degradation, the spread of disease, overpopulation, mass refugee movements, nationalism, terrorism, and nuclear catastrophe.[36] By deepening, I mean that the field is now more willing to consider the security of individuals and groups, rather than focusing narrowly on external threats to states.[37] These efforts have been prompted in part by the contributions of "critical" theorists—including feminists, postmodernists, and constructivists—who have probed the assumptions and political implications of the term "security" itself.[38]

Using the notions of broadening and deepening, it is possible to construct a matrix of the security studies field, as illustrated in Figure 1. The matrix con-

34. Stephen M. Walt, "The Renaissance of Security Studies," *International Studies Quarterly*, Vol. 35, No. 1 (March 1991), p. 212. For a critique of Walt's traditionalism, see Edward A. Kolodziej, "Renaissance in Security Studies? Caveat Lector!" *International Studies Quarterly*, Vol. 36, No. 4 (December 1992), pp. 421–438.
35. I borrow these terms from Richard Wyn Jones, *Security, Strategy, and Critical Theory* (Boulder, Colo.: Lynne Rienner, 1999).
36. See, for example, Richard H. Ullmann, "Redefining Security," *International Security*, Vol. 8, No. 1 (Summer 1983), pp. 129–153; Jessica Tuchman Mathews, "Redefining Security," *Foreign Affairs*, Vol. 68, No. 2 (Spring 1989), pp. 162–177; and Sean M. Lynn-Jones and Steven E. Miller, eds., *Global Dangers: Changing Dimensions of International Security* (Cambridge, Mass.: MIT Press, 1995).
37. See, for example, Robert L. Rothstein, ed., *After the Peace: Resistance and Reconciliation* (Boulder, Colo.: Lynne Rienner, 1999); Barbara F. Walter, "Designing Transitions from Civil War: Demobilization, Democratization, and Commitments to Peace," *International Security*, Vol. 24, No. 1 (Summer 1999), pp. 127–155; Krishna Kumar, ed., *Rebuilding Societies after Civil War: Critical Roles for International Assistance* (Boulder, Colo.: Lynne Rienner, 1997); and Donald L. Horowitz, *Ethnic Groups in Conflict* (Berkeley: University of California Press, 1985).
38. See, for example, Bill McSweeney, *Security, Identity, and Interests: A Sociology of International Relations* (Cambridge: Cambridge University Press, 1999); Keith Krause and Michael C. Williams, eds., *Critical Security Studies* (Minneapolis: University of Minnesota Press, 1997); David Campbell, *Writing Security: United States Foreign Policy and the Politics of Identity* (Manchester: Manchester University Press, 1998); and Barry Buzan, Ole Wæver, and Jaap de Wilde, *Security: A New Framework for Analysis* (Boulder, Colo.: Lynne Rienner, 1998).

Figure 1. A Matrix of Security Studies

What Is the Source of the Security Threat?

	Military	Military, Nonmilitary, or Both
States	**Cell 1** National security (conventional realist approach to security studies)	**Cell 2** Redefined security (e.g., environmental and economic security)
Societies, Groups, and Individuals	**Cell 3** Intrastate security (e.g., civil war, ethnic conflict, and democide)	**Cell 4** Human security (e.g., environmental and economic threats to the survival of societies, groups, and individuals)

Security for Whom?

tains four cells, each representing a different cluster of literature in the field. I assume that a "security threat" connotes some type of menace to survival. The top half of the map includes works that focus on security threats to states; the bottom half comprises works that consider security threats to societies, groups, and individuals. The left side of the matrix shows literature that focuses on military threats, and the right side on military or nonmilitary threats, or both. These divisions produce the following fourfold typology of the field:

- Cell 1 contains works that concentrate on military threats to the security of states. Conventional realists tend to adopt this perspective, which has traditionally dominated academic security studies, particularly in the United States.[39] Most of the articles published in *International Security*, for example, fall into this category.

---

39. See, for example, Walt, "The Renaissance of Security Studies"; Richard K. Betts, "Should Strategic Studies Survive?" *World Politics*, Vol. 50, No. 1 (October 1997), pp. 7–33; Michael E. Brown, Owen R. Coté, Jr., Sean M. Lynn-Jones, and Steven E. Miller, eds., *America's Strategic Choices*, rev. ed. (Cambridge, Mass.: MIT Press, 2000); David A. Baldwin, "Security Studies and the End of the Cold War," *World Politics*, Vol. 48, No. 1 (October 1995), pp. 117–141; and Joseph S. Nye, Jr., and

- Cell 2 contains works that address nonmilitary threats (instead of, or in addition to, military threats) to the national security of states, including environmental and economic challenges. Jessica Tuchman Mathews's much-cited 1989 article, "Redefining Security," is typical of this category. Mathews argues that foreign security policies should incorporate considerations of environmental destruction, among other things, but she still considers the state, rather than substate actors, to be the salient object of security.[40] Other examples of such work include the Palme Commission's 1982 report, *Common Security*, which argued that nuclear weapons posed a threat to the survival of all states;[41] investigations into the relationship between environmental degradation and international armed conflict;[42] and studies of foreign economic policy and international security.[43]
- Cell 3 includes works that focus on military threats to actors other than states: namely societies, groups, and individuals. The prevalence of intrastate violence since the end of the Cold War has given rise to a large literature on intrastate conflicts, in which substate groups are the principal belligerents.[44]

Sean M. Lynn-Jones, "International Security Studies: A Report of a Conference on the State of the Field," *International Security*, Vol. 12, No. 4 (Spring 1988), pp. 5–27.
40. Mathews, "Redefining Security." See also Ullmann, "Redefining Security"; and Joseph J. Romm, *Defining National Security: The Nonmilitary Aspects* (New York: Council on Foreign Relations, 1993).
41. Independent Commission on Disarmament and Security Issues, *Common Security: A Blueprint for Survival* (New York: Simon and Schuster, 1982).
42. See, for example, Thomas F. Homer-Dixon, *Environment, Scarcity, and Violence* (Princeton, N.J.: Princeton University Press, 1999); and Nils Peter Gleditsch, "Armed Conflict and the Environment: A Critique of the Literature," *Journal of Peace Research*, Vol. 35, No. 3 (May 1998), pp. 381–400. For an excellent bibliography, see Geoffrey D. Dabelko, ed., *Environmental Change and Security Project Report*, No. 6 (Summer 2000), pp. 232–238, also available at http://ecsp.si.edu/pdf/Report6–10.pdf (accessed on May 5, 2001).
43. See, for example, Jean-Marc F. Blanchard, Edward D. Mansfield, and Norrin M. Ripsman, eds., *Power and the Purse: Economic Statecraft, Interdependence, and National Security* (London: Frank Cass, 2000), originally published as a special issue of *Security Studies*, Vol. 9, Nos. 1–2 (Autumn 1999–Winter 2000), pp. 1–316; C. Fred Bergsten, "America's Two-Front Economic Conflict," *Foreign Affairs*, Vol. 80, No. 2 (March–April 2001), pp. 16–27; Richard N. Haass, ed., *Economic Sanctions and American Diplomacy* (New York: Council on Foreign Relations, 1998); and Jonathan Kirschner, "Political Economic in Security Studies after the Cold War," *Review of International Political Economy*, Vol. 5, No. 1 (Spring 1998), pp. 64–91.
44. See, for example, John Mueller, "The Banality of 'Ethnic War,'" *International Security*, Vol. 25, No. 1 (Summer 2000), pp. 42–70; Benjamin Valentino, "Final Solutions: The Causes of Mass Killing and Genocide," *Security Studies* Vol. 9, No. 3 (Spring 2000), pp. 1–59; Barbara F. Walter and Jack Snyder, eds., *Civil Wars, Insecurity, and Intervention* (New York: Columbia University Press, 1999); Beverly Crawford and Ronnie D. Lipschutz, eds., *The Myth of 'Ethnic Conflict': Politics, Economics, and 'Cultural' Violence* (Berkeley: International and Area Studies, University of California, 1998); Chaim Kaufmann, "Possible and Impossible Solutions to Ethnic Civil Wars," *International Security*,

In addition, studies of "democide," or the intentional killing by a state of its own citizens, also fall into this category.[45]

- Cell 4 is concerned with military or nonmilitary threats—or both—to the security of societies, groups, and individuals. Does poverty, for example, fuel violence within societies?[46] Are certain types of domestic political institutions more conducive to domestic peace?[47] Is the degree of urbanization of a society, or access to medical care, associated with the occurrence of civil violence?[48] What other societal conditions pose a particular danger to the survival of groups and individuals? All of these questions would fall into the category of research that I label "human security."

Vol. 20, No. 4 (Spring 1996), pp. 136–175; Donald M. Snow, *Uncivil Wars: International Security and the New Internal Conflicts* (Boulder, Colo.: Lynne Rienner, 1996); Michael E. Brown, ed., *Ethnic Conflict and International Security* (Princeton, N.J.: Princeton University Press, 1993); and Roy Licklider, ed., *Stopping the Killing: How Civil Wars End* (New York: New York University Press, 1993).

45. See, for example, R.J. Rummel, *Power Kills: Democracy as a Method of Non-Violence* (New Brunswick, N.J.: Transaction, 1997); Gerald W. Scully, "Democide and Genocide as Rent-Seeking Activities," *Public Choice*, Vol. 93, Nos. 1–2 (October 1997), pp. 77–97; and Matthew Krain, "State-Sponsored Mass Murder: The Onset and Severity of Genocides and Politicides," *Journal of Conflict Resolution*, Vol. 41, No. 3 (June 1997), pp. 331–360.

46. Steve Majstorovic, "Politicized Ethnicity and Economic Inequality," *Nationalism and Ethnic Politics*, Vol. 1, No. 1 (Spring 1995), pp. 33–53; Walker Connor, "Eco- or Ethno-Nationalism," in Connor, *Ethnonationalism: The Quest for Understanding* (Princeton, N.J.: Princeton University Press, 1994), pp. 145–164; Ted Robert Gurr, "Why Minorities Rebel: A Global Analysis of Communal Mobilization and Conflict since 1945," *International Political Science Review*, Vol. 14, No. 2 (April 1993), pp. 161–201; Saul Newman, "Does Modernization Breed Ethnic Conflict?" *World Politics*, Vol. 43, No. 3 (April 1991), pp. 451–478; James B. Rule, *Theories of Civil Violence* (Berkeley: University of California Press, 1988); Steven Finkel and James B. Rule, "Relative Deprivation and Related Theories of Civil Violence: A Critical Review," in Kurt Lang and Gladys Lang, eds., *Research in Social Movements, Conflicts, and Change* (Greenwich, Conn.: JAI, 1986), Vol. 9, pp. 47–69; Ted Robert Gurr, *Why Men Rebel* (Princeton, N.J.: Princeton University Press, 1970); and William Ford and John Moore, "Additional Evidence on the Social Characteristics of Riot Cities," *Social Science Quarterly*, Vol. 51, No. 2 (September 1970), pp. 339–348.

47. Håvard Hegre, Tanja Ellingsen, Nils Petter Gleditsch, and Scott Gales, "Towards a Democratic Civil Peace? Opportunity, Grievance, and Civil War, 1816–1992," paper presented to the workshop Civil Conflicts, Crime, and Violence in Developing Countries, World Bank, Washington, D.C., February 1999; Matthew Krain and Marissa Edson Myers, "Democracy and Civil War: A Note on the Democratic Peace Proposition," *International Interactions*, Vol. 23, No. 1 (June 1997), pp. 109–118; and Michael Engelhardt, "Democracies, Dictatorships, and Counterinsurgency: Does Regime Type Really Matter?" *Conflict Quarterly*, Vol. 12, No. 3 (Summer 1992), pp. 52–63.

48. These two factors, among others, are studied in Daniel C. Esty, Jack A. Goldstone, Ted Robert Gurr, Barbara Harff, Marc Levy, Geoffrey D. Dabelko, Pamela T. Surko, and Alan N. Unger, *State Failure Task Force Report: Phase II Findings* (McLean, Va.: Science Applications International Corporation, 1998). For a critique of this report, see Gary King and Langche Zeng, "Improving Forecasts of State Failure," paper prepared for the Midwest Political Science Association meeting in Chicago, Illinois, November 13, 2000, http://gking.harvard.edu/files/civil.pdf (accessed on May 5, 2001).

Using the term "human security" to describe this type of scholarship has several advantages. First, the contents of cell 4 echo many of the concerns of the human security coalition, so it makes intuitive sense to use this terminology. Second, employing human security as a label for a broad category of research eliminates the problem of deriving clear hypotheses from the human security concept itself—a concept that, I have argued, offers little analytical leverage because it is so sprawling and ambiguous. Consequently, scholars working in the "human security branch" of security studies would not need to adjudicate the merit or validity of human security per se, but rather they would focus on more specific questions that could be clearly defined (and perhaps even answered). Third, and relatedly, although many scholars in this branch of security studies may be interested in normative questions as well as empirical ones, the advantage of using human security as a descriptive label for a class of research is that the label would not presuppose any particular normative agenda.[49]

Fourth, mapping the field in this manner—with human security as one branch—helps to differentiate the principal nontraditional approaches to security studies from one another. With the broadening and deepening of security studies in recent years, it is no longer helpful or reasonable to define the field in dualistic terms: with the realist, state-centric, military-minded approach to security studies at the core and a disorderly bazaar of alternative approaches in the periphery. These alternative approaches actually fall into broad groupings and have become sufficiently important to merit their own classification scheme. Mapping the field in new ways can help us to understand how these approaches relate to more traditional approaches to security studies, and to one another. Finally, the very fashionability of the label "human security" could benefit scholars by drawing attention to existing works within cell 4 and opening up new areas of research in this branch of the field.

Of course, the boundaries between these four quadrants are not absolute. Environmental degradation, for example, may simultaneously pose a threat to the survival of states and substate actors, and could thus full into either cell 2 or cell 4.[50] The permeability of these boundaries, however, is not a significant

---

49. Scholars may conclude, for example, that certain socioeconomic conditions are not associated with any particular threats to human survival.
50. Steven J. Del Rosso, Jr., "The Insecure State: Reflections on 'The State' and 'Security' in a Changing World," *Dædalus*, Vol. 124, No. 2 (Spring 1995), p. 185.

problem for scholars because each quadrant represents a broad category of re-search—or a cluster of issues and questions, rather than a distinct causal hy-pothesis or theory—which would need to be more clearly specified.

Conclusion

Human security has been described as many different things: a rallying cry, a political campaign, a set of beliefs about the sources of violent conflict, a new conceptualization of security, and a guide for policymakers and academic re-searchers. As a rallying cry, the idea of human security has successfully united a diverse coalition of states, international agencies, and NGOs. As a political campaign, the human security coalition has accomplished a number of specific goals, such as the negotiation of the land mines convention. But as a new con-ceptualization of security, or a set of beliefs about the sources of conflict, hu-man security is so vague that it verges on meaninglessness—and consequently offers little practical guidance to academics who might be interested in apply-ing the concept, or to policymakers who must prioritize among competing pol-icy goals. Efforts to sharpen the definition of human security are a step in the right direction, but they are likely to encounter resistance from actors who believe that the concept's strength lies in its holism and inclusiveness. Definitional expansiveness and ambiguity are powerful attributes of human security, but only in the sense that they facilitate collective action by the mem-bers of the human security coalition. The very same qualities, however, hobble the concept of human security as a useful tool of analysis. On the other hand, human security could provide a handy label for a broad category of research—a distinct branch of security studies that explores the particular conditions that affect the survival of individuals, groups, and societies—that may also help to establish this brand of research as a central component of the security studies field.

Environmental Scarcities and Violent Conflict

Thomas F. Homer-Dixon

Evidence from Cases

Within the next fifty years, the planet's human population will probably pass nine billion, and global economic output may quintuple. Largely as a result, scarcities of renewable resources will increase sharply. The total area of high-quality agricultural land will drop, as will the extent of forests and the number of species they sustain. Coming generations will also see the widespread depletion and degradation of aquifers, rivers, and other water resources; the decline of many fisheries; and perhaps significant climate change.

If such "environmental scarcities" become severe, could they precipitate violent civil or international conflict? I have previously surveyed the issues and evidence surrounding this question and proposed an agenda for further research.[1] Here I report the results of an international research project guided by this agenda.[2] Following a brief review of my original hypotheses and the project's research design, I present several general findings of this research that led me to revise the original hypotheses. The article continues with an account of empirical evidence for and against the revised hypotheses, and it concludes with an assessment of the implications of environmentally induced conflict for international security.

Thomas F. Homer-Dixon is Assistant Professor of Political Science and Director of the Peace and Conflict Studies Program at the University of Toronto. From 1990 to 1993, he was co-director and lead researcher of the Project on Environmental Change and Acute Conflict.

Portions of this article have been drawn from Thomas Homer-Dixon, Jeffrey Boutwell, and George Rathjens, "Environmental Scarcity and Violent Conflict," *Scientific American*, February 1993; and from Homer-Dixon, "Environmental Scarcity and Global Security" *Headline Series* (New York: Foreign Policy Association, 1993). The author thanks the participants in the Project on Environmental Change and Acute Conflict, especially project co-directors Jeffrey Boutwell and George Rathjens. The Donner Canadian Foundation funded the article's preparation.

1. Thomas Homer-Dixon, "On the Threshold: Environmental Changes As Causes of Acute Conflict," *International Security*, Vol. 16, No. 2 (Fall 1991), pp. 76–116.
2. The three-year Project on Environmental Change and Acute Conflict brought together a team of thirty researchers from ten countries. It was sponsored by the American Academy of Arts and Sciences and the Peace and Conflict Studies Program at the University of Toronto.

In brief, our research showed that environmental scarcities are already contributing to violent conflicts in many parts of the developing world. These conflicts are probably the early signs of an upsurge of violence in the coming decades that will be induced or aggravated by scarcity. The violence will usually be sub-national, persistent, and diffuse. Poor societies will be particularly affected since they are less able to buffer themselves from environmental scarcities and the social crises they cause. These societies are, in fact, already suffering acute hardship from shortages of water, forests, and especially fertile land.

Social conflict is not always a bad thing: mass mobilization and civil strife can produce opportunities for beneficial change in the distribution of land and wealth and in processes of governance. But fast-moving, unpredictable, and complex environmental problems can overwhelm efforts at constructive social reform. Moreover, scarcity can sharply increase demands on key institutions, such as the state, while it simultaneously reduces their capacity to meet those demands. These pressures increase the chance that the state will either fragment or become more authoritarian. The negative effects of severe environmental scarcity are therefore likely to outweigh the positive.

General Findings

Our research was intended to provide a foundation for further work. We therefore focused on two key preliminary questions: does environmental scarcity cause violent conflict? And, if it does, how does it operate?

The research was structured as I proposed in my previous article. Six types of environmental change were identified as plausible causes of violent inter-group conflict:

- greenhouse-induced climate change;
- stratospheric ozone depletion;
- degradation and loss of good agricultural land;
- degradation and removal of forests;
- depletion and pollution of fresh water supplies; and
- depletion of fisheries.

We used three hypotheses to link these changes with violent conflict. First, we suggested that decreasing supplies of physically controllable environmental resources, such as clean water and good agricultural land, would provoke interstate "simple-scarcity" conflicts or resource wars. Second, we hypothesized that large population movements caused by environmental stress would induce "group-identity" conflicts, especially ethnic clashes. And third, we suggested that severe environmental scarcity would simultaneously increase economic deprivation and disrupt key social institutions, which in turn would cause "deprivation" conflicts such as civil strife and insurgency.

Two detailed case studies were completed for each of the three research hypotheses.[3] By selecting cases that appeared, *prima facie*, to show a link between environmental change and conflict, we sought to falsify the null hypothesis that environmental scarcity does not cause violent conflict. By carefully tracing the causal processes in each case, we also sought to identify how environmental scarcity operates, if and when it is a cause of conflict. The completed case studies were reviewed at a series of workshops of leading experts; in light of these findings, I revised the original hypotheses, identified common variables and processes across the cases, and examined the revised hypotheses in light of the case-study evidence. The project's conclusions were reviewed by a core team of experts. The following are four general findings of this research effort.

RESOURCE DEPLETION AND DEGRADATION

Of the major environmental changes facing humankind, degradation and depletion of agricultural land, forests, water, and fish will contribute more to social turmoil in coming decades than will climate change or ozone depletion.

When analysts and policymakers in developed countries consider the social impacts of large-scale environmental change, they focus undue attention on climate change and stratospheric ozone depletion.[4] But vast populations in the developing world are already suffering from shortages of good land, water, forests, and fish; in contrast, the social effects of climate change and ozone depletion will probably not be seen till well into the next century. If

---

3. On simple-scarcity conflicts, we examined water in the Jordan and Nile River basins and the Southern African region; on environmentally induced group-identity conflicts, we focused on Bangladesh-Assam and the Miskito Indians in Nicaragua; and on economic decline and civil strife, we studied the Philippines and China. Researchers in the project also investigated the 1989 conflict in the Senegal River basin, the 1969 Soccer War between El Salvador and Honduras, the rise of the Sendero Luminoso in Peru, migration and civil strife in Haiti, and migration from black homelands in South Africa.
4. For example, see David Wirth, "Climate Chaos," *Foreign Policy*, No. 74 (Spring 1989), pp. 3–22; and Neville Brown, "Climate, Ecology and International Security," *Survival*, Vol. 31, No. 6 (November/December 1989), pp. 519–532.

these atmospheric problems do eventually have an impact, they will most likely operate not as individual environmental stresses, but in interaction with other, long-present resource, demographic, and economic pressures that have gradually eroded the buffering capacity of some societies.

Mexico, for example, is vulnerable to such interactions. People are already leaving the state of Oaxaca because of drought and soil erosion. Researchers estimate that future global warming could decrease Mexican rainfed maize production up to forty percent. This change could in turn interact with ongoing land degradation, free trade (because Mexico's comparative advantage is in water-intensive fruits and vegetables), and the privatization of communal peasant lands to cause grave internal conflict.[5]

ENVIRONMENTAL SCARCITY
Environmental change is only one of three main sources of scarcity of renewable resources; the others are population growth and unequal social distribution of resources. The concept "environmental scarcity" encompasses all three sources.

Analysts often usefully characterize environmental problems as resource scarcities. Resources can be roughly divided into two groups: non-renewables, like oil and iron ore, and renewables, like fresh water, forests, fertile soils, and the earth's ozone layer. The latter category includes renewable "goods" such as fisheries and timber, and renewable "services" such as regional hydrological cycles and a benign climate.

The commonly used term "environmental change" refers to a human-induced decline in the quantity or quality of a renewable resource that occurs faster than it is renewed by natural processes. But this concept limits the scope of environment-conflict research. Environmental change is only one of three main sources of renewable-resource scarcity. The second, population growth, reduces a resource's per-capita availability by dividing it among more and more people.[6] The third, unequal resource distribution, concentrates a

---

5. Diana Liverman, "The Impacts of Global Warming in Mexico: Uncertainty, Vulnerability and Response," in Jurgen Schmandt and Judith Clarkson, eds., *The Regions and Global Warming: Impacts and Response Strategies* (New York: Oxford University Press, 1992), pp. 44–68; and Diana Liverman and Karen O'Brien, "Global Warming and Climate Change in Mexico," *Global Environmental Change*, Vol. 1, No. 4 (December 1991), pp. 351–364.
6. Peter Gleick provides a potent illustration of the effect of population growth on water scarcity in Table 3 of "Water and Conflict: Fresh Water Resources and International Security," *International Security*, Vol. 18, No. 1 (Summer 1993), p. 101.

resource in the hands of a few people and subjects the rest to greater scarcity.[7] The property rights that govern resource distribution often change as a result of large-scale development projects or new technologies that alter the relative values of resources.

In other words, reduction in the quantity or quality of a resource shrinks the resource pie, while population growth divides the pie into smaller slices for each individual, and unequal resource distribution means that some groups get disproportionately large slices.[8] Unfortunately, analysts often study resource depletion and population growth in isolation from the political economy of resource distribution.[9] The term "environmental scarcity," however, allows these three distinct sources of scarcity to be incorporated into one analysis. Empirical evidence suggests, in fact, that the first two sources are most pernicious when they interact with unequal resource distribution.

We must also recognize that resource scarcity is, in part, subjective; it is determined not just by absolute physical limits, but also by preferences, beliefs, and norms. This is illustrated by a debate about the role of population growth and resource scarcity as causes of the conflict between the Sandinista government and the Miskito Indians in Nicaragua.[10] Bernard Nietschmann argues that the Nicaraguan state's need for resources to sustain the country's economic and agricultural development caused environmental degradation to spread from the Pacific to the Atlantic coast of the country. As this happened, indigenous Miskitos in the east came into conflict with the central government. Sergio Diaz-Briquets responds that the Sandinistas expropriated Miskito lands because of ideology, not scarcity. The Atlantic coastal region was largely ignored by the Nicaraguan state under Somoza. Following the revolution, the Sandinistas had ample newly expropriated land to distribute to their followers; but the new government—guided by Marxism—saw the Miskitos as a backward people with a competing worldview and a precapitalist mode of production, whose land rightfully belonged to a state that was removing impediments to the historical progress of the working class.

---

7. The second and third types of scarcity arise only with resources that can be physically controlled and possessed, like fish, fertile land, trees, and water, rather than resources like the climate or the ozone layer.
8. Since population growth is often a main cause of a decline in the quality and quantity of renewable resources, it actually has a dual impact on resource scarcity, a fact rarely noted by analysts.
9. James Boyce, "The Bomb Is a Dud," *The Progressive*, September 1990, pp. 24–25.
10. Bernard Nietschmann, "Environmental Conflicts and Indigenous Nations in Central America," paper prepared for the Project on Environmental Change and Acute Conflict (May 1991); and Sergio Diaz-Briquets, "Comments on Nietschmann's Paper," ibid.

Figure 1. Resource Capture and Ecological Marginalization.

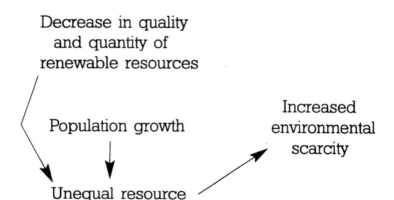

Resource Capture: Resource depletion and population growth cause unequal resource access.

The gap between the two views can be bridged by noting that scarcity is partly subjective. Marxist ideology encouraged the Sandinistas to adopt a strategy of state-directed industrialization and resource-use; this led them to perceive resources as more scarce than had the Somoza regime.

INTERACTION OF SOURCES OF ENVIRONMENTAL SCARCITY
The three sources of environmental scarcity often interact, and two patterns of interaction are particularly common: "resource capture" and "ecological marginalization" (see Figure 1).

A fall in the quality and quantity of renewable resources can combine with population growth to encourage powerful groups within a society to shift resource distribution in their favor. This can produce dire environmental scarcity for poorer and weaker groups whose claims to resources are opposed by these powerful elites. I call this type of interaction "resource capture." Unequal resource access can combine with population growth to cause migrations to regions that are ecologically fragile, such as steep upland slopes, areas at risk of desertification, and tropical rain forests. High population densities in these areas, combined with a lack of knowledge and capital to

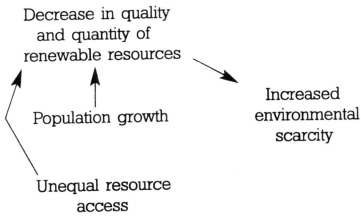

Decrease in quality
and quantity of
renewable resources

Population growth

Increased
environmental
scarcity

Unequal resource
access

Ecological Marginalization: Unequal resource access and population growth cause resource degradation and depletion.

protect local resources, causes severe environmental damage and chronic poverty. This process is often called "ecological marginalization."[11]

RESOURCE CAPTURE. Events in the Senegal River valley in 1989 illustrate resource capture. The valley demarcates the border between Senegal and Mauritania in West Africa. Senegal has fairly abundant agricultural land, but much of it suffers from high to severe wind and water erosion, loss of nutrients, salinization because of overirrigation, and soil compaction caused by intensification of agriculture.[12] The country has an overall population density of 38 people per square kilometer and a population growth rate of 2.8 percent; in 25 years the population will double.[13] In contrast, except for the Senegal Valley along its southern border and a few oases, Mauritania is

11. Jeffrey Leonard, "Overview," *Environment and the Poor: Development Strategies for a Common Agenda* (New Brunswick, N.J.: Transaction, 1989), p. 7. For a careful analysis of the interaction of population and land distribution in El Salvador, see chap. 2 in William Durham, *Scarcity and Survival in Central America: The Ecological Origins of the Soccer War* (Stanford, Calif.: Stanford University Press, 1979), pp. 21–62.
12. Global Assessment of Soil Degradation, *World Map on Status of Human-Induced Soil Degradation*, Sheet 2, Europe, Africa, and Western Asia (Wageningen, the Netherlands: United Nations Environment Programme [UNEP], International Soil Reference Centre, 1990).
13. Nafis Sadik, *The State of the World Population 1991* (New York: United Nations Population Fund, 1991), p. 24; World Resources Institute [WRI], *World Resources 1992–93* (New York: Oxford University Press, 1992), pp. 246 and 262.

largely arid desert and semiarid grassland.[14] Its population density is very low at about 2 people per square kilometer, but the growth rate is 2.9 percent. This combination of factors led the Food and Agriculture Organization (FAO) and two other organizations in a 1982 study to include both Mauritania and Senegal in their list of "critical" countries whose croplands cannot support their current and projected populations without a large increase in agricultural inputs, such as fertilizer and irrigation.[15]

Normally, the broad floodplains fringing the Senegal River support productive farming, herding, and fishing based on the river's annual floods. During the 1970s, however, the prospect of chronic food shortages and a serious drought encouraged the region's governments to seek international financing for the Manantali Dam on the Bafing River tributary in Mali, and the Diama salt-intrusion barrage near the mouth of the Senegal River between Senegal and Mauritania. These dams were designed to regulate the river's flow to produce hydropower, expand irrigated agriculture, and provide river transport from the Atlantic Ocean to landlocked Mali, which lies to the east of Senegal and Mauritania.

But the plan had unfortunate and unforeseen consequences. Anticipation of the new dams sharply increased land values along the river in areas where high-intensity agriculture would become feasible. The elite in Mauritania, which consists mainly of white Moors, then rewrote legislation governing land ownership, effectively abrogating the rights of black Africans to continue farming, herding, and fishing along the Mauritanian riverbank.[16]

---

14. Despite popular perception and the past claims of the United Nations Environment Programme, many experts now believe that the African Sahel (which includes southern Mauritania) is a robust ecosystem that does not exhibit extensive human-induced desertification. There is no clear southward march of the Sahara desert, and ecosystem recovery can be rapid if there is adequate rainfall and a reduction in grazing pressures. See "The Ebb and Flow of the Sahara," *New York Times*, July 23, 1991, p. B9. Overgrazing across the western Sahel, and the consequent migration of people from the region, appear to arise from the expansion of sedentary farming and population growth that together concentrate pastoralists on smaller areas of land (an example of ecological marginalization). In general, pastoralists are weak in the face of modern African states; state development since decolonization has often changed property rights at their expense. See Olivia Bennett, ed., *Greenwar: Environment and Conflict* (London: Panos, 1991), chap. 3, pp. 33–53.

15. G.M. Higgins, et al., *Potential Population Supporting Capacities of Lands in the Developing World*, Technical Report of Project INT/75/P13, "Land Resources of the Future," undertaken by the UN Food and Agriculture Organization (FAO) in collaboration with the International Institute for Applied Systems Analysis (IIASA) and the UN Fund for Population Activities (Rome, 1982), Table 3.5, p. 137.

16. Michael Horowitz, "Victims of Development," *Development Anthropology Network*, Bulletin of the Institute for Development Anthropology, Vol. 7, No. 2 (Fall 1989), pp. 1–8; and Horowitz, "Victims Upstream and Down," *Journal of Refugee Studies*, Vol. 4, No. 2 (1991), pp. 164–181.

There has been a long history of racism by white Moors in Mauritania towards their non-Arab, black compatriots. In the spring of 1989, the killing of Senegalese farmers by Mauritanians in the river basin triggered explosions of ethnic violence in the two countries. In Senegal, almost all of the 17,000 shops owned by Moors were destroyed, and their owners were deported to Mauritania. In both countries several hundred people were killed and the two nations nearly came to war.[17] The Mauritanian regime used this occasion to activate the new land legislation, declaring the Mauritanians who lived alongside the river to be "Senegalese," thereby stripping them of their citizenship; their property was seized. Some 70,000 of the black Mauritanians were forcibly expelled to Senegal, from where some launched raids to retrieve expropriated cattle. Diplomatic relations between the two countries have now been restored, but neither has agreed to allow the expelled population to return or to compensate them for their losses.

We see here the interaction of two sources of human-induced environmental scarcity: degradation of the land resource and population pressures helped precipitate agricultural shortfalls, which in turn encouraged a large development scheme. These factors together raised land values in one of the few areas in either country that offered the potential for a rapid move to high-intensity agriculture. A powerful elite then changed property rights and resource distribution in its own favor, which produced a sudden increase in resource scarcity for an ethnic minority, expulsion of the minority, and ethnic violence.

The water shortage on the occupied West Bank of the Jordan River offers a similar example of how population growth and excessive resource consumption can promote resource capture. While figures vary, Israel's average annual supply of renewable fresh water is about 1,950 million cubic meters (mcm).[18] Current Israeli demand, including that of settlements in the occupied territories and Golan Heights, exceeds this supply by about ten percent. The deficit is covered by overpumping aquifers. As a result, water tables in some parts of Israel and the West Bank have dropped. This can cause the

---

17. Jacques Belotteau, "Senegal-Mauritanie: les graves evenements du printemps 1989," *Afrique Contemporaine*, No. 152 (April 1989), pp. 41–42.
18. Miriam Lowi, "West Bank Water Resources and the Resolution of Conflict in the Middle East," Occasional Paper No. 1, Project on Environmental Change and Acute Conflict (September 1992); see also Lowi, "Bridging the Divide: Transboundary Resource Disputes and the Case of West Bank Water," *International Security*, Vol. 18, No. 1 (Summer 1993), pp. 113–138; and Natasha Beschorner, "Water and Instability in the Middle East," Adelphi Paper No. 273 (London: International Institute for Strategic Studies [IISS], Winter 1992/93).

exhaustion of wells and the infiltration of sea water from the Mediterranean.[19] Israel's population growth in the next thirty years, even without major immigration from the former Soviet Union, will probably cause the country's water demand to outstrip supply by at least forty percent.[20]

Over half of Israel's water comes from aquifers, and the rest from river flow, floodwater, and waste-water recycling. Two of the three main aquifers on which Israel depends lie principally underneath the West Bank, although their waters drain into Israel. About forty percent of the groundwater Israel uses (and therefore about a quarter of its sustainable supply) originates in occupied territory. To protect this important source, the Israeli government strictly limits water use by Jewish settlers and Arabs on the West Bank. But there is a stark differential in water access between the groups: on a per capita basis, settlers consume about four times as much as Arabs. Israel restricts the number of wells Arabs can drill in the territory, the amount of water Arabs are allowed to pump, and the times at which they can draw irrigation water. Since 1967, Arabs have not been permitted to drill new wells for agricultural purposes, although the Mekorot (the Israeli water company) has drilled more than thirty wells for settlers' irrigation.

Arab agriculture in the region has also suffered because some Arab wells have become dry or saline as a result of deeper Israeli wells drilled nearby. These Israeli water policies, combined with the confiscation of agricultural land for settlers as well as other Israeli restrictions on Palestinian agriculture, have encouraged many West Bank Arabs to abandon farming and move to towns.[21] Those who have done so have mostly become either unemployed or day laborers within Israel. The links between these processes and the recent unrest in the occupied territories are unclear; many political, economic, and ideological factors operate. But it seems reasonable to conclude that water scarcity and its consequent economic effects contributed to the grievances behind the *intifada* both on the West Bank and in Gaza.

---

19. There appears to be an impending crisis, for example, from salinization of aquifers beneath the Gaza Strip, where the pressure on water resources is "rapidly becoming intolerable"; Beschorner, "Water and Instability," pp. 14–15. The Gaza aquifers are connected to the coastal aquifer that is vital to Israel. Salinization can cause irreversible physical changes in aquifers; even if replenished with fresh water, their capacity is reduced. See Fred Pearce, "Wells of Conflict on the West Bank," *New Scientist*, June 1, 1991, pp. 37–38.
20. Lowi, "West Bank Water Resources," p. 34.
21. Since 1967, the irrigated area on the West Bank has dropped from 27 percent of the total cultivated area to 3.5–6 percent. Beschorner, "Water and Instability," pp. 14 and 78.

ECOLOGICAL MARGINALIZATION. The Philippines offers a good illustration of ecological marginalization. There, inequalities in access to rich agricultural lowlands combine with population growth to cause migration to easily degraded upland areas; erosion and deforestation contribute to economic hardship that spurs insurgency and rebellion.

Spanish and American colonial policies in the Philippines left behind a grossly unfair distribution of good cropland in lowland regions, an imbalance perpetuated since independence by a powerful landowning elite.[22] Since World War II, green-revolution technologies have greatly increased lowland production of grain for domestic consumption, and of cash crops such as sugar, coconut, pineapple, and bananas that help pay the country's massive external debt. This has raised demand for agricultural labor on large farms, but not enough to compensate for a population growth rate of 2.5 to 3.0 percent per annum. Together, therefore, inequalities in land access and growth in population have produced a surge in agricultural unemployment.

With insufficient rural or urban industrialization to employ this excess labor, there has been unrelenting downward pressure on wages.[23] Economically desperate, millions of poor agricultural laborers and landless peasants have migrated to shantytowns in already overburdened cities, such as Manila. Millions of others have moved to the least productive—and often most ecologically vulnerable—territories, such as steep hillsides.[24] In these uplands, settlers use fire to clear forested or previously logged land. They bring with them little knowledge or money to protect their fragile ecosystems, and their small-scale logging, production of charcoal for the cities, and slash-and-burn farming often cause horrendous environmental damage, particularly water erosion, landslides, and changes in the hydrological cycle.[25] This has set in motion a cycle of falling food production, the clearing of new plots,

---

22. The best cropland lies, for the most part, in the coastal plains of the archipelago's islands. Landowning and manufacturing elites are closely linked, and their relative economic power has actually grown since independence: the top 10 percent of the country's families controlled 37 percent of the nation's total income in 1985, up from 27 percent in 1956. See Richard Kessler, *Rebellion and Repression in the Philippines* (New Haven: Yale University Press, 1989), p. 18.
23. Using a standardized figure of 100 for 1972, average real wages dropped from 150 in the early 1950s to about 100 in 1980. Kessler, *Rebellion and Repression*, p. 26.
24. A full account can be found in Maria Concepción Cruz, et al., *Population Growth, Poverty, and Environmental Stress: Frontier Migration in the Philippines and Costa Rica* (Washington, D.C.: WRI, 1992).
25. World Bank, *Philippines: Environment and Natural Resource Management Study* (Washington, D.C.: World Bank, 1989). Erosion rates can exceed 300 tons per hectare per year, ten to twenty times the sustainable rate.

and further land degradation. There are few new areas in the country that can be opened up for agricultural production, so even marginally fertile land is becoming hard to find in many places, and economic conditions are often desperate for the peasants.[26]

The situation in the Philippines is not unique. Ecological marginalization occurs with striking regularity around the planet, affecting hundreds of millions of people in places as diverse as the Himalayas, Indonesia, Costa Rica, Brazil, and the Sahel.

SOCIAL AND TECHNICAL INGENUITY

Societies are more able to avoid turmoil if they can adapt to environmental scarcity so that it does not cause great suffering. Strategies for adaptation fall into two categories, and both depend on adequate social and technical ingenuity. First, societies can continue to rely on their indigenous resources but use them more sensibly and provide alternative employment to people who have limited resource access. For example, economic incentives like increases in resource prices and taxes can reduce degradation and depletion by encouraging conservation, technological innovation, and resource substitution. Family planning and literacy campaigns can ease population-growth induced scarcity. Land redistribution and labor-intensive rural industries can relieve the effects of unequal access to good cropland.

Second, the country might "decouple" itself from dependence on its own depleted environmental resources by producing goods and services that do not rely heavily on those resources; the country could then trade the products on the international market for the resources it no longer has at home. Such decoupling might, in fact, be achieved by rapidly exploiting the country's environmental resources and reinvesting the profits in capital, industrial equipment, and skills to permit a shift to other forms of wealth creation. For instance, Malaysia could use the income from over-logging its forests to fund a modern university system that trains electrical engineers and computer specialists for a high-technology industrial sector.

If either strategy is to succeed, a society must be able to supply enough ingenuity at the right places and times. Two kinds are key. Technical ingenuity is needed to develop, for example, new agricultural and forestry technologies that compensate for environmental loss. Social ingenuity is needed

26. Gareth Porter and Delfin Ganapin, Jr., *Resources, Population, and the Philippines' Future: A Case Study*, WRI Paper No. 4 (Washington, D.C.: World Resources Institute, 1988).

to create institutions and organizations that buffer people from the effects of scarcity and provide the right incentives for technological entrepreneurs. Social ingenuity is therefore often a precursor to technical ingenuity. The development and distribution of new grains adapted for dry climates and eroded soils, of alternative cooking technologies to compensate for the loss of firewood, and of water conservation technologies depend on an intricate and stable system of markets, legal regimes, financial agencies, and educational and research institutions.

In the next decades, the need for both technical and social ingenuity to deal with environmental scarcities will rise sharply. Population growth, rising average resource consumption, and persistent inequalities in access to resources ensure that scarcities will affect many environmentally sensitive regions with a severity, speed, and scale unprecedented in history. Resource-substitution and conservation tasks will be more urgent, complex, and unpredictable, driving up the need for technical ingenuity. Moreover, solving these problems through market and other institutional innovations (such as changes in property rights and resource distribution) will require great social ingenuity.

At the same time that environmental scarcity is boosting the demand for ingenuity, however, it may interfere with supply. Poor countries start at a disadvantage: they are underendowed with the social institutions—including the productive research centers, efficient markets, and capable states—that are necessary for an ample supply of both social and technical solutions to scarcity. Moreover, their ability to create and maintain these institutions may be diminished by the very environmental stress they need to address, because scarcity can weaken states, as we shall see, and it can engender intense rivalries between interest groups and elite factions.[27]

Evidence Bearing on the Hypotheses

The findings described above led me to revise the original three hypotheses by redefining the independent variable, "environmental scarcity." I narrowed the range of environmental problems that were hypothesized to cause conflict, so as to deemphasize atmospheric problems and focus instead on for-

---

27. For a full elaboration of the argument in this section, see Homer-Dixon, "The Ingenuity Gap: Can Developing Countries Adapt to Environmental Scarcity?" paper prepared for the Project on Environmental Change and Acute Conflict (March 1994).

ests, water, fisheries, and especially cropland. I expanded the scope of the independent variable to include scarcity caused by population growth and resource maldistribution as well as that caused by degradation and depletion. And I also incorporated into the variable the role of interactions among these three sources of scarcity.

Our research project produced the following empirical evidence bearing on the three hypotheses thus revised.

HYPOTHESIS 1: SIMPLE-SCARCITY CONFLICTS BETWEEN STATES

There is little empirical support for the first hypothesis that environmental scarcity causes simple-scarcity conflicts between states. Scarcities of renewable resources such as forests and croplands do not often cause resource wars between states. This finding is intriguing because resource wars have been common since the beginning of the state system. For instance, during World War II, Japan sought to secure oil, minerals, and other resources in China and Southeast Asia, and the 1991 Gulf War was at least partly motivated by the desire for oil.

However, we must distinguish between non-renewable resources such as oil, and renewable resources. Arthur Westing has compiled a list of twelve conflicts in the twentieth century involving resources, beginning with World War I and concluding with the Falklands/Malvinas War.[28] Access to oil or minerals was at issue in ten of these conflicts. Just five conflicts involved renewable resources, and only two of these—the 1969 Soccer War between El Salvador and Honduras, and the Anglo-Icelandic Cod War of 1972–73—concerned neither oil nor minerals (cropland was a factor in the former case, and fish in the latter). However, the Soccer War was not a simple-scarcity conflict between states; rather it arose from the ecological marginalization of Salvadorean peasants and their consequent migration into Honduras.[29] It is evidence in support, therefore, of our second and third hypotheses (below), but not for the first. And, since the Cod War, despite its name, involved very little violence, it hardly qualifies as a resource war.

States have fought more over non-renewable than renewable resources for two reasons, I believe. First, petroleum and mineral resources can be more

28. Arthur Westing, "Appendix 2. Wars and Skirmishes Involving Natural Resources: A Selection from the Twentieth Century," in Arthur Westing, ed., *Global Resources and International Conflict: Environmental Factors in Strategic Policy and Action* (Oxford: New York, 1986), pp. 204–210.
29. See Durham, *Scarcity and Survival*.

directly converted into state power than can agricultural land, fish, and forests. Oil and coal fuel factories and armies, and ores are vital for tanks and naval ships. In contrast, although captured forests and cropland may eventually generate wealth that can be harnessed by the state for its own ends, this outcome is more remote in time and less certain. Second, the very countries that are most dependent on renewable resources, and which are therefore most motivated to seize resources from their neighbors, also tend to be poor, which lessens their capability for aggression.

Our research suggests that the renewable resource most likely to stimulate interstate resource war is river water.[30] Water is a critical resource for personal and national survival; furthermore, since river water flows from one area to another, one country's access can be affected by another's actions. Conflict is most probable when a downstream riparian is highly dependent on river water and is strong in comparison to upstream riparians. Downstream riparians often fear that their upstream neighbors will use water as a means of coercion. This situation is particularly dangerous if the downstream country also believes it has the military power to rectify the situation. The relationships between South Africa and Lesotho and between Egypt and Ethiopia have this character.[31]

The Lesotho case is interesting. Facing critical water shortages, South Africa negotiated in vain with Lesotho for thirty years to divert water from Lesotho's mountains to the arid South African province of Transvaal. In 1986 South Africa gave decisive support to a successful military coup against Lesotho's tribal government. South Africa declared that it helped the coup because Lesotho had been providing sanctuary to guerrillas of the African National Congress. This was undoubtedly a key motivation, but within months the two governments reached agreement to construct the huge Highlands Water Project to meet South Africa's needs. It seems likely, therefore, that the desire for water was an ulterior motive behind South African support for the coup.[32]

---

30. Peter Gleick, "Water and Conflict," Occasional Paper No. 1, Project on Environmental Change and Acute Conflict (September 1992); and Gleick, "Water and Conflict: Fresh Water Resources and International Security," *International Security*, Vol. 18, No. 1 (Summer 1993), pp. 79–112.
31. In 1980, Egyptian President Anwar el-Sadat said, "If Ethiopia takes any action to block our right to the Nile waters, there will be no alternative for us but to use force"; quoted in Norman Myers, "Environment and Security," *Foreign Policy*, No. 74 (Spring 1989), p. 32. See also chap. 6, "The Nile River," in Thomas Naff and Ruth Matson, eds., *Water in the Middle East: Conflict or Cooperation?* (Boulder, Colo.: Westview, 1984), pp. 125–155.
32. "Pretoria Has Its Way in Lesotho," *Africa Report* (March–April, 1986), pp. 50–51; Patrick

However, our review of the historical and contemporary evidence shows that conflict and turmoil related to river water are more often internal than international. The huge dams that are often built to deal with general water scarcity are especially disruptive. Relocating large numbers of upstream people generates turmoil among the relocatees and clashes with local groups in areas where the relocatees are resettled. The people affected are often members of ethnic or minority groups outside the power hierarchy of their society, and the result is frequently rebellion by these groups and repression by the state. Water developments can also induce conflict over water and irrigable land among a country's downstream users, as we saw in the Senegal River basin.[33]

HYPOTHESIS 2: POPULATION MOVEMENT AND GROUP-IDENTITY CONFLICTS
There is substantial evidence to support the hypothesis that environmental scarcity causes large population movement, which in turn causes group-identity conflicts. But we must be sensitive to contextual factors unique to each socio-ecological system. These are the system's particular physical, political, economic, and cultural features that affect the strength of the linkages between scarcity, population movement, and conflict.

For example, experts emphasize the importance of both "push" and "pull" factors in decisions of potential migrants.[34] These factors help distinguish migrants from refugees: while migrants are motivated by a combination of push and pull, refugees are motivated mainly by push. Environmental scarcity is more likely to produce migrants than refugees, because it usually develops gradually, which means that the push effect is not sharp and sudden and that pull factors can therefore clearly enter into potential migrants' calculations.

Migrants are often people who have been weak and marginal in their home society and, depending on context, they may remain weak in the receiving society. This limits their ability to organize and to make demands. States play

---

Laurence, "A 'New Lesotho'?" *Africa Report* (January–February 1987), pp. 61–64; "Lesotho Water Project Gets Under Way," *Africa Report* (May–June 1988), p. 10. See also Charles Okidi, "Environmental Stress and Conflicts in Africa: Case Studies of African International Drainage Basins," paper prepared for the Project on Environmental Change and Acute Conflict (May 1992).
33. See Thayer Scudder, "River Basin Projects in Africa," *Environment*, Vol. 31, No. 2 (March 1989), pp. 4–32; and Scudder, "Victims of Development Revisited: The Political Costs of River Basin Development," *Development Anthropology Network*, Vol. 8, No. 1 (Spring 1990), pp. 1–5.
34. Astri Suhrke, "Pressure Points: Environmental Degradation, Migration, and Conflict," Occasional Paper No. 3, Project on Environmental Change and Acute Conflict (March 1993).

a critical role here: migrants often need the backing of a state (either of the receiving society or an external one) before they have sufficient power to cause conflict, and this backing depends on the region's politics. Without it, migration is less likely to produce violence than silent misery and death, which rarely destabilizes states.[35] We must remember too that migration does not always produce bad results. It can act as a safety valve by reducing conflict in the sending area. Depending on the economic context, it can ease labor shortages in the receiving society, as it sometimes has, for instance, in Malaysia. Countries as different as Canada, Thailand, and Malawi show the astonishing capacity of some societies to absorb migrants without conflict.

Even accounting for such contextual factors, events in Bangladesh and Northeast India provide strong evidence in support of the second hypothesis. In recent decades, huge numbers of people have moved from Bangladesh to India, producing group-identity conflicts in the adjacent Indian states. Only one of the three sources of environmental scarcity—population growth—seems to be a main force behind this migration. Even though Bangladesh's cropland is heavily used, in general it is not badly degraded, because the annual flooding of the Ganges and Brahmaputra rivers deposits nutrients that help maintain the fertility of the country's floodplains.[36] And while land distribution remains highly unequal, this distribution has changed little since an initial attempt at land reform immediately following East Pakistan's independence from the British.[37]

But the United Nations predicts that Bangladesh's current population of 120 million will nearly double, to 235 million, by the year 2025.[38] Cropland, at about 0.08 hectares per capita, is already desperately scarce. Population density is over 900 people per square kilometer (in comparison, population density in neigboring Assam is under 300 per square kilometer). Since virtually all of the country's good agricultural land has been exploited, population growth will cut in half the amount of cropland available per capita by 2025. Land scarcity and the brutal poverty and social turmoil it engenders have been made worse by flooding (perhaps aggravated by deforestation in

---

35. Ibid.
36. The relationship between flooding and soil fertility is ill-understood. See James Boyce, "Birth of a Megaproject: Political Economy of Flood Control in Bangladesh," *Environmental Management*, Vol. 14, No. 4 (July/August 1990), pp. 419–428, especially p. 424.
37. James Boyce, *Agrarian Impasse in Bengal: Institutional Constraints to Technological Change* (Oxford: Oxford University Press, 1987), p. 9.
38. Sadik, *The State of the World Population 1991*, p. 43.

the Himalayan watersheds of the region's major rivers); by the susceptibility of the country to cyclones; and by the construction by India of the Farakka Barrage, a dam upstream on the Ganges River.[39]

People have been moving around this part of South Asia in large numbers for centuries. But the movements are increasing in size. Over the last forty years, millions have migrated from East Pakistan or Bangladesh to the Indian states of Assam, Tripura, and West Bengal. Detailed data are scarce, since both India and Bangladesh manipulate their census data for political reasons, and the Bangladeshi government avoids admitting there is large out-migration, because the question causes friction with India. But by piecing together demographic information and experts' estimates, we concluded that migrants from Bangladesh have expanded the population of neighboring areas of India by 12 to 17 million, of which only 1 or 2 million can be attributed to migration induced by the 1971 war between India and Pakistan that created Bangladesh. We further estimate that the population of the state of Assam has been boosted by at least 7 million people, to its current total of 22 million.[40]

This enormous flux has produced pervasive social changes in the receiving regions. It has altered land distribution, economic relations, and the balance of political power between religious and ethnic groups, and it has triggered serious intergroup conflict. Members of the Lalung tribe in Assam, for instance, have long resented Bengali Muslim migrants: they accuse them of stealing the area's richest farmland. In early 1983, during a bitterly contested election for federal offices in the state, violence erupted. In the village of Nellie, Lalung people massacred nearly 1,700 Bengalis in one five-hour rampage.[41]

---

39. Controversy surrounds the question of whether Himalayan deforestation contributes to flooding; see Centre for Science and Environment (CSE), *Floods, Flood Plains, and Environmental Myths* (New Delhi: CSE, 1991), especially pp. 68–69. On the Farakka Barrage, Ashok Swain writes: "It has disrupted fishing and navigation [in Bangladesh], brought unwanted salt deposits into rich farming soil, affected agricultural and industrial production, changed the hydraulic character of the rivers and caused changes in the ecology of the Delta." See Swain, "Environmental Destruction and Acute Social Conflict: A Case Study of the Ganges Water Dispute," Department of Peace and Conflict Research, Uppsala University (November 1992), p. 24.
40. Sanjoy Hazarika, "Bangladesh and Assam: Land Pressures, Migration, and Ethnic Conflict," Occasional Paper No. 3, Project on Environmental Change and Acute Conflict (March 1993), p. 52–54.
41. "A State Ravaged," *India Today*, March 15, 1983, pp. 16–21; "Spillover Tension," *India Today*, March 15, 1983, pp. 22–23. The 1991 Indian Census showed that Assam's population growth rate has declined; the conflicts in Assam in the early 1980s appear to have encouraged many migrants from Bangladesh to go to West Bengal instead.

In Tripura, the original Buddhist and Christian inhabitants now make up less than 30 percent of the state's population. The rest are Hindu migrants from either East Pakistan or Bangladesh. This shift in the ethnic balance precipitated a violent insurgency between 1980 and 1988 that diminished only after the government agreed to return land to dispossessed Tripuris and to stop the influx of Bangladeshis. But, as the migration has continued, this agreement is in jeopardy.[42]

There are important features unique to this case. Within Bangladesh, key "push" factors include inheritance practices that divide cropland into smaller plots with each generation, and national and community water-control institutions that sharply limit agricultural output and keep peasants from gaining full benefit from some of the most fertile land in the world.[43] On the "pull" side, the standard of living in India is markedly better, and Indian politicians have often encouraged Bangladeshi migration to garner their votes. Furthermore, in the Ganges-Brahmaputra region, the concept of nation-state is often not part of the local culture. Many people think of the region as "greater Bengal," and state borders do not figure heavily in the calculations of some migrants, especially when there are receptive family, linguistic, and religious groups across the frontier. Finally, during the colonial period, the British used Hindus from Calcutta to administer Assam, and Bengali became the official language. As a result, the Assamese are particularly sensitive to their loss of political and cultural control in the state.

While such contextual factors are important, they cannot obscure the fact that land scarcity in Bangladesh, arising largely from population growth, has been a powerful force behind migration to neighboring regions and communal conflict there.[44]

HYPOTHESIS 3: ECONOMIC DEPRIVATION, INSTITUTIONAL DISRUPTION,

AND CIVIL STRIFE

Empirical evidence partially supports the third hypothesis that environmental scarcity simultaneously increases economic deprivation and disrupts key

---

42. Hazarika, "Bangladesh and Assam," pp. 60–61.
43. Boyce, *Agrarian Impasse.*
44. See Shaukat Hassan, "Environmental Issues and Security in South Asia," Adelphi Paper No. 262 (London: IISS, Autumn 1991), pp. 42–43; P.C. Goswami, "Foreign Immigration into Assam," in B.L. Abbi, ed., *Northeast Region: Problems and Prospects of Development* (Chandigarh, India: Centre for Research in Rural and Industrial Development), pp. 35–59; and Susanta Dass, *Spotlight on Assam* (Chanderpur, India: Premier Book Service, 1989).

social institutions, which in turn causes "deprivation" conflicts such as civil strife and insurgency. Environmental scarcity does produce economic deprivation, and this deprivation does cause civil strife. But more research is needed on the effects of scarcity on social institutions.

Resource degradation and depletion often affect economic productivity in poor countries and thereby contribute to deprivation. For example, erosion in upland Indonesia annually costs the country's agricultural economy nearly half a billion dollars in discounted future income.[45] The Magat watershed on the northern Filipino island of Luzon—a watershed representative of many in the Philippines—suffers gross erosion rates averaging 219 tons per hectare per year; if the lost nutrients were replaced by fertilizer, the annual cost would be over $100 per hectare.[46] Dryland degradation in Burkina Faso reduces the country's annual gross domestic product by nearly nine percent annually because of fuelwood loss and lower yields of millet, sorghum, and livestock.[47]

Vaclav Smil has estimated the combined effect of environmental problems on China's economic productivity.[48] The main burdens he identifies are reductions in crop yields caused by pollution of water, soil, and air; higher human morbidity from air pollution; farmland loss because of construction and erosion; nutrient loss and flooding due to erosion and deforestation; and timber loss arising from poor harvesting practices. Smil calculates the current cost to be at least 15 percent of China's gross national product, and he is convinced that the toll will rise steeply in the next decades.[49] Although China's economy is booming, much of the new wealth is concentrated in the

---

45. Robert Repetto, "Balance-Sheet Erosion—How to Account for the Loss of Natural Resources," *International Environmental Affairs*, Vol. 1, No. 2 (Spring 1989), pp. 103–137.
46. This estimate does not include the economic costs of lost rooting depth and increased vulnerability to drought, which may be even larger. See Wilfrido Cruz, Herminia Francisco, and Zenaida Conway, "The On-Site and Downstream Costs of Soil Erosion in the Magat and Pantabangan Watersheds," *Journal of Philippine Development*, Vol. 15, No. 1 (1988), p. 88.
47. Ed Barbier, "Environmental Degradation in the Third World," in David Pearce, ed., *Blueprint 2: Greening the World Economy* (London: Earthscan, 1991), Box 6.8, p. 90.
48. Vaclav Smil, "Environmental Change as a Source of Conflict and Economic Losses in China," Occasional Paper No. 2, Project on Environmental Change and Acute Conflict (December 1992).
49. It is hard to judge gross economic activity in China and convert these figures into dollars. Perhaps because of this, the World Bank has not increased its estimates of per capita annual GNP in line with the rapid expansion of the Chinese economy. Smil suggests that the Bank's current annual figure of $370/capita may be too low by a factor of four. This judgment is supported by recent re-evaluations of China's GNP by the International Monetary Fund. See World Bank, *World Development Report, 1992* (New York: Oxford University Press, 1992), p. 218; and Steven Greenhouse, "New Tally of World's Economies Catapults China into Third Place," *New York Times*, May 20, 1993, p. A1.

coastal provinces, especially around Hong Kong; many other parts of the country remain terribly poor.

I originally hypothesized that scarcity would undermine a variety of social institutions. Our research suggests, however, that one institution in particular—the state—is most important. Although more study is needed, the multiple effects of environmental scarcity, including large population movements and economic decline, appear likely to weaken sharply the capacity and legitimacy of the state in some poor countries.

First, environmental scarcity increases financial and political demands on governments. For example, to mitigate the social effects of loss of water, soil, and forest, governments must spend huge sums on industry and infrastructure such as new dams, irrigation systems, fertilizer plants, and reforestation programs. Furthermore, this resource loss can reduce the incomes of elites directly dependent on resource extraction; these elites usually turn to the state for compensation. Scarcity also expands marginal groups that need help from government by producing rural poverty and by displacing people into cities where they demand food, shelter, transport, energy, and employment. In response to swelling urban populations, governments introduce subsidies that drain revenues, distort prices, and cause misallocations of capital, which in turn hinders economic productivity. Such large-scale state intervention in the marketplace can concentrate political and economic power in the hands of a small number of cronies and monopolistic interests, at the expense of other elite segments and rural agricultural populations.

Simultaneously, if resource scarcity affects the economy's general productivity, revenues to local and national governments will decline. This hurts elites that benefit from state largesse and reduces the state's capacity to meet the increased demands arising from environmental scarcity. A widening gap between state capacity and demands on the state, along with the misguided economic interventions such a gap often provokes, aggravates popular and elite grievances, increases rivalry between elite factions, and erodes the state's legitimacy.

Key contextual factors affect whether lower economic productivity and state weakening lead to deprivation conflicts. Civil strife is a function of both the level of grievance motivating challenger groups and the opportunities available to these groups to act on their grievances. The likelihood of civil strife is greatest when multiple pressures at different levels in society interact to increase grievance and opportunity simultaneously. Our third hypothesis says that environmental scarcity will change both variables, by contributing to economic crisis and by weakening institutions such as the state. But numerous other factors also influence grievance and opportunity.

Contrary to common belief, there is no clear correlation between poverty (or economic inequality) and social conflict.[50] Whether or not people become aggrieved and violent when they find themselves increasingly poor depends, in part, upon their notion of economic justice. For example, people belonging to a culture that inculcates fatalism about deprivation—as with lower castes in India—will not be as prone to violence as people believing they have a right to economic wellbeing. Theorists have addressed this problem by introducing the variable "relative deprivation."[51] But there is little correlation between measures of relative deprivation and civil conflict.[52]

Part of the problem is that analysts have commonly used aggregate data (such as GNP/capita and average educational levels) to measure individual deprivation.[53] In addition, more recent research has shown that, to cause civil strife, economic crisis must be severe, persistent, and pervasive enough to erode the legitimacy or moral authority of the dominant social order and system of governance. System legitimacy is therefore a critical intervening variable between rising poverty and civil conflict. It is influenced by the aggrieved actors' subjective "blame system," which consists of their beliefs about who or what is responsible for their plight.[54]

Serious civil strife is not likely to occur unless the structure of political opportunities facing challenger groups keeps them from effectively expressing their grievances peacefully, but offers them openings for violence against authority.[55] The balance of coercive power among social actors affects the

---

50. Some of the best studies of this question have focused on the relationship between poverty and urban violence in the United States. See William Ford and John Moore, "Additional Evidence on the Social Characteristics of Riot Cities," *Social Science Quarterly*, Vol. 51, No. 2 (September 1970), pp. 339–348; and Robert Jiobu, "City Characteristics and Racial Violence," *Social Science Quarterly*, Vol. 55, No. 1 (June 1974), pp. 52–64.
51. People are said to be relatively deprived when they perceive a widening gap between the level of satisfaction they have achieved (usually defined in economic terms) and the level they believe they deserve. Deprivation is said to be relative to some subjective standard of equity or fairness; the size of the perceived gap depends upon the beliefs about economic justice held by the individual. See Ted Gurr, *Why Men Rebel* (Princeton: Princeton University Press, 1970).
52. Steven Finkel and James Rule, "Relative Deprivation and Related Theories of Civil Violence: A Critical Review," in Kurt and Gladys Lang, eds. *Research in Social Movements, Conflicts, and Change* (Greenwich, Conn.: JAI, 1986), pp. 47–69.
53. Ibid.
54. These beliefs are grounded in historical and economic experience. See, for example, James Scott, *The Moral Economy of the Peasant: Rebellion and Subsistence in Southeast Asia* (New Haven: Yale University Press, 1976), pp. 1–11.
55. Homer-Dixon, "On the Threshold," pp. 105–106 and 109–111.

probability of success and, therefore, the expected costs and benefits of different actions by the state, its supporters, and challenger groups. A state debilitated by corruption, by falling revenues and rising demand for services, or by factional conflicts within elites will be more vulnerable to violent challenges by political and military opponents; also vital to state strength is the cohesiveness of the armed forces and its loyalty to civil leadership.[56]

Challengers will have greater relative power if their grievances are articulated and actions coordinated through well-organized, well-financed and autonomous opposition groups. Since grievances felt at the individual level are not automatically expressed at the group level, the probability of civil violence is higher if groups are already organized around clear social cleavages, such as ethnicity, religion, or class. These groups can provide a clear sense of identity and act as nuclei around which highly mobilized and angry elements of the population, such as unemployed and urbanized young men, will coalesce. Conversely, if economic crisis weakens challenger groups more than the state, or affects mainly disorganized people, it will not lead to violence.

Factors that can influence both grievance and opportunity include the leadership and ideology of challenger groups, and international shocks and pressures such as changes in trade and debt relations and in costs of imported factors of production such as energy.[57] The rapid growth of urban areas in poor countries may have a similar dual effect: people concentrated in slums can communicate more easily than those in scattered rural villages; this may reinforce grievances and, by reducing problems of coordination, also increase the power of challenger groups. Research shows, however, surprisingly little historical correlation between rapid urbanization and civil strife;[58] and the exploding cities of the developing world have been remarkably quiescent in recent decades. This may be changing: India has lately witnessed ferocious urban violence, often in the poorest slums, and sometimes directed at new

---

56. See Farrokh Moshiri, "Revolutionary Conflict Theory in an Evolutionary Perspective," in Jack Goldstone, Ted Gurr, and Farrokh Moshiri, eds., *Revolutions of the Late Twentieth Century* (Boulder, Colo.: Westview, 1991), pp. 4–36; and Goldstone, "An Analytical Framework," ibid., pp. 37–51.
57. For a review of some of these factors, see Jack Goldstone, "Theories of Revolution: The Third Generation," *World Politics*, Vol. 32, No. 3 (April 1980), pp. 425–453.
58. Wayne Cornelius, Jr., "Urbanization As an Agent in Latin American Political Instability: The Case of Mexico," *American Political Science Review*, Vol. 63, No. 3 (September 1969), pp. 833–357; and Abdul Lodhi and Charles Tilly, "Urbanization, Crime, and Collective Violence in 19th-Century France," *American Journal of Sociology*, Vol. 79, No. 2 (September 1973), pp. 296–318.

migrants from the countryside.[59] In Egypt, fundamentalist opposition to the government is located in some of the most desperate sectors of Cairo and other cities such as Asyut.

The Philippines provides evidence of the links between environmental scarcity, economic deprivation, and civil strife. The country has suffered from serious strife for many decades, usually motivated by economic stress.[60] Today, cropland and forest degradation in the uplands sharply exacerbates this economic crisis. The current upland insurgency—including guerrilla attacks and assaults on military stations—is motivated by the poverty of landless agricultural laborers and farmers displaced into the remote hills, where the central government is weak.[61] During the 1970s and 1980s, the communist New People's Army and the National Democratic Front found upland peasants receptive to revolutionary ideology, especially where coercive landlords and local governments left them little choice between rebellion and starvation. The insurgency has waned somewhat since President Marcos left, not because economic conditions have improved much in the countryside, but because the democratically elected central government is more legitimate and the insurgent leadership is ideologically rigid.

Contextual factors are key to a full understanding of this case. Property rights governing upland areas are, for the most part, either nonexistent or very unclear. Legally these areas are a public resource, and their "open access" character encourages in-migration. Yet many upland peasants find themselves under the authority of concessionaires and absentee landlords who have claimed the land. Neither peasants, nor concessionaires, nor landlords, however, have secure enough title to have incentive to protect the land from environmental degradation. Increasing external debt encouraged the Marcos government, under pressure from international financial agencies, to adopt draconian stabilization and structural adjustment policies. These caused an economic crisis in the first half of the 1980s, which boosted

59. Sanjoy Hazarika, "Week of Rioting Leaves Streets of Bombay Empty," *New York Times*, January 12, 1993, p. A3.
60. The Huk rebellion in the late 1940s and early 1950s provides some of the best evidence for the link between economic conditions (especially unequal land distribution) and civil strife in the Philippines. See Benedict Kerkvliet, *The Huk Rebellion: A Study of Peasant Revolt in the Philippines* (Quezon City, Philippines: New Day Publishers, 1979); and E.J. Mitchell, "Some Econometrics of the Huk Rebellion," *American Political Science Review*, Vol. 63, No. 4 (December 1969), pp. 1159–1171.
61. Celso Roque and Maria Garcia, "Economic Inequality, Environmental Degradation and Civil Strife in the Philippines," paper prepared for the Project on Environmental Change and Acute Conflict (1993).

agricultural unemployment, reduced opportunities for alternative employment in urban and rural industries, and gave a further push to migration into the uplands.[62]

Finally, the insurgents gained adherents because they built on indigenous beliefs and social structures to help the peasants define their situation and focus their discontent. The most successful rebellions in Filipino history have drawn on peasants' millenarian vision—rooted in their Catholicism—of "an idealized pre-Spanish condition of wholeness."[63] The current insurgency has been particularly potent because it mingles "the spiritual search for liberation and the political search for independence, into the overarching quest for Filipino identity."[64] This has provided peasants with an alternative moral system to the traditional patron-client relationship between peasants and landowners. The feudal norms imposed obligations on landowners, which gave peasants rudimentary economic security, but disintegrated with the commercialization of agriculture and the urbanization of elites in the early and mid-twentieth century.[65]

Causal processes like those in the Philippines can be seen around the planet: population growth and unequal access to good land force huge numbers of rural people into cities or onto marginal lands. In the latter case, they cause environmental damage and become chronically poor. Eventually these people may be the source of persistent upheaval, or they may migrate yet again, stimulating ethnic conflicts or urban unrest elsewhere.

The rise of the Sendero Luminoso rebellion in Peru can be attributed to a subsistence crisis caused, in part, by such a process of ecological marginalization.[66] The country's mountainous southern highlands are not suitable for farming. The hills are steep, and the soil is thin and dry. Nonetheless, during

---

62. Maria Concepción Cruz and Robert Repetto, *The Environmental Effects of Stabilization and Structural Adjustment Programs: The Philippines Case* (Washington, D.C.: World Resources Institute, 1992). See also Francisco Lara, Jr., "Structural Adjustments and Trade Liberalization: Eating Away Our Food Security," *PPI Research Papers* (Quezon City: Philippine Peasant Institute [PPI], 1991); and Robin Broad, *Unequal Alliance, 1979–1986: The World Bank, the International Monetary Fund, and the Philippines* (Quezon City: Ateneo de Manila University Press, 1988).
63. Kessler, *Rebellion and Repression*, pp. 24–25.
64. Ibid.
65. Ibid, pp. 16–19. See also Reynaldo Clemena Ileto, *Pasyon and Revolution: Popular Movements in the Philippines, 1840–1910* (Manila: Ateneo de Manila University Press, 1979).
66. Cynthia McClintock, "Why Peasants Rebel: The Case of Peru's Sendero Luminoso," *World Politics*, Vol. 37, No. 1 (October 1984), pp. 48–84; and McClintock, "Peru's Sendero Luminoso Rebellion: Origins and Trajectory," in Susan Eckstein, ed., *Power and Popular Protest: Latin American Social Movements* (Berkeley: University of California Press, 1989), pp. 61–101.

the colonial period, Indian peoples in the region were displaced onto hillsides when Spanish settlers seized richer valley lands. In the 1970s, the Velasco government undertook a sweeping land-redistribution program. But people in the highlands benefited little, because the government was reluctant to break up large agricultural enterprises that generated much of the country's export earnings.

Natural population growth and a lack of good land or jobs elsewhere boosted population densities in the southern highlands. The department of Ayacucho saw density increase from 8.1 people per square kilometer in 1940 to 12.1 in 1980. Cropland availability dropped below .2 hectare per capita.[67] These densities exceed sustainable limits, given the inherent fragility of the region's land and prevailing agricultural practices. Cropland has therefore been badly degraded by erosion and nutrient depletion.

Cynthia McClintock notes that, "if population increases while the soil deteriorates, food production per-capita can be expected to decline."[68] Wealth in the region is almost entirely derived from subsistence agriculture. Family incomes—already among the lowest in Peru—dropped sharply in real terms in the 1970s and 1980s; in 1980, per-capita income in the Peruvian highlands was 82 percent of the 1972 level. This poverty resulted in declining caloric intake; in 1980 people in the southern highlands had less than 70 percent of the daily requirement set by the FAO. In 1983, a drought made the subsistence crisis even worse, and production of the staple crop of potatoes fell by 40–50 percent.

While government policies were partly responsible for the long-term income decline in the Peruvian highlands, the particularly harsh drop in the southern region was a result of population pressures, poor land, and the lack of alternative sources of income. The peasants' sense of deprivation was increased by the land reform in the 1970s, which raised their expectations in vain. There is thus a strong correlation between areas suffering severe poverty and areas of Sendero Luminoso strongholds: "the sine-qua-non element" of these strongholds is "the subsistence crisis in the country's southern highlands during the early 1980s."[69]

In terms of contextual factors, Ayacucho offered special opportunities to insurgents. It is physically remote, which reduced the government's control,

---

67. McClintock, "Why Peasants Rebel," pp. 61 and 63.
68. Ibid., p. 63.
69. Ibid., p. 82.

and it has a major university that served as an organizational base for radicals that became the core of Sendero. The university's remoteness also meant that students were disproportionately from the peasantry, and could therefore return to their communities with ease; moreover, they were less likely to find professional jobs on graduation. The relative power of the government was also weakened, ironically, by the land reform, which caused large landowners to leave the region. The Velasco regime did not fill the vacuum with new political and security institutions, in part because an economic downturn later in the decade reduced the government's resources for the task.

McClintock believes that the poverty of these regions condemns the country to chronic, long-term turmoil. The government may be civilian, but is unlikely to be very democratic, and will confront "virtually constant revolutionary and criminal violence."

A COMBINED MODEL

There are important links between the processes identified in the second and third hypotheses. For example, although population movement is sometimes caused directly by scarcity, more often it arises from the greater poverty caused by this scarcity. Similarly, the weakening of the state increases the likelihood not only of deprivation conflicts, but of group-identity conflicts.

It is useful, therefore, to bring the hypotheses together into one model of environment-conflict linkages (Figure 2). Decreases in the quality and quan-

Figure 2. Some Sources and Consequences of Environmental Scarcity.

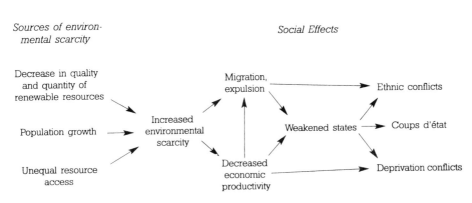

Figure 3. Environmental Scarcity in the Philippines.

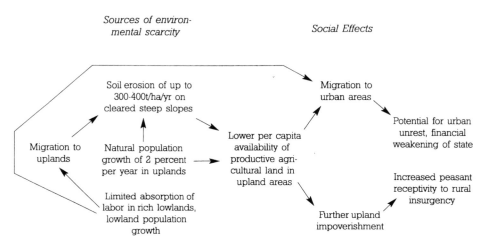

NOTE: The variables and linkages in Figure 3 map onto Figure 2, with the source of scarcity on the left and the forms of conflict on the right.

tity of renewable resources, population growth, and unequal resource access act singly or in various combinations to increase the scarcity, for certain population groups, of cropland, water, forests, and fish. This can reduce economic productivity, both for the local groups experiencing the scarcity and for the larger regional and national economies. The affected people may migrate or be expelled to new lands. Migrating groups often trigger ethnic conflicts when they move to new areas, while decreases in wealth can cause deprivation conflicts such as insurgency and rural rebellion. In developing countries, the migrations and productivity losses may eventually weaken the state which in turn decreases central control over ethnic rivalries and increases opportunities for insurgents and elites challenging state authority. Figure 3 shows how these linkages work in the Filipino case.

South Africa and Haiti illustrate this combined model. In South Africa, apartheid concentrated millions of blacks in some of the country's least productive and most ecologically sensitive territories, where population densities were worsened by high natural birth rates. In 1980, rural areas of the Ciskei homeland had 82 people per square kilometer, whereas the surrounding Cape Province had a rural density of 2. Homeland residents had little capital and few resource-management skills and were subject to corrupt and abusive local governments. Sustainable development in such a situation was impossible, and wide areas were completely stripped of trees for fuelwood, grazed down to bare dirt, and eroded of top soil. A 1980 report concluded that nearly 50 percent of Ciskei's land was moderately or severely eroded, and nearly 40 percent of its pasturage was overgrazed.[70]

This loss of resources, combined with a lack of alternative employment and the social trauma caused by apartheid, created a subsistence crisis in the homelands. Thousands of people have migrated to South African cities, which are as yet incapable of adequately integrating and employing these migrants. The result is the rapid growth of squatter settlements and illegal townships that are rife with discord and that threaten the country's move to democratic stability.[71]

In Haiti, the irreversible loss of forests and soil in rural areas deepens an economic crisis that spawns social strife, internal migration, and an exodus of "boat people." When first colonized by the Spanish in the late fifteenth century and the French in the seventeenth century, Haiti was treasured for its abundant forests. Since then, Haiti has become one of the world's most dramatic examples of environmental despoliation. Less than two percent of the country remains forested, and the last timber is being felled at four percent per year.[72] As trees disappear, erosion follows, worsened by the steepness of the land and by harsh storms. The United Nations estimates that at least 50 percent of the country is affected by topsoil loss that leaves the land "unreclaimable at the farm level."[73] So much soil washes off the slopes that the streets of Port-au-Prince have to be cleared with bulldozers in the rainy season.

Unequal land distribution was not a main cause of this catastrophe. Haiti gained independence in 1804 following a revolt of slaves and ex-slaves against

70. Francis Wilson and Mamphela Ramphele, *Uprooting Poverty: The South African Challenge* (New York: Norton, 1989); George Quail, et al., *Report of the Ciskei Commission* (Pretoria: Conference Associates, 1980), p. 73.
71. See Mamphela Ramphele and Chris McDowell, eds., *Restoring the Land: Environment and Change in Post-Apartheid South Africa* (London: Panos, 1991); and Chris Eaton, "Rural Environmental Degradation and Urban Conflict in South Africa," Occasional Paper of the Peace and Conflict Studies Program, University of Toronto, June 1992.
72. WRI, *World Resources, 1992–93*, p. 286.
73. *Global Assessment of Soil Degradation, World Map on Status of Human-Induced Soil Degradation*, Sheet 1, North and South America.

the French colonial regime. Over a period of decades, the old plantation system associated with slavery was dismantled, and land was widely distributed in small parcels.[74] As a result, Haiti's agricultural structure, unique to Latin America, has 73 percent of cropland in private farms of less than 4 hectares.[75]

But inheritance customs and population growth have combined to produce scarcity, as in Bangladesh. Land has been subdivided into smaller portions with each generation. Eventually the plots cannot properly support their cultivators, fallow periods are neglected, and greater poverty prevents investment in soil conservation. The poorest people leave for steeper hillsides, where they clear the forest and begin farming anew, only to exhaust the land in a few years.[76] Many peasants try to supplement their falling incomes by scavenging wood for charcoal production, which contributes to further deforestation.

These processes might have been prevented had a stable central government invested in agriculture, industrial development, and reforestation. Instead, since independence Haiti has endured a ceaseless struggle for power between black and mulatto classes, and the ruling regimes have been solely interested in expropriating any surplus wealth the economy generated. Today, over 60 percent of the population is still engaged in agriculture, yet capital is unavailable for agricultural improvement, and the terms of exchange for crop production favor urban regions.[77] The population growth rate has actually increased, from 1.7 percent in the mid-1970s to over 2 percent today: the UN estimates that the current population of 6.75 million will grow to over 13 million by 2025.[78] As the land erodes and the population grows, incomes shrink: agricultural output per capita has decreased ten percent in the last decade.[79]

Analysts agree that rising rural poverty has caused ever-increasing rural-rural and rural-urban migration. In search of work, agricultural workers move

74. Thomas Weil, et al., *Haiti: A Country Study* (Washington, D.C.: Department of the Army, 1982), pp. 28–33.
75. Anthony Catanese, "Haiti's Refugees: Political, Economic, Environmental," *Field Staff Reports*, No. 17 (Sausalito, Calif.: Universities Field Staff International, Natural Heritage Institute, 1990–91), p. 5.
76. Elizabeth Abbott, "Where Waters Run Brown," *Equinox*, Vol. 10, No. 59 (September/October 1991), p. 43.
77. Marko Ehrlich, et al., *Haiti: Country Environmental Profile, A Field Study* (Washington, D.C.: U.S. Agency for International Development, 1986), pp. 89–92.
78. WRI, *World Resources, 1992–93*, p. 246.
79. Ibid., p. 272.

from subsistence hillside farms to rice farms in the valleys. From there, they go to cities, especially to Port-au-Prince, which now has a population of over a million. Wealthier farmers and traders, and even those with slimmer resources, try to flee by boat.

These economic and migration stresses are undoubtedly contributing to civil strife. In the aftermath of the collapse of "Baby Doc" Duvalier's regime in 1986, the poor unleashed their vengeance on those associated with the regime, in particular on Duvalier's gangs of enforcers, the *tontons macoutes*. During his election campaign and his short tenure as president, Jean-Bertrand Aristide reportedly encouraged poor slum-dwellers to attack Haiti's elite. Fearful of uprisings, the current military regime has ferociously oppressed the country's poor and peasantry. Even if the present political stalemate is resolved, Aristide is returned to power, and international sanctions are lifted, Haiti will be forever bear the burden of its irreversibly ravaged environment, which may make it impossible to build a prosperous, just, and peaceful society.

THE CAUSAL ROLE OF ENVIRONMENTAL SCARCITY

Environmental scarcity often acts as a powerful long-term social stressor, but does it have any independent role as a cause of conflict? Many analysts assume that it is no more than a fully endogenous intervening variable linking political, economic, and social factors to conflict. By this view, environmental scarcity may be an important indicator that political and economic development has gone awry, but it does not merit, in and of itself, intensive research and policy attention at the expense of more fundamental political and economic factors.

But the cases reviewed here highlight three reasons why this view is wrong. First, as we saw in the Senegal and Jordan basins, environmental scarcity can itself be an important force behind changes in the politics and economics governing resource use. In both cases, scarcity caused powerful actors to increase in their own favor the inequities in the distribution of resources. Second, ecosystem vulnerability is often an important variable contributing to environmental scarcity, and this vulnerability is, at least in part, an independent physical factor: the depth of soils in the Filipino uplands and the vulnerability of Israel's aquifers to salt intrusion are not functions of human social institutions or behavior. Third, in many parts of the world— including regions of the Philippines, Haiti, Peru, and South Africa—environmental degradation has crossed a threshold of irreversibility. Even if enlightened social change removes the original political, economic, and cultural causes of the degradation, it will be a continuing burden on society. Once irreversible, in other words, environmental degradation becomes an exogenous variable.

Implications for International Security

Environmental scarcity has insidious and cumulative social impacts, such as population movement, economic decline, and the weakening of states. These can contribute to diffuse and persistent sub-national violence. The rate and extent of such conflicts will increase as scarcities worsen.

This sub-national violence will not be as conspicuous or dramatic as interstate resource wars, but it will have serious repercussions for the security interests of both the developed and the developing worlds. Countries under such stress may fragment as their states become enfeebled and peripheral regions are seized by renegade authorities and warlords. Governments of countries as different as the Philippines and Peru have lost control over outer territories; although both these cases are complicated, it is nonetheless clear that environmental stress has contributed to their fragmentation. Fragmentation of any sizeable country will produce large outflows of refugees; it will also hinder the country from effectively negotiating and implementing international agreements on collective security, global environmental protection, and other matters.

Alternatively, a state might keep scarcity-induced civil strife from causing its progressive enfeeblement and fragmentation by becoming a "hard" regime that is authoritarian, intolerant of opposition, and militarized. Such regimes are more prone to launch military attacks against neighboring countries to divert attention from internal grievances. If a number of developing countries evolve in this direction, they could eventually threaten the military and economic interests of rich countries.

A state's ability to become a hard regime in response to environmentally induced turmoil depends, I believe, on two factors. First, the state must have sufficient remaining capacity—despite the debilitating effects of scarcity—to mobilize or seize resources for its own ends; this is a function of the internal organizational coherence of the state and its autonomy from outside pressures. Second, there must remain enough surplus wealth in the country's ecological-economic system to allow the state, once it seizes this wealth, to pursue its authoritarian course. Consequently, the countries with the highest probability of becoming "hard" regimes, and potential threats to their neighbors, are large, relatively wealthy developing countries that are dependent on a declining environmental base and that have a history of state strength. Candidates include Indonesia and, perhaps, Nigeria.

Our research suggests that environmental pressures in China may cause the country's fragmentation.[80] This is not the received wisdom: most experts have been distracted by the phenomenal economic expansion in China's coastal areas; they have tended to project these trends onto the rest of the country and to neglect the dangers posed by resource scarcities.[81] The costs of misreading of the Chinese situation could be very high. China has over one-fifth of the world's population, a huge military with growing power-projection capability, and unsettled relations with some of its neighbors. The effects of Chinese civil unrest, mass violence, and state disintegration could spread far beyond its borders.

Chinese fertility rates peaked at the height of the cultural revolution between 1969 and 1972. Population growth will peak at about 17 million per year in the mid-1990s, as the babies born during the cultural revolution reach their reproductive years. In the late 1980s and early 1990s, specialists tempered their optimism about Chinese ability to bring population growth down to replacement rate.[82] Market liberalization in the countryside undermined the one-child policy. In rural areas state coercion seemed less effective, and peasants enriched by market reforms could more easily pay fines. In some provinces, therefore, it became common for families to have two or three children. The most recent evidence, however, suggests that Chinese authorities have renewed their commitment to controlling population growth. In response to often extremely coercive measures by low-level officials, fertility rates have fallen below two children per woman for the first time.[83] But

80. Smil, "Environmental Change as a Source of Conflict and Economic Losses in China"; Jack Goldstone, "Imminent Political Conflict Arising from China's Environmental Crises," Occasional Paper No. 2, Project on Environmental Change and Acute Conflict (December 1992).
81. See, for example, Barber Conable and David Lampton, "China: The Coming Power," *Foreign Affairs*, Vol. 72, No. 5 (Winter 1992/93), pp. 133–149. In their assessment of the pressures on contemporary China, the authors devote only half a sentence to demographic and environmental stresses.
82. Griffith Feeney, et al., "Recent Fertility Dynamics in China: Results from the 1987 One Percent Population Survey," *Population and Development Review*, Vol. 15, No. 2 (June 1989), pp. 297–321; Shanti Conly and Sharon Camp, "China's Family Planning Program: Challenging the Myths," *Country Study Series*, No. 1 (Washington, D.C.: Population Crisis Committee, 1992).
83. Nicholas Kristof, "China's Crackdown on Births: A Stunning, and Harsh, Success," *New York Times*, April 25, 1993, p. A1.

experts are not sure that this accomplishment can be sustained for long, and even if it is, China's population will continue to grow well into the next century.

Only two poor populous countries in the world have less arable land per capita than China: Egypt and Bangladesh. In fact, 300 million people in China's interior have even less arable land than the Bangladeshis. China has little scope to expand irrigated and arable land, although it might be able to increase the intensity of irrigation in some places. Consequently, continued population growth and loss of cropland mean that China will have 25 percent less arable land per capita by 2010. Moreover, the remaining land will often be of declining quality: every year the country loses as much nitrogen and phosphorous from soil erosion as it applies in inorganic fertilizer. Vaclav Smil notes that many experts and senior authorities in China are frightened by the environmental situation, believing the country has already crossed key thresholds of unsustainability. Grain is a constant preoccupation of the leadership, and imports even into rich areas may soon be necessary. Already, tens of millions of Chinese are trying to migrate from the country's interior and northern regions, where water and fuelwood are desperately scarce and the land is often badly damaged, to the booming coastal cities. Smil expects bitter disputes among these regions over migration and water sharing.

Jack Goldstone has estimated the consequences of these stresses for social stability. He notes that population and resource pressures led to widespread civil violence in China during the Ming and Qing dynasties.[84] The current regime recognizes that such pressures will cause mounting grievances in the worst-affected regions. "The rapidly growing population of the north and west cannot be fed and employed within those regions," Goldstone writes. "There is not sufficient land, nor sufficient water, to provide for the additional hundreds of millions that will be born in the next decades."[85] If large-scale migration out of the region is blocked, deprivation conflicts in the northwest are likely. Coupled with merchant and worker resistance in the major cities, they would probably lead to the fall of the central government. If the migration is diverted into China's southern countryside, deprivation and group-identity conflicts are likely to result there.

The only realistic policy is to permit movement to the wealthy coastal cities. Coastal areas must therefore be allowed to continue their rapid eco-

---

84. For a full analysis, see Jack Goldstone, *Revolution and Rebellion in the Early Modern World* (Berkeley: University of California Press, 1991).
85. Goldstone, "Imminent Political Conflicts Arising from China's Environmental Crises," p. 52.

nomic growth to absorb surplus labor. But, Goldstone argues, the Beijing government will have great difficulty maintaining economic and political control over this process. Economic liberalization helps to mobilize the population by dissolving long-standing social relations, and this weakens the Communist Party's ability to micro-manage Chinese society. Moreover, the Party is divided from the very non-Party elites that are rapidly expanding because of economic growth, including student, business, and professional groups. Further growth will depend on private domestic investment, which will encourage these elites, and also workers in private industry, to demand democratization and responsiveness of the regime. The Party has also been weakened by deep internal disagreements over the rate and degree of economic and political liberalization; suspicions about the reliability of the Army; and worker discontent that remains high throughout the country.

Divisions within the regime and among elites, combined with an increasingly mobilized population, create greater opportunities for challenges to central authority. But resource and population pressures force the regime to pursue policies, such as further economic liberalization, that only weaken it more. Goldstone believes that long-term stability would be more likely if China were to begin serious democratization soon, but he is not sanguine. Central authorities will probably refuse to recognize their loosening grip on the society, and this will eventually prompt secessionist movements in Moslem lands to the west and Tibet in the South. Sichuan may also seek independence. "Once the glue of unified communist rule dissolves, China may once again, as it has so often in its history following the fall of unifying dynasties, experience a decade or even century-long interregnum of warring among regional states."[86]

Conclusions

Our research shows that environmental scarcity causes violent conflict. This conflict tends to be persistent, diffuse, and sub-national. Its frequency will probably jump sharply in the next decades as scarcities rapidly worsen in many parts of the world. Of immediate concern are scarcities of cropland, water, forests, and fish, whereas atmospheric changes such as global warm-

---

86. Ibid., p. 54.

ing will probably not have a major effect for several decades, and then mainly by interacting with already existing scarcities.

The degradation and depletion of environmental resources is only one source of environmental scarcity; two other important sources are population growth and unequal resource distribution. Scarcity often has its harshest social impact when these factors interact. As environmental scarcity becomes more severe, some societies will have a progressively lower capacity to adapt. Of particular concern is the decreasing capacity of the state to create markets and other institutions that promote adaptation. The impact of environmental scarcity on state capacity deserves further research.

Countries experiencing chronic internal conflict because of environmental stress will probably either fragment or become more authoritarian. Fragmenting countries will be the source of large out-migrations, and they will be unable to effectively negotiate or implement international agreements on security, trade and environmental protection. Authoritarian regimes may be inclined to launch attacks against other countries to divert popular attention from internal stresses. Any of these outcomes could seriously disrupt international security. The social impacts of environmental scarcity therefore deserve concerted attention from security scholars.

Security, Stability, and International Migration | *Myron Weiner*

$\mathbf{M}$igration and refugee issues, no longer the sole concern of ministries of labor or of immigration, are now matters of high international politics, engaging the attention of heads of states, cabinets, and key ministries involved in defense, internal security, and external relations. Certainly the most dramatic high-politics event involving international migration in recent years was the exodus of East Germans to Austria through Czechoslovakia and Hungary in July and August 1989; it precipitated the decision of the German Democratic Republic to open its western borders, a massive migration westward followed by the fall of the East German government, and the absorption of East Germany by the Federal Republic of Germany. It was flight, not an invasion, that ultimately destroyed the East German state.[1]

Examples abound of migration flows—both of economic migrants affected by the push and pull of differentials in employment opportunities and income, and of refugees from the pushes of domestic turmoil and persecution—that have generated conflicts within and between states and have therefore risen to the top of the political agenda. Among these examples are the rise of right-wing anti-migrant political parties throughout Western Europe; the conflict between the United States and Great Britain over the forcible repatriation of refugees from Hong Kong; the U.S.-Israeli controversy over the settlement of Soviet Jews on the West Bank; the placement of Western migrants by Iraq at strategic locations in order to prevent air strikes; the anxieties in Western Europe over a possible influx of migrants from Eastern Europe and the former Soviet Union; a threat by Palestinian radicals that they would launch terrorist attacks against airlines that carried Soviet Jews to Israel; an

Myron Weiner is Ford International Professor in the Department of Political Science at the Massachusetts Institute of Technology. He was director of the Center of International Studies at MIT from 1987 to 1992.

For helpful comments on an earlier draft of this paper I am grateful to Rogers Brubaker, Karen Jacobsen, Robert Jervis, Stephen Krasner, Robert Lucas, Rosemarie Rogers, and Sharon Russell.

1. Timothy Garton Ash, "The German Revolution," *The New York Review of Books*, December 21, 1989, pp. 14–17, provides an informed eye-witness account of how the exodus of East Germans in the summer and fall of 1989 led to the dismantling of the Berlin Wall and the absorption of the East German state into West Germany.

invasion of Rwanda by armed Tutsi refugees in Uganda aimed at overthrowing the Hutu-dominated government; the successful defeat of the Kabul regime, after thirteen years of warfare, by the Afghan mujaheddin. One could go on, drawing examples from the daily press to make three points:

First, international migration shows no sign of abating. Indeed, with the end of the Cold War there has been a resurgence of violent secessionist movements that create refugee flows,[2] while barriers to exit from the former Soviet Union and Eastern Europe have been lifted. The breakup of empires and countries into smaller units has created minorities who now feel insecure.[3] Vast differentials in income and employment opportunities among countries persist, providing the push and pull that motivate economic migrants.[4] Environmental degradation, droughts, floods, famines, and civil conflicts compel people to flee across international borders.[5] And new global

---

2. On secessionist movements, see Allen Buchanan, *Secession: The Morality of Political Divorce from Fort Sumter to Lithuania and Quebec* (Boulder, Colo.: Westview Press, 1991). This otherwise excellent analysis by a political philosopher does not deal with the problem of minorities that remain in successor states.

3. Democratization and political liberalization of authoritarian regimes have enabled people to leave who previously were denied the right of exit. An entire region of the world, ranging from Central Europe to the Chinese border, had imprisoned those who sought to emigrate. Similar restrictions continue to operate for several of the remaining communist countries. If and when the regimes of North Korea and China liberalize, another large region of the world will allow its citizens to leave. See Alan Dowty, *Closed Borders: The Contemporary Assault on Freedom of Movement* (New Haven: Yale University Press, 1987), which provides a useful account of how authoritarian states engaged both in restricting exodus and in forced expulsions. For an analysis of the right to leave and return, see H. Hannum, *The Right to Leave and Return in International Law and Practice* (London: Martinus Nijhoff, 1987). As has happened twice before in this century, the breakup of an empire is producing large-scale ethnic conflict and emigration. With the withdrawal of Soviet power from Eastern Europe and the disintegration of the Soviet state itself, conflicts have erupted between Turks and Bulgarians in Turkey; Romanians and Hungarians in Transylvania; Armenians and Azeris in the Caucasus; Albanians, Croatians, Slovenians, Bosnians, and Serbs in former Yugoslavia; Slovaks and Czechs in Czechoslovakia; and among a variety of ethnic groups in Georgia, Moldova, Ukraine, and in the new states of Central Asia. There is a high potential for continued emigration of minorities among each of these states. See F. Stephen Larrabee, "Down and Out in Warsaw and Budapest: Eastern Europe and East-West Migration," *International Security*, Vol. 16, No. 4 (Spring 1992), pp. 5–33.

4. A long-term decline in the birth rate in advanced industrial countries combined with continued economic growth may lead employers to seek low-wage laborers from abroad. Transnational investment in manufacturing industries may reduce some manpower needs, but the demand for more workers in the service sector seems likely to grow, barring technological breakthroughs that would replace waiters, bus conductors, nurses, and household help. Employers in Japan, Singapore, and portions of the United States and Western Europe are prepared to hire illegal migrants, notwithstanding the objections of their governments and much of the citizenry. So long as employer demand remains high, borders are porous, and government enforcement of employer sanctions is limited, illegal migration seems likely to continue and in some countries to increase.

5. There have already been mass migrations within and between countries as a result of

networks of communication and transportation provide individuals with information and opportunities for migration.[6]

Second, more people want to leave their countries than there are countries willing or capable of accepting them. The reluctance of states to open their borders to all who wish to enter is only partly a concern over economic effects. The constraints are as likely to be political, resting upon a concern that an influx of people belonging to another ethnic community may generate xenophobic sentiments, conflicts between natives and migrants, and the growth of anti-migrant right-wing parties.

Third, it is necessary to note that while the news media have focused on South/North migration and East/West migration, this focus is narrow and misleading. The movement of migrant workers from North Africa to Western Europe, migration from Asia and Latin America to the United States and Canada, and the increase in the number of people from the Third World and Eastern Europe claiming refugee status in the West represent simply one dimension of the global flows. Only a fraction of the world's seventeen million refugees are in the advanced industrial countries and only a small portion of global migration has flowed to Western Europe (where migrants total 5 percent of the population) or to the United States. Most of the movement has been from one developing country to another; the world's largest refugee flows have been in Africa, South Asia, Southeast Asia, and most recently in the Persian Gulf.[7] In South Asia alone, 35 to 40 million people

---

desertification, floods, toxic wastes (chemical contamination, nuclear reactor accidents, hazardous waste), and threats of inundation as a result of rising sea levels. According to one estimate, two million Africans were displaced in the mid-1980s as a result of drought. See Jodi L. Jacobson, *Environmental Refugees: A Yardstick of Habitability*, Worldwatch Paper No. 86 (Washington, D.C.: Worldwatch Institute, 1988).

6. Information concerning employment opportunities and changes in immigration and refugee laws is quickly transmitted to friends and relatives. Not only do many people in the Third World view the United States and Europe as potential places for migration, but differences and opportunities *within* the Third World are also becoming better known. Indonesians, for example, are seeking (illegal) employment in peninsular Malaysia, Sabah, and Sarawak. Malaysians and others are aware of opportunities in Singapore. Oil-rich Brunei attracts workers from Malaysia, the Philippines, Thailand, and Indonesia. Taiwan, Hong Kong, and South Korea export manpower, but also attract illegal immigrant workers drawn by their reputation for employment at high wages. Migrants continue to be attracted to the oil-producing countries of the Middle East. For one account of large-scale migration among Third World countries, see Michael Vatikiotis, "Malaysia: Worrisome Influx; Foreign Workers Raise Social, Security Fears," *Far Eastern Economic Review*, August 6, 1992, p. 21, which describes the concerns in Malaysia over the influx of an estimated one million migrants from Indonesia.

7. An estimated 5.5 million people from forty countries were temporarily or permanently displaced by the Gulf War. The largest single group was an estimated 1–1.5 million Yemenis who were forced to leave Saudi Arabia to return to Yemen. The other main displaced peoples

have crossed international borders within the region.[8] In the Middle East, wars and civil conflicts have led to large-scale population flows from Iraq, Kuwait, Israel, Saudi Arabia, Iran, and Lebanon. In Africa, civil wars and famines have produced some of the largest refugee populations to be found anywhere in the world.[9] Attention has been given by economists to the ways in which economic differentials between countries influence migration,[10] and by some political scientists to the ways in which conflicts within countries lead to refugee flows.[11] But little systematic comparative attention has been given to the ways in which international population movements create conflicts within and between states, that is, to population flows as an independent rather than as a dependent variable. A study of these effects is necessary to understand why states and their citizens often have an aversion to international migration even when there are economic benefits.

These features of population movements—a growth propelled by economic differentials, internal political disorder, and global networks of communication and transportation; the political as well as economic constraints on the admission of migrants and refugees; and the truly global character of migration—suggest the need for a security/stability framework for the study of international migration that focuses on state policies toward emigration and immigration as shaped by concerns over internal stability and international

---

were Kurds, Kuwaitis, Palestinians, and South Asians. See Elizabeth N. Offen, "The Persian Gulf War of 1990–91: Its Impact on Migration and the Security of States" (M.S. dissertation, Department of Political Science, MIT, June 1992).

8. For data on South Asia, including a description of the major bilateral flows that have led to conflict, see Myron Weiner, "Security, Migration, and Conflict," in *Defense Intelligence Journal* (forthcoming).

9. *World Refugee Survey, 1992* (Washington: D.C.: U.S. Committee for Refugees, 1992). The World Refugee Survey is the best single source for annual world-wide data on both refugees and internally displaced persons, with brief accounts by country of source and destination.

10. See Sidney Klein, ed., *The Economics of Mass Migration in the Twentieth Century* (New York: Paragon House, 1987); Brinley Thomas, *Migration and Economic Growth: A Study of Great Britain and the Atlantic Economy* (Cambridge: Cambridge University Press, 1954); Charles P. Kindleberger, *Europe's Postwar Growth: The Role of Labor Supply* (Cambridge: Harvard University Press, 1967), chap. 9; Theodore W. Schultz, "Migration: An Economist's View," in William H. McNeill and Ruth S. Adams, eds., *Human Migration: Patterns and Policies* (Bloomington: Indiana University Press, 1987), pp. 377–386. These and other works by economists deal with the benefits and costs as well as the determinants of migration. For a useful bibliography on the economics of migration, see Julian L. Simon, *The Economic Consequences of Immigration* (New York: Basil Blackwell, 1989).

11. Aristide R. Zolberg, Astri Suhrke, and Sergio Aguayo, *Escape from Violence: Conflict and the Refugee Crisis in the Developing World* (New York: Oxford University Press, 1989); and Michael R. Marrus, *The Unwanted: European Refugees in the Twentieth Century* (New York: Oxford University Press, 1985), are among the most comprehensive treatments of the major world regions that have produced refugees in this century.

security. Such a framework should consider political changes within states as a major determinant of international population flows, and migration, including refugee flows, both as cause and as consequence of international conflict.

A security/stability framework can be contrasted with an international political economy framework, which explains international migration primarily by focusing on global inequalities, the economic linkages between sending and receiving states including the movement of capital and technology and the role played by transnational institutions, and structural changes in labor markets linked to changes in the international division of labor. The two frameworks have much in common. Both turn our attention from individual decision-making by migrants to the larger social, political, and economic context within which individuals act; both are interactive frameworks emphasizing the linkage between migration processes and other global processes; and both pay close attention to the behavior of states and to the importance of borders, although the security/stability framework gives somewhat greater importance to state decision-making than does a political economy approach, which often regards the state as a weak actor buffeted by larger global forces.

The two frameworks direct us to study different aspects of international migration, to ask different questions, to offer different explanations for international flows, and to create different conceptual tools for analysis. While they are at times complementary, the frameworks often yield different outcomes. A more narrowly economic perspective, for example, may lead the analyst to regard the movement of people from a poor country to a rich country as mutually advantageous (the one benefiting from remittances, the other from needed additions to its labor force), whereas a security/stability perspective of the same migration flow may lead one to point to the political risks associated with changes in the ethnic composition of the receiving country, and the attending international strains that result if there are clashes between natives and migrants. Alternately, an economic perspective might lead the analyst to conclude that migration results in a brain drain from the sending country while worsening unemployment and creating housing shortages in the receiving country, while a security/stability framework might lead the analyst looking at the same migration flow to argue that internal security and international peace can be enhanced because the migrants are an ethnic minority unwelcomed in their home country but readily accepted by another country. The movement of people may be acceptable to both countries even though each incurs an economic loss. Thus, cost/benefit analyses may yield different assessments and policies, depending upon which framework is chosen.

Much of the contemporary literature on international migration focuses on global economic conditions as the key determinants of population movements.[12] Differentials in wages and employment opportunities—a high demand for labor in one country and a surplus in another—stimulate the movement of labor. According to economic theories of migration, individuals will emigrate if the expected benefits exceed the costs, with the result that the propensity to migrate from one region or country to another is viewed as being determined by average wages, the cost of travel, and labor market conditions. Accordingly, it is argued, changes in the global economy, such as a rise in the world price of oil or shifts in terms of trade and international flows of capital, will increase the demand for labor in some countries and decrease it in others. Moreover, the development strategies pursued by individual countries may lead to high growth rates in some and low growth rates and stagnation in others. Uneven economic development among states and a severe maldistribution of income within states may induce individuals and families to move across international boundaries to take advantage of greater opportunities.

These economic explanations go a long way toward explaining a great deal of international population movements, but they neglect two critical political elements. The first is that international population movements are often impelled, encouraged, or prevented by governments or political forces for reasons that may have little to do with economic conditions. Indeed, much of the international population flows, especially within Africa and South

---

12. On the political economy of international migration see, for a neo-Marxist perspective, Saskia Sassen, *The Mobility of Labor and Capital: A Study in International Investment and Labor Flow* (Cambridge: Cambridge University Press, 1988); Alejandro Portes and John Walton, *Labor, Class, and the International System* (New York: Academic Press, 1981); Stephen Adler, *International Migration and Dependence* (Westmead: Saxon House, 1977); and Stephen Castles and Godula Kosack, *Immigrant Workers and Class Structure in Western Europe* (London: Oxford University Press, 1973). For other political economy interpretations, see Kindleberger, *Europe's Postwar Growth*; Michael Piore, *Birds of Passage: Migrant Labor in Industrial Societies* (Cambridge: Cambridge University Press, 1979); Wolf R. Bohning, *The Migration of Workers in the United Kingdom and the European Community* (London: Oxford University Press, 1972); and Wolf R. Bohning, *Studies in International Labour Migration* (London: Macmillan, 1984). Two recent works by economists on migration to the United States do not deal with the political or security dimensions of international migration. See Simon, *The Economic Consequences of Immigration*; and George J. Borjas, *Friends or Strangers: The Impact of Immigrants on the U.S. Economy* (New York: Basic Books, 1990).

Asia, are determined only marginally, if at all, by changes in the global or regional political economy. And secondly, even when economic conditions create inducements for people to leave one country for another, it is governments that decide whether their citizens should be allowed to leave and governments that decide whether immigrants should be allowed to enter, and their decisions are frequently based on non-economic considerations. Moreover, governments vary in their capacity to control entry. States that are capable of defending themselves against missile, tank, and infantry attacks are often unable to defend themselves against the intrusion of thousands of illegals infiltrating across a border in search of employment or safety. Governments want to control the entry of people and regard their inability to do so as a threat to sovereignty. Any effort, therefore, to develop a framework for the analysis of transnational flows of people must also take into account the political determinants and constraints upon these flows.[13]

A security/stability framework complements rather than replaces an economic analysis by focusing upon the role of states in both creating and responding to international migration. The object of this article is to identify some of the circumstances in which security/stability considerations become paramount in how states deal with issues of international migration. I do so in three ways, first, by identifying types of international movements generated by considerations of state security and stability, as distinct from those flows largely shaped by the regional or international political economy. I provide a brief description of forced and induced emigrations as examples of politically-driven population movements with international repercussions.

---

13. Among the studies that focus on the political determinants of refugee flows, the most comprehensive is Zolberg, Suhrke, and Aguayo, *Escape from Violence*. Few other studies so directly consider the relationship between population flows and the political processes within and between states that create them. For a study of the *effects* of migration, especially on foreign policy, see the particularly useful set of essays edited by Robert W. Tucker, Charles B. Keely, and Linda Wrigley, *Immigration and U.S. Foreign Policy* (Boulder, Colo.: Westview Press, 1990). Also see Michael S. Teitelbaum, "Immigration, Refugees and Foreign Policy," *International Organization*, Vol. 38, No. 3 (Summer 1984), pp. 429–450. For an examination of how refugee flows affect and are affected by international relations, see Gilbert Loescher and Laila Monahan, eds., *Refugees and International Relations* (New York: Oxford University Press, 1989); and Leon Gordenker, *Refugees in International Politics* (London: Croom Helm, 1987). It should be noted that the standard works in international relations and in the political economy of international relations do not discuss international migration and refugee flows. See, for example, Robert O. Keohane and Joseph S. Nye, Jr., *Power and Interdependence* (Boston: Little, Brown, 1977); Robert Gilpin, *The Political Economy of International Relations* (Princeton: Princeton University Press, 1987); Kenneth Waltz, *Theory of International Politics* (Reading, Mass: Addison-Wesley, 1979); Stephen D. Krasner, *Defending the National Interest* (Princeton: Princeton University Press, 1978); Robert O. Keohane, *After Hegemony* (Princeton: Princeton University Press, 1984).

Secondly, I identify those circumstances when international migration is regarded as a threat to a country's security and stability. This leads us to consider how and when refugees and economic migrants come to be regarded as threatening by receiving and sending countries. And thirdly, I consider the various ways states react when faced with population movements they regard as a threat to their international security and internal stability.

Forced and Induced Emigrations: A Global Perspective

It would be inaccurate to use the passive voice to describe much of the world's population flows. They do not merely happen; more often they are made to happen. We can identify three distinct types of forced and induced emigrations in the contemporary world.

First, governments may force emigration as a means of achieving cultural homogeneity or asserting the dominance of one ethnic community over another. Such flows have a long and sordid world-wide history. The rise of nationalism in Europe was accompanied by state actions to eject religious communities that did not subscribe to the established religion, and ethnic minorities that did not belong to the dominant ethnic community. In the fifteenth century the Spanish crown expelled the Jews. In the sixteenth century the French expelled the Huguenots. In the seventeenth and eighteenth centuries the British crown induced Protestant dissenters to settle in the American colonies. And in the early decades of the twentieth century minorities throughout Eastern Europe—Bulgarians, Greeks, Jews, Turks, Hungarians, Serbs, Macedonians—were put to flight.[14]

Contemporary population movements in post-independence Africa, the Middle East, South Asia, and Southeast Asia are similarly linked to the rise of nationalism and the emergence of new states. The boundaries of many of the new post-colonial regimes divided linguistic, religious, and tribal communities, with the result that minorities, fearful of their future and often faced with discrimination and violence, migrated to join their ethnic brethren in a neighboring country. Many Third World countries also expelled their ethnic minorities, especially when the minorities constituted an industrious

---

14. See Eugene M. Kulischer, *Europe on the Move: War and Population Changes, 1917–47* (New York: Columbia University Press, 1948), pp. 248–249.

class of migrant origin in competition with a middle-class ethnic majority.[15] Governments facing unemployment within the majority community and conflicts among ethnic groups over language and educational opportunities often regarded the expulsion of a prosperous, well-placed minority as a politically popular policy. Minorities have often been threatened by the state's antagonistic policies toward their religion, their language and their culture, as the state sought to impose a hegemonic ethnic or religious identity upon its citizens.[16] Economically successful minorities have often been told that others would be given preferences in employment, a policy of discrimination which effectively made it difficult for minorities to compete on the basis of merit.[17] Many governments expelled their minorities or created conditions that induced them to leave, and thereby forced other countries, on humanitarian grounds or out of cultural affinity, to accept them as refugees. The list of expulsions is long: Chinese from Vietnam, Indians and Pakistanis from East Africa, Tamils from Sri Lanka, Bahais from Iran, Kurds from Turkey, Iran and Iraq, Ahmediyas from Pakistan, Chakmas from Bangladesh, and in Africa the Tutsi from Rwanda, Eritreans and others from Ethiopia, and non-Arab peoples from the south in Sudan, to name a few.[18] To this list from the Third World, we must now add the minorities in each of the successor states of Yugoslavia.[19]

Secondly, governments have forced emigration as a means of dealing with political dissidents and class enemies. The ancient Greeks were among the

---

15. In 1969 Kenya announced that eighty thousand noncitizen Asians must leave and in 1972 Uganda expelled its Indian population, most of whom were part of the country's middle class. See Zolberg, Suhrke, and Aguayo, *Escape from Violence*, pp. 65–66.
16. Sri Lanka is an example. See Stanley J. Tambiah, *Ethnic Fratricide and the Dismantling of Democracy* (Chicago: University of Chicago Press, 1987); and Stanley J. Tambiah, *Buddhism Betrayed? Religion, Politics, and Violence in Sri Lanka* (Chicago: University of Chicago Press, 1992).
17. Two examples are Malaysia, where the government adopted a policy of giving preferences in employment and education to Malays over Chinese, and Sri Lanka, where government gave preference to Sinhalese over Tamils. For these and other examples see Donald L. Horowitz, *Ethnic Groups in Conflict* (Berkeley: University of California Press, 1985), pp. 185–228.
18. Ibid., pp. 198–199, 200–201, 208–209.
19. The war for "ethnic cleansing" in Yugoslavia is the latest example of governments seeking to move populations to move in an effort to establish ethnic hegemony over a territory; in this particular instance it is combined with an effort to force a change in the borders themselves by establishing Serbian demographic and military preponderance in areas of Croatia and Bosnia-Herzegovina that could then be incorporated into Serbia. For an account see Misha Glenny, "Yugoslavia: The Revenger's Tragedy," *The New York Review of Books*, Vol. 34, No. 14 (August 13, 1992), pp. 37–43. Glenny notes that majority-minority conflicts in Kosovo and Macedonia, accompanied by similar refugee flights, could lead to military action by Albania, Bulgaria, Greece, or Turkey.

earliest to strip dissidents of citizenship and cast them into exile. Socrates himself was offered the option of going into exile rather than being executed. Contemporary authoritarian governments have expelled dissidents or allowed them to go into exile as an alternative to imprisonment. Exiles from the Third World—from Ethiopia, Iran, Cuba, South Korea, Nicaragua, Vietnam, Chile—have largely replaced exiles from Europe in the United States.[20]

Governments may expel not just a handful of dissidents, but a substantial portion of the population hostile to the regime. Revolutionary regimes often see large-scale emigration of a social class as a way of transforming the country's social structure. The exodus of more than a half million members of the Cuban middle class was regarded by the Castro regime as a way of disposing of a social class hostile to socialism. In 1971 the Pakistani government sought to weaken the insurgency in East Pakistan by forcing large numbers of Bengali Hindus out of the country. The Vietnamese government justified expulsions as a way of eliminating a bourgeois social class opposed to the regime. The Khmer Rouge regime killed or forced into exile citizens tainted with French and other western cultural influences in an effort to reduce Cambodia's cultural and economic ties with the West. And in Afghanistan, the Soviet and Afghan military forced populations hostile to the regime to flee to Pakistan and Iran.[21]

A third type of forced emigration can be described as part of a strategy to achieve a foreign policy objective. Governments may, for example, force emigration as a way of putting pressure on neighboring states, although they may deny any such intent. The refugee-receiving country, however, often understands that a halt to unwanted migration is not likely to take place unless it yields on a demand made by the country from which the refugees come. In 1981, for example, the United States government believed that the government of Haiti was encouraging its citizens to flee by boat to Florida to press the United States to substantially increase its economic aid. (It did.)[22]

20. On exile politics see the articles in *Third World Quarterly*, Vol. 9, No. 1 (London: Third World Foundation, January 1987); and Yossi Shain, *The Frontier of Loyalty: Political Exiles in the Age of the Nation-State* (Middletown, Conn.: Wesleyan University Press, 1989).
21. For accounts of forced migration as an instrument of both domestic and foreign policy, see Michael S. Teitelbaum, "Forced Migration: The Tragedy of Mass Expulsions," in Nathan Glazer, ed., *Clamor at the Gates: The New Migration* (San Francisco: ICS Press, 1985); and Peter H. Koehn, *Refugees from Revolution: U.S. Policy and Third-World Migration* (Boulder, Colo.: Westview Press, 1991).
22. As part of its effort to halt Haitian migration to the United States, the Reagan administration promised increased amounts of foreign aid to improve the conditions that purportedly promoted the flow. For an account of how the United States utilized its aid program to persuade the

In the 1980s, Pakistani officials believed that Soviet pressure on Afghans to flee was intended in part to force Pakistan to seek a settlement with the Afghan regime and to withdraw military aid to the insurgents.[23] The Malaysian government feared that the government of Vietnam sought to destabilize it by forcing Malaysia to accept Chinese refugees.[24] The Federal Republic of Germany believed that the German Democratic Republic was permitting Tamil refugees to enter through the Berlin border to force the FRG to establish new rules of entry that would tacitly recognize the East German state or, alternatively, as a bargaining ploy for additional financial credits (which the FRG subsequently granted in return for a halt to the flow).

In the eighteenth and nineteenth centuries, colonization was an instrument of foreign economic policy that served to extend control over a territory. The British settled their colonies in the western hemisphere, in southern and eastern Africa, and in the Pacific; the French settled North Africa; the Portuguese populated Angola and Brazil; the Russians moved into nearby territories in the east, south, and southwest.[25]

The imperial powers also moved populations from one territory to another in pursuit of their own economic interests. Slaves were transported from Africa to the Caribbean and to North and South America. After the abolition of slavery, the British established a system of indentured labor that enabled them to satisfy the labor needs in their colonies (especially on British-owned plantations) by moving Indians to East Africa, Mauritius, the Caribbean, and Fiji.[26] The colonial powers also encouraged the migration of entrepreneurial

---

Haitian government to prosecute those engaged in trafficking in illegal migrants and to pledge not to mistreat return migrants, see Jorge Domínguez, "Immigration as Foreign Policy in U.S.-Latin American Relations," in Robert Tucker, Charles B. Keely, and Linda Wrigley, eds., *Immigration and U.S. Foreign Policy* (Boulder, Colo.: Westview Press, 1990). Also see Gil Loescher and John A. Scanlan, *Calculated Kindness: Refugees and America's Half-Open Door, 1945 to the Present* (New York: Free Press, 1986).

23. U.S. Department of State, *Afghanistan: Eight Years of Soviet Occupation* (Washington, D.C.: U.S. Government Printing Office, December 1987).

24. For an account of Malaysian and Thai government responses to refugees from Vietnam, see Loescher and Scanlan, *Calculated Kindness*, p. 135. Also see Lesleyanne Hawthorne, *Refugee: The Vietnamese Experience* (London: Oxford University Press, 1982).

25. For a political analysis of Russian colonization policy, see Alexandre A. Bennigsen and S. Enders Wimbush, "Migration and Political Control: Soviet Europeans in Soviet Central Asia," in McNeill and Adams, *Human Migration*.

26. For accounts of how the British settled South Asians in British colonies in Burma, Uganda, Kenya, Malawi, Mauritius, Guyana, Malaysia, South Africa, Fiji, and in the Caribbean, see Hugh Tinker, *The Export of Indian Labour Overseas 1830–1920* (London: Oxford University Press, 1974); and Hugh Tinker, *The Banyan Tree: Overseas Emigrants from India, Pakistan, and Bangladesh* (Oxford: Oxford University Press, 1977).

communities, traders, and money lenders whom they regarded as politically pliable, e.g., Indians to the Gulf, Lebanese to West Africa, and Chinese to Southeast Asia.

While the colonization of distant territories rarely led to enduring political or economic control, the colonization of nearby territories has almost always had permanent consequences. Americans moved westward into Mexican and Indian territories. The Chinese colonized non-Han areas. The Russians colonized the Ukraine, Moldavia, the Baltic states, and portions of Muslim-populated Soviet Central Asia. And the Germans moved eastward in central Europe. These flows displaced the local populations and transformed the politics of the areas that were colonized.

With independence from European colonialism, many newly-established regimes sought to "decolonize" themselves by pressing for the exodus of populations they regarded as imposed upon them by the imperial power. With few exceptions, white settlers were pressed to return home. French settlers vacated Algeria; most Portuguese left Angola and Mozambique; many British left Zimbabwe. The new regimes often pressed for the exodus of those who had been brought in by the imperial rulers as indentured servants, although they were now free laborers and many had become prosperous businessmen and members of the middle class. Uganda forced South Asians to leave.[27] Sri Lanka pressed for the departure of Tamil tea estate workers. The Fijian military overthrew an elected government dominated by Indian descendants of estate workers, and native Melanesian Fijians rioted against Indians in an apparent effort to force them to leave the island.[28] A similar process of rejection may soon be at work in the former Soviet republics, where millions of Russian "colons" are regarded as illegitimate settlers imposed by the Soviet regime.[29]

Forced emigration can be an instrument by which one state seeks to destabilize another, force recognition, stop a neighboring state from interfering

27. M. Mamdani, *From Citizen to Refugee: Ugandan Asians Come to Britain* (London: Pinter Publishers, 1973).
28. Colonel Sitveni Rabuka, a Melanesian, took over the government and arrested all cabinet members. The coup was endorsed by the Great Council of Chiefs and was quickly followed by race riots and attacks on Indian property. For an account of the 1987 coup, see the *Far Eastern Economic Review*, June 4, 1987, p. 38. It is estimated that in 1987 Fiji's population of 714,000 was 48.6 percent of Indian origin and 46.2 percent of Melanesian origin. For an account of subsequent emigration by many Indians from Fiji see the *Far Eastern Economic Review*, June 28, 1990, p. 15.
29. Rogers Brubaker, "Ethnopolitical Migration from and among Soviet Successor States," in Myron Weiner, ed., *International Migration and Security* (forthcoming).

in its internal affairs, prod a neighboring state to provide aid or credit in return for stopping the flow, or extend its own political and economic interests or those of a dominant ethnic group through colonization or decolonization. An examination of both historical and contemporary population movements thus demonstrates that countries of emigration have more control over international population flows than is usually accounted for by political analysts, and that what often appears to be spontaneous emigration and refugee movements may represent deliberate emigration policies on the part of sending countries. To view refugee flows as simply the unintended consequences of internal upheavals or economic crises is to ignore the eagerness of some governments to reduce or eliminate from within their own borders selected social classes and ethnic groups, and to affect the politics and policies of their neighbors.[30]

When is Migration a Threat to Security and Stability?

Migration can be perceived as threatening by governments of either population-sending or population-receiving communities. The threat can be an attack by armed refugees; migrants can be a threat to either country's political stability; or migrants can be perceived as a threat to the major societal values of the receiving country.

"Security" is a social construct with different meanings in different societies. An ethnically homogeneous society, for example, may place a higher value on preserving its ethnic character than does a heterogeneous society and may, therefore, regard a population influx as a threat to its security. Providing a haven for those who share one's values (political freedom, for example) is important in some countries, but not in others; in some countries, therefore, an influx of "freedom fighters" may not be regarded as a threat to security. Moreover, even in a given country, what is highly valued may not be shared by elites and counter-elites. The influx of migrants regarded as radicals may be feared by a monarch, but welcomed by the opposition. One ethnic group may welcome migrants, while another is vehemently opposed to them. The business community may be more willing than the general public to import migrant workers.

---

30. For a useful bibliographical guide to the vast literature on refugees, see *Displaced Peoples and Refugee Studies: A Resource Guide*, edited by the Refugee Studies Programme, University of Oxford (London: Hans Zell Publishers, 1990).

Similarly, countries differ in whether or not they regard the mistreatment of their citizens abroad as a threat that calls for state action. While some countries are prepared to take armed action in defense of their overseas citizens, others prefer not to antagonize a government that has enabled its citizens to find employment and a country that is a source of much-needed remittances.

Any attempt to classify types of threats from immigration quickly runs into distinctions between "real" and "perceived" threats, or into absurdly paranoid notions of threat or mass anxieties that can best be described as xenophobic and racist. But even these extreme notions are elements in the reaction of governments to immigrants and refugees. It is necessary to find an analytical stance that, on the one hand, does not dismiss fears, and, on the other, does not regard all anxieties over immigration and refugees as a justification for exclusion.

Before turning to an analysis of how, why, and when states may regard immigrants and refugees as potential threats, it is first necessary to note that some obvious explanations for the response of population-receiving countries are of limited utility. One example is economic absorptive capacity. It is plausible, for example, that a country with little unemployment, a high demand for labor, and the financial resources to provide the housing and social services required by immigrants should regard migration as beneficial, while a country low on each of these dimensions should regard migration as economically and socially destabilizing. Nevertheless, using these criteria, one might expect Japan to welcome migrants and Israel to reject them, when in fact the opposite is the case.[31]

A second plausible but unsatisfactory explanation is the volume of immigration. A country faced with a large-scale influx should feel more threatened than a country experiencing a small influx of migrants. From this perspective one might have expected the Federal Republic of Germany to regard a trickle of Sri Lankan Tamils in the mid-1980s with equanimity, but to move swiftly to halt the 1989 influx of 2,000 East Germans daily, or for the countries of Africa to feel more threatened by the onrush of refugees and hence less receptive than the countries of Western Europe confronted with a trickle from the Third World. Again, however, the opposite has been the case.

---

31. In fact, when Soviet Jewish migration reached 200,000 in one year, there were "euphoric expectations of a million-and-a-half newcomers within two or three years," wrote the editor of the Jerusalem *Post*. David Bar-Illan, "Why Likud Lost—And Who Won," *Commentary*, Vol. 94, No. 2 (August 1992), p. 28.

Economics does, of course, matter. Even a country willing to accept immigrants when its economy is booming is more likely to close its doors in a recession. But economics does not explain many of the differences between countries, nor does it explain the criteria countries employ to decide whether a particular group of migrants or refugees is acceptable or is regarded as threatening. Similarly, volume can matter, but again it depends upon who is at the door.

The third and most plausible explanation for the willingness of states to accept or reject migrants is ethnic affinity. A government and its citizens are likely to be receptive to those who share the same language, religion, or race, while it might regard as threatening those with whom such an identity is not shared. But what constitutes "ethnic affinity" is, again, a social construct that can change over time. Australians and Americans, for example, redefined themselves so that Asians are no longer excluded as unassimilable peoples. Many West Europeans now regard East Europeans as fellow-Europeans, more acceptable as migrants than people from North Africa. Who is or is not "one of us" is historically variable. To many nineteenth-century American Protestants, Jews and Catholics were not "one of us," and today, for many Europeans, Muslims are not "one of us." Moreover, what constitutes cultural affinity for one group in a multi-ethnic society may represent a cultural, social, and economic threat to another: note, for example, the hostile response of some African-Americans in Florida to Cuban migrants,[32] Indian Assamese response to Bangladeshis, and Pakistan Sindhi response to Biharis. Cultural affinity—or its absence—clearly plays a critical role in how various communities within countries respond to a population influx; this is a theme to which we shall return.

We can identify five broad categories of situations in which refugees or migrants may be perceived as a threat to the country that produces the emigrants, to the country that receives them, or to relations between sending and receiving countries. The first is when refugees and migrants are regarded as a threat—or at least a thorn—in relations between sending and receiving countries, a situation that arises when refugees and migrants are opposed to the regime of their home country. The second is when migrants or refugees

---

32. The ambivalent attitude of African-Americans toward immigration is described by Lawrence H. Fuchs, "The Reactions of Black Americans to Immigration," in Virginia Yans-McLaughlin, ed., *Immigration Reconsidered: History, Sociology and Politics* (New York: Oxford University Press, 1990).

are perceived as a political threat or security risk to the regime of the host country. The third is when immigrants are seen as a cultural threat or, fourth, as a social and economic problem for the host society. And the fifth—a new element growing out of recent developments in the Gulf—is when the host society uses immigrants as an instrument of threat against the country of origin.

REFUGEES AND IMMIGRANTS AS OPPONENTS OF THE HOME REGIME

Conflicts create refugees, but refugees can also create conflicts. An international conflict arises when a country classifies individuals as refugees with a well-founded fear of persecution,[33] thereby accusing and condemning their country of origin for engaging in persecution. The mere granting of asylum can create an antagonistic relationship. Thus, the January 1990 debate in Congress over whether Chinese students should be permitted to remain in the United States because of the persecutions in China was regarded by the People's Republic of China as "interference" in its internal affairs. President Bush was prepared to permit graduating students and other Chinese in the United States to remain by extending their visas, but not to grant asylum, while many Congressmen wanted to grant formal asylum status in order to condemn China. Moreover, to classify individuals as refugees with a well-founded fear of persecution is also to acknowledge that they have a moral (as distinct from a political) right to oppose their country's regime. The view of the United Nations High Commission for Refugees (UNHCR) is that the granting of refugee status does not necessarily imply criticism of the sending by the receiving country, but such a view contradicts the conception of the

---

33. The language is from the 1951 United Nations Convention Relating to the Status of Refugees, subsequently modified in a 1967 protocol. The Convention states that a refugee is a person who "owing to a well-founded fear of being persecuted for reasons of race, religion, nationality, membership of a particular social group or political opinion, is outside the country of his nationality and is unable, or unwilling to avail himself of the protection of that country." This definition is the centerpiece of most Western law dealing with refugees. Some critics (see Zolberg, Suhrke, and Aguayo, *Escape from Violence*) believe that the definition is too narrow because it excludes those who only flee from violence. For a defense of the United Nations definition, see David A. Martin, "The Refugee Concept: On Definitions, Politics, and the Careful Use of Scarce Resources," in Howard Adelman, ed., *Refugee Policy: Canada and the United States* (Toronto: York Lanes Press, 1991), pp. 30–51. A wider definition of refugee was adopted in 1969 by the Organization of African Unity in its Refugee Convention, according to which the term refugee applies to every person who "owing to external aggression, occupation, foreign domination or events seriously disturbing public order in either part or the whole of his country of origin or nationality, is compelled to leave his place of habitual residence in order to seek refuge in another place outside his country of origin or nationality."

refugee as one with a fear of *persecution*.[34] Moreover, democratic regimes generally allow their refugees to speak out against the regime of their country of origin, allow them access to the media, and permit them to send information and money back home in support of the opposition. The host country's decision to grant refugee status thus often creates an adversary relationship with the country that produces the refugees. The receiving country may have no such intent, but even where its motives are humanitarian the mere granting of asylum can be sufficient to create an antagonistic relationship. In the most famous asylum episode in this century, Iranian revolutionaries took violent exception to the U.S. decision to permit the shah of Iran to enter the U.S. for medical reasons; many Iranians regarded it as a form of asylum and used it as an occasion for taking American hostages.

A refugee-receiving country may actively support the refugees in their quest to change the regime of their country of origin. Refugees are potentially a tool in inter-state conflict. Numerous examples abound: the United States armed Cuban refugees in an effort to overthrow the Castro regime at the Bay of Pigs; the United States armed Contra exiles from Nicaragua; the Indian government armed Bengali "freedom fighters" against the Pakistan military; the Indian government provided military support for Tamil refugees from Sri Lanka to give the Indian government leverage in the Tamil-Sinhalese dispute; Pakistan, Saudi Arabia, China, and the United States armed Afghan refugees in order to force Soviet troops to withdraw from Afghanistan; the Chinese provided arms to Khmer Rouge refugees to help overthrow the Vietnamese-backed regime in Cambodia; and Palestinian refugees received Arab support against Israelis. Refugee-producing countries may thus have good reason for fearing an alliance between their adversaries and the refugees.

Non-refugee immigrants can also be a source of conflict between receiving and sending countries. A diaspora made up primarily of refugees is, of course, likely to be hostile to the regime of the country from which they fled. But even economic migrants may become hostile, especially if they live in democratic countries while the government of their homeland is repressive. Thus, many overseas Chinese lost their sympathy for China's government in 1989 when the regime became repressive at Tiananmen Square. Thereafter, many overseas Chinese supported dissidents within China and pressed their

---

34. For an analysis of the UNHCR's concept of protection, see Leon Gordenker, *Refugees in International Politics* (New York: Columbia University Press, 1987), pp. 27–46.

host governments to withdraw support for China. The Beijing government came to regard many overseas Chinese as a source of support for dissidents.[35] There are numerous examples of diasporas seeking to undermine the regime of their home country: South Koreans and Taiwanese in the United States (who supported democratic movements at home), Iranians in France (Khomeini himself during the reign of the Shah, and opponents of Khomeini's Islamic regime thereafter), Asian Indians in North America and the UK (after Indira Gandhi declared an emergency), Indian Sikhs (supporting secession), and dissident Sri Lankan Tamils and Northern Irish Catholics among others.[36]

The home country may take a dim view of the activities of its citizens abroad, and hold the host country responsible for their activities. But host countries, especially if they are democratic, are loath to restrict migrants engaged in lawful activities, especially since some of the migrants have already become citizens. The home country may even plant intelligence operators abroad to monitor the activities of its migrants,[37] and may take steps to prevent further emigration. The embassy of the home country may also provide encouragement to its supporters within the diaspora. The diaspora itself may become a focal point of controversy between the home and host countries, among contending groups within the diaspora, or between sections of the diaspora and the home government.[38] Thus, struggles that might overwise take place only within a country become internationalized if the country has a significant overseas population.

---

35. They have some cause to do so: in March 1990 the Chinese government sealed Tiananmen Square after receiving word that overseas Chinese, using fax machines, had called upon dissidents to protest peacefully by gathering in large numbers in the Square. For a history of Communist China's relationship with its diaspora, see Stephen FitzGerald, *China and the Overseas Chinese: A Study of Peking's Changing Policy 1949–1970* (Cambridge: Cambridge University Press, 1972).

36. For an analysis of the role played by Asian migrants and their descendants in the United States in supporting movements for democratization or for self-determination in their "home" countries, see Myron Weiner, "Asian Immigrants and U.S. Foreign Policy," in Tucker, Keely, and Wrigley, *Immigration and U.S. Foreign Policy*, pp. 192–213; for an analysis of the political role of other diasporas in the United States, see Yossi Shain, "Democrats and Secessionists: U.S. Diasporas as Regime Destabilizers," in Weiner, *International Migration and Security.*

37. On the role played by the Taiwanese security apparatus in attempts to thwart support for Taiwanese independence sentiments within the Taiwanese community in the United States, see Weiner, "Asian Immigrants and U.S. Foreign Policy," p. 197.

38. Examples include conflicts between Turkish Muslim fundamentalists and their opponents within Germany and, earlier, among Indians in Britain who were divided in their attitude toward Prime Minister Indira Gandhi's government after she declared an emergency in 1975 and arrested members of the opposition.

REFEREES AND IMMIGRANTS AS A POLITICAL RISK TO THE HOST COUNTRY
Governments are often concerned that refugees to whom they give protection may turn against them if they are unwilling to assist the refugees in their opposition to the government of their country of origin. Paradoxically, the risk may be particularly high if the host country has gone so far as to arm the refugees against their country of origin. Guns can be pointed in both directions, and the receiving country takes the risk that refugees will seek to dictate the host country's policies toward the sending country. For example, the decision by Arab countries to provide political support and arms to Palestinian refugees from Israel created within the Arab states a population capable of influencing their own foreign policies and internal politics. Palestinians, for example, became a political force within Lebanon in ways that subsequently made them a political and security problem for Lebanon, Syria, Jordan, Israel, France, and the United States. The support of Iraqi invaders by Palestinians in Kuwait was an asset to Iraq since some of the 400,000 Palestinians in Kuwait held important positions in the Kuwaiti administration. The decision after the war by the Kuwaiti government to expel Palestinians reflected its view that Palestinians had become a security threat.[39] Throughout the Middle East, governments must consider the capacity of the Palestinians to undermine their regimes should they adopt policies that are unacceptable to the Palestinians. Similarly, the arming of Afghan refugees in Pakistan limited the options available to the government of Pakistan in its dealings with the governments of Afghanistan and the Soviet Union. The Pakistani government armed the Afghans in order to pressure the Soviets to withdraw their forces and to agree to a political settlement, but the Pakistani government was also constrained by the knowledge that it could not sign an agreement with the Soviet or Afghan governments that was unacceptable to the armed Afghans in Pakistan.

Refugees have launched terrorist attacks within their host country, illegally smuggled arms, allied with the domestic opposition against host-government policies, participated in drug traffic, and in other ways eroded governments' willingness to admit refugees. Palestinians, Sikhs, Croats, Kurds, Armenians, Sri Lankan Tamils, and Northern Irish, among others, have been regarded

---

39. For an analysis of the changing attitudes of Kuwaitis toward Palestinian migrants and toward foreign workers in general, see Jill Crystal, *Kuwait: The Transformation of an Oil State* (Boulder, Colo.: Westview Press, 1991), pp. 166–169.

with suspicion by intelligence and police authorities of other countries and their requests for asylum have been scrutinized not only for whether they have a well-founded fear of persecution, but for whether their presence might constitute a threat to the host country.

Such fears, it should be noted, are sometimes exaggerated, and governments have often gone to extreme lengths to protect themselves against low-level threats[40] but these fears are nonetheless not always without foundation, especially in the context of an increase in international terrorism.

MIGRANTS PERCEIVED AS A THREAT TO CULTURAL IDENTITY

How and why some migrant communities are perceived as cultural threats is a complicated issue, involving initially how the host community defines itself. Cultures differ with respect to how they define who belongs to or can be admitted into their community. These norms govern whom one admits, what rights and privileges are given to those who are permitted to enter, and whether the host culture regards a migrant community as potential citizens. A violation of these norms (by unwanted immigrants, for example) is often regarded as a threat to basic values and in that sense is perceived as a threat to national security.

These norms are often embedded in the law of citizenship that determines who, by virtue of birth, is entitled as a matter of right to be a citizen, and who is permitted to become a naturalized citizen. The main distinction is between citizenship laws based on *jus sanguinis,* whereby a person wherever born is a citizen of the state of his parents, and those based on *jus soli,* the rule that a child receives its nationality from the soil or place of birth. The ties of blood descent are broader than merely parentage, for they suggest a broader "volk" or people to whom one belongs in a fictive relationship. The Federal Republic of Germany, for example, has such a legal norm. Under a law passed in 1913—and still valid—German citizenship at birth is based exclusively on descent (*jus sanguinis*); thus the children of migrants born in Germany are not thereby automatically entitled to citizenship (no *jus soli*). The Basic Law (Germany's postwar "Constitution") also accords citizenship

---

40. One of the more extreme responses was the McCarran-Walter Immigration Act passed by the U.S. Congress in 1952, which excluded any aliens who might "engage in activities which would be prejudicial to the public interest, or endanger the welfare, safety or security of the United States." The Immigration and Naturalization Service interpreted the act to go beyond barring known or suspected terrorists to exclude writers and politicians known to be critical of the United States.

to those Germans who no longer live in Germany and who may no longer speak German but came (or are descended from those who came) from Germany, including the territories from which Germans were expelled after the war.[41] Thus, thousands of immigrants who entered the Federal Republic from East Germany or from Poland after the Second World War were regarded as German citizens returning "home." Other countries share a similar concept. Israel, for example, has a Law of Return, under which all Jews, irrespective of where they presently live, are entitled to "return" home to reclaim, as it were, their citizenship. Nepal also has a law which entitles those who are of Nepali "origin," though they may have lived in India, Singapore, Hong Kong or elsewhere for several generations, to reclaim their citizenship by returning home.

Where such notions of consanguinity dominate citizenship law, the political system is capable of distinguishing between an acceptable and unacceptable influx, without regard either to the numbers or to the condition of the economy into which the immigrants move. In general, countries with norms of consanguinity find it difficult to incorporate ethnically alien migrants, including refugees, into citizenship. These countries are also likely to have political groups that advocate sending immigrants home even though expulsion may impose severe economic consequences for the host as well as the home countries.

A norm of indigenousness may also be widely shared by a section of a country's population and even incorporated into its legal system. This norm prescribes different rights for those who are classified as indigenous and those who, irrespective of the length of time they or their ancestors resided in the country, are not so classified. An indigenous people asserts a superior claim to land, employment, education, political power, and the central national symbols that is not accorded to others who live within the country. The indigenous—called *bhoomiputras* in Malaysia, "sons of the soil" in India, and native peoples in some societies—may assert exclusive rights denied to others, often resting on the notion that they as a people exist only within one country, while others have other homes to which they can return. Thus, the Sinhalese in Sri Lanka, the Malays (the *bhoomiputras*) in Malaysia, the Assamese in Assam, and the Melanesians in Fiji, among others, subscribe to

---

41. Kay Hailbronner, "Citizenship and Nationhood in Germany," in William Rogers Brubaker, ed., *Immigration and the Politics of Citizenship in Europe and North America* (Lanham, Md.: University Press of America, 1989).

an ideology of indigenousness which has, in various guises, been enshrined in the legal system and which shapes the response of these societies to immigrants. The *bhoomiputras* in Malaysia regarded the influx of Chinese and others from Vietnam as a fundamental threat, indeed so threatening as to lead the government to sink Vietnamese boats carrying refugees. Similarly, the Assamese rejected the influx of Bengalis, Indian-born Nepalis, and Marwaris from other parts of India (as well as immigrants from Nepal and Bangladesh), fearing that any resulting demographic change would threaten their capacity to maintain the existing legal arrangement under which native Assamese are provided opportunities in education and employment not accorded other residents of the state.[42] Nativism, a variant of the norm of indigenousness, played an important role in shaping the U.S. Immigration Act of 1924, particularly its national origins clause providing for national quotas. This legislation, and the political sentiment that underlay it, resulted in a restrictive policy toward refugees throughout the 1930s and early 1940s. After the war, however, the older American tradition of civic pluralism became politically dominant. It shaped the 1965 Immigration Act, which eliminated national quotas and gave preferences to individuals with skills and to family unification. The numbers and composition of migrants then significantly changed. From the mid-1960s to the later 1980s, between five hundred thousand and one million migrants and refugees entered each year, with nearly half the immigrants coming from Asia.

Citizenship in the United States is acquired by birth or by naturalization. Originally, American law permitted naturalization only to "free white persons," but subsequent acts permitted naturalization without regard to race. Apart from the usual residence requirements, U.S. naturalization law requires applicants to demonstrate their knowledge of the American Constitution and form of government, and to swear allegiance to the principles of the U.S. Constitution. Political knowledge and loyalty, not consanguinity, are thus the norms for membership. It is in part because the United States has political rather than ethnic criteria for naturalization that the United States has been more supportive of immigration and in the main has felt less threatened by immigration than most other countries.

For much of its history a low level of threat perception has also characterized the French response to immigration. While a concern for cultural unity

---

42. For an analysis, with examples, of the notion of indigenousness as providing the basis of group legitimacy, see Donald L. Horowitz, *Ethnic Groups in Conflict* (Berkeley: University of California Press, 1985), pp. 202–216.

is a central element in the French conception of nationhood, the French have also had a political conception of citizenship derived from the revolutionary origins of the notion of citizenship. The French, as Rogers Brubaker has written, are universalist and assimilationist in contrast with the *Volk*-centered Germans.[43] The result is that the French have been more willing to naturalize immigrants than have the Germans and more open to political refugees than most other West European countries. Even so, France has a strong anti-migrant movement, the National Front, led by Jean-Marie Le Pen, a North African–born Frenchman who has won considerable support for his position that guest-workers from North Africa, and their French-born children, should "return" home to North Africa.

Legal definitions of citizenship aside, most societies react with alarm when there is an unregulated large-scale illegal migration of people who do not share their culture and national identity. Examples abound. Illegal migration into the Sabah state of Malaysia from the Philippines and Indonesia—an estimated 400,000 or more of Sabah's 1.4 million population—has created anxieties there. The government of Malaysia is particularly uneasy since the Philippines lays claim to Sabah and some Filipino leaders insist that, so long as the dispute continues, Malaysia has no right to consider Filipinos as illegal aliens. Should the Filipinos acquire citizenship, it has been noted, they might win a third or more of Sabah's parliamentary seats and pursue a merger with the Philippines. The Philippines might thereby acquire through colonization what it is unable to win through diplomatic or military means.[44]

Colonization as a means of international conquest and annexation can in fact be the deliberate intent of a state. The government of Morocco, for example, moved 350,000 civilians into Western Sahara in an effort to claim and occupy disputed territory. The Israeli government has provided housing subsidies to its citizens to settle on the West Bank. Since the annexation of the Turkic regions of central Asia in the nineteenth century, the Czarist and

---

43. William Rogers Brubaker, ed., "Introduction," in Brubaker, *Immigration and the Politics of Citizenship in Europe and North America*, p. 8.
44. Concern over colonization, it should be noted, can also be an internal affair in multi-ethnic societies. Territorially-based ethnic groups may consider an influx of people from other parts of the country as a cultural and political threat. Hence, the Moros in Mindanao revolted at the in-migration of people from other parts of the Philippines, Sri Lanka's Tamils oppose settlement by Sinhalese in "their" region, Nicaragua Miskito Indians object to the migration of non-Miskito peoples into "their" territory on the Atlantic coast, and a variety of India's linguistic communities regard in-migration as a form of colonization. In some cases such settlements can provoke an internal conflict between migrants and indigenes, with international consequences.

Soviet regimes have encouraged Russian settlement, while a similar policy of settling Han people has been pursued by the Chinese government in Sinkiang province and other areas.

Many governments are concerned that migration may lead to xenophobic popular sentiments and to the rise of anti-migrant political parties that could threaten the regime. Under such circumstances governments may pursue anti-migration policies in anticipation of public reactions.

MIGRANTS PERCEIVED AS A SOCIAL OR ECONOMIC BURDEN

Societies may react to immigrants because of the economic costs they impose or because of their purported social behavior such as criminality, welfare dependency, delinquency, etc. Societies may be concerned because the people entering are so numerous or so poor that they create a substantial economic burden by straining housing, education, and transportation facilities. In advanced industrial societies, services provided by the welfare state to migrant workers, permanent migrants, or refugees may generate local resentment. In less developed countries, refugees may illegally occupy private or government lands; their goats, sheep, and cattle may decimate forests and grazing land; they may use firewood, consume water, produce waste, and in other ways come to be regarded as an ecological threat. The willingness to bear these costs is likely to be low if the host government believes that the government of the sending country is engaged in a policy of population "dumping," by exporting its criminals, unwanted ethnic minorities, and "surplus" population at the cost of the receiving country. The United States, for example, distinguished between those Cubans who fled the Communist regime in the 1960s, whom it welcomed, and Cuban convicts removed from prisons and placed on boats for the United States in the 1970s, whom it did not.[45] After the 1947 partition, India accepted Hindus from Pakistan who preferred to live in India, but regarded as destabilizing and threatening the forced exodus of East Pakistanis in the early 1970s, which India saw as a Pakistani effort to turn West Pakistan into the majority province by "dumping" East Pakistanis into India. Governments also distinguish between situ-

---

45. For an account of the history of Cuban migration to the United States from 1959 until the Mariel boatlift in 1980, see Gil Loescher and John A. Scanlan, "U.S. Foreign Policy, 1959–1980: Impact on Refugee Flow from Cuba," *Annals*, Vol. 467 (May 1983), pp. 114–137. Also see Jorge I. Domínguez, "Immigration as Foreign Policy in U.S.-Latin American Relations," in Tucker, Keely, and Wrigley, *Immigration and U.S. Foreign Policy*; and Felix Roberto Masud-Piloto, *With Open Arms: Cuban Migration to the United States* (Totowa, N.J.: Rowman and Littlefield, 1988).

ations in which ethnic minorities are permitted to leave (e.g., Jews from the Soviet Union) and those from which minorities are forced to flee (e.g., Bulgarian Turks or Sri Lankan Tamils), and are therefore more likely to accept the former than the latter.

In the eighteenth and nineteenth centuries, several European governments promoted emigration as a way of easing the social and political burdens that might result from poverty and crime. It has been estimated that between 1788 and 1868 England exiled 160,000 of its criminals to Australia as a convenient way to get rid of prisoners and reduce the costs of maintaining prisons.[46] In the middle of the nineteenth century, the British regarded emigration as a form of famine relief for Ireland. In seven famine years, from 1849 to 1856, one and a half million Irish emigrated, mostly across the Atlantic.[47] In Germany, from which 1,500,000 emigrated between 1871 and 1881, local officials believed that "a large body of indigent subjects constitute a social danger and a serious burden on meager public funds; better let them go."[48] Reacting to these policies, one American scholar wrote in 1890 that "there is something almost revolting in the anxiety of certain countries to get rid of their surplus population and to escape the burden of supporting the poor, the helpless and the depraved."[49] His reaction foreshadowed some of the popular concerns over Third World migration that grew in Western Europe in the latter part of this century.

The fears of western countries notwithstanding, however, population dumping has not been a significant element in the flow of migrants from the Third World to advanced industrial countries. To the extent that population dumping has occurred, it has largely been of ethnic minorities; flights—at least before the Yugoslav crisis—have primarily been to neighboring developing countries rather than to advanced industrial countries.

Forced population movements of ethnic minorities took place in Eastern Europe during the interwar period, placing enormous economic and social strains upon the receiving countries, taking a heavy toll upon the migrants themselves, and worsening relations among states. But because there was

---

46. Robert Hughes, *The Fatal Shore* (New York: Knopf, 1987).

47. H.J.M. Jonston, *British Emigration Policy 1815–1830: Shovelling out Paupers* (Oxford, UK: Clarendon Press, 1972).

48. Mack Walker, *Germany and the Emigration 1860–1885* (Cambridge: Harvard University Press, 1964).

49. Richmond Mayo-Smith, *Emigration and Immigration: A Study in Social Science* (New York: Charles Scribner and Sons, 1890); reprinted 1986, pp. 197–198.

an element of exchange, and minorities moved to states in which their ethnic community was a majority, settlement was possible and violent international conflict was avoided. In 1922–23 Greeks fled Turkey and Turks fled Greece. An estimated 1.5 million people from both nations were involved. In a related population exchange, in 1923 the Greek government, in an effort to Hellenize its Macedonian region, forced the exodus of its Bulgarian population. As the Bulgarian refugees moved into Greek-speaking areas of Bulgaria, the local Greek population fled southward to Greece.[50] The world's largest population exchange was in South Asia, where fourteen million people moved between India and Pakistan between 1947 and 1950. But since both countries respected the wishes of each other's ethnic minorities to settle in the country in which they constituted a majority, the exchange took place without causing a conflict between the two countries.[51] Similarly, the forced exit of Jews from North Africa to Israel in the 1950s was not a source of international conflict, since the refugees were welcomed by Israel. In contrast, however, the flight of Arabs from Israel in 1948 led to an interminable conflict between Israel and its Arab neighbors since the Arab states did not recognize the legitimacy of the new state.[52]

Government officials, otherwise concerned with the plight of refugees, may fear that a decision to grant refugee status to a small number of individuals might open the floodgate beyond what society is prepared to accept. One reason states hesitate to grant refugee and asylum status to those fleeing because of economic and even violent conditions at home—as distinct from having a personal "well-founded fear of persecution"—is the concern that the number of asylum requests would then increase. States prefer restrictive criteria in order to keep the influx small. Since laws of asylum are often imprecise and the policy that states will admit refugees with a well-founded fear of persecution is subject to varied interpretations, individuals who wish to enter a country but cannot do so under existing guestworker and migration laws may resort to claiming political asylum. Western European governments are thus torn between a humanitarian sentiment toward refugees and the

---

50. Michael R. Marrus, *The Unwanted: European Refugees in the Twentieth Century* (New York: Oxford University Press, 1985).
51. The population exchange proved to be violent, as the various communities slaughtered one another. However, it was neither the exchange nor the killings that led to war between India and Pakistan. The Indo-Pakistan war of 1947–48 was over the disputed territory of Kashmir.
52. Benny Morris, *The Birth of the Palestinian Refugee Problem, 1947–1949* (Cambridge: Cambridge University Press, 1987).

recognition that the more generous the law of asylum, the greater the number of applicants. As the number of asylum-seekers grows, governments become more restrictive, insisting on evidence that the individual does indeed have a well-founded fear of persecution, not "merely" a fear of being killed in a violent civil conflict. A major increase in asylum applications to Switzerland in 1986 and 1987, for example, led to passage of a referendum imposing a ceiling on the number of entries under the laws of asylum. In recent years Western Europe has become more restrictive as the requests for asylum have increased. Policy makers argue that to admit even a small number of refugees who enter because of political conditions or violence at home would be to open the door to larger numbers than their society is prepared to admit.

MIGRANTS AS HOSTAGES: RISKS FOR THE SENDING COUNTRY
Recent actions of the governments of Iran, Iraq, and Libya all demonstrate how migrants can be used as an instrument of statecraft in order to impose restraints upon the actions of the home government. Following the invasion of Kuwait on August 2, 1990, the government of Iraq announced a series of measures using migrants as instruments for the achievement of political objectives. The Iraqis declared that Westerners living in Iraq and Kuwait would be forcibly held as a shield against armed attack, in an effort to deter the United States and its allies from launching airstrikes against military facilities where hostages might be located. The Iraqi government then indicated its willingness to treat the migrants of those countries that did not send troops to Saudi Arabia, such as India, more favorably than the migrants of those countries that did, such as Pakistan and Bangladesh. The Iraqi government subsequently declared that food would not be provided for Asian migrants (including Indians) unless their countries sent food supplies and medicines in violation of the United Nations embargo.

While the Iraqi strategy of using their control over migrants for international bargaining is thus far unique, the mere presence of migrants in a country from which they could be expelled has been for some time an element affecting the behavior of the migrants' home country. Since the late 1970s the countries of South Asia have been aware of their dependence upon migration to the Gulf and have recognized that any sudden influx of returning migrants would create a major problem for domestic security as remittances came to an end, balance of payments problems were created, families dependent upon migrant income were threatened with destitution, and large numbers of people were thrown into labor markets where there already existed substantial unemployment. Since the Gulf War, all of these fears have materialized. Sending governments aware of these potential consequences have hesitated to criticize host governments for the treatment of migrant workers.[53] When workers have been expelled for strikes and other agitational activities, the home governments have sought to pacify their migrants—and the host government—in an effort to avoid further expulsions. Governments have often remained silent even when workers' contracts have been violated. Thus, the understandable reaction of some governments with migrants in Kuwait and Iraq was to see first whether it was possible for their migrants to remain, and to assure the security of their citizens, rather than to support international efforts against Iraqi aggression.

More recently there were reports that Libya threatened to expel migrants of any home government that voted for the UN Security Council resolution invoking sanctions against Libya for its failure to extradite two men accused of terrorism in the Pan American flight which fell over Lockerbie, Scotland. The target of Libya's threat was clearly Egypt, which had one million citizens working and living in Libya.

A security threat, as Robert Jervis has reminded us, is often a matter of perception.[54] What are the enemy's capabilities? What are its intentions? Perceptions similarly shape decision-makers' assessments of whether refugees and migrants constitute a security threat. Time and again we have seen how different are the assessments that various governments make of the threat posed by a population influx. With the rise of anti-migrant right wing parties in France, Germany, Italy, Switzerland, and elsewhere in Europe, European governments have virtually halted migration and made entry difficult for refugees from Third World countries; in contrast, the United States, Canada, and Australia, all traditional immigration countries, have strong pro-immigrant constituencies that have sustained pro-immigration policies even in the midst of substantial unemployment.[55] Moreover, perceptions of

53. For a description of working conditions of South Asian migrants in the Persian Gulf, and the reluctance of South Asian governments to protest the mistreatment of migrants, see Myron Weiner, "International Migration and Development: Indians in the Persian Gulf," *Population and Development Review*, Vol. 8, No. 1 (March 1988), pp. 1–36. For accounts of the benefits to Asian countries of migration to the Gulf see Godfrey Gunatilleke, ed., *Migration of Asian Workers to the Arab World* (Tokyo: United Nations University, 1986); and Rashid Amjad, ed., *To the Gulf and Back: Studies in the Economic Impact of Asian Labour Migration* (Geneva: International Labor Organization, 1989).
54. Robert Jervis, *Perception and Misperception in International Politics* (Princeton: Princeton University Press, 1976).
55. These countries have their anti-immigrant sentiments as well. Patrick Buchanan, candidate

risk change. Prior to the invasion by Iraq, Kuwait had a larger number of guest workers than native workers, yet did not feel insecure in their presence. But as a result of the invasion and the support to Iraq reportedly given by some migrant communities, the government and citizens of Kuwait now have a different assessment of the political risks of foreign workers and are concerned both with their numbers and national origin. Moreover, a country's concern that a refugee influx is the result of population "dumping" by its neighbor—clearly a matter of perception of intentions—is likely to be greatest when there is a history of enmity between sending and receiving countries, as in the case of Pakistan and India. Countries almost always feel threatened if their neighbor seeks to create a more homogeneous society by expelling its minorities—the phrase now is "ethnic cleansing"[56]—but we have also seen that there can be circumstances when a population "exchange" or an orderly "return" of an ethnic minority can be regarded as non-threatening by the receiving country.

How governments assess one another's intentions with respect both to economic migrants and political refugees is thus critical to how conflictual population movements may become. A government is more likely to accommodate a refugee flow from a neighboring country if it believes that the flight is the unfortunate and unintended consequences of a civil conflict than if it believes that the flight of the refugees is precisely what is intended.[57] Similarly, a government's response to reports that its citizens abroad are maltreated will depend upon whether it believes that the host country is culpable.

But perception is not everything. As we have seen, there are genuine conflicts of interests among countries on matters of migrants and refugees.

---

for president in the 1992 Republican primaries, was opposed to migration, particularly for what he regarded as its impact on employment and on welfare. The Australian debate is more pertinent to this article for its focus on the security dimensions of migration: Australian advocates of migration have argued that Australia's security is improved by opening its doors to migrants from Asia; opponents have been concerned with multiculturalism and population growth. See Katharine Betts, *Ideology and Immigration: Australia 1976 to 1987* (Victoria: Melbourne University Press, 1988); and Robert Birrell, Douglas Hill, and Jon Nevill, eds., *Populate and Perish? The Stresses of Population Growth in Australia* (Sidney: Fontana/Australian Conservation Foundation, 1984).

56. The older expression "unmixing of peoples" was reportedly used by Lord Curzon to describe the situation during the Balkan Wars; Marrus, *The Unwanted*, p. 41.

57. The European community stiffened its views toward Serbia when it became clear that Serbs were seeking to force the exodus of Croatians and Bosnians; many German officials then concluded that their willingness to accommodate refugees was enabling the Serbs to achieve their objective of clearing areas of non-Serbs.

Countries quarrel over each other's entry and exit rules as some countries want those whom another will not let go, while some countries force out those whom others do not want.[58] How states react to international population flows can itself be a source of international conflict.

State Responses to Population Movements

How do states react when they are confronted with an unwanted population influx, either of economic migrants or of refugees? For the foreseeable future the numbers of people who wish to leave or are forced to leave their countries will continue to exceed substantially the numbers that other countries are willing to accept. What strategies are available to states confronted with a rising demand for entrance? One possible response is to increase immigration. For many industrial countries, migration is advantageous, providing more young people to offset low national birthrates, manpower for service sector jobs that local people do not want, skilled manpower for labor-short occupations, and new investments by energetic, entrepreneurial newcomers. "The absorptive capacity of West European countries," wrote *The Economist*, "though not as great as that of America or Australia, is still bigger than timid people think. European politicians who run scared of racist or anti-immigrant feeling will be doing their countries no favours. Their guiding principle as they map out Europe's immigration plans should not be 'How few can we get away with letting in?', but rather, 'How many can we possibly take without creating unbearable social strain?'"[59]

But even countries that are relatively open to economic migrants and to refugees will not be able to admit all who want to enter. Sealing borders is one response, but rarely wholly effective even in the case of islands. Control is difficult for any country with large coastlines or land borders. Regulation of employers (including penalties for employing illegals) and the use of identity cards has made a difference in the countries of Western Europe, but is not a useful option for a country with large numbers of small firms, a poorly developed administrative structure, and officials who are easily cor-

---

58. For an analysis of how the congruence or incongruence of rules of entry and exit influence the patterns of conflict and cooperation among states, see Myron Weiner, "On International Migration and International Relations," *Population and Development Review*, Vol. 11, No. 3 (September 1985), pp. 441–455.

59. *Economist*, "The Would-be Europeans," August 4, 1990, p. 15. The *Economist* adds, "For West Europeans it will be easier to absorb East Europeans than North Africans."

rupted. Moreover, however opposed the government and a majority of the population are to illegal migration, there are often elements within the society who welcome refugees and migrant workers: employers, ethnic kinfolk, political sympathizers, or officials willing to accept bribes. Finally, even if a country is able to fine-tune the number and characteristics of the economic migrants it admits, how can it cope with a massive influx of refugees in flight from a neighboring country?

Faced with unwanted flows whose entrance they cannot control, governments have increasingly turned to strategies for halting emigration.[60] We can identify three such strategies.

The first is to pay to avoid what one does not want. It has been suggested that an infusion of aid and investment, an improvement in trade, the resolution of the debt crisis, and other measures that would improve income and unemployment in low-income countries would reduce the rate of emigration. Meritorious as these proposals are, there is no evidence that they can reduce emigration in the short run. Indeed, high rates of emigration have often been associated with high economic growth rates. It was so for Great Britain in the nineteenth century, and in recent years for South Korea, Taiwan, Turkey, Algeria, and Greece. Only after an extended period of economic growth and a significant rise in wages do we see a substantial reduction in pressures for emigration.[61] Economic aid, however, may not be intended to remedy a country's high unemployment or low economic growth rate, but rather as payment to a government to halt a refugee flow. As noted earlier, United States economic assistance to Haiti halted a growing refugee flow (although

---

60. For a somewhat different view than is presented here, arguing that the challenge of migration can best be dealt with as part of dealing with other global issues, see Jonas Widgren, "International Migration and Regional Stability," *International Affairs,* Vol. 66, No. 4 (October 1990), pp. 749–766: "The long-term solutions to the migration challenge are the same as those outlined for all the other burning global problems that we face: stabilizing world population at a reasonable level, reinstalling human rights, reinforcing democracy, peacefully settling regional conflicts, halting environmental degradation, allowing for continued economic growth, abolishing trade protectionism, alleviating poverty, relieving the debt burden, increasing sound development aid, strengthening UN cooperation—and in general maintaining peace, regionally and globally" (p. 766). To the extent states regard migration and refugee flows as threats to their security, more direct and immediate measures will be taken.
61. For an attempt to deal with the relationship between migration, investment, and trade, see *Authorized Migration: An Economic Development Response* (Washington, D.C.: Report of The Commission for the Study of International Migration and Cooperative Economic Development, 1990). The bipartisan Commission, created by Congress in the Immigration Reform and Control Act of 1986, concluded that "any serious cooperative effort to reduce migratory pressure at their source must be pursued over decades, even in the face of intermediate contrary results" (p. xvi).

it resumed again in early 1992, following a coup); similarly, the flow of Sri Lankan refugees to West Germany from East Germany was reduced when the Federal Republic of Germany agreed to provide credits to the German Democratic Republic. In the Haitian case, government-to-government aid was intended by the donor country to persuade the recipient of the aid to halt the exodus; in the German case, the aid was intended to persuade the recipient of the aid to cease providing transit to unwanted refugees.

Assistance can also be used by governments to persuade other governments to retain refugees. Thus, the United States and France have been willing to provide economic assistance to Thailand if the Thais would hold Vietnamese refugees rather than permit these refugees to seek entrance into the United States and France.[62] The United Nations High Commission for Refugees and other international agencies, largely financed by the West and Japan, provide resources to refugee receiving countries—especially in Africa—not only as an expression of humanitarian concerns, but also as a means of enabling refugees to remain in the country of first asylum rather than attempting to move elsewhere, such as to advanced industrial countries.[63] International financial support has also been important in inducing refugees to return home when a conflict subsides. Funds for transportation, resettlement, and mine clearance are often critical for a successful speedy repatriation process.

Secondly, where generosity does not work or is not financially feasible, receiving countries may employ a variety of threats to halt emigration. Diplomatic pressures, including coercive diplomacy, may be exerted. The Indian government, for example, pressured the government of Bangladesh to halt Bangladeshi land settlement in the Chittagong Hill tracts, which had led local Chakma tribals to flee into India. The Indian government is in a position to damage Bangladeshi trade and to affect the flow of river waters if the Bangladesh government is not accommodating. When Burmese Muslim refugees

---

62. John R. Rogge, "Thailand's Refugee Policy: Some Thoughts on Its Origin and Future Direction," in Howard Adelman and C. Michael Lanphier, ed., *Refuge or Asylum: A Choice for Canada* (Toronto: York Lanes Press, 1990), pp. 150–171. Rogge describes how the Thais came to regard the influx from Vietnam as a security threat (pp. 162–163).

63. In 1991–92 the United States sought to use its financial leverage to induce the government of Israel not to settle Soviet Jews on the West Bank, arguing that the settlement policy was damaging to the peace negotiations between Israel, the Palestinians, and Israel's neighboring Arab states. The Israeli Labor Party's opposition to settlements, and the implication that the suspension of settlements would lead the United States to provide guarantees for $10 billion in bank loans, may have been a factor in the Labor victory. See Bar-llan, "Why Likud Lost—And Who Won," p. 28.

moved from the Arakan region of Burma into Bangladesh as a result of a Burmese government policy of settling non-Muslim Burmese in Arakan, the Bangladesh government threatened to arm the Burmese Muslim refugees if settlement was not halted. In both cases the threats worked to reduce or, for a while, halt the flow. In another example, the Arab League representative to the United Nations argued that the influx of Soviet Jews into Israel could constitute a threat to international peace and security under the UN charter.[64] Palestinians threatened international carriers who agreed to carry Soviet Jews to Israel, an instance of intervention by a third party which did not want an unimpeded flow between a sending and receiving country.

Coercive diplomacy to induce a country to halt actions that are forcing people to flee may be more effective when there are collective international sanctions. But thus far it has been exceedingly difficult for counties burdened by refugee flows to persuade the international community that sanctions should be imposed on the country producing the refugees.

Thirdly, there is the extreme sanction of armed intervention to change the political conditions within the sending country. In 1971 an estimated ten million refugees fled from East Pakistan to India following the outbreak of a civil war between the eastern and western provinces of Pakistan. This refugee flow was regarded by India as the result of a deliberate policy by the Pakistan military to resolve Pakistan's own internal political problems by forcing East Pakistan's Hindu population into India. Many Indian officials believed that the Pakistan government was seeking to change the demographic balance in favor of West Pakistan by shifting millions of East Pakistanis to India. The Indian government responded by sending its armed forces into Pakistan; its occupation of East Pakistan forced the partition of the country, and within months India had sent the refugees home.

In two other instances in South Asia, armed support for refugees was an instrument of policy by the receiving country. The Pakistani government armed some of the three million Afghan refugees who entered Pakistan following the April 1978 communist coup in Kabul and the subsequent Soviet invasion of Afghanistan in December 1979. The aim of the Pakistan government was for the armed Afghans to force a Soviet withdrawal, bring down the Soviet-supported Communist regime, and repatriate the refugees. The other instance of intervention was the initial Indian support for the Tamil

---

64. *New York Times,* February 8, 1990.

Tigers, a militant group fighting against the Sri Lankan government. The Indian government supported Tamil Tiger refugees in India and enabled arms to flow into Sri Lanka in an effort to force a political settlement between the Tamils and the Sri Lankan government, but the result was that the ethnic conflict worsened and the refugee exodus continued, prompting direct intervention by the Indian military.

The high level of threat or violence among the countries of South Asia to deal with unwanted refugee flows may foreshadow similar behavior elsewhere. The factors at work in South Asia include the ethnic affinity between the migrants and the people of the region into which they have migrated (a factor affecting the decision of refugees to flee and also increasing the anger of the receiving population), the adversarial relationship among some of the countries in the region, the porosity of borders, and the lack of administrative, military, and political capacity to enforce rules of entry. Faced with large unwanted population movements whose entry they cannot control, governments in the region have looked for ways to influence the exit policies of their neighbors.

The Kurdish revolt in Iraq after the Gulf war provides another example of the use of force to deal with an unwanted refugee flow. As Kurdish refugees entered Turkey, the government of Turkey made clear its unwillingness to add to its own Kurdish population and used its troops to seal the borders. The United States, Great Britain, and other allies in the war used their military power to force Iraq to place the Kurdish region under allied protection; the intervention enabled an estimated 1.5 million Kurds who had fled to Iran and Turkey to return, and the Kurds to form their own government.[65]

With the outbreak of war among the successor states of Yugoslavia, and a large outpouring of Croatian and Bosnian refugees to Germany, Hungary, Austria, and other former Yugoslav states, there were calls for armed intervention by NATO or by the United Nations.[66]

---

65. Allied intervention to protect the Kurds is a rare instance of a UN-sanctioned military intervention to protect a minority within a country. For a useful account of the history of the efforts by the Kurds to create a state of their own, see Gerard Chaliand, ed., *People Without a Country: The Kurds and Kurdistan* (London: Zed Press, 1980). The Kurds have reportedly created their own government in the territory within the allied protected security zone; "Kurds Creating a Country on the Hostile Soil of Iraq," *New York Times*, August 12, 1992, p. 1.
66. For useful brief historical as well as contemporary accounts of refugee movements throughout the Balkans, see Minority Rights Group, *Minorities in the Balkans*, Report No. 82 (London: Minority Rights Group, October 1989).

In each of these instances the high profile and highly conflictual nature of population movements has affected which institutions make exit and entry rules and engage in international negotiations. Decisions on such matters have come to be dealt with, not by ministries of labor, border control officials, or the courts, but at the highest levels of government, in the foreign and defense ministries, the security and intelligence agencies, and by heads of government. The very form and intensity of response to unwanted migrations is itself an indication that such population flows are regarded as threats to security or stability. These responses also suggest that states do not regard refugee flows and emigration as purely an internal matter, despite the assertions of the United Nations and other international agencies that countries do not have the right to interfere in the internal affairs of states that produce refugees, even when there is a perceived threat to the security and stability of countries upon whom the burden of unwanted refugees falls.

While the notion of sovereignty is still rhetorically recognized, a variety of "internal" actions by states are increasingly regarded as threats by other states. Thus, the spewing of nuclear waste and other hazardous materials into the atmosphere and the contamination of waterways which then flow into other countries is no longer regarded as an internal matter. In the same spirit, a country that forces its citizens to leave or creates conditions which induce them to leave has internationalized its internal actions.

A conundrum for Western liberal democratic regimes, however, is that they are reluctant to insist that governments restrain the exit of citizens simply because they or others are unwilling to accept them. Western liberal democracies believe in the right of emigration by individuals, but they simultaneously believe that governments retain the right to determine who and how many shall be permitted to enter. Liberal regimes may encourage or even threaten countries that produce refugees and unwanted immigrants in an effort to change the conditions that induce or force people to leave, but they are often reluctant to press governments to prevent people from leaving, or to force people to return home against their will. They do not want regimes to prevent political dissidents or persecuted minorities from leaving their country; rather, they want governments to stop their repression.

Advanced industrial countries that admit immigrants prefer an immigration policy that creates the fewest domestic or international political problems. One policy option is to admit those who best satisfy the requirements of the receiving country: those who have skills needed in the labor market, or capital to create new businesses, or relatives who would facilitate their integration into the society.[67] But a limited, largely skill-based immigration policy for Western Europe or the United States would still leave large numbers of people banging on the doors, seeking to enter as refugees or, failing that, as illegals.

An alternative policy based upon the needs of immigrants and refugees, though morally more attractive, is more difficult to formulate, more difficult to implement, and legally and politically more contentious. But no policy, short of the obliteration of international boundaries and sovereign states, can deal with the vast numbers of people who want to leave their country for another where opportunities are greater and life is safer. A moral case can be made for giving preference to those in flight, even at the cost of limiting the number of immigrants admitted to meet labor needs or to enable families to reunite. If countries have a ceiling on the number of people they are willing to admit, there is a strong moral argument for providing admissions first to those who are persecuted or whose lives are in danger, and have few places to go. But for reasons indicated above, only a narrow definition of what constitutes a refugee, with a case-by-case review, will enable states to put a cap on what they regard as potentially unlimited flows.

As a matter of political realism, then, a significant increase in the flow of refugees or of unwanted illegal economic migrants is likely to lead the governments of population-receiving countries to consider various forms of intervention to change the domestic factors that force or induce people to leave their homeland. If a people violate the boundaries of a neighboring country, then they and their government should expect others to intervene in their internal affairs.

---

67. See Ben J. Wittenberg and Karl Zinsmeister, "The Case for More Immigration," *Commentary*, Vol. 89, No. 4 (1990), 19–25; and Simon, *The Economic Consequences of Immigration*.

A Surplus of Men, A Deficit of Peace

Valerie M. Hudson and Andrea Den Boer

Security and Sex Ratios in Asia's Largest States

International security and stability rest in large measure on the internal security of nations. Analysts have long examined factors such as arms transfers and ethnic violence in this regard, but the list now includes variables that were not traditionally viewed as related to national security. Unemployment rates, water tables and river flows, infant mortality, migration patterns, infectious disease epidemiology, and a whole host of other variables that tap into the general stability of a society are now understood to affect security. To understand the long-term security dynamics of a region, one must inquire into what Thomas Homer-Dixon and others have termed the "environmental security" of the nations therein.[1]

Our own research is surely located in that field of inquiry, yet we contemplate a variable that has been by and large neglected even by scholars of environmental security. One overlooked wellspring of insecurity, we argue, is exaggerated gender inequality. Security scholarship is theoretically and empirically impoverished to the extent that it fails to inquire into the relationship between violence against women and violence within and between societies. We believe that our research demonstrates that the long-term security trajectory of a region is affected by this relationship.

Admittedly, there is probably no society in which women do not experience some gender inequality, meaning subordinate status or inferior treatment in political, legal, social, or economic matters. Indeed, what would constitute a perfect society between men and women is a controversial topic with which we are not concerned here. However, *exaggerated* gender inequality is hard to miss: We define it to be present when, because of gender, one child is allowed to live while another is actively or passively killed.[2] Offspring sex

Valerie M. Hudson is Professor of Political Science at Brigham Young University and a faculty affiliate of the David M. Kennedy Center for International and Area Studies. Her research centers on foreign policy decisionmaking, national security policy, and the international political economy of gender. Andrea Den Boer is currently completing her Ph.D. at the University of Kent at Canterbury in England. Her research explores the relationship between identity, community, justice, and violence as found in the writings of the philosopher Emmanuel Levinas. This article contains an abridgment of material found in the authors' book manuscript, "Bare Branches: Causes and Consequences of the Masculinization of Asia's Sex Ratios."

1. Thomas F. Homer-Dixon, *Environment, Scarcity, and Violence* (Princeton, N.J.: Princeton University Press, 1999).
2. "Passive killing" refers to such phenomena as withholding food from a newborn or abandoning a newborn in the wild. Though not an active killing, such as smothering a child, the intent to kill is clear, and so is termed passive killing.

selection,[3] almost universally used to favor male offspring, indicates that the life of a female in the society is not only not valued but actually despised. There can be no greater evidence of the extremely unequal and subordinate status of women in a society than the presence of prevalent offspring sex selection therein.

If violence against women within a society bears any relationship to violence within and between societies, then it should be possible to see that relationship at work in societies where violence against women is exaggerated—that is, where offspring sex selection is prevalent. Specifically, internal instability is heightened in nations displaying exaggerated gender inequality, leading to an altered security calculus for the state. Possibilities of meaningful democracy and peaceful foreign policy are diminished as a result.

We first quantify the scale on which sex ratios are being altered in Asia, then estimate the number of resulting surplus young adult males currently present in Asia's two largest states, China and India, as well as projected to the year 2020. Next, we discuss behavioral syndromes associated with surplus young adult male groups, and investigate the role of such groups in instability and violence within and between societies in several historical cases. Finally, we ask whether these same phenomena are beginning to be seen in China and India today, and raise broader issues of governance and foreign policy in high sex-ratio societies.

Modern Prevalence of Offspring Sex Selection

The practice of offspring sex selection can be found in a large variety of historical cultures from all continents. In virtually all cases, the selection was in favor of male infants. Here we concentrate on the modern incidence of offspring sex selection and seek to quantify its scale.

Two statistics set the stage for our discussion: the birth sex ratio and the overall sex ratio. Normal birth sex ratios range between 105 and 107 male births per 100 female births. This normal range holds across racial groups, though there may be some parental age-related or diet-related variations within such groups. The overall sex ratio (i.e., the sex ratio across all ages) tends toward 1:1 or less, reflecting a combination of increased female mortality from childbearing, but longer female life span.

---

3. Offspring sex selection should not to be confused with the term "sex selection" as used by evolutionary biologists to refer to the calculus by which males and females choose mates; "offspring sex selection" refers to the selective rearing of children based on sex. Female infanticide and sex-selective abortion are two examples of offspring sex selection.

OVERALL SEX RATIOS

Ansley Coale suggests that the sex ratio for a stationary population (as determined by Western model life tables) is between 97.9 and 100.3 males per 100 females.[4] (In the remainder of the article, the ratio is expressed as the number of males per 100 females—that is, 105:100 is rendered as 105 and the "100" should be assumed after each such number throughout the article.) A population with a young age structure may have a slightly higher overall sex ratio than a population with an older age structure. Table 1 provides sex ratios for overall populations by continent.

As Table 1 shows, the sex ratio favors the male population only in Oceania (slightly) and in Asia. A glance at overall sex ratios and population sizes for each country in Asia indicates that the highest sex ratios are found in Afghanistan, Bangladesh, Bhutan, Brunei, China, India, the Maldives, Nepal, Pakistan, and Taiwan. The large populations found in several of these countries mean that the majority of "missing" females can be attributed to them.

Examining the seven countries listed in Table 2, we find that from 66 to 86 million of the missing females in Asia are attributable to them alone, with two countries in particular contributing the majority of missing females due to their high sex ratios and large population size: China and India together contribute between 62 and 68 million of the missing females in Asia. This is, however, but a rough estimation of the effects of sex-selective abortion, female infanticide, differential mortality rates, and other discriminatory practices against females. More than a decade ago, Amartya Sen asserted that the number of missing Asian females had already surpassed 100 million.[5]

BIRTH SEX RATIOS

Birth sex ratios are a very valuable piece of information but are sometimes difficult to obtain. They are also relatively unreliable for several reasons. First, birth registration in very large or predominantly rural countries may not be accurate because of the number of births occurring outside of a hospital. Indeed, for this very reason some nations do not even report a birth sex ratio. Second, birth sex ratios may be highly politicized and subject to bureaucratic "adjustment" in some cultures. Third, birth sex ratios may mask troubling phenomena. For example, though the 1992 overall birth sex ratio for South Korea was

---

4. Ansley Coale, "Excess Female Mortality and the Balance of the Sexes in the Population: An Estimate of the Number of 'Missing Females,'" *Population and Development Review*, Vol. 17, No. 3 (September 1991), p. 518.
5. Amartya Sen, "More Than 100 Million Women Are Missing," *New York Review of Books*, December 20, 1990, pp. 61–66.

Table 1. Overall Sex Ratios by Continent, 2001.

Continent	Male Population	Female Population	Overall Sex Ratio
Africa	411,253,443	411,986,267	99.8
Asia	1,907,090,382	1,829,783,975	104.2
Europe	351,404,742	377,571,861	93.1
North America	239,028,087	247,004,746	96.8
Oceania	15,563,506	15,473,003	100.6
South America	173,486,299	177,333,047	97.8

SOURCE: U.S. Bureau of the Census, *International Data Base,* IDB Aggregation, Table 094, http://www.census.gov/ipc/www/idbnew.html/.

reported as an abnormally high 114, the sex ratio for fourth children born in that same year was an astounding 228.6.[6] Another example is that birth sex ratios may be lower than the sex ratios of early childhood. In India the birth sex ratio is reported to be 111–114; however, the sex ratio for ages 0–6 has dropped precipitously in the last ten years, and in some states the early childhood sex ratio is higher than the reported birth sex ratio. In Punjab, for example, the 0–6 sex ratio is now greater than 126, while its birth sex ratio is reported to be 122.8. Despite the incomplete picture afforded by birth sex ratios, we present such information as we have on the countries of Asia in Table 3.

All of the birth sex ratios for the countries listed in Table 3 are significantly higher than the 105–107 range considered normal across racial groups. Though in times past, methods of offspring sex selection included active and passive female infanticide, for these birth sex ratios to hold, prenatal offspring sex selection favoring males must be widespread. Indeed the evidence suggests that such is the case. Even accounting for underregistration and adoption of females, the skewness of these sex ratios is very real and is worsening over time. Tradition can be a stubborn force, slow to die or change. Laws on the books may simply be ignored in favor of misogynist tradition. Although prenatal sex tests are illegal in China, and in most states in India, such testing is nevertheless ubiquitous in both nations. Sex-selective abortion is illegal in both China and India, as, of course, is infanticide. As one scholar notes, "The sudden increases in sex ratios in East Asian societies are impressive—in each country,

6. Chai Bin Park and Nam-Hoon Cho, "Consequences of Son Preference in a Low-Fertility Society: Imbalance of the Sex Ratio at Birth in Korea," *Population and Development Review,* Vol. 21, No. 1 (March 1995), p. 66, Table 6.

Table 2. Selected Asian Countries and Missing Female Populations, 2001.

Country	Male Population	Female Population	Actual Sex Ratio	Coale's Expected Sex Ratio	Calculated Missing Females Assuming Coale's Ratio	Modern Expected Sex Ratio	Calculated Missing Females Assuming Modern Expected Ratio
Afghanistan	13,814,607	12,998,450	106.3	103.0	413,790	100.0	816,157
Bangladesh	67,372,369	63,897,491	105.4	102.5	1,831,649	100.0	3,474,878
China	653,550,000	612,280,000	106.7	101.0	34,799,200	100.0	40,635,000
India	508,625,036	471,516,674	107.2	102.0	27,135,322	100.0	37,108,362
Nepal	12,135,861	11,562,560	105.0	102.5	277,304	100.0	573,301
Pakistan	69,232,082	65,903,113	105.1	102.5	1,640,382	100.0	3,328,969
Taiwan	11,237,506	10,670,629	105.3	101.0	455,615	100.0	566,877
Total					**66,553,262**		**86,498,544**

SOURCES: All figures are from the U.S. Bureau of the Census, International Data Base, with the exception of the sex ratio figure for India, which has been taken from the 2001 census, *Provisional Population Totals: India, Census of India, 2001,* Paper 1, http://www.censusindia.net/results (and the number of females in the population, as well as total population, has then been determined by this sex ratio), and the sex ratio for China, which was taken from "Major Figures of the 2000 Population Census," National Bureau of Statistics, People's Republic of China, March 28, 2001.

Table 3. Reported Birth Sex Ratios for Selected Asian Nations.

Country	Reported Birth Sex Ratio	Year and Source of Information
China	121.0	1993 and 1994 State Family Planning Commission of China, *Zhongguo shengyu nianjin, 1996* [China birth planning yearbook, 1996]
	113.8–115.4	1989–90, Zeng et al., 1993
	115.62	1994.10.1–1995.9.30; State Statistical Bureau of China (SSB) (1.04 percent sample)
	116.57	October 1, 1995, SSB (1.04 percent sample)
	118.65	April 1, 1995, SSB (1.04 percent sample)
	120.0	1999, Chinese Academy of Social Sciences
	131–400	Anecdotal reports for particular regions/towns by journalists and scholars, 1995–2000
Taiwan	110.2	1990, Gu and Roy, 1995
South Korea	109.6	2001, National Statistical Office of South Korea, July 2001
	114.0	1990, Park and Cho, 1995
	116.9	1992, Park and Cho, 1995
	117.9	1990, first births only, Park and Cho, 1995
India	111.0	1996–98, SRS data, reported in Premi, 2001
	113.7	1993–95, Jhunjhunwala, 2001
	112.2	1981–91, hospital births, Office of the Registrar General, 1991
	123.3	1996–98, SRS data for the state of Haryana, reported in Premi, 2001
	132.0	1993, one hospital in Punjab, Booth et al., 1994
	156.0	1990, town of Rohtak near New Delhi, *Far Eastern Economic Review,* 1991

SOURCES: State Family Planning Commission of China, *China Birth Planning Yearbook* (Beijing, 1996); Yi Zeng, Tu Ping, Gu Baochang, Xu Yi, Li Bohua, and Li Youngping, "Causes and Implications of the Recent Increase in the Reported Sex Ratio at Birth in China," *Population and Development Review*, Vol. 19, No. 2 (June 1993), pp. 283–302; State Statistical Bureau, *China Population Statistics Yearbook* (Beijing: China Statistics Press, 1996), 1.04 percent samples for October 1994, April 1995, and October 1995; personal communication with the director of the Chinese Academy of Social Sciences via e-mail based on article in the *Nando Times* entitled "China Reportedly Has 20 Percent More Males Than Females," January 7, 1999; Gu Baochang and Krishna Roy, "Sex Ratio at Birth in China, with Reference to Other Areas in Asia: What We Know," *Asia-Pacific Population Journal,* Vol. 10, No. 3 (September 1995), pp. 17–42; *2001 Report of the National Statistical Office of South Korea* (Seoul, July 2001); Chai Bin Park and Nam-Hoon Cho, "Consequences of Son Preference in a Low Fertility Society: Imbalance of the Sex Ratio At Birth in Korea," *Population and Development Review,* Vol. 21, No. 1 (March 1995), pp. 59–84; Mahendra Premi, "The Missing Girl Child," Economic and Political Weekly, May 26, 2001, pp. 1875–1880; Bharat Jhunjhunwala, "Sex Ratio Riddles," *Statesman* (India), June 2, 2001; Office of the Registrar General of India, *Compendium of India's Fertility and Mortality Indicators Based on the SRS* (Delhi: Controller of Publications, 1991); Beverly E. Booth, Manorama Verma, and Rajbir Singh Beri, "Fetal Sex Determination in Infants in Punjab, India: Correlations and Implications," *British Medical Journal,* Vol. 304 (1994), pp. 1259–1261; and Hamish McDonald, "Unwelcome Sex," *Far Eastern Economic Review,* December 26, 1991, pp. 18–19.

within a single year the sex ratio has jumped to a high level that has subsequently been sustained. This suggests that people have been anxiously awaiting the availability of sex-control technology . . . and that couples actively use such technology, regardless of fertility level."[7]

The Chinese government has begun to address the problem of sex selection more seriously in recent years. Indeed Zeng Yi, director of the Demography Institute at Beijing University, freely admits, "The loss of female births due to illegal prenatal sex determination and sex-selective abortion and female infanticide will affect the true sex ratio at birth and at young ages, creating an unbalanced population sex structure in the future and resulting in potentially serious social problems."[8] A vast demographic shift is taking place in Asia because of these new technologies. The scale on which sex ratios are being skewed in Asia is arguably unprecedented in human history. Furthermore, it is worthwhile to remember that China and India alone comprise more than 38 percent of the world's population. This peculiarly Asian phenomenon may have ramifications beyond that region.

The Other Side of the Ratio: Surplus Males

Selection against female offspring produces an excess proportion of males in society: surplus males. Given the long history of son preference in China, it is not surprising that the Chinese have a special term for such surplus males: *guang gun-er* (also transliterated as *guanggun, guangguer,* or *guanguen*), alternatively translated as "bare sticks" or "bare branches," indicating those male branches of a family tree that would never bear fruit because no marriage partner might be found for them.

Given our focus on security, we are most interested in bare branches who are in the age group 15–34/35, as this is the male age group that commits the preponderance of violence within a society. How many young adult bare branches are there now, and how many are there expected to be in the next two decades in the two most populous nations on earth, China and India? Generally speaking we will be seeing 29–33 million young surplus males in China in twenty years and 28–32 million young surplus males in India at that same time (see Tables 4 and 5). (These are very conservative estimates, using birth sex ratios

---

7. Ibid., p. 79.
8. Zeng Yi, Tu Ping, Gu Baochang, Xu Yi, Li Bohua, and Li Youngping, "Causes and Implications of the Recent Increase in the Reported Sex Ratio at Birth in China," *Population and Development Review*, Vol. 19, No. 2 (June 1993), p. 296.

Table 4. Surplus Males, Aged 15–34, China.

Year	Surplus Males	Source of Information
1990	14,857,587	U.S. Bureau of the Census, International Data Base
2020	29,207,874	Calculated using birth sex ratio of 111.3 for 1985–89; 118.2 for 1990–94; 115.4 for 1995–99; and 115.0 for 2000–04, with adjusted Life Table Survival Ratio (LTSR)
2020	33,059,694	Calculated as above, without adjusting LTSR

SOURCE: U.S. Bureau of the Census, *International Data Base*, IDB Aggregation, Table 094, http://www.census.gov/ipc/www/idbnew.html/.

that are lower than arguably should be used. For example, if the Chinese Academy of Social Sciences' figure of 120:100 male-to-female births were substituted, there would be closer to 40 million young surplus males in 2020 in China.)

Who are these young surplus males? First, they are not equivalent to the bachelors of the West. Single men in the West are not surplus males: Indeed they can and often do form semipermanent attachments to women and produce children in that context. Surplus males, on the other hand, do not have such possibilities. In a marriage market where women are scarce and thus able to "marry up," certain characteristics of young surplus males are easily and accurately predicted. They are liable to come from the lowest socioeconomic class, be un- or underemployed, live a fairly nomadic or transient lifestyle with few ties to the communities in which they are working, and generally live and socialize with other bachelors. In sum, these young surplus males may be considered, relatively speaking, losers in societal competition.

The behavior of young surplus males also follows a broadly predictable pattern. Theory suggests that compared with other males in society, bare branches will be prone to seek satisfaction through vice and violence, and will seek to capture resources that will allow them to compete on a more equal footing with others. These theoretical predictions are substantiated by empirical evidence so vast and so compelling as to approach the status of social science verity.[9] Cross-culturally, an overwhelming percentage of violent crime is per-

---

9. The literature here is immense. We cite only a few illustrative works: D. Benton, "Do Animal Studies Tell Us Anything about the Relationships between Testosterone and Human Aggression?" in Graham C.L. Davey, ed., *Animal Models of Human Behavior* (Chichester, U.K.: Wiley, 1983), pp. 281–298; Marie France Bouissou, "Androgens, Aggressive Behavior, and Social Relationships in Higher Mammals," *Hormone Research*, Vol. 18 (1983), pp. 43–61; John M.W. Bradford and D. McLean, "Sexual Offenders, Violence, and Testosterone: A Clinical Study," *Canadian Journal of*

Table 5. Surplus Males, Aged 15–35, India.

Year	Surplus Males	Source of Information
1991	7,267,923	*Census of India, 1991*
2006	16,509,449	Calculated using *Census of India, 1991*
2020	28,326,000	Calculated using birth sex ratio of 109.65 M:F
2020	31,671.000	Calculated using birth sex ratio of 112.23 M:F

SOURCE: Office of the Registrar General, *Census of India, 1991* (New Delhi, 1994).

petrated by young, unmarried, low-status males. As Margo Wilson and Martin Daly note, "Men are not poorer than women, but they help themselves to other people's property more often, and they are evidently readier to use violence to do so."[10]

Some may question whether marital status plays an important role in such behavioral dispositions, but this is another widely confirmed research finding.[11] David Courtwright notes, "It is when young men cannot or do

Psychiatry, Vol. 29, No. 4 (June 1984), pp. 335–343; Kerrin Christiansen and Rainier Knussmann, "Androgen Levels and Components of Aggressive Behavior in Men," *Hormones and Behavior,* Vol. 21, No. 2 (June 1987), pp. 170–180; James M. Dabbs Jr. and Robin Morris, "Testosterone, Social Class, and Antisocial Behavior in a Sample of 4,462 Men," *Psychological Science,* Vol. 1 (1990), pp. 209–211; Bruce B. Svare, ed., *Hormones and Aggressive Behavior* (New York: Plenum, 1983); Jane Shibley Hyde, "Gender Differences in Aggression," in Jane Shibley Hyde and Marcia C. Linn, eds., *The Psychology of Gender: Advances through Meta-Analysis* (Baltimore, Md.: Johns Hopkins University Press, 1986); Kenneth E. Moyer, "Sex Differences in Aggression," in Richard C. Friedman, Ralph M. Richart, and Raymond L. Vande Wiele, eds., *Sex Differences in Behavior* (New York: Wiley, 1974), pp. 335–372; and Dolf Zillmann, *Connections between Sex and Aggression* (Hillsdale, N.J.: Erlbaum, 1984).

Regarding the youthfulness of these aggressors, see, for example, Dan Olweus, Ake Mattsson, Daisy Schalling, and Hans Loew, "Circulating Testosterone Levels and Aggression in Adolescent Males: A Causal Analysis," *Psychosomatic Medicine,* Vol. 50, No. 3 (May–June 1988), pp. 261–272; Margo Wilson and Martin Daly, "Competitiveness, Risk Taking, and Violence: The Young Male Syndrome," *Ethology and Sociobiology,* Vol. 6, No. 1 (1985), pp. 59–73; Derral Cheatwood and Kathleen J. Block, "Youth and Homicide," *Justice Quarterly,* Vol. 7, No. 2 (1990), pp. 265–292; and Christian G. Mesquida and Neil I. Wiener, "Human Collective Aggression: A Behavioral Ecology Perspective," *Ethology and Sociobiology,* Vol. 17, No. 4 (1996), pp. 247–262. The vast majority of homicides are committed by males aged 15–35. Within that age group, males aged 20–29 commit most of the homicides. See Wilson and Daly, "Competitiveness, Risk Taking, and Violence."

10. Wilson and Daly, "Competitiveness, Risk Taking, and Violence," p. 66.

11. See Mesquida and Wiener, "Human Collective Aggression"; Martin Daly and Margo Wilson, *Sex, Evolution, and Behavior* (North Scituate, Mass.: Duxbury Press, 1978); David T. Courtwright, *Violent Land: Single Men and Social Disorder from the Frontier to the Inner City* (Cambridge, Mass.: Harvard University Press, 1996); Theodore D. Kemper, *Social Structure and Testosterone: Explorations of the Socio-Bio-Social Chain* (New Brunswick, N.J.: Rutgers University Press, 1990); Robert Wright, *The Moral Animal* (New York: Pantheon, 1994); Laura Betzig, "Despotism and Differential Reproduction: A Cross-Cultural Correlation of Conflict Asymmetry, Hierarchy, and Degree of Polygyny,"

not marry that socially disruptive behavior is intensified."[12] Robert Wright explains:

An unmarried man between 24 and 35 years of age is about three times as likely to murder another male as is a married man the same age. Some of this difference no doubt reflects the kinds of men that do and don't get married to begin with, but . . . a good part of the difference may lie in "the pacifying effect" of marriage. Murder isn't the only thing an "unpacified" man is more likely to do. He is also more likely to incur various risks—committing robbery, for example—to gain the resources that may attract women. He is more likely to rape. Abuse of drugs and alcohol . . . compound the problem by further diminishing his chances of ever earning enough money to attract women by legitimate means.[13]

Why should this be so? Allan Mazur and his coauthors have determined that T (serum testosterone) levels in men who court and then marry drop relative to men who do not: "T levels fall during the years surrounding marriage. Changing T levels may explain the low criminality found among married men. . . . Married men, living stably with their wives, are less prone to crime than unmarried men. Married men are less likely than single men of the same age to kill an unrelated male."[14] According to Mazur, T has been found to be significantly related to a variety of antisocial behaviors, including trouble with the law, alcohol and substance abuse, violent behavior, and other types of rebellion and rule breaking. When T falls, so does the propensity to engage in these behaviors.[15] According to Mazur's analysis, the more men in the society

---

Ethology and Sociobiology, Vol. 3, No. 4 (1982), pp. 209–221; Martin Daly and Margo Wilson, *Homicide* (Hawthorne, N.Y.: Aldine de Gruyter, 1988); Martin Daly and Margo Wilson, "Killing the Competition: Female/Female and Male/Male Homicide," *Human Nature*, Vol. 1, No. 1 (1990), pp. 81–107; Napoleon Chagnon, "Is Reproductive Success Equal in Egalitarian Societies?" in Chagnon and William Irons, eds., *Evolutionary Biology and Human Social Behavior: An Anthropological Perspective* (North Scituate, Mass.: Duxbury Press, 1979); David Buss, *The Evolution of Desire: Strategies of Human Mating* (New York: Basic Books, 1994); Frank A. Pedersen, "Secular Trends in Human Sex Ratios: Their Influence on Individual and Family Behavior," *Human Nature*, Vol. 2, No. 3 (1991), pp. 271–291; and Randy Thornhill and Nancy Thornhill, "Human Rape: An Evolutionary Analysis," *Ethology and Sociobiology*, Vol. 4, No. 3 (1983), pp. 137–173.

12. Courtwright, *Violent Land*, p. 202.
13. Wright, *The Moral Animal*, p. 100.
14. Allan Mazur and Joel Michalek, "Marriage, Divorce, and Male Testosterone," *Social Forces*, Vol. 77, No. 1 (September 1998), p. 1.
15. See Allan Mazur and Alan Booth, "Testosterone and Dominance in Men," *Behavioral and Brain Science*, Vol. 21, No. 3 (June 1998), pp. 353–397. There have been numerous debates over the effects of testosterone on behavior. Some suggest that it is testosterone's transformation into estradiol that provides these effects. Others dispute that any effect exists at all. See, for example, David France, "Testosterone, the Rogue Hormone, Is Getting a Makeover," *New York Times*, February 17, 1999, p. G3.

who are unable to marry, even though they would be willing to marry, the higher their circulating T and the greater amount of antisocial, violent, and criminal behavior they will exhibit, generally speaking, than if they were able to marry.

When bare branches congregate, the potential for more organized aggression increases substantially. For example, experiments have shown that the "risky shift" is more pronounced in groups of males than in groups of females.[16] The advocacy of risky choices by men in group situations appears to enhance their social prestige. As Courtwright puts it, "Men who congregate with men tend to be more sensitive about status and reputation. Even if they are not intoxicated with drink or enraged by insult, they instinctively test one another, probing for signs of weakness. . . . Disreputable, lower-class males . . . exercised much greater influence in bachelor communities like bunkhouses and mining camps. They both tempted and punished, for to fail to emulate their vices was to fail, in their own terms, to be a man."[17]

In this "least common denominator" theory, the behavior of men in groups —most particularly young, single, low-status males—will not rise above the behavior of the worst-behaved individual. Together, they will take larger risks and be more violent than they otherwise would individually.

The sheer number of bare branches, coupled with the distinctive outcast subculture that binds them together and their lack of "stake" in the existing social order, predispose them to organized social banditry. The potential for intrasocietal violence is increased when society selects for bare branches, as certain Asian societies do. It is possible that this intrasocietal violence may have intersocietal consequences as well.

It is important to note that we are not claiming that the presence of significant numbers of bare branches *causes* violence; violence can be found in all societies, regardless of sex ratio. Indeed, to give but one example, the sex ratio of Rwanda in 1994 was normal. Rather the opportunity for such violence to emerge and become relatively large-scale is heightened by socially prevalent selection for bare branches. We see this factor as having an amplifying or aggravating effect. To use a natural metaphor, the presence of dry, bare branches

---

16. Norris R. Johnson, James G. Stemler, and Deborah Hunter, "Crowd Behavior as "Risky Shift": A Laboratory Experiment," *Sociometry*, Vol. 40, No. 2 (June 1977), pp. 183–187. Playing off Irving Janis's seminal work on groupthink, it has been noted that individuals in a cohesive group take greater risks than any one of them would individually. This has been repeatedly confirmed in experimental research.
17. Courtwright, *Violent Land*, pp. 42–43.

cannot cause fire in and of itself, but when the sparks begin to fly, those bare branches provide kindling sufficient to turn the sparks into a fire larger and more dangerous than otherwise.

Three Illustrative Historical Cases

One useful way of examining this relationship between young adult surplus males and societal violence is to see how it developed in certain historical episodes where the presence of large numbers of young surplus males can be documented. The cases that follow are meant to be suggestive, not exhaustive, for we are not historians. However, because historians generally have not classified social conflict according to the involvement of bare branches, we have had to probe source material ourselves to detect their presence.

THE NIEN REBELLION

The Nien Rebellion of 1851–63, finally quelled in 1868, originated with an organized group of bandits from the poor area of Huai-pei in northern China.[18] This region has a very harsh environment, and during the first half of the nineteenth century, experienced flood, drought, or locust invasion on an average of every three to four years. Many died of starvation. The response of the people of Huai-pei to this period of famine and stress was female infanticide. Nineteenth-century statistics for the Huai-pei region reveal that there was an overall average of 129 men for every 100 women,[19] an extremely high sex ratio.

A significant number of Huai-pei males may have gone unmarried and had no hope of marrying. The best scholarly estimates suggest that in this period, "poorer men had to delay their marriages by six years in comparison with richer men, and that *twenty-five percent of men were unable to marry at all*."[20] This accords with estimates of female infanticide in the late imperial period reaching levels of approximately 300 per 1,000.[21] James Lee and Wang Feng concur: "Among peasant families in north-eastern China in the century after 1774, be-

---

18. This account of the Nien is adapted from the work of Elizabeth Perry, specifically Perry, *Rebels and Revolutionaries in North China, 1845–1945* (Stanford, Calif.: Stanford University Press, 1980).
19. Ibid., p. 51. For purposes of comparison, the sex ratio in Dodge City, Kansas, in 1880 was "only" 124. Courtwright, *Violent Land*, p. 58.
20. David Ownby, "Approximations of Chinese Bandits: Perverse Rebels or Frustrated Bachelors?" in Jeffrey Wasserstrom and Usam Brownell, eds., *Chinese Masculinities/Femininities* (Berkeley: University of California Press, forthcoming), p. 20 (emphasis added). See also David Ownby, *Brotherhoods and Secret Societies in Early and Mid-Qing China* (Stanford, Calif.: Stanford University Press, 1996).
21. Ownby, "Approximations of Chinese Bandits," p. 19.

tween one-fifth and one-quarter of all females were killed as children."[22] The scarcity of marriageable women was deepened by polygamy and concubinage practiced by rich men, present in an estimated 10 percent of Chinese marriages of the period.[23] Although individual peasant families were pursuing a rational policy in preferring to rear sons who were expected to augment household income, the social impact of this policy was a serious surplus of poor, young single males. As one scholar explains, "Families adopted the practice of female infanticide to increase family income and security, but the long-term aggregate result was a skewed demography in which there was a large surplus of young men. These young men became natural recruits for bandit gangs and local militia—thus providing resources for the emergence of collective strategies of predation and protection."[24]

These were the young men dubbed the "bare sticks" or "bare branches" because they would not have families: Their parents had killed the girls who should have grown up to be their wives. One Chinese official, Chen Shengshao, wrote in 1827, "Since marrying off women is hard, people raise few women. Since affording to marry is difficult, there are many bachelors."[25] Chen goes on to note that it was the high price of marriage that led "homeless bandits" to "kidnap, steal, and feud."[26]

James Watson of Harvard University and David Ownby of the University of Montreal have both articulated the link between permanent, involuntary bachelorhood caused by high sex ratios and violence in historical China. Watson coined the phrase "bachelor subculture" to help explain how antisocial behavior becomes the norm for these men. Ownby explains that "in the eyes of most Chinese an unmarried man is not truly an adult, not truly a man."[27] He suggests that the theory of "protest masculinity," wherein men unable to fulfill gender expectations are driven toward "hypermasculine displays in order to prove to others, as well as to themselves, that they are indeed "real men," may apply.[28] Watson provides evidence for this linkage in a study of

---

22. "6.3 Brides," *Economist*, December 19, 1998, p. 57. See also James Z. Lee and Wang Feng, *One Quarter of Humanity: Malthusian Mythology and Chinese Realities, 1700–2000* (Cambridge, Mass.: Harvard University Press, 1999).

23. Ownby, *Brotherhoods and Secret Societies in Early and Mid-Qing China.*

24. Daniel Little, *Understanding Peasant China: Case Studies in the Philosophy of Social Science* (New Haven, Conn.: Yale University Press, 1989), p. 172.

25. Chen Shengshao, Wensulu 1827, as quoted in Ownby, "Approximations of Chinese Bandits," p. 19.

26. Chen Shengshao, Wensulu 1827, as quoted in Ownby, "Approximations of Chinese Bandits," p. 22.

27. Ownby, "Approximations of Chinese Bandits," p. 20.

28. Ibid.

militias composed, he finds, of almost exclusively bare branches. He explains that

A strategy that [bare branches] sometimes use to enhance their male image is to make a regular practice of challenging the public face of other men. Face is essentially an attribute of married men who have families to protect and obligations to fulfill. Unmarried men have little face to preserve because they do not command much respect in the community. . . . By definition, therefore, bachelors remain perpetual adolescents who cannot play a full role in society. Taking this argument to its logical conclusion an unmarried youth can have no face and is therefore dangerous. . . . These "bare sticks" had nothing to lose except their reputations for violence.[29]

Ownby points out that the term "bare branches or "bare sticks" "refers to both violent, petty criminals as well as to bachelors" and quotes a nineteenth-century Western missionary as describing the "sublime ideal" of the "bare sticks" as making it "a sport and a matter of pride to defy the laws and the magistrates, and commit all kinds of crimes. To give and receive wounds with composure; to kill others with the most perfect coolness; and to have no fear of death for yourself."[30] Ownby goes on to suggest that most bandits in historical China were, in fact, bare branches. Watson details that most bare branches in his study were semiliterate and were third, fourth, or fifth sons whose families were too poor to offer them an inheritance. In many cases, these noninheriting sons were "pushed out" (*tuei chu*) of their fathers' houses in their teens, and came to live in bachelor houses with groups of other unmarried youths.[31] In their early twenties, they would move out of the bachelor house and in with a collective of men—a dormitory of workers, a monastery or religious brotherhood, or the local militia. In each case, they would spend much of their leisure time learning and practicing the martial arts. These collectives, whatever their character, often led to the formation of bandit gangs, by means of which bare branches could gain a measure of face and wealth that would otherwise be unobtainable in a society where marriage was the mark of maturity.

In the case of the bare branches of Huai-pei born in the early nineteenth century, not only were these young men never going to settle down, but most of them were not able to secure labor. Eventually, enough of these "rational bachelors" began to view banditry as an alternative lifestyle that would enable

29. James L. Watson, "Self-Defense Corps, Violence, and the Bachelor Subculture in South China: Two Case Studies," proceedings of the Second International Conference on Sinology, Academia Sinica, Taipei, Republic of China, June 1989, p. 216.
30. Ownby, "Approximations of Chinese Bandits," p. 22.
31. Watson, "Self-Defense Corps," p. 213.

them to contribute to family income.[32] They started as salt smugglers, an activity made profitable because of the high tax placed by the government on salt. In 1815 a county magistrate classified the troublemakers of the area into three categories: bare sticks, smugglers, and bandits. The overlap between the three groups was great.[33] One commentator noted, "They do not fear the imperial laws, nor do they submit to the discipline of their fathers or elder brothers."[34]

Initially these bandits were not out to topple the Qing dynasty; they were just looting to make a living. They began as small, autonomous groups but eventually organized. Li Ji notes, "In 1855, most of the 'Nien Zi' met at Zhi Heji (a small county in An Hui province) and united to form a powerful armed force—'Nien Jun.' The goal of the army was to overthrow the Qing Dynasty."[35] The Nien grew in influence, and their threat expanded. At the peak of the rebellion, as many as 100,000 bare sticks were participants. Active in Hupeh, Honan, Shantung, Kiangsu, and Anhui regions, the Nien became very powerful. In 1862 the governor of Anhui "reported that there were at least two thousand Nien forts in Huai-pei, each with one to three thousand inhabitants. The Nien apparently were in at least nominal control of a population of some two to six million people."[36] The imperial government was compelled to adopt foreign arms and modernize its army along Western lines, which allowed the army to finally gain the advantage and defeat the Nien over a period of several years ending in 1868.

An interesting resemblance of modern China to the era of the Nien is a contemporary echo of the Chinese official noted above who stated in 1815 that the social problems of his area stemmed from bare sticks, smugglers, and bandits. Recent analysis notes, "According to figures from authoritative departments, China has an indigent population of 80 million, a migrant population of 80 million, and will soon have 80 million single men."[37] Our analysis tells us that the overlap between these three populations is very large. China is recreating the vast army of bare sticks that plagued it during the nineteenth century.

---

32. See James Tong, "Rational Outlaws: Rebels and Bandits in the Ming Dynasty, 1368–1644," in Michael Taylor, ed., *Rationality and Revolution* (Cambridge: Cambridge University Press, 1988).
33. Perry, *Rebels and Revolutionaries in North China*, p. 102.
34. Kung-ch'uan Hsiao, *Rural China: Imperial Control in the Nineteenth Century* (Seattle: University of Washington Press, 1967), p. 458.
35. Li Ji, "Discussions on the Gender Imbalance in China and the Entailed Social Problems," Foreign Affairs College, Beijing, 1999, p. 11.
36. Perry, *Rebels and Revolutionaries in North China*, p. 127.
37. See Meng Ren, "Confronting Three Populations of 80 Million," *Inside China Mainland*, Vol. 19, No. 1 (January 1997), pp. 78–81.

MEDIEVAL PORTUGAL

Though medieval Portugal contained certain causal factors not present in China or India,[38] James Boone's case study demonstrates that when governments become aware of the bare branch threat, they consciously seek to minimize that threat through foreign policy initiatives.[39]

Medieval Portugal invested heavily in firstborn sons to maintain familial accumulation of resources over generations. It comes as no surprise, then, that the adult sex ratio of the time was approximately 112:100. In addition to low-status bare branches, the case of medieval Portugal is interesting because it also had *high-status* bare branches—second-, third- and higher-birth-order sons of nobility ("cadet sons") who could not inherit, and thus could not marry.

As Boone notes, this confluence of factors bred extreme political instability for Portugal; the cadet sons and the lower-class bare branches began to band together in small armies. These bare-branch bands affected governmental policy in two ways: (1) in times of political upheaval, they generally backed—by force of arms—usurpers who promised to redistribute societal resources in their favor; and (2) in less turbulent times, the government consciously pursued policies to disperse them to foreign lands, usually in causes of expansionist warfare and colonization. Boone cites the case of Joao I, the illegitimate half-brother of a Portuguese monarch, who took the throne after the monarch's death with the help of the cadet sons and their bare-branch bands. But then Joao I discovered that the piracy and robbery they caused threatened his own monarchy. Having obtained Papal consent, and at great cost and deficit, Joao I sponsored the Reconquista—an attack on the North African coast. Boone cites another scholar working from primary sources: "It was above all the *cadets*, who lacked land and other sources of revenue within the country who desired war, which would permit them to accede to a situation of social and material independence."[40] Indeed Georges Duby notes, "It is obvious that it was the

---

38. Primogeniture was not universally practiced in India—it was more prevalent among upper castes. Primogeniture was not practiced for the most part in China, although it is reported that firstborn sons were more likely to receive land as an inheritance and younger sons were more likely to receive movable property. In some cases, all sons received some land, but the firstborn received more land than his brothers. Of course, the second factor in the Portuguese case, landed nobility, is not a major factor in either modern-day China or modern-day India.

39. The case study is adapted from James L. Boone, "Noble Family Structure and Expansionist Warfare in the Late Middle Ages," in Rada Dyson-Hudson and Michael A. Little, eds., *Rethinking Human Adaptation: Biological and Cultural Models* (Boulder, Colo.: Westview, 1983); and James L. Boone, "Parental Investment and Elite Family Structure in Preindustrial States: A Case Study of Late Medieval–Early Modern Portuguese Genealogies," *American Anthropologist*, Vol. 88, No. 4 (December 1986), pp. 859–878.

40. Boone, "Noble Family Structure and Expansionist Warfare," p. 94 (emphasis in original).

bands of 'youths' excluded by so many social prohibitions from the main body of settled men, fathers of families and heads of houses, with their prolonged spells of turbulent behavior making them an unstable fringe of society, who created and sustained the crusades."[41]

The expansionist strategy worked, to a certain extent. Boone notes that by the mid-sixteenth century, almost 25 percent of adult noble males would die in expansionist or civil warfare. It may be useful, however, to step back and contemplate the significant cost to society and government of creating the bare branches in the first place. Political turbulence was continual, the drain on the economy due to the required expansionist warfare was seriously detrimental to both the government and the population in general, and the loss of life and property due to the bare branch bands (and the loss of life of the bare branches themselves) was considerable. The reproductive strategy chosen—that of high sex ratio—coupled with primogeniture ensured, in Boone's words, "political instability, warfare, and territorial expansion."[42]

MARTIAL RELIGIOUS BROTHERHOODS IN HISTORICAL CHINA

In Western society, monks of centuries past are stereotypically viewed as having been peaceful, generally older men who spent their time engaged in good works, or perhaps copying manuscripts. In Chinese history, monks were very much involved in worldly affairs. Indeed the life course of "monk" or "religious zealot" was one means by which bare-branch youths could seek to raise their status in society. This choice of vocation did not necessarily preclude continuance of what we have recognized as typical bare-branch behavior.[43] To be more specific, martial prowess and the amassing of unearned wealth were not infrequently associated with some monasteries and other quasi-religious brotherhoods, and this had political ramifications.

Probably the most famous example is the Shaolin fighting monks, who, having saved the life of the emperor Tai Tsung in the Tang era, were given land to build a monastery that eventually housed 2,500 martial monks. But later in Chinese history, the power of monasteries would grow, especially Buddhist monasteries favored by the powerful eunuchs. In the late A.D. 800s, official figures show "over a quarter of a million monastics, who controlled some 4,600 monasteries, 40,000 pagodas, and untold thousands of temples, including

---

41. Georges Duby, *The Chivalrous Society*, trans. Cynthia Postan (London: Edward Arnold, 1977), p. 120, as cited in ibid.
42. Boone, "Parental Investment and Elite Family Structure," p. 871.
43. Indeed certain sects of monks did not practice celibacy, though they also did not marry. We have here in mind the Taoist monks.

slaves and attendants, much of the nation's best lands, and much wealth, all existing tax free."[44] By the late 1400s, there were more than 1.5 million monks, with one official calculating that the rice needed to feed them all "could easily supply the entire capital population for over one year."[45] David Robinson has found participation of martial monks as mercenaries in quelling rebellions alongside imperial troops throughout the sixteenth century.[46]

Monastic orders coexisted with more heterodox quasi-religious brotherhoods, many of them secret. The migratory fluidity induced by hardship and lack of opportunity led many young men, typically bare branches of Watson's "bachelor subculture," to the ranks of these brotherhoods.[47] Fei-ling Davis identifies those likely to belong to secret brotherhoods as dispossessed peasants, unemployed artisans, laborers and porters, disbanded soldiers, smugglers, and victims of disasters, all of whom came to be known as the "floating population" (*you-min*) due to their mobility and their poverty.[48]

Sometimes the practice of martial arts was an explicit element of these secret brotherhoods. Indeed boxing exhibitions were a primary way to seek recruits. Once a young man expressed a desire to become a pupil of the boxing instructor, he would be carefully groomed to become a member of the society itself. The poorer the area, the more likely young male devotees would be found. In the late 1800s, a letter by a former magistrate noted, "The road passed through Chiping. The area is bitterly poor, but in hundreds of villages they are studying United-in-Righteousness Boxing."[49] According to chroniclers of the time, we can identify some hallmarks of bare-branch behavior among these boxing enthusiasts: "In this area there are many vagabonds and rowdies (*wu-lai gun-tu*) who draw their swords and gather crowds. They have established societies of various names: the Obedient Swords (Shun-dao hui), Tiger-tail Whip (Hu-wei bian), the Yi-he Boxers, and Eight Trigrams sect (Ba-gua jiao). They are overbearing in the villages and oppress the good people."[50]

---

44. Mary M. Anderson, *Hidden Power: The Palace Eunuchs of Imperial China* (Buffalo, N.Y.: Prometheus Books, 1990), p. 162.

45. Ibid., p. 226.

46. David M. Robinson, "The Management of Violence in the Mid-Ming Capital Region," Colgate University, 1998.

47. Quoted in Ownby, *Brotherhoods and Secret Societies in Early and Mid-Qing China*, p. 20. See Watson, "Self-Defense Corps."

48. Fei-ling Davis, *Primitive Revolutionaries of China: A Study of Secret Societies in the Late Nineteenth Century* (Honolulu: University of Hawaii Press, 1977), p. 90.

49. Joseph Esherick, *The Origins of the Boxer Uprising* (Berkeley: University of California Press, 1987), p. 223.

50. Quoted in ibid., p. 46.

Occasionally, members of these secret brotherhoods became bandits and rebels. In 1898 the governor of Shandong reported, "This year the spring rains were late and the grain prices rose. In addition it was a time of troop reduction and consolidation. Dispersed braves and habitual outlaws from elsewhere . . . combined with unemployed vagrants into a mob of several hundreds. . . . Armed with foreign rifles and weapons, they plundered neighboring villages on the pretext of borrowing grain, and extorted horses, weapons, and ammunition."[51] Another contemporary commentator noted, "In the provinces of Chihli, Honan, and Shantung, *chiao-fei* [religious bandits] spread their creeds one to another. . . . Once famine occurs they, relying on their numerical strength, plunder collectively in broad daylight, calling their marauding activities 'equalizing the food.'"[52] We propose that several major rebellions might usefully be investigated to assess the role of bare branches, including the Eight Trigrams Rebellion, the Boxer Rebellion, and the Black Flag Army's activities.

Sometimes the fate of these rebellious bare branches was not eventual defeat and violent death, but rather astounding success. Taizu, the Grand Progenitor of the Ming dynasty had, for most of his life, been "a vagrant, a beggar, a member of a millenarian sect, and a rebel."[53] After the Ming slashed the number of government employees in 1629, "Li Zicheng, who eventually emerged as the rebel leader who drove the Ming from Beijing, was among those unemployed workers who threw his lot in with the rebels."[54] Throughout Chinese history, a standing pool of marginal men were available for violent work, and they sometimes changed the destiny of the nation. According to Gensho Nishimara, most of this pool were *wulai*, meaning young male "floaters" who prided themselves on being "tough."[55] Ueda Makato calls the *wulai* urban vagabonds who depended on violence to make a living, often forming "enforcers guilds."[56] In the Ming, government reports blamed much of the crime in Beijing on the "unregistered ones"—gangs made up of bare sticks, whose members were called "fierce tigers."[57] The fate of these criminals was not always bleak. For example, according to Ownby, the common folk saying "If you

---

51. Quoted in ibid., pp. 176–177.
52. Quoted in Hsiao, *Rural China*, p. 447.
53. Robinson, "Management of Violence," p. 8.
54. David M. Robinson, "Banditry and Rebellion in the Capital Region during the Mid-Ming (1450–1525)," Ph.D. dissertation, Princeton University, 1995, p. 490.
55. Gensho Nishimara, "Ryu Roku Ryu Nana no ran ni tsuite," *Toyoshi kenkyu*, Vol. 32, No. 4 (1974), pp. 44–86.
56. Ueda Makato, "Minmatsu Shinso: Konan no toshino burai o meguru shakui kankei, dako to kyakufu," *Shigaku zasshi*, Vol. 90, No. 12 (1981), pp. 1619–1653.
57. Robinson, "Banditry and Rebellion," pp. 126–127.

want to become an official, carry a big stick" has reference to the traditional practice of awarding the bandits with official posts as a means of co-opting them.[58]

Martial ethos, poverty, mobility, anonymity, and congregation with other young bachelors in a similar situation—these common attributes were found in those who made up the backbone of Chinese brotherhoods. As Ownby notes, "Secret societies were reinterpreted by scholars in the 1970s and 1980s as marginal, frequently criminal gangs, little different from 'pure' bandits as we usually think of them. . . . Other bandit gangs, whether they qualify as secret societies or not (the distinction is a fine one in many cases), engaged in religious practices as well, . . . [such as] initiation ceremonies and invulnerability rituals."[59] These brotherhoods, whether orthodox or heterodox, were to pose grave security problems for the central government. As one seventeenth-century commentator put it, "Heretical teachings start by inciting, deluding, and gathering people, but end by planning rebellion."[60] Given the high sex ratios of its society, perhaps the grave suspicion with which the current Chinese government views movements such as the Falun Gong is not entirely unfounded in light of this history.

In conclusion, there is both strong theory and persuasive historical evidence that the bare branches of high sex-ratio societies can contribute significantly to intrasocietal violence. In some cases, this domestic threat has led governments to create foreign policy initiatives designed to disperse bare branches. The strategies that bare branches choose to better their position in society erode the stability of the societies in which they live. As we have seen, governments do become aware of the potentially violent dynamics of their high sex-ratio populations and struggle, sometimes successfully and sometimes unsuccessfully—but always at great cost—to implement policies to counteract the destabilization caused.

The Security Logic of High Sex-Ratio Societies

The repercussions of artificially high sex ratios pose grave problems of insecurity for a society which, in turn, create vexing policy dilemmas for govern-

---

58. Ownby, "Approximations of Chinese Bandits," p. 18.
59. Ibid. Indeed Ownby goes on to note that during the civil war, both national and communist forces courted bandits, with communists being willing to swear "blood oaths and pretend[ing] to adopt bandit/secret society codes of brotherhood and loyalty—attempting, of course, to assimilate such values to Leninist discipline."
60. Quoted in Barend J. ter Harr, *The White Lotus Teachings in Chinese Religious History* (Leiden, the Netherlands: E.J. Brill, 1992), p. 237.

ments. As Boone puts it, "Reproductive strategies have an important effect on the development of state political organization, and . . . there is a fundamental contradiction between individual (or familial) reproductive interests and the social reproduction of the state political structure."[61] It is to these issues that we now turn.

STATE POLITICAL ORGANIZATION IN HIGH SEX-RATIO SOCIETIES

High sex-ratio societies will tend to develop authoritarian political systems over time, for these are better equipped to deal with possible large-scale intrasocietal violence created by society's selection for bare branches. As Christian Mesquida and Neil Weiner note, "Choice of political system made by the members of a population is somewhat restricted by the age composition of its male population."[62] Robert Wright is even more blunt: "Few things are more anxiety-producing for an elite governing class than gobs of [unmarried] and childless men with at least a modicum of political power. . . . Extreme polygyny [which is the functional equivalent of a high sex ratio] often goes hand in hand with extreme political hierarchy, and reaches its zenith under the most despotic regimes. . . . Leaving lots of men without wives is not just inegalitarian: it's dangerous. . . . A nation, in which large numbers of low-income men remain mateless, is not the kind of country many of us would want to live in."[63]

If Wright, Boone, Mesquida, and Wiener are right, then we can expect high sex-ratio societies to be governable only by authoritarian regimes.[64] Indeed, in an intriguing empirical study of 186 societies, Laura Betzig finds the correlation between despotism and polygyny to be 0.72, significant at the 0.01 level.[65] Though analysts have high hopes for increasing democratization in such nations as China, India, and Pakistan, we would argue that the longer-term prospects are not good when gender elements of security are factored in. These are traditionally high sex-ratio societies whose birth sex ratios have undergone a strikingly upward climb since approximately 1985 when prenatal sex-selection

---

61. Boone, "Parental Investment and Family Structure," p. 859.
62. Mesquida and Weiner, "Human Collective Aggression," p. 257.
63. Wright, *The Moral Animal*, pp. 98–101.
64. It is hard to concur with William T. Divale and Marvin Harris that "warfare perpetuate[s] and propagate[s] itself because it [is] an effective method for sustaining the material and ideological restrictions on the rearing of female infants." Nevertheless, we understand how their analysis of 448 populations could result in the conclusion that "we are most likely to find unbalanced sex ratios when warfare is present." See Divale and Harris, "Population, Warfare, and the Male Supremacist Complex," *American Anthropologist*, Vol. 78, No. 3 (September 1976), pp. 531, 528.
65. Laura Betzig, *Despotism and Differential Reproduction: A Darwinian View of History* (New York: Aldine de Gruyter, 1986), p. 94.

techniques became widely available. Fortunately for the case of South Korea, stringent enforcement of anti-sex-selective abortion laws since identification of the problem in the early 1990s has led to a much improved sex ratio, hopefully auguring well for the continuance of democracy in that country. Speaking more generally about Asia, however, we are on the cusp of the time period wherein these larger proportions of bare branches will become socially active. As they do, we believe that governments in such societies will begin their predicted shift toward greater authoritarianism. In countries with high sex-ratio societies that are not ethnically homogeneous, such as India, this shift may start as rule by the majority ethnic group which group will, in turn, actually promote interethnic violence.

Indeed, governments of high sex-ratio societies must often cultivate a political style crafted to retain the allegiance and respect of its bare branches. This tends to be a swaggering, belligerent, provocative, martial style—to match that of the bare branches themselves. In the rhetoric accompanying such a posture, there is inevitably an "other," who is weak and contemptible and whose attempt to find a place in society or in the international order must be opposed. The society is then enjoined to muster its strength so that these "insults" can be answered with appropriate action. Though all governments at one time or another may engage in these types of tactics, they take on a particular urgency for governments of high sex-ratio societies. These governments understand that its bare branches are a formidable club—if it is in your hand it can be very useful, but if it is poised over your head, it may constitute a greater threat than external enemies.

STRATEGIES FOR CONTROLLING INTRASOCIETAL VIOLENCE IN HIGH SEX-RATIO
SOCIETIES

There is only one short-term strategy for dealing with a serious bare-branch problem: Reduce their numbers. There are several traditional ways to do so: Fight them, encourage their self-destruction, or export them. Longer-range strategies to address the problem, such as decreasing offspring sex selection, are also viable (and laudable), but are not likely to improve the government's situation for a generation or more. Furthermore, though economic prosperity is useful in placating disgruntled members of society, including bare branches, no amount of wealth will turn surplus males into nonsurplus males. At most, it can only rearrange which males end up at the bottom of the hypergynous heap. (Hypergyny is the practice of brides marrying upward in social class, which inevitably leaves lowest-class men without wives.) Prosperity is thus no panacea in this situation, though economic downturns are likely to trigger violent resource capture by bare branches.

Governments will always seek to suppress societal violence that threatens their authority. Indeed the government may actually recruit bare branches into military or police units that are used to fight bare-branch criminals. As we have shown in the historical studies, however, significant societal dislocation may be caused by large-scale suppression tactics.

Another approach is to simply let bare branches destroy each other, either turning a blind eye when rivals dispatch one another or encouraging ethnic divisions that will lead to intergroup violence. Once again, however, the level of societal dislocation may in the end threaten the government, as it will appear that the government has lost control over the level of violence in society. A second variant of this strategy is to provide large, dangerous public works that pay well. Building intercontinental railways or huge new dams, reclaiming vast tracts of swampland or desert—if done the old-fashioned way using primarily manual labor—can both occupy and sustain bare branches, while also ensuring significantly increased mortality among that population subgroup. Nevertheless, there may be a limit to how many such works can be undertaken by a given society.

Finally, governments seek to send bare branches elsewhere. "Elsewhere," in the government's perspective, may include distant frontier regions of the country or may in fact be other countries. This may be a peaceful export of colonists to a frontier or an exodus of migrant workers to other nations. There is, however, a martial variant of this strategy as well: a strategy that has been consciously used in history to reduce bare-branch numbers. If the bare branches threaten national security if they live at home, the government may prefer to let them die in some glorious national cause far from home instead. As Boone puts it, "Many males at the lower end of the scale lead lives of enforced celibacy in what for them is a seller's market and are furthermore engaged in production, construction, and military occupations that tend to raise their mortality rates through occupational hazards and unhealthful conditions. Their poor socioeconomic position and reproductive prospects make them perennial aspirants in large-scale expansionist and insurgent military campaigns through which they might hope to achieve higher positions."[66] Mesquida and Weiner have recently put some empirical flesh on these propositions. In their

---

66. Boone, "Parental Investment," p. 862.

examination of collective violence in human societies, they report, "Our analyses of interstate and intrastate episodes of collective aggression since the 1960s indicate the existence of a consistent correlation between the ratio of males 15 to 29 years of age per 100 males 30 years of age and older, and the level of coalitional aggression as measured by the number of reported conflict related deaths."[67] They go on to explain:

Young males participate in collective aggression to acquire the resources needed to attract a mate, and we should expect a great majority of the militants to come from that section of the population with fewest resources. . . . It is likely then that controlling elites astutely underwrite such risky undertakings as territorial expansion or colonization, especially when the alternative is having the aggressive tendencies of the male citizens directed at themselves. . . . Tentatively, we would like to propose that this intergenerational competition for reproductive resources, when exacerbated by the presence of a relatively large number of resourceless young males, might result in the emergence of male collective aggression, which occasionally expresses itself as expansionist warfare. . . . The presence of a relatively large number of young men makes coalitional aggression more probable, particularly when resources needed to attract a mate are insufficiently available or poorly distributed.[68]

Boone suggests that in medieval Portugal, the presence of significant numbers of bare branches ("cadet males") necessitated territorial expansion by the state. He documents the creation of "a highly competitive, volatile situation at the societal level with respect to the problem of excess cadet males. Rulers must choose between dispersing these individuals, for example, in expansionist campaigns, or facing disorder and overthrow on the home front."[69] Furthermore, "territorial expansion does not necessarily arise as an adaptive response on the part of a polity to expand its resource base or to solve productive deficiencies facing the population at large: expansionist warfare often results from attempts by individuals or coalitions to maintain control by directing the competition of their immediate subordinates away from themselves and against neighboring territories. These strategies . . . may be maintained at a considerable resource deficit seen from the point of view of the general population."[70] In sum, insights from theory and history portend that the increasing skewness of Asia's sex ratios mitigate against both democracy and peace in that region.

---

67. Mesquida and Wiener, "Human Collective Aggression," p. 247.
68. Ibid., pp. 256–260.
69. Boone, "Parental Investment," p. 868.
70. Boone, "Noble Family Structure," p. 81.

The Bare Branches of Today's Asia

Because prenatal offspring sex selection only became widely prevalent from about 1985, we currently stand at the threshold of time in which bare branches will come to represent a greater proportion of the population in certain Asian societies than heretofore, and become a significant factor in contemporary governmental calculations. Nevertheless, there are signs that our expectations regarding the societal instability to be created by increasing numbers of surplus males are already beginning to be fulfilled.

CHINA

About 97 percent of all unmarried persons aged 28–49 in China are male.[71] Data show that approximately 74 percent of unmarried males failed to graduate from high school.[72] About 97 percent of rural unmarried males did not graduate from high school, and about 40 percent are illiterate.[73] Ye Wenzhen and Lin Qingguo note the predictably hypergynous result, "The existence of lots of unmarried men after marriage age should attribute to the rational 'marrying up' of women at marriage age, and the relatively low social-economic situation of the unmarried men."[74]

Chinese transients are overwhelmingly young and male and of low status, and they do tend to congregate. Though we do not have data on marital status of transients, we assert that when data are collected on the subject, it will be found that most are unmarried. Reliable estimates indicate that in the *liudong renkou* (the "floating population") of 100–150 million persons, 80 percent are under age 35 and about 72–75 percent are male.[75] One 1993 sample finds 81.8

---

71. Ping Zhang, "Issues and Characteristics of the Unmarried Population," *Chinese Journal of Population Science*, Vol. 2, No. 1 (1990), pp. 87–97. Ping's figure of 94 percent is a little low, because he only examines single persons aged 28–49. His figures are also from 1987. Reasonable adjustments to his figures based on our own demographic statistics yield a percentage of about 97 percent.
72. Ibid.
73. Ibid.
74. Ye Wenzhen and Lin Qingguo, "The Reasons and Countermeasures for Demographic Phenomena in China," *Chinese Demography*, Vol. 4 (1998), as quoted in Ren Feng, "Bare Branches among Rural Migrant Laborers in China: Causes, Social Implications, and Policy Proposals," Foreign Affairs College, Beijing, May 24, 1999, p. 12.
75. Age data are from "HIV/AIDS—What the Chinese Experts Say," http://www.usembassy-china.org.cn/english/sandt/webaids3.htm (accessed July 10, 1998). Sex data are from Zhao Yi, *The Population, Resources, Environment, Agriculture, and Continuous Development of 21st-Century China* (Shan Xi: Economic Publishing House, 1997), p. 144; Zang Xiaohui, Wu Zhingang, and Chen Liangbiao, "Age Difference among the Rural Labor Force in Interregional Migration," *Population Science of China*, Vol. 9, No. 3 (1997), pp. 193–202; and Bruce Gilley, "Irresistible Force," *Far Eastern Economic Review*, April 4, 1996, pp. 18–22. Another revealing statistic is that approximately 82 percent of men remaining unmarried between the ages of 30 and 44 are registered residents of rural

percent of migrants to be male.[76] The floating population is expected to surpass 200 million persons in the next decade.[77]

The transients have not been smoothly integrated into urban life, and they do tend to congregate for social support. *Inside China Mainland* reports that "the increase in migrants has placed an added burden on already overloaded city infrastructures. On the outskirts of major towns, unplanned settlements have sprung up, where not only is public order and safety a problem, but where counterfeit goods and pornography are produced, and where the sex trade is prominent."[78] The periodical goes on to note that "over two million migrants are living in that nation's train stations, warehouses and along the tracks."[79] We assert that these are probably bachelor subculture communities. Transient workers find bewildering differences when they first come to cities, "often experiencing disdain or exclusion from urbanites."[80]

The development of a large floating population was always a harbinger of increasing social unrest in historical China. The ranks of the "floating people" (*liu min*) were full of the poor, the unemployed, and the vagrant, all of whom were noted to be prone to violence. Indeed a common governmental reaction to this phenomenon throughout history was periodic registration drives, in which floaters would be registered and placed in an administration unit, where they would be under the daily supervision of a government employee. This response, dating back at least four or five *centuries*,[81] has recently been adopted by the current government, which is also demolishing unlicensed markets and migrant housing and placing strict limits on the number of registered migrants a company can hire. Beijing authorities recently enunciated the goal of reducing legal migrants by at least 15 percent, while hoping to slash illegal migration.[82]

Given that the 100–150 million floating population of China is overwhelmingly young, male, and low status—characteristics that we have demonstrated

areas. China Statistical Publishing House, *China Population Statistics Yearbook (1994)*, pp. 36–53. Of all persons remaining unmarried between the ages of 30 and 44, more than 94 percent are male.
76. Ji Dangsheng and Shao Qin, *The Tendency and Management of Chinese Population Movement* (Beijing: Beijing Publishing House, 1996), p. 99.
77. Li Jingnen, "Challenge to Chinese Population Theory Research on the Period of the 21st Century," *Chinese Population Science*, n.s. 4 (1998), p. 10.
78. Meng, "Confronting Three Populations of 80 Million," p. 79.
79. Ibid., p. 80.
80. Quote from Ji Yang, "Transient Workers: A Special Social Group," and "Educating Transient Workers," *Beijing Review*, June 3–9, 1996, pp. 20–21.
81. Robinson, "Banditry and Rebellion"; see, for example, p. 16.
82. Erik Eckholm, "As Beijing Pretties Up, Migrants Face Expulsion," *New York Times*, April 18, 1999.

to be hallmarks of bare branches—can the typical bare-branch behavioral syndrome be found among China's floaters? The answer is an unequivocal yes.

Though crime data for China are very sketchy, and statistics vary from source to source, a clear pattern begins to emerge: Migrants are responsible for an inordinate amount of crime in China today. According to one source, in economically developed regions, migrants account for more than 50 percent of all arrests. "In the Jingdiao area of Shanghai's Pudong region, . . . migrants now account for over 90 percent of crimes, compared to 30 percent in 1990." The same source notes that "among all cases solved by railway authorities in 1994 concerning criminal acts and public order, 82 percent were committed by migrants, while 69% of criminals apprehended were migrants."[83] *Beijing Review* reports that "outsiders were responsible for 80 percent of criminal offenses in the capital. Similarly, it was found that 80 percent of the people arrested in the southern Pearl River delta and other coastal regions came from other provinces."[84]

Duan Chengyang reports, "In 1994, . . . the rate of committing crime among the rural migrant laborers was 1.3 percent, which was four times the national average. In Shanghai, Beijing, and other very large cities, the criminal cases committed by the rural migrant laborers accounted for more than half of the total criminal cases in these cities. Guangzhou even reached 80 percent."[85] Yet another scholar indicates that migrants "are said to be responsible for between one-third to 70 percent of all criminal activities in Chinese cities, with offenses ranging from theft, robbery, prostitution, to drug peddling, extortion, and murder." Other sources estimate that migrants account for 90 percent of criminals in Hangzhou.[86] Zhang Haiyang notes, "Generally speaking, the rural laborers are less educated, are extremely heterogeneous in composition, and lack the sense of law. When their requests cannot be satisfied, they tend to commit crimes."[87]

Yingyi Situ and Liu Weizheng, comparative criminologists, provide the following analysis and statistics:

83. Meng, "Confronting Three Populations of 80 Million," p. 80.
84. Tan Li, " The Population Flow into Big Cities," *Beijing Review*, July 18–24, 1994, p. 17.
85. Duan Chengyang, "Floating Population and Its Effects on Rural and Urban Socioeconomic Development," *Population Research*, Vol. 22, No. 4 (1998), as quoted in Ren, "Bare Branches among Rural Migrant Laborers in China," p. 16.
86. Linda Wong, "China's Urban Migrants—The Public Policy Challenge," *Pacific Affairs*, Vol. 67, No. 3 (Autumn 1994), p. 340.
87. Zhang Haiyang, "On Flowing Population in Qiqiha'er: Current Conditions and Management," *Plan Study*, n.s. 5 (1997), p. 23.

The influx of rural people has caused a variety of problems for the cities. Besides the extreme pressure derived from the shortage of living space, transportation, water, electricity, and gas supplies, the worst problem is crime. According to recent statistics from the Administers of Public Security, 569,000 of the offenders arrested by the police in 1994 were transient people. In Beijing, 44% of the crimes solved by the police were committed by transients. In Shanghai, this rate has been continually rising from 10% in the mid-1980s to 60%, even 80% in some districts, by 1995. In Xiamen, 62% of the crimes in general, and 82% of the felonies, were committed by transients. In Guangdong province, 90% of the prostitutes and drug traffickers were temporary residents. Burglary was the most serious crime in Guangzhou city in 1994, with 80% of it being committed by transients. Apparently, whereas the regular city residents are responsible for a portion of the crimes, the new migrants constitute a large majority of the problem in the major Chinese cities. Moreover, our study found that many crimes committed by transient people are senseless and ruthless. An argument over a word can lead to a cold-blooded fight; burglars often kill the victims or witnesses on the scene if the offense is observed; highway robbery, rape, and kidnapping usually end with the victims' death; and a complaint about the poor quality of goods sold by transient vendors can cause injury in a severe physical assault.[88]

Notable is the specific mention of details so characteristic of bare-branch behavior: senseless, ruthless violence over words, insults, and injured pride.

Other rebellious activity has been noted as well. One source notes that in 1996 there were 12,000 labor strikes and protests, mostly carried out by migrant workers with grievances over pay.[89] The 2001 entry of China into the World Trade Organization is thus a double-edged sword. On the one hand, entry into the WTO is liable to facilitate long-term Chinese prosperity. On the other hand, the concessions made by China will fall heavily on workers in both agriculture and heavy industry. Chi Lo, a senior Asian economist based in Hong Kong, expects urban employment to double as a result.[90] And another study suggests, "Millions of farmers . . . would have to leave their homes and find new jobs in urban areas."[91] One anonymous Western economist predicted a "blood bath" for Chinese farmers as a result of China's accession to the WTO.[92] It is important to remember that these two groups—farmers and

88. Yingyi Situ and Liu Weizheng, "Transient Population, Crime, and Solution: The Chinese Experience," *International Journal of Offender Therapy and Comparative Criminology,* Vol. 40, No. 4 (December 1996), p. 295.
89. Meng, "Confronting Three Populations of 80 Million," p. 78.
90. Paul Eckert, "China's Monumental Leap," Reuters, November 21, 1999, http://www.desnews.com/cgi-bin/libstory-state?dn99&9911220265.
91. Ibid.
92. Erik Eckholm, "One Giant Step for Mr. Jiang's China," *New York Times,* November 21, 1999, sec. 4, p. 4.

heavy-industry workers—are groups with a heavy representation of bare branches. What WTO accession means for China, then, is that more bare branches will join the ranks of the unemployed. In the short term, then, the potential for instability may be worse than economists estimate. We hope it is not worse than the Chinese government estimates. Indeed we could not help but note that press reports indicate that one major source of recruits for the Falun Gong is the unemployed.[93]

Observers of the larger picture seem intuitively aware of the propensities of bare-branch syndrome behavior to disrupt society. One source refers to the migrant workers as "a volatile social factor," another asserting that "the challenge facing Chinese officials—central, provincial and urban alike—is to keep this giant [migrant] work force happy, or at least satisfied with their lot. If they fail, public order will deteriorate as restless migrants tire of being treated as second-class citizens."[94] This deterioration is reflected in the fact that crime in China is increasing significantly over time. In 1998, criminal cases rose 22 percent, explosions increased 9 percent, and murders increased almost 6 percent.[95]

In a very interesting development that bears continued scrutiny, the Chinese government has increased the number of troops assigned to the People's Armed Police by fourteen divisions, to about 1 million men total. The mission of the People's Armed Police is to maintain internal stability, in particular by quelling incidents of domestic unrest and rioting typically caused by economic complaints regarding unemployment and taxes. According to policy analysts John Corbett and Dennis Blasko, "By increasing the size of the People's Armed Police, the leadership in Beijing implicitly acknowledges that internal unrest is a greater threat to the regime's survival and Chinese economic modernization than is foreign invasion."[96]

In a move fraught with ominous historical parallels, however, many of the new members of the People's Armed Police are what one expert termed "the dregs."[97] As noted, the use of bare branches by various Chinese dynasties to control other bare branches typically backfired. The abuses, corruption, and violence of the "co-opted" bare branches came to rival those of the bare-branch bandits they were supposed to be controlling. Keeping these "troops" close to

---

93. Eckert, "China's Monumental Leap."
94. First quote from Li, "Population Flow into Big Cities," p. 17; second quote from Gilley, "Irresistible Force," p. 18.
95. "Chinese Saw Crime Jump 22% in First 9 Months of 1998, Report Says," Reuters, February 10, 1999, http://www.desnews.com/cgi-bin/libstory-state?dn99&9902101255.
96. Quoted in Erik Eckholm, "A Secretive Army Grows to Maintain Order in China," *New York Times*, March 28, 1999, sec. 1, p. 6.
97. Quoted in ibid.

rich metropoles proved to be a very unwise strategy. In Robinson's study of mid-Ming banditry and rebellion, he finds that many of the foremost bandit and rebel leaders were formerly in the imperial military. Indeed some were *still* in the military while engaging in pillage and brigandage. As Robinson puts it, "Managing these men of force was a delicate balance, and the price of failure could be very high. The same factors that made these men attractive to military officers, civil officials, and local gentry were precisely those that made them most dangerous—skill in arms, physical bravery, a willingness to use violence, a band of followers, and ties that extended beyond the confines of local society. Allied with proper authorities, these men were a potent addition to the forces of order. If, however, relations between these men and the powers that be broke down, they became a frightening avatar of social chaos."[98]

INDIA

Much the same analysis can be made concerning India today, where the bare branches are to be found primarily in the north and northwest states.[99] Interestingly, these states are referred to as India's "Wild West," and hold almost half of India's population, as well as the highest fertility rates in the country and the highest sex ratios.

Power in these states, especially Uttar Pradesh (UP) and Bihar, comes from the organized criminal gangs (*goondas*) embedded deeply in their societies. Private armies abound, and corruption has led to the development of a kleptocracy, in which gangs are now elected officials in state government. More than 10 percent of Bihar's legislators are well-known criminals. In Uttar Pradesh, 132 of 424 members of the Vidhan Sabha are "suspected criminals."[100] In commenting on the pervasiveness of violent crime in Uttar Pradesh and Bihar, one journalistic account notes, "In Uttar Pradesh, kidnapping is a way of life, especially in the western UP. Most gangs are politically connected." Regarding Bihar, the account continues, "Kidnapping is one of the main growth industries. Two people are snatched for ransom every day."[101]

Indeed there is a statistically significant relationship between violent crime rates and the sex ratio in Indian states. Sen notes that "extensive interdistrict contrasts . . . show a strong—and statistically very significant—relation be-

---

98. Robinson, "The Management of Violence," p. 35.
99. *Census of India, 1991*, Series 1, Part 2-B(i), Primary Census Abstract General Population, Vol. 1.
100. Farzand Ahmed and Subhash Mishra, "Stooping to Conquer," *India Today International*, November 10, 1997, p. 22.
101. Samar Halarnkar, Sayantan Chakravarty, and Smruti Koppikar, "Fear in the City," *India Today International*, October 6, 1997, p. 14.

tween the female-male ratio in the population and the scarcity of violent crimes. Indeed, the inverse connection between murder rates and the female-male ratio in the population has been observed by many researchers."[102] Using 1981 crime statistics, Philip Oldenburg was able to show a striking correlation in Indian states and also in districts of Uttar Pradesh between the sex ratio and the murder rate. The calculated Pearson's r was -0.72 (sex ratio defined as number of females per 100 males). Indeed the states with the worst sex ratios—the states of the north and northwest of India—are termed by Oldenburg "the Bermuda Triangle for girls."[103]

Jean Dreze and Reetika Khera replicated Oldenburg's research, correlating murder rates (1980–82) with the female-to-male sex ratio (1981), in addition to other variables such as urbanization, poverty rate, literacy rate, and so forth. The strongest correlation found was between murder and sex ratio, which were inversely related. As the authors note, "This correlation is very robust: no matter which other variables are included or excluded from the regression, we found that the female-male ratio remained highly significant, always with a negative sign. Further, the size of the coefficient of the female-male ratio is quite large."[104] We updated the above analyses by using the 1991 census data and the most recent murder rate available (1997) and found the same strong relationship, yielding $p \leq .07$. This is prima facie evidence that this linkage has persisted in India through the late 1990s.

The robust and persistent link to be found in the Indian case leads us to the same conclusion as Dreze and Khera: "What seems clear is that there is a strong link of some kind between gender relations and criminal violence (not just violence against women, but violence in the society as a whole). . . . This issue may be crucial in understanding criminal violence in many societies."[105]

Conclusions

Francis Fukuyama has wondered whether the democratic peace phenomenon is better explained by the status of women in democracies than by the existence of democratic institutions themselves.[106] Our analysis takes this one step

---

102. Amartya Sen, *Development as Freedom* (New York: Alfred A. Knopf, 1999), p. 200.
103. Philip Oldenburg, "Sex Ratio, Son Preference, and Violence in India: A Research Note," *Economic and Political Weekly*, Vol. 27, Nos. 49 and 50 (1992), pp. 2657–2662.
104. Jean Dreze and Reetika Khera, "Crime, Gender, and Society in India: Insights from Homicide Data," *Population and Development Review*, Vol. 26, No. 2 (June 2000), p. 342.
105. Ibid., p. 347.
106. Francis Fukuyama, "Women and the Evolution of World Politics," *Foreign Affairs*, Vol. 77, No. 5 (September/October 1998), pp. 24–40.

further. In a way, the very type of government to which a nation can aspire may be tied to the status of women in society. When that status is very low, the possibilities for a full and meaningful democracy and for a peaceful foreign policy are distinctly less. High sex-ratio societies, denoting a very low status for women, cannot be expected to emulate normal sex-ratio societies either in terms of their form of government or in terms of their tendency toward peacefulness. Any attempts at that emulation may prove, historically speaking, to be short-lived. And any attempts by scholars from normal sex-ratio societies to project their own security logic onto a high sex-ratio society will lead to miscalculation. High sex-ratio societies simply have a different security calculus.

Our analysis does not lend itself to precise prediction. Nevertheless, a few broad prognostications can be put forward. First, the prognosis for the development of full democracy in China is poor. The prognosis for the maintenance of a viable democracy in India (or Pakistan for that matter) is troubled. These are all high sex-ratio societies, and their governments will be hard-pressed to deal with the ever-increasing numbers of bare branches that will arise in the next few decades. A move toward authoritarianism is much more likely, according to our analysis. As mentioned, we would also expect, in the case of India (and Pakistan), an increase in sectarian and ethnic violence.

Second, the prognosis for a conflict such as that over Kashmir between India and Pakistan is likewise poor. India and Pakistan, both high sex-ratio societies, are unlikely to settle the conflict peacefully. Though there may be occasional movements toward a settlement, we predict that the conflict will either remain a protracted war of attrition or, possibly, become an open interstate war. Each society has plenty of bare branches to spare in such a conflict—and the respective governments might be happy to spare them. Likewise, any compromise or conciliation will probably be viewed as humiliating by a high sex-ratio society. We found it noteworthy that the 1999 Pakistani pullback from Kashmir was followed in short order by a military coup in that nation.

We are tempted to suggest that the same logic would apply to the China-Taiwan controversy, but the international ramifications are much broader there, and deterrence may remain effective in this situation. Nevertheless, it should never be forgotten by policymakers on either side of the Pacific that the worst-case scenario implies that China may have close to 40 million young adult bare branches to spare in twenty years, and that the government may at that point ardently wish to see them give their lives in pursuit of a national interest. The alternative is to allow them to remain a threat to national interest, which may increasingly be seen as an untenable policy position by the government.

The bottom line is that the politics of handling significant numbers of bare branches are liable to become a more pronounced and more explicit part of government calculation in these nations. The relationship we see is not straightforward cause and effect: Strife and war obviously take place within and between normal sex-ratio cultures as well. Nevertheless, exaggerated gender inequality, as we have seen, may provide an aggravating catalyst to the mix of insecurity factors leading to conflict. All we have found suggests that high sex-ratio societies in contexts of unequal resource distribution and generalized resource scarcity breed chronic violence and persistent social disorder and corruption. Though these phenomena certainly exist as well in societies without high sex ratios, the bare branches of high sex-ratio societies present an unmistakable aggravating and amplifying effect, leading to disruption on a larger scale than might be possible in societies with lower sex ratios.

In conclusion, exaggerated gender inequality is a potentially serious source of scarcity and insecurity. As Barbara Miller has argued, a normal sex ratio is a "public good," and governments that fail to preserve that public good do their societies a disservice with tangible negative consequences.[107] The scale on which sex ratios are being artificially altered in Asia today is, generally speaking, unprecedented in human history. What are the consequences of this vast demographic shift? What happens to societies that explicitly *select* for increasing and disproportionate numbers of bare branches? We suggest that societies with young adult sex ratios of approximately 120 and above are inherently unstable, and both China and India are, at this writing, nearing that level and will probably surpass that level in the next two decades.[108] We stand at the thresh-

---

107. Barbara D. Miller, "Female-Selective Abortion in Asia: Patterns, Policies, and Debates," *American Anthropologist*, Vol. 103, No. 4 (December 2001), pp. 1083–1095.

108. In the historical time periods we examined, sex ratios of greater than 120 have been noted. With regard to China and India, such very high sex ratios were usually regionally or temporally bounded (a particular region would embrace female infanticide for a time). Never before in history, however, have entire nations engaged in such high rates of offspring sex selection. It is the new, cheap technology that allows for this heightened and nationwide prevalence. Thus the scale (in terms of what percentage of the country's population is practicing offspring sex selection) is unprecedented in human history. Also, never before have China and India had such huge populations. For example, China's population at the turn of the twentieth century was about 460 million persons. Today it is more than 1.2 billion persons. The combination of these two factors means that the sheer number of bare branches being created in Asia is also unprecedented in human history. Yet, given the pockets of high sex ratios in history, we can also say with some confidence that societies that reach and exceed 120 males per 100 females in the young-adult age group are inherently unstable.

old of a time in which these young surplus males will increasingly figure into the deliberations of Asian governments. Not only the nations of Asia, but the nations of the world will want to pay close attention to the ramifications of Asia's spiraling sex ratios and the policy choices they force upon Asian governments. How ironic it would be if women's issues, so long ignored in security studies as simply irrelevant, became a central focus of security scholars in the twenty-first century.

HIV/AIDS and the Changing Landscape of War in Africa

Stefan Elbe

Since the discovery of AIDS more than two decades ago, 60 million people have been infected with HIV, the virus that causes AIDS, and more than 20 million have died from AIDS-related illnesses. The HIV/AIDS pandemic has become a humanitarian and human security issue of almost unimaginable magnitude, representing one of the most pervasive challenges to human well-being and survival in many parts of the world.[1] It has taken a particularly heavy toll on sub-Saharan Africa, where AIDS is now the primary cause of death.[2] In light of this magnitude, HIV/AIDS is not only having devastating effects on the individuals and families touched by the illness; it is also beginning to have much wider social ramifications. In some African countries, HIV prevalence rates have reached between 20 and 30 percent of the adult population. In these countries HIV/AIDS is giving rise to a vast array of economic, social, and political problems.

An important development overlooked by scholars in this regard is the growing impact of HIV/AIDS on the nature and conduct of armed conflict in Africa.[3] As the director of the Joint United Nations Program on HIV/AIDS

Stefan Elbe is a Lecturer in International Relations at the University of Warwick and a Visiting Fellow at the International Institute for Strategic Studies in London.

---

1. For discussions of "human security," see United Nations Development Programme, *Human Development Report, 1994: New Dimensions of Human Security* (New York: Oxford University Press, 1994); Roland Paris, "Human Security: Paradigm Shift or Hot Air?" *International Security*, Vol. 26, No. 2 (Fall 2001), pp. 87–102; Jenny Hadingham, "Human Security and Africa: Polemic Opposites," *South African Journal of International Affairs*, Vol. 7, No. 2 (Winter 2000), pp. 113–121; and Caroline Thomas, *Global Governance, Development, and Human Security* (London: Pluto Press, 2000). With specific reference to HIV/AIDS, see Ulf Kristoffersson, "HIV/AIDS as a Human Security Issue: A Gender Perspective," paper prepared for the Expert Group Meeting, Windhoek, Namibia, November 13–17, 2000; Deepika Grover, "Local Responses to AIDS in South Africa: Gender/ Human Insecurity and Social Organising in the Context of Dwindling Social Resources," paper presented at the annual meeting of the International Studies Association, Chicago, Illinois, February 21–24, 2001; and Pieter Fourie and Martin Schönteich, "Africa's New Security Threat: HIV/ AIDS and Human Security in Southern Africa," *African Security Review*, Vol. 10, No. 4 (2001), pp. 29–57.
2. Joint United Nations Programme on HIV/AIDS (UNAIDS), *AIDS Epidemic Update* (Geneva: UNAIDS, December 2001), p. 2.
3. For recent studies on the security dimensions of infectious diseases in general, see National Intelligence Council, *National Intelligence Estimate: The Global Infectious Disease Threat and Its Implications for the United States* (Washington, D.C.: National Intelligence Council, January 2000); Chemical and Biological Arms Control Institute (CBACI) and Center for Strategic and International Studies (CSIS), *Contagion and Conflict: Health as a Global Security Challenge* (Washington, D.C.,

(UNAIDS) recently noted, "Conflict and HIV are entangled as twin evils."[4] Armed conflicts certainly facilitate the spread of HIV/AIDS, but the virus also leaves its distinctive mark on the nature and conduct of war in regions where prevalence rates are already high. Historically, novel social developments have tended to influence the ways in which societies wage war, and HIV/AIDS has proven no different. "Over the past five years," one analyst has noted, "HIV/AIDS has changed the landscape of war more than any other single factor."[5] To date, however, academic attention to this relatively new aspect has not been commensurate with the increasingly significant role that HIV/AIDS has played in recent armed conflicts in Africa.[6] The question for scholars is: What happens when a sexually transmitted, lethal illness such as AIDS is introduced into the social environment in which these conflicts take place?

This article argues that HIV/AIDS is increasingly influencing three components of armed conflicts in Africa: their combatants, how the conflicts are conducted, and their social significance. The argument developed over the next five sections is that although these influences may at times be subtle, together they are elevating the social cost of armed conflict in Africa to new levels.

The first section presents an overview of the AIDS epidemic in Africa. The second section explains how armed forces in Africa, embedded within this

and Stanford, Calif.: CBACI and CSIS, January 2000); Jonathan Ban, *Health, Security, and U.S. Global Leadership* (Washington, D.C.: CBACI, 2001); Andrew T. Price-Smith, *The Health of Nations: Infectious Disease, Environmental Change, and Their Effects on National Security and Development* (Cambridge, Mass.: MIT Press, 2001); and Patrick W. Kelley, "Transnational Contagion and Global Security," *Military Review*, Vol. 80, No. 3 (May–June 2000), pp. 59–64.

4. Peter Piot, speech delivered to the UN Security Council special session "The Situation in Africa: The Impact of AIDS on Peace and Security," New York, New York, January 10, 2000, p. 1.

5. Graça Machel, "The Impact of Armed Conflict on Children: A Critical Review of Progress Made and Obstacles Encountered in Increasing Protection for War-Affected Children," paper presented at the International Conference on War-Affected Children, Winnipeg, Canada, September 10–17, 2000, p. 15.

6. For studies of the broader security implications of HIV/AIDS, see Rodger Yeager and Stuart Kingma, "HIV/AIDS: Destabilising National Security and the Multi-National Response," *International Review of the Armed Forces Medical Services*, Vol. 74, Nos. 1–3 (2001), pp. 3–12; Greg Mills, "AIDS and the South African Military: Timeworn Cliché or Timebomb?" in Michael Lange, ed., *HIV/AIDS: A Threat to the African Renaissance?* Occasional Paper (Johannesburg, South Africa: Konrad Adenauer Foundation, 2000); Lindy Heinecken, "Strategic Implications of HIV/AIDS in South Africa," *Conflict, Security, and Development*, Vol. 1, No. 1 (2001), pp. 109–113; Roxanne Bazergan, "UN Peacekeepers and HIV/AIDS," *World Today*, Vol. 57, No. 5 (May 2001), pp. 6–8; Lindy Heinecken, "Living in Terror: The Looming Security Threat to Southern Africa," *African Security Review*, Vol. 10, No. 4 (2001), pp. 7–17; and Stefan Elbe, *The Strategic Dimensions of HIV/AIDS*, Adelphi Paper (Oxford: Oxford University Press for the International Institute for Strategic Studies, forthcoming); United States Institute of Peace (USIP), *AIDS and Violent Conflict in Africa* (Washington, D.C.: USIP, October 15, 2001); International Crisis Group (ICG), *HIV/AIDS as a Security Issue* (Washington, D.C., and Brussels: ICG, June 19, 2001); and Marcella David, "Rubber Helmets: The Certain Pitfalls of Marshalling Security Council Resources to Combat AIDS in Africa," *Human Rights Quarterly*, Vol. 23, No. 3 (August 2001), pp. 560–582.

larger social context, have become a high-risk group for the transmission of HIV/AIDS. The third section illustrates how the virus has been used as a weapon of war in some regions of the African continent. As a result, the social ramifications of these conflicts have begun to extend far beyond the battlefield, leading, as the fourth section argues, to a significant increase in the number of eventual AIDS-related war casualties. The article concludes by suggesting that the emerging symbiosis between HIV/AIDS and armed conflict in Africa can be reversed only if the combatants, as a high-risk group and vector of the illness, participate in local and international efforts to reduce its spread. To this end, it also suggests several policy recommendations.

HIV/AIDS in Africa

Armed conflicts in Africa are increasingly occurring in environments of widespread HIV/AIDS prevalence. To appreciate this important change in the broader social context of these conflicts, it is useful to consider the magnitude of the AIDS pandemic in Africa over the past two decades. Logistical, political, and human rights constraints complicate the task of collecting accurate data. Nevertheless, UNAIDS and the World Health Organization estimate that, in several sub- Saharan countries, between a fifth and a third of the adult populations are living with HIV/AIDS. In sub-Saharan Africa approximately 28.5 million persons are HIV positive, an estimated 3.5 million of whom became infected in 2001 alone.[7] At the same time, it is exceedingly difficult to generalize about the effects of HIV/AIDS in Africa, and important regional variations need to be considered.

Within sub-Saharan Africa, southern Africa has the largest proportion of people living with HIV and AIDS. South Africa alone is estimated to have around 5 million infected citizens, or roughly 20 percent of the adult population of the country. Officially, this is also the largest absolute number of HIV infections in any state in the world. Moving northward, in Botswana 38.8 percent of the adult population is thought to have contracted the virus, while in Mozambique 13 percent of adults are estimated to be living with the virus. Namibia has an adult prevalence rate of around 22.5 percent, while in Zimbabwe the figure is close to 34 percent. In Angola, where systematic testing began only recently, the adult HIV prevalence rate is 5.5 percent. In neighboring Zambia, approximately 1.2 million people are living with HIV, which trans-

---

7. UNAIDS, *A Global Overview of the Epidemic* (Geneva: UNAIDS, July 2002), p. 22. Subsequent HIV prevalence figures are taken from this study.

lates into an adult prevalence rate of nearly 21.5 percent. In central Africa, the Democratic Republic of Congo has an adult prevalence rate of around 5 percent, the threshold at which it becomes extremely difficult to prevent a larger, more widespread AIDS epidemic. In Burundi the adult prevalence rate is 8.3 percent, while in neighboring Rwanda it is estimated to be nearly 9 percent. In Tanzania 1.5 million people are living with HIV.

In eastern Africa, too, HIV prevalence rates continue to be very high, having reached 15 percent of the adult population in Kenya in 2001. Ethiopia is thought to have around 2.1 million infected persons. Uganda, by contrast, has been able to stabilize and even reduce its prevalence rate following the creation of programs designed to prevent the spread of HIV; the rate of HIV infection in Uganda fell from around 14 percent in the early 1990s to roughly 5 percent in 2001. In western Africa, Nigeria has 3.5 million HIV-infected persons and a 5.8 percent adult prevalence rate. Côte d'Ivoire has an estimated 690,000 adults living with HIV and an adult prevalence rate of nearly 10 percent. In Sierra Leone, the rate has increased to 7 percent not least due to the conflict between the government and the Revolutionary United Front.[8] Importantly, however, infection rates in five west African countries (Burkina Faso, Congo, Nigeria, Sierra Leone, and Togo) are close to or slightly above the crucial 5 percent threshold.

Data on HIV prevalence rates in northern Africa are scarce. Local studies indicate that HIV is spreading among the populations in both northern and southern Sudan. In southern Sudan, in particular, the rates are increasing partly because of the ongoing hostilities between the government and the separatist Sudanese Popular Liberation Army and partly because of the region's proximity to other countries with high infection rates such as Kenya, Uganda, and Zaire.[9] In southern Algeria around 1 percent of pregnant women who visit antenatal clinics test positive for the AIDS virus.[10] In Libya a court recently dismissed charges brought against nine Libyan citizens, six Bulgarian health workers, and a Palestinian who had been detained since early 1999. They had been accused of involvement in a foreign intelligence plot to destabilize Libya by intentionally infecting 393 children at the Al-Fateh Children's Hospital in Benghazi, northeast of Tripoli, with HIV-contaminated blood.[11] Still, northern Africa remains the least affected region on the continent.

---

8. See Simon Robinson, "Battle Ahead," *Time,* July 16, 2001, p. 31.
9. Gustavo Capdevila, "UN Issues Call for Emergency Aid," Inter Press, February 18, 1997.
10. UNAIDS, fact sheet "HIV/AIDS in Africa," Geneva, Switzerland, December 2000.
11. "Libya Court Rejects HIV Plot Charges," BBC News, February 17, 2002.

These figures are best seen as indicators of broad trends, not as an exact reflection of the prevailing reality. Nevertheless, this brief survey underscores the immense magnitude of the AIDS epidemic in Africa, which has the misfortune of hosting not only a significant number of the world's armed conflicts but also its most serious AIDS pandemic.

HIV/AIDS in Africa's Armed Forces

The HIV/AIDS pandemic has already begun to diminish the operational efficiency of many of Africa's armed forces. Indeed these forces are at its core. Prevalence rates of sexually transmitted diseases among military personnel usually exceed those of the civilian population by a factor of two to five. In many African militaries, this is also true with regard to HIV.[12] These higher prevalence rates result from a variety of factors: Soldiers, for example, are of a sexually active age; they are highly mobile and away from home for long periods of time; they often valorize violent and risky behavior; they have greater opportunities for casual sexual relations; and they may seek to relieve themselves from the stress of combat through sexual activity. These same factors make soldiers more vulnerable to other sexually transmitted diseases that can increase their chances of contracting HIV through unprotected sex.

Recently, the defense ministries of several countries in sub-Saharan Africa documented HIV prevalence rates among their armed forces that averaged between 10 and 20 percent. In some countries, however, where the AIDS virus has been present for more than ten years, the prevalence rates have climbed to as high as 50 to 60 percent.[13] The U.S. National Intelligence Council lists the following figures for HIV prevalence in selected military populations in sub-Saharan Africa: Angola 40–60 percent, Congo-Brazzaville 10–25 percent, Côte d'Ivoire 10–20 percent, Democratic Republic of Congo 40–60 percent, Eritrea 10 percent, Nigeria 10–20 percent, and Tanzania 15–30 percent.[14] These figures were provided to the council by the U.S. Defense Intelligence Agency. It remains unclear, however, how they were obtained and, in light of their considerable margins, whether they are based on actual testing or anecdotal evidence. Regardless, they are compatible with a recent South African defense intelligence assessment that arrived at the following figures: Angola 50 per-

12. UNAIDS, fact sheet, "AIDS and the Military," Geneva, Switzerland, May 1998, p. 2.
13. Lindy Heinecken, "AIDS: The New Security Frontier," *Conflict Trends*, Vol. 3, No. 4 (2000), pp. 12–15.
14. National Intelligence Council, *The Global Infectious Disease Threat*.

cent, Botswana 33 percent, Democratic Republic of Congo 50 percent, Lesotho 40 percent, Malawi 50 percent, Namibia 16 percent, South Africa 15–20 percent, Swaziland 48 percent, Zambia 60 percent, and Zimbabwe 55 percent.[15]

These two sets of figures jibe with media reports from these countries. With regard to southern Africa, Mosiuoa Lekota, the South African defense minister, has stated that 17 percent of his country's soldiers are HIV positive,[16] although some recent reports place the figure closer to 50–60 percent.[17] The Namibian defense minister, Erkki Nghimtina, has claimed that nearly one-third of Namibia's 15,000-strong National Defense Force are living with HIV/AIDS.[18] In Botswana the military infection rate is reported to be around one-third,[19] while in parts of the Zimbabwean armed forces, the figure may have reached 75–80 percent as early as 1993.[20] In Zambia the figures for HIV infection in the defense forces are so high that authorities have decided not to disclose them.[21] One report also suggests that Malawi's key public services, including the military, would see a reduction in their workforces of between 25 and 50 percent by 2005 due to the spread of HIV/AIDS.[22]

Further northward, public sources have reported HIV prevalence rates of 22 percent in the armed forces of the Central African Republic, and as high as 50 percent of the troops in Angola and the Democratic Republic of Congo.[23] Other reports have suggested that the Congolese armed forces have a 14 percent infection rate and that AIDS is now the number one cause of death among these forces. According to Congolese Col. Prosper Kinzonzi, the equivalent of three

---

15. Heinecken, "Living in Terror," p. 11.

16. "17 Percent of South African Soldiers HIV-positive: Minister," Agence France-Presse, September 15, 2000.

17. Jean Le May, "More Than Half of South Africa's Army 'May Have HIV,'" *Independent* (London), July 15, 2002.

18. "HIV/AIDS Rife in Namibia Defence Forces," Panafrican News Agency, February 16, 2001.

19. Heinecken, "AIDS: The New Security Frontier."

20. Mills, "AIDS and the South African Military," p. 69. Paul Kirk, however, reports prevalence rates of 75 percent of the armed forces of Malawi and 80 percent of the armed forces of Zimbabwe. Kirk, "Sixty Percent of Army May Be HIV-Positive," *Daily Mail and Guardian* (Johannesburg), March 31, 2000.

21. Masautso Chipako, "Who Will Deliver the Military from High AIDS Figures?" *Times of Zambia,* June 26, 1999.

22. "HIV/AIDS Devastating Military," UN Integrated Regional Information Network, March 3, 2001; and Martin Foreman and Thomas Scalway, *Men and HIV in Malawi* (London: Panos Institute, November 2000). This is also supported by statements from Gen. Joseph Chimbayo, the commander of the Malawi army. See Michelle Sieff, "HIV/AIDS: Under Siege," *World Today*, Vol. 57, No. 5 (May 2001), p. 5.

23. Sven Groennings, ed., *HIV/AIDS Strategy in Latin America and Africa: Military and Civil-Military Policies and Issues*, Occasional Paper No. 1 (Geneva: Civil Military Alliance to Combat HIV and AIDS, April 1997), cited in Martin Foreman, *AIDS and Men—Old Problem, New Angle,* HIV/AIDS Briefing No. 6 (London: Panos Institute, December 1998).

companies died from AIDS-related illnesses between 1989 and 1993.[24] In Sierra Leone, more than 21 percent of the 1,099 candidates recently screened for military service tested positive for the AIDS virus. Another 1,000 soldiers who showed signs of disease over the past three years were found to be HIV positive. According to Maj. James Samba, the rate of infection among Sierra Leone's 12,000-strong military force is between a quarter and a third.[25] Given the sensitive nature of such information and that data of this kind are often considered a matter of national security, accurate figures are hard to obtain. Although this means that these figures must be treated with caution, it underscores the perceived relationship between HIV/AIDS and security.

Nor are the impacts of these high prevalence rates only of marginal relevance. According to Maj. Gen. Matshwenyego Fisher, chief of staff of the Botswana defense force, "AIDS in the military as well as in the national environment is no longer an academic issue; it is a reality that has to be tackled with all the vigor and effort that is commensurate with its ramifications."[26]

These high rates are influencing at least four aspects of operational efficiency among Africa's armed forces. First, they are generating the need for additional resources for the recruitment and training of soldiers to replace those who have fallen ill, have died, or are expected to die in the near future from HIV/AIDS. Additional resources are also required to provide health care for soldiers who are sick or dying.

Second, the spread of HIV/AIDS is affecting important staffing decisions. High HIV prevalence rates eventually lead to (1) a decrease in the available conscription pool from which to draw new recruits, (2) deaths among officers higher up the chain of command, and (3) a loss of highly specialized and technically trained staff who cannot be easily or quickly replaced.

Third, the presence of HIV/AIDS can hinder the ability of soldiers to carry out their duties. It can result in increased absenteeism and reduced morale, as healthy soldiers must assume heavier workloads until replacements are found for those who are sick or have already died. Another factor is the emotional impact on soldiers of watching their comrades die slow, painful deaths. Fears of caring for injured soldiers in light of the possibility of contracting the virus, and the question of how to secure blood supplies during military operations, are similarly becoming concerns for the efficient execution of deployments.

---

24. Lyne Mikangou, "AIDS the Number One Cause of Death in the Army," Inter Press, January 10, 2000.

25. James Astill, "War Injects AIDS into Sierra Leone," *Daily Mail and Guardian* (Johannesburg), May 21, 2001.

26. Quoted in UNAIDS, "AIDS and the Military," p. 7.

Fourth, HIV/AIDS is generating new political and legal challenges for civil-military relations in terms of how to deal with this issue in the ranks and how to treat persons living with the virus.[27] The Namibian military, for example, recently lost a lengthy court case involving its decision to exclude HIV-positive persons from the armed forces. The court found the military's decision to be unconstitutional.

Although the combined impact of these factors is unlikely to prevent militaries from engaging in combat activities altogether, they are beginning to take a toll on operational efficiency. Lindy Heinecken, of the South African Centre for Military Studies, has noted that high HIV/AIDS prevalence rates have meant that the armed forces in some African countries have been unable to deploy a full contingent on short notice, in some cases not even half of their troops.[28] It is an assessment shared by Greg Mills, director of the South African Institute of International Affairs, who when writing about sending a peacekeeping mission to Congo noted that "the high rate of infection in SADC [Southern African Development Community] armies . . . calls into question the nature and size of their potential contribution" to such a mission.[29] Although this impact may not necessarily be detrimental to the capabilities of armed forces in the region, it does pose important new challenges. Moreover, it illustrates one way in which HIV/AIDS has already begun to have implications for the security sectors of countries with high prevalence rates.

HIV/AIDS also has consequences for international security more generally because, as mentioned above, many of these armed forces contribute to international peacekeeping operations. HIV/AIDS presents novel political problems for these operations, as it becomes widely known that peacekeepers contribute to the spread of HIV/AIDS where and when they are deployed. This has already begun to affect the perceptions of countries hosting such operations as well as of those states contributing to them.[30] The Cambodian government, for example, places considerable blame for its country's high level of HIV prevalence on the United Nations Transition Authority in Cambodia, even though there is no epidemiological data to determine how significant a factor it is in relation to other possible sources of the epidemic. How much these perceptions will strengthen in the years to come remains to be seen, but clearly they have created concerns and political tensions that need to be ad-

---

27. For an elaboration of these points, see Elbe, *The Strategic Dimensions of HIV/AIDS*, chap. 2.
28. Heinecken, "Strategic Implications of HIV/AIDS in South Africa," p. 110.
29. Mills, "AIDS and the South African Military," p. 70.
30. See Elbe, *The Strategic Dimensions of HIV/AIDS*, chap. 3.

dressed.[31] Moreover, they are likely to raise questions about the West's strategy of devolving peacekeeping operations in Africa to the regional level.[32]

Thus, in addition to its potential long-term destabilizing impact, the HIV/AIDS pandemic poses a range of novel challenges for those charged with carrying out decisions to deploy armed force—be it in offensive, defensive, or peacekeeping operations. Moreover, as one of the high-risk groups for contracting HIV/AIDS, armed forces will have an important, long-term role in efforts to address the AIDS pandemic. In terms of the complex role that HIV/AIDS has played in recent African armed conflicts, however, this marks only the first phase of a much more destructive cycle that has emerged over the past decade.

HIV/AIDS as a Weapon of War

While HIV/AIDS is diminishing the operational efficiency of many armed forces in Africa, it is also providing them with a novel psychological and biological weapon of war, the use of which has been threatened when hostilities have broken out. One of the most striking aspects of recent armed conflicts in Africa is the deliberate targeting of civilians and the widespread use of rape, which has been employed as a systematic tool of warfare in conflicts in Liberia, Mozambique, Rwanda, and Sierra Leone. Although official statistics are not yet available, human rights workers from Sierra Leone have reported that during the country's eight-year civil war, armed rebels and insurgent forces raped thousands of women.[33] Human Rights Watch has documented the systematic nature of the sexual violence perpetrated against women by rebel forces, noting how the latter "planned and launched operations in which they rounded up girls and women, brought them to rebel command centers and then subjected them to individual and gang-rape."[34] In the Rwandan conflict, observers have suggested that between 200,000 and 500,000 women were raped.[35] In some areas, especially in and around the capital, Kigali, the vast majority of fe-

---

31. See U.S. General Accounting Office, *UN Peacekeeping: United Nations Faces Challenges in Responding to the Impact of HIV/AIDS on Peacekeeping Operations* (Washington, D.C.: Government Printing Office, December 2001).
32. Mills, "AIDS and the South African Military," p. 70.
33. Douglas Farah, "A War against Women," *Washington Post*, April 11, 2000, p. 1.
34. "Sierra Leone: Getting Away with Murder, Mutilation, Rape," *Human Rights Watch Report*, Vol. 11, No. 3a (July 1999), http://www.hrw.org/reports/1999/sierra.
35. Manuel Carballo, Carolyn Mansfield, and Michaela Prokop, *Demobilization and Its Implications for HIV/AIDS*, Linking Complex Emergency Response and Transition Initiative (CERTI) Crisis and Transition Tool Kit, October 2000, p. 16, n. 5; and Lisa Sharlach, "Rape as Genocide: Bangladesh, the Former Yugoslavia, and Rwanda," *New Political Science*, Vol. 22, No. 1 (March 2000), p. 98.

male survivors were victims of rape.[36] Though not a new phenomenon, rape is an important manifestation of how recent conflicts have been waged, and how conflicts can spread beyond combatants to civilian populations.

Diseases, too, have long been used as weapons of war. During the bubonic plague in Europe, attackers catapulted infected dead bodies over city walls with the aim of infecting and weakening both the enemy and the city's inhabitants. The weaponization of naturally occurring and man-made biological agents in the course of the twentieth century and the renewed threat of bioterrorism underscore the continuing relevance of biological agents in warfare. Evidence from recent armed conflicts in Africa suggests that militaries and armed militias have begun to sporadically appropriate HIV as a psychological, and perhaps even biological, weapon of war.[37] Indeed UNAIDS officials have claimed that "there have been documented instances in which AIDS has been used as an instrument of war."[38] More specifically, they have noted that "soldiers involved in conflicts in the Great Lakes Region of Africa reportedly raped women of 'the enemy side' with the stated intent of infecting them with HIV."[39]

It is of course notoriously difficult to determine when the transmission of HIV is deliberate, especially in environments where orders are mostly communicated orally. Moreover, the true motivation of the perpetrators is most likely known only to them, and they are unlikely to admit their culpability. At the same time, there is documented testimony from female survivors of rape in Rwanda that the transmission of HIV was a deliberate act. According to some accounts, HIV-positive Hutu men would tell the women they were raping that they would eventually suffer an agonizing death from AIDS.[40] Margaret Owen has noted that both radio communications and testimony from Tutsi rape victims confirm the deliberate nature of these acts. According to Owen, some of the rapists allegedly taunted: "We are not killing you. We are giving you something worse. You will die a slow death."[41] Similar stories have been recounted

---

36. Sharlach, "Rape as Genocide," p. 98.

37. Vivienne Nathanson, "Preventing and Limiting Suffering Should Conflict Break Out: The Role of the Medical Profession," *International Review of the Red Cross*, September 30, 2000, pp. 601–615.

38. UNAIDS, "UN Security Council Meeting on HIV/AIDS in Africa: Briefing Pack," January 10, 2000, p. 7.

39. UNAIDS press release, "AIDS Becoming Africa's Top Human Security Issue, UN Warns," January 10, 2000, p. 1.

40. Sharlach, "Rape as Genocide," p. 99. See also Andrew Lawday, *HIV and Conflict: A Double Emergency* (London: Save the Children, 2002), pp. 5, 11.

41. Margaret Owen, "Widows Expose HIV War Threat," *Worldwoman News*, June 12, 2001, p. 1.

by Joseph Karemera, the Rwandan minister of health, who has stated that captured women were taken to HIV-positive soldiers specifically to be raped,[42] as well as by Chantal Kayitesi, of the Rwandan Association of Genocide Widows.[43] In these cases, the transmission of HIV would not appear to be a "one-off" or merely accidental feature of war.

It seems likely, then, that the deliberate transmission of HIV/AIDS has been used in Africa at a minimum as a psychological weapon of war to induce further anxiety among females in societies that have become war zones. Because these societies attach a high social stigma to those who may carry the virus, testifying on these matters is extremely difficult. Indeed, given this stigma, it seems unlikely that victims of rape would lie about having experienced such a horrific event.

Preliminary evidence suggests that the HIV prevalence rate among rape survivors is high. Two-thirds of a recent sample of 1,200 Rwandan genocide widows tested positive for HIV.[44] Although it has not yet been proven, it is possible that the virus was deliberately spread: Soldiers could have already known that they were HIV positive from having been tested or from having an infected spouse. Another possibility is that they already had some other opportunistic infection that would have increased their chances of contracting HIV. Moreover, given the brutality of other offenses committed during the Rwandan genocide, it seems unlikely that soldiers would have refrained from an act such as rape on humanitarian grounds. Given the duration of the conflict and the deliberate targeting of the civilian population during the hostilities, it could have even been seen as a "useful" strategy.

Similar accusations have been levied by a Congolese minister who claims that, during the conflict in the Democratic Republic of Congo, Ugandan troops used HIV/AIDS as a weapon in cities under their control.[45] Again, however, these allegations have not yet been proven. It is conceivable, for example, that the Ugandan government may have decided to deploy HIV-positive soldiers rather than healthy troops precisely because of their shorter life expectancies. This could have been seen as a way to reduce the spread of the virus at home.

42. "HIV/AIDS as a Weapon of War," newsletter of the Civil-Military Alliance to Combat HIV/ AIDS, Vol. 1, No. 2 (April 1995), p. 3.
43. Sharlach, "Rape as Genocide," p. 99.
44. "Genocide Widows Die of AIDS," *New Vision* (Kampala), December 11, 2001.
45. Mulegwa Zihindula, "Rape: A Weapon of War," General Board of Global Ministries news archives, December 10, 1998. See also United Nations Security Council, 4087th meeting, January 10, 2000, Official Records of the Security Council, S/PV. 4087 (Resumption 1), p. 40.

Any such decision, however, would have had to have been made in awareness of the social consequences for civilians in those regions where the soldiers were deployed. In Sierra Leone, for example, Amnesty International has already reported the first AIDS-related deaths resulting from HIV infections transmitted during rape.[46]

Regardless of whether the spread of HIV through rape can be proven to have been deliberate, the virus's very existence makes this practice all the more problematic on human rights and social grounds. It also further blurs the distinction between (1) rape and deliberate killing and (2) civilians and combatants. Practically speaking, the question of intent is secondary. The likelihood of contracting HIV during rape is, after all, considerable given the violent nature of the act and the fact that it often creates wounds through which the virus can enter into the bloodstream.[47] This chance of transmission is multiplied when victims are raped repeatedly. In the first instance, therefore, it does not matter whether the transmission was deliberate, because transmission occurred nonetheless—and with lethal consequences. Even in those cases where HIV transmission did not occur, the psychological stress would still have been considerable.

Finally, HIV/AIDS can be used as a weapon of war independent of the practice of rape. One highly disconcerting example involved the apartheid regime in South Africa. In 1998, following the transition to democracy, the country's Truth and Reconciliation Commission heard testimony that the regime may have planned to use HIV against its political enemies. "In at least one case," a South African newspaper reports, "the Civil Co-operation Bureau is thought to have been involved in collecting infected blood—possibly from a dying double agent—to be used in 'an operation.'"[48] Bacteriologist Mike Odendaal has stated that the head of the Roodeplaat Research Laboratories near Pretoria, which functioned as a front company for the apartheid military, had given him a bottle with HIV-infected blood taken from a man who had died of AIDS in a military hospital. Odendaal testified that he had received orders to freeze-dry the blood for Wouter Basson, a chemical-warfare specialist who allegedly wanted to use it "against a political opponent." Basson's defense counsel denied the allegation, claiming as ridiculous the suggestion that anyone would

---

46. Amnesty International, "Sierra Leone: Rape and Other Forms of Sexual Violence against Girls and Women," AFR 51/035/2000, June 26, 2000, p. 2.
47. Sharlach, "Rape as Genocide," p. 99.
48. Tvette Van Breda, "AIDS Link to CCB Probed," *Sunday Times* (South Africa), June 21, 1998, http://www.suntimes.co.za/1998/06/21/news/news11.htm.

"grab the enemy, inject him with the [HIV] infected blood, and he would only die 14 years later."[49]

It is not necessary, however, to go to such extremes to weaponize HIV. Willie Nortje and Andries van Heerden, security officers under the apartheid regime, requested amnesty from the Truth and Reconciliation Commission for their part in a different plan. They tried to use four HIV-positive freedom fighters from the African National Congress and the Pan Africanist Congress, who had switched sides to work for the state security forces, to spread HIV/AIDS among sex workers in two Hillbrow hotels in the 1990s. Nortje and Van Heerden apparently hoped that the sex workers would then spread the virus to their other clients.[50]

Such appropriations of HIV/AIDS by armed forces in Africa reflect the virus's increasing significance as a weapon of war. Combatants have sought to use the psychological and lethal effects of HIV/AIDS to gain strategic advantages over their opponents. For this reason, too, a concerted response to the global AIDS pandemic can be successful only if the security sectors have an important role. This is all the more important because HIV/AIDS not only changes the way in which armed conflicts are conducted but also increases the number of persons who will eventually die as a result of these conflicts.

HIV/AIDS and the Casualties of War

HIV/AIDS also affects armed conflicts by significantly increasing the number of eventual war-related casualties. In many African conflicts, indirect casualties of war already exceed munitions-related ones. In the Democratic Republic of Congo, for example, it was estimated that 2.5 million more deaths occurred between August 1998 and March 2001 than would have had there been no conflict. Three hundred fifty thousand of these deaths are thought to have resulted from direct acts of violence; the vast majority of the rest were caused by disease and malnutrition.[51] Given that AIDS is a lethal illness and that armed conflicts further frustrate the ability of individuals and communities to stem the spread of HIV, hostilities in regions with high prevalence rates generate

---

49. "Apartheid Scientists Kept HIV-Infected Blood for 'Political Enemy,'" Agence France-Presse, May 24, 2000.
50. "Apartheid Forces Spread AIDS," Agence France-Presse, November 12, 1999. See also Tom Mangold and Jeff Goldberg, *Plague Wars: A True Story of Biological Warfare* (London: Macmillan, 1999), p. 253.
51. Les Roberts, *Mortality in Eastern Democratic Republic of Congo* (New York: International Rescue Committee, 2001), p. 3.

large numbers of additional civilian casualties of war that are not munitions related. In this way, HIV/AIDS can push conflicts further toward their social
limits, wagering the existence not only of the combatants but also of entire segments of society. In addition to the practice of rape, there are at least four other
ways in which armed conflicts facilitate increases in the number of HIV trans-
missions that will eventually lead to AIDS-related deaths.

First, armed conflicts strain already poorly equipped medical facilities. In
some African countries, only around 40 percent of people have access to such
facilities in peacetime. Armed conflicts, like AIDS itself, place additional
strains on this infrastructure and its personnel. Medical facilities that remain
operational in wartime frequently lack vital resources such as clean water,
trained staff, medicines, and basic equipment. At times they may already be
substantially filled with AIDS patients.[52] Health and medical centers can be
targets of looting and are often singled out for attack to demoralize the civilian
population.[53] Again, the eastern part of the Democratic Republic of Congo has
been particularly vulnerable in this regard, with a large number of its hospitals
having been destroyed during the hostilities.[54] While resources have been used
to fight off rebel groups from neighboring countries, even basic HIV/AIDS
prevention measures have been lacking.[55] In Sierra Leone the supply of con-
doms to residents of Freetown was disrupted during the January 1999 rebel
invasion, and community- and school-based education programs were discon-
tinued.[56]

Second, civilians are at greater risk of becoming infected with HIV/AIDS because of the demographic disruptions caused by armed conflicts. These disruptions put individuals in situations where they are much more vulnerable to
contracting the virus. In refugee camps, for example, women may trade sex for
vital goods such as food, water, money, shelter, and firewood; some may even
be sold into sexual slavery by family members or spouses.[57] In other cases, the
configuration of the camps themselves may encourage such activities. Water
taps and latrines are often situated at considerable distances from the refugees'

52. Oxfam International, *No End in Sight: The Human Tragedy of the Conflict in the Democratic Republic of Congo* (London: Oxfam International, August 6, 2001).
53. Jordan S. Kassalow, "Why Health Is Important to U.S. Foreign Policy," paper prepared for the
Council on Foreign Relations, New York and Washington, D.C., April 2001.
54. Oxfam International, *No End in Sight.*
55. See Mark Lynas, *No Excuses: Facing Up to Sub-Saharan Africa's AIDS Orphans Crisis* (London:
Christian Aid, May 14, 2001), chap. 2.
56. Lansana Fofana, "Sierra Leone: Conflict Spurs the Spread of HIV/AIDS," Inter Press, July 5,
1999.
57. Rodger Yeager and Donna Ruscavage, *HIV Prevention and Behavior Change in International Military Populations*, CERTI Crisis and Transition Tool Kit, September 2000, http://www.certi.org.

dwellings, which means that women and girls risk being raped on their way to and from these facilities. Others may be pressed into performing sexual favors for self-appointed guards.[58] To date, however, relatively little attention has been paid to the problem of HIV/AIDS in refugee camps, although there are signs that this is slowly changing.[59]

Third, armed conflicts can increase the spread of HIV into rural areas, where mortality rates are likely to rise as a result. During the Rwandan conflict, infection rates in rural areas more than doubled.[60] Between 1989 and 1998, rural infection rates in Burundi increased from 1 percent to 20 percent—for a variety of reasons, including the erection of refugee camps and continued adherence to traditional practices such as polygamy and ritual scarification with unsterilized equipment.[61] In some cases, this process has been reversed. During the conflict in Sudan, for example, rural inhabitants have moved to urban centers, where there are higher rates of infection.[62] In both cases, the increased intermingling between urban and rural populations has facilitated the spread of HIV/AIDS.

Finally, armed conflicts contribute to increases in AIDS-related deaths by encouraging an inversion of priorities, as combatants and civilians are forced to deal with more immediate and more pressing needs, allowing them to avoid thinking about the potential consequences of HIV infection. As a result, HIV/AIDS does not receive the attention that it merits. Pascale Crussard, director of CARE's AIDS program in Gitarama, Rwanda, sums it up this way, "The priority for these people . . . is not AIDS. It's security. When people can die tomorrow from a machete wound, I'm not sure they think much about AIDS, from which they could die in 10 years."[63]

This is true at both the individual and the collective levels. Countries involved with armed conflicts have fewer resources with which to educate their populations about HIV prevention. Ileka Atoki, the Democratic Republic of Congo's ambassador to the United Nations, noted the extraordinary difficulty

---

58. Judy A. Benjamin, "Conflict, Post-Conflict, and HIV/AIDS—The Gender Connections," remarks presented at the World Bank, Washington, D.C., March 8, 2001.

59. "UNHCR Tackles HIV/AIDS in Refugee Camps," UN Integrated Regional Information Network, August 9, 2001, http://www.irinnews.org.

60. Millicent Obaso, remarks presented at the United States Institute for Peace Current Issues Briefing Panel "Plague upon Plague: AIDS and Violent Conflict in Africa," Washington, D.C., May 8, 2001.

61. "Burundi: Rural Population Increasingly Affected by HIV-AIDS," UN Integrated Regional Information Network, April 14, 2000.

62. Nhial Bol, "AIDS on the Increase in the Military, Report Says," Inter Press, July 10, 1997.

63. Quoted in James C. McKinley Jr., "Ravaged by War and Massacre, Rwanda Faces Scourge of AIDS," *New York Times*, May 28, 1998, p. 1.

of combating HIV/AIDS in 1991 when his country was being pillaged, and again in 1994, when it became the unwilling host to millions of refugees from neighboring Rwanda.[64] The situation was similar in Sierra Leone. As Gabriel Madiye, head of Sierra Leone's only hospice for persons living with HIV/AIDS, once remarked, "Here is a country going through a civil war. If you recognize that we have a war and AIDS, which one are you going to put a premium on? War's impact is immediate. AIDS is a silent war."[65] On both the individual and collective levels, then, armed conflicts create other priorities that further undermine efforts to prevent the diffusion of HIV/AIDS among civilians. The longer this is ignored, the more widespread the pandemic will become.

In the aggregate, then, armed conflicts and their participants constitute an important vector of HIV/AIDS, a virus responsible for killing more than ten times as many people in Africa as the conflicts themselves.[66] Although these hostilities generate conditions that increase the difficulty of gathering epidemiological data, it is possible to corroborate this link. An epidemiological study carried out by two Cambridge University geographers in Uganda, for example, concluded that "the apparent geographical pattern of clinical AIDS in Uganda partially reflects the diffusion of HIV associated with civil war during the first six years of the post-Amin period."[67] It is likely that the war to overthrow the Ugandan dictator Idi Amin in the late 1970s played a major role in the emergence of AIDS as a widespread phenomenon in the region. When the last Tanzanian soldiers were returning from Uganda after Amin's overthrow, AIDS cases began to appear on both sides of the border.[68] It might be a while, however, before the full extent of the longer-term impact of these more recent armed conflicts can be documented, although it is already evident that they are having similar effects.

For scholars of armed conflict, the recognition that HIV/AIDS is being spread by soldiers presents a new challenge. The increase in HIV/AIDS–related cases is pushing these conflicts closer to their logical limits, giving rise to questions about the viability of war as a means of addressing social conflict. Today African civilians who manage to survive an armed conflict may still face

---

64. United Nations press release, SC/6781, January 10, 2000.
65. Quoted in Robinson, "Battle Ahead," p. 31.
66. Sandra Thurman, "Joining Forces to Fight HIV and AIDS," *Washington Quarterly*, Vol. 24, No. 1 (Winter 2001), pp. 191–192.
67. Matthew Smallman-Raynor and Andrew D. Cliff, "Civil War and the Spread of AIDS in Central Africa," *Epidemiology and Infection*, No. 107 (August 1991), p. 78.
68. Edward Hooper, *The River: A Journey Back to the Source of HIV and AIDS* (London: Penguin, 2000), p. 44.

the prospect of slow, painful deaths years after the hostilities have ended—a situation that many Rwandans are currently confronting. These casualties may eventually outnumber those resulting from the conflicts themselves and may, in the long run, pose far greater social and medical challenges.[69] Thus, the growing influence of HIV/AIDS in conflicts in Africa may present the same stark choice that Western Europe faced half a century ago, albeit for different reasons: Abolish war as an instrument for addressing political differences or gradually be abolished yourself. Whatever the short-term gains produced by armed conflicts, the presence of HIV/AIDS is rendering them increasingly irrational and counterproductive in the long term.

Conclusion

HIV/AIDS has played an increasingly significant role in recent armed conflicts in Africa. It has evolved from a virus that disproportionately affected the armed forces and weakened their operational efficiency to one that has begun to enter into the strategic calculations of combatants as a weapon of war. Given that armed conflicts facilitate the spread of HIV/AIDS, however, the presence of HIV/AIDS is raising the social stakes of these conflicts to new levels. Just as the emergence of industrial and nuclear warfare in the twentieth century wagered the existence not only of combatants but of entire societies, so too is the introduction of HIV/AIDS into armed conflicts in Africa gradually escalating the social costs of war as a way to resolve differences.

This emerging symbiosis between HIV/AIDS and armed conflict can be reversed only if Africa's armed forces, as a high-risk group and vector of the illness, contribute to international efforts to reduce its spread. Success requires their involvement. Only then can local, regional, and international agencies arrange to deliver preventive measures and treatments, to raise awareness in the armed forces about the role they play in the larger pandemic, and to devote serious and sustained national and international efforts to addressing the issue of HIV/AIDS. If the international community is to find a remedy for the global AIDS pandemic, the armed forces in Africa will have to be encouraged through economic and political means to make a contribution to this objective. This of course is a tall order, but not an impossible one. Indeed, in countries such as Thailand and Uganda, considerable decreases were achieved in their

---

69. For studies of the impact on HIV/AIDS on postconflict transitions, see Johanna Mendelson Forman and Manuel Carballo, "A Policy Critique of HIV/AIDS and Demobilization," *Conflict, Security, and Development*, Vol. 1, No. 2 (2001), pp. 73–92.

overall HIV prevalence rates in no small measure because their militaries chose to cooperate on this issue in an open and responsible manner. Perhaps for this reason more than any other, the AIDS pandemic should be understood not only as a global health issue but also as an international security issue.

POLICY RECOMMENDATIONS

If Africa is to successfully address the spread of HIV/AIDS, its leaders and the international community more generally must increase their level of cooperation and develop a broader approach to which the security sector can contribute. The strategy to best address the security dimensions of HIV/AIDS documented in this article would be one that is implemented simultaneously along three axes.

First, greater efforts are needed to improve health care standards and emergency responses to armed conflicts. In these situations, the role of HIV/AIDS is often not considered. HIV/AIDS prevention and treatment should become more high-profile components of such responses, including procedures to ensure the safety of blood supplies, wider availability of contraceptive devices, and more effective treatment of sexually transmitted diseases that increase the probability of contracting HIV during sexual relations. Such efforts could be enhanced through the provision of basic health care for those already living with HIV/AIDS and by ensuring the use of sterile equipment during medical procedures. Progress in these areas is possible: The UN high commissioner for refugees, for example, has already allocated funds to fight the spread of HIV/AIDS in Zambian refugee camps.[70]

Second, the armed forces themselves should be involved in combating the HIV/AIDS pandemic. In Africa these forces should be encouraged to implement education programs that discuss the illness in an open and serious manner, as well as work to reduce the stigma attached to the illness. Militaries, given their rigid, hierarchical nature and captive audiences, lend themselves to these tasks. Military leaders should also strive to make voluntary and confidential testing widely available, in addition to offering counseling both before and after testing. They should also reevaluate military practices that expose soldiers to HIV transmission, making changes where possible. Crucially, however, the armed forces should address the issue of HIV/AIDS with due consideration of the human rights issues involved. People living with the virus are not the enemy but rather the only hope for achieving viable improvements in the future. Consequently, they should be included in these efforts. Moreover,

---

70. "UNHCR to Help Refugees Fight AIDS at Camps," *Africa News Service*, October 26, 2000.

armed forces with advanced medical facilities should continue research for a viable and affordable AIDS vaccine. Indeed, Western militaries have an interest in conducting research on strands of the virus that predominate in regions of Africa to which these militaries might someday be deployed. In this way, they could also serve as an important counterbalance to pharmaceutical companies that focus their research primarily on HIV strands found in Western Europe and North America.

Third, an effective strategy for the security sector with regard to HIV/AIDS should incorporate a greater appreciation for the wider efforts already being made to combat the pandemic, such as making cheaper drugs available for African countries and contributing to the Global Fund to Fight AIDS, Tuberculosis, and Malaria. These efforts must be sustained because the causes of the AIDS pandemic are rooted in a much broader set of economic, political, and structural conditions that must be addressed if the pandemic is ever to be contained. The security sector should recognize the convergence of interests regarding the HIV/AIDS pandemic and support this wider endeavor.

Collateral Damage | *Sarah Kenyon Lischer*

Humanitarian Assistance as a Cause of Conflict

During the 1994–96 refugee crisis in the Democratic Republic of Congo (then Zaire), Hutu perpetrators of the Rwandan genocide established military training bases adjacent to the Rwandan Hutu refugee camps. The militants stockpiled weapons, recruited and trained refugee fighters, and launched cross-border attacks against the new Tutsi-led regime in Rwanda. The militant leaders gloated about their manipulation of the Hutu refugees and their plan to complete the genocide of the Tutsi. From the camps, the genocidal Hutu leader Jean Bosco Barayagwiza boasted that "even if [the Tutsi-led Rwandan Patriotic Front] have won a military victory they will not have the power. We have the population."[1] In late 1996, the growing strength of the militant groups provoked a Rwandan invasion of Zaire and attacks against the refugees. Until the invasion disrupted their operations, international humanitarian organizations regularly delivered food and supplies to the refugee camps and military bases. The chief executive of the American charity CARE, Charles Tapp, admitted at the time, "We are going to be feeding people who have been perpetrating genocide."[2]

Since the refugee crisis, eastern Congo has become the epicenter of a regional war in which more than a dozen states and rebel groups have fought each other and plundered the region's resources. An estimated 3.3 million people have died as a result of the war, mostly from preventable diseases and malnutrition.[3]

Sarah Kenyon Lischer is an Assistant Professor of Government at Sweet Briar College. In 2002–03, she was a Research Fellow at the Belfer Center for Science and International Affairs (BCSIA), John F. Kennedy School of Government, Harvard University.

For their helpful comments, the author thanks Gerard McHugh, Barry Posen, Jeremy Pressman, Stephen Van Evera, the members of the BCSIA International Security Program brown bag seminar, the participants in the Third Annual New Faces Conference at Duke University (September 2002), and two anonymous reviewers.

1. African Rights, *Rwanda: Death, Despair, and Defiance*, rev. ed. (London: African Rights, 1995), p. 1094.
2. Quoted in ibid., p. 1091.
3. Mahmoud Kassem, "Final Report of the Panel of Experts on the Illegal Exploitation of Natural Resources and Other Forms of Wealth of the Democratic Republic of the Congo" (New York: United Nations Security Council, October 16, 2002); and International Rescue Committee, "Mortality in the Democratic Republic of Congo: Results of a Nationwide Survey" (New York: IRC, April 2003).

The conflict in Rwanda, and the resulting regionwide destabilization, traces its roots to ethnic polarization between Hutu and Tutsi that occurred at the end of the colonial period in 1959, which spurred thousands of Tutsi to flee the country. Over the decades, hundreds of thousands of Tutsi established themselves in neighboring Uganda and formed their own political entity, the Rwandan Patriotic Front. The army of the RPF invaded Rwanda on October 1, 1990, in an attempt to topple the Hutu-dominated government of President Juvénal Habyarimana. Neither side was able to win a military victory, however. Negotiations to end the stalemated civil war resulted in the Arusha accords, a power-sharing agreement between the Habyarimana government and the RPF signed in 1993. Despite the presence of a United Nations peacekeeping contingent, Hutu hard-liners prepared for genocide, which began with the mysterious downing of President Habyarimana's plane. Experts generally agree that between 500,000 and 800,000 Tutsi and some moderate Hutu perished at the hands of the killers, often referred to as *génocidaires*.[4] The genocide ended when the RPF defeated the Rwandan government forces and took control of the capital, Kigali, on July 4, 1994. By that time, nearly 2 million Hutu refugees had fled at the instigation of an estimated 20,000 Hutu soldiers and 50,000 militia members, who joined the refugees in exile.

A major catalyst for the regional insecurity in Central Africa was this internationally supported refugee population, which included tens of thousands of unrepentant genocide perpetrators. Between 1994 and 1996, international donors spent $1.3 billion to sustain this population.[5] These same donors refused to fund efforts to disarm the militants, much less send peacekeeping troops to do so.

Following the massive misuse of humanitarian aid in the Rwandan refugee camps, a cottage industry of critics has exposed the sometimes perverse effects of humanitarian aid and discovered that humanitarian organizations are often motivated by the same nonaltruistic incentives that affect other organizations.[6]

---

4. On the Rwandan genocide, see Gérard Prunier, *The Rwanda Crisis: History of a Genocide* (New York: Columbia University Press, 1995); African Rights, *Rwanda: Death, Despair, and Defiance*; Philip Gourevitch, *We Wish to Inform You That Tomorrow We Will Be Killed with Our Families* (New York: Farrar, Straus and Giroux, 1998); Mahmood Mamdani, *When Victims Become Killers* (Princeton, N.J.: Princeton University Press, 2001); Alan J. Kuperman, *The Limits of Humanitarian Intervention: Genocide in Rwanda* (Washington, D.C.: Brookings, May 2001); and Alison Des Forges, *Leave None to Tell the Story: Genocide in Rwanda* (New York: Human Rights Watch, 1999).
5. David Rieff, *A Bed for the Night: Humanitarianism in Crisis* (New York: Simon and Schuster, 2002), p. 187.
6. See Fiona Terry, *Condemned to Repeat? The Paradox of Humanitarian Action* (Ithaca, N.Y.: Cornell University Press, 2002); Alexander Cooley and James Ron, "The NGO Scramble: Organizational Insecurity and the Political Economy of Transnational Action," *International Security*, Vol. 27, No. 1

Despite the barrage of attention, it remains unclear how and why humanitarian relief exacerbates conflict. The chroniclers of international humanitarian aid's unintended consequences often suggest that the entire system is malignant. On the other side, defenders of the relief regime absolve humanitarian organizations of all wrongdoing, arguing that other parties—including perpetrators of violence, their allies, and powerful donor states—are far more culpable for the spread of conflict in a refugee crisis.[7]

This article uses deductive reasoning and extended examples to explain the conditions under which humanitarian assistance to refugees can exacerbate conflict. It argues that two often-ignored aspects of the political context are essential for explaining conflict. The first aspect is the level of politicization, or political cohesion, of the refugee group at the outset of the crisis. A highly politicized group is more likely to view humanitarian aid as a resource with which to further its political and military goals vis-à-vis the sending state. It is possible to gauge a group's likely initial level of political cohesion from the circumstances surrounding the refugees' flight.

The second significant aspect of the political context is the state response to the crisis. Specifically, the misuse of aid is likely when the receiving state is unwilling or unable to impose political order and demilitarize the refugees. Demilitarization may entail the use of police or the army from the receiving state, external intervenors, or a multilateral peace enforcement unit. In the absence of state-imposed security, it is more likely that militants will use humanitarian assistance as a tool of war. A hostile or incapable receiving state erodes the potential for nonpolitical humanitarian action.

Notwithstanding the possible political and military effects of refugee relief, humanitarian organizations usually characterize their activities as impartial and neutral. Impartiality is understood as the consideration of need as the only criterion in aid distribution. Neutrality means that organizations do not take sides in the conflict. The emphasis on impartial and neutral intentions can lead to a "type of groupthink . . . where the group perceives itself as having a

---

(Summer 2002), pp. 5–39; Alex de Waal, *Famine Crimes: Politics and the Disaster Relief Industry* (Bloomington: Indiana University Press, 1998); Mary B. Anderson, *Do No Harm: How Aid Can Support Peace—or War* (Boulder, Colo.: Lynne Rienner, 1999); Neil S. MacFarlane, *Humanitarian Action: The Conflict Connection*, Occasional Paper No. 43 (Providence: Thomas J. Watson Jr. Institute for International Studies, Brown University, 2001); and Tony Vaux, *The Selfish Altruist: Relief Work in Famine and War* (London: Earthscan, 2001).
7. Refugee studies scholar Otto Hieronymi suggests using a hierarchy of responsibility to understand the role of humanitarian organizations in fueling conflict. He places humanitarian organizations at the bottom of the hierarchy, after perpetrators, their supporters, and the international community. Personal communication, March 27, 2002.

particular inherent morality. This prevents the group from considering the con-sequences of its actions."[8] In reality, the humanitarian assistance may be deliv-ered with impartial and neutral intent, but the effects of the humanitarian actions always have political, and sometimes even military, repercussions.

The political context explanation leads to policy recommendations to reduce or prevent the use of humanitarian aid as a tool of war. Faced with a situation in which refugees have strong political cohesion and states demonstrate little willingness or capability to enforce security, humanitarian organizations that want to decrease the misuse of refugee relief have two policy options. These options, which can be combined or used separately, are to improve the security situation and reduce the availability of humanitarian assistance. Options for improving security include hiring private guards and training local police forces. In extreme situations, aid organizations may consider closing refugee camps or completely withdraw from the relief effort.

The next section of the article details the ways in which humanitarian assis-tance to refugees can exacerbate conflict. The second and third sections explain the political conditions that increase the likelihood that aid contributes to war. I create three categories of refugee groups that describe the groups' initial lev-els of political cohesion. I then analyze how state responses to a refugee crisis can facilitate the misuse of humanitarian assistance. The fourth section sug-gests how aid organizations can leverage their resources to improve security during refugee crises. The article concludes with a discussion of the practical and ethical challenges involved in the humanitarian provision of security and the withdrawal of assistance.

How Refugee Relief Exacerbates Conflict

There are four main mechanisms through which humanitarian aid in refugee crises can exacerbate conflict. Refugee relief can feed militants; sustain and protect the militants' supporters; contribute to the war economy; and provide legitimacy to combatants. The conditions under which these mechanisms func-tion include a high level of political cohesion among the refugees and low state capability or willingness to provide security. After describing these four mech-anisms, I explain the relevant political conditions.

---

8. Kurt Mills, "Neo-Humanitarianism: The Role of International Humanitarian Organizations in the Emerging Global Order," paper presented at the annual meeting of the International Studies Association, New Orleans, Louisiana, March 24–27, 2002, p. 16.

FEEDING MILITANTS

At the most basic level, direct assistance to militants, both inadvertent and intentional, relieves them of having to find food themselves. Inadvertent distribution occurs when militants hide among the refugees. For example, at the beginning of the Rwanda crisis in 1994, many aid workers were unaware of the genocide that preceded it. Hutu militants implemented a successful propaganda effort that painted the Hutu as victims and ignored the genocide. David Rieff quotes an American engineer who arrived in Goma, Zaire, technically prepared but politically ignorant: "I went to Goma and worked there for three solid months. But it was only later, when I finally went to Rwanda on a break, that I found out about the genocide, and realized, 'Hey, I've been busting my butt for a bunch of ax murderers!'"[9]

In some cases, nongovernmental organizations (NGOs) have intentionally provided food directly to militants. In the Zaire camps, some NGOs rationalized that if the Hutu militants did not receive aid, they would steal it from the refugees. Another rationale was strict adherence to the humanitarian imperative of impartiality without any determination of whether the recipients included hungry warriors. Fabrizio Hochchild, a United Nations High Commissioner for Refugees official, summed up this logic in his defense of UNHCR action during the Rwanda crisis: "Even the guilty need to be fed."[10]

SUSTAINING AND PROTECTING THE MILITANTS' SUPPORTERS

Even if assistance does not directly help to sustain the militants, it can support their war aims by succoring their families and civilian supporters. Humanitarian assistance relieves militants from providing goods and services for their supporters. Rebels may live outside of the camps, but they will frequently send their families there to live in relative safety. Ironically, militants often present themselves as a state-in-exile, even though humanitarian organizations provide many of the functions of the state. As Mary Anderson explains, "When external aid agencies assume responsibility for civilian survival, warlords tend to define their responsibility and accountability only in terms of military control."[11]

---

9. Rieff, *A Bed for the Night*, p. 184.
10. Quoted in ibid., p. 54.
11. Anderson, *Do No Harm*, p. 49; see also Kathleen Newland, "Refugee Protection and Assistance," in P.J. Simmons and Chantal de Jonge Oudraat, eds., *Managing Global Issues: Lessons Learned* (Washington, D.C.: Carnegie Endowment for International Peace, 2001), p. 522.

CONTRIBUTING TO THE WAR ECONOMY

Militants may use relief resources to finance their conflicts. It is not uncommon for refugee leaders to levy a war tax on the refugee population, commandeering a portion of all rations and salaries. Refugee leaders can also divert aid when they control the distribution process. Among Rwandan refugees, militant leaders diverted large amounts of aid by inflating population numbers and pocketing the excess. Alain Destexhe, secretary-general of Médecins sans Frontières (Doctors without Borders, or MSF), warned that "food represents power, and camp leaders [in Goma, Zaire] who control its distribution divert considerable quantities towards war preparations."[12]

Often armed groups raid warehouses and international compounds to steal food, medicine, and equipment. Thousands, sometimes millions, of dollars of relief resources, including vehicles and communication equipment, are stolen every year. In the mid-1990s, aid organizations curtailed their operations in Liberia after the theft of $20 million in equipment during that country's civil war.[13] The International Committee of the Red Cross (ICRC) reported that "the level of diversion by the factions had reached a systematic and planned level, that it was integrated into the war strategy. . . . It had become obvious that the factions were opening the doors to humanitarian aid, up to the point where all the sophisticated logistics had entered the zones: cars, radios, computers, telephones. When all the stuff was there, then the looting would start in a quite systematic way."[14]

Defenders of aid organizations are quick to point out that, in many cases, humanitarian assistance forms a negligible part of the resources available to combatants.[15] There are two responses to this argument. First, even a relatively small role for aid does not absolve humanitarian organizations of responsibility. Absolute amounts matter, as well as relative measures: The $20 million of equipment stolen in Liberia during the mid-1990s was $20 million that aid agencies did not have for other crises regardless of the relative importance of aid resources in Liberia's conflict. Second, the nonmonetary benefits of humanitarian aid as a resource of war must also be considered. The legitimacy con-

---

12. Cooley and Ron, "The NGO Scramble," pp. 30–31.
13. MacFarlane, "Humanitarian Action," p. 17; and Terry, *Condemned to Repeat?*
14. ICRC, "ICRC Conditionality: Doctrine, Dilemma, and Dialogue," in Nicholas Leader and Joanna Macrae, eds., *Terms of Engagement: Conditions and Conditionality in Humanitarian Action*, Report No. 6 (London: Humanitarian Policy Group, Overseas Development Institute, 2000), p. 25.
15. MacFarlane, "Humanitarian Action," p. 23.

ferred by humanitarian activity can bolster the strength of a rebel group, regardless of the cash value of the aid.

PROVIDING LEGITIMACY TO COMBATANTS

Humanitarian assistance shapes international opinion about the actors in a crisis. To raise money from Western publics and governments, aid agencies tend to present oversimplified stories that emphasize the helplessness and victimization of the refugees.[16] Aid to the Rwandan refugees established a perception of the Hutu refugees as needy victims, obscuring their role as perpetrators of genocide against the Tutsi.

Aid also provides international legitimation of a group's political goals. The ruling party in Angola, the Movimento Popular da Libertação de Angola (MPLA), repeatedly used humanitarian assistance to bolster its political standing during the country's civil war in the 1990s. One member of the opposition explained: "The greatest problem is that people confuse humanitarian assistance as assistance from the MPLA party. The MPLA have taken advantage of this situation and many people think that what [aid] arrives has been given by the MPLA, not by the international aid organizations nor [sic] the government. . . . We [the União Nacional para a Independência Total de Angola (UNITA)–Renovada faction] don't have access to distribution of humanitarian aid, this is going to affect with certainty the electoral constituency of the future."[17] Rebel groups also manipulate aid agencies to increase their legitimacy and profile in the international media. To gain access to a needy population, humanitarian agencies are often forced to negotiate with unsavory rebel or government groups. The very act of negotiation solidifies the reputation of the group as powerful and legitimate.

Despite the proven political uses of humanitarian aid, many impassioned arguments suggest that impartiality and neutrality are both possible and desirable. Rieff makes a principled argument that humanitarianism "is neutral or it is nothing."[18] More practically, aid workers fear becoming targets in the conflict and losing access to the needy population if combatants view their work as political. Advocates of strict neutrality rarely admit that by giving aid in a so-called impartial and neutral manner, their actions may benefit one or

---

16. Cooley and Ron, "The NGO Scramble."
17. Integrated Regional Information Network (IRIN), "Angola: IRIN Interview with Eugenio Manuvakola," March 14, 2002.

more combatants and lead to wider war.[19] In reality, however, any humanitarian action in a conflict zone will have political, and possibly military, consequences regardless of the nonpolitical intentions of the provider.

Assessing Refugees' Potential for Militarization

The four mechanisms outlined above do not operate in all refugee crises, which leads to the following question: Under what conditions does a refugee population have a high propensity to use humanitarian assistance as a resource for war? The best way to determine the initial likelihood for violence is to examine the origin of the refugee crisis. The origin determines the political cohesion of the refugees and their initial level of military organization. The greater the level of political cohesion among the refugees, the more likely they (or their leaders) will attempt to divert refugee relief in support of their political and military goals.

I create three categories of refugee groups according to the origin of the crisis. These categories are situational refugees, persecuted refugees, and state-in-exile refugees (see Table 1). The impetus for their exile, their initial levels of political organization, and their requirements for return to the sending state differentiate these groups and indicate their initial propensity for militarization.[20] The following sections describe the three types of groups and their propensities to use humanitarian assistance as a tool of war.[21]

SITUATIONAL REFUGEES

Situational refugees have the least propensity to use humanitarian assistance for waging war. They have little political cohesion and thus little motivation to divert refugee relief in support of militarization. Typically, situational refugees

---

18. Rieff, *A Bed for the Night*, p. 330.
19. On the nonneutrality of famine aid, see David Keen, "Engaging with Violence: A Reassessment of Relief in Wartime," in Joanne Macrae et al., eds., *War and Hunger: Rethinking International Responses to Complex Emergencies* (London: Zed Books, 1994), pp. 209–221.
20. Militarization describes noncivilian attributes of refugee-populated areas, including inflows of weapons, military training, and recruitment. Militarization also includes actions of refugees and exiles who engage in noncivilian activity outside the refugee camp, yet who depend on assistance from refugees or international organizations.
21. Before moving to the analysis of these groups, I echo the caveat offered by Myron Wiener in his classification of causes of refugee flows: "Though it is usually possible to determine the predominant reason for a refugee flow, it is often a judgment call as to whether to classify a particular conflict as ethnic or non-ethnic [for example]. The nature of the conflict also sometimes changes. . . . [And] some of the conflicts are mixed." Weiner, "Bad Neighbors, Bad Neighborhoods: An Inquiry into the Causes of Refugee Flows," *International Security*, Vol. 21, No. 1 (Summer 1996), p. 18.

Table 1. Types of Refugee Groups.

Type of Refugees	Origin of Flight	Requirements for Voluntary Return	Initial Political Organization	Propensity to Use Humanitarian Aid for War
Situational refugees	War, chaos, deprivation	Peace and stability	None or very loose	Unlikely
Persecuted refugees	Group-based persecution	Credible guarantees of protection	Weak; may grow in exile	Somewhat likely
State-in-exile refugees	Defeat in civil war	New government or military victory	Strong; often grows in exile	Very likely

report that they left their homes in a panic when combatants threatened to kill them or destroy their livelihoods. For example, a report on the ongoing war in eastern Congo noted that massive displacement occurred because "the pressure in the villages is so great that people can't live their lives."[22] Similarly, an observer of the 1996 civil war in Congo (then Zaire) reported that "fear and instability in the region [eastern Zaire] are so great that many inhabitants have fled their villages even without being directly attacked."[23] Basically, situational refugees, such as the refugees from Congo, find themselves in the wrong place at the wrong time. Their villages become the front lines in a war in which the local residents have little interest. If these refugees become involved in violence, it is usually as victims of attacks or as pawns of militant leaders.

The willingness of situational refugees to return home depends on a cessation of the war, rather than any specific political or military outcome. The goals of these refugees are to earn a livelihood and return to their previous way of life. An essential difference between situational refugees and other groups is that situational refugees express a willingness to return to their country as soon as they can live in peace, regardless of the outcome of the conflict.

The less politicized nature of situational refugees stems in part from the type of conflict they seek to escape. In many instances, these conflicts garner very low levels of popular support.[24] Often one finds that all combatants have engaged in such high levels of brutality toward their own people that they have alienated any potential supporters. In the Liberian civil war, for example, both the government forces and the rebels, especially the Liberians United for Reconciliation and Democracy (LURD) group, prey on civilians. Refugees from Liberia explained the seemingly wanton brutality that caused their flight: "[LURD rebels] burned the whole town. Everyone fled into the bushes. . . . Government troops were behind us. They came into the bush and took our clothes and materials."[25] For situational refugees, such as the Liberians, the origin of the crisis reduces the likelihood that they will use refugee relief to exacerbate conflict.

An example where the origin of the crisis explains an unexpected nonviolent outcome is the flight of more than 1 million Mozambican refugees to neighbor-

---

22. Nigel Marsh of World Vision, quoted in "DRC: People Running for Their Lives in the East," IRIN report, November 16, 2000, http://www.reliefweb.int.
23. Sheldon Yett, *Masisi: Down the Road from Goma—Ethnic Cleansing and Displacement in Eastern Zaire*, Issue Brief (Washington, D.C.: U.S. Committee for Refugees, June 1996), p. 5.
24. This is different from many ethnic conflicts, for example, in which every person must choose a side, either willingly or unwillingly.
25. Human Rights Watch, *Liberian Refugees in Guinea: Refoulement, Militarization of Camps, and Other Protection Concerns* (New York: Human Rights Watch, November 2002), p. 20.

ing Malawi during the Mozambican civil war in the 1980s. Despite the large size of the refugee population, its location on the border, and their poor living conditions, humanitarian aid to the refugees in Malawi did not become a tool in the war. The refugee camps did not become militarized, and few cross-border attacks occurred.

During the civil war, the Marxist/Socialist Mozambican government battled the South African–supported Resistencia National Moçambicana (RENAMO) rebels in a brutal contest to rule the state. RENAMO attempted to make the country ungovernable, and to that end terrorized the population and demolished much of Mozambique's infrastructure, including schools, clinics, and roads. Unlike many African civil wars, the conflict lacked a strong ethnic or communal component. The main effect of the conflict was to destroy the peace and threaten the lives of civilians caught in the crossfire. Refugees streamed out of the country to escape the horror and devastation. At their height, Mozambican refugees constituted 10 percent of the population in Malawi and lived mostly in villages and camps less than ten miles from the Mozambique border.

For the most part, the refugees engaged in little political or military activity in support of either side. Observers noted that "RENAMO made no attempt to win over the support of the Mozambican people."[26] RENAMO seemingly had no political goals and focused only on destroying the government, at whatever cost to Mozambicans. In a U.S. State Department study, refugees expressed overwhelmingly negative attitudes toward RENAMO and neutral attitudes toward the Mozambican government.[27] These situational refugees desired a return to peace and stability.[28] One refugee asserted that "we can't possibly go [home] until we are absolutely certain that the hostilities have subsided."[29] Once the combatants reached a peace agreement in 1992, hundreds of thousands of refugees voluntarily returned to Mozambique without demanding any additional political preconditions or guarantees.

---

26. Burton Bollag, "Destabilization: The Human Cost," *Refugees*, July–August 1988, p. 20.
27. Interviews with 200 refugees revealed 96 percent with a very or somewhat negative attitude toward RENAMO and 1 percent with a positive attitude. Seventy-two percent of refugees expressed "no complaint" about government forces, Frente de Libertação de Moçambique, or FRELIMO, but only 11 percent characterized their attitude as positive. Robert Gersony, "Summary of Mozambican Refugee Accounts of Principally Conflict-Related Experience in Mozambique," report submitted to Bureau of Refugee Programs, U.S. Department of State, April 1988.
28. In one study, 65 percent of respondents cited security as their main priority for return. The other 35 percent cited various economic and social factors. Khalid Koser, "Information and Repatriation: The Case of Mozambican Refugees in Malawi," *Journal of Refugee Studies*, Vol. 10, No. 1 (March 1997), pp. 11, 5.
29. Sandy Kuwali, "Escape to Nsanje," *Southern African Economist*, February/March 1989, p. 11.

PERSECUTED REFUGEES

Some refugee populations flee due to targeted persecution or oppression. Persecuted refugees seek to escape ethnic cleansing, genocide, or other violent policies that target them for their ethnic, religious, language, or political affiliations. The experience of persecution helps to create politically cohesive refugee groups that are more easily organized for military activity. Humanitarian assistance to persecuted refugees is more likely to exacerbate conflict than is aid to situational refugees.

During the 1992–95 war in Bosnia, for example, combatants tried to expel all members from the opposing ethnic group to create ethnically homogeneous areas. In repeated instances, Muslim residents fled in terror when Serb militias entered a town. Often an attack on a Muslim neighbor convinced other Muslims to flee before they too experienced a direct attack. One Bosnian Muslim refugee described the impetus to flight: "First [the Serbs] sent written notices saying that Muslims and Croats had to leave the area immediately. Our neighbors came and warned us to go, because they said that if they tried to help us they would also be killed."[30] Thus the war created groups of refugees united by the experience of ethnically based persecution and determined not to return home until the risk of persecution ended.

For these refugees, the political outcome of the conflict bears directly on their willingness to return home. The goals of persecuted refugees often include political change, for example, demands for power sharing or other credible guarantees that their group will not be persecuted if its members return home. One displaced Bosnian Muslim reported that her family would return home "only if as Bosniacs they would be free and equal citizens in Republika Srpska."[31]

The coalescing event of group persecution increases refugees' receptivity to political or military activity. In many instances, refugee or rebel leaders draw on the experience of persecution (and often exaggerate it) to rally support for military activity. Due to the causes of their flight, persecuted refugees are more vulnerable to propaganda and manipulation than are situational refugees. Refugees who have experienced persecution also fear repeated attacks by the sending state. Therefore they will be more willing to take measures perceived as defensive or preventive. These refugees may find that ambitious leaders manipulate a defensive desire for survival for offensive purposes.

---

30. Amnesty International, "Bosnia-Herzegovina: All the Way Home—Safe 'Minority Returns' as a Just Remedy and for a Secure Future," Report No. EUR 63/02/98, February 1998, sec. 2.
31. Ibid.

Persecuted refugees also face a higher probability of cross-border attacks by the sending state than do situational refugees. The cause of their flight demonstrates that the sending state views the refugees as a threat for reasons of ethnicity, religion, or political affiliation. Thus, even if the refugees do not organize politically or militarily while in exile, they remain vulnerable to continued attacks. The sending state will likely view the internationally supported refugee camps as threats to its security.

In some cases, a group of persecuted refugees becomes more violence prone, as political and military organization builds. This is especially likely for long-term refugees who see no hope of return until radical change occurs in their homeland. As time passes, a leadership may emerge that unites the refugees behind a program of political and military action.[32] For example, the Palestinian refugees who were expelled to neighboring states following the 1948 war constituted a persecuted refugee group. Over time, organized militant groups, such as the Palestinian National Liberation Movement (Fatah) in the late 1950s and the Palestinian Liberation Organization in 1964, emerged among the refugees. Under the leadership of these organizations, militarized refugee populations engaged in cross-border warfare against Israel. For aid agencies, this suggests that protracted refugee relief may help to build and sustain a militarized population.

The Burundian Hutu population in Tanzania offers an example of persecuted refugees who have used humanitarian aid in support of political violence. Since 1993 a brutal ethnic civil war in Burundi has led to the deaths of hundreds of thousands of civilians and the displacement of many more. The conflict pits the Tutsi-dominated government and army against an array of Hutu rebel forces. Both sides have targeted civilians based on their ethnicity. The government has rounded up Hutu villagers into "regroupment" camps to prevent the rebels from gaining support. The rebels, conversely, have sought to create a vast population of Hutu refugees to undermine the legitimacy of the Tutsi government and provide cover for rebel activity. As of December 2002, 370,000 Hutu refugees from Burundi lived in camps near the Tanzanian-Burundian border.

The ethnic polarization that led to the refugee flows has allowed Hutu leaders to mobilize support in the camps, as has the tacit support of the Tanzanian government for the Hutu rebel activity. Tanzania hotly denies the Burundian

---

32. For more on the phenomenon of refugee groups that become militarized after their flight from danger, see Howard Adelman, "Why Refugee Warriors Are Threats," *Journal of Conflict Studies*, Spring 1998, pp. 49–69.

government's accusations that rebels operate freely in the refugee camps, but observers confirm that Burundian Hutu refugees engage in both political and military activity. Many extremist political parties with military wings have developed in the camps. Rebel groups recruit young men from the camps for military training and subsequent cross-border raids.[33] As one analyst recognized, "This should come as no surprise, considering the traumatic experiences which caused [the refugees'] flight."[34] The Burundian army has threatened to retaliate by attacking the camps, leading to a Tanzanian military buildup on the border.[35]

Humanitarian assistance has exacerbated the conflict by feeding militants, sheltering the militants' followers, supporting the war economy, and bolstering the rebels' legitimacy. It is an open secret that the militant parties enforce a war tax on refugees, either in food or cash.[36] The presence of the camps sustains the militants' dependents and followers, freeing the rebel parties from providing support. The refugee camps themselves do not function as military bases, but they are highly politicized. When a UNHCR team assessed the security situation in the camps, it found a high level of political activity (including political meetings).[37] This allows the rebel parties to strengthen their legitimacy and following among the refugees.

STATE-IN-EXILE REFUGEES

The third, and most violence-prone, group includes both refugees and a highly organized political and military leadership. This type of population is a "state-in-exile" refugee group.[38] In some instances, the leadership has organized the refugees as a strategy of war. Such leaders hold aggressive goals, which might

---

33. Gérard Prunier, *Rwanda: Update to End of July 1995*, Writenet Country Papers (Geneva: Refworld, UNHCR, August 1995), sec. 3.1.
34. Jean-François Durieux, "Preserving the Civilian Character of Refugee Camps: Lessons from the Kigoma Refugee Programme in Tanzania," *Track Two*, Vol. 9, No. 3 (November 2000), p. 31.
35. Real and perceived persecution fuels the refugees' fear. See, for example, IRIN, "Burundi: Tutsi Group Threatens to Attack Refugees in Camps in Tanzania," IRIN Update 1,014 for the Great Lakes, September 19, 2000.
36. Aid workers have noticed correlations between higher levels of malnutrition and increased rebel political activity in camps, both due to greater taxation.
37. Emile Segbor, UNHCR official, interview, Geneva, Switzerland, July 15, 1998.
38. My concept of a state-in-exile population is similar to what Aristide R. Zolberg, Astri Suhrke, and Sergio Aguayo term a "refugee-warrior community." They describe such groups as "highly conscious refugee communities with a political leadership structure and armed sections engaged in warfare for a political objective." See Zolberg, Suhrke, and Aguayo, *Escape from Violence* (Oxford: Oxford University Press, 1989), pp. 275–278. The term "state-in-exile group" is a more accurate description than "refugee-warriors" and does not carry the same possibly pejorative connotation.

include a radical change in the government of the sending state. Because such outflows include many civilians, states and international agencies often designate them as refugee populations. The Rwandan Hutu refugees in eastern Zaire provide a recent example of the state-in-exile phenomenon. These refugees fled Rwanda in 1994 under pressure from the leaders of the genocide, who used the refugees as a valuable resource for their militant purposes.

Of the three categories of refugee groups, state-in-exile refugees are the most likely to use humanitarian relief as a resource of war. Indeed the leaders often intend that the refugee crisis, and resulting international assistance, will facilitate their war aims. The strong political organization exercised by the leaders enables them to divert large amounts of assistance to support the conflict. In the Zaire crisis, humanitarian aid to the refugees essentially functioned as the infrastructure for the state-in-exile.

State-in-exile refugees usually return home either in victory or due to forced repatriation, rejecting power-sharing or amnesty offers from the sending state. For example, the Rwandan Hutu refugees in Zaire refused all attempts by the Rwandan government to orchestrate their return, leading to the judgment that "the extremists were not opposed to return as such, merely to a return that they did not control."[39]

State-in-exile refugees present a greater threat to the sending state than do other types of groups, thus increasing the chance of preventive cross-border attacks against the refugees. Large, politically active refugee populations serve as an indictment of the sending state regime and a constant threat to its security. State-in-exile refugees challenge the legitimacy of the sending state's government, providing fodder for domestic and international critics.

Although state-in-exile refugees exist within a strong, politicized leadership structure, many of the refugees may have little desire to become involved in violence. The nature of the group makes it more likely, however, that these refugees will serve as a political and military resource for their leaders. By maintaining an iron grip on the information that reaches the refugees, as well as controlling the distribution of humanitarian aid, the leaders convince many refugees of threats to their safety and the need to mobilize. Leaders emphasize real and imagined injustices to foster fear of return among the refugees. In the Rwandan Hutu camps, leaders successfully nurtured a belief in Hutu victimhood, distorting or erasing the genocide that preceded the refugee flight. Hutu leaders also played on fears created by real injustices in Rwanda, such as the

---

39. African Rights, *Rwanda: Death, Despair, and Defiance*, p. 1098.

1995 massacre of unarmed displaced Hutu by the Rwandan Patriotic Army at Kibeho camp.

An example of a state-in-exile is the population of more than 3 million Afghan refugees who fled to Pakistan after the Marxist military coup in Afghanistan in 1978 and subsequent Soviet invasion in 1979. The well-funded Afghan rebels who lived among the refugees eventually forced a Soviet retreat and took over the country.[40] During their exile, the refugees lived in more than 300 settlements along the border with Afghanistan. The seven main rebel groups recruited new refugee arrivals as members and fighters. The government of Pakistan (and its sponsor, the United States) condoned this arrangement and allowed the rebel leaders free reign among the refugees. Pakistan channeled military aid to the resistance parties that was "crucial to the parties' growth and development."[41]

Pressured by major donors, UNHCR did not protest the militarization of the refugee areas, to which the agency continued to deliver assistance. International assistance allowed the resistance parties to focus their resources on waging war in Afghanistan, rather than providing goods and services for the refugee population. The assistance clearly benefited the anticommunist rebels and their supporters by sustaining fighters and their dependents, contributing to the war economy, and boosting the legitimacy of the militant leaders.

Throughout the more than ten years that the refugees lived in Pakistan, cross-border military activity occurred frequently. The Afghan rebels organized attacks from Pakistan to destabilize and ultimately overthrow the Soviet-backed government in Kabul. The rebels even brought Soviet prisoners of war into Pakistan after their attacks.[42] The Soviet-backed Afghan government responded with hundreds of bombing raids across the border that targeted the refugee settlements.

The organization and goals of the Afghan refugees clearly indicate that this was a state-in-exile population. Many of the refugees fled due to Soviet attacks on their villages, and once in Pakistan became card-carrying (literally) members of one of the resistance parties.[43] As the idea of a state-in-exile took hold

---

40. The United States alone provided more than $2 billion in aid to the exiles between 1982 and 1991, including antiaircraft guns and other heavy weapons. UNHCR, *The State of the World's Refugees: Fifty Years of Humanitarian Action* (Oxford: Oxford University Press, 2000), p. 120.
41. Anthony Hyman, "The Afghan Politics of Exile," *Third World Quarterly*, Vol. 9, No. 1 (January 1987), p. 73.
42. Ibid., p. 75.
43. One difference from other state-in-exile groups is that the Afghan resistance was fractured into many rival groups, all sharing the goal of toppling the Kabul regime. Under pressure from donors,

among the population, observers noted a rise in openly expressed nationalism among the refugees.[44] The U.S. State Department reported in 1984 that "opposition to the communist government grew quickly and spontaneously. . . . Virtually all elements of the population were involved."[45] The refugees did not return to Afghanistan until the withdrawal of the Soviet forces in 1989 and the defeat of the Soviet-backed Najibullah regime in 1992.[46]

International humanitarian aid provided the infrastructure of the anticommunist Afghan state-in-exile. In 1982 UNHCR alone spent $77 million in Pakistan, supplying tents, health care, clothes, water, fuel, and supplementary food (tea and sugar).[47] Later the bill for humanitarian assistance would total $400 million per year. As a World Food Programme official stated in 1983: "WFP takes the lead from donor governments, and if the donors and the [government of Pakistan] aren't worried about the workings of the food distribution mechanism, including possible diversion, the WPF will not modify its own program."[48] Strong sympathy for the refugees as resisters of a communist, anti-Islamic regime prevailed among the donors, the Pakistani officials, and the humanitarian organizations. For example, mujaheddin recruits did not lose their right to food rations upon return to the camps from a stint in battle. In the Afghan state-in-exile, as in the Rwandan camps, international humanitarian assistance contributed to the spread of conflict.

State Responses to Militarized Refugee Crises

State responses to a militarized, or potentially militarized, crisis determine the level of misuse of humanitarian assistance. State-in-exile refugee groups will

---

the resistance attempted to present a united front internationally, but their unity crumbled after the Soviet withdrawal in 1989.

44. Tom Rogers, "Harbouring Instability: Pakistan and the Displacement of Afghans," K.M. de Silva and R.J. May, eds., *Internationalization of Ethnic Conflict* (New York: St. Martin's, 1991), p. 73.

45. Craig Karp, *Afghan Resistance and Soviet Occupation*, Special Report No. 118 (Washington, D.C.: U.S. Department of State, December 1984), p. 2.

46. Continued civil war among the rival rebel groups in Afghanistan hindered the return of many refugees, although almost 2 million returned in 1992. U.S. Committee for Refugees, *World Refugee Survey, 1993* (Washington, D.C.: U.S. Committee for Refugees, 1993), pp. 87, 95.

47. The World Food Programme played the primary role in coordinating food aid. For statistics, see Department of State, U.S. embassy, Pakistan, "Afghan Refugee Situation—An Overview," confidential cable by Barrington King, December 9, 1982, Digital National Security Archive item number AF01408, pars. 10–12.

48. Comment reported in Department of State, U.S. embassy, Pakistan, "Visit of WFP Emergency Unit Director to Pakistan," cable by Barrington King, September 2, 1983, Digital National Security Archive item number AF01494, par. 7.

use humanitarian assistance as a strategy of war in the absence of preventive state action. Persecuted refugee groups, especially those with opportunistic leaders, are also likely to use aid as a political and military resource unless they are constrained by the receiving state. An effective state response includes separating militants from refugees, protecting aid supplies from theft, securing the border, and disarming and reintegrating willing militants into the civilian population. Possible preventive forces include the police or army in the receiving state, an external intervenor, or a multilateral peace enforcement unit. In the absence of such a force, humanitarian aid is likely to exacerbate conflict. In a weak or hostile state, humanitarian aid cannot remain neutral or impartial. Minimizing humanitarian "collateral damage" requires favorable conditions of political order in the receiving state.

RESPONSES OF THE RECEIVING STATE

According to international law, the refugee-receiving state bears primary responsibility for ensuring the safety of the refugees and maintaining the civilian nature of the refugee-populated area.[49] The duties of the receiving state include disarming and demobilizing any noncivilian exiles who wish to integrate into the refugee camp, preventing the flow of arms to refugee areas, protecting refugees from attack and intimidation, and separating people who do not qualify for international protection (e.g., war criminals) from the refugees.[50] In the optimal case, the receiving state provides physical and legal protection to the refugees while humanitarian organizations provide material assistance. This represents an ideal, but not likely, scenario. In situations where receiving states do not meet their obligations, humanitarian organizations cannot operate in a neutral or impartial manner. With a weak or unwilling receiving state, combatants will more likely use aid as a tool of war.

Two types of receiving states are likely to impair the neutrality and impartiality of aid organizations. The first is a state that lacks the ability to impose

---

49. The Organization for African Unity (OAU) Convention states that "Signatory States undertake to prohibit refugees residing in their respective territories from attacking any member state of the OAU." OAU, *Convention Governing the Specific Aspects of Refugee Problems in Africa*, 1969, art. 3. The Organization of American States (OAS) also urges the institution "of appropriate measures in the receiving countries to prevent the participation of the refugees in activities directed against the country of origin." OAS, *Cartegena Declaration on Refugees*, 1984. In a more recent document, the Security Council reaffirmed "the primary responsibility of States to ensure [refugee] protection, in particular by maintaining the security and civilian character of refugee and internally displaced person camps." UN Security Council Resolution 1265, adopted September 17, 1999, UN Doc. S/RES/1265 (1999).
50. UN Doc. S/RES/1265 (1999), par. 6.

political order on its territory. Such a state does not have the capability to police the refugee camps, patrol the borders, and enforce international and domestic law against militarization. A lack of capability is common in refugee
crises because the majority of receiving states are developing countries with
extremely limited resources, including for their own citizens. In these states,
institutions such as the police and judiciary often lack adequate funding and
competence to deal with a large influx of refugees. In this case, the receiving
state may wish to prevent violence but is unable to do so. If an external donor
or ally is willing to assist, violence becomes less likely. Without external assistance, however, the conflict may spread to the weak receiving state. In such a
state, humanitarian organizations have little control over whether their resources become tools of war.

Guinea from 2000 to 2002 provides an example of a weak receiving state that
sought external assistance to improve the security of its refugee population.
The government of Guinea, host to more than 400,000 refugees, was unable to
prevent repeated cross-border attacks from rebels in both Liberia and Sierra
Leone. After numerous attacks against the refugees and local Guineans, the
government consented to a relocation effort, funded by external donors, that
moved thousands of vulnerable refugees from the insecure border with Liberia
and Sierra Leone.[51]

The second type of receiving state is one that actively sympathizes with one
of the parties to the conflict. The state may have the capability to impose political order, but the order it imposes clashes with international laws promoting
the civilian and humanitarian nature of refugee populations. A receiving state
that sympathizes with the refugees' goals may allow, or even abet, military
activity by the refugees. The state may pressure (or coerce) humanitarian organizations to divert assistance to combatants and loyalists.

Ethnic ties between the refugees and groups in the receiving state can
increase domestic pressure to overlook refugee-instigated violence. Ethnic alliances between the refugees and the receiving state could also pressure the
government to repel cross-border attacks initiatated by the sending state. Conversely, alliances between the receiving and sending states could encourage
the receiving state to allow cross-border attacks against the refugees. In such a
situation, the receiving state usually refuses international help that would im-

---

51. International Council of Voluntary Agencies, "Refugee Camps on the Border: A Recipe for
Disaster in West Africa," December 22, 2000. For more on this situation, see Human Rights Watch,
Guinea: Refugees Still at Risk, Vol. 13, No. 5 (July 2001), pp. 1–21.

prove security in the refugee areas, regarding intervention as an unwelcome infringement of its sovereignty. Humanitarian organizations are then at the mercy of the hostile receiving state, which will likely use the international humanitarian assistance to further its war aims.

INTERACTION WITH THE SENDING STATE

Humanitarian aid workers and refugees also face possible cross-border attacks from the sending state. If a sending state perceives a refugee group as a threat, it is likely to oppose the establishment of internationally funded refugee camps. The sending state will interpret the camps as an international condemnation of its legitimacy and ability to control its borders. It may also fear that the refugee camps will supply militants with resources (including recruits, supplies, and international legitimacy).

The sending state response will depend, in part, on its relationship with the receiving state. The sending state will be less likely to attack the refugees if the receiving state is willing and able to prevent militarization. In addition, a capable receiving state is more able to deter opportunistic attacks by the sending state.

If the receiving state is incapable of controlling military activity among the refugees, it will become an attractive target for the sending state. Rwanda invaded Zaire in 1996 to establish a zone of security on the border and to fulfill larger political and economic objectives (such as overthrowing President Mobutu Sese Seko and installing a friendlier regime). In this context, Rwanda viewed the international humanitarian support of the refugees as a contributing factor toward its insecurity. It also viewed the decrepit Mobutu regime as an easy target for change.

Another possible scenario is an alliance between the sending and receiving states, in which the receiving state allows cross-border attacks against the refugees. For example, in the mid-1990s the government of Ivory Coast supported the Liberian opposition party, National Patriotic Front of Liberia, and forced Liberian refugees to live in unprotected border villages subject to lethal cross-border attacks by the NPFL.[52] In extreme cases, humanitarian organizations might decide that the lack of receiving state cooperation merits closing the camps.

---

52. Amnesty International, "In Search of Safety: The Forcibly Displaced and Human Rights in Africa," Report AFR 01/05/97, June 20, 1997, sec. 4.

It is also possible that a predatory sending state will attack the refugees regardless of their levels of militarization. Examples include attacks against Rwandan Hutu refugees in Burundi in 1994. Unlike the refugees in Zaire, these Rwandan Hutus were not militarized and lived in fear of the Burundian Tutsi military. The Burundian military allowed cross-border attacks by Rwandan Tutsi forces that killed more than 250 Hutu refugees. Similarly, the Guinean military has allowed Liberian LURD rebels unimpeded access to the defenseless Liberian refugee camps in Guinea. Rebels enter the camps, forcibly recruit fighters, and steal supplies in full view of the Guinean camp guards.[53] In such situations, humanitarian organizations can do little except publicize the refugees' plight and plead for protection. The refugees and international humanitarian workers become targets, even if the humanitarian assistance is not fueling a war effort. There is also a risk that attacks against the refugees will have a radicalizing effect, convincing them to support rebel organizations to protect themselves.

EXTERNAL RESPONSES

A worst-case scenario occurs when the receiving state ignores or abets militants who are using humanitarian assistance as a tool of war. Such a situation requires a powerful external intervenor to impose order. The intervenor could be a regional state, a powerful donor state, or a multilateral peace enforcement unit. The level of coercion required depends on the attitude of the receiving state (e.g., actively hostile or merely apathetic) and the capability of the militants.

During the Rwandan refugee crisis, no external actor was willing to pay the political and military price of separating the Rwandan militants from the refugees. Initial UN plans to separate them fell through when aid agencies realized that they would have to move 60,000 to 100,000 militia and army members (with their families) at an estimated cost of $90 million to $125 million. Such a move would have required high levels of coercion, because the militants would have refused to separate willingly from their power base—the refugee population.

External support for a militarized refugee population exacerbates the abuse of humanitarian assistance. In this situation, the chances of demilitarization are minimal. For example, the U.S. commitment to the militarized Afghan refu-

---

53. Human Rights Watch, *Liberian Refugees in Guinea*.

gees in the 1980s greatly limited the scope for action of both UNHCR and regional states (e.g., Pakistan) that benefited from U.S. donations. Aid agencies dared not jeopardize their funding by refusing to supply the mujaheddin fighters who controlled the refugees.

BUILDING OF STATE CAPACITY

When states fail to provide protection, one option for demilitarization is a partnership between the receiving state and international humanitarian actors to provide security. Security partnerships usually consist of international funding and training for local forces (police or army, or both). Obviously, a successful security partnership requires the willingness of the receiving state to use or improve its capability. This is a controversial option for humanitarian organizations, which generally view security provision as beyond their responsibility, but it has been used in desperate situations.

Refugee crises in Zaire and Tanzania offer two models of security partnerships, both of which fell short of demilitarizing the refugee areas. In Zaire in 1994, UNHCR hired 1,500 elite soldiers from President Mobutu's presidential guard as a last resort when no international force was forthcoming. The Zairian force, called the Contingent Zairois pour la Sécurité dans les Camps, deployed in February 1995. The objectives of the force were to provide security in the camps for the refugees and relief workers. The force had no mandate to disarm the militants. UNHCR paid the soldiers $3 per day plus food, lodging, and clothes.[54]

The Zairian force received mixed reviews. The first contingent of soldiers that arrived in early 1995 was relatively well disciplined. Later contingents actually contributed to insecurity as their discipline and morale broke down. The soldiers became involved in crime and extortion, victimizing the refugees rather than protecting them. By the time of the Rwandan invasion in 1996, many of the Zairian soldiers were fighting with the Hutu militias against the Tutsi invaders. The Zairian experience suggests that an ill-disciplined force may be worse than no force at all. Throughout the crisis, UNHCR had little or no control over these forces, even as it financed their presence.

A second model for security partnership was undertaken in Tanzania in the late 1990s to deal with security threats associated with more than 500,000

---

54. Joel Boutroue, "Missed Opportunities: The Role of the International Community in the Return of the Rwandan Refugees from Eastern Zaire," Rosemarie Rogers Working Paper Series (Cambridge, Mass.: Center for International Studies, Massachusetts Institute of Technology, 1998).

Burundian and Congolese refugees. Security problems included military activity by Burundian rebel groups, violence between rebel factions, and criminal activity within and around refugee camps. Under the arrangement, called the "security package," UNHCR agreed to train, equip, and pay nearly 300 police officers to work in the refugee areas.[55] The memorandum of understanding signed between UNHCR and Tanzania outlined the goals of the package: "It is expected that the additional police presence will considerably reduce the level of insecurity, criminality, and safeguard the civilian and humanitarian character of the refugee camps."[56] Despite Tanzania's willingness, inappropriate police behavior and inadequate capability bedeviled the security package. The police were singularly unsuccessful in separating militants from the refugees.[57]

The level of political order in the receiving state determines the success of a security partnership. Tanzania was a stable, peaceful country that sought international recognition for assisting refugees. Yet even in Tanzania, bureaucratic incompetence, corruption, and political maneuvering limited the security partnership. Chaotic or hostile receiving states will further complicate attempts at security partnerships. Such inhospitable environments require more external security assistance, and perhaps coercion, if such security programs are to be implemented. In these cases, humanitarian organizations may have little opportunity to improve the security situation on their own.

When All Else Fails . . . Humanitarian Aid as Leverage

Recent crises, such as the Rwandan refugee crisis in Zaire, have seen a colossal failure of state actions to prevent militarization. In such contexts, impartial and indiscriminate humanitarian assistance becomes a building block for successful rebel movements. In its retrospective on the Rwanda crisis, the human rights organization African Rights asserted, "To deliver humanitarian assistance in a no-questions asked, open-ended manner is to deliver the extremists their strongest remaining card."[58] Unconditional assistance can worsen the se-

---

55. UNHCR paid the officers a stipend of about $280 per month—approximately three times their normal wages. The U.S. government provided funding to UNHCR to implement the security package.
56. "Memorandum of Understanding between the Tanzanian Ministry of Home Affairs and UNHCR," September 28, 1999.
57. In 2001, for example, 40 percent of militants escaped from detention. The police detained or fined 143 combatants in the first half of 2001. Jeff Crisp, "Lessons Learned from the Implementation of the Tanzania Security Package," Evaluation and Policy Analysis Unit, UNHCR, May 2001.
58. African Rights, *Rwanda: Death, Despair, and Defiance*, p. 1100.

curity situation for refugees, local residents, and relief workers by enriching and legitimizing militant elements. The negative impact of humanitarian assistance in militarized refugee crises raises the question of when aid should be reduced or withdrawn. Even with only minimal state support, humanitarian organizations can use their resources as leverage to improve security. In some hostile crises, however, the least harmful outcome will entail withdrawing humanitarian assistance.

Humanitarian organizations have two assets, or forms of leverage, with which they can affect outcomes. They have the moral clout that comes from the charitable, altruistic nature of their work. They also have the tangible asset of material resources. Organizations have these assets in different amounts, depending on their reputations, wealth, and mandates. They can use this leverage to influence various stakeholders, including the UN Security Council, receiving states, donor states, and militant refugee leaders.

Moral clout enables humanitarian organizations to lobby policymakers and use the media to gain support for their positions. Organizations currently use their moral clout to publicize the need for material assistance in a crisis. Newspapers regularly report on the amount of tents, food, medicine, and so on that humanitarian organizations need in a crisis. Issues of physical protection receive much less attention, from both UNHCR and the media. By directing more resources toward physical protection of refugees and aid workers, aid agencies can increase public awareness of the issue. Kathleen Newland writes that "UNHCR, other states, and refugee advocates must rely on diplomatic pressure, persuasion, and incentives to encourage reluctant states to implement provisions for international protection."[59] Humanitarian organizations can trade on their altruist credentials to emphasize the need for security measures in refugee crises.

The idea of using moral clout to encourage intervention by the UN Security Council or other external party is not without precedent. In the lead-up to U.S. military intervention in Somalia in 1992, NGOs explicitly stated the need for better security for humanitarian operations. In a press conference, a group of prominent U.S. NGOs threatened to withdraw from Somalia unless security was improved.[60] More recently, a number of NGOs encouraged the 1999 NATO intervention in Kosovo.[61]

59. Newland, "Refugee Protection and Assistance." p. 530.
60. Alex de Waal, "Dangerous Precedents? Famine Relief in Somalia, 1991–93," in Macrae et al., *War and Hunger,* p. 154.
61. Within the NGO community, debate continues over the appropriateness of advocating military intervention. MSF received criticism for championing the Kosovo intervention but later withdrew

Humanitarian organizations' second asset, material resources, has a great impact on the war-torn areas that receive assistance. In resource-poor environments, militant leaders depend on humanitarian assistance to sustain their followers. In Angola, rich with oil, or Sierra Leone, rich with diamonds, combatants also fund conflict through smuggling natural resources. Yet even when militants have other resources, humanitarian assistance can provide valuable legitimacy to their cause. Thus the value of humanitarian assistance provides leverage for humanitarian organizations to improve the security situation.

Using humanitarian aid as leverage entails making aid contingent on security improvements. Possible security requirements include disarmament of refugees, separation of militants, and adequate police protection of the refugee-populated area. Adequate border security also limits cross-border attacks by the sending state or the refugees. An MSF official cautions that humanitarian organizations should take action to preserve "humanitarian space" but not to enforce respect for human rights.[62] The leverage would not be used to press for major changes in the government of the receiving state or structure of peacekeeping operations. In practice, that means NGOs should act to prevent situations in which aid is diverted or used to endanger the recipients.

In the Rwandan refugee crisis in Zaire, aid agencies used assistance as leverage on several occasions, but always in an ad hoc manner. For example, individual NGOs, such as MSF–France, withdrew from the Rwandan refugee camps to protest their militarization. The MSF director, Jacques de Milliano, claimed, "In refugee camps there are killers walking around making plans for new attacks. We don't want to be part of that system."[63] Tellingly, however, not all country chapters of MSF withdrew from the camps. This illustrates how even within an organization there are different understandings of its mission.[64] In isolated instances, aid workers made assistance contingent on demilitariza-

from the relief effort to protest NATO's inability to protect the Serb minority. This highlights the problem of unintended consequences of intervention. Roberto Belloni, former Organization for Security and Cooperation in Europe official, personal communication, November 21, 2003. See also Belloni, "Kosovo and Beyond: Is Humanitarian Intervention Transforming International Society?" *Human Rights and Human Welfare*, Vol. 2, No. 1 (Winter 2002), p. 42; and Christian Jennings, "UN Has Failed Kosovo Minorities," *Independent*, August 17, 2000.

62. Françoise Bouchet-Saulnier, "The Principles and Practices of 'Rebellious Humanitarianism,'" Médecins sans Frontières International Activity Report, 2000, http://www.odihpn.org.

63. Quoted in "Aid Agency to Abandon 'Killers' in Hutu Camps," *Herald* (Glasgow), August 29, 1995, p. 6.

64. I thank Kurt Mills for this insight. Personal communication, March 27, 2002.

tion. On the whole, however, millions of dollars of humanitarian assistance sustained the militant Hutu state-in-exile during the refugee crisis.

Conditionality is not necessarily an all-or-nothing proposition. There are gradations in levels of assistance and numbers of agencies involved. In extreme cases, all humanitarian organizations may withdraw; in other situations, selected organizations will do so. Sometimes essential life-saving services remain (such as hospital workers and emergency feeding centers). For example, the World Food Programme scaled back its services in Afghanistan in the 1990s to the bare minimum in an attempt to promote respect for human rights.

As a last resort, humanitarian organizations can consider shutting down the refugee camps. This is a drastic step that would occur when the harm caused by the camps overwhelms the benefits of refugee assistance. Myron Weiner warned, "Sometimes it may be necessary to close refugee camps because they are used by warrior refugees intent on pursuing armed conflict." According to Weiner, forcible return may be necessary when "camps are used by military forces as a staging area for resuming the war (by recruiting boys and young men in the camps, extracting resources from camp refugees, and using camps as a safe haven) and . . . refugees have become hostages to warriors and are therefore unable to choose whether or not to repatriate."[65] UNHCR also recognizes that, in extraordinary circumstances, forced return and camp closure may be the least harmful policy. UNHCR reasons that, in forced returns, "the risk of undermining the principle of voluntariness must be weighed against the ability to save people's lives."[66]

ETHICAL AND PRACTICAL CHALLENGES

Even though a logical requirement for refugee relief is that the assistance must do more good than harm, putting that into practice is difficult for many reasons.[67] First, aid organizations cannot easily determine the harm being done or what would happen in the absence of humanitarian assistance. Thus they face an ethical dilemma involving an uncertain trade-off between short-term suffering and long-term benefits. Practically, humanitarian organizations fear losing funding if they withdraw from an area in crisis.

Aid workers' greatest fear is that people will suffer and perhaps die if aid is withdrawn or reduced. In the short term, making assistance contingent on

---

65. Myron Weiner, "The Clash of Norms: Dilemmas in Refugee Policies," *Journal of Refugee Studies*, Vol. 11, No. 4 (December 1998), pp. 10, 17.
66. UNHCR, *Protecting Refugees: A Field Guide for NGOs* (Geneva: UNHCR, 1999), pt. 2.
67. For the best statement of this idea, see Anderson, *Do No Harm*.

physical protection is often viewed as an unacceptable trade-off because it punishes legitimate refugees for the behavior of the militants. Denying immediate assistance to people in need is seen as a violation of humanitarian principles.

Part of the concern about refugees' suffering is that the benefits of physical protection are less tangible than those of assistance. It is easy to see that providing food and medicine can prevent deaths. It is less easy to demonstrate (especially to the public back home) how demilitarization will prevent deaths. Also, physical protection is perceived as a more political issue than is material assistance. Donors want to provide food and medicine to needy children, not train local police. Donors, and humanitarian organizations, often fail to recognize that material assistance is also a political act. This misperception of physical protection as a secondary or irrelevant goal is not an insurmountable obstacle, but it requires a concerted effort to educate governments and the public about the importance of security during a refugee crisis.

In militarized crises, the culture of relief agencies may impede conditionality policies. Humanitarian organizations closely guard their independence, and each agency reserves the right to act as it sees fit: "Agencies have differing and sometimes competing mandates, and are often reluctant to coordinate the type of detailed information regarding their operations that is required to plan and conduct effective emergency security operations."[68] Some analysts question the value of this independence when taken to extreme levels: "Is a point reached where the right of each agency and donor government to make its own ethical judgment in fact makes the impact of the system 'dysfunctional'? To what extent do different mandates justify different compromises?"[69] The lack of coordination and competition between agencies does not lend itself to a clear-headed analysis of the situation. Ideally, there would exist some overarching framework that could help guide organizations when making these difficult decisions.[70]

A humanitarian organization's attitude toward conditionality also depends on its mission. Organizations that focus purely on material assistance generally view their actions as separate from the political sphere. The sentiments of one

---

68. Sean Greenaway and Andrew J. Harris, "Humanitarian Security: Challenges and Responses," paper presented to the Forging Peace Conference, Harvard University, Cambridge, Massachusetts, March 13–15, 1998, sec. 5.
69. Nicholas Leader and Joanna Macrae, "New Times, Old Chestnuts," in Leader and Macrae, *Terms of Engagement*, p. 12.
70. Arthur C. Helton presents a plan for a humanitarian coordinating body in his article "Rescuing the Refugees," *Foreign Affairs*, Vol. 81, No. 2 (March/April 2002).

aid worker in eastern Zaire illustrate this attitude: "I know some of them [refugees] have killed a lot of people. But I don't care about the past. My job is to feed everyone irrespective of the past."[71] Other organizations have multiple (and sometimes conflicting) missions. Médecins sans Frontières provides medical assistance and also acts as a vocal witness to human rights abuses. The ICRC describes its mission as helping victims and promoting respect for international humanitarian law.[72] Agencies whose missions include refugee protection or promotion of human rights are more receptive to using some limited form of conditionality.

Even if all relevant organizations agreed that their actions were causing significantly more harm than good, that would not necessarily lead to a withdrawal. Agencies are still faced with a coordination problem because no organization knows what the others will do. Each organization rationally assumes that if it pulls out of a crisis, it will lose "market share" because other organizations will stay. Thus it is easy for an organization to rationalize its passivity on both ethical and practical grounds. An individual organization may see it as futile and self-defeating to withdraw. In most past cases of withdrawal, a replacement organization quickly took over. For example, before MSF withdrew from Ethiopia in the 1980s due to government abuses of aid, the organization negotiated for a replacement NGO to step in. Practically, if one agency withdraws and others do not, the withdrawing agency has lost its contracts and may lose funding. The ethical gesture may doom the organization in the long run.

UNHCR faces additional obstacles to withholding assistance because it is beholden to the governments that finance it. Amnesty International noted: "This dependence on governments can sometimes constrain UNHCR from taking a strong and public stance on protection issues and may affect the vigor with which it discharges its protection mandate."[73] It has often been repeated that donor governments use UNHCR as a shield. By sending UNHCR to the crisis area, governments claim to take action while avoiding political and military commitments to resolve the crisis. This means that UNHCR could face stiff resistance from donors if it demands a peacekeeping force to demilitarize the refugee situation. UNHCR also has concerns about losing its relevance and status as the preeminent refugee relief agency.[74]

---

71. Quoted in African Rights, *Rwanda: Death, Despair, and Defiance*, p. 1092.
72. ICRC, "ICRC Conditionality," p. 23.
73. Amnesty International, "In Search of Safety," sec. 1.
74. On the challenges facing UNHCR, see Gil Loescher, *The UNHCR and World Politics: A Perilous Path* (Oxford: Oxford University Press, 2001), chap. 10.

Despite the constraints described above, UNHCR could coordinate humanitarian action in situations where most organizations agree that their efforts are exacerbating the conflict. In the refugee relief regime, UNHCR is the dominant actor. Its leadership in protesting abuse of aid is likely to effect a somewhat unified response. Because of coordination problems that commonly afflict NGOs, they will not be able to encourage changes as well among donor governments or refugee-receiving states without UNHCR leadership. For example, Human Rights Watch noted that UNHCR passivity in the face of abuses in Guinea inhibited smaller organizations from protesting: "UNHCR generally plays an intermediary role between international nongovernmental humanitarian agencies and the authorities of the refugee-hosting country; but in Guinea UNHCR appeared unwilling to do so, creating a climate in which aid workers were also unwilling or unable to speak out. UNHCR's failure to press for access to the border region in particular posed a major obstacle to the work of its partner agencies."[75] It is probable that agencies that feel too helpless to seek change might follow the UNHCR lead, should it take one. In addition, UNHCR has an even stronger ethical reason to act than most NGOs—UNHCR is tasked with ensuring refugees' protection.

Critics of a UNHCR leadership role suggest that UNHCR can easily be replaced. The common example given is Kosovo in 1999, where NATO stepped in to care for the refugees. It is misleading to claim that the Kosovo situation would be the rule in most of the world, however. In most areas affected by refugee crises, NATO has no desire to engage. Crises in Europe are the exception. In reality, there is little alternative to UNHCR as the main actor in refugee relief.

Conclusion

The Rwandan refugee crisis of 1994–96 offers an extreme example of humanitarian aid becoming a cause of conflict. In that situation, the political context strongly indicated that humanitarian assistance would contribute to the spread of conflict. The refugees arrived as a state-in-exile, with the leaders loudly proclaiming their genocidal intentions. The receiving state, Zaire, expressed support for the Hutu militants and also lacked the ability to control the national border. External states refused to demilitarize the militants or enforce border security. The combination of these factors left humanitarian organizations on their own in a hostile environment.

---

75. Human Rights Watch, *Liberian Refugees in Guinea*, p. 22.

Humanitarian organizations faced three choices: ignore the militarization, attempt to improve security, or reduce the level of assistance available for manipulation. For the most part, these organizations and their donors ignored the military activity and poured millions of dollars into eastern Zaire. The international humanitarian assistance had the effect of feeding militants, supporting the war economy, sustaining the militants' dependents, and legitimizing the refugees/rebels as victims. The internationally supported camps functioned as the infrastructure of the state-in-exile and the rear bases for the genocidal Hutu fighters.

The Rwandan refugee crisis in Zaire is often regarded as an anomaly among humanitarian emergencies. Numerous aid workers strenuously argue that eastern Zaire was a unique and incomparable situation.[76] Sadako Ogata, then UN High Commissioner for Refugees, claimed, "Probably never before has my Office found its humanitarian concerns in the midst of such a lethal quagmire of political and security interests."[77] The Zaire crisis, however, was not unique and can be fruitfully compared to other refugee situations. Treating the Zaire situation as an aberration obscures the general patterns that explain how humanitarian assistance can cause conflict.

Two general political factors emerge from the above analysis. The first factor is the origin of the refugee crisis. Refugees fleeing as a state-in-exile or from targeted persecution will have greater political cohesion than refugees fleeing the general destruction caused by war. State-in-exile and persecuted groups are more likely to coalesce around militarist leaders and view refugee relief as an instrument of war.

The second political factor is the response of the refugee-receiving state and third-party states. In an ideal setting, states would respond to a militarized refugee group by disarming the militants and preventing cross-border attacks between the refugees and the sending state. Often receiving states lack the ability to impose political order, especially in far-flung border areas that host refugees. In other cases, the receiving state is sympathetic to the militant refugees and frustrates attempts at demilitarization. Under such conditions, humanitarian organizations will find it difficult (if not impossible) to ensure their resources are used in a neutral and impartial manner.

---

76. UNHCR officials, interviews, Geneva, Switzerland, July 1998.
77. Quoted in Dennis McNamara, statement to House International Relations Committee, Subcommittee on International Operations and Human Rights, hearing on "Rwanda: Genocide and the Continuing Cycle of Violence," May 5, 1998, p. 9.

In evaluating their actions during militarized refugee crises, humanitarian organizations usually absolve themselves by focusing on the failures of states to enforce international law. Transferring blame to states, even if it rightfully belongs there, does not solve the difficult issue of a militarized refugee crisis, however. Even if states and the UN Security Council fail to act, or act in a way to encourage violence, refugee relief agencies still bear responsibility for their actions. Ignoring the militarization has political effects, just as confronting it does. Either actively or passively, the refugee relief regime can contribute to the spread of conflict.[78]

To avoid this result, humanitarian organizations (such as UN agencies, the ICRC, and NGOs) cannot ignore the political and military context in which they provide their services. Despite the desire for neutrality, it is virtually impossible for material assistance to have a neutral effect in a conflict situation. Recognizing that fact, aid organizations should press for external political and military intervention when faced with a militarized refugee crisis. Even without external assistance, it is possible, in some cases, to improve the receiving state's capability to impose political order. In extreme situations where the negative effects of assistance outweigh the benefits, humanitarian agencies must consider withdrawing or reducing assistance. In the long run, if agencies do not leverage their resources, they risk losing their moral clout when refugee assistance contributes to conflict. The travesty in the Rwandan refugee camps highlighted the urgent need to design refugee relief programs with a better understanding of their political and military impacts. In militarized refugee crises, purity of intention cannot prevent the spread of conflict.

---

78. Based on his experience during the Ethiopian famine, Rony Brauman explains how NGO inaction and/or silence constitute a political position. Brauman, "Refugee Camps, Population Transfers, and NGOs," in Jonathan Moore, ed., *Hard Choices, Moral Dilemmas in Humanitarian Intervention* (Lanham, Md.: Rowman and Littlefield, 1998), pp. 177–194.

Part III:
Transnational Actors and Security

Market Civilization and Its Clash with Terror

Michael Mousseau

Clausewitz's dictum that war is politics by other means is a reminder that the primary goal of the war against terror is not to defeat and eliminate those who aim to attack the United States and its allies. Rather it is to enhance the security of the American people and their allies. These goals are the same only if terrorist organizations such as al-Qaeda are isolated groups of criminals that need only be found and dealt with swiftly. But if al-Qaeda and its associated groups represent the values and beliefs of substantial numbers of people, and all signs indicate that this is the case, then defeating these groups will not end the struggle against terror. Only by changing the values and beliefs of supporters of terrorist groups can the United States and its allies expect to achieve this objective.

To win the war against terror, the United States and its allies must have both a military strategy and a political strategy. Achieving political victory requires an understanding of the social basis of terror—that is, the values and beliefs that legitimate the use of extreme and indiscriminate violence against the civilian populations of out-groups. Such understanding will not reveal much about terror groups that seem to lack social support, such as the Basque terrorists in Spain, but it will help to reduce the influence of those groups that appear to enjoy widespread support, such as al-Qaeda. Seeking to understand the motivations of terrorists, however, should not be confused with empathizing with them or acquiescing on issues that terrorists and their supporters claim motivate them.

Some scholars have sought to link poverty with terror. Poverty, they argue, fosters terror because it creates a sense of hopelessness, restricts educational opportunity, and produces frustration over inequality.[1] The direct causal linkages between poverty and terror are more elusive than scholars suggest, how-

Michael Mousseau is Associate Professor of International Relations at Koç University in Istanbul, Turkey.

It is with profound gratitude that the author dedicates this article to the memory of Stuart A. Bremer (1944–2002), whose brilliance, affection, and scholarly leadership will be deeply missed by his many students and colleagues.

1. For a summary of these views, see Martha Crenshaw, "The Causes of Terrorism," in Charles W. Kegley Jr., ed., *International Terrorism: Characteristics, Causes, Controls* (New York: St. Martin's, 1990), pp. 113–126. For recent examples, see Samuel P. Huntington, "The Age of Muslim Wars," *Newsweek*, December 17, 2001, pp. 42–48; and James D. Wolfensohn, "Making the World a Better and Safer Place: The Time for Action Is Now," *Politics*, Vol. 22, No. 2 (May 2002), pp. 118–123.

ever. Indeed I am unaware of any comprehensive explanation in print for how poverty causes terror. Nor has there been any demonstrated correlation between the two.[2] Nevertheless, there has been a chorus of calls to increase foreign aid as a tool in the fight against terror.[3] Absent an understanding of the social origins of this phenomenon, however, there is little reason to believe that greater foreign aid will have any significant positive effect. It may even increase the terrorist threat.

In this article, I argue that the social origins of terror are rooted less in poverty—or in growing discontent with U.S. foreign policy—and more in the values and beliefs associated with the mixed economies of developing countries in a globalizing world. I show how liberal-democratic values and beliefs are embedded in the economic infrastructure that prevails in market democracies, and how collective-autocratic values and beliefs are embedded in clientalist economies. As a result of globalization, these values and beliefs are increasingly clashing in the mixed market–clientalist economies of the developing world, triggering intense antimarket resentment directed primarily against the epitome of market civilization: the United States. This study builds on several generations of research in anthropology, economics, political science, and sociology; it explains much of the historical record of sectarian terror around the globe and, most important, suggests how the United States and its allies can combat it.

The article is organized as follows. After reviewing the literature on rational and cultural explanations for terror, I show how market democracies constitute a global civilization based not on interstate trade but on common liberal values and beliefs that thrive in market economies. I then discuss the clash of these liberal values and beliefs with the values and beliefs embraced in many parts of the developing world. I next demonstrate how clientalist values are a necessary condition for the resort to terrorist violence. I conclude with recommendations for developing a political strategy to win the war on terror.

Rational and Cultural Explanations for Terror

The academic literature offers two explanations, one rational and the other cultural, for why some societies support terrorism. The first view holds that ter-

---

2. Alan B. Krueger and Jitka Maleckova, "The Economics and the Education of Suicide Bombers: Does Poverty Cause Terrorism?" *New Republic*, June 24, 2002, pp. 27–33.
3. Many of these calls are made in the media. In the academic literature, see Ivo H. Daalder and James M. Lindsay, "Nasty, Brutish, and Long: America's War on Terrorism," *Current History*, December 2001, pp. 403–408; and Wolfensohn, "Making the World a Better and Safer Place."

rorism is a rational strategy for dealing with particular socioeconomic grievances in societies where the "paths to legal expression of opposition are blocked."[4] "Governments that fail to meet the basic welfare and economic needs of their peoples and suppress their liberties," argues Samuel Huntington, "generate violent opposition to themselves and to Western governments that support them."[5] In the context of the current war on terror, the Arab world is said to need "a managed political opening . . . that introduces pluralism into . . . political life."[6]

Rational explanations of the origins and social support of terror accord well with mainstream views in academia. Realism, for instance, assumes that values and beliefs play no role in the origin or resolution of conflict,[7] and thus the resort to terror is a predictable strategy of the weak. Liberal institutionalists argue that democracies are more likely than other kinds of states to resolve their internal (and external) differences through peaceful means.[8] In addition, they predict that societies in autocracies are more likely to experience violence and to support terror as an acceptable political tool. Although many developing countries have not produced widespread support for terrorism, such support does seem to be more pervasive in the developing world, especially in those countries lacking stable democratic institutions (e.g., Egypt, Indonesia, and Pakistan).

Rational models for explaining the social support of terror have several major weaknesses. The historical record, for instance, does not accord with the proposition that democracies are less likely to condone terror. India, as some observers suggest, has been democratic for more than half a century, yet the threat of sectarian violence seems omnipresent. Nor does the evidence support the notion that poverty or illiteracy increases the threat of terror.[9] If economic deprivation were the culprit, then a century or two ago most societies around the world should have supported terrorist activity, because they were generally worse off (in terms of diet, health care, leisure time, and material wealth) than most societies are today. In addition, it is perhaps noteworthy that fifteen of the nineteen hijackers who struck at the World Trade Center and the Penta-

4. Crenshaw, "The Causes of Terrorism," p. 116.
5. Huntington, "The Age of Muslim Wars," p. 48.
6. Larry Diamond, as cited in Thomas L. Friedman, "The Free-Speech Bind," *New York Times,* Mach 27, 2002, p. A23.
7. Kenneth N. Waltz, *Theory of International Politics* (New York: McGraw-Hill, 1979).
8. Larry Diamond, "Introduction: In Search of Consolidation," in Diamond, Marc F. Plattner, Yun-han Chu, and Hung-mao Tien, eds., *Consolidating the Third Wave Democracies* (Baltimore, Md.: Johns Hopkins University Press, 1997), pp. xiii–xlvii.
9. Krueger and Maleckova, "The Economics and the Education of Suicide Bombers."

gon on September 11, 2001, were from Saudi Arabia, one of the richest countries in the world. Most of them were highly educated and appeared to have had ample opportunities for building materially rewarding lives.

These facts suggest that rational explanations for the social origins and support of terrorism are inadequate. The September 11 hijackers were motivated by something deeper—something that fundamentally distinguished them from their victims. Put simply, terrorists and their supporters do not think like their victims. From the cultural perspective, terrorists are not merely engaged in a rational strategy of the weak. Rather there is something about ingrained habits and historical traditions that renders terrorism a socially acceptable method for addressing grievances in some societies, but not others.[10] When such traditions are combined with social, economic, or political grievances, individuals can be "socialized into violence from early childhood," particularly when they experience violence in their formative years.[11]

From a cultural perspective, the creation of a political strategy to combat terror must begin with an examination of terrorists' values and beliefs. What motivates them? What values do they claim justify their actions? Because all the September 11 hijackers were from Islamic countries, and all seemed to express religious motivations, the cultural approach would suggest that there is something inherent in Islamic beliefs and values that yields the social approval of terror. For instance, some observers argue that because the Koran offers instructions "for even the minutiae of everyday life," Islamic culture has tremendous difficulty dealing with change and lacks "a tradition of self-criticism." As a result, some analysts suggest that Muslims tend to be "defensive and insecure"; they are also likely to blame bad news on "exterior, malevolent powers."[12]

Like rational theories, cultural theories that seek to explain terrorism's origins and base of support have significant weaknesses. For instance, traditional cultural mores are a constant, not a variable, and thus cultural explanations cannot sufficiently account for variation in levels of social support for terror across time and place. More specifically, Islamic values and beliefs cannot explain why the Muslim world did not produce suicidal mass murderers in, for instance, the 1950s, or why millions of Muslims around the world joined others in expressing shock and horror at the events of September 11. Further,

10. Crenshaw, "The Causes of Terrorism," p. 115.
11. Martha Crenshaw, "Thoughts on Relating Terrorism to Historical Contexts," in Crenshaw, ed., *Terrorism in Context* (University Park: Pennsylvania State University Press, 1992), p. 74.
12. Hume Horan, "Those Young Arab Muslims and Us," *Middle East Quarterly*, Vol. 9, No. 4 (Fall 2002), pp. 53–54.

the social support of terror has a tradition in non-Islamic societies (e.g., Catholics and Protestants in Northern Ireland), demonstrating that Muslim culture alone does not sufficiently explain this phenomenon.

Rational approaches have an advantage over cultural approaches because they focus on observable circumstances—poverty, economic inequality, illiteracy, and lack of democracy—that allow scholars to predict when and where social support for terror is likely to emerge. Explanations linking poverty and its related conditions with terror, however, are nebulous. Cultural approaches have an advantage over rational approaches because they are based on the seemingly apparent fact that those who engage in or support suicidal mass murder do not think like people in out-groups (in this case, people in the United States and the rest of the Western world). None of these approaches, however, helps scholars to predict—and thus expose and eradicate—the kinds of values and beliefs that support terror.

To grasp the origins of socially approved terror, scholars need an approach that combines the rationalist identification of observable circumstances with the culturalist emphasis on learning why people think and act as they do. In short, scholars must be able to predict when and where the use of indiscriminate violence against out-groups is likely to be socially approved and when and where it is not. Only then can potential terrorist targets devise a political strategy for eliminating this growing menace.

The Rise of Market Civilization

Many scholars of politics have suggested that there is a growing need to be able to predict variation in peoples' values and beliefs,[13] a need illustrated most dramatically by the September 11 terrorist attacks. In this view, political scientists do not have to start from scratch: Anthropologists, economic historians, and sociologists have been at this task for years. Anthropologists have long sought to explain the relationship between economic conditions and values and beliefs;[14] economic historians have for years linked certain economic conditions with particular sets of values and beliefs, identifying at least two primary kinds of socioeconomic integration in history—clientalism and mar-

---

13. Robert O. Keohane, "Governance in a Partially Globalized World," *American Political Science Review*, Vol. 95, No. 1 (March 2001), pp. 1–15; and Alexander Wendt, *Social Theory of International Politics* (Cambridge: Cambridge University Press, 1999).
14. See Marvin Harris, *Cultural Materialism: The Struggle for a Science of Culture* (Walnut Creek, Calif.: AltaMira Press, 2001 [1979]); and Maxine L. Margolis, "Introduction to the Updated Edition," in Marvin Harris, *The Rise of Anthropological Theory: A History of Theories of Culture*, updated ed. (Walnut Creek, Calif.: AltaMira Press, 2001), pp. vii–xiii.

kets;[15] and sociologists have documented the social implications of clientalist exchange.[16]

In clientalist economies, the obligations of cooperating parties are implied (rather than made explicit) and take the form of reciprocity, or gift giving. Exchange occurs through the giving of gifts, which reinforces a sense of trust and enduring obligation among the parties. Enforcement of obligations comes with the threat of punishment: Violations of trust lead to severed relationships. Clientalist economies can be complex;[17] and with specialization, patrons emerge who have more to give than others, creating a surplus of obligations accompanied by increased influence. Because reciprocal obligations are only implied and are socially enforced, patrons rather than states regulate economic cooperation. Examples of clientalist socioeconomies include feudal Europe, and in the contemporary period, mafias and the complex systems of patronage that characterize the politics of redistribution in most developing countries.[18]

Because economic relations are enduring, clientalist economies are based on explicit social linkages, such as kinship and ethnicity. These linkages render in-groups more important than out-groups, making clientalist communities more inward looking than market communities in terms of identity, values, and beliefs. Clientalist communities are also organized hierarchically: Patrons, such as lords, dons, and uncles, receive gifts from clients as expressions of loyalty in exchange for life-long protection.[19]

In market economies, in contrast, the mutual obligations of cooperating parties are made explicit in the form of contracts. The quid pro quo nature of the

---

15. A third mode of integration, sharing, is common among hunting and gathering societies, but is not discussed here because it has not been a prominent mode of exchange in any state. See Janet L. Abu-Lughod, *Before European Hegemony: The World System, A.D. 1250–1350* (New York: Oxford University Press, 1989); Karl Polanyi, *The Great Transformation: The Political and Economic Origins of Our Time* (Boston: Beacon, 1957 [1944]); Marshall D. Sahlins, *Stone Age Economics* (Hawthorne: Aldine de Gruyter, 1972); and David W. Tandy and Walter C. Neale, "Karl Polanyi's Distinctive Approach to Social Analysis and the Case of Ancient Greece: Ideas, Criticisms, Consequences," in Colin A.M. Duncan and Tandy, eds., *From Political Economy to Anthropology: Situating Economic Life in Past Societies* (London: Black Rose, 1994), pp. 19–20.
16. See, for instance, Marcel Mauss, *The Gift: The Form and Reason for Exchange in Archaic Societies* (New York: W.W. Norton, 2000 [1924]).
17. Polanyi, *The Great Transformation*, pp. 49–50.
18. See S.N. Eisenstadt and René Lemarchand, *Political Clientalism: Patronage and Development* (Thousand Oaks, Calif.: Sage, 1981); and Luis Roniger and Ayþe Güneþ-Ayata, eds., *Democracy, Clientelism, and Civil Society* (Boulder, Colo.: Lynne Rienner, 1994).
19. For further discussion of the rules and norms of gift exchange, see Christopher A. Gregory, *Gifts and Commodities* (San Diego, Calif.: Academic Press, 1983); and Monica Prasad, "The Morality of Market Exchange: Love, Money, and Contractual Justice," *Sociological Perspectives*, Vol. 42, No. 2 (Summer 1999), pp. 181–214.

cooperation implies no obligation among the parties beyond that expressed in the contract. Unlike in clientalist economies, therefore, in market economies, strangers and even enemies can cooperate in prescribed ways.[20] Because contracts cannot be negotiated without explicit assertions of self-interest, their extensive use renders such assertions socially approved. Moreover, a contract imposes an equitable relationship on the parties.[21] The implications of this are profound: The norm of cooperating with strangers on the basis of legal equality is the logical prerequisite for respecting the rule of common law. Because contractual obligations are explicit, a state can enforce them, and a market economy can emerge if a state is willing and able to enforce contracts with impartiality. In these ways, markets develop and the liberal values of individualism, universalism, tolerance, and equity emerge concurrently with the rule of common law and democratic governance.[22] Examples of market economies include classical Athens and, in the contemporary period, Sweden and the United States.[23]

The market economy and its liberal belief system also account for the rise of science over faith-based forms of knowledge. Science is anchored in the notion that (1) some facts are universal (universalism), (2) any person can challenge another's assertions of fact, including those of his or her leader (freedom and equity), and (3) truth is sought through the competition of ideas (tolerance). The opposite of science is truth determined by an authority sanctioned by loyalty and faith—the norm in clientalism.

All societies have some combination of clientalist and market exchange. For markets to prevail, however—for a majority of people to engage regularly in making contracts—a complex division of labor associated with economic development is necessary. At lower levels of development and thus incomes, individuals engage in fewer exchanges, and the few big-ticket exchanges that do

---

20. In this way, the initial emergence of market norms allows for increased specialization and thus greater economic production, which in turn can stimulate a mutually reinforcing cycle of market-integrated growth. See Michael Mousseau, "Market Prosperity, Democratic Consolidation, and Democratic Peace," *Journal of Conflict Resolution,* Vol. 44, No. 4 (August 2000), p. 478.
21. William J. Booth, "On the Idea of the Moral Economy," *American Political Science Review,* Vol. 88, No. 3 (September 1994), pp. 653–667; and Ronald Inglehart, *Culture Shift in Advanced Industrial Society* (Princeton, N.J.: Princeton University Press, 1990), p. 46.
22. For further discussion of this process, see Mousseau, "Market Prosperity, Democratic Consolidation, and Democratic Peace"; and Michael Mousseau, "Globalization, Markets, and Democracy: An Anthropological Linkage," in Mehdi Mozaffari, ed., *Globalization and Civilizations* (London: Routledge, 2002), pp. 97–124.
23. Rondo Cameron, *A Concise Economic History of the World: From Paleolithic Times to the Present,* 3d ed. (New York: Oxford University Press, 1997), pp. 32–35.

occur—such as getting a job, buying a home, or purchasing expensive consumer goods—are less likely to be mediated by the market (with price determined by supply and demand): More often than not, these will be seen as exchanges of gifts among members of an in-group (with price determined by privileged discount). As a result, developing countries tend to have political cultures characterized by intergroup conflict (deep in-group/out-group feelings), less respect for individual freedom, stronger religious beliefs, greater respect for loyalty and hierarchy than for the rule of law, and extensive informal patronage networks (known for, among other things, high levels of corruption).[24]

Sociologists and economic historians have documented the association of gift giving and contracting norms with, respectively, collectivist and individualist value orientations.[25] Anthropologists and archaeologists have long considered economic conditions to be a leading influence on cultural mores and institutional structures.[26] Rational choice theorists and others acknowledge that values affect political behavior[27]; and most agree that, for stability, democracy requires a liberal political culture.[28] The chain of causation is well established: The evidence linking economic development with liberal values is so overwhelming that the proposition has no serious detractors,[29] nor does the

---

24. Mousseau, "Market Prosperity, Democratic Consolidation, and Democratic Peace"; and Mousseau, "Globalization, Markets, and Democracy."
25. Abu-Lughod, *Before European Hegemony*; Fernand Braudel, *Afterthoughts on Material Civilization and Capitalism*, trans. Patricia Ranum (Baltimore, Md.: Johns Hopkins University Press, 1979), p. 63; Emile Durkheim, *The Division of Labour in Society* (Basingstoke, U.K.: Macmillan, 1984 [1893]); Polanyi, *The Great Transformation*; and Tandy and Neale, "Karl Polanyi's Distinctive Approach."
26. Harris, *Cultural Materialism*; and Margolis, "Introduction to the Updated Edition."
27. Keohane, "Governance in a Partially Globalized World"; Margaret Levi, *Consent, Dissent, and Patriotism* (Cambridge: Cambridge University Press, 1997); James D. Morrow, *Game Theory for Political Scientists* (Princeton, N.J.: Princeton University Press, 1994); Elinor Ostrom, *Governing the Commons: The Evolution of Institutions for Collective Action* (New York: Cambridge University Press, 1990); and Tom R. Tyler, *Why People Obey the Law* (New Haven, Conn.: Yale University Press, 1990).
28. Gabriel A. Almond and Sidney Verba, *The Civic Culture: Political Attitudes and Democracy in Five Nations* (Princeton, N.J.: Princeton University Press, 1963); Robert Alan Dahl, *Democracy and Its Critics* (New Haven, Conn.: Yale University Press, 1989); Samuel P. Huntington, "Will More Countries Become Democratic?" *Political Science Quarterly*, Vol. 99, No. 2 (Summer 1984), pp. 193–218; and Seymour Martin Lipset, "Some Social Requisites of Democracy: Economic Development and Political Legitimacy," *American Political Science Review*, Vol. 53, No. 1 (March 1959), pp. 69–105.
29. Braudel, *Afterthoughts on Material Civilization and Capitalism*; Geert Hofstede, *Culture's Consequences: Comparing Values, Behaviors, Institutions, and Organizations across Nations*, 2d ed. (Thousand Oaks, Calif.: Sage, 2001 [1980]); and Ronald Inglehart and Wayne E. Baker, "Modernization, Cultural Change, and the Persistence of Traditional Values," *American Sociological Review*, Vol. 65, No. 1 (February 2000), pp. 19–52.

stabilizing impact of development on democracy.[30] Indeed virtually every economically developed democracy in history has been a market democracy.

Although the disciplines of anthropology, economics, political science, and sociology have all addressed different aspects of the relationship between market economies and society, none has examined this relationship in its entirety. Anthropologists and archaeologists typically link cultural mores not to modes of exchange but to environmental conditions;[31] some economists have argued that the social implications of markets invalidate the core assumptions of neoclassical liberalism,[32] and others have addressed the role of social capital in economic growth;[33] political scientists have focused on how development, not the market economy, stabilizes democracy;[34] and sociologists have highlighted the social, but apparently not the political, consequences of gift exchange.[35]

Findings from these four disciplines help to explain the rise of market civilization and its supremacy in the contemporary era. Surveys and other works have established that the inhabitants of high-income countries—most of which have developed market economies—share common liberal values;[36] other studies confirm that elected leaders seek to promote domestic values in making foreign policy.[37] If median voters in market democracies have liberal values

---

30. Ross E. Burkhart and Michael S. Lewis-Beck, "Comparative Democracy: The Economic Development Thesis," *American Political Science Review,* Vol. 88, No. 4 (December 1994), pp. 111–131; and Adam Przeworski and Fernando Limongi, "Modernization: Theories and Facts," *World Politics,* Vol. 49, No. 2 (January 1997), pp. 155–183.
31. See, for example, R. Brian Ferguson, *Yanomami Warfare: A Political History* (Sante Fe, N.M.: School of American Research Press, 1995).
32. See Polanyi, *The Great Transformation.*
33. Stephen Knack and Philip Keefer, "Does Social Capital Have an Economic Payoff? A Cross-country Investigation," *Quarterly Journal of Economics,* Vol. 112, No. 4 (November 1997), pp. 1251–1288.
34. Lipset, "Some Social Requisites of Democracy"; and Dietrich Rueschemeyer, Evelyne Huber Stephens, and John D. Stephens, *Capitalist Development and Democracy* (Chicago: University of Chicago Press, 1992).
35. Mauss, *The Gift;* and Prasad, "The Morality of Market Exchange."
36. Braudel, *Afterthoughts on Material Civilization and Capitalism;* Yun-han Chu, Fu Hu, and Chung-in Moon, "South Korea and Taiwan: The International Context," in Diamond et al., *Consolidating the Third Wave of Democracies,* pp. 267–294; Hofstede, *Culture's Consequences;* and Inglehart and Baker, "Modernization, Cultural Change, and the Persistence of Traditional Values."
37. George C. Edwards III and B. Dan Wood, "Who Influences Whom? The President, Congress, and the Media," *American Political Science Review,* Vol. 93, No. 2 (June 1999), pp. 327–345; Ronald H. Hinckley, *Peoples, Polls, and Policymakers: American Public Opinion and National Security* (New York: Lexington, 1992); Jeffrey W. Knopf, "How Rational Is the 'Rational Public'? Evidence from U.S. Public Opinion on Military Spending," *Journal of Conflict Resolution,* Vol. 42, No. 5 (October 1998),

and median voters in all other types of democracies do not, then only the elected leaders of the market democracies are likely to have liberal values and a political incentive to pursue a liberal foreign policy course. In this way, the common liberal values of their electorates constrain leaders of market democracies (but not leaders of other types of democracies) to pursue common aims in foreign affairs: for instance, to respect and promote international law, human rights, and an equitable global order.

Proponents of the democratic peace note the apparent dearth of militarized conflict among democratic nations.[38] It now appears, however, that this peace is limited to the advanced market democracies.[39] Democratic dyads where at least one state lacked a developed market economy and that have had a history of militarized confrontation include India and Pakistan, Greece and Turkey, and Ecuador and Peru. Moreover, market democracies—but not other types of democracies—tend to cooperate with each other against other states.[40] They also tend to express common positions in the United Nations General Assembly.[41] Of course, leaders of market democracies do not agree on everything, but they do agree on the fundamentals: how the world should be organized—politically, economically, and socially—and what constitutes proper governmental behavior both internally and externally. When differences surface among market democracies, the discourse is bounded by mutual respect for state rights (equity) and the primacy of international law—just as the domestic political behavior of the governments of these democracies is culturally

pp. 544–571; Timothy J. McKeown, "The Cuban Missile Crisis and Politics as Usual," *Journal of Politics*, Vol. 62, No. 1 (February 2000), pp. 70–87; Benjamin I. Page and Robert Y. Shapiro, *The Rational Public: Fifty Years of Trends in Americans' Policy Preferences* (Chicago: University of Chicago Press, 1992); and Douglas A. Van Belle and Steven W. Hook, "Greasing the Squeaky Wheel: News Media Coverage and U.S. Development Aid, 1977–1992," *International Interactions*, Vol. 26, No. 3 (July–September 2000), pp. 321–346.
38. Stuart A. Bremer, "Dangerous Dyads: Conditions Affecting the Likelihood of Interstate War, 1816–1965," *Journal of Conflict Resolution*, Vol. 36, No. 2 (June 1992), pp. 309–341; Bruce M. Russett, *Grasping the Democratic Peace: Principles for a Post–Cold War World* (Princeton, N.J.: Princeton University Press, 1993); and James Lee Ray, *Democracy and International Conflict: An Evaluation of the Democratic Peace Proposition* (Columbia: University of South Carolina Press, 1995).
39. Mousseau, "Market Prosperity, Democratic Consolidation, and Democratic Peace"; and Michael Mousseau, Håvard Hegre, and John R. Oneal, "How the Wealth of Nations Conditions the Liberal Peace," *European Journal of International Relations*, Vol. 9, No. 4 (June 2003), in press.
40. Michael Mousseau, "An Economic Limitation to the Zone of Democratic Peace and Cooperation" *International Interactions*, Vol. 28, No. 2 (April–June 2002), pp. 137–164.
41. Michael Mousseau, "The Nexus of Market Society, Liberal Preferences, and Democratic Peace: Interdisciplinary Theory and Evidence," *International Studies Quarterly*, Vol. 47, No. 3 (September 2003), in press.

bounded by respect for individual rights and the primacy of democratic law. There is, in short, a market civilization.

The Clash against Market Civilization

Few if any states have predominantly clientalist economies. Most economies are heavily integrated with the market (market democracies) or include some mixture of clientalism and markets (developing countries). Although in many developing countries contracts are officially enforced and regulated, in-group linkages can diminish impartiality. In addition, because clientalist exchange is informal, it lies beyond the regulatory capacity of the state. In this mixed economy, the clash of clientalist and market cultures can lead to illiberal and unstable democracy, military dictatorship, state failure, sectarian violence, or some combination thereof—and bitter anti-Americanism.

In clientalist societies, cooperation occurs with the exchange of gifts, and trust is based on life-long friendships within in-groups. In market societies, loyalty to the in-group is downgraded, as cooperation with strangers is encouraged; trust is based not on friendship but on the perceived universal principle of the sanctity of contractual exchange. Individuals from market cultures thus seek out cooperation universally. From the clientalist perspective, however, those with market values are from out-groups and thus are untrustworthy. Moreover, by expressing self-interest, individuals with market values are viewed as selfish; they appear to have no culture and are seemingly interested in little beyond the crude pursuit of material gain.

Cultures change slowly; so when endogenous factors cause a rise in contractual exchange, a clientalist society's economic norms diverge from prevailing cultural values and beliefs. When this happens, individuals with deeply embedded clientalist values have difficulty grasping new market norms; they perceive that those who are driven by self-interest not only lack strong social ties but have no values at all. This perception is partly true: A society that undergoes economic change may experience a period when there is no common culture, as clientalist linkages break down before market values emerge.

During this period of social anarchy, a zero-sum culture may emerge in which strangers pursue their interests without any regard for shared values—market or clientalist. This explains the circumstances in many developing-world societies today: that is, widespread disrespect for the rule of law (everyone wants the law to apply to someone else); social chaos, as many act without regard for others (e.g., unwillingness to wait in line or obey rules); and the apparent lack of empathy for anyone outside one's in-groups (family, friends, and coworkers).[42] From the market perspective, these conditions seem uncivil and are often assumed to be a consequence of local indigenous culture (i.e., a "supposed" function of Arab culture, Asian culture, and so on). Academics from market cultures have assumed that what people in these countries need is more education,[43] a democratic form of government,[44] or time to develop.[45] As I have sought to show, however, this behavior may not be associated with any particular indigenous culture, form of government, or inherent backwardness. Rather, it may reflect the breakdown of clientalist linkages in economies that, facing severe and persistent economic shocks, have not replaced their clientalist values with market values.

Although great differences remain across the developing world, traditional clientalist protections tend to be strongest in rural areas. Urban communities, on the other hand, are more likely to be in flux, with new patron-client networks (e.g., political parties, unions, and mafias) increasingly replacing traditional patron-client networks (e.g., clans and villages). Strangers in these communities, lacking in both empathy and mutual respect, frequently interact on the basis of few if any common values and beliefs. Meanwhile, in-groups compete over state resources in a zero-sum way—with winners taking all. This helps to explain (1) the high frequency of political violence in developing countries; (2) why democratic institutions in such countries seem to do so poorly in producing public goods, such as roads and security; and (3) why the absence of a strong state often results in chronic instability, civil conflict, and in some cases state failure.

No economic transition can erase a society's collective history or memory, nor can it eliminate the role of external influences, ethnic diversity, and historical animosity among competing factions. Moreover, the breakdown of traditional clientalist linkages is not the only source of social anarchy in developing countries: War and state failure can also be factors, as witnessed in Afghanistan and Somalia, where both rural and urban areas remain in tremendous

---

42. As documented by Hofstede, *Culture's Consequences*.
43. Daniel Lerner, *The Passing of Traditional Society: Modernizing in the Middle East* (New York: Free Press, 1958); and Alex Inkeles and David Smith, *Becoming Modern: Individual Change in Six Developing Countries* (Cambridge, Mass.: Harvard University Press, 1974).
44. Diamond, "Introduction: In Search of Consolidation."
45. Talcott Parsons, "Evolutionary Universals in Society," *American Sociological Review*, Vol. 29, No. 3 (June 1964), pp. 339–357.

flux. Likewise, mineral wealth in a developing economy with weak market norms probably works to reinforce the influence of traditional clientalist in-groups, as patrons spread their riches in return for pledges of loyalty. For the majority of countries without mineral wealth, however, the mire of under-development and economic displacement has meant a rise in social anarchy and civil insecurity.

For many individuals living in this rough-and-tumble Hobbesian world, the new zero-sum culture has a thoroughly Western or American character, as seen on television, in movies, and in other forms of popular culture exported from Europe and the United States. Lacking market values and beliefs, millions of people in developing countries believe that the breakdown of traditional clientalist relationships and the emergence of zero-sum anarchy are results of a growing Westernization or Americanization of their societies, and they deeply resent it. Moreover, a society with clientalist values and beliefs but with fading protections from in-groups is extremely vulnerable to any in-group system that promises to put an end to its deep sense of insecurity. This explains the al-lure of alternative value systems in developing countries that support ethnic sectarianism, extreme nationalism, or various types of religious funda-mentalism.

A brief examination of the impact of economic change in the contemporary period confirms this view. Contractual exchange in the modern period began in northwestern Europe in the 1450s,[46] precipitating for the next 200 years the social and institutional changes brought about during the Protestant Reforma-tion. For three centuries after that, many states in Europe (e.g., England and Holland) began to develop market economies—by enforcing contracts, subsi-dizing private enterprise, and breaking up clientalist linkages.[47] Only in the twentieth century, however, did the majority of Europeans possess the re-sources to engage regularly in contractual exchange. The combination of nine-teenth-century industrialization and mass migration to the United States greatly increased the demand for, and thus the wages of, labor in Europe. As a result, Europe's majority, once clients in a clientalist world, became buyers in a new market world.[48]

The political repercussions of this socioeconomic transition were vast: Euro-

---

46. Braudel, *Afterthoughts on Material Civilization and Capitalism*, p. 24.
47. As documented by Polanyi, *The Great Transformation*.
48. See Simona Piattoni, ed., *Clientelism, Interests, and Democratic Representation: The European Expe-rience in Historical and Comparative Perspective* (Cambridge: Cambridge University Press, 2001).

pean peasants gave up their way of life—including traditional in-group protection—only to arrive in cities in the midst of rapid economic change and seemingly devoid of common values and beliefs. Like their counterparts in the nineteenth century, today's migrants confront a bewildering array of zero-sum conditions and Hobbesian anarchy. In both cases, the refugees created by these socioeconomic disruptions sought economic and political protection by joining new forms of clientalist in-groups; and in both cases, they seem to have perceived the rise of market exchange as lacking any redeeming social value. The consequences were the same in both cases: Just as many Europeans in the last century were drawn to clientalist in-groups that championed antimarket (i.e., socialist, communist, or fascist) values, many of today's refugees have been pulled toward antimarket socialist, nationalist, or religious political organizations. I say organizations because these clientalist in-groups are not civic-oriented political parties: They offer all-encompassing social, economic, and political programs in exchange for absolute loyalty.

In the midst of industrial change, many Europeans joined ethnic sectarian groups, including some that identified European Jewry as the cause of their social anarchy. Frequently, European Jews were merchants and thus tended to behave according to market norms by, among other things, expressing self-interest through the use of contracts. Faced with the increasing destruction of their traditional clientalist linkages and rising social anarchy, many other Europeans began to equate the proliferation of zero-sum values with Jewish values. Seeking support in socially collapsing societies, some political leaders unleashed antimarket passions by encouraging pogroms against the seemingly "cultureless" (but really just liberal) Jews. One such leader, Adolf Hitler, was himself from a poor migrant section of Vienna—as were many of his followers. While Germany was in the midst of a rapid transition toward a market economy in the 1920s, hyperinflation eliminated the savings of the nascent middle class. This caused a widespread loss of faith in contracts, a revival of clientalist values, and an antimarket fury that legitimated the mass murder of out-groups. This explains why the Nazis replaced the failing market with a state-directed economy, and why the Germans (and others) became Hitler's willing executioners."[49] In fact, across Europe and across time, the strength of anti-Semitism seems to correlate negatively, and the stability of democracy positively, with the intensity of the market economy. One indication of this is the

49. Daniel J. Goldhagen, *Hitler's Willing Executioners: Ordinary Germans and the Holocaust* (New York: Alfred A. Knopf, 1996).

availability of jobs that offer a living wage. Significantly, just one generation after the U.S. imposition and subsidization of a market economy in West Germany following the end of World War II, West Germans were well on their way toward developing a liberal political culture.[50]

Europe's transition to a market economy in the nineteenth and early twentieth centuries led to the rise of antimarket socialist, communist, and fascist movements as well as sectarian terror. Similarly, the transition toward a market economy in many contemporary developing countries is associated with antimarket socialist, ethnofascist, hypernationalist, and religious fundamentalist movements—as well as sectarian terror. Examples include the Marxist guerrillas in Latin America, such as the FARC in Colombia and the Shining Path in Peru; increasing ethnic identification, and popularity of hypernationalist political parties, in parts of Russia and Turkey; and the rise of religious fundamentalism in India and much of the Islamic world. Although the character of these movements varies, the catalyst is the same: bitter opposition to market (liberal) values. Herein lays the source of today's widespread anti-Americanism and anti-Westernism: The liberal way of life in the United States and the rest of the West—its cold materialism, from the clientalist perspective—is being broadcast to homes around the world, many of which are transitioning to market economies. In this way, just as the Jews symbolized emerging market norms in Europe a century ago, today, with modern technology, American and Western culture symbolizes the dreaded market norms linked with globalization.

The Resort to Terror

Those on the lowest rung of the economic ladder are the most vulnerable to the negative consequences associated with globalization. Those with the most to lose, however, are patrons and their lieutenants who hold privileged positions in the old clientalist hierarchies. This is why leaders of terrorist organizations frequently come from privileged backgrounds. To maintain the clientalist structure that carries with it higher social status, these leaders seek to rally their client base by appealing to some antimarket ideology. Because it is in a

---

50. See Ronald Inglehart, *Modernization and Postmodernization: Cultural, Economic, and Political Change in Forty-three Societies* (Princeton, N.J.: Princeton University Press, 1997), p. 175. Of course, the socioeconomic transition cannot explain the long history of anti-Semitism in Europe, much of which predates the rise of markets.

client's interest to have a powerful patron, leaders attract and maintain followers by demonstrations of strength. In this way, the mass murder of Westerners
serves two purposes: It reflects the leader's power, and it taps into widespread
antimarket fury.

Islam itself is not responsible for the social approval of terror. Patrons fearing the loss of their privileged status—such as Osama bin Laden—find an
antimarket ideology useful to attract followers. They manipulate Islam to
serve their own ends, just like their counterparts in Europe did a century ago
by contorting Christianity to justify terror and mass murder.[51] In fact, Islam
emerged in Mecca, the center of sixth-century Mediterranean and South Asian
trade, and the Koran stress the market values of universalism, equity, contractual exchange, and a degree of tolerance toward outsiders (non-Muslims).[52]
The market economy in this region declined before market norms—and liberal
culture—intensified and expanded throughout the Islamic world, but the liberal origins of Islam demonstrate that religion can be interpreted, and manipulated, to suit anyone's purposes.

In societies steeped in market values, it is difficult to comprehend how anyone can engage in the mass murder of out-groups, or how anyone can support
it. Individuals with market values believe that each person is responsible only
for his or her actions. Just as those who are not parties to contracts cannot be
made obligated to them, individuals cannot be assumed to be responsible for
any and all behavior of other members of their apparent in-group. It therefore
seems absurd to blame individuals for the alleged bad behavior of others, and
this is the social origin of the presumption of individual innocence in market
societies. From the clientalist perspective, in contrast, no one is innocent: Individuals share responsibility for the actions of others within the in-group; if followers do not support their leaders, then they are betraying the entire in-
group. From the clientalist perspective, all in-group members are privileged
and all out-group members are enemies or, at best, outsiders unworthy of em-

---

51. Although Osama bin Laden is from Saudi Arabia, I do not contend that Saudi Arabia has an
emerging market economy. On the contrary, its oil wealth has served to reinforce its clientalist linkages, as patron sheiks spread their wealth in return for loyalty. With globalization and satellite television, however, patrons have reason to feel threatened by the perceived omnipresence of zero-
sum norms and Americanization, a fear that fuels resentment toward the West and, more
specifically, the presence of U.S. troops on Saudi soil. Support for al-Qaeda appears in tribal linkages in Saudi Arabia and Yemen, as well as in poor Muslim countries facing the social anarchy of
development, such as Egypt, Indonesia, and Pakistan.
52. Ali A. Mazrui, *Cultural Forces in World Politics* (Portsmouth, N.H.: Heinemann, 1990).

pathy. A paucity of empathy is necessary for doing harm to, and tolerating the suffering of, all out-group members. This is why international human rights are a concern promoted mostly by market democracies. It is also why widespread social support for both terrorism and sectarian violence frequently arises in developing countries but not in countries with deeply integrated markets.[53]

Clientalist values also lie at the core of the social approval of suicidal mass murder. From the market perspective, all behavior should have some immediate utility for the parties to a contract. It is thus difficult to comprehend the efficacy of suicide. But in cultures where the individual is less important than the group and the absence of science increases devotion to insular beliefs, suicide—under conditions of extreme socioeconomic disruption—may emerge as a socially approved way of expressing ultimate loyalty to the in-group. In this way, cultural insularism, characterized by the absence of a market economy, is a necessary condition for the social approval of suicidal mass murder and sectarian violence.

Cultural insularism combined with a particular grievance—such as the negative consequences associated with globalization—can create a deadly mix for Americans and other Westerners. Although latent anti-Americanism and anti-Westernism exist throughout much of the developing world, these are most likely to rise to the surface during economic crises—when nascent middle classes lose their status and turn against emerging liberal values. This is what is happening, for example, in Indonesia where the recent collapse of the local currency has eliminated the savings of the middle class, just as hyperinflation devastated the savings of Germany's middle class seventy-five years ago. Recent terrorist acts against Indonesian Christians (as symbols of the West) and Westerners directly (the November 2002 bombing of a disco in Bali) are reminiscent of Germany's middle class turning against those it identified with market values, such as European Jews and the West. The West, in this sense, means market civilization.

---

53. The closest possible exceptions that I am aware of are the socially approved lynchings of African Americans by white Southerners in the 1920s and 1930s and the sectarian murders during the Troubles in Northern Ireland. In my view, however, the economies of neither the Southern states in the United States nor Northern Ireland were primarily integrated with contracts—and this helps to explain the sectarian terror. Of course, this is an empirical issue that could be explored in future research.

The Eradication of Terror

Terrorism has both expressed and underlying causes. Expressed causes are those that terrorists assert themselves. Emic analysis, in which subjects are asked to explain why they behave as they do, identifies expressed causes. It does not explain, however, why some acts inflame passions while others go unnoticed. For instance, hundreds have died in recent violence between Hindus and Muslims in India, including many Muslims. Yet these killings have elicited "an emotionally muted headline in the Arab media." When Israelis kill Muslims, however, as has occurred in the most recent round of Middle East violence, "it inflames the entire Muslim world."[54] To understand these different responses, scholars must engage not only in emic but also in etic analysis: They need to be able to interpret the behavior of their subjects. Why do so many Indonesians, for instance, empathize with the plight of the Palestinians but seem to express little outrage over the deaths of Indian Muslims? The reason is Israel's identification with the United States and emerging markets. Although identification with Islam may be an expressed cause of this rage, the underlying cause is not Islam but rather a deeply embedded antimarket and thus anti-American passion—a fury that extends beyond the Islamic world and whose origins are not understood even by those espousing hatred for the West.

This sense of rage against market civilization and its shared liberal values and beliefs—a rage that can be inflamed with the addition of any immediate cause—lies just beneath the surface in many developing countries. This is not to say that all or even the majority of people living in the developing world share this wrath, but that the potential for a clash is ever-present. Once policymakers understand this, they can begin to develop the kinds of political strategies needed to eliminate the terrorist threat.

Since the terrorist attacks of September 11, three myths have emerged regarding the direction that these strategies should take; all three threaten to derail efforts to eradicate terror. The first myth is that to win the hearts and minds of people around the world in the struggle against terror, the United States must do more to signal its friendly intentions—for instance, by increasing economic aid and explaining U.S. policies more clearly.[55] This view is mistaken.

---

54. Thomas L. Friedman, "The Core of Muslim Rage," *New York Times,* March 6, 2002, p. A21.
55. Articles representing influential American think tanks that take this view include Daalder and Lindsay, "Nasty, Brutish, and Long"; and Peter G. Peterson, "Diplomacy and the War on Terrorism," *Foreign Affairs,* Vol. 81, No. 5 (September–October 2002), pp. 74–96.

The rage against the United States as the leading symbol of the West is so deeply embedded in some societies that many will interpret whatever the United States does with malign intent. If the United States offers to increase economic aid, it is seen as imperialist; if it does not, it is neglectful. If the United States intervenes to protect Muslims, as it did in the 1999 Kosovo conflict, critics will rail against U.S. "imperialism" (there must be oil there) or, at best, charge that the United States intentionally delayed the intervention because Americans really hate Muslims. Consider that in clientalist cultures the notion of science—universal truth—is incomprehensible.[56] For this reason, even many educated people in the developing world believe in such nonsense as the notion that 4,000 Jews were warned not to go to work at the World Trade Center on September 11:[57] These people believe what they want to believe, regardless of the evidence before them. In fact, for those enraged against the United States for its perceived zero-sum values, friendly acts will have no positive effect. The implication of this is liberating: In terms of underlying causes, the United States need not worry about how societies that produce or harbor terrorists perceive its actions in the war against terrorism. Given that whatever the United States (and other market democracies) do will be interpreted as malevolent, they may as well behave as they see fit.

The second myth associated with September 11 is that terror arises in the absence of democracy,[58] and therefore the United States should push harder for democratic change in developing countries. This view is also flawed. Stable democracies emerge when people want them to, when they share the liberal values and beliefs that prevail in market economies. It is understandable that scholars, policymakers, and pundits in market democracies value democracy and consider it a cure-all against evil: In market civilization, democratic institutions are a deeply embedded value. There is little evidence, however, that democracy causes liberal values. History shows that democracy without lib-

---

56. The notion of science should not be confused with the use of advanced technology or education. Science is a process of discovery that assumes that some facts are universal, anyone can challenge another's assertions of fact, and truth is sought through the free competition of ideas. One can be taught the discoveries of advanced physics but still have no concept of challenging assertions of fact scientifically. This is why communist and developing nations can import and modify advanced technology, but the market democracies will always be in the avant-garde of developing knowledge.

57. Thomas L. Friedman, "Global Village Idiocy," *New York Times,* May 12, 2002, sec. 4, p. 15; see also Horan, "Those Young Arab Muslims and Us," p. 54.

58. For example, Crenshaw, "The Causes of Terrorism"; Friedman, "The Free-Speech Bind"; Huntington, "The Age of Muslim Wars"; and Nicholas D. Kristof, "What Is Democracy Anyway?" *New York Times,* May 3, 2002, p. A23.

eral values results in illiberal democracy and the rise to power of antidemocratic regimes that frequently display antimarket and clientalist—and therefore terrorist—orientation, such as the Bolsheviks in Russia and the Nazis in Germany.

The third myth to emerge after September 11 is that if people who detest the United States only had greater exposure to American values, their hatred would dissipate.[59] This view is premised on the assumption that because Americans know they are nice people, others will feel the same way if only they get to know them better. This view is also inaccurate. Anti-American rage is the result of people knowing Americans too well. The problem is that they just do not like what they see, because from the clientalist perspective, American values reflect a degeneration of culture and the ascendance of zero-sum norms. Ironically, the notion that modern culture means no culture is also a common assumption of many academic models of global politics.[60] As I have deduced from my analysis of the market economy, however, modern culture does possess values—the values of contractual exchange. The task for the United States in the struggle against terrorism then is not to expose more of itself but to counteract the ill effects of too much exposure by more subtly demonstrating the redeeming aspects of market culture.

To win the war against terrorism, the United States and other market democracies must remove the underlying cause of terror: the deeply embedded antimarket rage brought on by the forces of globalization. To do this, the market democracies have only one option: to boost developing countries out of the mire of social anarchy and into market development. Most developing countries cannot make this transition alone, because their leaders are likely to hold clientalist rather than market values and beliefs. Furthermore, maintaining their grasp on power typically involves redistributing state resources among winning coalitions of clientalist in-groups. In this way, current forms of foreign aid may actually reinforce values and beliefs that condone terror, as recipient governments use the aid to pay off supporters and reinforce clientalist linkages. In fact, studies report that much foreign aid pays the salaries of bureaucrats and those working for aid agencies.[61] Because these jobs are frequently

---

59. See, for instance, Friedman, "Global Village Idiocy."
60. See, for instance, Bruce Bueno de Mesquita, James D. Morrow, Randolph M. Siverson, and Alastair Smith, "An Institutional Explanation of the Democratic Peace," *American Political Science Review*, Vol. 93, No. 4 (December 1999), pp. 791–807; and Waltz, *Theory of International Politics*.
61. See "Dubious Aid," *Canada and the World Backgrounder*, Vol. 65, No. 6 (May 2000), p. 27.

obtained through clientalist linkages, current forms of aid can actually promote the very clientalist values that can legitimate the resort to terror.

Because governments of developing countries are unlikely to get out of the mire of social anarchy and into market development themselves, an outside power is needed to act as a sort of Leviathan: to push the governments of target countries to establish the prerequisites of a market economy. These include impartial enforcement of contracts and common law; destruction of clientalist linkages (corruption); subsidization of private enterprises (with fair bidding practices); widespread equitable subsidization of small loans so people can purchase homes or start small businesses; and redistribution to widen the scope of opportunities for market engagement. In the 1980s, Ronald Reagan's administration encouraged cuts in the number of state-owned enterprises in a variety of countries. State ownership of enterprises is not the problem, however: The problem is when state ownership prevents an enterprise from competing fairly in the market. In recent years the International Monetary Fund has begun to enforce rules of equity in banking practices.[62] For the most part, however, policymakers have placed greater emphasis on balancing budgets, supporting democratization,[63] and reducing poverty.[64] It is not deregulated markets, democracy, or an absence of poverty that produces liberal values, however, but rather a market economy.[65] Thus, to reduce the social support of terror, market democracies should use economic aid as both a means and an incentive for governments in developing countries (1) to create and enforce bodies of common law that are vital to the functioning of a market economy, and (2) to equitably subsidize local private enterprises with the goal of widespread employment. The latter is critical during the transition period: The availability of living-wage jobs in the market alleviates insecurity and prevents antimarket rage.

Given the deep distrust of U.S. motives among the millions living in the social anarchy of underdevelopment, other market democracies must share the burden of pulling them out of this mire. One option would be to create an in-

---

62. Ajit Singh, "Aid, Conditionality, and Development," *Development and Change*, Vol. 33, No. 2 (2002), pp. 299–300.
63. James K. Boyce, "Unpacking Aid," *Development and Change*, Vol. 33, No. 2 (2002), p. 242.
64. Graham Bird, "A Suitable Case for Treatment? Understanding the Ongoing Debate about the IMF," *Third World Quarterly*, Vol. 22, No. 5 (October 2001), pp. 823–848.
65. A market economy is not a free market. A market economy is one in which the majority of people routinely engage in contractual exchange. Thus a market economy may be highly regulated (e.g., Sweden) and, in theory at least, be publicly owned. A free market, in contrast, refers to a deregulated or partially regulated economy that can coexist with underdevelpment (e.g., Kenya).

ternational organization with substantial powers to monitor compliance with aid conditions, run by the donor states yet unconstrained by their independent interests. In this way, multilateralism could legitimate the indirect external control of the economies of recipient states during their transitions. Multilateral action would also allow the United States to keep a lower profile and include its allies as partners in the war against terror.

The historical record shows that market democracies easily cooperate and establish legal regimes among themselves.[66] The European Union and the North Atlantic Treaty Organization are just two of the many regimes that bind these countries together. Although differences do occur, they are mostly at the level of tactics and not over major goals. Sharing preferences and bounded by the logic of contractual exchange, market democracies manage their relationships and resolve their disputes with other market democracies through a combination of mutual respect (equity), common law, and in the absence of law, negotiation and compromise. As German Chancellor Gerhard Schröder described his country's recent rift with the United States, "Between friends, there can be factual differences."[67] Like West Germany after World War II, developing countries whose market economies are subsidized are likely to one day have market economies, at which time their newly emerged liberal values will reinforce their market-democratic institutions, and there will be no further need of foreign assistance. The social basis of terror against the United States and its allies could thus be eradicated.

Conclusion

Until now there have been two general approaches to understanding the motivations behind terrorism, one rational and the other cultural. Rational explanations focus on the role of political and economic grievances and assume that certain observable factors associated with poverty such as economic inequality, illiteracy, and lack of democracy cause terror. None of these approaches, however, has established a direct causal link between any of these factors and terror. Nor does there appear to be a correlation between poverty and terror.

Cultural explanations, in contrast, focus not on political or economic conditions but on the notion that the values and beliefs of terrorists and their sup-

---

66. Mousseau, "An Economic Limitation to the Zone of Democratic Peace and Cooperation."
67. Quoted in Steven Erlanger, "Moves by Germany to Mend Relations Rebuffed by Bush," *New York Times*, September 24, 2002, p. A1.

porters are vastly different from those of their targets. Typically, however, these explanations identify indigenous culture as the causal variable, which makes this approach unsuitable for predicting variation in social support for terror within cultures across both time and place. To grasp the origins of terror and why some support it, scholars need an approach that combines the rationalist identification of observable circumstances with the culturalist emphasis on the way people think.

In this article I drew on several generations of research in anthropology, economics, political science, and sociology to show how the values and beliefs that support terror—a lack of empathy for out-groups, an emphasis on community over the individual, and an incomprehension for objective truth and individual innocence—arise from the clientalist economic linkages that are commonplace in many developing countries. In contrast, values that work against terror—individualism, tolerance, equity, and the rule of common law—arise with a market economy. Because all market economies in the contemporary period have been developed economies, there appears to be a link between underdevelopment and terror. As I have argued, however, the real culprit is social anarchy produced by globalization and the difficulties attending the transition to a market economy. Just as millions in the last century turned to antimarket and sectarian values during the rise of market economies in Europe, today millions in the developing world support antimarket and sectarian values reflected in support for ethnofacism, sectarian murder, and fundamentalist religions—anything that offers psychic comfort in the face of volatile social anarchy.

It follows that there is a market civilization based on common liberal values and beliefs, and that this civilization is in conflict with much of the developing world. Direct and expressed causes bring this conflict to the surface at particular times and places. Beneath the surface, however, lies a deeply embedded clash of cultures: market civilization versus the rest. A number of scholars have noted signs of this conflict but have typically identified indigenous culture, not the market economy, as exogenous.[68] The problem with this view is that it

---

68. The most prominent argument for this view in recent years appears in Samuel P. Huntington, *The Clash of Civilizations and the Remaking of World Order* (New York: Simon and Schuster, 1996). For empirical challenges to this thesis, see Errol Anthony Henderson and Richard Tucker, "Clear and Present Strangers: The Clash of Civilizations and International Conflict," *International Studies Quarterly*, Vol. 45, No. 2 (June 2001), pp. 317–338; and Bruce M. Russett, John R. Oneal, and Michaelene Cox, "Clash of Civilizations, or Realism and Liberalism Déjà Vu? Some Evidence," *Journal of Peace Research*, Vol. 37, No. 5 (September 2000), pp. 583–609. For Huntington's response to Russett, Oneal, and Cox, see Samuel P. Huntington, "Try Again: A Reply to Russett, Oneal, and Cox," ibid., pp. 609–610.

assumes that liberal values emerge from Western indigenous culture. Although this view is pervasive,[69] it runs contrary to the historical record. For instance, a generation after Max Weber wrote about the virtues of the Protestant ethic,[70] millions of Protestants in the West conspired to murder millions of Jews.[71] The Nazis are just one prominent example of Western barbarism; white Southern Protestants in the United States who participated in lynchings in the early twentieth century are another. To many, it may seem as though liberal values are inherently Western, but this notion rests on a biased selection of the evidence. It ignores cases of Western barbarity. Empirical research across several disciplines demonstrates that it is market development that correlates with liberal values.[72] Although this conclusion may be unsettling for many scholars of global politics, it offers a better accounting of global history. More important, it carries a liberating implication for progressive leaders in the developing world: The rise of markets and liberal culture will not make a developing country any more Western than the rise of a market economy in England made the British any more Dutch.

Nevertheless, there is nothing in this thesis that argues against other possible sources of anti-Americanism and anti-Westernism. Realists and world systems theorists might focus on the projection of U.S. military power from the core into the periphery as the source of anti-Americanism; liberal institutionalists may focus on what they consider the unilateralist turn that U.S. foreign policy recently seems to have taken. These sources of anti-Americanism, however, exist primarily on the surface and are present mostly in the West and at universities. Antiglobalization protesters within market democracies, for instance, frequently express anti-American and antimarket sentiments. These protesters, however, call for greater global equality—a deeply embedded lib-

---

69. See, for example, Francis Fukuyama, "The Primacy of Culture," *Journal of Democracy*, Vol. 6, No. 1 (January 1995), pp. 7–14; and Ronald Inglehart, "The Renaissance of Political Culture," *American Political Science Review*, Vol. 82, No. 4 (December 1988), pp. 1203–1230.
70. Max Weber, *The Protestant Ethic and the Spirit of Capitalism*, trans. Talcott Parsons (New York: Charles Scribner's Sons, 1958 [1904–05]).
71. See Goldhagen, *Hitler's Willing Executioners*.
72. For the observation that a rise in markets liberalizes values, see Braudel, *Afterthoughts on Material Civilization and Capitalism*. There is extensive cross-national data linking economic development and liberal values, with the overwhelming majority of observed cases of development being cases of market-oriented development. See Hofstede, *Culture's Consequences*; and Inglehart and Baker, "Modernization, Cultural Change, and the Persistence of Traditional Values." For specific empirical confirmation that it is market development—and not other kinds of development—that promotes liberal values, see Michael Mousseau, "Market Culture and Peace among Nations: It's the Market Democracies That Ally," paper presented at the annual meeting of the American Political Science Association, Boston, Massachusetts, August 26–September 1, 2002.

eral preference. Although these protesters may also express resentment of the market, they do so for the same reason that many people in developing countries resent the market: They are typically young students with little direct experience in the marketplace. Regardless, such anti-Americanism appears only among a minority of the West, and few would suggest that antiglobalization protesters would support the mass murder of Americans and other Westerners—a preference that requires a radically different set of values than those associated with market democracies.

Once the rise of market civilization and its clash with the rest is understood, political strategies for winning the war against terror can be developed. Just as the United States imposed and subsidized the emergence of market economies in Germany and Japan after World War II—effectively liberalizing their cultures—market democracies today must subsidize the rise of markets in developing countries. This does not mean deregulating their economies, which would do little to inhibit clientalist linkages or encourage trust in contractual exchange. Nor is wealth the source of liberal values: Saudi Arabia is one of the world's wealthiest states, but it has a predominantly clientalist economy, which is why it produces terrorists. Rather, it is through the establishment of market economies that the United States and its allies can be made safe from terror.

Behind the Curve | Audrey Kurth Cronin

Globalization and International Terrorism

$\mathbf{T}$he coincidence between the evolving changes of globalization, the inherent weaknesses of the Arab region, and the inadequate American response to both ensures that terrorism will continue to be the most serious threat to U.S. and Western interests in the twenty-first century. There has been little creative thinking, however, about how to confront the growing terrorist backlash that has been unleashed. Terrorism is a complicated, eclectic phenomenon, requiring a sophisticated strategy oriented toward influencing its means and ends over the long term. Few members of the U.S. policymaking and academic communities, however, have the political capital, intellectual background, or inclination to work together to forge an effective, sustained response. Instead, the tendency has been to fall back on established bureaucratic mind-sets and prevailing theoretical paradigms that have little relevance for the changes in international security that became obvious after the terrorist attacks in New York and Washington on September 11, 2001.

The current wave of international terrorism, characterized by unpredictable and unprecedented threats from nonstate actors, not only is a reaction to globalization but is facilitated by it; the U.S. response to this reality has been reactive and anachronistic. The combined focus of the United States on state-centric threats and its attempt to cast twenty-first-century terrorism into familiar strategic terms avoids and often undermines effective responses to this nonstate phenomenon. The increasing threat of globalized terrorism must be met with flexible, multifaceted responses that deliberately and effectively exploit avenues of globalization in return; this, however, is not happening.

Audrey Kurth Cronin is Specialist in International Terrorism at the Congressional Research Service at the Library of Congress. The article was written when she was Visiting Associate Professor at the Edmund A. Walsh School of Foreign Service and a Research Fellow at the Center for Peace and Security Studies, Georgetown University.

I am grateful for helpful comments and criticisms on previous drafts from Robert Art, Patrick Cronin, Timothy Hoyt, James Ludes, and an anonymous reviewer. I have been greatly influenced by conversations and other communications with Martha Crenshaw, to whom I owe a huge debt. None of these people necessarily agrees with everything here. Also beneficial was a research grant from the School of Foreign Service at Georgetown University. My thanks to research assistants Christopher Connell, William Josiger, and Sara Skahill and to the members of my graduate courses on political violence and terrorism. Portions of this article will be published as "Transnational Terrorism and Security: The Terrorist Threat to Globalization," in Michael E. Brown, ed., *Grave New World: Global Dangers in the Twenty-first Century* (Washington, D.C.: Georgetown University Press, forthcoming).

As the primary terrorist target, the United Sates should take the lead in fashioning a forward-looking strategy. As the world's predominant military, economic, and political power, it has been able to pursue its interests throughout the globe with unprecedented freedom since the breakup of the Soviet Union more than a decade ago. Even in the wake of the September 11 terrorist attacks on the World Trade Center and the Pentagon, and especially after the U.S. military action in Afghanistan, the threat of terrorism, mostly consisting of underfunded and ad hoc cells motivated by radical fringe ideas, has seemed unimportant by comparison. U.S. strategic culture has a long tradition of downplaying such atypical concerns in favor of a focus on more conventional state-based military power.[1] On the whole, this has been an effective approach: As was dramatically demonstrated in Afghanistan, the U.S. military knows how to destroy state governments and their armed forces, and the American political leadership and public have a natural bias toward using power to achieve the quickest results. Sometimes it is important to show resolve and respond forcefully.

The United States has been far less impressive, however, in its use of more subtle tools of domestic and international statecraft, such as intelligence, law enforcement, economic sanctions, educational training, financial controls, public diplomacy, coalition building, international law, and foreign aid. In an ironic twist, it is these tools that have become central to the security of the United States and its allies since September 11. In an era of globalized terrorism, the familiar state-centric threats have not disappeared; instead they have been joined by new (or newly threatening) competing political, ideological, economic, and cultural concerns that are only superficially understood, particularly in the West. An examination of the recent evolution of terrorism and a projection of future developments suggest that, in the age of globalized terrorism, old attitudes are not just anachronistic; they are dangerous.

Terrorism as a phenomenon is not new, but for reasons explained below, the threat it now poses is greater than ever before. The current terrorist backlash is manifested in the extremely violent asymmetrical response directed at the United States and other leading powers by terrorist groups associated with or inspired by al-Qaeda. This backlash has the potential to fundamentally threaten the international system. Thus it is not just an American problem. Unless the United States and its allies formulate a more comprehensive re-

---

1. The issue of U.S. strategic culture and its importance in the response to international terrorism is explored in more depth in Audrey Kurth Cronin, "Rethinking Sovereignty: American Strategy in the Age of Terror," *Survival*, Vol. 44, No. 2 (Summer 2002), pp. 119–139.

sponse to terrorism, better balanced across the range of policy instruments, the results will be increasing international instability and long-term failure.

The article proceeds in five main sections. First, it provides a discussion of the definition, history, causes, and types of terrorism, placing the events of September 11, 2001, in their modern context. Second, it briefly describes key trends in modern terrorism, explaining how the phenomenon appears to be evolving. Third, it analyzes the implications of these trends for the stability and security of the international community generally, and the United States and its allies more specifically. Fourth, the article outlines the prospects of these trends. It concludes with a range of policy recommendations suggested by the analysis.

Definition, Origins, Motivations, and Types of Modern Terrorism

The terrorist phenomenon has a long and varied history, punctuated by lively debates over the meaning of the term. By ignoring this history, the United States runs the risk of repeating the plethora of mistakes made by other major powers that faced similar threats in the past. This section begins with an explanation of the definition of terrorism, then proceeds to an examination of terrorism's origins, major motivations, and predominant types.

DEFINITION OF TERRORISM

Terrorism is notoriously difficult to define, in part because the term has evolved and in part because it is associated with an activity that is designed to be subjective. Generally speaking, the targets of a terrorist episode are not the victims who are killed or maimed in the attack, but rather the governments, publics, or constituents among whom the terrorists hope to engender a reaction—such as fear, repulsion, intimidation, overreaction, or radicalization. Specialists in the area of terrorism studies have devoted hundreds of pages toward trying to develop an unassailable definition of the term, only to realize the fruitlessness of their efforts: Terrorism is intended to be a matter of perception and is thus seen differently by different observers.[2]

Although individuals can disagree over whether particular actions constitute terrorism, there are certain aspects of the concept that are fundamental.

---

2. On the difficulty of defining terrorism, see, for example, Omar Malik, *Enough of the Definition of Terrorism!* Royal Institute of International Affairs (London: RIIA, 2001); and Alex P. Schmid, *Political Terrorism: A Research Guide* (New Brunswick, N.J.: Transaction Books, 1984). Schmid spends more than 100 pages grappling with the question of a definition, only to conclude that none is universally accepted.

First, terrorism always has a political nature. It involves the commission of outrageous acts designed to precipitate political change.[3] At its root, terrorism is about justice, or at least someone's perception of it, whether man-made or divine. Second, although many other uses of violence are inherently political, including conventional war among states, terrorism is distinguished by its nonstate character—even when terrorists receive military, political, economic, and other means of support from state sources. States obviously employ force for political ends: When state force is used internationally, it is considered an act of war; when it is used domestically, it is called various things, including law enforcement, state terror, oppression, or civil war. Although states can terrorize, they cannot by definition be terrorists. Third, terrorism deliberately targets the innocent, which also distinguishes it from state uses of force that inadvertently kill innocent bystanders. In any given example, the latter may or may not be seen as justified; but again, this use of force is different from terrorism. Hence the fact that precision-guided missiles sometimes go astray and kill innocent civilians is a tragic use of force, but it is not terrorism. Finally, state use of force is subject to international norms and conventions that may be invoked or at least consulted; terrorists do not abide by international laws or norms and, to maximize the psychological effect of an attack, their activities have a deliberately unpredictable quality.[4]

Thus, at a minimum, terrorism has the following characteristics: a fundamentally political nature, the surprise use of violence against seemingly random targets, and the targeting of the innocent by nonstate actors.[5] All of these attributes are illustrated by recent examples of terrorism—from the April 2000 kidnapping of tourists by the Abu Sayyaf group of the Philippines to the various incidents allegedly committed by al-Qaeda, including the 1998 bombings of the U.S. embassies in Kenya and Tanzania and the September 11 attacks. For the purposes of this discussion, the shorthand (and admittedly imperfect) definition of terrorism is the threat or use of seemingly random violence against innocents for political ends by a nonstate actor.

---

3. Saying that terrorism is a political act is not the same as arguing that the political ends toward which it is directed are necessarily negotiable. If violent acts do not have a political aim, then they are by definition criminal acts.
4. The diabolical nature of terrorism has given resonance to Robert Kaplan's view that the world is a "grim landscape" littered with "evildoers" and requiring Western leaders to adopt a "pagan ethos." But such conclusions deserve more scrutiny than space allows here. See Steven Mufson, "The Way Bush Sees the World," *Washington Post*, Outlook section, February 17, 2002, p. B1.
5. R.G. Frey and Christopher W. Morris, "Violence, Terrorism, and Justice," in Frey and Morris, eds., *Violence, Terrorism, and Justice* (Cambridge: Cambridge University Press, 1991), p. 3.

ORIGINS OF TERRORISM

Terrorism is as old as human history. One of the first reliably documented instances of terrorism, however, occurred in the first century B.C.E. The Zealots-Sicarri, Jewish terrorists dedicated to inciting a revolt against Roman rule in Judea, murdered their victims with daggers in broad daylight in the heart of Jerusalem, eventually creating such anxiety among the population that they generated a mass insurrection.[6] Other early terrorists include the Hindu Thugs and the Muslim Assassins. Modern terrorism, however, is generally considered to have originated with the French Revolution.[7]

The term "terror" was first employed in 1795, when it was coined to refer to a policy systemically used to protect the fledgling French republic government against counterrevolutionaries. Robespierre's practice of using revolutionary tribunals as a means of publicizing a prisoner's fate for broader effect within the population (apart from questions of legal guilt or innocence) can be seen as a nascent example of the much more highly developed, blatant manipulation of media attention by terrorist groups in the mid- to late twentieth century.[8] Modern terrorism is a dynamic concept, from the outset dependent to some degree on the political and historical context within which it has been employed.

DECOLONIZATION AND ANTIGLOBALIZATION: DRIVERS OF TERRORISM?

Although individual terrorist groups have unique characteristics and arise in specific local contexts, an examination of broad historical patterns reveals that the international system within which such groups are spawned does influence their nature and motivations. A distinguishing feature of modern terrorism has been the connection between sweeping political or ideological concepts and increasing levels of terrorist activity internationally. The broad political aim has been against (1) empires, (2) colonial powers, and (3) the U.S.-led international system marked by globalization. Thus it is important to understand the general history of modern terrorism and where the current threat fits within an international context.

---

6. Walter Laqueur, *Terrorism* (London: Weidenfeld and Nicolson, 1977, reprinted in 1978), pp. 7–8; and David C. Rapoport, "Fear and Trembling: Terrorism in Three Religious Traditions," *American Political Science Review*, Vol. 78, No. 3 (September 1984), pp. 658–677.
7. David C. Rapoport, "The Fourth Wave: September 11 in the History of Terrorism," *Current History*, December 2001, pp. 419–424; and David C. Rapoport, "Terrorism," *Encyclopedia of Violence, Peace, and Conflict* (New York: Academic Press, 1999).
8. Ironically, Robespierre's tactics during the Reign of Terror would not be included in this article's definition of terrorism, because it was state terror.

David Rapoport has described modern terrorism such as that perpetuated by al-Qaeda as part of a religiously inspired "fourth wave." This wave follows three earlier historical phases in which terrorism was tied to the breakup of empires, decolonization, and leftist anti-Westernism.[9] Rapoport argues that terrorism occurs in consecutive if somewhat overlapping waves. The argument here, however, is that modern terrorism has been a power struggle along a continuum: central power versus local power, big power versus small power, modern power versus traditional power. The key variable is a widespread perception of opportunity, combined with a shift in a particular political or ideological paradigm. Thus, even though the newest international terrorist threat, emanating largely from Muslim countries, has more than a modicum of religious inspiration, it is more accurate to see it as part of a larger phenomenon of antiglobalization and tension between the have and have-not nations, as well as between the elite and underprivileged within those nations. In an era where reforms occur at a pace much slower than is desired, terrorists today, like those before them, aim to exploit the frustrations of the common people (especially in the Arab world).

In the nineteenth century, the unleashing of concepts such as universal suffrage and popular empowerment raised the hopes of people throughout the western world, indirectly resulting in the first phase of modern terrorism. Originating in Russia, as Rapoport argues, it was stimulated not by state repression but by the efforts of the czars to placate demands for economic and political reforms, and the inevitable disappointment of popular expectations that were raised as a result. The goal of terrorists was to engage in attacks on symbolic targets to get the attention of the common people and thus provoke a popular response that would ultimately overturn the prevailing political order. This type of modern terrorism was reflected in the activities of groups such as the Russian Narodnaya Volya (People's Will) and later in the development of a series of movements in the United States and Europe, especially in territories of the former Ottoman Empire.

The dissolution of empires and the search for a new distribution of political power provided an opportunity for terrorism in the nineteenth and twentieth centuries. It climaxed in the assassination of Archduke Franz Ferdinand on June 28, 1914, an event that catalyzed the major powers into taking violent action, not because of the significance of the man himself but because of the sus-

9. Rapoport, "The Fourth Wave."

picion of rival state involvement in the sponsorship of the killing. World War I, the convulsive systemic cataclysm that resulted, ended the first era of modern terrorism, according to Rapoport.[10] But terrorism tied to popular movements seeking greater democratic representation and political power from coercive empires has not ceased. Consider, for example, the Balkans after the downfall of the former state of Yugoslavia. The struggle for power among various Balkan ethnic groups can be seen as the final devolution of power from the former Ottoman Empire. This postimperial scramble is also in evidence elsewhere—for example, in Aceh, Chechnya, and Xinjiang, to mention just a few of the trouble spots within vast (former) empires. The presentation of a target of opportunity, such as a liberalizing state or regime, frequently evokes outrageous terrorist acts.

According to Rapoport, a second, related phase of modern terrorism associated with the concept of national self-determination developed its greatest predominance after World War I. It also continues to the present day. These struggles for power are another facet of terrorism against larger political powers and are specifically designed to win political independence or autonomy. The mid-twentieth-century era of rapid decolonization spawned national movements in territories as diverse as Algeria, Israel, South Africa, and Vietnam.[11] An important by-product was ambivalence toward the phenomenon in the international community, with haggling over the definition of terrorism reaching a fever pitch in the United Nations by the 1970s.

The question of political motivation became important in determining international attitudes toward terrorist attacks, as the post–World War II backlash against the colonial powers and the attractiveness of national independence movements led to the creation of a plethora of new states often born from violence. Arguments over the justice of international causes and the designation of terrorist struggles as "wars of national liberation" predominated, with consequentialist philosophies excusing the killing of innocent people if the cause in the long run was "just." Rapoport sees the U.S. intervention in Vietnam, and especially the subsequent American defeat by the Vietcong, as having catalyzed a "third wave" of modern terrorism; however, the relationship between the Vietnam conflict and other decolonization movements might just as easily be considered part of the same phase. In any case, the victory of the

10. Ibid., pp. 419–420.
11. Ibid., p. 420.

Vietcong excited the imaginations of revolutionaries throughout the world and, according to Rapoport, helped lead to a resurgence in terrorist violence. The Soviet Union underwrote the nationalist and leftist terrorist agendas of some groups, depicting the United States as the new colonial power—an easy task following the Vietnam intervention—and furthering an ideological agenda oriented toward achieving a postcapitalist, international communist utopia. Other groups, especially in Western Europe, rejected both the Soviet and capitalist models and looked admiringly toward nationalist revolutionaries in the developing world.[12] Leftist groups no longer predominate, but the enduring search for national self-determination continues, not only in the areas mentioned above but also in other hot spots such as the Basque region, East Timor, Sri Lanka, and Sudan.

Terrorism achieved a firmly international character during the 1970s and 1980s,[13] evolving in part as a result of technological advances and partly in reaction to the dramatic explosion of international media influence. International links were not new, but their centrality was. Individual, scattered national causes began to develop into international organizations with links and activities increasingly across borders and among differing causes. This development was greatly facilitated by the covert sponsorship of states such as Iran, Libya, and North Korea, and of course the Soviet Union, which found the underwriting of terrorist organizations an attractive tool for accomplishing clandestine goals while avoiding potential retaliation for the terrorist attacks.

The 1970s and 1980s represented the height of state-sponsored terrorism. Sometimes the lowest common denominator among the groups was the concept against which they were reacting—for example, "Western imperialism"—rather than the specific goals they sought. The most important innovation, however, was the increasing commonality of international connections among the groups. After the 1972 Munich Olympics massacre of eleven Israeli athletes, for example, the Palestinian Liberation Organization (PLO) and its associated groups captured the imaginations of young radicals around the world. In Lebanon and elsewhere, the PLO also provided training in the pre-

---

12. Adrian Gulke, *The Age of Terrorism and the International Political System* (London: I.B. Tauris, 1995), pp. 56–63.
13. This is not to imply that terrorism lacked international links before the 1970s. There were important international ties between anarchist groups of the late nineteenth century, for example. See David C. Rapoport, "The Four Waves of Modern Terrorism," in Audrey Kurth Cronin and James Ludes, eds., *The Campaign against International Terrorism* (Washington, D.C.: Georgetown University Press, forthcoming).

ferred techniques of twentieth-century terrorism such as airline hijacking, hostage taking, and bombing.

Since the September 11 attacks, the world has witnessed the maturation of a new phase of terrorist activity, the jihad era, spawned by the Iranian Revolution of 1979 as well as the Soviet defeat in Afghanistan shortly thereafter. The powerful attraction of religious and spiritual movements has overshadowed the nationalist or leftist revolutionary ethos of earlier terrorist phases (though many of those struggles continue), and it has become the central characteristic of a growing international trend. It is perhaps ironic that, as Rapoport observes, the forces of history seem to be driving international terrorism back to a much earlier time, with echoes of the behavior of "sacred" terrorists such as the Zealots-Sicarii clearly apparent in the terrorist activities of organizations such as al-Qaeda and its associated groups. Religious terrorism is not new; rather it is a continuation of an ongoing modern power struggle between those with power and those without it. Internationally, the main targets of these terrorists are the United States and the U.S.-led global system.

Like other eras of modern terrorism, this latest phase has deep roots. And given the historical patterns, it is likely to last at least a generation, if not longer. The jihad era is animated by widespread alienation combined with elements of religious identity and doctrine—a dangerous mix of forces that resonate deep in the human psyche.

What is different about this phase is the urgent requirement for solutions that deal both with the religious fanatics who are the terrorists and the far more politically motivated states, entities, and people who would support them because they feel powerless and left behind in a globalizing world. Thus if there is a trend in terrorism, it is the existence of a two-level challenge: the hyperreligious motivation of small groups of terrorists and the much broader enabling environment of bad governance, nonexistent social services, and poverty that punctuates much of the developing world. Al-Qaeda, a band driven by religious extremism, is able to do so much harm because of the secondary support and sanctuary it receives in vast areas that have not experienced the political and economic benefits of globalization. Therefore, the prescription for dealing with Osama bin Laden and his followers is not just eradicating a relatively small number of terrorists, but also changing the conditions that allow them to acquire so much power. Leaving aside for the moment the enabling environment, it is useful to focus on the chief motivations of the terrorists themselves, especially the contrasting secular and spiritual motivations of terrorism.

LEFTIST, RIGHTIST, ETHNONATIONALIST/SEPARATIST, AND "SACRED" TERRORISM

There are four types of terrorist organizations currently operating aound the world, categorized mainly by their source of motivation: left-wing terrorists, right-wing terrorists, ethnonationalist/separatist terrorists, and religious or "sacred" terrorists. All four types have enjoyed periods of relative prominence in the modern era, with left-wing terrorism intertwined with the Communist movement,[14] right-wing terrorism drawing its inspiration from Fascism,[15] and the bulk of ethnonationalist/separatist terrorism accompanying the wave of decolonization especially in the immediate post–World War II years. Currently, "sacred" terrorism is becoming more significant.[16] Although groups in all categories continue to exist today, left-wing and right-wing terrorist groups were more numerous in earlier decades. Of course, these categories are not perfect, as many groups have a mix of motivating ideologies—some ethnonationalist groups, for example, have religious characteristics or agendas[17]—but usually one ideology or motivation dominates.

Categories are useful not simply because classifying the groups gives scholars a more orderly field to study (admittedly an advantage), but also because different motivations have sometimes led to differing styles and modes of behavior. Understanding the type of terrorist group involved can provide insight into the likeliest manifestations of its violence and the most typical patterns of its development. At the risk of generalizing, left-wing terrorist organizations, driven by liberal or idealist political concepts, tend to prefer revolutionary, antiauthoritarian, antimaterialistic agendas. (Here it is useful to distinguish between the idealism of individual terrorists and the frequently contradictory motivations of their sponsors.) In line with these preferences, left-wing organizations often engage in brutal criminal-type behavior such as kidnapping, murder, bombing, and arson, often directed at elite targets that symbolize authority. They have difficulty, however, agreeing on their long-term

---

14. Groups such as the Second of June Movement, the Baader-Meinhof Gang, the Red Brigades, the Weathermen, and the Symbionese Liberation Army belong in this category.
15. Among right-wing groups would be other neo-Nazi organizations (in the United States and Europe) and some members of American militia movements such as the Christian Patriots and the Ku Klux Klan.
16. The list here would be extremely long, including groups as different as the Tamil Tigers of Sri Lanka, the Basque separatist party, the PLO, and the Irish Republican Army (IRA) and its various splinter groups.
17. Bruce Hoffman notes that secular terrorist groups that have a strong religious element include the Provisional IRA, Armenian factions, and perhaps the PLO; however, the political/separatist aspect is the predominant characteristic of these groups. Hoffman, "Terrorist Targeting: Tactics, Trends, and Potentialities," *Technology and Terrorism* (London: Frank Cass, 1993), p. 25.

objectives.[18] Most left-wing organizations in twentieth-century Western Europe, for example, were brutal but relatively ephemeral. Of course, right-wing terrorists can be ruthless, but in their most recent manifestations they have tended to be less cohesive and more impetuous in their violence than leftist terrorist groups. Their targets are often chosen according to race but also ethnicity, religion, or immigrant status, and in recent decades at least, have been more opportunistic than calculated.[19] This makes them potentially explosive but difficult to track.[20] Ethnonationalist/separatist terrorists are the most conventional, usually having a clear political or territorial aim that is rational and potentially negotiable, if not always justifiable in any given case. They can be astoundingly violent, over lengthy periods. At the same time, it can be difficult to distinguish between goals based on ethnic identity and those rooted in the control of a piece of land. With their focus on gains to be made in the traditional state-oriented international system, ethnonationalist/separatist terrorists often transition in and out of more traditional paramilitary structures, depending on how the cause is going. In addition, they typically have sources of support among the local populace of the same ethnicity with whom their separatist goals (or appeals to blood links) may resonate. That broader popular support is usually the key to the greater average longevity of ethnonationalist/separatist groups in the modern era.[21]

---

18. An interesting example is France's Action Directe, which revised its raison d'être several times, often altering it to reflect domestic issues in France—anarchism and Maoism, dissatisfaction with NATO and the Americanization of Europe, and general anticapitalism. See Michael Dartnell, "France's Action Directe: Terrorists in Search of a Revolution," *Terrorism and Political Violence*, Vol. 2, No. 4 (Winter 1990), pp. 457–488.

19. For example, in the 1990s Germany and several other European countries experienced a rash of random arson attacks against guest houses and offices that provided services to immigrants, many of whom were Middle Eastern in origin. Other examples include the violence associated with groups such as Europe's "football hooligans." A possible American example of the opportunistic nature of right-wing terrorism may be the anthrax letter campaign conducted in October 2001. See Susan Schmidt, "Anthrax Letter Suspect Profiled: FBI Says Author Likely Is Male Loner; Ties to Bin Laden Are Doubted," *Washington Post*, November 11, 2001, p. A1; and Steve Fainaru, "Officials Continue to Doubt Hijackers' Link to Anthrax: Fla. Doctor Says He Treated One for Skin Form of Disease," *Washington Post*, March 24, 2002, p. A23.

20. It is interesting to note that, according to Christopher C. Harmon, in Germany, 1991 was the first year that the number of indigenous rightist radicals exceeded that of leftists. Harmon, *Terrorism Today* (London: Frank Cass, 2000), p. 3.

21. For example, in discussing the longevity of terrorist groups, Martha Crenshaw notes only three significant terrorist groups with ethnonationalist ideologies that ceased to exist within ten years of their formation (one of these, EOKA, disbanded because its goal—the liberation of Cyprus—was attained). By contrast, a majority of the terrorist groups she lists as having existed for ten years or longer have recognizable ethnonationalist ideologies, including the IRA (in its many

All four types of terrorist organizations are capable of egregious acts of barbarism. But religious terrorists may be especially dangerous to international security for at least five reasons.

First, religious terrorists often feel engaged in a Manichaean struggle of good against evil, implying an open-ended set of human targets: Anyone who is not a member of their religion or religious sect may be "evil" and thus fair game. Although indiscriminate attacks are not unique to religious terrorists, the exclusivity of their faith may lead them to dehumanize their victims even more than most terrorist groups do, because they consider nonmembers to be infidels or apostates—as perhaps, for instance, al-Qaeda operatives may have viewed Muslims killed in the World Trade Center.

Second, religious terrorists engage in violent behavior directly or indirectly to please the perceived commands of a deity. This has a number of worrisome implications: The whims of the deity may be less than obvious to those who are not members of the religion, so the actions of violent religious organizations can be especially unpredictable. Moreover, religious terrorists may not be as constrained in their behavior by concerns about the reactions of their human constituents. (Their audience lies elsewhere.)

Third, religious terrorists consider themselves to be unconstrained by secular values or laws. Indeed the very target of the attacks may be the law-based secular society that is embodied in most modern states. The driving motivation, therefore, is to overturn the current post-Westphalian state system—a much more fundamental threat than is, say, ethnonationalist terrorism purporting to carve out a new secular state or autonomous territory.

Fourth, and related, religious terrorists often display a complete sense of alienation from the existing social system. They are not trying to correct the system, making it more just, more perfect, and more egalitarian. Rather they are trying to replace it. In some groups, apocalyptic images of destruction are seen as a necessity—even a purifying regimen—and this makes them uniquely dangerous, as was painfully learned on September 11.[22]

---

forms), Sikh separatist groups, Euskadi Ta Askatasuna, the various Palestinian nationalist groups, and the Corsican National Liberation Front. See Crenshaw, "How Terrorism Declines," *Terrorism and Political Violence*, Vol. 3, No. 1 (Spring 1991), pp. 69–87.

22. On the characteristics of modern religious terrorist groups, see Bruce Hoffman, *Inside Terrorism* (New York: Columbia University Press, 1998), especially pp. 94–95; and Bruce Hoffman, "Terrorism Trends and Prospects," in Ian O. Lesser, Bruce Hoffman, John Arguilla, Michelle Zanini, and David Ronfeldt, eds., *Countering the New Terrorism* (Santa Monica, Calif.: RAND, 1999), especially pp. 19–20. On the peculiar twists of one apocalyptic vision, see Robert Jay Lifton, *Destroying the*

Fifth, religious terrorism is especially worrisome because of its dispersed popular support in civil society. On the one hand, for example, groups such as al-Qaeda are able to find support from some Muslim nongovernmental foundations throughout the world,[23] making it truly a global network. On the other hand, in the process of trying to distinguish between the relatively few providers of serious support from the majority of genuinely philanthropic groups, there is the real risk of igniting the very holy war that the terrorists may be seeking in the first instance.

In sum, there are both enduring and new aspects to modern terrorism. The enduring features center on the common political struggles that have characterized major acts of international terrorism. The newest and perhaps most alarming aspect is the increasingly religious nature of modern terrorist groups. Against this historical background, the unique elements in the patterns of terrorist activity surrounding September 11 appear starkly.

Key Trends in Modern Terrorism

By the late 1990s, four trends in modern terrorism were becoming apparent: an increase in the incidence of religiously motivated attacks, a decrease in the overall number of attacks, an increase in the lethality per attack, and the growing targeting of Americans.

Statistics show that, even before the September 11 attacks, religiously motivated terrorist organizations were becoming more common. The acceleration of this trend has been dramatic: According to the RAND–St. Andrews University Chronology of International Terrorism,[24] in 1968 none of the identified international terrorist organizations could be classified as "religious"; in 1980, in the aftermath of the Iranian Revolution, there were 2 (out of 64), and that number had expanded to 25 (out of 58) by 1995.[25]

World to Save It: Aum Shinrikyo, Apocalyptic Violence, and the New Global Terrorism (New York: Henry Holt, 1999).

23. There is a long list of people and organizations sanctioned under Executive Order 13224, signed on September 23, 2001. Designated charitable organizations include the Benevolence International Foundation and the Global Relief Foundation. The list is available at http://www.treas.gov/offices/enforcement/ofac/sanctions/t11ter.pdf (accessed November 26, 2002).
24. The RAND–St. Andrews University Chronology of International Terrorism is a databank of terrorist incidents that begins in 1968 and has been maintained since 1972 at St. Andrews University, Scotland, and the RAND Corporation, Santa Monica, California.
25. Hoffman, *Inside Terrorism*, pp. 90–91; and Nadine Gurr and Benjamin Cole, *The New Face of Terrorism: Threats from Weapons of Mass Destruction* (London: I.B. Tauris, 2000), pp. 28–29.

Careful analysis of terrorism data compiled by the U.S. Department of State reveals other important trends regarding the frequency and lethality of terrorist attacks. The good news was that there were fewer such attacks in the 1990s than in the 1980s: Internationally, the number of terrorist attacks in the 1990s averaged 382 per year, whereas in the 1980s the number per year averaged 543.[26] But even before September 11, the absolute number of casualties of international terrorism had increased, from a low of 344 in 1991 to a high of 6,693 in 1998.[27] The jump in deaths and injuries can be partly explained by a few high-profile incidents, including the bombing of the U.S. embassies in Nairobi and Dar-es-Salaam in 1998;[28] but it is significant that more people became victims of terrorism as the decade proceeded. More worrisome, the number of people killed per incident rose significantly, from 102 killed in 565 incidents in 1991 to 741 killed in 274 incidents in 1998.[29] Thus, even though the number of terrorist attacks declined in the 1990s, the number of people killed in each one increased.

Another important trend relates to terrorist attacks involving U.S. targets. The number of such attacks increased in the 1990s, from a low of 66 in 1994 to a high of 200 in the year 2000.[30] This is a long-established problem: U.S. nationals consistently have been the most targeted since 1968.[31] But the percentage of international attacks against U.S. targets or U.S. citizens rose dramatically over the 1990s, from about 20 percent in 1993–95 to almost 50 percent in 2000.[32] This is perhaps a consequence of the increased role and profile of the United States in the world, but the degree of increase is nonetheless troubling.

The increasing lethality of terrorist attacks was already being noticed in the late 1990s, with many terrorism experts arguing that the tendency toward more casualties per incident had important implications. First it meant that, as had been feared, religious or "sacred" terrorism was apparently more dangerous than the types of terrorism that had predominated earlier in the twentieth

---

26. Statistics compiled from data in U.S. Department of State, *Patterns of Global Terrorism*, published annually by the Office of the Coordinator for Counterterrorism, U.S. Department of State.
27. Ibid. For a graphical depiction of this information, created on the basis of annual data from *Patterns of Global Terrorism*, see Cronin, "Rethinking Sovereignty," p. 126.
28. In the 1998 embassy bombings alone, for example, 224 people were killed (with 12 Americans among them), and 4,574 were injured (including 15 Americans). U.S. Department of State, *Patterns of Global Terrorism*, 1998.
29. Ibid. For a graphical depiction of deaths per incident, created on the basis of annual data from *Patterns of Global Terrorism*, see Cronin, "Rethinking Sovereignty," p. 128.
30. Ibid.
31. Hoffman, "Terrorist Targeting," p. 24.
32. U.S. Department of State, *Patterns of Global Terrorism*, various years.

century. The world was facing the resurgence of a far more malignant type of terrorism, whose lethality was borne out in the larger death toll from incidents that increasingly involved a religious motivation.[33] Second, with an apparent premium now apparently placed on causing more casualties per incident, the incentives for terrorist organizations to use chemical, biological, nuclear, or radiological (CBNR) weapons would multiply. The breakup of the Soviet Union and the resulting increased availability of Soviet chemical, biological, and nuclear weapons caused experts to argue that terrorist groups, seeking more dramatic and deadly results, would be more drawn to these weapons.[34] The 1995 sarin gas attack by the Japanese cult Aum Shinrikyo in the Tokyo subway system seemed to confirm that worry. More recently, an examination of evidence taken from Afghanistan and Pakistan reveals al-Qaeda's interest in chemical, biological, and nuclear weapons.[35]

In addition to the evolving motivation and character of terrorist attacks, there has been a notable dispersal in the geography of terrorist acts—a trend that is likely to continue. Although the Middle East continues to be the locus of most terrorist activity, Central and South Asia, the Balkans, and the Transcaucasus have been growing in significance over the past decade. International connections themselves are not new: International terrorist organizations inspired by common revolutionary principles date to the early nineteenth century; clandestine state use of foreign terrorist organizations occurred as early as the 1920s (e.g., the Mussolini government in Italy aided the Croat Ustasha); and complex mazes of funding, arms, and other state support for international terrorist organizations were in place especially in the 1970s and 1980s.[36] During the Cold War, terrorism was seen as a form of surrogate warfare and

33. Examples include Bruce Hoffman, *"Holy Terror": The Implications of Terrorism Motivated by a Religious Imperative*, RAND Paper P-7834 (Santa Monica, Calif.: RAND, 1993); and Mark Juergensmeyer, "Terror Mandated by God," *Terrorism and Political Violence*, Vol. 9, No. 2 (Summer 1997), pp. 16–23.
34. See, for example, Steven Simon and Daniel Benjamin, "America and the New Terrorism," *Survival*, Vol. 42, No. 1 (Spring 2000), pp. 59–75, as well as the responses in the subsequent issue, "America and the New Terrorism: An Exchange," *Survival*, Vol. 42, No. 2 (Summer 2000), pp. 156–172; and Hoffman, "Terrorism Trends and Prospects," pp. 7–38.
35. See Peter Finn and Sarah Delaney, "Al-Qaeda's Tracks Deepen in Europe," *Washington Post*, October 22, 2001, p. A1; Kamran Khan and Molly Moore, "2 Nuclear Experts Briefed Bin Laden, Pakistanis Say," *Washington Post*, December, 12, 2001, p. A1; James Risen and Judith Miller, "A Nation Challenged: Chemical Weapons—Al Qaeda Sites Point to Tests of Chemicals," *New York Times*, November 11, 2001, p. B1; Douglas Frantz and David Rohde, "A Nation Challenged: Biological Terror—2 Pakistanis Linked to Papers on Anthrax Weapons," *New York Times*, November 28, 2001; and David Rohde, "A Nation Challenged: The Evidence—Germ Weapons Plans Found at a Scientist's House in Kabul," *New York Times*, December 1, 2001.
36. Laqueur, *Terrorism*, pp. 112–116.

seemed almost palatable to some, at least compared to the potential prospect of major war or nuclear cataclysm.[37] What has changed is the self-generating nature of international terrorism, with its diverse economic means of support allowing terrorists to carry out attacks sometimes far from the organization's base. As a result, there is an important and growing distinction between where a terrorist organization is spawned and where an attack is launched, making the attacks difficult to trace to their source.

Reflecting all of these trends, al-Qaeda and its associated groups[38] (and individuals) are harbingers of a new type of terrorist organization. Even if al-Qaeda ceases to exist (which is unlikely), the dramatic attacks of September 2001, and their political and economic effects, will continue to inspire similarly motivated groups—particularly if the United States and its allies fail to develop broad-based, effective counterterrorist policies over the long term. Moreover, there is significant evidence that the global links and activities that al-Qaeda and its associated groups perpetuated are not short term or anomalous. Indeed they are changing the nature of the terrorist threat as we move further into the twenty-first century. The resulting intersection between the United States, globalization, and international terrorism will define the major challenges to international security.

The United States, Globalization, and International Terrorism

Whether deliberately intending to or not, the United States is projecting uncoordinated economic, social, and political power even more sweepingly than it is in military terms. Globalization,[39] in forms including Westernization, secularization, democratization, consumerism, and the growth of market capitalism, represents an onslaught to less privileged people in conservative cultures repelled by the fundamental changes that these forces are bringing—or angered by the distortions and uneven distributions of benefits that result.[40] This

---

37. Ibid., pp. 115–116.
38. Groups with known or alleged connections to al-Qaeda include Jemaah Islamiyah (Indonesia, Malaysia, and Singapore), the Abu Sayyaf group (Philippines), al-Gama'a al-Islamiyya (Egypt), Harakat ul-Mujahidin (Pakistan), the Islamic Movement of Uzbekistan (Central Asia), Jaish-e-Mohammed (India and Pakistan), and al-Jihad (Egypt).
39. For the purposes of this article, globalization is a gradually expanding process of interpenetration in the economic, political, social, and security realms, uncontrolled by (or apart from) traditional notions of state sovereignty. Victor D. Cha, "Globalization and the Study of International Security," *Journal of Peace Research*, Vol. 37, No. 3 (March 2000), pp. 391–393.
40. With respect to the Islamic world, there are numerous books and articles that point to the phenomenon of antipathy with the Western world, either because of broad cultural incompatibility or

is especially true of the Arab world. Yet the current U.S. approach to this growing repulsion is colored by a kind of cultural naïveté, an unwillingness to recognize—let alone appreciate or take responsibility for—the influence of U.S. power except in its military dimension. Even doing nothing in the economic, social, and political policy realms is still doing something, because the United States is blamed by disadvantaged and alienated populations for the powerful Western-led forces of globalization that are proceeding apace, despite the absence of a focused, coordinated U.S. policy. And those penetrating mechanisms of globalization, such as the internet, the media, and the increasing flows of goods and peoples, are exploited in return. Both the means and ends of terrorism are being reformulated in the current environment.

THE MEANS

Important changes in terrorist methods are apparent in the use of new technologies, the movement of terrorist groups across international boundaries, and changes in sources of support. Like globalization itself, these phenomena are all intertwined and overlapping but, for ease of argument, they are dealt with consecutively here.

First, the use of information technologies such as the internet, mobile phones, and instant messaging has extended the global reach of many terrorist groups. Increased access to these technologies has so far not resulted in their widely feared use in a major cyberterrorist attack: In Dorothy Denning's words, terrorists "still prefer bombs to bytes."[41] Activists and terrorist groups have increasingly turned to "hacktivism"—attacks on internet sites, including

---

a specific conflict between Western consumerism and religious fundamentalism. Among the earliest and most notable are Samuel P. Huntington, "The Clash of Civilizations?" *Foreign Affairs*, Vol. 72, No. 3 (Summer 1993); Benjamin R. Barber, *Jihad vs. McWorld: Terrorism's Challenge to Democracy* (New York: Random House, 1995); and Samuel P. Huntington, *The Clash of Civilizations and the Remaking of World Order* (New York: Simon and Schuster, 1996).
41. For more on cyberterrorism, see Dorothy Denning, "Activism, Hacktivism, and Cyberterrorism: The Internet as a Tool for Influencing Foreign Policy," paper presented at Internet and International Systems: Information Technology and American Foreign Policy Decision-making Workshop at Georgetown University, http://www.nautilus.org/info-policy/workshop/papers/denning.html (accessed January 5, 2003); Dorothy Denning, "Cyberterrorism," testimony before the U.S. House Committee on Armed Services, Special Oversight Panel on Terrorism, 107th Cong., 1st sess., May 23, 2001, available on the Terrorism Research Center website, http://www.cs.georgetown.edu/?denning/infosec/cyberterror.html (accessed January 5, 2003); Jerold Post, Kevin Ruby, and Eric Shaw, "From Car Bombs to Logic Bombs: The Growing Threat of Information Terrorism," *Terrorism and Political Violence*, Vol. 12, No. 2 (Summer 2000), pp. 97–122; and Tom Regan, "When Terrorists Turn to the Internet," *Christian Science Monitor*, July 1, 1999, http://www.csmonitor.com (accessed January 5, 2003).

web defacements, hijackings of websites, web sit-ins, denial-of-service attacks, and automated email "bombings"—attacks that may not kill anyone but do attract media attention, provide a means of operating anonymously, and are easy to coordinate internationally.[42] So far, however, these types of attacks are more an expense and a nuisance than an existential threat.

Instead the tools of the global information age have led to enhanced efficiency in many terrorist-related activities, including administrative tasks, coordination of operations, recruitment of potential members, communication among adherents, and attraction of sympathizers.[43] Before the September 11 attacks, for example, members of al-Qaeda communicated through Yahoo email; Mohammed Atta, the presumed leader of the attacks, made his reservations online; and cell members went online to do research on subjects such as the chemical-dispersing powers of crop dusters. Although not as dramatic as shutting down a power grid or taking over an air traffic control system, this practical use of technology has significantly contributed to the effectiveness of terrorist groups and the expansion of their range.[44] Consider, for example, the lethal impact of the synchronized attacks on the U.S. embassies in 1998 and on New York and Washington in 2001, neither of which would have been possible without the revolution in information technology. When he was arrested in 1995, Ramzi Yousef, mastermind of the 1993 World Trade Center attack, was planning the simultaneous destruction of eleven airliners.[45]

The internet has become an important tool for perpetuating terrorist groups, both openly and clandestinely. Many of them employ elaborate list serves, collect money from witting or unwitting donors, and distribute savvy political messages to a broad audience online.[46] Groups as diverse as Aum Shinrikyo, Israel's Kahane Chai, the Popular Front for the Liberation of Palestine, the Kurdistan Worker's Party, and Peru's Shining Path maintain user-friendly

---

42. Ibid. Dorothy Denning cites numerous examples, among them: In 1989, hackers released a computer worm into the NASA Space Physics Analysis Network in an attempt to stop a shuttle launch; during Palestinian riots in October 2000, pro-Israeli hackers defaced the Hezbollah website; and in 1999, following the mistaken U.S. bombing of the Chinese embassy in Belgrade during the war in Kosovo, Chinese hackers attacked the websites of the U.S. Department of the Interior, showing images of the three journalists killed during the bombing.
43. Paul R. Pillar, *Terrorism and U.S. Foreign Policy* (Washington, D.C.: Brookings, 2001), p. 47.
44. Ibid.
45. Simon Reeve, *The New Jackals: Ramzi Yousef, Osama bin Laden, and the Future of Terrorism* (Boston: Northeastern University Press, 1999), p. 260.
46. Dorothy Denning, "Cyberwarriors: Activists and Terrorists Turn to Cyberspace," *Harvard International Review*, Vol. 23, No. 2 (Summer 2001), pp. 70–75. See also Brian J. Miller, "Terror.org: An Assessment of Terrorist Internet Sites," Georgetown University, December 6, 2000.

official or unofficial websites, and almost all are accessible in English.[47] Clandestine methods include passing encrypted messages, embedding invisible graphic codes using steganography,[48] employing the internet to send death threats, and hiring hackers to collect intelligence such as the names and addresses of law enforcement officers from online databases.[49] All of these measures help to expand and perpetuate trends in terrorism that have already been observed: For example, higher casualties are brought about by simultaneous attacks, a diffusion in terrorist locations is made possible by internet communications, and extremist religious ideologies are spread through websites and videotapes accessible throughout the world.

More ominous, globalization makes CBNR weapons increasingly available to terrorist groups.[50] Information needed to build these weapons has become ubiquitous, especially through the internet. Among the groups interested in acquiring CBNR (besides al-Qaeda) are the PLO, the Red Army Faction, Hezbollah, the Kurdistan Workers' Party, German neo-Nazis, and the Chechens.[51]

Second, globalization has enabled terrorist organizations to reach across international borders, in the same way (and often through the same channels) that commerce and business interests are linked. The dropping of barriers through the North American Free Trade Area and the European Union, for instance, has facilitated the smooth flow of many things, good and bad, among countries. This has allowed terrorist organizations as diverse as Hezbollah, al-Qaeda, and the Egyptian al-Gama'at al-Islamiyya to move about freely and establish cells around the world.[52] Movement across borders can obviously en-

---

47. Miller, "Terror.org," pp. 9, 12.
48. Steganography is the embedding of messages usually in pictures, where the messages are disguised so that they cannot be seen with the naked eye. See Denning, "Cyberwarriors."
49. I am indebted to Dorothy Denning for all of this information. The Provisional IRA hired contract hackers to find the addresses of British intelligence and law enforcement officers. See Denning, "Cyberterrorism"; and Denning, "Cyberwarriors."
50. There are many recent sources on CBNR. Among the best are Jonathan B. Tucker, ed., *Toxic Terror: Assessing Terrorist Use of Chemical and Biological Weapons* (Cambridge, Mass.: MIT Press, 2000); Joshua Lederberg, *Biological Weapons: Limiting the Threat* (Cambridge, Mass.: MIT Press, 1999); Richard A. Falkenrath, Robert D. Newman, and Bradley A. Thayer, *America's Achilles' Heel: Nuclear, Biological, and Chemical Terrorism and Covert Attack* (Cambridge, Mass.: MIT Press, 1998); Gurr and Cole, *The New Face of Terrorism*; Jessica Stern, *The Ultimate Terrorists* (Cambridge, Mass.: Harvard University Press, 1999); and Brad Roberts, ed., *Terrorism with Chemical and Biological Weapons: Calibrating Risks and Responses* (Alexandria, Va.: Chemical and Biological Arms Control Institute, 1997).
51. See Falkenrath, Newman, and Thayer, *America's Achilles' Heel*, pp. 31–46.
52. A clear example of this phenomenon was the uncovering in December 2001 of a multinational plot in Singapore by the international terrorist group Jemaah Islamiyah to blow up several Western targets, including the U.S. embassy. A videotape of the intended targets (including a description of

able terrorists to carry out attacks and potentially evade capture, but it also complicates prosecution if they are apprehended, with a complex maze of extradition laws varying greatly from state to state. The increased permeability of the international system has also enhanced the ability of nonstate terrorist organizations to collect intelligence (not to mention evade it); states are not the only actors interested in collecting, disseminating, and/or acting on such information. In a sense, then, terrorism is in many ways becoming like any other international enterprise—an ominous development indeed.

Third, terrorist organizations are broadening their reach in gathering financial resources to fund their operations. This is not just an al-Qaeda phenomenon, although bin Laden's organization—especially its numerous business interests—figures prominently among the most innovative and wealthy pseudocorporations in the international terrorist network. The list of groups with global financing networks is long and includes most of the groups identified by the U.S. government as foreign terrorist organizations, notably Aum Shinrikyo, Hamas, Hezbollah, and the Tamil Tigers. Sources of financing include legal enterprises such as nonprofit organizations and charities (whose illicit activities may be a small or large proportion of overall finances, known or unknown to donors); legitimate companies that divert profits to illegal activities (such as bin Laden's large network of construction companies); and illegal enterprises such as drug smuggling and production (e.g., the Revolutionary Armed Forces of Colombia—FARC), bank robbery, fraud, extortion, and kidnapping (e.g., the Abu Sayyaf group, Colombia's National Liberation Army, and FARC).[53] Websites are also important vehicles for raising funds. Although no comprehensive data are publicly available on how lucrative this avenue is, the proliferation of terrorist websites with links or addresses for contributions is at least circumstantial evidence of their usefulness.

The fluid movement of terrorists' financial resources demonstrates the growing informal connections that are countering the local fragmentation caused elsewhere by globalization. The transit of bars of gold and bundles of dollars

---

the plans in Arabic) was discovered in Afghanistan after al-Qaeda members fled. Thus there are clear connections between these organizations, as well as evidence of cooperation and coordination of attacks. See, for example, Dan Murphy, "'Activated' Asian Terror Web Busted," *Christian Science Monitor*, January 23, 2002, http://www.csmonitor.com (accessed January 23, 2002); and Rajiv Changrasekaran, "Al Qaeda's Southeast Asian Reach," *Washington Post*, February 3, 2002, p. A1.
53. Rensselaer Lee and Raphael Perl, "Terrorism, the Future, and U.S. Foreign Policy," issue brief for Congress, received through the Congressional Research Service website, order code IB95112, Congressional Research Service, Library of Congress, July 10, 2002, p. CRS-6.

across the border between Afghanistan and Pakistan as U.S. and allied forces were closing in on the Taliban's major strongholds is a perfect example. Collected by shopkeepers and small businessmen, the money was moved by operatives across the border to Karachi, where it was transferred in the millions of dollars through the informal *hawala* or *hundi* banking system to the United Arab Emirates.[54] There it was converted into gold bullion and scattered around the world before any government could intervene. In this way, al-Qaeda preserved and dispersed a proportion of its financial resources.[55] In addition to gold, money was transferred into other commodities—such as diamonds in Sierra Leone and the Democratic Republic of Congo, and tanzanite from Tanzania—all while hiding the assets and often making a profit,[56] and all without interference from the sovereign governments that at the time were at war with al-Qaeda and the Taliban.[57]

As this example illustrates, globalization does not necessarily require the use of high technology: It often takes the form of traditional practices used in innovative ways across increasingly permeable physical and commercial borders. Terrorist groups, whose assets comparatively represent only a small fraction of the amount of money that is moved by organized crime groups and are thus much more difficult to track, use everything from direct currency transport (by couriers) to reliance on traditional banks, Islamic banks, money changers (using accounts at legitimate institutions), and informal exchange (the *hawala* or *hundi* system).

This is by no means a comprehensive presentation of global interpenetration of terrorist means, and some of the connections described above have existed for some time and in other contexts. The broad strategic picture, however, is of

---

54. Roger G. Weiner, "The Financing of International Terrorism," Terrorism and Violence Crime Section, Criminal Division, U.S. Department of Justice, October 2001, p. 3. According to Weiner, the *hawala* (or *hundi*) system "relies entirely on trust that currency left with a particular service provider or merchant will be paid from bank accounts he controls overseas to the recipient specified by the party originating the transfer." Ibid. See also Douglas Frantz, "Ancient Secret System Moves Money Globally," *New York Times*, October 3, 2001, http://www.nytimes.com (accessed October 3, 2001).

55. International efforts to freeze bank accounts and block transactions between suspected terrorists have hindered, at least to some degree, al-Qaeda's ability to finance attacks; however, a proportion remains unaccounted for. "Cash Moves a Sign Al-Qaeda Is Regrouping," *Straits Times*, March 18, 2002, http://www.straitstimes.asia1.com.sg (accessed March 18, 2002).

56. U.S. Department of State, *Patterns of Global Terrorism, 2001*. According to the U.S. Department of State, Hezbollah also may have transferred resources by selling millions of dollars' worth of Congolese diamonds to finance operations in the Middle East.

57. Douglas Farah, "Al Qaeda's Road Paved with Gold," *Washington Post*, February 17, 2002, pp. A1, A32.

an increasing ability of terrorist organizations to exploit the same avenues of communication, coordination, and cooperation as other international actors, including states, multinational corporations, nongovernmental organizations, and even individuals. It would be naïve to assume that what is good for international commerce and international communication is not also good for international terrorists[58]—who are increasingly becoming opportunistic entrepreneurs whose "product" (often quite consciously "sold") is violence against innocent targets for a political end.

THE ENDS

The objectives of international terrorism have also changed as a result of globalization. Foreign intrusions and growing awareness of shrinking global space have created incentives to use the ideal asymmetrical weapon, terrorism, for more ambitious purposes.

The political incentives to attack major targets such as the United States with powerful weapons have greatly increased. The perceived corruption of indigenous customs, religions, languages, economies, and so on are blamed on an international system often unconsciously molded by American behavior. The accompanying distortions in local communities as a result of exposure to the global marketplace of goods and ideas are increasingly blamed on U.S.-sponsored modernization and those who support it. The advancement of technology, however, is not the driving force behind the terrorist threat to the United States and its allies, despite what some have assumed.[59] Instead, at the heart of this threat are frustrated populations and international movements that are increasingly inclined to lash out against U.S.-led globalization.

As Christopher Coker observes, globalization is reducing tendencies toward instrumental violence (i.e., violence between states and even between communities), but it is enhancing incentives for expressive violence (or violence that is ritualistic, symbolic, and communicative).[60] The new international terrorism is

---

58. Pillar, *Terrorism and U.S. Foreign Policy*, p. 48.
59. Many in the United States focus on the technologies of terrorism, with a much less developed interest in the motivations of terrorists. Brian M. Jenkins, "Understanding the Link between Motives and Methods," in Roberts, *Terrorism with Chemical and Biological Weapons*, pp. 43–51. An example of a study that focuses on weapons and not motives is Sidney D. Drell, Abraham D. Sofaer, and George W. Wilson, eds., *The New Terror: Facing the Threat of Biological and Chemical Weapons* (Stanford, Calif.: Hoover Institution, 1999).
60. Christopher Coker, *Globalisation and Insecurity in the Twenty-first Century: NATO and the Management of Risk*, Adelphi Paper 345 (London: International Institute for Strategic Studies, June 2002), p. 40.

increasingly engendered by a need to assert identity or meaning against forces of homogeneity, especially on the part of cultures that are threatened by, or left behind by, the secular future that Western-led globalization brings.

According to a report recently published by the United Nations Development Programme, the region of greatest deficit in measures of human development—the Arab world—is also the heart of the most threatening religiously inspired terrorism.[61] Much more work needs to be done on the significance of this correlation, but increasingly sources of political discontent are arising from disenfranchised areas in the Arab world that feel left behind by the promise of globalization and its assurances of broader freedom, prosperity, and access to knowledge. The results are dashed expectations, heightened resentment of the perceived U.S.-led hegemonic system, and a shift of focus away from more proximate targets within the region.

Of course, the motivations behind this threat should not be oversimplified: Anti-American terrorism is spurred in part by a desire to change U.S. policy in the Middle East and Persian Gulf regions as well as by growing antipathy in the developing world vis-à-vis the forces of globalization. It is also crucial to distinguish between the motivations of leaders such as Osama bin Laden and their followers. The former seem to be more driven by calculated strategic decisions to shift the locus of attack away from repressive indigenous governments to the more attractive and media-rich target of the United States. The latter appear to be more driven by religious concepts cleverly distorted to arouse anger and passion in societies full of pent-up frustration. To some degree, terrorism is directed against the United States because of its engagement and policies in various regions.[62] Anti-Americanism is closely related to antiglobalization, because (intentionally or not) the primary driver of the powerful forces resulting in globalization is the United States.

Analyzing terrorism as something separate from globalization is misleading and potentially dangerous. Indeed globalization and terrorism are intricately intertwined forces characterizing international security in the twenty-first century. The main question is whether terrorism will succeed in disrupting the

---

61. The indicators studied included respect for human rights and human freedoms, the empowerment of women, and broad access to and utilization of knowledge. See United Nations Development Programme, Arab Fund for Economic and Social Development, *Arab Human Development Report, 2002: Creating Opportunities for Future Generations* (New York: United Nations Development Programme, 2002).
62. Martha Crenshaw, "Why America? The Globalization of Civil War," *Current History,* December 2001, pp. 425–432.

promise of improved livelihoods for millions of people on Earth. Globalization is not an inevitable, linear development, and it can be disrupted by such unconventional means as international terrorism. Conversely, modern international terrorism is especially dangerous because of the power that it potentially derives from globalization—whether through access to CBNR weapons, global media outreach, or a diverse network of financial and information resources.

Prospects for the Future

Long after the focus on Osama bin Laden has receded and U.S. troops have quit their mission in Afghanistan, terrorism will be a serious threat to the world community and especially to the United States. The relative preponderance of U.S. military power virtually guarantees an impulse to respond asymmetrically. The lagging of the Arab region behind the rest of the world is impelling a violent redirection of antiglobalization and antimodernization forces toward available targets, particularly the United States, whose scope and policies are engendering rage. Al-Qaeda will eventually be replaced or redefined, but its successors' reach may continue to grow via the same globalized channels and to direct their attacks against U.S. and Western targets. The current trajectory is discouraging, because as things currently stand, the wellspring of terrorism's means and ends is likely to be renewed: Arab governments will probably not reform peacefully, and existing Western governments and their supporting academic and professional institutions are disinclined to understand or analyze in depth the sources, patterns, and history of terrorism.

Terrorism is a by-product of broader historical shifts in the international distribution of power in all of its forms—political, economic, military, ideological, and cultural. These are the same forms of power that characterize the forces of Western-led globalization. At times of dramatic international change, human beings (especially those not benefiting from the change—or not benefiting as much or as rapidly from the change) grasp for alternative means to control and understand their environments. If current trends continue, widening global disparities, coupled with burgeoning information and connectivity, are likely to accelerate—unless the terrorist backlash, which is increasingly taking its inspiration from misoneistic religious or pseudoreligious concepts, successfully counters these trends. Because of globalization, terrorists have access to more powerful technologies, more targets, more territory, more means of recruitment, and more exploitable sources of rage than ever before. The West's twentieth-century approach to terrorism is highly unlikely to mitigate any of these long-term trends.

From a Manichean perspective, the ad hoc and purportedly benign intentions of the preponderant, secular West do not seem benign at all to those ill served by globalization. To frustrated people in the Arab and Muslim world, adherence to radical religious philosophies and practices may seem a rational response to the perceived assault, especially when no feasible alternative for progress is offered by their own governments. This is not to suggest that terrorists should be excused because of environmental factors or conditions. Instead, Western governments must recognize that the tiny proportion of the population that ends up in terrorist cells cannot exist without the availability of broader sources of active or passive sympathy, resources, and support. Those avenues of sustenance are where the center of gravity for an effective response to the terrorist threat must reside. The response to transnational terrorism must deal with the question of whether the broader enabling environment will increase or decrease over time, and the answer will be strongly influenced by the policy choices that the United States and its allies make in the near future.

Conclusions and Policy Prescriptions

The characteristics and causes of the current threat can only be analyzed within the context of the deadly collision occurring between U.S. power, globalization, and the evolution of international terrorism. The U.S. government is still thinking in outdated terms, little changed since the end of the Cold War. It continues to look at terrorism as a peripheral threat, with the focus remaining on states that in many cases are not the greatest threat. The means and the ends of terrorism are changing in fundamental, important ways; but the means and the ends of the strategy being crafted in response are not.

Terrorism that threatens international stability, and particularly U.S. global leadership, is centered on power-based political causes that are enduring: the weak against the strong, the disenfranchised against the establishment, and the revolutionary against the status quo. Oversimplified generalizations about poverty and terrorism, or any other single variable, are caricatures of a serious argument.[63] The rise in political and material expectations as a result of the in-

---

63. A number of recent arguments have been put forth about the relationship between poverty and terrorism. See, for example, Anatol Lieven, "The Roots of Terrorism, and a Strategy against It,"

formation revolution is not necessarily helpful to stability, in the same way that rising expectations led terrorists to take up arms against the czar in Russia a century ago. Indeed the fact that so many people in so many nations are being left behind has given new ammunition to terrorist groups; produced more sympathy for those willing to take on the United States; and spurred Islamic radical movements to recruit, propagandize, and support terrorism throughout many parts of the Muslim world. The al-Qaeda network is an extremist religious terrorist organization, its Taliban puppet regime was filled with religious zealots, and its suicide recruits were convinced that they were waging a just holy war. But the driving forces of twenty-first-century terrorism are power and frustration, not the pursuit of religious principle. To dismiss the broad enabling environment would be to focus more on the symptoms than the causes of modern terrorism.

The prescriptions for countering and preventing terrorism should be twofold: First, the United States and other members of the international community concerned about this threat need to use a balanced assortment of instruments to address the immediate challenges of the terrorists themselves. Terrorism is a complex phenomenon; it must be met with short-term military action, informed by in-depth, long-term, sophisticated analysis. Thus far, the response has been virtually all the former and little of the latter. Second, the United States and its counterterrorist allies must employ a much broader array of longer-term policy tools to reshape the international environment, which enables terrorist networks to breed and become robust. The mechanisms of globalization need to be exploited to thwart the globalization of terrorism.

In the short term, the United States must continue to rely on capable military forces that can sustain punishing air strikes against terrorists and those who harbor them with an even greater capacity for special operations on the ground. This requires not only improved stealthy, long-range power projection capabilities but also agile, highly trained, and lethal ground forces, backed up

---

Prospect (London), October 2001, http://www.ceip.org/files/Publications/lieventerrorism.asp?from=pubdate (accessed November 17, 2002); and Daniel Pipes, "God and Mammon: Does Poverty Cause Militant Islam?" *National Interest*, No. 66 (Winter 2001/02), pp. 14–21. This is an extremely complex question, however, and much work remains to be done. On the origins of the new religious terrorism, see Hoffman, *Inside Terrorism*; and Mark Juergensmeyer, *Terror in the Mind of God: The Global Rise of Religious Violence* (Berkeley: University of California Press, 2000). Important earlier studies on the sources of terrorism include Martha Crenshaw, "The Causes of Terrorism," *Comparative Politics*, July 1981, pp. 379–399; Martha Crenshaw, *Terrorism in Context* (University Park: Pennsylvania State University Press, 1995); and Walter Reich, ed., *Origins of Terrorism: Psychologies, Ideologies, Theologies, States of Mind*, 2d ed. (Washington, D.C.: Woodrow Wilson Center for International Scholars, 1998).

with greater intelligence, including human intelligence supported by individuals with language skills and cultural training. The use of military force continues to be important as one means of responding to terrorist violence against the West, and there is no question that it effectively preempts and disrupts some international terrorist activity, especially in the short term.[64]

Over time, however, the more effective instruments of policy are likely to remain the nonmilitary ones. Indeed the United States needs to expand and deepen its nonmilitary instruments of power such as intelligence, public diplomacy, cooperation with allies, international legal instruments, and economic assistance and sanctions. George Kennan, in his 1947 description of containment, put forth the same fundamental argument, albeit against an extremely different enemy.[65] The strongest response that the United States can muster to a serious threat has to include political, economic, and military capabilities—in that order; yet, the U.S. government consistently structures its policies and devotes its resources in the reverse sequence.

The economic and political roots of terrorism are complex, increasingly worrisome, and demanding of as much breadth and subtlety in response as they display in their genesis. The United States must therefore be strategic in its response: An effective grand strategy against terrorism involves planning a global campaign with the most effective means available, not just the most measurable, obvious, or gratifying. It must also include plans for shaping the global environment after the so-called war on terrorism has ended—or after the current political momentum has subsided.

The United States, working with other major donor nations, needs to create an effective incentive structure that rewards "good performers"—those countries with good governance, inclusive education programs, and adequate social programs—and works around "bad performers" and intervenes to assist so-called failed states. Also for the longer term, the United States and its allies need to project a vision of sustainable development—of economic growth, equal access to basic social needs such as education and health, and good governance—for the developing world. This is particularly true in mostly Muslim countries whose populations are angry with the United States over a perceived double standard regarding its long-standing support for Israel at the expense

---

64. For more discussion on the traditional elements of U.S. grand strategy, especially military strategy, see Barry R. Posen, "The Struggle against Terrorism: Grand Strategy, Strategy, and Tactics," *International Security*, Vol. 26, No. 3 (Winter 2001/02), pp. 39–55.
65. George F. Kennan, "The Sources of Soviet Conduct," *Foreign Affairs*, Vol. 25, No. 4 (July 1947), pp. 575–576.

of Palestinians, policies against the regime of Saddam Hussein at the expense of some Iraqi people, and a general abundance of American power, including the U.S. military presence throughout the Middle East. Whether these policies are right or wrong is irrelevant here; the point is that just as the definition of terrorism can be subjective and value laden, so too can the response to terrorism take into account perceptions of reality. In an attempt to craft an immediate military response, the U.S. government is failing to put into place an effective long-term grand strategy.

This is not just a problem for the U.S. government. The inability to develop a strategy with a deep-rooted, intellectually grounded understanding of the history, patterns, motivations, and types of terrorism is reflective of the paucity of understanding of the terrorist phenomenon in the academic community. Terrorism is considered too policy-oriented an area of research in political science,[66] and it operates in an uncomfortable intersection between disciplines unaccustomed to working together, including psychology, sociology, theology, economics, anthropology, history, law, political science, and international relations. In political science, terrorism does not fit neatly into either the realist or liberal paradigms, so it has been largely ignored.[67] There are a few outstanding, well-established senior scholars in the terrorism studies community—people such as Martha Crenshaw, David Rapoport, and Paul Wilkinson—but in the United States, most of the publicly available work is being done in policy-oriented research institutes or think tanks that are sometimes limited by the narrow interests and short time frames of the government contracts on which they depend. Some of that research is quite good,[68] but it is not widely known within the academy. The situation for graduate students who wish to study terrorism is worse: A principal interest in terrorism virtually guarantees exclusion from consideration for most academic positions. This would not necessarily be a problem if the bureaucracy were more flexible and creative than the academy is, but as we know from the analysis of the behavior of U.S. agencies shortly before September 11, it is not. In the United States, academe is no more strategic in its understanding of terrorism than is the U.S. government.

---

66. See the extremely insightful article by Bruce W. Jentleson, "The Need for Praxis: Bringing Policy Relevance Back In," *International Security*, Vol. 26, No. 4 (Spring 2002), pp. 169–183.
67. I am indebted to Fiona Adamson for this observation.
68. Important terrorism scholars in the think tank community include Walter Laqueur (Center for Strategic and International Studies), Brian Jenkins (RAND), Bruce Hoffman (RAND) and, from the intelligence community, Paul Pillar. This list is illustrative, not comprehensive.

The globalization of terrorism is perhaps the leading threat to long-term stability in the twenty-first century. But the benefit of globalization is that the international response to terrorist networks has also begun to be increasingly global, with international cooperation on law enforcement, intelligence, and especially financial controls being areas of notable recent innovation.[69] If globalization is to continue—and there is nothing foreordained that it will—then the tools of globalization, including especially international norms, the rule of law, and international economic power, must be fully employed against the terrorist backlash. There must be a deliberate effort to move beyond the current episodic interest in this phenomenon: Superficial arguments and short attention spans will continue to result in event-driven policies and ultimately more attacks. Terrorism is an unprecedented, powerful nonstate threat to the international system that no single state, regardless of how powerful it may be in traditional terms, can defeat alone, especially in the absence of long-term, serious scholarship engaged in by its most creative minds.

---

69. On these issues, see Cronin and Ludes, *The Campaign against International Terrorism.*

The NGO Scramble

Alexander Cooley and James Ron

Organizational Insecurity and the Political Economy of Transnational Action

$\mathbf{S}$cholarly assessments of transnational actors are largely optimistic, suggesting they herald an emerging global civil society comprising local civic groups, international organizations (IOs), and international nongovernmental organizations (INGOs). This new civil society, moreover, is widely assumed to rest upon shared liberal norms and values that motivate INGO action and explain their supposedly benign influence on international relations.[1]

Alexander Cooley is Assistant Professor of Political Science at Barnard College, Columbia University. James Ron is Canada Research Chair in Conflict and Human Rights, Department of Sociology, McGill University.

A version of this article was presented at the annual meeting of the International Studies Association, New Orleans, Louisiana, March 24–27, 2002. The authors are grateful for comments by Peter Andreas, Mark Blyth, Mlada Bukovansky, Elisabeth Jay Friedman, Kevin Hartigan, Patrick Jackson, Paula Duarte Lopes, Larry Minear, Dominique Morel, Emma Naughton, Hendrik Spruyt, Jacques Stroun, Kellee Tsai, Peter Uvin, members of the nongovernmental organization community who have chosen to remain anonymous, and three anonymous reviewers for *International Security*.

---

1. For recent works, see John Boli and George M. Thomas, eds., *Constructing World Culture: International Nongovernmental Organizations since 1875* (Stanford, Calif.: Stanford University Press, 1999); Ann Marie Clark, *Diplomacy of Conscience: Amnesty International and Changing Human Rights Norms* (Princeton, N.J.: Princeton University Press, 2001); Martha Finnemore, *National Interests in International Society* (Ithaca, N.Y.: Cornell University Press, 1996); Margaret E. Keck and Kathryn Sikkink, *Activists beyond Borders: Advocacy Networks in International Politics* (Ithaca, N.Y.: Cornell University Press, 1998); Audie Klotz, *Norms in International Relations: The Struggle against Apartheid* (Ithaca, N.Y.: Cornell University Press, 1996); David Holloran Lumsdaine, *Moral Vision in International Politics: The Foreign Aid Regime, 1949–1989* (Princeton, N.J.: Princeton University Press, 1993); Thomas Risse, Stephen C. Ropp, and Kathryn Sikkink, *The Power of Human Rights: International Norms and Domestic Change* (New York: Cambridge University Press, 1999); Paul Kevin Wapner, *Environmental Activism and World Civic Politics* (Buffalo: State University of New York Press, 1995); and Paul Kevin Wapner, "The Normative Promise of Nonstate Actors: A Theoretical Account of Global Civil Society," in Wapner, Lester Edwin Ruiz, and Richard A. Falk, eds., *Principled World Politics: The Challenge of Normative International Relations* (Lanham, Md.: Rowman and Littlefield, 2000).
   Other scholars do not dispute the normative motivations of IOs and INGOs, but provide critical analysis of their emergence, strategies, and effectiveness. See, for example, Ann Marie Clark, Elisabeth J. Friedman, and Kathryn Hochstetler, "The Sovereign Limits of Global Civil Society: A Comparison of NGO Participation in UN World Conferences on the Environment, Human Rights, and Women," *World Politics*, Vol. 51, No. 1 (October 1998), pp. 1–35; Michael Edwards and David Hulme, eds., *Beyond the Magic Bullet: NGO Performance and Accountability in the Post–Cold War World* (West Hartford, Conn.: Kumarian, 1996); Chaim D. Kaufmann and Robert A. Pape, "Explaining Costly International Moral Action: Britain's Sixty-Year Campaign against the Atlantic Slave Trade," *International Organization*, Vol. 53, No. 4 (Autumn 1999), pp. 631–668; James Ron, "Varying Methods of State Violence," *International Organization*, Vol. 51, No. 2 (Spring 1997), pp. 275–300;

Although not entirely misplaced, this view does not adequately address the organizational insecurity, competitive pressures, and fiscal uncertainty that characterize the transnational sector. Powerful institutional imperatives can subvert IO and INGO efforts, prolong inappropriate aid projects, or promote destructive competition among well-meaning transnational actors. Attempts by IOs and INGOs to reconcile material pressures with normative motivations often produce outcomes dramatically at odds with liberal expectations.

This article develops a political economy approach to the study of contemporary transnational networks. We argue that many aspects of IO and INGO behavior can be explained by materialist analysis and an examination of the incentives and constraints produced by the transnational sector's institutional environment. We advance two theoretical propositions. First, the growing number of IOs and INGOs within a given transnational sector increases uncertainty, competition, and insecurity for all organizations in that sector. This proposition disputes the liberal view that INGO proliferation is, in and of itself, evidence of a robust global civil society. Second, we suggest that the marketization of many IO and INGO activities—particularly the use of competitive tenders and renewable contracting—generates incentives that produce dysfunctional outcomes. This claim disputes the popular assumption that market-based institutions in the transnational sector increase INGO efficiency and effectiveness.

In advancing these arguments, we do not criticize the normative agendas, moral character, or nominal goals of individual transnational groups. Rather we suggest that dysfunctional organizational behavior is likely to be a rational response to systematic and predictable institutional pressures. In many cases, uncooperative local actors will take advantage of the transnational sector's perverse incentives to further their own opportunistic agendas.

In making our argument, we draw on the New Economics of Organization (NEO), a body of theory that focuses on the incentives and institutional outcomes generated by contractual relations, incomplete information, transaction costs, and property rights.[2] By applying these concepts to the environment in

---

and Jack Snyder and Karen Ballentine, "Nationalism and the Marketplace of Ideas," *International Security*, Vol. 21, No. 2 (Fall 1996), pp. 5–40.

2. Thráinn Eggertsson, *Economic Behavior and Institutions* (New York: Cambridge University Press, 1990); Geoffrey M. Hodgson, *Economics and Institutions: A Manifesto for a Modern Institutional Economics* (Philadelphia: University of Pennsylvania Press, 1988); Douglass O. North, *Institutions, Institutional Change, and Economic Performance* (New York: Cambridge University Press, 1990); and Oliver Williamson, *The Economic Institutions of Capitalism: Firms, Markets, and Relational Contracting* (New York: Free Press, 1985). A rich literature applies the NEO to international institutions and or-

which contemporary transnational actors operate, we identify sources of organizational insecurity and explain patterns of behavior that liberal theories of transnationalism either fail to acknowledge or cannot address conceptually. INGOs compete to raise money and secure contracts. These contracts, moreover, are often performance based, renewable, and short term, creating counterproductive incentives and acute principal-agent problems. Opportunism and dysfunctional outcomes are particularly rife when groups seek control over the same project, a phenomenon known as the "multiple-principals problem." Indeed we find that nonprofit INGOs respond to contractual incentives and organizational pressures much like firms do in markets.

To test our model, we examine three cases of transnational assistance. Although our theory is broadly rationalist, our method is necessarily qualitative and case based. Because we seek to go beyond the images, public documents, and prepared statements of IOs and INGOs, our three studies draw on in-depth interviews that seek to uncover hidden behavioral imperatives. The first case is based on more than thirty discussions with for-profit corporations operating in Kyrgyzstan under contracts from Western governments, international financial institutions, and the United Nations (UN). The case shows how reliance on one-year renewable contracts by Western donors created incentives for contracting INGOs to downplay government subversion of economic reforms, withhold information about ineffective projects, and tolerate bureaucratic opportunism. Our second case shows how inter-INGO competition in Goma, Democratic Republic of Congo (former Zaire), undercut the collective action necessary to protest misuse of refugee aid. This case draws on thirty-five dis-

---

ganizations. Here we extend those insights to explain relations among international aid donors, INGO contractors, and aid recipients.

For NEO applications to international relations, see Alexander Cooley, "Imperial Wreckage: Property Rights, Sovereignty, and Security in the Post-Soviet Space," *International Security,* Vol. 25, No. 3 (Winter 2000/01), pp. 100–127; Jeffry Frieden, "International Investment and Colonial Control: A New Interpretation," *International Organization,* Vol. 48, No. 4 (Autumn 1994), pp. 559–593; David A. Lake, *Entangling Relations: American Foreign Policy in Its Century* (Princeton, N.J.: Princeton University Press, 1999); Lisa L. Martin, *Democratic Commitments: Legislatures and International Cooperation* (Princeton, N.J.: Princeton University Press, 2000); Helen V. Milner, *Interests, Institutions, and Information: Domestic Politics and International Relations* (Princeton, N.J.: Princeton University Press, 1997); Hendrik Spruyt, *The Sovereign State and Its Competitors* (Princeton, N.J.: Princeton University Press, 1994); Roland Vaubel, "A Public Choice View of International Organizations," in Vaubel and Thomas Willett, eds., *The Political Economy of International Organizations* (Boulder, Colo.: Westview, 1991); Celeste A. Wallander, "Institutional Assets and Adaptability: NATO after the Cold War," *International Organization,* Vol. 54, No. 4 (Autumn 2000), pp. 705–735; and Beth V. Yarbrough and Robert M. Yarbrough, *Cooperation and Governance in International Trade: A Strategic Organizational Approach* (Princeton, N.J.: Princeton University Press, 1992).

cussions with staffers from "Refugee Help," a respected nonprofit organization with a budget in the tens of millions of dollars.[3] The final case draws on events in wartime Bosnia, showing how inter-IO and INGO competition empowered local military commanders seeking to resist international efforts to protect prisoners of war (POWs). Here we make use of some 100 interviews with members of the International Committee of the Red Cross (ICRC), the UN, INGOs, and Bosnian military officers.[4]

Although three qualitative cases cannot provide a definitive test of our claims, they fulfill important criteria of social inquiry and suggest a global trend. First, our cases include both for-profit and nonprofit transnational actors, providing a "most likely" and "least likely" test of our claims. Second, each case is drawn from a different geographic region, allowing us to control for local cultural factors, identity-based action, and other potential regional idiosyncrasies. Finally, each case involves a different sector of the transnational world: economic technical assistance, humanitarian aid/refugee relief, and POW monitoring. Controlling for for-profit status, geographical setting, and issue area, we observe dynamics consistent with a political economy approach.

Some INGOs may resist material pressures, either because of idiosyncratic funding patterns, unique organizational cultures, or remarkable leaders or coalitions. Others may even define themselves in opposition to the mainstream, condemning their rivals' marketized or "corporate" mentalities. For sure, normative aspirations may sometimes overcome material constraints. As a general rule, however, the transnational environment is pushing INGOs and IOs toward greater competition, regardless of their normative starting points or orientations. By identifying these institutional pressures and imperatives, we hope to encourage scholars and policymakers to think theoretically and systematically about the transnational world's political economy. This is particularly important given the enormous relief and reconstruction efforts currently under way in Afghanistan, as well as the mass influx of IOs and INGOs into Central Asia. It is vital that the international community devise workable solutions to the "NGO scramble."

The next section examines the conventional wisdom espoused by analysts of transnationalism and global civil society. We then build on insights from NEO theory to examine how the tender process, renewable contracts, and the pres-

---

3. James Ron, *Human Rights vs. Humanitarian Relief in the Goma Refugee Camps* (Refugee Help, 1999). Permission to use the material was conditioned on using "Refugee Help" as a pseudonym.
4. James Ron, *Compete or Collaborate? The ICRC and Other Protection-Related Agencies in the Former Yugoslavia* (Geneva: ICRC, 1996). Permission to use the interviews was conditioned on informants' anonymity.

ence of multiple contractors create self-interested and competitive incentives antithetical to liberal expectations. After presenting our three empirical cases, we conclude with a theoretical summary and discussion of policy implications.

A "Civil" Global Society? Organizational Density and Marketization

Liberal scholars and Western aid donors view two key trends in transnational activity—increasing organizational density and growing marketization—as important contributions to a global civil society. Because they assume that transnational behavior is shaped chiefly by liberal norms, they believe that the more IOs and INGOs exist, the better. Moreover, marketization of aid funding, through the creation of competitive project tenders, is supposed to boost efficiency. Competition cuts waste, curbs corruption, and allows new INGOs to become transnational players. We question the optimism embedded in both propositions, suggesting that more is not always better and that marketization can produce dysfunctional incentives and results.

The notion that growth in the transnational sector heralds a more benign global civil society is fast achieving doctrinal status. An influential article by Jessica Mathews, for example, charts the rise of a liberal world polity based on transnational NGOs and argues that this trend deepens global democracy by "disrupt[ing] hierarchies" and spreading "power among more people and groups," thereby promoting an unprecedented "power shift" from states to liberal private organizations. NGOs "breed new ideas, advocate, protest, and mobilize public support," Mathews says, and "shape, implement, monitor, and enforce national and international commitments."[5] P.J. Simmons is similarly upbeat, noting that "unprecedented levels" of INGO activity have produced startling liberal triumphs, including agreement on the international ban on land mines and greater World Bank accountability.[6] And in a widely acclaimed study of transnational activism, Margaret Keck and Kathryn Sikkink argue that world politics have been fundamentally transformed by liberal transnational networks that "multiply the channels of access to the international system," most notably in the environmental and human rights fields.[7]

---

5. Jessica T. Mathews, "Power Shift," *Foreign Affairs*, Vol. 76, No. 1 (January/February 1997), pp. 52–53.
6. P.J. Simmons, "Learning to Live with NGOs," *Foreign Policy*, No. 112 (Fall 1998), pp. 82–96. On the land-mine issue, see also Richard Price, "Reversing the Gun Sights: Transnational Civil Society Targets Land Mines," *International Organization*, Vol. 52, No. 3 (Summer 1998), pp. 613–644.
7. Keck and Sikkink, *Activists beyond Borders*, p. 1.

There is little doubt that the transnational world is increasingly dense. Between 1960 and 1996, the number of INGOs grew from 1,000 to 5,500.[8] This growth has been particularly dramatic in the transnational aid sector, as private aid agencies expanded their operations by 150 percent from 1985 to 1995, affecting the lives of 250 million people worldwide.[9] In 1992 the total amount of assistance to the developing world channeled through INGOs was $8 billion, representing 13 percent of all development assistance.[10] War-related relief in particular is growing rapidly. In 1989 the U.S. Agency for International Development (USAID) spent $297 million on humanitarian relief, a figure that rose to $1.2 billion four years later, in large part due to the relief effort in Bosnia.[11] Increasing organizational density is also evident from the number of INGOs operating near or within zones of armed conflict. In 1980, for example, there were 37 foreign relief agencies in a major Cambodian refugee camp along the Thai border. By 1995, more than 200 INGOs were present in Goma; and in 1996, 240 INGOs were active in Bosnia,[12] requiring some thirty coordination meetings per week.[13] In our interviews, most professional aid officials expressed concern with this trend, viewing it as indication of the relief market's low barriers to entry.

The explosion in INGO numbers stems in part from shifts in donor strategies, which increasingly rely on private transnational groups as contractors and intermediaries.[14] USAID, for example, disburses 25–30 percent of its budget through private groups, as do the governments of Sweden, Switzerland, Norway, and the European Union (EU).[15] In 2000 the UN High Commission for Refugees' (UNHCR) budget was $1 billion, most of which was disbursed through competitive INGO contracts.[16] "Willy nilly," Simmons notes, "the UN

---

8. Taken from the *Yearbook of International Organizations, 1996,* as cited in Simmons, "Learning to Live with NGOs," p. 89.
9. This United Nations Development Programme (UNDP) estimate is cited in Roger Charlton and Roy May, "NGOs, Politics, Projects, and Probity: A Policy Implementation Perspective," *Third World Quarterly,* Vol. 16, No. 2 (June 1995), p. 240.
10. Simmons, "Learning to Live with NGOs," p. 87.
11. Andrew S. Natsios, "NGOs and the UN System in Complex Humanitarian Emergencies: Conflict or Cooperation?" *Third World Quarterly,* Vol. 16, No. 3 (September 1995), p. 406.
12. Ian Smillie, *Relief and Development: The Search for Synergy* (Providence: War and Humanitarianism Project, Brown University, 1998), p. 42; and interviews with Refugee Help officials, August–November 1998.
13. Interview with ICRC head of office, Sarajevo, April 12, 1996.
14. For background and analysis, see Ruben Berrios, *Contracting for Development: The Role of For-Profit Contractors in U.S. Foreign Development Assistance* (Westport, Conn.: Praeger, 2000).
15. Ian Smillie, "NGOs and Development Assistance: A Change in Mind-Set?" *Third World Quarterly,* Vol. 18, No. 3 (September 1997), p. 564.
16. Philippe Rekacewicz, "How the Burden of the World's Refugees Fall on the South," *Le Monde Diplomatique* [English version], (April 2001), p. 19.

and nation-states are depending more on NGOs to get things done."[17] This increased reliance on competitive contract tenders has stimulated further INGO growth, because as the number of tenders increase, so do contractors' ranks.[18]

The growing reliance on INGOs and the marketization of transnationalism is propelled by searing critiques of project failures, demands for accountability by domestic politicians, and broad neoliberal agendas.[19] Western, Japanese, and other aid donors are increasingly issuing short-term, renewable contracts for discrete aid projects, requiring aid contractors to bid competitively and demonstrate concrete results.[20] As one study of Bosnian assistance noted, for example, "virtually all donor grant mechanisms had a time frame of one year or less. Some were for six months or even three."[21] Donors, moreover, seek to fund projects, not administrative overhead, hoping that this will push INGO contractors to rationalize procedures, demonstrate effectiveness, and slash

---

17. Simmons, "Learning to Live with NGOs," p. 87. On the growing influence of NGOs on UN activities, see also Kathryn Hochstetler, Ann Marie Clark, and Elisabeth J. Friedman, "Sovereignty in the Balance: Claims and Bargains at the UN Conferences on the Environment, Human Rights, and Women," *International Studies Quarterly*, Vol. 44, No. 4 (December 2000), pp. 591–614; Natsios, "NGOs and the UN System in Complex Humanitarian Emergencies"; Peter Willets, "From 'Consultative Arrangements' to 'Partnership': The Changing Status of NGOs in Diplomacy at the UN," *Global Governance*, Vol. 6, No. 2 (April–June 2000), pp. 191–212; and Thomas George Weiss and Leon Gordenker, eds., *NGOs, the United Nations, and Global Governance* (Boulder, Colo.: Lynne Rienner, 1996).
18. Although some transnational sectors have assumed oligopolistic qualities, the increase in tenders has boosted overall INGO numbers for several reasons. First, there are often low barriers to entry in the humanitarian market, which has no binding set of regulatory agencies or rules. Moreover, because many donors are governments, they tend to give preference to INGOs from their own countries, spurring greater growth. Thus, for example, major aid groups such as Save the Children are often divided into multiple and independent national branches. Specific countries also have greater connections to conflicts for historical reasons. For instance, Portuguese aid groups are particularly active in Angola, a former colony. Finally, the individual country offices of INGOs continue to press for financial self-sufficiency. Thus each country branch of the same NGO behaves as an autonomous entity, and these subunits may actually vie for the same contracts.
19. Recent critiques of humanitarian, relief, and human rights groups include Ben Barber, "Feeding Refugees, or War? The Dilemma of Humanitarian Aid," *Foreign Affairs*, Vol. 76, No. 4 (July/August 1997), pp. 8–14; Edward N. Luttwak, "Give War a Chance," *Foreign Affairs*, Vol. 78, No. 4 (July/August 1999), pp. 36–44; Snyder and Ballentine, "Nationalism and the Marketplace of Ideas"; and Alex de Waal, *Famine Crimes: Politics and the Disaster Relief Industry in Africa* (Bloomington: James Currey and Indiana University Press, 1997). For a critique of the development sector, see Peter Uvin, *Aiding Violence: The Development Enterprise in Rwanda* (West Hartford, Conn.: Kumarian, 1998). For two sensationalist critiques, see Graham Hancock, *The Lords of Poverty: The Power, Prestige, and Corruption of the International Aid Business* (New York: Atlantic Monthly Press, 1989); and Michael Maren, *The Road to Hell: The Ravaging Effects of Foreign Aid and International Charity* (New York: Free Press, 1997).
20. On the marketization of humanitarian relief, see Smillie, *Relief and Development*, pp. 35–51; and Ian Smillie, *The Alms Bazaar* (London: IT Publications, 1995).
21. Ian Smillie and Goran Todorovic, "Reconstructing Bosnia, Constructing Civil Society," in Smillie, ed., *Patronage or Partnership: Local Capacity Building in Humanitarian Crises* (Bloomfield, Conn.: Kumarian, 2001), p. 31.

overhead. They view marketization as a way to curb waste, improve professionalism, and enhance project implementation.[22] Marketization can also generate support within donor countries by reassuring skeptical legislators that
foreign assistance is being spent responsibly and efficiently.

The proliferation of IOs and INGOs operating in the same sector, along with
the marketization of their activities, is radically transforming certain sectors of
the humanitarian relief world. The UN system itself has become increasingly
complex, with four major agencies—the United Nations Development
Programme, the United Nations Children's Fund, the World Food Programme,
and UNHCR—operating independently with separate budgets and staffs.
These are joined by at least 40 large aid and relief INGOs and two separate Red
Cross groupings, the ICRC and the International Federation of Red Cross and
Red Crescent Societies.[23] In addition, hundreds of smaller INGOs are seeking
entry to the aid and relief market, hoping to raise funds for future work by
raising their flag in media-saturated humanitarian "hot spots." Although the
global INGO relief market is dominated by eight agencies, each of their country offices is forced to compete heavily for individual contracts in particular
conflict settings.[24]

Western technical assistance programs in Eastern Europe and the former
socialist states contribute to also an increasingly lucrative, crowded, and
marketized transnational sector. Cumulative technical assistance from the EU
to the former Soviet states totaled $2.804 billion from 1991 to 1996; U.S. assis-
tance from 1992 to 1997 totaled $10.967 billion.[25] Most of these disbursements
funded projects implemented by well-known for-profit multinationals. In 1995
alone, contracts worth $476 million were awarded to just four corporations—
Arthur Andersen, Booz Allen and Hamilton, Chemonics, and KPMG/Peat
Marwick—for economic restructuring efforts.[26] Indeed, the annual value of

22. Charlton and May, "NGOs, Politics, Projects, and Probity," p. 244. See also Berrios, *Contracting for Development*, pp. 23–34.
23. Natsios, "NGOs and the UN System in Complex Humanitarian Emergencies," p. 416.
24. The eight large relief INGOs are APDOVE (Association of Protestant Development Organizations in Europe), CARE, CIDSE (Coopération internationale pour le développement et la soli-
darité), Eurostep, Médecins sans Frontières, Oxfam, Save the Children, and World Vision. Each
controls a budget of more than $500 million. Together they account for more than half of the
world's relief market. Simmons, "Learning to Live with NGOs," p. 92.
25. Janine Wedel, *Collision and Collusion: The Strange Case of Western Aid to Eastern Europe* (New
York: St. Martin's, 1998), pp. 203–204.
26. Nancy Lubin, "U.S. Assistance to the Newly Independent States: When Good Things Come in
Smaller Packages," in Bruce Parrott and Karen Dawisha, eds., *The International Dimension of Post-
Communist Transitions in Russia and the New States of Eurasia* (Armonk, N.Y.: M.E. Sharpe, 1997),
p. 351.

technical assistance and INGO projects to many post-Soviet states exceeds that of financial assistance from established multilateral lenders such as the International Monetary Fund (IMF).[27]

INGO and IO insiders are increasingly concerned by this growth of actors and marketization. According to a recent UN-commissioned study, for example, coordination efforts among war-relief IOs and INGOs are being systematically undermined by the growing number of humanitarian groups vying for contracts.[28] "Competitiveness," the report states, is "built into the system" of war-related aid, while competition within the UN relief system, according to one senior UN official, is even fiercer than in the private sector. The results have been deeply corrosive.[29]

Our research on transnational aid of all kinds reveals dysfunctions beyond coordination failure, however, including disincentives to protest aid diversion and empowerment of uncooperative aid recipients. Density and marketization have created new relationships and incentives between transnational and local actors, but analysts have largely relegated these endogenous sources of dysfunctional IO and INGO behavior to industry-specific literatures.[30]

Organizational Environments, Contracting, and NGO Incentives

When an organization's survival depends on making strategic choices in a market environment characterized by uncertainty, its interests will be shaped, often unintentionally, by material incentives. We assume that IOs and INGOs behave similarly to other organizations, internalizing the values, goals, and methods of their institutional environment through imitation and isomorphism.[31] The more that nonprofit groups attempt to secure and maintain contracts under market-generated pressures, the more they will copy the struc-

27. For comparative data, see Alexander Cooley, "International Aid to the Former Soviet States: Agent of Reform or Guardian of the Status Quo?" *Problems of Post-Communism*, Vol. 47, No. 4 (July/August 2000), p. 38. It is becoming increasingly difficult to disentangle the value of monetary and nonmonetary disbursements, given that many developmental and restructuring credits granted by financial institutions such as the World Bank and the Asian Development Bank are now accompanied by mandatory technical assistance projects.

28. Nicola Reindorp and Peter Wiles, *Humanitarian Coordination: Lessons from Recent Field Experience* (London: Overseas Development Institute, 2001). The study was commissioned by the UN's Office for the Coordination of Humanitarian Affairs.

29. Ibid., p. 9.

30. For a rare exception, see Michael N. Barnett and Martha Finnemore, "The Politics, Power, and Pathologies of International Organizations," *International Organization*, Vol. 53, No. 4 (Autumn 1999), pp. 699–732.

31. James G. March and Johan P. Olsen, *Rediscovering Institutions: The Organizational Basis of Politics* (New York: Free Press, 1989); Walter W. Powell and Paul J. DiMaggio, eds., *The New Institutionalism*

tures, interests, and procedures of their for-profit counterparts.[32] The influence of material incentives is further bolstered by the organizational structures of aid INGOs emulating private-sector models. Most large nonprofit groups have developed elaborate structures for handling public relations, fund-raising, internal audits and accounting, human resources, and the like. Thus, as a theory created to study organizational behavior under market conditions, the NEO is particularly suited to today's transnational setting. Because IOs and INGOs engage in competitive and contractual relations, we analyze their behavior with tools specifically developed for that purpose.

Transnational organizations are embedded in market-based institutions created by contracts between donors and INGO contractors, or between contractors and recipients. Donors typically seek the effective implementation of their projects; contractors are tacitly preoccupied with organizational survival.[33] In unstable or competitive markets, aid contractors cannot take their survival as a given.[34] INGOs are in the business of implementing programs. Securing new contracts—or renewing existing ones—is the best way to remain solvent.[35] In this respect, the dependence of major U.S. relief groups on short-term, renewable government contracts is notable. In 1995, for instance, U.S. government contracts constituted 62 percent of CARE-USA's total revenue and 54 percent for Save the Children–USA.[36] In turn, principal-agent problems, competitive contract tenders, and the presence of multiple principals exacerbate INGO insecurity and create organizational imperatives that promote self-interested action, inter-INGO competition, and poor project implementation.

---

in Organizational Analysis (Chicago: University of Chicago Press, 1991); and Richard W. Scott, *Organizations: Rational, Natural, and Open Systems* (New York: Prentice Hall, 1997).

32. For institutional isomorphism, see Powell and DiMaggio, *The New Institutionalism*. For applications to U.S. corporations, see Neil Fligstein, *The Transformation of Corporate Control* (Cambridge, Mass.: Harvard University Press, 1990); for Chinese firms, see Doug Guthrie, *Dragon in a Three-Piece Suit* (Princeton, N.J.: Princeton University Press, 1999); and for political organizations, see Hendrik Spruyt, *The Sovereign State and Its Competitors*.

33. We recognize that implementing projects may not always rank highest on the list of donor's preferences. Other factors are clearly at work, including international profile, organizational prestige, and even fiscal survival, depending on the donor's funding sources. We believe, however, that the project implementation motive is a reasonable simplifying assumption for generating hypotheses about behavior.

34. The contractors' predicament differs from that of most donors, which tend to be permanent international organizations or part of a donor state's bureaucracy.

35. David C. Korten, *Getting to the Twenty-First Century* (West Hartford, Conn.: Kumarian, 1996), p. 102.

36. Data are from USAID, cited in Smillie, *Relief and Development*, p. 43.

PRINCIPAL-AGENT PROBLEMS

Short-term contracting can lead to acute agency problems. Relations between donors, contractors, and recipients can be modeled as a double set of "principal-agent" problems wherein the donor is a "principal" and contractors are "agents." At the lower half of the hierarchy, the contractor functions as the principal and the aid recipient is the agent.[37] As in all relations of authority, an agent's fulfillment of a principal's directives cannot be taken for granted,[38] and donor-principals face the problems of hidden action and information.[39] Because contractor-agents often have de facto control over a project's resources, they will try and guide the project so that it promotes their own goals, which may or may not be identical to those of the donor.[40] If the project is not going according to the donor's plan, contractors or recipients—or possibly both—may conceal, withhold, or distort information harmful to their interests.[41] More important, most projects are renewed after an initial evaluation, giving contractor-agents little incentive to report failing or inappropriate projects. If contractor-agents were to be entirely truthful about implementation problems, they might hurt their chances of contract renewal and threaten their own organizational survival.

Relations between contractors and project recipients are also characterized by agency problems. It is more difficult, however, to impute a priori a project recipient's preferences than it is those of a contractor. Recipients may genuinely welcome all project support and use aid resources for the purposes for

---

37. Terry M. Moe, "The New Economics of Organization," *American Journal of Political Science*, Vol. 28, No. 4 (November 1984), p. 756. On the dynamics of more complex, multilevel hierarchies, see Steven Solnick, *Stealing the State: Control and Collapse in Soviet Institutions* (Cambridge, Mass.: Harvard University Press, 1998).
38. For overviews of agency theory, see Kathleen M. Eisenardt, "Agency Theory: An Assessment and Review," *Academy of Management Review*, Vol. 14, No. 1 (January 1989), pp. 57–74; Gary Miller, *Managerial Dilemmas: The Political Economy of Hierarchy* (New York: Cambridge University Press, 1992); and John W. Pratt and Richard J. Zeckhauser, *Principals and Agents: The Structure of Business* (Boston: Harvard Business School Press, 1985). Many of the monitoring mechanisms employed by donors endogenize agency problems. For instance, all USAID contractors must compile detailed monthly reports that list their activities and, at the end of year, present a list of "objectives accomplished." In both cases, USAID must rely extensively on information exclusively provided by contractors.
39. Miller, *Managerial Dilemmas*, especially pp. 138–178.
40. David Sappington, "Incentives in Principal-Agent Relationships," *Journal of Economic Perspectives*, Vol. 5, No. 2 (Spring 1991), pp. 45–66.
41. This is especially true in remote locations, where contractors acquire specialized information typically unavailable to the donor. North, *Institutions, Institutional Change, and Economic Performance*, pp. 54–60; and Hendrik Spruyt, "Oversight, Control, and Resistance in Translocal Organizations," paper presented at the annual meeting of the International Studies Association, San Diego, California, April 16–20, 1996.

which they were intended. On the other hand, without adequate monitoring, recipients may appropriate the contractor's resources for opportunistic gain. One of our key hypotheses is that when faced with pressure to renew existing contracts, aid contractors will be reluctant to report recipients' opportunistic behavior unless donors can credibly guarantee that they will not terminate or reduce funding for the project.[42] Two other institutional features can exacerbate these agency problems: competitive bidding and multiple principals.

COMPETITIVE BIDDING

The competitive nature of short-term contracts acts as a powerful institutional constraint on IO and INGO contractors. Donors initiate projects with a semipublic tender, which contractors then bid on.[43] In war-related relief, three- to six-month contracts are the norm, with contractors constantly facing threats of layoffs, cutbacks, and capacity reductions. Contractors incur significant start-up costs to service a new contract—hiring staff, renting offices, and leasing new equipment—and can recoup their expenses only by securing additional contracts. Because alternative contractors threaten to appropriate projects, INGOs are under constant pressure to renew, extend, or win new contracts, regardless of the project's overall utility. Some INGO headquarters order their country offices to become financially self-sufficient, exacerbating the competitive dynamic. Securing new funding is an ever-expanding part of the INGO's function, pushing other concerns—such as ethics, project efficacy, or self-criticism—to the margins.[44]

THE MULTIPLE-PRINCIPALS PROBLEM

A final institutional constraint arises when multiple donors or contractors compete for the same project. If IOs and INGO were members of a purely

---

42. This is a variant of the "ratchet problem." See Solnick, *Stealing the State*, pp. 27–29.
43. The process is not entirely open or fully competitive, of course. Large aid contractors with strong reputations and connections have a better chance of securing contracts than small or little-known rivals. See Berrios, *Contracting for Development*, pp. 35–51.
44. Contracts, moreover, generate economies of scale, creating incentives for acquiring and maintaining large projects. Staff, materials, and logistics are expensive but fixed costs, whereas overhead, or "administrative recovery," is calculated as a fixed percentage of the contract's value. As non-earmarked funds, administrative recovery is a significant source of revenue. As the contract's value increases, fixed costs decline while the administrative recovery percentage remains constant. Overhead fees, in other words, are rents of increasing return generated by project size and continuity. On rents and rent seeking, see James M. Buchanan, Robert D. Tollison, and Gordon Tullock, eds., *Toward a Theory of the Rent-Seeking Society* (College Station: Texas A&M University Press, 1980).

normatively driven and robust global civil society, we might expect them to cooperate, pool resources, and share information. There are good theoretical reasons, however, to believe that the opposite may occur due to the multiple-principals problem. The more contractors there are, the more each organization's position within the market seems insecure.[45] As a result, some organizations may seek to undermine competitors, conceal information, and act unilaterally. Rather than burden and cost sharing, this generates project duplication, waste, incompatible goals, and collective inefficiencies.[46] In addition, competing multiple contractors often dilute the coherence of their collective project goals, advice, and strategies.

The presence of multiple contractors also increases recipients' ability to play contractors and donors off against each other. Recipients can use cross-cutting advice and strategies offered by multiple principals to pick and choose among the project elements they most like, disregarding projects that are more disruptive. This is especially likely when recipients seek concessions or payoffs from one or more principals and can threaten to withdraw their cooperation as a bargaining tactic.

Calls for IO and INGO coordination are ubiquitous in the humanitarian aid literature, prompting periodic creation of new UN coordination studies and agencies.[47] Recurring coordination problems, however, are not caused solely by poor communication, lack of professionalism, or a dearth of coordinating bodies. They are also—and perhaps chiefly—produced by a crowded and highly competitive aid market in which multiple organizations compete for contracts from the same donors. Interorganizational discord is a predictable outcome of existing material incentives.

---

45. For the multiple-principals problems in matrix organizations, see Stanley Davis and Paul Lawrence, *Matrix* (Reading, Mass.: Addison-Wesley, 1979). On multiple principals and bureaucratic appointments, see Pablo Spiller and Santiago Urbiztondo, "Political Appointees vs. Career Civil Servants: A Multiple Principals Theory of Political Bureaucracies," *European Journal of Political Economy,* Vol. 10, No. 3 (October 1994), pp. 465–497. For an application of the concept to defense appropriations, see Deborah D. Avant, *Political Institutions and Military Change: Lessons from Peripheral Wars* (Ithaca, N.Y.: Cornell University Press, 1994).
46. Philippe Aghion and Jean Tirole, "Formal and Real Authority in Organizations," *Journal of Political Economy,* Vol. 105, No. 1 (February 1997), pp. 20–22. See also Jean Tirole, "The Internal Organization of Government," *Oxford Economic Papers,* Vol. 46, No. 1 (January 1994), pp. 1–29.
47. See, for example, Natsios, "NGOs and the UN System in Complex Humanitarian Emergencies"; Reindorp and Wiles, *Humanitarian Coordination;* Cyril Ritchie, "Coordinate? Cooperate? Harmonize? NGO Policy and Operational Coalitions," *Third World Quarterly,* Vol. 16, No. 3 (September 1995), pp. 513–524; and Marc Sommers, *The Dynamics of Coordination* (Providence: War and Humanitarianism Institute, Brown University, 2000).

In sum, our analysis draws on the NEO to identify the political economy of relations among transnational actors. Agency problems, competitive contracts, and multiple principals generate incentives promoting self-interested behavior, intense competition, and poor project implementation. Our cases illustrate these claims in practice.

Case Study #1: Technical Assistance in Kyrgyzstan

In Kyrgyzstan both the multiple-principals problem and competitive bidding constrained aid INGOs, empowering recipient bureaucracies to evade reforms promoted by donors and preventing contractors from publicly protesting these evasions. This case might be considered a relatively easy test of our assumptions, because the INGOs involved were Western for-profit corporations, not nonprofit groups.

TECHNICAL ASSISTANCE

Since the collapse of the Soviet Union, international donors have assisted former Soviet-bloc countries with their economic, political, and social transitions. Although much of this effort has been monetary, the last decade also saw an explosion in funding INGOs via the establishment of technical assistance programs (TAPs). Broadly speaking, most TAPs target state agencies and seek to introduce parliamentary legislation that will strengthen institutional capacity, increase bureaucratic transparency, formalize accountability procedures, and routinize decisionmaking procedures. Prominent donors in this sector include USAID, the EU, UNDP, the World Bank, and the Asian Development Bank (ADB).

TAPs have been at the heart of external efforts to assist building market-based economies. Contracted technical assistance providers are typically established for-profit corporations with expertise in the legalities and logistics of capitalist institutions. Projects include designing privatization programs and constructing capital markets, standardizing trade and exchange-rate regimes, enacting banking reforms, formulating property laws, introducing international accounting standards and commercial laws, reforming tax codes, and re-designing entitlements programs. As a result, donors expect that state institutions will be better equipped to manage and govern the nascent market economy.

PROJECTS IN KYRGYZSTAN

Kyrgyzstan portrays itself as one of the most liberalizing of the former Soviet republics and is often touted by multilateral organizations as a model of successful reform.[48] Since 1994 the small Central Asian state has received $80–120 million annually (5–10 percent of annual gross domestic product) in technical assistance, along with substantial financial assistance from multilateral lenders. Per capita, Kyrgyzstan has received the second-most USAID technical assistance of all the post-Soviet states, with disbursements totaling $42 million in 1997, $36.5 million in 1998, and $30 million in the years since.[49] Other major donors include the EU through the Technical Assistance to the Commonwealth of Independent States (TACIS) program (providing ECU 28 million up to 1996 and 40 million ECU in 1997 alone),[50] and UNDP ($15 million between 1994 and 1997).[51]

At first glance, this plethora of assistance seems to have had an unprecedented impact on Kyrgyz legislation. Fifty-five percent of bills under consideration in the spring of 1998 were either formulated or drafted by IOs and INGOs acting as technical assistance providers. In the area of economic policy, foreign specialists sponsored 65 percent of all bills relating to tax reform, the budget, privatization, finance, business, banking, and trade.[52]

---

48. For examples of these generally optimistic assessments made by the international community, see International Monetary Fund, *Kyrgyz Republic: Recent Economic Developments,* IMF Staff Country Report No. 98/8 (Washington, D.C.: IMF, 1998); and World Bank, *From Plan to Market: World Development Report, 1996* (New York: Oxford University Press 1996). More recent assessments are less upbeat.
49. Of the $36.5 million allocated for technical assistance in 1998, $1.5 million was earmarked for fiscal reform; $14.5 million for private enterprise and corporate governance institution building; $4 million for citizens' initiatives and democracy and civil society promotion; $3 million for financial reform; $2 million for local government; $3 million for the social sector; and another $8.5 million for "cross-cutting initiatives." Full details of USAID project disbursements can be found at http://www.usaid.gov/regions/europe_eurasia/car/kgpage.html.
50. European Commission, *Evropeiskaya Kommissiya: Programma TACIS Godovoi Otchet za 1996 god* [European Commission: TACIS Program annual report for 1996] (Brussels: European Community, 1997), p. 24.
51. UNDP internal memo provided by central office in Bishkek, Kyrgyzstan.
52. Among the donors involved were the USAID contractors Barents Group, Booz Allen and Hamilton, CARANA Corporation, International Business and Technical Consultants, International City/County Management Association, KPMG/Peat Marwick, and Pragma Corporation. In addition, contractors from the German Technical Agency, the World Bank, ADB, and TACIS also formulated the original versions of some bills. Parliament of the Kyrgyz Republic (Jogorku Kanesh), "Bills under Consideration" (Bishkek: Jogorku Kanesh, 1998). A comprehensive list of the donors responsible for each article of legislation can be found in Alexander Cooley, "Depending Fortunes: Aid, Oil, and the Formation of the Post-Soviet States," Ph.D. dissertation, Columbia University, 1999, pp. 174–177.

ACTUAL RESULTS: INCOMPLETE INSTITUTIONAL REFORM

Yet while the volume of legislation seems impressive, the bills' final text diverges significantly from the original donor-drafted versions. Kyrgyz parliamentary committees, the assembly, the president's office, or some combination thereof have all amended the reform laws to protect their interests. The substance and wording of final bills dealing with land reform, budgetary laws, new tax codes, and other issues bear little resemblance to the original, INGO-formulated drafts.

The "modernizing" tax code of 1996, for example, produced by Barents Group (the USAID-contracted INGO), the World Bank, and the EU, is littered with exemptions inserted to safeguard the interests of regional administrators, prominent social factions, and organized crime. Indeed the code finally adopted in 1996 was substantially altered after eighteen months of circulation in government circles from the Barents Group–proposed version. One major change was the addition of several new rates of personal taxation. Whereas the original draft proposed a two-tiered taxation rate, the final legislation delineates six different brackets of taxation rates, scaled progressively according to income level, but with a host of new deductions.[53] Other changes include permission for parliament to exempt politically loyal regions from taxation and ambiguous additions to the foreign investment laws.[54] As a result of these and other loopholes, tax revenues actually decreased after the code's adoption.[55] Despite the tax initiative's failure, however, fiscal reform projects are an ongoing part of Western donor efforts in the country. In 2001 USAID renewed the Barents Group project on fiscal reform for the eighth consecutive year.

As with the issue of taxes, the extent of donor involvement in promoting change may seem high because of the volume of donor-sponsored legislation. The actual legislation, however, diverges frequently from donor intent, and

53. *The Tax Law of the Kyrgyz Republic,* Bishkek, April 14, 1997 (amended version); and interviews with relevant TAP officials, March–April 1998, Bishkek, Kyrgyzstan.
54. Scott Horton and Temirbek Kenenbaev, "Kyrgyzstan Struggles to Modernize Its Tax Law," *Central Asia Monitor,* Vol. 5, No. 2 (1997), pp. 26–30.
55. As the IMF noted, "An increasing number of discretionary tax exemptions to value added tax (VAT), customs, and excise duties has eroded the tax base following the introduction of the new tax code on July 1, 1996." IMF, *Kyrgyz Republic: Recent Economic Developments,* p. 14. VAT areas that were granted subsequent exemptions included organized gambling, financial services, and selected agricultural producers. The more politically motivated amendments for exemptions from the income tax include income derived from the extraction of precious metals, inheritances, and interest income as well as "income from the sale of apartments, houses, cars, jewelry and artwork." Ibid., pp. 83, 87. Contrast these IMF observations with the optimism with which USAID describes the project and its selective use of performance indicators. See USAID website, http://www.usaid.gov/country/ee/kg/116–012.html.

many of the laws passed have not produced the intended institutional changes.[56] Contrary to public proclamations by the Kyrgyz government, donors, and INGOs, institutional change has not been rapidly forthcoming. Instead entrenched state and social interests have drained most substance from these reform initiatives.

CONTRACTOR INCENTIVES FOR TOLERATING OPPORTUNISM

While uncooperative Kyrgyz bureaucracies and political factions are responsible for the watering down of TAPs, their continuation is explained by the institutional environment in which INGO contractors and recipients operate. The contracting system forces INGOs to tolerate legislative backsliding. Because donors often ask recipients whether the contractor's project should be renewed, contractors are likely to permit and even conceal recipient obstructions so as to curry favor with recipients.[57] Among the dozens of projects initiated through 1999, we uncovered only one project voluntarily terminated by contractors for recipient noncompliance.[58] The short-term contract renewal requirement, coupled with the contractor's desire to survive, trumps most other concerns, including effective project implementation and frank discussion of project problems.

Contractors also provide recipients with perks to maintain good relations. TAPs do not offer cash payments, but they do provide scarce assets to resource-strapped bureaucracies. Office computers, vehicles, and telecommunications are included in most TAP budgets, but the equipment is frequently embezzled by recipients or resold on the black market. Many TAPs also offer their recipients foreign trips, justifying these expenditures as "institutional instruction." In 1997, for example, Kyrgyz judges were flown to Paris and Riga, parliamentarians to Washington, privatization officials to New York, health-care administrators to Denmark, and oblast administrators to Switzerland. The cost of such trips can exceed $100,000 each, while some seminars can top $30,000.[59] One contractor acknowledged that these were de facto bribes, say-

---

56. On the similar weakening of USAID legislative initiatives in the case of post-Soviet Georgia, see Charles King, "Potemkin Democracy: Four Myths about Post-Soviet Georgia," *National Interest*, No. 64 (Spring 2001), pp. 98–100.
57. For an insider's account of how contractors collude with bureaucracies to renew ineffective projects in Kazakhstan, see Mathew Bivens, "Aboard the Gravy Train: In Kazakhstan, the Farce That Is USAID," *Harper's*, August 1997, pp. 69–76.
58. The project was the TACIS project on Civil Service Reform, subcontracted to the legal firm Eurostar.
59. Interviews with TAP contractors, Bishkek, Kyrgyzstan, March and April 1998.

ing, "the trips are a very good bargain for us . . . allowing us to continue [the project] with the cooperation of important ministry members."[60] Contractors also budget money for "local operating costs" or "local consulting services"— work that is often given to groups with strong ties to officials involved in the project, some of whom then collect a hefty premium for their recommendations.[61] Both recipients and INGO contractors, however, conceal these and other project problems from donors to help ensure renewal of their contracts.[62]

MULTIPLE PRINCIPALS: INSTITUTIONAL REFORM STALLED

The presence of several donors in the same sector also precipitated multiple-principals problems. Project implementation has often been delayed or halted as a result of interdonor and INGO competition. This lack of coordination is not a product of ill will or poor organizational culture. Rather, it is generated by an increasingly marketized aid environment in which IOs and INGOs feel required to demonstrate their ability to spend monies and win influence, regardless of broader project outcomes.

For instance, during discussions over how to restructure the state-owned energy company, KyrgyzEnergo, IOs and INGOs submitted contradictory proposals. Whereas USAID preferred to completely dismantle the state monopoly and privatize by function, TACIS and the European Bank for Reconstruction and Development wanted to keep the company intact and find a foreign partner to help it initiate gradual reforms.[63] Unsure of its position, the World Bank shifted support from USAID to the European donors. Although the first proposals for KyrgyzEnergo reform were drafted in 1995, legislation on the matter was not finalized until 2000, in part because Kyrgyz officials stalled as donors vied for influence.[64] Similar confusion is evident in agriculture, where efforts to reform farmer cooperatives stalled as contractors for Swiss Aid, TACIS, the

---

60. Interview with a director of a capital-market-formation TAP, Bishkek, Kyrgyzstan, March 17, 1998.
61. See also Bivens, "Aboard the Gravy Train," pp. 72–75.
62. In fact, most INGOs are explicitly instructed by management at home to submit all project-related memos and evaluations to their home office for clearance before forwarding them to their relevant USAID or EU country directors.
63. Interviews with foreign staff members of TAPs, March and April 1998; and various TAP reports on energy reform. See the reform options discussed in Haglar Bailey, *International Experiences with Privatization and Restructuring in the Energy Sector and Alternatives for the Kyrgyz Republic* (Bishkek: USAID, 1996).
64. Although even as of early 2002, the planned denationalization and restructuring had yet to be completed.

World Bank, and the German Technical Agency each independently tried to implement a strikingly different program.[65] In land reform, a World Bank plan to lease property to peasants was halted by a disagreement with TACIS over basic monitoring and statistical gathering procedures.[66]

In other cases, donors simply refused to meet with each other, duplicating work and wasting valuable time, resources, and opportunities for cooperation. For example, in the area of pension reform, the contractors for USAID, the World Bank, and ADB all drafted separate proposals. These IOs and INGOs were operating on renewable, one-year contracts; and as one TAP official acknowledged, it would have been better to have pooled resources and coordinated efforts rather than to have each spent six months gathering data and drawing up individual action plans.[67] The same dysfunctions characterized the budget reform process.[68]

Aid specialists often discuss coordination failures, but many of these studies do not acknowledge the systematic bias toward interorganizational competition. Although aid donors and contractors are rhetorically committed to cooperation and broadly shared goals, they are pushed into competition by their institutional environment, which pits actors within similar sectors against one another in a struggle for survival and contract renewal.

INSTITUTIONAL INCENTIVES AND INGO OPERATIONS IN KYRGYZSTAN

Kyrgyzstan's technical assistance projects have largely been ineffective. Although the roots of project failure may lie within the Kyrgyz state and its uncooperative or "predatory" tendencies, the issue of why projects continue to receive international funding is best explained by the political economy of the donor-contractor-recipient relationship.[69] With their organizational survival depending on contract renewal, TAP contractors have little incentive to protest

65. World Bank, *Kyrgyz Republic: Agricultural Support Services Project*, Report No. 17312-KG (Washington, D.C.: World Bank, 1998), pp. 9–10; and Gennady Zhalkubayev, "Agricultural Reform: Not a Step without the World Bank," *Central Asian Post*, April 20, 1998, p. 3. For details, see Cooley, "Depending Fortunes," p. 194.
66. TACIS, *Policy and Agro-Business Support Projects: Addendum Report on Land Reform and Agricultural Legislation* (Bishkek: TACIS Office Kyrgyzstan, 1996), p. 5.
67. Interview with foreign staff member of a TAP working on a fiscal reform TAP in the ministry of finance, Bishkek, Kyrgystan, April 16, 1998.
68. Cooley, "Depending Fortunes," pp. 199–204.
69. On predatory states and corrupt bureaucracies, see Peter Evans, "The State As Problem and As Solution: Predation, Embedded Autonomy, and Structural Change," in Stephen Haggard and Robert Kaufman, eds., *The Politics of Economic Adjustment* (Princeton, N.J.: Princeton University Press, 1992).

abuse of donor resources, to discontinue ineffective projects, or to cooperate with one another. Indeed the more they conceal abuses and failures, the more likely they are to receive renewed contracts.

Contrary to the expectations of global civil society scholars, the evidence from Kyrgyzstan does not suggest that transnational NGOs have successfully promoted liberalization and reform in Central Asia.[70] Despite the enormous amount of ongoing IO and INGO activity, the Kyrgyz Republic is widely seen to have moved backward on promoting economic and political liberalization.[71] These findings are consistent with observations made by other scholars studying the transnational sector's shortcomings in multiple postsocialist states.[72]

The Kyrgyz case provides a relatively easy test of our assumptions, because the INGO contractors involved are for-profit corporations. We might expect for-profit groups to seek to promote their own interests, even at the expense of a donor's overall goals. What is surprising, however, is the tendency of nonprofit groups to behave similarly, despite their different normative orientation. In many situations, INGOs will act like their for-profit counterparts as long as their financial survival is at stake. The following two cases of humanitarian relief and POW monitoring provide evidence for this claim.

---

70. On this point, see also Fiona Adamson, "International Democracy Assistance in Uzbekistan and Kyrgyzstan: Building Civil Society from the Outside?" in Sarah E. Mendelson and John K. Glenn, eds., *The Power and Limits of NGOs: A Critical Look at Building Democracy in Eastern Europe and Eurasia* (New York: Columbia University Press, 2002); and Michael Dobbs, "Investment in Freedom Is Flush with Peril: From Kazakhstan, a Cautionary Tale," *Washington Post,* January 25, 2001, p. A1. On the problems of environmental NGOs in Central Asia, see Pauline Jones Luong and Erika Weinthal, "The NGO Paradox: Democratic Goals and Non-Democratic Outcomes in Kazakhstan," *Europe-Asia Studies,* Vol. 51, No. 7 (November 1999), pp. 1267–1284.

71. For instance, the Freedom House indicator for economic and political freedom in Kyrgyzstan has dropped to its lowest level since independence. See Freedom House Country Ratings, available at http://www. freedomhouse.org/ratings.

72. See Lubin, "U.S. Assistance to the Newly Independent States"; and Nancy Lubin and Monica Ware, *Aid to the Former Soviet Union: When Less Is More* (New York: JNA Associates, 1996). For a critical, but highly provocative, view of Western INGO involvement in the economic reform process in Russia and Ukraine, see Wedel, *Collision and Collusion.* Even scholars who are generally supportive of INGO efforts have pointed to mixed results. For instance, for candid assessments of the state of democracy promotion in post-socialist countries, see Thomas Carothers, *Aiding Democracy Abroad: The Learning Curve* (Washington, D.C.: Carnegie Endowment for International Peace, 1999); Thomas Carothers, *Assessing Democracy Assistance: The Case of Romania* (Washington, D.C.: Carnegie Endowment for International Peace, 1996); Mendelson and Glenn, *The Power and Limits of NGOs;* Sarah E. Mendelson, "Democracy Assistance and Political Transition in Russia: Between Success and Failure," *International Security,* Vol. 25, No. 4 (Summer 2001), pp. 68–106; and Jack Snyder, *From Voting to Violence: Democratization and Nationalist Conflict* (New York: W.W. Norton, 2001), pp. 189–264. See also Gideon Rose, "Democracy Promotion and American Foreign Policy: A Review Essay," *International Security,* Vol. 25, No. 3 (Winter 2000/01), pp. 186–203.

Case Study #2: Competitive Bidding and Refugee Relief in Goma

Competition and an overabundance of organizations helped to cause a myriad of problems during refugee relief operations around Goma, a town in the Democratic Republic of Congo, formerly known as Zaire. From 1994 to 1996, representatives from more than 200 relief organizations traveled to Goma to secure UN contracts seeking to aid desperate Rwandan refugees. Contrary to the "more is better" hypothesis, however, the presence of multiple international aid groups did not produce optimal outcomes. In particular, competitive contract bidding created powerful disincentives for Refugee Help, a respected private Western relief organization, to strongly protest aid diversion by Hutu militants and suspected war criminals. Refugee Help's reluctance in this respect is particularly striking, given its stated commitment to a deeply ethical view of global affairs.

HUMANITARIAN AID IN GOMA

In the summer of 1994, 1.5 million Rwandans of ethnic Hutu origin fled to Tanzania and eastern Zaire.[73] In April of that year, extremist Hutu groups had launched a deadly campaign of genocide against ethnic Tutsis, but a reversal of military fortunes pushed Hutu soldiers and civilians alike into exile. NGOs, including Refugee Help, moved quickly to provide refugee relief in four major Zairean and Tanzanian camp complexes, often working on relief contracts provided by the United Nations High Commission for Refugees.[74] UNHCR representatives extended dozens of tenders for short-term contracts dealing with food distribution, camp administration, airport off-loading, transportation, warehousing, and medical and sanitation services.

Conditions were particularly atrocious in and around Goma, where camps housed 800,000 ill and malnourished refugees, making it one of the largest-ever concentrations of human misery.[75] As a result of the genocide and mass

73. Gérard Prunier, *The Rwandan Crisis: History of a Genocide* (New York: Columbia University Press, 1997). For broader discussions of war and refugees, see Alan Dowty and Gil Loescher, "Refugee Flows as Grounds for International Action," *International Security*, Vol. 21, No. 1 (Summer 1996), pp. 43–71; Barry R. Posen, "Military Responses to Refugee Disasters," ibid., pp. 72–111; and Myron Weiner, "Bad Neighbors, Bad Neighborhoods: An Inquiry into the Causes of Refugee Flows," ibid., pp. 5–42.
74. David Millwood, ed., *The International Response to Conflict and Genocide: Lessons from the Rwanda Experience* (Copenhagen: Steering Committee of the Joint Evaluation of Emergency Assistance to Rwanda, 1996), especially Vol. 3.
75. The intense suffering of refugees in Goma was captured in multiple media reports, including Steve Fainaru, "When Death Becomes Casual: Defying Solutions, Rwandan Tragedy Overwhelms the Senses," *Boston Globe*, July 31, 1994, p. 1.

civilian flight, Goma attracted unprecedented press and Western and international donor interest.[76] Two hundred NGOs made their way to Goma in 1994 and 1995, competing for more than $1 billion in relief-related contracts, making the Goma relief operation one of the highest profile and best-funded relief operations in history.[77] Established NGOs specializing in general camp administration and food distribution were joined by dozens of intermediate and smaller groups specializing in niche activities such as public-health education, sanitation, firewood provision, community development, psychological counseling, and unaccompanied child protection.

GOMA'S HYPERCOMPETITIVE RELIEF MARKET

The combination of vast sums of donor money, short-term contracts, and an overabundance of NGOs created an unstable and competitive environment for Refugee Help and others. NGOs constantly renegotiated old contracts whose due dates were fast approaching, while competitors kept lobbying the UNHCR for new contracts. "It's perhaps embarrassing to admit," one midlevel Refugee Help manager recalled, "but much of the discussion between headquarters and the field focused on contracts: securing them, maintaining them, and increasing them. The pressure was on: 'Get more contracts!'"[78] When headquarters staff visited the field, another manager recalled, "They mostly asked about contracts. How many did we have? When were they up? What were the chances that they would be renewed? Were there any competitors?"[79] "Contract fever" was in the air, and most of the international relief groups found themselves slipping into a deeply competitive frame of mind.

Refugee Help was by no means the only Goma-based NGO to react this way. As one journalist noted after a 1995 visit, Goma had become a "three-ring circus of financial self-interest, political abuse and incompetence" where aid had become "big, big money," and any NGO "worth its salt . . . recognized that it had to be in Rwanda."[80] As a result, he said, aid INGOs "parachuted" by the

76. Contrary to the initial impression given by some Western media reports, the Goma refugees were not victims of the Rwandan genocide, which had chiefly targeted persons of Tutsi ethnicity. Rather the refugees were largely of Hutu origin, who had fled when the Hutu-led Rwandan government and militia allies were defeated by the predominantly Tutsi Rwandan Patriotic Front.
77. International donors spent $1.4 billion on relief contracts for Goma from April to December 1994 alone. Millwood, *The International Response to Conflict and Genocide*, Vol. 3, pp. 24–45.
78. Interview in North America with former senior Refugee Help staffer, October 1, 1998. Precise interview locations and NGO informant names have been withheld to protect anonymity.
79. Telephone interview with former Refugee Help camp manager, October 8, 1998.
80. John Vidal, "Blood Money," *Guardian*, April 5, 1995, p. T2.

hundreds into Goma, creating "chaos and madness."[81] Another Western reporter described Goma as an "aid agency supermarket" in which aid groups "blare[d] out their names and logos like soft drink manufacturers," plastering everything from water pumps to T-shirts with advertisements.[82] Competition was fierce, he wrote, and aid groups were desperate to be involved in the Goma relief effort so that they could bolster their fund-raising capacities back home.[83]

There is no doubt that Refugee Help and other like-minded groups sincerely wanted to provide relief to the refugees. The human needs were tremendous, and the NGOs were able to do much good. Normative considerations aside, however, Refugee Help's material stakes were also high; at the peak of the crisis, some 13 percent of Refugee Help's headquarters costs were funded by Goma-related administrative recovery. No major organization concerned about self-preservation could risk losing such an important source of funding, and Refugee Help was no different. In addition, a major presence in Goma created a foothold for future work in the country and allowed for the possible expansion of Refugee Help's global capacities. This latter consideration was particularly important; if Refugee Help could secure more contracts in Goma, it could then deepen its reservoir of trained staff, purchase relief hardware (such as trucks and radios), and expand its stocks of emergency material, allowing Refugee Help to respond quickly to emergencies elsewhere. Typically, major relief contracts were secured only after an NGO first demonstrated a significant field presence. Refugee Help's long-term prospects, therefore, depended on its ability to use current contracts to boost capacity for future operations. Goma, in other words, was important both for the enormity of the suffering that Refugee Help could alleviate and for its boost to Refugee Help's competitiveness in the global relief market.

AID DIVERSION AND ETHICAL DILEMMAS

Although relief groups were saving lives in Goma, their efforts soon drew harsh criticism from Western human rights groups and the new Rwandan gov-

---

81. Ibid.
82. Richard Dowden, "Battle of Logos and T-Shirts Rages in Refugee Camps: Aid Agencies Scramble for Cash," *Independent*, September 4, 1994, p. 11. See also Chris McGreal, "Aid with Biblical Strings Attached," *Guardian*, December 17, 1994, p. 11; and Colin Smith, "Aid Agencies Feud as Rwandans Die," *Sunday Times*, August 7, 1994.
83. Dowden, "Battle of Logos and T-Shirts Rages in Refugee Camps"; and Luttwak, "Give War a Chance," p. 43.

ernment.[84] Hutu armed forces responsible for the genocide had regrouped near Goma, recruiting among the refugees, importing weapons, and organizing military training. Soon the number of armed Hutu militants swelled to more than 50,000.[85] Over time, the refugee camps became de facto safe havens for Hutu fighters, some of whom were suspected war criminals. They also came to serve as rear bases for cross-border guerrilla operations against Tutsi civilians and the Tutsi-led Rwandan government. The fighters sold some relief items on the open market and used the camp population as a source of political legitimacy. Critics increasingly accused the UNHCR and its aid contractors of indirectly fueling the conflict and unwittingly aiding Hutu war criminals.[86] As a relatively important component of Goma's international relief machinery, Refugee Help found itself implicated in an acute ethical dilemma.

WEAK PROTEST AND COLLECTIVE ACTION

Given the competitive nature of Goma's INGO environment, officials in Refugee Help's headquarters were reluctant to encourage self-critical analysis or to publicly protest aid diversions. Refugee Help managers who fended off competitors, renewed UNHCR contracts, and ensured smooth delivery systems were valued for their work. Those interested in exploring the potentially unethical by-products of Refugee Help's relief activities, however, received little encouragement. "Nobody told me to stop looking into that kind of thing," one former Refugee Help emergency manager said, "but I was never asked to work on it either."[87] Competition created incentives for contract renewal and growth, not self-reflection or protest.

In the camps, NGO staffers were frustrated with both the UNHCR and the Zairean government's refusal to crack down on Hutu militants. Although there was little the UNHCR could do without Zairean cooperation or a UN-supplied military force, its representatives might have launched a stronger and more public advocacy effort. Specifically, UNHCR representatives might have

---

84. Barber, "Feeding Refugees, or War?"; Philip Gourevitch, *We Wish to Inform You That Tomorrow We Will Be Killed with Our Families: Stories from Rwanda* (New York: Picador, 1999); Rakiya Omar, *Death, Despair, and Defiance* (London: African Rights, 1995); and Prunier, *The Rwandan Crisis*.

85. Human Rights Watch/Arms Project, *Rearming with Impunity: International Support for the Perpetrators of the Rwandan Genocide* (New York: Human Rights Watch, 1995).

86. See Gourevitch, *We Wish to Inform You That Tommorow We Will Be Killed with Our Families*; Prunier, *The Rwandan Crisis*; and newspaper reports, including Robert Block, "Wolves Lie Down with the Lambs: Killers Are on the Loose among the Refugee Camps in Zaire," *Independent*, July 24, 1994, p. 14; Chris McGreal, "Hutu Extremist Holds UN and Refugees to Ransom," *Guardian*, December 5, 1994, p. 11; and Paul Jelinek, "Foreign Aid Fattens Exiled Hutu Regime: Agencies Aghast as Rwandans Plot Return to Power," *Toronto Star*, December 4, 1994, p. A18.

87. Interview in North America with former senior Refugee Help staffer, October 1, 1998.

pressed the issue with greater public vigor in the media, the UN Security Council, and interested publics. The UNHCR, however, was eager to ensure a smooth, problem-free relief operation and was not keen to do anything that might jeopardize its contracts, or undermine broader international support for the Goma aid effort. A vigorous and public UNHCR protest against Hutu militants living in the refugee camps would have reduced international support for relief efforts. It might have also transformed Goma into an unmanageable, even dangerous, quagmire. The UNHCR thus quietly lobbied the UN Security Council, but dared not raise its voice too loudly. As a result, Hutu militants continued to use the camps for their own purposes.

Although many Refugee Help staffers recognized the ethical dilemmas involved in the Goma aid effort, the organization as a whole made few systematic efforts to address the problem. Refugee Help never convened an internal conference or debate on the issue, and never wrote an internal position paper probing the dilemma. When asked, Refugee Help officials attributed this in part to the frantic pace of work, including Goma's prevailing "contract fever," concern about losing aid contracts, and fear of inspiring a violent reaction by Hutu extremists.

Even if it had launched an introspective effort, Refugee Help might have still chosen to continue in Goma, because it was helping thousands of refugees. Were it not for Goma's highly competitive environment, however, Refugee Help might have taken steps to address the urgent ethical concerns. In addition to conducting an internal analysis, the group might have tried to push the UNHCR or Western powers into a more publicly principled stand. Given the multitude of potential NGO competitors already in Goma, however, Refugee Help staffers felt that they had to exercise caution. After all, if Refugee Help earned a reputation as a loud-mouthed troublemaker, the UNHCR might push it aside and award lucrative relief contracts to less-vocal aid groups. This was especially true given the eagerness of other aid contractors in Goma to offer similar relief services at a similar or lower cost.

Competition among international relief groups also undercut the potential for Refugee Help–led collective action. For example, Refugee Help might have tried to organize a protest coalition with other groups, threatening to temporarily cease food distributions if the Zairean government or international agencies did not drive the militias out. Given inter-NGO competition, however, Refugee Help could not be sure that other relief groups would join in. Some might have agreed to protest, but others might not have, preferring instead to take over Refugee Help's contracts. In fact, during a security crisis in one of the Goma camps, another Western relief group did signal its willingness to immediately take over Refugee Help's contract if the latter so much as temporarily ceased aid distribution.

Finally, competition and the ready presence of rival NGOs made Refugee Help feel powerless. Given that many other groups were willing and able to assume Refugee Help's aid contracts, what difference would it make if the group withdrew in protest? Refugee Help was not irreplaceable, and it therefore had little bargaining power. As one staffer opined, "No one would have paid any attention if we left. They would have just carried on without us."[88] Given the presence of multiple competitors, withdrawal—the ultimate act of protest by a high-profile relief organization—seemed an empty gesture.

Comparing today's multitude of relief NGOs to previous eras, one expert notes a decline in NGOs' ability to resist Goma-like problems of aid diversion: "Competition for turf and difficulties of coordination . . . make [today's] humanitarian actors easy targets for political actors seeking access to the scarce resources they control."[89] When there were only a few aid providers in a war zone, NGOs could vigorously protest recipient opportunism. Today NGOs are more cautious, fearing they might be pushed aside by rival groups.

Organizational survival was a particularly pressing concern for NGOs situated in Goma's competitive and uncertain environment. Individual Refugee Help officials realized Goma's ethical dilemmas, but the organization focused firmly on securing and renewing contracts. Had competitive pressures not been so heavy, Refugee Help might have publicly protested, vigorously lobbied, openly organized, and even threatened to withdraw.

Not all NGOs allowed themselves to be caught up in Goma's "contract fever." The Belgian chapter of Médecins sans Frontières (MSF), for example, resolved to avoid competition and forgo Goma-related revenue, refusing to bid on new Goma contracts and replacing its relief operations with an advocacy campaign pushing for limits on the Hutu militant camp presence.[90] According to MSF's secretary-general, "Food represents power, and camp leaders [in Goma] who control its distribution divert considerable quantities towards war preparations," as well as "skim off a percentage of the wages earned by the

---

88. Interview in North America with senior Refugee Help staffer, August 25, 1998.
89. Neil MacFarlane, *Politics and Humanitarian Action* (Providence: War and Humanitarianism Project, Brown University, 2000), p. 45.
90. Mark Frohardt, Diane Paul, and Larry Minear, *Protecting Human Rights: The Challenge to Humanitarian Organizations* (Providence: War and Humanitarianism Project, Brown University, 2000), pp. 72–73.

thousands of refugees employed by relief agencies."[91] The majority of aid groups, however, chose to stay on. Indeed MSF's experience is the exception that proves the rule: It was able to protest aid abuse only by opting out of the Goma contract system altogether. As long as relief groups remained embedded in Goma's competitive humanitarian market, institutional pressures forced them to tone down their criticism. These dynamics were not unique to Goma, and are present in other war zones where donor interest attracts multiple relief groups.

In Afghanistan, for example, a similarly competitive NGO environment evolved in the town of Herat, when in 1996 Taliban forces banned girls from attending school. Development and relief NGOs were unable to develop a common response, largely due to inter-NGO competition. Two leading aid groups suspended their education programs in the area, but the Taliban were not deterred, according to journalist Ahmed Rashid, because they realized that "other UN agencies were not prepared to take a stand against them on the gender issue," and because IOs and INGOs in Herat could not mount a sustained negotiating effort. "As each UN agency tried to cut its own deal with the Taliban," Rashid writes, "the UN compromised its principles, while Taliban restrictions on women only escalated."[92] As had been true in Goma, intra-NGO competition hindered collective protest and empowered local armed forces.

More broadly, the Goma case, like that of Kyrgyzstan, highlights the role of material struggles within the transnational world, rather than the harmonious and liberalizing civil society of globalization theory. What is striking, however, is that as a result of institutional conditions, nonprofit humanitarian groups were pushed to behave like their for-profit counterparts in the technical assistance sector.

Case Study #3: Multiple Principals and Bosnia's POWs

Competition also created uncertainty among IOs and INGOs in the former Yugoslavia, and again empowered uncooperative local recipients.[93] Instead of

---

91. MSF Secretary-General Alain Destexhe, quoted in Patrick Bishop, "Aid Workers Pull Out of Refugee Camps," *Daily Telegraph*, February 14, 1995, p. 13.
92. Ahmed Rashid, *Taliban: Militant Islam, Oil, and Fundamentalism in Central Asia* (New Haven, Conn.: Yale University Press, 2001), p. 113.
93. For two very different perspectives on the causes of war in the former Yugoslavia, see V.P. Gagnon Jr., "Ethnic Nationalism and International Conflict: The Case of Serbia," *International Security*, Vol. 19, No. 3 (Winter 1994/95), pp. 130–166; and Susan Woodward, *Balkan Tragedy: Crisis and Dissolution after the Cold War* (Washington, D.C.: Brookings, 1995).

technical assistance or refugee care, however, this case involves the promotion of international humanitarian law, with specific reference to the protection of POWs.[94]

From 1992 to 1995, the ICRC saw its position as the lead international guarantor of POW rights eroded by competition from UN forces and European Community monitors, both of which sought to protect Bosnian POWs. These multiple principals unduly empowered Bosnian Serb, Croat, and Muslim military commanders, helping them to evade international prisoner monitoring by playing the three international groups off against one another.[95]

POW MONITORING IN BOSNIA

The ICRC's lead role in prisoner monitoring was established by the Fourth Geneva Convention, which entrusts the Swiss group with responsibility for implementation of international humanitarian law.[96] The convention stipulates that warring parties must permit ICRC delegates to register and privately interview all war prisoners and to transmit messages from them to their families. Private, one-on-one prisoner interviews and prisoner tracking help to protect prisoners from abuse, disappearance, or murder.[97] If ICRC delegates learn of abusive conditions during their interviews, they are obligated to confide their findings to prison commanders, local authorities, and senior state officials.[98]

ICRC delegates collect information on prison commanders, evaluating their compliance with the Fourth Geneva Convention. The ICRC's relationship with warring states is highly legalistic, including the signing of an agreement granting the organization the right to visit prisons in accordance with convention and internal ICRC guidelines. Because the ICRC cannot certify compliance with the Geneva Convention without physically inspecting prisons, access is required.

---

94. For the laws of war, see Frits Kalshoven, *Constraints on the Waging of War* (Geneva: ICRC, 1991); and Theodor Meron, *Human Rights and Humanitarian Norms As Customary Law* (New York: Oxford University Press, 1989).
95. Strictly speaking, there was less of a monetized "market" in Bosnia than in Goma, where all relief operations were generated through competitive contract tenders. With the exception of the ICRC, IOs did not receive funds explicitly for prisoner-of-war visitation, although their funding overall was tied to their usefulness and productivity. This, in turn, required that they demonstrate engagement with key humanitarian issues, including prisoner protection.
96. David P. Forsythe, *Humanitarian Politics: The International Committee of the Red Cross* (Baltimore, Md.: Johns Hopkins University Press, 1977).
97. See International Committee of the Red Cross, *ICRC Action on Behalf of Prisoners* (Geneva: ICRC, 1997).
98. In extreme cases, the ICRC may break confidentiality.

When fighting began in Croatia during the summer of 1991, the ICRC was recognized by combatants, IOs, and Western powers as the sole agency responsible for safeguarding war prisoner rights. To ensure its leading role, the ICRC signed an agreement with Croatian republican authorities, the Yugoslav federal army, Bosnian republican authorities, and other combatants.[99] Although the ICRC did not gain access to all Bosnian prisons, it initially faced no rivals in the monitoring business. Other IOs and NGOs engaged in humanitarian relief work, but none dealt with POWs.

When the fighting in Bosnia began in 1992, however, the UN Protection Force (UNPROFOR) initially sent to protect aid convoys, gradually began to conduct its own inspections of POW camps.[100] The UN soldiers were stationed throughout the Bosnian Croat and Muslim enclaves and were aware of intense international concern for Bosnian POWs, especially following reports of Bosnian Serb prison camp atrocities.[101] UNPROFOR officers were eager to ensure that similar abuses did not occur in their zones of responsibility and hoped to show skeptical donors that they were effective protectors of POWs. After being heavily criticized for not blocking Bosnian ethnic cleansing early on, UN officers were eager to show journalists, Western publics, donor governments, and other significant audiences that they could protect Bosnia's war victims.[102] The agency's normative agenda was thus joined by concern for its image and survival.

A second international organization, the European Community Monitoring Mission (ECMM), was also increasingly keen to protect POWs. The ECMM was an observer mission funded by the European Community, with a vague mission to monitor and reduce violence in the former Yugoslavia. Like its UN counterpart, the ECMM was searching for high-visibility opportunities to prevent human rights abuses. The ICRC had a clear mandate under the Geneva Convention, and UNPROFOR was in Bosnia because of a UN Security Council resolution. The ECMM, by contrast, had been sent there only on the European Community's say so, and thus had less international legal backing. Originally

---

99. For ICRC operations in the former Yugoslavia, including its signed agreements with Bosnian military and militia officers, see Michel Mercier, *Crimes without Punishment: Humanitarian Action in Former Yugoslavia* (London: Pluto, 1995).
100. The UN Peace Forces were sent to Croatia in 1991 and became known as UNPROFOR in 1992. In 1995 the contingent was split into UNCRO (UN Confidence Restoration Operation) for Croatia and UNPROFOR for Bosnia.
101. Roy Gutman, *Witness to Genocide* (New York: Macmillan, 1993).
102. David Rieff, *Slaughterhouse: Bosnia and the Failure of the West* (New York: Simon and Schuster, 1995).

designed by European mediators seeking to monitor long-failed cease-fires, the ECMM was verging on irrelevance. Continued fighting in Bosnia and elsewhere made its work virtually irrelevant, while UNPROFOR's overwhelming presence threatened to marginalize it. POW camp inspections, the ECMM hoped, might justify its existence, enhance its credibility with donors, and secure future funding.

Theorists of global civil society would expect multiple international monitors with similar principled beliefs to cooperate and enhance Bosnian prisoner welfare. Our model, however, suggests the opposite: More organizations should create multiple-principals problems, empowering local military commanders to subvert external monitoring. This is ultimately what happened.

Before the UN and ECMM interventions, Bosnian military commanders had relied exclusively on the ICRC for certification of their Geneva Convention compliance. ICRC certification, however, was often burdensome to POW prison commanders, because its inspection procedures required unimpeded access to all prison areas and detainees as well as private, one-on-one interviews with prisoners, allowing ICRC representatives to obtain accurate information from persons who might otherwise fear to speak out. ICRC delegates were also trained to conduct thorough evaluations of prisoners' mental and physical condition. The art of ICRC prison inspection had been developed over decades and was closely monitored by internal supervisors.

The UN and ECMM inspectors, by contrast, were poorly trained, rendering their efforts far less effective. Neither organization provided specialized prison inspection training, and neither regarded prison visits as a core function. UN and ECMM staffers typically did not insist on full access and confidential interviews, and thus could not guarantee that the information they received was accurate or that prisoners would not suffer retaliation. More important, the UN and ECMM did not register the prisoners they interviewed, and thus could not track detainees as they were released or transferred. As a result, the UN and ECMM could not know if a prisoner was tortured or killed for speaking freely. Prisoners meeting with the ICRC, conversely, were registered and tracked until their release, upon which they were reinterviewed about their experiences.

The presence of multiple international monitors threatened the welfare of POWs by empowering POW prison commanders to resist proper inspections. Prison authorities preferred the UN and ECMM visits to those of the ICRC, because the latter were more intrusive. Openness to international monitoring was a public relations gain, but UN or ECMM visits were quicker, simpler, and less likely to provoke difficult questions about the fate of individual prisoners or the conditions in which POWs were held. With three organizations eager to act as principals for the international community, Bosnian commanders, as agents, could pick and choose.

The three-way competition for prison inspections also helped Bosnian commanders to play one IO off against another. When ICRC representatives demanded access to a POW camp, commanders often balked, saying that they had already been visited by the UN or ECMM. Indeed some prison commanders made that argument even if the UN or ECMM had not visited the prison. In the chaos of war and with high turnover rates among international aid personnel, the "prior visitation" argument was plausible.

All three international groups identified themselves to Bosnian commanders as international community representatives seeking to promote humanitarian law. Publicly, all three had normative and complementary agendas. Their organizational environment and interests, however, made cooperation difficult. Here, more organizations did not generate higher rates of prisoner welfare, and competitive pressures did not enhance the efficiency of POW monitoring. Instead of leading to greater POW protection, the multiplicity of concerned transnational organizations empowered prison authorities seeking to evade the requirements of international humanitarian law.

The competitive aid market in Bosnia was not restricted to POW monitoring, however, and INGO competition in Bosnia created other dysfunctions following the signing of the 1995 Dayton peace accords.[103] According to one source, local humanitarian NGOs were "quick to fall into competition with each other, vying for donor attention and funding," chasing whatever new donor funds and priorities emerged in a desperate "search for security and employment." Although many Bosnian groups originally were concerned with helping war victims overcome psychological trauma, they shifted their attention to reconstruction and public infrastructure following the reordering of international donor priorities. "Because funding was drying up in one programming area," observers argue, "NGOs, in order to survive, were being drawn to new areas where they had no special expertise and little interest." Contrary to the expectations of liberal globalization theorists, the transnational market for aid in

---

103. The following quotes are drawn from Smillie and Todarovic, "Reconstructing Bosnia," pp. 28–31.

Bosnia led to opportunism and poor project implementation, despite the normative inclinations of local NGO staffers.

Conclusion

Scholars need to rethink their approach to the emerging world of transnational action. To date, most theorists have seen transnational groups as harbingers of a new, liberal, and robust civil society, but our theory and case studies demonstrate that this view may be overly optimistic. The evidence we have compiled suggests that scholars should also analyze the transnational world with tools drawn from political economy. We should recognize the powerful, if often unacknowledged, role of material incentives, competitive struggles, and tacit collusion with uncooperative government officials or local militias. Given the structure of today's transnational world, organizations may find financial considerations more pressing than liberal norms.

Relying on insights from New Economics of Organization, a body of theory that examines the incentives generated by market institutions and contractual relations, we uncovered a tacit system of material constraints that shaped INGO actions and, on occasion, subverted nominal agendas. Focusing on the diverse world of transnational aid, we found that across the board, competitive environments create institutions that not only systematically shape the behavior of donors, INGO contractors, and recipients but also inhibit cooperation.

There is no doubt that many of today's INGOs are motivated by normative agendas. Insecurity and competition, however, often pushes them to behave in rational and rent-seeking ways. As scholars of institutional isomorphism have long suspected, organizational environments have powerfully homogenizing effects on their constituent units.[104] When placed in competitive, market-like settings, nonprofit groups are likely to behave like their for-profit counterparts. Consequently, there should be little disagreement over whether our approach is ontologically appropriate, given that the transnational actors in question are responding to actual market incentives. Donors, INGO contractors, and recipients behave in manners consistent with agency theory precisely because they have entered into contractual relations and thus have disparate preferences.

The transnational sector has opened new channels for political access and action, but its dynamics are often inconsistent with the views of scholars who

---

104. George Ritzer, *The MacDonaldization of Society* (Newbury Park, Calif.: Pine Forge Press, 2000).

argue that the growing number of INGOs will create a liberal and normatively driven transnational civil society. In fact, organizational density and marketization pose formidable challenges to the consolidation of such a transnational civil society. More is not always better, tenders do not always promote efficiency, and competition does not solely reduce waste. As the volume and intensity of transnationalism grow, scholars should pay as much attention to the tacit material relations among transnational actors as they do to their nominal liberal agendas.

More studies are needed across regions and sectors to test the generalizability of our propositions. It is likely that different conflicts create different types of humanitarian markets, and that different markets will lead to variations in organizational behavior. In some cases, conflicts may take place near or within strong states capable of creating barriers to entry, limiting the penetration of transnational actors and reducing interorganizational competition. Elsewhere, competition could be reduced by declining donor interest or tacit donor agreements to divide the aid market. In still other cases, a single donor or aid contractor may dominate the aid market for historical or political reasons, crowding rivals out and creating a more stable transnational hierarchy. Although our analysis is likely to hold true at the most general level, there will be important regional and sectoral variations in transnational markets.

Our analysis highlights structural contradictions within the transnational world, rather than the dispositions or morality of specific transnational actors. Opportunism may be a rational response to institutional configurations of material interests, not an inherent characteristic of individual INGOs. This is an important finding for a field marred by accusations of immorality and corruption. Although we do not ignore individual organizational responsibility, we believe that many problems within the transnational sector, including aid diversion and poor project implementation, are institutionally conditioned.

Donors and contractors can address these problems in concrete ways. INGOs, for example, can bolster their ability to resist competitive pressures by locating alternative sources of funding beyond established Western governments and IOs. Here, faith-based groups are of particular interest because of their access to less competitive funding. The relief and development group Catholic Relief Services (CRS), for example, has rejected contracts offered by Western governments or UN donors when it believes that the projects are misguided. More often than not, CRS country offices can do so because they have access to alternative funds from Catholic dioceses in Europe and the

United States.[105] Lutheran World Services, World Vision, the Middle East Council of Churches, and other faith-based groups are in a similarly enviable position.

Donors can reduce organizational uncertainty and create healthier incentives by extending the length of contracts and encouraging INGOs to speak openly about their problems. Because short-term, renewable contracts create powerful agency problems, donors could provide longer-term, general-use funds for reputable INGOs that would then be free to make better choices and constructively confront failing projects.[106] Once released from the pressures of "contract fever," INGOs could focus on their work, adjusting their strategies midstream or protesting aid diversion where appropriate. Most important, new structural incentives would make it easier for INGOs on the ground to cooperate rather than to compete. If INGOs knew that their organizational survival did not depend on their rival's failure, they would have reason to share information, pool resources, and generate broad coalitions.

Reforming the institutions underlying the "NGO scramble" is all the more pressing in light of ongoing efforts to provide humanitarian relief and reconstruction aid to Afghanistan. Our analysis suggests that a large amount of assistance does not guarantee project effectiveness, especially in uncertain and chaotic postconflict environments. If efforts to rebuild Afghanistan and aid the Afghani people are to succeed, Western donors and IOs must design humanitarian market institutions with greater care, avoid creating a competitive aid frenzy, and provide long-term contracts to respected groups with regional experience. Similarly, donors seeking to rebuild Afghanistan's infrastructure and public institutions—a process that will inevitably be long and arduous—should consider granting INGOs nonrevocable contracts so that they can publicly confront problems of aid abuse and political interference and change ineffective project strategies without fearing for their fiscal survival.[107]

Once established, transnationals are organizations like any other. To survive in a competitive world, they must justify their existence to donors, secure new

---

105. Interview in North America with a senior CRS staffer, September 17, 2001.
106. For the importance of administrative overhead, see Raymond Bonner, "Post-Mortem for Charities: Compassion Wasn't Enough in Rwanda," *New York Times*, December 18, 1994, p. 3.
107. Alexander Cooley and James Ron, "Coming to the Aid of Afghan People," *Toronto Star*, October 29, 2001, p. A19; Alexander Cooley and James Ron, "Afghan Relief Business Bears Watching," *Baltimore Sun*, October 15, 2001, p. A11; and Barnett Rubin, "Putting an End to Warlord Government," *New York Times*, January 15, 2002, p. A21.

contracts, and fend off competitors. Under specific institutional conditions, these imperatives will produce dysfunctional results. In the 1990s scholars established the importance of transnational networks and organizations for global politics; now we should turn our attention to the material incentives shaping their actions.

Corporate Warriors | *P.W. Singer*

The Rise of the Privatized Military Industry and Its Ramifications for International Security

A failing government trying to prevent the imminent capture of its capital, a regional power planning for war, a ragtag militia looking to reverse its battlefield losses, a peacekeeping force seeking deployment support, a weak ally attempting to escape its patron's dictates, a multinational corporation hoping to end constant rebel attacks against its facilities, a drug cartel pursuing high-technology military capabilities, a humanitarian aid group requiring protection within conflict zones, and the world's sole remaining superpower searching for ways to limit its military costs and risks.[1] When thinking in conventional terms, security studies experts would be hard-pressed to find anything that these actors may have in common. They differ in size, relative power, location in the international system, level of wealth, number and type of adversaries, organizational makeup, ideology, legitimacy, objectives, and so on.

There is, however, one unifying link: When faced with such diverse security needs, these actors all sought external military support. Most important is where that support came from: not from a state or even an international organization but rather the global marketplace. It is here that a unique business form has arisen that I term the "privatized military firm" (PMF). PMFs are profit-driven organizations that trade in professional services intricately linked to warfare. They are corporate bodies that specialize in the provision of military skills—including tactical combat operations, strategic planning, intelligence gathering and analysis, operational support, troop training, and military technical assistance.[2] With the rise of the privatized military industry, actors in

P.W. Singer is an Olin Fellow in the Foreign Policy Studies Program at the Brookings Institution.

This article was written while the author was a fellow at the Belfer Center for Science and International Affairs at Harvard University. He would like to thank the BCSIA International Security Program, the MacArthur Transnational Security Program, Graham Allison, Robert Bates, Doug Brooks, Laura Donohue, Samuel Huntington, Susan Morrison, Benjamin Runkle, and the many military industry interviewees for their help in the research and writing process.

1. I am referring here to the Strasser regime in Sierra Leone, the Ethiopian military, the Croat army, the West African ECOMOG (Economic Community Cease-fire Monitoring Group) peacekeeping force, Papua New Guinea, British Petroleum, the Rodridguez cartel, Worldvision, and the United States.
2. Many analysts have referred to some of these new firms as "private military companies" (PMCs). This term, however, is used to describe only firms that offer tactical military services while ignoring firms that offer other types of military services, despite sharing the same causes,

the global system can access capabilities that extend across the entire military spectrum—from a team of commandos to a wing of fighter jets—simply by becoming a business client.

PMFs represent the newest addition to the modern battlefield, and their role in contemporary warfare is becoming increasingly significant. Not since the eighteenth century has there been such reliance on private soldiers to accomplish tasks directly affecting the tactical and strategic success of military engagement. With the continued growth and increasing activity of the privatized military industry, the start of the twenty-first century is witnessing the gradual breakdown of the Weberian monopoly over the forms of violence.[3] PMFs may well portend the new business face of war.

This is not to say, however, that the state itself is disappearing. The story is far more complex than that. The power of PMFs has been utilized as much in support of state interests as against them. As Kevin O'Brien writes, "By privatizing security and the use of violence, removing it from the domain of the state and giving it to private interest, the state in these instances is both being strengthened and disassembled."[4] With the growth of the privatized military industry, the state's role in the security sphere has become deprivileged, just as it has in other international arenas such as trade and finance.

The aim of this article is to introduce the privatized military industry. It seeks to establish a theoretical structure in which to study the industry and explore its impact on the overall risks and dynamics of warfare. The first section discusses the emergence and global spread of PMFs, their distinguishing features, and the reasons behind the industry's rise. The second section examines the organization and operation of this new player at the industry level of analysis (as opposed to the more common focus in the literature on individual firms). This allows the classification of the industry's key characteristics and variation. The third section offers a series of propositions that suggest potential consequences of PMF activity for international security. It also demonstrates how critical issue areas, such as alliance patterns and civil-military relations, must be reexamined in light of the possibilities and complications that this nascent industry presents.

---

dynamics, and consequences. The term private military firm is not only intended to be broader, and thus encompass the overall industry rather than just a subsector, but is also more theoretically grounded, pointedly drawing from the business economics "theory of the firm" literature.
3. Max Weber, *Theory of Social and Economic Organization* (New York: Free Press, 1964), p. 154.
4. Kevin O'Brien, "Military-Advisory Groups and African Security: Privatised Peacekeeping," *International Peacekeeping*, Vol. 5, No. 3 (Autumn 1998), p. 78.

The Emergence of the Privatized Military Industry

The activity and significance of the privatized military industry have grown tremendously in recent years, yet its full scope and long-term impact remain underrealized. This section explains the emergence of this phenomenon. It begins by exploring how widespread and important the PMF business has become. It then briefly examines the history of past profit-motivated actors in the military realm, with an eye toward establishing the distinguishing factors of this latest corporate form. Finally, it lays out the causal synergy of forces that led to the PMF industry's rise, including changes in the market of security after the end of the Cold War, transformations in the nature of warfare, and normative shifts toward privatization and broader outsourcing trends.

THE GLOBAL REACH OF THE PRIVATIZED MILITARY INDUSTRY
Since the end of the Cold War, PMF activity has surged around the globe. PMFs have operated in relative backwaters, key strategic zones, and rich and poor states alike (see Figure 1). In Saudi Arabia, for example, the regime's military relies almost completely on a multiplicity of firms to provide a variety of services—from operating its air defense system to training and advising its land, sea, and air forces. Even Congo-Brazzaville, with less strategic importance and wealth, once depended on a foreign corporation to train and support its military—in this case from the Israeli firm Levdan. PMFs have also influenced the outcomes of numerous conflicts. They are credited, for example, with being or having been determinate actors in wars in Angola, Croatia, Ethiopia-Eritrea, and Sierra Leone.

The privatized military industry's reach extends even to the world's remaining superpower. Every major U.S. military operation in the post–Cold War era (whether in the Persian Gulf, Somalia, Haiti, Zaire, Bosnia, or Kosovo) has involved significant and growing levels of PMF support. The 1999 Kosovo operations illustrate this trend. Before the conflict, PMFs supplied the military observers who made up the U.S. contingent of the international verification mission assigned to the province. When the air war began, other PMFs not only supplied the logistics and much of the information warfare aspects of the NATO campaign against the Serbs, but they also constructed and operated the refugee camps outside Kosovo's borders.[5] In the follow-on KFOR peacekeeping operation, PMFs expanded their role to include, for example, provision of

5. Craig A. Copetas, "It's Off to War Again for Big U.S. Contractor, " *Wall Street Journal*, April 14, 1999, p. A21.

Figure 1. The Global Activity of the Privatized Military Industry, 1991–2001.

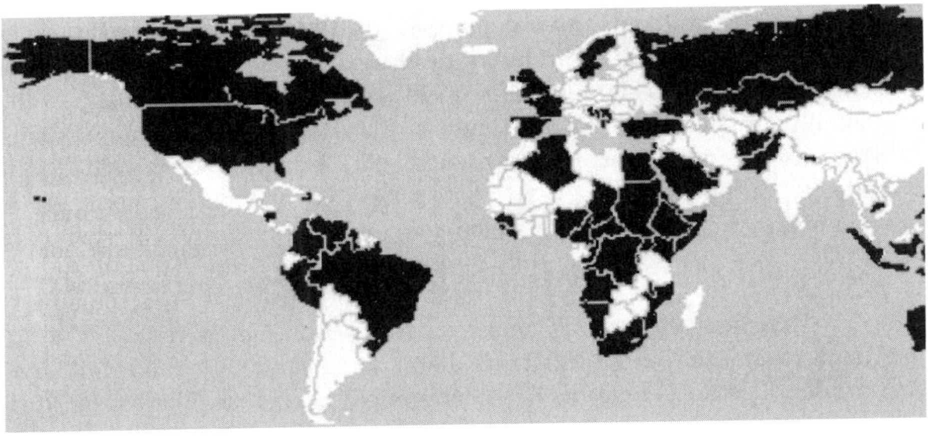

NOTE: Areas of PMF activity appear in bold.

critical aerial surveillance for the force.[6] The U.S. military has also employed PMFs to perform a range of other services—from military instruction in more than 200 ROTC programs to operation of the computer and communications systems at NORAD's Cheyenne Mountain base, where the U.S. nuclear response is coordinated.[7]

The general point is that individuals, corporations, states, and international organizations are increasingly relying on military services supplied not by public institutions but by the private market. Unfortunately, our understanding of this market is limited theoretically, conceptually, and even geographically. Much of what has been written on PMFs focuses on individual company case studies and is confined to specific regions (usually in Africa), not on the industry more broadly.[8] Moreover, there have been no theoretically grounded

---

6. Robert Wall, "Army Leases Eyes to Watch Balkans," *Aviation Week and Space Technology*, October 30, 2000, p. 68.
7. MPRI web site, http://www.mpri.com; and Steven Saint, "NORAD Outsources," *Colorado Springs Gazette*, September 1, 2000, p. A1.
8. Examples include David Isenberg, *Soldiers of Fortune Ltd.: A Profile of Today's Private Sector Corporate Mercenary Firms*, Center for Defense Information monograph, November 1997; David Shearer, *Private Armies and Military Intervention*, Adelphi Paper 316 (London: International Institute for Strategic Studies, February 1998); Peter Lock, "Military Downsizing and Growth in the Security Industry in Sub-Saharan Africa," *Strategic Analysis*, Vol. 22, No. 9 (December 1998), pp. 1393–1426; and Thomas Adams, "The New Mercenaries and the Privatization of Conflict," *Parameters*, Vol. 29, No. 2 (Summer 1999), pp. 103–116.

frameworks of analysis to elucidate the variation in PMF activities or their impact, no attempts to examine the industry from either an economic or a political perspective, no comparative analyses of PMFs with firms in other industries or within the PMF industry itself, and no explorations of what the presence of these firms signifies for security studies. In addition, much of the existing literature on the industry is highly polarized, aimed at either extolling PMFs or condemning their mere existence.[9] And because the firms and their opponents are usually focused on promoting their agendas, rather than on broadening understanding, they often misuse this literature for their own ends.

PRIVATE MILITARIES IN HISTORY: DISTINGUISHING THE CORPORATE WAVE

A general assumption about warfare is that it is engaged in by public militaries (i.e., armies of citizens) fighting for a common political cause. This assumption, however, is an idealization. Throughout history, participants in war have often been for-profit private entities, loyal to no one government. Indeed the state monopoly over violence is the exception in history rather than the rule.[10] Every empire, from Ancient Egypt to Victorian England, utilized contract forces. As Jeffrey Herbst notes, "The private provision of violence was a routine aspect of international relations before the twentieth century."[11]

In the grand scheme, the modern state is a relatively new form of governance, appearing only in the last 400 years, and did itself draw extensively from private military sources to consolidate its power.[12] Even in the modern period, when states began to predominate, organized private militaries remained active players. For example, the overwhelming majority of forces in the Thirty Years' War (1618–48) and the ensuing half-century of fighting were privately contracted, as were the generals who led them.[13] Like the post–Cold War period, the seventeenth century was a time of systemic transition, when

---

9. Examples include Doug Brooks, "Write a Cheque, End a War," *Conflict Trends*, No. 6 (July 2000), http://www.accord.org.za/web.nsf; Ken Silverstein, "Privatizing War," *Nation*, July 7, 1998, http://past.thenation.com/issue/970728/0728silv.htm; and Abdel-Fatau Musah and Kayode Fayemi, *Mercenaries: An African Security Dilemma* (London: Pluto Press, 2000).
10. Janice Thomson, *Mercenaries, Pirates, and Sovereigns: State Building and Extraterritorial Violence in Early Modern Europe* (Princeton, N.J.: Princeton University Press, 1994).
11. Jeffrey Herbst, "The Regulation of Private Security Forces," in Greg Mills and John Stremlau, eds., *The Privatisation of Security in Africa* (Pretoria: South Africa Institute of International Affairs, 1999), p. 117.
12. William H. McNeill, *The Pursuit of Power: Technology, Armed Force, and Society since A.D. 1000* (Chicago: University of Chicago Press, 1982).
13. Anthony Mockler, *Mercenaries* (London: Macdonald and Company, 1969), p. 14; and Fritz Redlich, *The German Military Enterpriser and His Work Force: A Study in European Economic and Social History* (Wiesbaden, Germany: Franz Steiner Verlag, 1964).

governments were weakened and military services were available on the open market. During the following era of colonial expansion, trading entities such as the Dutch and English East Indies Companies operated as near-sovereign powers, commanding armies and navies larger than those in Europe, negotiating their own treaties, governing their own territory, and even minting their own money.[14] These firms dominated in non-European areas considered beyond the accepted boundaries of the sovereign system, such as on the Indian subcontinent, where local capabilities were weak and transnational companies the most efficiently organized units to be found—again, similar to many areas of the world today.

By the twentieth century, the state system and the concept of state sovereignty had spread across the globe. Norms against private armies had begun to build in strength as well. Once organized into large integrated enterprises, the primary players in the private military trade became freelancing ex-soldiers (what we conceive of today as mercenaries), motivated essentially by personal gain. Mercenaries, it should be noted, are conventionally understood to be individual-based in unit of operation and thus ad hoc in organization (*Les Affreux*, the Terrible Ones, of the Congo conflict in the 1960s are the archetype). They work for only one client and, focused as they are on combat, provide only one service: guns for hire. Although their trade is technically banned by international law, mercenaries remain active in nearly every ongoing conflict. But because of their ad hoc nature, they lack cohesion and discipline, and thus their strategic impact is limited.[15]

Today's PMFs represent the evolution of private actors in warfare. The critical analytic factor is their modern corporate business form. PMFs are hierarchically organized into incorporated and registered businesses that trade and compete openly on the international market, link to outside financial holdings, recruit more proficiently than their predecessors, and provide a wider range of military services to a greater variety and number of clients. Corporatization not only distinguishes PMFs from mercenaries and other past private military ventures, but it also offers certain advantages in both efficiency and effectiveness.

---

14. James Tracey, *The Rise of Merchant Empires* (New York: Cambridge University Press, 1990), p. 39.
15. John Keegan, "Private Armies Are a Far Cry from the Sixties Dogs of War," *Electronic Telegraph*, May 13, 1998, http://www.telegraph.co.uk; Gus Constantine, "Mercenaries' Roles Different since Cold War," *Washington Times*, March 6, 1997, p. A13; and Anthony Mockler, *The New Mercenaries: The History of the Hired Soldier from the Congo to the Seychelles* (London: Sidgewick and Jackson, 1985).

PMFs operate as companies first and foremost, focusing on their relative advantages in the provision of military services. As business units, they are often tied through complex financial arrangements to other firms, both within and beyond their own industry. Many of the most active firms—such as MPRI (which boldly proclaims in its advertisements to have "the greatest corporate assemblage of military expertise in the world"), Armorgroup, and Vinnell—are subsidiaries of larger corporations listed on public stock exchanges. For military-oriented multinational corporations (MNCs) such as Dyncorp and TRW, the addition of military services to their list of offerings helps them to maintain profitability in times of shrinking public contracts. For companies such as mining and energy MNCs that are not directly involved in security issues, links with PMFs provide an effective way to manage their political risks abroad.

Corporatization also means that PMFs are business profit-, rather than individual profit-, driven endeavors. Instead of relying on the ad hoc, black-market structuring and payment system associated with mercenaries, PMFs maintain permanent corporate hierarchies. As a result, they can make use of complex corporate financing—ranging from the sale of stock shares to intrafirm trade—and can engage in a wider variety of deals and contracts. In comparison, mercenaries tend to demand payment in hard cash and cannot be relied on beyond the short term. Thus for PMFs, it is not the people who matter but the structure they are within. A number of PMF employees have also been mercenaries at one time or another. However, the processes of their hire, their relationships to clients, and their impacts on conflicts were all very different when they worked for military firms.

Also unlike mercenaries, privatized military firms compete on the open global market. PMFs are considered legal entities that are contractually bound to their clients. In many cases, they are at least nominally tied to their home states through laws requiring registration and licensing of foreign contracts. Rather than denying their existence, as many mercenaries do, most PMFs publicly advertise their services, including on the World Wide Web.[16]

Finally, PMFs offer a much wider array of services to a greater variety of clients than do mercenaries. As one executive notes, PMFs are "structured organizations with professional and corporate hierarchies. . . . We cover the full spectrum—training, logistics, support, operational support, post-conflict reso-

16. See, for example, http://www.airscan.com/, http://www.icioregon.com/, http://www.mpri.com, http://www.sandline.com, and http://www.vinnell.com.

lution."[17] Moreover, PMFs can work for multiple clients in multiple markets/theaters at once—something mercenaries could never do.

REASONS BEHIND MILITARY PRIVATIZATION

The confluence of three momentous dynamics—the end of the Cold War and the vacuum this produced in the market of security, transformations in the nature of warfare, and the normative rise of privatization—created a new space and demand for the establishment of the privatized military industry. Importantly, few changes appear to loom in the near future to counter any of these forces. As such, the industry is distinctly representative of the changed global security environment at the start of the twenty-first century.

THE GAP IN THE MARKET OF SECURITY. Massive disruptions in the supply and demand of capable military forces after the end of the Cold War provided the immediate catalyst for the rise of the privatized military industry. With the end of superpower pressure from above, a raft of new security threats began to appear after 1989, many involving emerging ethnic or internal conflicts. Likewise, nonstate actors with the ability to challenge and potentially disrupt world society began to increase in number, power, and stature. Among these were local warlords, terrorist networks, international criminals, and drug cartels. These groups reinforce the climate of insecurity in which PMFs thrive, creating new demands for such businesses.[18]

Another factor is that the Cold War was a historic period of hypermilitarization. Its end thus sparked a chain of military downsizing around the globe. In the 1990s, the world's armies shrank by more than 6 million personnel. As a result, a huge number of individuals with skill sets uniquely suited to the needs of the PMF industry, and who were often not ready for the transition to civilian life, found themselves looking for work. Complete units were cash-

---

17. Timothy Spicer, founder of Sandline and now chief executive officer of SCI, quoted in Andrew Gilligan, "Inside Lt. Col. Spicer's New Model Army," *Sunday Telegraph*, November 22, 1998, p. A1.
18. Many groups are also suspected of having benefited from hiring some of the industry's more unsavory private firms. Examples include Angolan rebels and certain Mexican and Colombian drug cartels. The increased activity of PMFs also illustrates that many of these firms have no compunction about challenging state interests, even those of great powers, as long as the price is right. André Linard, "Mercenaries SA," *Le Monde Diplomatique*, August 1998, p. 31, http://www.monde diplomatique.fr/1998/08/Linard/10806.html; Christopher Goodwin, "Mexican Drug Barons Sign Up Renegades from Green Berets," *Sunday Times*, August 24, 1997, p. A1; Patrick J. Cullen, "Keeping the New Dogs of War on a Tight Leash," *Conflict Trends*, No. 6 (July 2000), http://www.accord.org.za/publications/ct6/issue6.htm; and Xavier Renou, "Promoting Destabilization and Neoliberal Pillage," paper presented at the Globalization and Security Conference, University of Denver, Colorado, November 11, 2000.

iered, and many of the most elite units (such as the South African 32d Reconnaissance Battalion and the Soviet Alpha special forces unit) simply kept their structure and formed their own private companies. Line soldiers were not the only ones left jobless; it is estimated that 70 percent of the former KGB joined the industry's ranks.[19] Meanwhile, massive arms stocks opened up to the market: Machine guns, tanks, and even fighter jets became available to anyone who could afford them.[20] Thus downsizing fed both supply and demand, as new threats emerged and demobilization created fresh pools of PMF labor and capital.

At the same time, the ability of states to respond to many of today's threats has declined. Shorn of their superpower support, a number of states have suffered breakdowns in governance. This has been particularly true in developing areas, where many regimes possess sovereignty in name only and lack any real political authority or capability.[21] The result has been failing states and the emergence of new areas of instability. Given their often poorly organized local militaries and police forces, the security apparatuses of these regimes can be exceptionally deficient, resulting in near military vacuums. Moreover, the almost complete absence of functioning state institutions has meant that outsiders have begun to assume a wider range of political roles customarily reserved for the state. Among these is the provision of security.[22]

The traditional response for dealing with areas of instability used to be outside intervention, typically by one of the great powers. The end of the Cold War, however, reordered these states' security priorities. The great powers are no longer automatically willing to intervene abroad to restore stability. Devoid of ideological or imperial value, conflicts in many developing regions have ceased to pose serious threats to the national interests of these powers. In addition, public support is more difficult to garner unless there is a clear national security threat. As a result, intervention into potential quagmires against diffuse enemies has become less palatable and the potential costs less bearable. Unless strong domestic support can be built, casualty figures beyond single digits are routinely seen as a political, and thus a military, defeat.[23]

19. Lock, "Military Downsizing and Growth in the Security Industry in Sub-Saharan Africa."
20. Bonn International Center for Conversion, *An Army Surplus—The NVA's Heritage,* BICC Brief No. 3 (1997), http://www.bicc.de/weapons/.
21. Examples range from Albania and Afghanistan to Somalia and Sierra Leone. Robert H. Jackson, *Quasi-states: Sovereignty, International Relations, and the Third World* (New York: Cambridge University Press, 1990).
22. William Reno, *Warlord Politics and African States* (London: Lynne Rienner, 1998).
23. James Adams, *The Next World War: Computers Are the Weapons and the Front Line Is Everywhere* (New York: Simon and Schuster, 1998), p. 279.

PMFs aim to fill this void. They are eager to present themselves as businesses with a natural niche in an often-complicated, post–Cold War world order. As one company executive explains, "The end of the Cold War has allowed conflicts long suppressed or manipulated by the superpowers to re-emerge. At the same time, most armies have gotten smaller and live footage on CNN of United States soldiers being killed in Somalia has had staggering effects on the willingness of governments to commit to foreign conflicts. We fill the gap."[24]

TRANSFORMATIONS IN THE NATURE OF WARFARE. Concurrent with the reordering of the security market are two other critical underlying trends. First, warfare itself has been undergoing revolutionary change at all levels. At high-intensity levels of conflict, the military operations of great powers have become more technologic and thus more reliant on civilian specialists to run their increasingly sophisticated military systems. At low-intensity levels, the primary tools of warfare have not only diversified but, as stated earlier, have become more available to a broader array of actors. Increasingly, the motivations behind many conflicts in the developing world are either criminalized or driven by the profit motive in some way. Both directly and indirectly, these parallel changes have heightened demand for services provided by the privatized military industry.

Until recently, wars were decided by Clausewitzian clashes of great numbers of men fighting on extended fronts. With the growing access to sophisticated technology, however, strategic consequences can now be achieved by relative handfuls, sometimes even by individual soldiers not on the battlefield. According to this concept of the "revolution in military affairs," the nature of the professional soldier and the execution of high-intensity warfare is changing.[25] Fewer individuals are doing the actual fighting, while massive support systems are required to maintain the world's most modern forces.

The requirements of high-technology warfare have also dramatically increased the need for specialized expertise, which often must be drawn from the private sector. For example, recent U.S. military exercises reveal that its Army of the Future will be unable to operate without huge levels of technical and logistics support from private firms.[26] Other advanced powers are also set-

---

24. Timothy Spicer, quoted in Gilligan, "Inside Lt. Col. Spicer's New Model Army," p. A1.
25. "The RMA Debate" web site at http://www.comw.org/rma/bib.html, hosted by the Project on Defense Alternatives, is an excellent resource on this issue.
26. Adams, *The Next World War*, p. 113; and Steven J. Zamparelli, "Contractors on the Battlefield: What Have We Signed Up For?" U.S. Air War College Research Report, March 1999, http://www.au.af.mil/au/database/research/ay1999/awc/99-254.htm.

ting out to privatize key military services. Great Britain, for instance, recently contracted out its aircraft support units, tank transport units, and aerial refueling fleet—all of which played vital roles in the 1999 Kosovo campaign.[27] Another change in the postmodern battlefield requiring greater civilian involvement is the growing importance of information dominance (particularly when the military's ability to retain individuals with highly sought-after and well-paying information technology skills is well-nigh impossible). As one expert notes, "The U.S. army has concluded that in the future it will require contract personnel, even in the close fight area, to keep its most modern systems functioning. This applies especially to information-related systems. Information-warfare, in fact, may well become dominated by mercenaries."[28]

At the same time, the motivations behind warfare also seem to be in flux. This has been particularly felt at low-intensity levels of conflict, where weak state regimes are facing increasing challenges on a variety of fronts. The state form triumphed centuries ago because it was the only one that could harness the men, machinery, and money required to take full advantage of the tools of warfare.[29] This monopoly of the nation-state, however, is over. As a result of changes in the nature of weapons technology, individuals and small groups can now easily purchase and wield relatively massive amounts of power. This plays out in numerous ways, the most disruptive of which may be the global spread of cheap infantry weapons, the primary tools of violence in low-intensity warfare. Their increased ease of use and devastating potential are reshaping local balances of power. Almost any group operating inside a weak state can now acquire at least limited military capabilities, thus lowering the bar for creating viable threats to the status quo.[30]

Importantly, this shift encourages the proliferation and criminalization of local warring groups. According to Stephen Metz, "With enough money anyone can equip a powerful military force. With a willingness to use crime, nearly anyone can generate enough money."[31] As a result, conflicts in a number of places (Colombia, Congo, Liberia, Tajikistan, etc.) have lost any of the ideologi-

27. Simon Sheppard, "Soldiers for Hire," *Contemporary Review*, August 1999, http://www.findarticles.com/m2242/1603_275/55683933/p1/article.jhtml.
28. Adams, "The New Mercenaries and the Privatization of Conflict," p. 115.
29. Charles Tilly, ed., *The Formation of National States in Western Europe* (Princeton, N.J.: Princeton University Press, 1975).
30. Michael Klare, "The Kalashnikov Age," *Bulletin of the Atomic Scientists*, Vol. 55, No. 1 (January/February 1999), http://www.bullatomsci.org/issues/1999/jf99/jf99klare.html.
31. Stephen Metz, *Armed Conflict in the Twenty-first Century: The Information Revolution and Postmodern Warfare*, Strategic Studies Institute report (Carlisle, Pa.: U.S. Army War College, April 2000), p. 24, http://carlisle-www.army.mil/usassi/ssipubs/pubs2000/conflict/conflict.htm.

cal motivation they once possessed and instead have degenerated into conflicts among petty groups fighting to grab local resources. Warfare itself thus becomes self-perpetuating, as violence generates personal profit for those who wield it most effectively (which often means most brutally), while no one group can eliminate the others.[32] PMFs thrive in such profit-oriented conflicts, either working for these new conflict groups or reacting to the humanitarian disasters they create.

THE POWER OF PRIVATIZATION AND THE PRIVATIZATION OF POWER. Finally, the last few decades have been characterized by a normative shift toward the marketization of the public sphere. As one analyst puts it, the market-based approach toward military services is "the ultimate representation of neoliberalism."[33]

The privatization movement has gone hand in hand with globalization: Both are premised on the belief that the principles of comparative advantage and competition maximize efficiency and effectiveness. Fueled by the collapse of the centralized systems in the Soviet Union and in Eastern Europe, and by successes in such places as Thatcherite Britain, privatization has been touted as a testament to the superiority of the marketplace over government. It reflects the current assumption that the private sector is both more efficient and more effective. Harvey Feigenbaum and Jeffrey Henig sum up this sentiment: "If any economic policy could lay claim to popularity, at least among the world's elites, it would certainly be privatization."[34] Equally, in modern business, outsourcing has become a dominant corporate strategy and a huge industry in its own right. Global outsourcing expenditures will top $1 trillion in 2001, having doubled in just the past three years alone.[35]

Thus, turning to external, profit-motivated military service providers has become not only a viable option but the favored solution for both public institutions and private organizations. The successes of privatization programs and outsourcing strategies have given the market-based solution not only the stamp of legitimacy, but also the push to privatize any function that can be

---

32. Max Singer and Aaron Wildavsky, *The Real World Order: Zones of Peace/Zones of Turmoil* (Chatham, Mass.: Chatham House, 1993); Michael Ignatieff, *The Warrior's Honor: Ethnic War and the Modern Conscience* (New York: Holt and Company, 1997); and Janice Gross Stein, Michael Bryans, and Bruce Jones, *Mean Times: Humanitarian Action in Complex Political Emergencies—Stark Choices, Cruel Dilemmas* (Toronto: University of Toronto Program on Conflict Management and Negotiations, 1999).
33. Kevin O'Brien, "Military-Advisory Groups and African Security: Privatised Peacekeeping," *International Peacekeeping*, Vol. 5, No. 3 (Autumn 1998), p. 89.
34. Harvey Feigenbaum and Jeffrey Henig, "Privatization and Political Theory," *Journal of International Affairs*, Vol. 50, No. 2 (Winter 1997), p. 338.
35. "Outsourcing 2000," *Fortune*, May 29, 2000, pullout section.

handled outside government. As a result, the momentum of privatization has spread to areas that were once the exclusive domain of the state. The last decade, for example, was marked by the cumulative externalization of functions that were once among the nation-state's defining characteristics, including those involving schools, welfare programs, prisons, and defense manufacturers (e.g., Aerospatiale in France and British Aerospace). In fact, the parallel to military service outsourcing is already manifest in the domestic security market, where in states as diverse as Britain, Germany, the Philippines, Russia, and the United States, the number of private security forces and the size of their budgets greatly exceed those of public law-enforcement agencies.[36]

That the norm of privatization would cross into the realm of military services is not surprising. As Sinclair Dinnen notes, "The current revival in private military security is broadly consistent with the prevailing orthodoxy of economic rationalism, with its emphasis on 'downsizing' government and large-scale privatization."[37] The privatized military industry has thus drawn on precedents, models, and justifications from the wider "privatization revolution," allowing private firms to become potential, and perhaps even the preferred, providers of military services.

Organization and Operation of the Privatized Military Industry

This section explores the structure of the privatized military marketplace. It then develops a system of classification that captures the key internal variation of this marketplace.

INDUSTRY CHARACTERISTICS

The privatized military industry is not an overly capital-intensive sector, particularly compared to such traditional industries as manufacturing. Nor does it require the heavy investment needed to maintain a public military structure (which ranges from bases in important congressional districts to untouchable pension plans). The barriers to entry are relatively low, as are the economies of scale. Whereas state militaries require regular, substantial budget outlays

---

36. For example, the U.S. security industry has grown dramatically in the last decade, with three times as many persons employed by private security firms than by public law-enforcement agencies and $22 billion more being spent in the private sphere than in the public sector. Edward J. Blakely and Mary Gail Snyder, *Fortress America: Gated Communities in the United States* (Washington, D.C.: Brookings, 1997), p. 126.
37. Sinclair Dinnen, "Trading in Security: Private Security Contractors in Papua New Guinea," in Dinnen, Ron May, and Anthony J. Regan, eds., *Challenging the State: The Sandline Affair in Papua New Guinea* (Canberra: National Centre for Development Studies, 1997), p. 11.

to sustain themselves, PMFs need only a modicum of financial and intellectual capital. All the necessary tools are readily available on the open market, often at bargain prices from the international arms bazaar. The labor input—predominantly former soldiers with skill sets unique to the industry—is also relatively inexpensive and widely available. Spurring their recruitment is the comparatively low pay and declining prestige of many state militaries: PMF employees tend to receive two to ten times as much as they did in the military, often allowing the best and brightest to be lured away with relative ease.

The expansion of the privatized military industry has been acyclical, with revenues continually rising. This is another way of saying that economic and political crises are fueling demand beyond the sector itself. The secretive nature of the industry prevents exact data collection, but best estimates suggest annual revenues of as much as $200 billion. Over the next few years, revenues are expected to increase about 85 percent in industrial countries and 30 percent in developing countries, a further indication of the industry's robust health and growing power.[38]

Many PMFs operate as "virtual companies." Similar to internet firms that limit their expenditure on fixed (brick and mortar) assets, most PMFs do not maintain standing forces but rather draw from databases of qualified personnel and specialized subcontractors on a contract-by-contract basis.[39] This globalization of resource allocation builds greater efficiency with less operational slack.

The overall number of firms in the industry is in the high hundreds, with market caps ranging from a few hundred thousand dollars to 20 billion dollars. A rapid consolidation of the industry into larger transnational firms, however, is under way. The 1997 merger of the London-based Defense Systems Limited with the U.S. firm Armor Holdings and the purchase of MPRI by L-3 in 2000 exemplify this trend. Having made twenty global acquisitions in the last three years, Armor Holdings is notable for having been named among *Fortune* magazine's 100 fastest-growing companies in both 1999 and 2000, one of the few non-high-technology firms to do so.[40]

---

38. Lock, "Military Downsizing and Growth in the Security Industry in Sub-Saharan Africa"; Gumisai Mutume, "Private Military Companies Face Crisis in Africa," *Inter Press Service*, December 11, 1998; and correspondence with investment firm analysts, September 2000. Despite the lack of transparency, we can determine some subsector revenues, such as the $400 million mine countermeasures market and the $2 billion spent on privatized military training within the United States in 1999.
39. "Can Anybody Curb Africa's Dogs of War?" *Economist*, January 16, 1999, pp. 41–42.
40. "100 Fastest-Growing Companies," *Fortune*, September 2000, http://www.fortune.com/fortune/fastest/csnap/0,7130,45,00.html.

Figure 2.   The "Tip of the Spear" Typology: PMFs Distinguished by Range of Services and Force Levels.

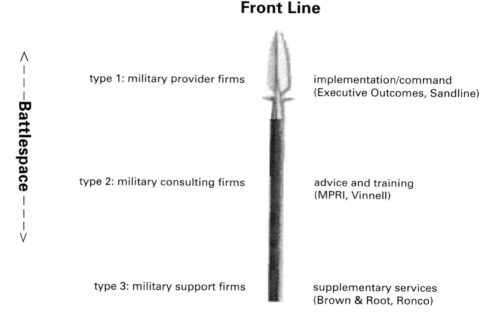

The reason for this industry consolidation centers on the global branding necessary to compete in the world market. Large international companies have social capital and established records that allow them to increase their market share rapidly, while more easily offering a wider range of services to tackle complex security situations. There remains a niche, however, for aggressive smaller firms that can make informal deals that bigger firms cannot. Such companies can more easily insinuate themselves into the political networks of local regimes or utilize the barter system of payment. Larger firms, with their highly scrutinized accounting procedures and close monitoring by institutional investors, are restricted from engaging in such practices.

INDUSTRY CLASSIFICATION: THE TIP-OF-THE-SPEAR TYPOLOGY

Not all PMFs look alike, nor do they serve the same market. The privatized military industry is organized according to the range of services and levels of force that its firms are able to offer. Figure 2 illustrates the organization of firm types, drawn in part from an analogy prevalent in military thought—the "tip of the spear" metaphor. According to this typology, units in the armed forces are distinguished by their location in the battlespace in terms of level of impact, training, prestige, and so on. Importantly, this categorization is also correlated with how business chains in the outsourcing industry as a whole break down, thus allowing useful cross-field parallels and lessons to be drawn. The industry is divided into three types: (1) military provider firms, (2) military consulting firms, and (3) military support firms.

TYPE 1. Military provider firms focus on the tactical environment. They offer services at the forefront of the battlespace, engaging in actual fighting or direct command and control of field units, or both. In many cases, they are utilized as "force multipliers," with their employees distributed across a client's force to provide leadership and experience. Clients of type 1 firms tend to be those with comparatively low military capabilities facing immediate, high-threat situations. PMFs such Executive Outcomes and Sandline that offer special forces–type services are classic examples of military provider firms. Other firms with battlefield capabilities include Airscan, which can perform aerial military reconnaissance. Nonmilitary corollaries to type 1 firms include sales brokers, who represent manufacturers that have outsourced their retail forces, and "quick fill" contractors in the computer programming industry.

TYPE 2. Military consulting firms provide advisory and training services. They also offer strategic, operational, and organizational analysis that is often integral to the function or restructuring of armed forces. Their ability to bring to bear a greater amount of experience and expertise than almost any standing force can delegate on its own represents the primary advantage of military consulting firms over in-house operations. MPRI, for example, has on call the skill sets of more than 12,000 former military officers, including four-star generals.

The critical difference between type 1 and type 2 firms is the "trigger finger" factor; the task of consultants is to supplement the management and training of their clients' military forces, not to engage in combat. Although type 2 firms can reshape the strategic and tactical environments, the clients bear the final battlefield risks. Type 2 customers are usually in the midst of force restructuring or aiming for a transformative gain in capabilities. Their needs are not as immediate as those of type 1 clients, and their contract requirements are longer term and often more lucrative. Examples of type 2 firms include Levdan, Vinnell, and MPRI. The best nonmilitary corollaries are management consultants, with similar subsector divisions. Some firms, such as McKinsey, focus on strategic issues (as does MPRI) while others, such as Accenture, focus on more technical issues (as does SAIC).

TYPE 3. Military support firms provide rear-echelon and supplementary services. Although they do not participate in the planning or execution of direct hostilities, they do fill functional needs that fall within the military sphere—including logistics, technical support, and transportation—that are critical to combat operations. The most common clients of type 3 firms are those engaged in immediate, but long-duration, interventions (i.e., standing forces and organizations requiring a surge capacity).

Whereas type 1 and type 2 firms tend to resemble what economists refer to as "free-standing" companies (i.e., companies originally established for the purpose of utilizing domestic capital advantages to serve targeted external markets), type 3 firms bear a greater similarity to traditional MNCs.[41] Seeking to maximize their established commercial capabilities, these firms typically expand into the new military support market after having achieved dominance in their earlier ventures. For example, Ronco, which was once only a development assistance company, has moved into demining. Meanwhile, the Brown & Root Services division of Halliburton, which originally focused on domestic construction for large-scale civilian projects, has found the military engineering sector to be profitable as well. Brown & Root has augmented U.S. forces in Somalia, Haiti, Rwanda, and Bosnia, and most recently secured a $1 billion contract to support U.S. forces in Kosovo. Besides the dual-market firms listed above, civilian corollaries to type 3 firms include supply-chain management firms.

Implications of the Privatized Military Industry for International Security

Although there have been numerous descriptions of PMFs and their activities, propositions about the consequences of the privatized military industry for international security are meager. Questions such as what types of firms are likely to cause what kinds of consequences, and under what conditions, are largely undiscussed. This section offers a series of general hypotheses that highlight some of the potential impacts of this industry on international security.[42] Each is deductively sound; has survived plausibility probes; and in most

---

41. Mira Wilkins, *The Free-Standing Company in the World Economy, 1830–1996* (Oxford: Oxford University Press, 1998), p. 3.
42. This approach consciously mimics the productive paths taken by Robert Jervis and Stephen Van Evera in explicating the impacts of misperception and nationalism on international security. Jervis, "Hypotheses on Misperception," in Robert J. Art and Jervis, eds., *International Politics: Anarchy, Force, Political Economy, and Decision Making*, 2d ed. (Glenview, Ill.: Scott Foresman, 1985),

cases has anecdotal or historical support, or both. Taken together they set the stage for further empirical examination and, in some cases, generate policy prescriptions. Finally, they suggest explanations and predictions that a conventional security studies approach, not taking into account the potential impact of the industry, cannot generate.

The likely consequences of PMF activity fall into three broad categories, each briefly analyzed below (see also Table 1). The first subsection examines the introduction of business contractual dilemmas into the security environment. The second investigates the potential impact of military market dynamics and disruptions on security relations. The third explores the policy impact of PMFs acting as alternative military actors.

CONTRACTUAL DILEMMAS
The pull between economic incentives and political exigency has created a variety of intriguing dilemmas for the privatized military industry. At issue are divided loyalties and different goals. Clear tensions exist between a PMF client's security objectives and a firm's desire to maximize profit. Put another way, the public good and a private company's good often conflict. A firm may claim that it will act only in its client's best interests, but this may not always be true. Because in these arrangements the locus of judgment shifts from the client to the PMF, the PMF becomes the agent enacting decisions critical to the security of the principal. Thus, in many cases a distinctive twist on conventional principal-agent concerns emerges. In addition, concerns that arise in any normal contracting environment—for example, incomplete information and monitoring, loss of control, and the difficulties of aligning incentives—are further complicated when the business takes place within the military environment.

INCOMPLETE INFORMATION AND MONITORING DIFFICULTIES. Problems of incomplete information and monitoring generally accompany any type of outsourcing. These difficulties are intensified in the military realm, however, because few clients have experience in contracting with security agents. In most cases, there is either little oversight or a lack of clearly defined requirements, or both. Add in the fog of war, and proper monitoring becomes extremely difficult. Moreover, PMFs are usually autonomous and thus require extraterritorial monitoring, which is always problematic. And at times, the actual con-

---

pp. 510–526; and Van Evera, "Hypotheses on Nationalism and War," *International Security*, Vol. 18, No. 4 (Spring 1994), pp. 5–39.

Table 1. The Impact of the Privatized Military Industry on International Security.

Hypotheses	Effects by Firm Type	Conflicts Involving PMFs
1. The privatized military industry introduces contractual dilemmas into international security.		
A. Military outsourcing heightens incomplete information and monitoring difficulties.	Cheating—1, 2, 3 Performance at less than peak efficiency/ Prolonged conflict—1, 3	Bosnia, Ethiopia, Haiti, Kosovo
B. Military outsourcing risks critical losses of control.	Cut and run—1, 3 Takeover/defection—1	Congo, Persian Gulf, Sierra Leone
C. Military outsourcing introduces novel incentive measures.	Faustian bargains—1 Strategic privatization—1	Angola, Papua New Guinea, Sierra Leone
2. The privatized military industry introduces market dynamics and disruptions into international security.		
A. The market makes power more fungible.	Easier to initiate war—1, 2, 3 Surge capacity—1, 3 Force multiplier—1, 2, 3	Croatia, Ethiopia, Kosovo, Saudi Arabia
B. A dynamic market complexifies the balance of power.	Balance less predictable—1, 2 Deterrence more intricate—1, 2 Arms control more difficult—1, 2	Congo, Croatia, Ethiopia
C. The market alters alliance behavior.	Shifts patron-client relations—1, 2, 3 Burden sharing less necessary—1, 3 New forms of military assistance—1, 2	Bosnia, Croatia, Macedonia, Papua New Guinea
D. The market empowers nonstate actors.	Antistate groups able to access state-like capabilities—1, 2, 3 International organizations less restricted by member state shortfalls—1, 3	Angola, Congo, Colombia, East Timor, Liberia
E. The market affects the respect for human rights within conflicts.	Moral hazard, adverse selection, and diffusion of responsibility vs. market constraints and reputational concerns—1, 2	Angola, Croatia, Peru, Sierra Leone
3. The privatized military industry introduces alternative military actors into the policymaking process.		
A. PMFs alter local civil-military balances.	Threatens balance by displacement, jealousy concerns—1, 2 Reinforces balance through profession-alization, focus, deterrence—1, 2, 3	Croatia, Nigeria, Papua New Guinea, Sierra Leone
B. PMFs may be used to circumvent public policy limitations.	Executive branch evades legislative limits—2, 3 Use of policy proxies may backfire—1, 2	Bosnia, Colombia, Sierra Leone, United States

sumer may not be the contracting party: Some states, for example, pay PMFs to supply personnel on their behalf to international organizations.

Another difficulty is the firms' focus on the bottom line: PMFs may be tempted to cut corners to increase their profits. No matter how powerful the client, this risk cannot be completely eliminated. During the Balkans conflict, for example, Brown & Root is alleged to have failed to deliver or severely overcharged the U.S. Army on four out of seven of its contractual obligations.[43]

A further manifestation of this monitoring difficulty is the danger that PMFs may not perform their missions to the fullest. PMFs have incentives not only to prolong their contracts but also to avoid taking undue risks that might endanger their own corporate assets. The result may be a protracted conflict that perhaps could have been avoided if the client had built up its own military forces or more closely monitored its private agent. This was certainly true of mercenaries in the Biafra conflict in the 1970s, and many suspect that this was also the case with PMFs in the Ethiopia-Eritrea conflict in 1997–99. In the latter instance, the Ethiopians essentially leased a small but complete air force from the Russian aeronautics firm Sukhoi—including Su-27 jet fighter planes, pilots, and ground staff. Some contend, though, that this private Russian force failed to prosecute the war fully—for example, by rarely engaging Eritrea's air force, which itself was rumored to have hired Russian and Ukrainian pilots.[44]

A CRITICAL LOSS OF CONTROL. As PMFs become increasingly popular, so too does the danger of their clients becoming overly dependent on their services. Reliance on a private firm means that an integral part of one's strategic success is vulnerable to changes in market costs and incentives. This dependence can result in two potential risks to the security of the client: (1) the agent (the firm) might leave its principal (the client) in the lurch, or (2) the agent might gain dominance over the principal.

A PMF may have no compunction about suspending its contract if a situation becomes too risky in either financial or physical terms. Because they are typically based elsewhere, and in the absence of applicable international laws to enforce compliance, PMFs face no real risk of punishment if they or their employees defect from their contractual obligations. Industry advocates dismiss these claims by noting that firms failing to fulfill the terms of their con-

---

43. Two others were partially taken over by U.S. military personnel, and the remaining one was given to another company. General Accounting Office, *Contingency Operations: Opportunities to Improve the Logistics Civil Augmentation Program*, GAO/NSIAD-97-63, February 1997; and Gregory Piatt, "Balkans Contracts Too Costly," *European Stars and Stripes*, November 14, 2000, p. 4.
44. Kevin Whitelaw, "The Russians Are Coming," *U.S. News and World Report*, March 15, 1999, p. 46; and Adams, "The New Mercenaries and the Privatization of Conflict."

tracts would sully their reputation, thus hurting their chances of obtaining future contracts. Nevertheless, there are a number of situations in which short-term considerations could prevail over long-term market punishment. In game-theoretic terms, each interaction with a private actor is *sui generis*. Exchanges in the international security market may take the form of one-shot games rather than guaranteed repeated plays.[45] Sierra Leone faced such a situation in 1994, when the type 1 firm that it had hired (the Gurkha Security Guards, made up primarily of Nepalese soldiers) lost its commander in a rebel ambush. Reports suggest that the commander was later cannibalized. The firm decided to break its contract, and its employees fled the country, leaving its client without an effective military option until it was able to hire another firm.[46]

The loss of direct control as a result of privatization carries risks even for strong states. For U.S. military commanders, an added worry of terrorist targeting or the potential use of weapons of mass destruction is that their forces are more reliant than ever on the surge capacity of type 3 support firms. The employees of these firms, however, cannot be forced to stay at their posts in the face of these or other dangers.[47] Because entire functions such as weapons maintenance and supply have become completely privatized, the entire military machine would break down if even a modest number of PMF employees chose to leave.

In addition to sometimes failing to fulfill their contractual obligations, type 1 firms may pose another risk. In weak or failed states, PMFs, which are often the most powerful force on the local scene, may take steps to protect their own interests. Thus early termination of a contract, dissatisfaction with the terms of payment, or disagreements over specific orders could lead to unpleasant repercussions for a weak client. Indeed the corporate term "hostile takeover" may well take on new meaning when speaking of the privatized military industry. The precedent does exist—from the *condottieri*, who took over their client regimes in the Middle Ages, to participants in the 1969 Mercenary Revolt in Zaire. More recently, there is continued suspicion that in 1996 Executive Outcomes helped to oust the leader of Sierra Leone, head of the regime that had hired it, in favor of a local general with whom the firm's executives had a better working relationship.[48]

---

45. Avinash K. Dixit and Susan Skeath, *Games of Strategy* (New York: W.W. Norton, 1999), pp. 259–263.
46. The firm has since lost most of its business. As for its employees in Sierra Leone, they must have been happy just to have made it out alive.
47. Zamparelli, "Contractors on the Battlefield."
48. Confidential interviews, spring 2001.

NOVEL INCENTIVE MEASURES. Another risk of outsourcing is that a firm's motivations for fighting may differ from those of its client. This is particularly a problem for clients that contract type 1 firms. These clients are often those most in need yet least able to pay and thus at the highest risk of default. In a number of cases, this imbalance has led to the creation of curious structures that attempt to align client and firm incentives. In a sort of Faustian bargain, a client locks in a firm's loyalties by mortgaging valuable public assets, usually to business associates of the PMF. This often takes place through veiled privatization programs.[49] To be paid, a firm must protect its new, at-risk assets, effectively tying its fortunes to those of its client. This was how cash-poor regimes in Angola, Papua New Guinea, and Sierra Leone allegedly compensated their PMFs—specifically, by selling off mineral and oil rights to related companies. Rebel groups in Sierra Leone and Angola are also rumored to have reached similar arrangements with rival corporations. In the long term, however, potentially valuable resources for the nation as a whole are lost forever to meet short-term exigencies.

"Strategic privatization," in which the asset being traded as payment is located within an opponent's territory (e.g., a lucrative mine), provides an added variation. Even if during an intrastate conflict the regime is not in military control of certain public assets, as the internationally recognized sovereign, it can still legally privatize and sell them to a PMF or its associates in return for the PMF's services. In this case, the PMF must then seek out and attack the government's opponent in order to secure payment. This represents a modern parallel to Michael Doyle's notion of "imperialism by invitation," whereby parties that control ties to the international market acquire more power than their local rivals.[50] The Angolan government has been most effective in using this strategy, selling concessions that have placed mining companies and their type 1 protectors astride its opponent's lines of communication, thus adding to the government's recent strategic gains.

These are only a few of the complications to consider when outsourcing military services. Other questions include: How would bankruptcies or mergers affect the continuation of services to a client? What would happen in the event of a foreign takeover of the parent company if the new owners are opposed to a PMF's operations? Would an optimum strategy for a losing opponent be a financial takeover of the corporate boardroom rather than

49. Khareen Pech and Yusef Hassan, "Sierra Leone's Faustian Bargain," *Weekly Mail and Guardian*, May 20, 1997, p. 1.
50. Michael W. Doyle, *Empires* (Ithaca, N.Y.: Cornell University Press, 1986).

engagement on the battlefield? Each scenario leads to different empirical expectations other than using one's own military, and each requires internally focused contractual monitoring mechanisms to address such contingencies.

MARKET DYNAMICS AND DISRUPTIONS

A standard conception of international security is that states are the only relevant actors in world politics. Other players are discounted as not having strategic relevance in both political calculations and conflict outcomes.[51] This conception, however, does not anticipate what happens when states are operating in a real market with all its dynamic shifts and uncertainties, rather than within a simplified microeconomic model (such as the "state as microeconomic firm" model that neorealism uses to derive its findings).[52] Military market dynamics and disruptions can potentially complexify international security. When military powers are no longer exclusively sovereign states but include "interdependent players caught in a network of trans-national transactions," familiar concepts such as the simplified "balance of power" lose some of their analytical muscle.[53]

Some might argue that the rise of the privatized military industry represents no great change for international security; rather, the industry is merely another resource that states can use to enhance their power. Although true in the sense that states can benefit from hiring PMFs, this claim ignores the fact that the privatized military industry is also an independent, globalized supplier operating beyond any one state's domain. State and nonstate actors alike, including MNCs and even drug cartels, can access formerly exclusive state military capabilities. Where state structures are weak, the result is a direct challenge to the local basis of sovereign authority. Even when PMFs are hired by strong states, the locus of judgment can shift beyond these states' control and their military agents' motivations can become warped, with all of the change and uncertainty that these processes entail. The very act of military outsourcing also runs counter to other key tenets of international relations

---

51. John J. Mearsheimer, "The False Promise of International Institutions," *International Security*, Vol. 19, No. 3 (Winter 1994/95), pp. 5–49.
52. Kenneth N. Waltz, *Theory of International Politics* (New York: McGraw-Hill, 1979); and Richard D. Auster and Morris Silver, *The State as a Firm: Economic Forces in Political Development* (Boston: Martinus Nijhoff, 1979).
53. Jean-Marie Guéhenno, "The Impact of Globalisation on Strategy," *Survival*, Vol. 40, No. 4 (Winter 2000), p. 6.

theory, such as the assertion that states seek to maximize their power through self-sufficiency in order to minimize their reliance on others.[54]

The following five subsections explore the interplay of the marketization of violence and the overall global security environment. Each considers an area in which the dynamics of and potential disruptions from a marketplace that includes PMFs might affect international security. These are (1) the ability of PMFs to transform limited economic power into military might, (2) the complications they present for estimating the balance of power, (3) the changes that the market offers for alliance relations, (4) PMFs' ability to empower nonstate actors, and (5) the impact of PMFs on the respect for human rights.

THE NEW FUNGIBILITY OF POWER. The military privatization phenomenon means that military resources are available on the open market. Where once the creation of a military force required huge investments in both time and resources, today the entire spectrum of conventional forces can be obtained in a matter of weeks, if not days. The barriers to acquiring military strength are thus lowered, making power more fungible than ever. For example, economically rich but population-poor states such as those in the Persian Gulf now hire PMFs to achieve levels of power well beyond what they otherwise could. The same holds for new states and even nonstate groups that lack the institutional support or expertise to build capable military forces. With the help of PMFs, not only can clients add to their existing military forces and obtain highly specialized capacities (e.g., expertise in information warfare), but they may even be able to skip a whole generation of war skills. The result, however, may be a return to the dynamics of sixteenth-century Europe, where wealth and military capability went hand in hand: *Pecunia nervus belli* (Money nourishes war).[55]

This ability to transform money into force also means a renewal of Kantian fears over the dangers of lowering the costs of war. Economic assets can now be rapidly transformed into military threats, making economic power more threatening, which runs contrary to liberalist assumptions Likewise, modern liberalism tends to assume only what is positive about the profit motive. It views the spread of capitalism and globalism as diminishing the incentives for

---

54. Waltz, *Theory of International Politics*, p. 88; and Andrew L. Ross, "Arms Acquisition and National Security: The Irony of Military Strength," in Edward E. Azar and Chun-in Moon, eds., *National Security in the Third World: The Management of Internal and External Threats* (Hants, Nova Scotia: Edward Elgar, 1988), p. 154.
55. Or as the French put it, *Pas d'argent, pas de Suisses!* (No money, no Swiss! referring to the common mercenary units of the sixteenth century). Michael Howard, *War in European History* (London: Oxford University Press, 1976), p. 38.

violent conflict and the rise of global civil society as an immutable good thing.[56] The emergence of a new type of private transnational firm that relies instead on the existence of conflict for its profits counters the assumption that nonstate actors are generally peace orientated.

NEW COMPLEXITIES IN THE BALANCE OF POWER. The privatized military industry lies beyond any one state's control. Further, the layering of market uncertainties atop the already-thorny issue of net assessment creates a variety of complications for determining the balance of power, particularly in regional conflicts. Calculating a rival's capabilities or force posture has always been difficult. In an open market, where the range of options is even more variable, likely outcomes become increasingly hard to discern. As the Serbs, Eritreans, Rwandans, and Ugandans (whose opponents hired PMFs prior to successful offensives) all learned, not only can once-predictable deterrence relationships rapidly collapse, but the involvement of PMFs can quickly and perhaps unexpectedly tilt local balances of power.

In addition, arms races could move onto the open market and begin to resemble instant bidding wars. (In the Ethiopia-Eritrea conflict, a new spin on the traditional arms race emerged when both countries competed first on the global military leasing market before taking to the battlefield.) The result is that the pace of the race is accelerated, and "first-mover" advantages are heightened. Indeed such changes could well influence the likelihood of war initiation.[57] Conventional arms control is also made more difficult with the existence of this market, because actual force capacities can be lowered without reducing the overall threat potential.

On the other hand, the privatized military industry can act to reduce the tendency toward conflict in certain situations. The announcement of the hiring of a PMF, for example, may make adversaries think twice about initiating war or be more apt to settle an ongoing conflict, by changing the expected costs of victory.[58] Effective corporate branding might thus have a deterrent effect. Like-

56. Jessica Mathews, "Power Shift: The Rise of Global Civil Society," *Foreign Affairs*, Vol. 76, No. 1 (January/February 1997), pp. 50–66; Richard Rosecrance, "A New Concert of Powers," *Foreign Affairs*, Vol. 71. No. 2 (Spring 1992), pp. 64–82; and Norman Angell, *The Great Illusion*, 2d ed. (New York: G.P. Putnam's Sons, 1933), pp. 33, 59–60, 87–89.
57. Randolph Siverson and Paul Diehl, "Arms Races, the Conflict Spiral, and the Onset of War," in Manus I. Midlarsky, ed., *Handbook of War Studies* (Boston: Unwin Hyman, 1989), pp. 195–218; Samuel P. Huntington, "Arms Races: Prerequisites and Results," in Robert J. Art and Kenneth N. Waltz, *The Use of Force: Military Power and International Politics* (Lanham, Md.: University Press of America, 1988), pp. 637–647; and Stephen Van Evera, *The Causes of War: Power and the Roots of Conflict* (Ithaca, N.Y.: Cornell University Press, 1999), especially chaps. 2, 3.
58. James D. Fearon, "Rationalist Explanations for War," *International Organization*, Vol. 49, No. 3 (Summer 1995), pp. 379–414.

wise, hiring races in one region might suppress potential races elsewhere, by reducing slack in the market and raising the price for services.

ALLIANCE BEHAVIOR PRIVATIZED. During and after the Cold War, the relationships between strong states (patrons) and weaker, security-dependent states (clients)—often located in the developing world—have been critical.[59] The control that patrons have exerted over their clients has usually resulted from a bargain, whereby the patrons provide military aid and advisers necessary to their clients' security. This support, however, comes at a price. As Olav Stokke notes, it is "used as a lever to promote objectives set by the donor, which the recipient government would not have otherwise agreed to."[60]

Accessibility to the privatized military market fundamentally alters this patron-client relationship. Instead of having to accede to the demands of their patrons, weaker states can now purchase the military skills, training, and capabilities that they need for their security on the open market. As a result, the patron's leverage is diminished,[61] and by becoming clients of a different sort, weaker states are no longer bound by their patrons' prerogatives. Papua New Guinea, for example, hired a PMF in 1997 when its patron, Australia, attempted to restrict its military assistance because of human rights concerns. As explained by Papua New Guinea's prime minister, "We have requested the Australians support us in providing the necessary specialist training and equipment. . . . They have consistently declined and therefore I had no choice but to go to the private sector."[62]

Studies of alliance behavior also point to functional differentiation as a method of institutionalizing alliances.[63] Traditionally, states in alliances have divided up their military tasks, making them more dependent on one another

---

59. Stephen R. David, "Explaining Third World Alignment," *World Politics*, Vol. 43, No. 2 (January 1991), pp. 233–256; and Jack S. Levy and Michael M. Barnett, "Alliance Formation, Domestic Political Economy, and Third World Security," *Jerusalem Journal of International Relations*, Vol. 14, No. 4 (December 1992), pp. 19–40.

60. Olav Stokke, "Aid and Political Conditionality: Core Issues and the State of the Art," in Stokke, ed., *Aid and Political Conditionality* (London: Frank Cass, 1995), p. 12.

61. For a more in-depth study of this point, see Christopher Spearin, "The Commodification of Security and Post–Cold War Patron Client Balancing," paper presented at the Globalization and Security Conference, University of Denver, Colorado, November 11, 2000.

62. Julius Chan, quoted in Sinclair Dinnen, "Militaristic Solutions in a Weak State: Internal Security, Private Contractors, and Political Leadership in Papua New Guinea," *Contemporary Pacific*, Vol. 11, No. 2 (Fall 1999), p. 286. As explored in the section on alterations in the civil-military balance, Papua New Guinea gained the outside support that it sought, but at the price of prompting an army mutiny.

63. Celeste A. Wallander and Robert O. Keohane, "Risk, Threat, and Security Institutions," in Helga Haftendorn, Keohane, and Wallander, *Imperfect Unions: Security Institutions over Time and Space* (Oxford: Oxford University Press, 1999).

in the process. Now PMFs can perform some of these tasks, thus decreasing this reliance and perhaps weakening the ties that bind allied states. For example, if an ally defects or chooses not to participate in a military action, its tactical functions could instead be performed by a PMF. As another illustration, many of the capacities that NATO members rely on the United States to supply for external deployment (e.g., lift capacity, logistics, and even intelligence gathering and analysis) could be adequately supplied by type 3 firms, perhaps by the very firms that already supply these functions to the U.S. military. As a result, allied states may be less restrained by a potential veto on their out-of-area operations than is generally assumed.

The PMF market also makes available new forms of aid and alliances. Because PMFs allow the easy transformation of financial resources into military might, allies can provide military aid in the guise of simple cash infusions. For example, in 1995, after the war in the former Yugoslavia, moderate Arab states wanted to assist the Bosnian Muslim government and at the same time counter the radicalizing influence of Iranian military aid. They did so not by sending their own military personnel to the region but rather by paying a PMF—MPRI—to train the Bosnian army. The rationale for this new form of aid is that it lowers potential risks for donors by reducing the likelihood of their becoming embroiled in their allies' fighting. In addition, the pool of possible donors of military assistance need no longer be restricted to states. With an equal ability to pay, nonstate actors—including even rich individuals—can become valuable allies, able to bolster local forces and even tilt military balances from a distance.[64]

NONSTATE ACTORS EMPOWERED. The unrestricted access to military services ushered in by the rise of the privatized military industry has clearly enhanced the role of nonstate groups, which at one time had been at a significant disadvantage in a system dominated by states. PMFs provide these groups with new options and new paths to power not imagined until very recently. As a result, states may eventually become like dinosaurs toward the end of the Cretaceous period: powerful but cumbersome, not yet superseded, but no longer the unchallenged masters of their environment.[65]

Some PMF executives contend that their firms work just for states, and more specifically, only for those with reputable governments. They argue that PMFs

---

64. An example is Rakesh Saxena, a private businessman who in 1997, while under indictment for stealing money from the Thai central bank, financed the Sandline operation in Sierra Leone that helped to defeat the local rebel-military coup alliance.
65. Metz, *Armed Conflict in the Twenty-first Century,* p. 13.

will not do business with unsavory customers because it could harm their ability to obtain future contracts. Both the structure of the market and the record so far, however, argue against this. Much the way that PMFs may decide to break contracts for their own interests, under certain conditions high, single-shot payoffs might prove too great a temptation in client choice. In the current unregulated market, the firms decide for whom they work. Thus far, they have contracted with all types of clients, the only limitation being the affordability of their services.

Itinerate type 1 firms having difficulty succeeding in a competitive market are the most likely to work with violent nonstate entities. Rebel groups in Angola, Sierra Leone, and Congo have all contracted with type 1 PMFs to receive training and assistance in the use of advanced military technologies. International criminal organizations, including Colombian drug cartels, are also reported to have paid for assistance in counterintelligence, electronic warfare, and the use of sophisticated weaponry from what might be referred to as "rogue firms." One such firm, Hod Hahanit, which was staffed by former Israeli army officers, even trained Colombian paramilitaries who were later involved in the assassination of two Colombian presidential candidates and the bombing of a civilian airliner.[66] The increased military capabilities of these and other nonstate groups have had other consequences, including a widening of conflicts and a lessening of weak states' ability to put down internal opposition.

Perhaps less pernicious, the market also offers a greater array of military options for more reputable nonstate actors. Normally, the intervention options of international and regional organizations are limited by the weaknesses of their member states. The use of type 1 and type 3 firms, however, can compensate for such shortfalls, allowing these organizations to undertake operations that they would not be able to otherwise. Take, for instance, ECOWAS, an organization of relatively poor West African states whose militaries are severely limited in certain specializations considered critical for external intervention, particularly air support and logistics. In both Liberia and Sierra Leone, ECOWAS forces were nonetheless able to deploy, primarily because of assistance from PMFs such as International Charters. Likewise, United Nations operations, already growing dependent on type 3 firms for logistics, air transport, demining,

---

66. The firm's president was later fined $13,400 by an Israeli court. Linard, "Mercenaries SA"; Goodwin, "Mexican Drug Barons"; Cullen, "Keeping the New Dogs of War on a Tight Leash"; "Who Is Yair Klein and What Is He Doing in Colombia and Sierra Leone?" *Democracy NOW!* program, Pacifica Radio, June 1, 2000; and Peace Brigades International, *Informacion Catorce Dias*, February 23–March 8, 1998.

and security consultation, have been urged by some PMF industry advocates to hire type 1 firms to act as "enforcers" in stiffening the backs of threatened UN peacekeeping forces.[67] If hired, such firms would likely be able to supply much more capable military personnel, but any gains in efficiency come at the risk of increasing problems of control, monitoring, and defection.

HUMAN RIGHTS AND THE MARKET. Certain tensions also exist regarding the impact of PMFs on the respect for human rights during conflict. On one hand, PMFs point to particular market incentives for engaging in good behavior: Their long-term profits are partly dependent on their public image. PMFs also emphasize the positive impact that they might have in helping to professionalize local forces or in supplanting client forces that cannot end conflicts.

Issues of moral hazard, adverse selection, and the potential for the diffusion of responsibility, however, battle with these positive proclivities. Just as in other areas of commerce, war is a business in which nice firms do not always finish first. Thus PMF aspirations of corporate responsibility and the desire to cultivate a "good guy" image may be overridden by the need to fulfill a contract or by the desire to be seen as the kind of firm "that gets things done." In other words, considerations of the commonweal are matters of morality, while the bottom line is fundamentally amoral.

Thus, although it is incorrect to assume that PMFs kill just for money, there are certain situations in which human rights may be transgressed for the corporate interest. Possible examples include Executive Outcomes personnel using indiscriminate force in Sierra Leone and Angola.[68] The firm is also known to have used fuel air explosives (FAEs or vacuum bombs) in its Angola operations.[69] International bodies regard the use of FAEs as a transgression against human rights, because they inflict particularly torturous injuries and are prone to indiscriminate use.[70] But they are also highly effective, which explains why a firm would choose to use them.

---

67. Brooks, "Write a Cheque, End a War"; and Jonathan Broder, "Mercenaries: The Future of U.N. Peacekeeping?" *Fox News*, June 26, 2000. Transcript available at http://www.foxnews.com/world/062300/un_broder.sml.

68. Musah and Fayemi, *Mercenaries: An African Security Dilemma*; Xavier Reneou, "Promoting Destabilization and Neoliberal Pillage: The Utilization of Private Military Companies for Peacekeeping and Peace Enforcement Activities in Africa," paper presented at the Globalization and Security Conference, University of Denver, Colorado, November 11, 2000; and Elizabeth Rubin, "An Army of One's Own," *Harper's*, February 1997, pp. 44–55.

69. Alex Vines, "Mercenaries and the Privatisation of Security in Africa in the 1990s," in Mills and Stremlau, *The Privatization of Security in Africa*, p. 54.

70. With the destructive power comparable to a low-yield nuclear weapon, an FAE releases a fuel-infused blast that ruptures the lungs, killing victims in an excruciatingly painful manner. Human Rights Watch, "Backgrounder on Russian Fuel Air Explosives," February 2000, http://www.hrw.org/press/2000/02/chech0215b.htm.

There may also be an adverse selection mechanism at work in the industry that attracts disreputable players looking for the cover of legitimacy. PMFs provide a new outlet for individuals who may be naturally drawn to mercenary work or have been forced out of the public sphere. It is not reassuring, for example, that many of the major actors in the Iran-Contra illegal arms trade and the BCCI bank fraud scandals are currently affiliated with the industry. As employers, PMFs want to hire individuals who will be effective, even if this sometimes means casting a blind eye on past human rights abuses. As a result, many members of the most ruthless military and intelligence units once affiliated with either the communist regime in the Soviet Union or the apartheid regime in South Africa have found employment in the industry. Even when firms scrupulously screen prospective employees (which is easier said than done, given that most CVs do not have an "atrocities committed" section), it is still difficult to monitor troops in the field. If employees do commit violations, there is little incentive for firms to report them. A firm that does so risks scaring off both clients and prospective employees.

The ultimate problem with PMFs is that they diffuse responsibility. Questions about who monitors, regulates, and punishes employees or companies that go astray are still to be fully answered. That many of these firms are chartered in offshore accounts complicates matters even further. Traditionally, a state's security institutions are responsible for enforcing the laws within its sovereign territory. However, it is usually the very weakness of these institutions that results in the hire of a PMF. Furthermore, even if external legal action or sanction were attempted, it is doubtful whether any firm would ever allow its employees to be tried in a weak client state's judicial system.[71]

Moreover, even when a PMF operates with good intent, there is no assurance that its employees and their military skills will not be used in ways unanticipated by either the PMF or its client. For example, a number of soldiers in the Croatian army who received MPRI military training subsequently resigned to join the rebel Kosovo Liberation Army (KLA). Among those who resigned was the KLA's commander. Many of these same soldiers have since become involved in the Macedonian conflict across the border.

In sum, privatization provides no greater assurance of moral military behavior. It may even produce countervailing incentives. Just as state institutions can serve both good and evil ends, so too can PMFs.

---

71. For example, Dyncorp employees implicated in facilitating prostitution rings in Bosnia were spirited away to avoid local prosecution. Antony Barnett and Solomon Hughes, "British Firm Accused in UN 'Sex Scandal,'" *Guardian*, July 29, 2001, p. A1; and private correspondence, May 2000.

THE POLICY IMPACT OF ALTERNATIVE MILITARY ACTORS
The rise of the privatized military industry suggests that government agencies are no longer the exclusive mechanism for executing foreign and military policy. In effect, PMFs provide a neoliberal "third way" in the military sphere. This new variable could affect the civil-military balance and result in new means to evade public policy restrictions.

ALTERATIONS IN THE CIVIL-MLITARY BALANCE. Civil-military relations theory is a story of institutional balance, where proper civilian control over the military vies with military professionals' need for autonomy to do their jobs properly.[72] The privatized military industry represents a third-party influence on this balance.

The case of Sandline's operation in Papua New Guinea illustrates how PMFs can alter the traditional civil-military balance. As noted earlier, in 1997 the beleaguered government of Papua New Guinea hired Sandline to help defeat a local rebellion after its ally Australia refused to help. As payment, the government sold off a valuable mine inside rebel territory that it had privatized without public authorization. Before Sandline could fully deploy, however, Papua New Guinea's regular army, which itself had not been paid in months, returned to barracks in a mutiny over the contract. The government was toppled and the contract terminated.

Variation in the impact of PMFs on civil-military relations is determined by firm type and the timing of their deployment. Types 1 and 2 tend to pose the greatest threat to the institutional balance, because they supplant core military positions and functions. In particular, the hire of PMFs would be destabilizing if any of the following conditions applies: (1) their line employees receive higher pay than local soldiers for performing similar tasks, (2) clients provide PMF employees with vastly better equipment, (3) these employees are kept separate and distinct from local forces, or (4) PMF officers are placed in command positions, or their presence blocks normal promotion tracks. PMFs are particularly attractive to vulnerable leaders, because they make possible the removal of politically unreliable or untrustworthy military officers. Of course, local militaries know this and may seek to preempt such action if PMFs are slow to deploy.

72. Kenneth W. Kemp and Charles Hudlin, "Civilian Supremacy over the Military: Its Nature and Limits," *Armed Forces and Society*, Vol. 19, No. 1 (Fall 1992), pp. 7–26; and Samuel P. Huntington, *The Soldier and the State: The Theory and Politics of Civil-Military Relations* (Cambridge, Mass.: Harvard University Press, 1957).

Under certain conditions, PMFs can help to stabilize the civil-military balance. During an impending breakdown in civil-military relations, for example, the quick insertion of a type 1 PMF can tilt the balance of power toward the civilian side by helping to deter or defeat a military coup (Executive Outcomes stopped at least two coups in Sierra Leone in 1996). In peacetime, type 2 firms may engage in long-term restructuring programs designed to bring militaries under greater civilian control. For example, MPRI's contract with the Nigerian government is intended both to help build up the local military's esprit de corps and to strengthen civilian oversight mechanisms. Although they have less direct influence than the other types of PMFs, type 3 firms can reinforce the civil-military balance in a limited way. By assuming certain tasks, they can pull local officers out of functional areas such as logistics and supply that often lend themselves to corruption, which not surprisingly complicates civil-military relations. By limiting the military to more core military tasks, type 3 firms also help to distinguish between the scope of civilian expertise and that of the military profession.

SKIRTING OF PUBLIC POLICY LIMITATIONS. Another rationale for outsourcing is political expediency. In the United States, for example, the executive branch has used private military means to circumvent limits placed on it by the legislature or by public opinion. This proposition applies to all three firm types, but with vastly different ramifications. Much of the push behind the use of type 3 firms by the U.S. military in recent contingency operations resulted from two factors: congressional limits on troop numbers and the reluctance of the Clinton administration to deal with the potential political costs of calling up the National Guard and Reserves, who otherwise would have been required.[73] Although using private military support to circumvent legislative limits was technically against Congress's mandate, no members objected because it was in keeping with their original intent to minimize the number of U.S. troops put at risk (e.g., 9,000 fewer U.S. troops deployed in Bosnia because of military support outsourcing). Recourse to type 1 and type 2 PMFs can have more negative implications for the democratic principle of checks and balances, however. It may allow the executive branch to gain too much autonomy and power, which could lead to the authorization of public-private activities against the intent of Congress.

---

73. General Accounting Office, "Contingency Operations"; and Col. Donald T. Wynn, "Managing the Logistics-Support Contract in the Balkans Theater," *Engineer*, July 2000, http://call.army.mil/call/trngqtr/tq4–00/wynn.htm.

The rationale for using PMFs instead of official covert action is that they give the cover of plausible deniability that public forces lack. If an operation goes awry, the activities of a firm are easier for a government to deny and the blame simpler to shift. The current involvement of U.S.-based PMFs in the civil war in Colombia illustrates this point. Dyncorp is officially engaged there in "antidrug" operations. However, the firm utilizes armed reconnaissance planes and helicopter gunships, designed for counterguerrilla warfare, and has been involved in several firefights with local rebels. Dyncorp has lost several planes and employees to rebel fire, but there has been no public outcry in response to these losses.[74]

Another possible advantage of using PMFs is that it may allow the executive branch to avoid public debate or legislative controls, and therefore undertake what it sees as a much more "rational" foreign policy.[75] As Arthur S. Miller avers, however, this is not always for the best: "Democratic government is *responsible* government—which means *accountable* government—and the essential problem in contracting out is that responsibility and accountability are greatly diminished." He goes on the say that the use of private firms places "the influence over, and sometimes even control of, important decisions one step further away from the public and their elected representatives."[76]

Without public debate and monitoring, the actions of PMFs not only may prove embarrassing but could have far more negative repercussions. In Colombia, for example, Airscan has been implicated in coordinating the bombing of a village in which eighteen civilians (including nine children) were killed. And in Peru, employees of Aviation Development Corporation who were working on aerial surveillance operations for the U.S. Central Intelligence Agency mistakenly directed the shoot down of a private passenger plane that was later found to be carrying a family of missionaries. An American mother and her seven-month-old daughter were killed in the attack.[77] In addition, PMF operations might backfire and ultimately involve the client in direct

74. Tod Robberson, "Shedding Light on a Dark War," *Dallas Morning News*, May 3, 2001, p. A1, http://www.dallasnews.com/world/355876_andean_03int.A.html; and Jeremy McDermott, "U.S. Crews Involved in Colombian Battle," *Scotsman*, February 23, 2001, p. A1.

75. Theodore Lowi, "Making Democracy Safe for the World: On Fighting the Next War," in G. John Ikenberry, ed., *American Foreign Policy: Theoretical Essays* (New York: HarperCollins, 1989), pp. 258–292.

76. Quoted in John D. Hanrahan, *Government by Contract* (New York: W.W. Norton, 1983), p. 317 (emphasis in original).

77. William Arkin, "The Underground Military," *Washington Post*, May 7, 2001, p. A1, http://www.washingtonpost.com/wp-dyn/articles/A44024-2001May4.html; and Karl Penhaul, "Americans Blamed in Colombia Raid," *San Francisco Chronicle*, June 15, 2001, p. A1, http://www.sfgate.com/cgibin/article.cgi?file?/c/a/2001/06/15/MN219178.DTL.

fighting without the requisite public debate. Many worry, for example, that the extensive use of private firms in dubious operations in Colombia risks widening the war there. As one congressional staffer put it, "What you have here is a 1964 model of Vietnam."[78]

Conclusion

The privatized military industry entered the security arena only recently, but it has already created a host of new opportunities and challenges. States, international institutions, nonstate organizations, corporations, and even individuals can now lease military capabilities from the global market. This change will affect international relations in critical ways, ranging from the introduction of market dynamics and disruptions into security relations to the policy impact of alternative military agents. It may also necessitate far-reaching reassessments in both policymaking and theory building.

In terms of policy, just as Western militaries recently had to develop a system for working with NGOs during humanitarian operations, so too they should begin to consider how to deal with PMFs, which they will increasingly encounter in the field. At the decisionmaking level, governments and international organizations must develop standard contracting policies and establish vetting and monitoring systems attuned to PMFs, including the assurance of legislative oversight. A policy that defers to the market will not curb threats to peace.

The rise of this new security actor also opens up a variety of theoretical pathways for future research. Most fundamental, the emergence of PMFs challenges one of the basic premises of the study of international security: that states possess a monopoly over the use of force and that the study of security can therefore be based on the principle that states constitute the sole unit of analysis. Outdated assumptions about the exclusive role of the state in the military sphere should be reexamined. A broadening of civil-military theory to allow for the influence of third parties is an example of how this can be done without threatening the core of the theory. Similarly, consideration of the impact of the broader military outsourcing market would make theories of deterrence, conventional arms races, and conflict formation more reflective of the real world. Likewise, corporate branding and marketing might well become relevant in future conflicts and thus merit research from a security perspective.

---

78. Quoted in Joshua Hammer and Michael Isikoff, "The Narco-Guerilla War," *Newsweek*, August 9, 1999, p. 42.

In sum, the rise of the privatized military industry raises possibilities and dilemmas that are not only compelling and fascinating in an academic sense but are also driven by real-world relevance. It is thus paramount that our understanding of this new player in international security continues to be developed.

Suggestions for Further Reading

I. General

Ayoob, Mohammed. *The Third World Security Predicament: State Making, Regional Conflict, and the International System.* Boulder, Colo.: Lynne Rienner Publishers, 1995.

Baldwin, David A. "Security Studies and the End of the Cold War," *World Politics,* Vol. 48, No. 1 (October 1995), pp. 117–141.

Betts, Richard K. "Should Strategic Studies Survive?" *World Politics,* Vol. 50, No. 1 (October 1997), pp. 7–33.

Brown, Michael E., ed. *Grave New World: Security Challenges in the 21st Century.* Washington, D.C.: Georgetown University Press, 2003.

Buzan, Barry, Ole Wæver, and Jaap de Wilde. *Security: A New Framework for Analysis.* Boulder, Colo.: Lynne Rienner Publishers, 1998.

Carter, Ashton B., William J. Perry, and John D. Steinbruner. *A New Concept of Cooperative Security.* Washington, D.C.: Brookings Institution, 1992.

Crocker, Chester A., Fen Osler Hampson, and Pamela Aall, eds. *Turbulent Peace: The Challenges of Managing International Conflict.* Washington, D.C.: U.S. Institute of Peace Press, 2001.

Croft, Stuart, and Terry Terriff, eds. *Critical Reflections on Security and Change.* London: Frank Cass & Co., 2000.

Cusimano, Maryann K., ed. *Beyond Sovereignty: Issues for a Global Agenda.* New York: Wadsworth, 2000.

Fawcett, Louise, and Yezid Sayigh, eds. *The Third World beyond the Cold War: Continuity and Change.* Oxford: Oxford University Press, 1999.

Finel, Bernard I., and Kristin M. Lord, eds. *Power and Conflict in the Age of Transparency.* New York: Palgrave Macmillan, 2000.

Freedman, Lawrence. "International Security: Changing Targets?" *Foreign Policy,* No. 110 (Spring 1998), pp. 48–63.

Harkavy, Robert E., and Stephanie G. Neuman. *Warfare and the Third World.* New York: Palgrave Macmillan, 2001.

Huntington, Samuel P. *The Clash of Civilizations and the Remaking of the World Order.* New York: Simon & Schuster, 1996.

Inbar, Efraim, and Gabriel Sheffer, eds. *The National Security of Small States in a Changing World.* London: Frank Cass, 1997.

de Jonge Oudraat, Chantal, and P.J. Simmons, eds. *Managing Global Issues: Lessons Learned.* Washington, D.C.: Carnegie Endowment for International Peace, 2001.

Kolodziej, Edward A. "Renaissance in Security Studies? Caveat Lector!" *International Studies Quarterly,* Vol. 36, No. 4 (December 1992), pp. 421–438.

Kugler, Richard L., and Ellen L. Frost, eds. *The Global Century: Globalization and National Security,* two volumes. Washington, D.C.: National Defense University Press, 2001.

Mathews, Jessica T. "Redefining Security," *Foreign Affairs,* Vol. 68, No. 2 (Spring 1989), pp. 162–177.

McNeill, William. *The Pursuit of Power: Technology, Armed Force, and Society since A.D. 1000.* Chicago: University of Chicago Press, 1982.

Mearsheimer, John J. *The Tragedy of Great Power Politics*. New York: W.W. Norton, 2001.

Miller, Steven E. "*International Security* at Twenty-Five: From One World to Another," *International Security*, Vol. 26, No. 1 (Summer 2001), pp. 5–39.

Nye, Joseph S. Jr. and Sean M. Lynn-Jones. "International Security Studies: A Report of a Conference on the State of the Field," *International Security*, Vol. 12, No. 4 (Spring 1988), pp. 5–27.

Schultz, Richard H. Jr., Roy Godson, and George H. Quester, eds. *Security Studies for the 21ˢᵗ Century*. Washington, D.C.: Brassey's, 1997.

Ullman, Richard H. "Redefining Security," *International Security*, Vol. 8, No. 1 (Summer 1983), pp. 129–153.

Walt, Stephen P. "The Renaissance of Security Studies," *International Studies Quarterly*, Vol. 35, No. 2 (June 1991), pp. 211–239.

Waltz, Kenneth N. "Structural Realism after the Cold War," *International Security*, Vol. 25, No. 1 (Summer 2000), pp. 5–41.

Wolfers, Arnold. "'National Security' as an Ambiguous Symbol," *Political Science Quarterly*, Vol. 67, No. 4 (December 1952), pp. 481–502.

II. Weapons and Security

Allison, Graham T., Owen R. Coté Jr., Richard A. Falkenrath, and Steven E. Miller. *Avoiding Nuclear Anarchy: Controlling the Threat of Loose Russian Nuclear Weapons and Fissile Material*. Cambridge, Mass.: MIT Press, 1996.

Bohlen, Avis. "The Rise and Fall of Arms Control," *Survival*, Vol. 45, No. 3 (Autumn 2003), pp. 7–34.

Boutwell, Jeffrey, and Michael T. Klare, eds. *Light Weapons and Civil Conflict: Controlling the Tools of Violence*. Lanham, Md.: Rowman and Littlefield, 1999.

Brodie, Bernard, and Fawn M. Brodie, *From Crossbow to H-Bomb*, revised edition. Bloomington, Ind.: Indiana University Press, 1973.

Campbell, Kurt. "Nuclear Proliferation beyond Rogues," *Washington Quarterly*, Vol. 26, No. 1 (Winter 2002–03), pp. 7–15.

Chyba, Christopher. "Toward Biological Security," *Foreign Affairs*, Vol. 81, No. 3 (May–June 2002), pp. 122–136.

Cirincione, Joseph, ed. *Repairing the Regime: Preventing the Spread of Weapons of Mass Destruction*. New York: Routledge, 2000.

Croddy, Eric. *Chemical and Biological Warfare: A Comprehensive Survey for the Concerned Citizen*. New York: Copernicus Books, 2001.

Durch, William J. *Constructing Regional Security: The Role of Arms Transfers, Arms Control, and Reassurance*. New York: Palgrave Macmillan, 2000.

Feiveson, Harold A., ed. *The Nuclear Turning Point: A Blueprint for Deep Cuts and De-Alerting of Nuclear Weapons*. Washington, D.C.: Brookings Institution, 1999.

Husbands, Jo L. "The Proliferation of Conventional Weapons and Technologies," in Michael E. Brown, ed., *Grave New World: Security Challenges in the 21ˢᵗ Century*. Washington, D.C.: Georgetown University Press, 2003, pp. 62–90.

Johnson, Dana J., Scott Pace, and C. Bryan Gabbard. *Space: Emerging Options for National Power*. Santa Monica, Calif.: RAND Corporation, 1998.

Krepon, Michael, with Christopher Clary. *Space Assurance or Space Dominance? The Case Against Weaponizing Space.* Washington, D.C.: Henry L. Stimson Center, 2003.

Lambeth, Benjamin S. *Mastering the Ultimate High Ground: Next Steps in the Military Uses of Space.* Santa Monica, Calif.: Rand Corporation, 2003.

Larsen, Jeffery A., ed. *Arms Control: Cooperative Security in a Changing Environment.* Boulder, Colo.: Lynne Rienner Publishers, 2002.

Lavoy, Peter R., Scott D. Sagan, and James J. Wirtz. *Planning the Unthinkable: How New Powers Will Use Nuclear, Biological, and Chemical Weapons.* Ithaca, N.Y.: Cornell University Press, 2000.

Lederberg, Joshua, ed. *Biological Weapons: Limiting the Threat.* Cambridge, Mass.: MIT Press, 1999.

Litwak, Robert S. "Non-proliferation and the Dilemmas of Regime Change," *Survival*, Vol. 45, No. 4 (Winter 2003–04), pp. 7–32.

Litwak, Robert S. *Rogue States and U.S. Foreign Policy: Containment after the Cold War.* Baltimore: Johns Hopkins University Press, 2000.

Lumpe, Lora, ed. *Running Guns: The Global Black Market in Small Arms.* London: Zed Books, 2000.

Miller, Judith, Stephen Engelberg, and William Broad. *Germs: Biological Weapons and America's Secret War.* New York: Simon and Schuster, 2001.

Nolan, Janne E., Bernard I. Finel, and Brian D. Finlay, eds. *Ultimate Security: Combating Weapons of Mass Destruction.* New York: The Century Foundation, 2003.

O'Hanlon, Michael. *Technological Change and the Future of Warfare.* Washington, D.C.: Brookings Institution, 2000.

Pierre, Andrew J., ed. *Cascade of Arms: Managing Conventional Weapons Proliferation.* Washington, D.C.: Brookings Institution, 1997.

Price, Richard M. *The Chemical Weapons Taboo.* Ithaca, N.Y.: Cornell University Press, 1997.

Sagan, Scott D., and Kenneth N. Waltz. *The Spread of Nuclear Weapons: A Debate.* New York: W.W. Norton, 1995.

Shields, John M., and William C. Potter, eds. *Dismantling the Cold War: U.S. and NIS Perspectives on the Nunn-Lugar Cooperative Threat Reduction Program.* Cambridge, Mass.: MIT Press, 1997.

Utgoff, Victor, ed. *The Coming Crisis: Nuclear Proliferation, U.S. Interests, and World Order.* Cambridge, Mass.: MIT Press, 2000.

III. Nonmilitary Aspects of Security

Berger, Peter, and Samuel P. Huntington, eds. *Many Globalizations: Cultural Diversity in the Contemporary World.* Oxford: Oxford University Press, 2002.

Brower, Jennifer, and Peter Chalk. *The Global Threat of New and Reemerging Infectious Diseases: Reconciling U.S. National Security and Public Health Policy.* Santa Monica, Calif.: Rand Corporation, 2003.

Cohen, Roberta, and Francis M. Deng. *Masses in Flight: The Global Crisis of Internal Displacement.* Washington, D.C.: Brookings Institution, 1998.

Denning, Dorothy E. *Information Warfare and Security*. Reading, Mass.: Addison-Wesley, 1999.

Eberstadt, Nicholas. "The Future of AIDS," *Foreign Affairs*, Vol. 81, No. 6 (November-December 2002), pp. 22–45.

Frazier, Thomas W., and Drew C. Richardson, eds. *Food and Agricultural Security: Guarding Against Natural Threats and Terrorist Attacks Affecting Health, National Food Supplies, and Agricultural Economics*. New York: New York Academy of Sciences, 1999.

Friedman, Thomas. *The Lexus and the Olive Tree: Understanding Globalization*. New York: Farrar, Straus, Giroux, 1999.

Harris, Martha. "Energy and Security," in Michael E. Brown, ed., *Grave New World: Security Challenges in the 21st Century*. Washington, D.C.: Georgetown University Press, 2003, pp. 157–177.

Homer-Dixon, Thomas F. *Environment, Scarcity, and Violence*. Princeton, N.J.: Princeton University Press, 1999.

Keely, Charles B. "Demographic Developments and Security," in Michael E. Brown, ed., *Grave New World: Security Challenges in the 21st Century*. Washington, D.C.: Georgetown University Press, 2003, pp. 197–212.

Klare, Michael T. *Resource Wars: The New Landscape of Global Conflict*. New York: Metropolitan Books, 2001.

McNeill, J.R. *Something New Under the Sun: An Environmental History of the Twentieth-Century World*. New York: Norton, 2000.

Moran, Theodore H. *American Economic Policy and National Security*. New York: The Brookings Institution, 1993.

O'Meara, Patrick, Howard D. Mehlinger, and Matthew Krain, eds. *Globalization and the Challenges of a New Century*. Bloomington, Ind.: Indiana University Press, 2000.

Rattray, Gregory J. *Strategic Warfare in Cyberspace*. Cambridge, Mass.: MIT Press, 2001.

Romm, Joseph J. *Defining National Security: The Nonmilitary Aspects*. New York: Council on Foreign Relations Press, 1993.

Rosecrance, Richard N. *The Rise of the Virtual State: Wealth and Power in the Coming Century*. New York: Basic Books, 1999.

Rotberg, Robert I. "The New Nature of Nation-State Failure," *Washington Quarterly*, Vol. 25, No. 3 (Summer 2002), pp. 86–96.

Shapiro, Andrew L.. "Think Again: The Internet," *Foreign Policy*, No. 115 (Summer 1999), pp. 14–27.

Singer, P.W. "AIDS and International Security," *Survival*, Vol. 44, No. 1 (Spring 2002), pp. 145- 158.

Stares, Paul B. *Global Habit: The Drug Problem in a Borderless World*. Washington, D.C.: Brookings Institution, 1996.

United Nations Development Program. "New Dimensions of Human Security," in *Human Development Report, 1994*. New York: United Nations, 1994, pp. 22–40.

U.S. Central Intelligence Agency. *The Global Infectious Disease Threat and Its Implications for the United States*. Washington, D.C.: U.S. Central Intelligence Agency, January 2000.

U.S. National Intelligence Council. *Global Trends 2015*. Washington, D.C.: U.S. Central Intelligence Agency, December 2000.

Weiner, Myron. *International Migration and Security.* Boulder, Colo.: Westview Press, 1993.

Weiner, Myron, and Sharon Stanton Russell. *Demography and National Security.* New York: Berghahn, 2001.

Wolf, Martin. "Will the Nation-State Survive Globalization?" *Foreign Affairs,* Vol. 80, No. 1 (January-February 2001), pp. 178–190.

IV. Transnational Actors and Security

Barber, Benjamin R. *Jihad vs. McWorld: Terrorism's Challenge to Democracy.* New York: Ballantine, 1996.

Booth, Ken, and Tim Dunne, eds. *Worlds in Collision: Terror and the Future of Global Order.* New York: Palgrave Macmillan, 2002.

Boulden, Jane, and Thomas G. Weiss, eds. *Terrorism and the UN: Before and After September 11.* Bloomington, Ind.: Indiana University Press, 2004.

Cronin, Audrey Kurth. "Rethinking Sovereignty: American Strategy in the Age of Terrorism," *Survival,* Vol. 44, No. 2 (Summer 2002), pp. 119–139.

Cronin, Audrey Kurth, and James L. Ludes, eds. *Attacking Terrorism: Elements of a Grand Strategy.* Washington, D.C.: Georgetown University Press, 2004.

Falkenrath, Richard A., Robert D. Newman, and Bradley A. Thayer. *America's Achilles' Heel: Nuclear, Biological, and Chemical Terrorism and Covert Attack.* Cambridge, Mass.: MIT Press, 1998.

Findlay, Mark. *The Globalisation of Crime.* Cambridge: Cambridge University Press, 2000.

Florini, Ann M., ed. *The Third Force: The Rise of Transnational Civil Society.* Washington, D.C.: Carnegie Endowment for International Peace, 2000.

Godson, Roy. "Transnational Crime, Corruption, and Security," in Michael E. Brown, ed., *Grave New World: Security Challenges in the 21st Century.* Washington, D.C.: Georgetown University Press, 2003, pp. 259–278.

Godson, Roy, and Phil Williams. "Strengthening Cooperation Against Transnational Crime," *Survival,* Vol. 40, No. 3 (Autumn 1998), pp. 66–88.

Heymann, Philip B. *Terrorism and America: A Commonsense Strategy for a Democratic Society.* Cambridge, Mass.: MIT Press, 1998.

Hoffman, Bruce. *Inside Terrorism.* New York: Columbia University Press, 1998.

de Jonge Oudraat, Chantal. "Combating Terrorism," *Washington Quarterly,* Vol. 26, No. 4 (Autumn 2003), pp. 163–176.

Kaufman, Edward. "A Broadcasting Strategy to Win Media Wars," *Washington Quarterly,* Vol. 25, No. 2 (Spring 2002), pp. 115–127.

Kenney, Michael. "From Pablo to Osama: Counter-Terrorism Lessons from the War on Drugs," *Survival,* Vol. 45, No. 3 (Autumn 2003), pp. 187–206.

Mathews, Jessica T. "Power Shift," *Foreign Affairs,* Vol. 76, No. 1 (January-February 1997), pp. 50–66.

O'Sullivan, Meaghan L. *Shrewd Sanctions: Statecraft and State Sponsors of Terrorism.* Washington, D.C.: Brookings Institution, 2003.

Owen, Diana. "Transnational Media Organizations and Security," in Michael E. Brown, ed., *Grave New World: Security Challenges in the 21ˢᵗ Century.* Washington, D.C.: Georgetown University Press, 2003, pp. 233–258.

Pillar, Paul. *Terrorism and U.S. Foreign Policy.* Washington, D.C.: Brookings Institution, 2001.

Roberts, Adam. "Counter-Terrorism, Armed Force and the Laws of War," *Survival,* Vol. 44, No. 1 (Spring 2002), pp. 7–32.

Rudman, Warren B., et al. *Emergency Responders: Drastically Underfunded, Dangerously Unprepared.* New York: Council on Foreign Relations, 2003.

Stern, Jessica. *The Ultimate Terrorists.* Cambridge, Mass.: Harvard University Press, 1999.

Tanter, Raymond. *Rogue Regimes: Terrorism and Proliferation,* revised edition. New York: St. Martin's Press, 1999.

Tucker, Jonathan B., ed. *Toxic Terror: Assessing Terrorist Use of Chemical and Biological Weapons.* Cambridge, Mass.: MIT Press, 2000.

Williams, Phil, and Dimitri Vlassis, eds. *Combating Transnational Crime: Concepts, Activities and Responses.* London: Frank Cass, 2001.

Winer, Jonathan M., and Trifin J. Roule. "Fighting Terrorist Finance," *Survival,* Vol. 44, No. 3 (Autumn, 2002), pp. 87–103.

Wolfsthal, Jon B., and Tom Z. Collina. "Nuclear Terrorism and Warhead Control in Russia," *Survival,* Vol. 44, No. 2 (Summer 2002), pp. 71–83.

International Security

The Robert and Renée Belfer Center for
Science and International Affairs
John F. Kennedy School of Government
Harvard University

Articles in this reader were previously published in **International Security**, a quarterly journal sponsored and edited by the Robert and Renée Belfer Center for Science and International Affairs at the John F. Kennedy School of Government at Harvard University, and published by MIT Press Journals. To receive subscription information about the journal or find out more about other readers in our series, please contact MIT Press Journals at Five Cambridge Center, Fourth Floor, Cambridge, MA, 02142-1493 or at www.mitpress.com.